W9-ADA-909

FOOD
FOR
FIFTY

FOOD FOR FIFTY

6th. ed.

Bessie Brooks West
**Professor Emeritus of Dietetics,
Restaurant and Institutional Management
Formerly Head of Department
Kansas State University**

Grace Severance Shugart
**Professor Emeritus of Dietetics,
Restaurant and Institutional Management
Formerly Head of Department
Kansas State University**

Maxine Fay Wilson
**Associate Professor of Restaurant,
Hotel and Institutional Management
Purdue University**

John Wiley & Sons
New York   Chichester   Brisbane   Toronto

Library of Congress Cataloging in Publication Data:

West, Bessie Brooks, 1890–
    Food for 50.

    Previous ed. by S. F. Fowler and others.
    Includes indexes.
    1. Quantity cookery.   2. Menus.   I. Shugart,
Grace Severance, joint author.   II. Wilson, Maxine Fay,
joint author.   III. Fowler, Sina Faye. Food for 50.
IV. Title.

TX820.F65 1979   641.57   78-21921
ISBN 0-471-02688-3

Preface

The sixth edition of *Food for Fifty,* as was the first, is planned to supplement *Food Service in Institutions,* now in its fifth edition.

This edition of *Food for Fifty* has been designed to meet the changing needs of the persons responsible for planning, preparing, and serving food in the various types of institution foodservices. To accomplish this and to increase its effectiveness for students in foodservice management, the introduction to each food section has been enlarged and brought up to date. New recipes have been included, and metric measurements have been added to each recipe. The sections on menu planning and special meals have been updated.

We wish to express our indebtedness and appreciation to all those who have helped in the preparation of the sixth edition of this publication.

Bessie Brooks West

Grace Severance Shugart

Maxine Fay Wilson

Contents

Tables

Part

General
Information

General
Information

Information in this section is presented as a guide for ordering food, adjusting recipes, or converting weights of ingredients as given in recipes to measures. Information also is included to assist in conversion from present U.S. weights and measures to metric.

Tables 1.1 and 1.2 are guides for amounts of food to buy and prepare for 50 persons. Tables 1.3 to 1.13 contain tables of weights, measures, and equivalents to assist in adjusting recipes. U.S. measures of weight and volume and their metric equivalents are given in Tables 1.3 and 1.4. In Table 1.7, a selected number of commonly used foods are listed in weights up to 1 lb with measure equivalents. Tables 1.9 and 1.10 are direct reading tables for enlarging or decreasing recipes. Amounts are given in weights and measures for 25 to 500 portions. Table 1.11 gives ingredient amounts in measure for portion yields of 8 to 96.

Tables 1.13 to 1.21 include preparation and serving guides, such as dipper and ladle equivalents, fruit and vegetable yields, and food equivalents, substitutions, and proportions. Cooking temperatures are included in Tables 1.21 to 1.25; metric temperature equivalents in Table 1.23. Use of spices and seasonings in food are found in Table 1.26, and a Glossary of Food Terms begins on p. 78.

Amounts of Food to Serve 50

Table 1.1 suggests amounts of food AS PURCHASED to serve approximately 50 persons. Table 1.2, which begins on p. 23, gives amounts of PREPARED foods needed for 50 servings.

The quantity of any item ordered or prepared must be adjusted to the particular requirements of the group to be served. Rarely is 50 the exact number to be served, nor do all groups require the same amount of food for a given number. The amounts given in these tables are based on average servings, with the knowledge that there will need to be an adjustment to fit each situation. For example, 2 2-lb loaves of bread would provide not more than 56 slices of bread. The order must be increased to 4 loaves if 2 slices per portion are desired. Inexperienced employees may find it difficult to obtain the exact number of portions indicated for a given quantity, so a small increase in allowance for these items may be desirable. Odd amounts, such as 4¼ doz rolls, would need to be adjusted to the next whole unit. If the number to be served is a few less or more than 50, the order would be for 4 or 5 doz.

The weight of ingredients in a package, or the number of slices of bread in a loaf, may vary with different suppliers. The count of peaches or other fruit and the weight of berries in a can varies with the pack. Information usually may be obtained from the purveyor as to the count or weight of foods in a container.

Table 1.1 AMOUNTS OF FOOD **AS PURCHASED** TO SERVE 50

Food	Weight or Measure	U.S.		Metric		Miscellaneous Information
		Serving Portion	Amount to Serve 50	Serving Portion	Amount to Serve 50	
BAKERY PRODUCTS						
Biscuits, to bake	8-oz can	1 biscuit	5-7 cans	1 biscuit	5-7 227-g cans	8-10 biscuits per can
Bread, loaf						
Small	1 lb	1-2 slices	3-4 loaves	1-2 slices	3-4 454-g loaves	16 slices per loaf
Sandwich	1½ lb	1-2 slices	3 loaves	1-2 slices	3 680-g loaves	24 thin slices per loaf
Pullman	2 lb	1 slice	1½ loaves	1 slice	1½ 908-g loaves	36 slices per loaf
Cake						
Angel food	10-in. round	12-14 cuts per cake	3-4 cakes	12-14 cuts per cake	3-4 cakes	
Fruit	Varies	2½ oz	8-10 lb	70 g	3.63-4.54 kg	
Cupcakes	doz	1 each	4½ doz	1 each	4½ doz	
Layer	2 layer 9 in.	14-16 cuts per cake	3-4 cakes	2 layer 9 in.	14-16 cuts per cake	
Sheet	12 × 20 in.	2 × 2½ in. (1¾ oz)	1 pan	2 × 2½ in. (50 g)	1 pan	Cut 6 × 8 (48 servings) Cut 5 × 8 (40 servings)
Cookies						
Cream filled	lb	2 cookies	3 lb	2 cookies	1.36 kg	19 per lb (454 g)
Vanilla wafers	lb	2 wafers	1 lb	2 wafers	454 g	113 per lb (454 g)
Crackers						
Graham	lb	2 crackers	1¾-2 lb	2 crackers	794-908 g	60-65 per lb (454 g)
Soda	lb	2 crackers	1½-2 lb	2 crackers	680-908 g	82 per lb (454 g)
Saltines	lb	4 crackers	1¾ lb	4 crackers	794 g	112 per lb (454 g)
Pies	8 in.	6 cuts per pie	8-9 pies	6 cuts per pie	8-9 pies	

Food	Unit	Size of serving	Amount for 50	Size of serving	Amount for 50	Notes
Rolls						
Dinner	doz	1½-2	6-8½ doz	1½-2	6-8½ doz	
Hard	doz	1-1½	4½-6½ doz	1-1½	4½-6½ doz	
Buns	doz	1	4½ doz	1	4½ doz	
Sweet	doz	1	4½ doz	1	4½ doz	
BEVERAGES						
Cider	gal	½ c	1½ gal	120 mL	5.68 L	Makes 2½ gal (9.46 L)
Cocoa						
Unsweetened	1-lb pkg	6-oz c	8 oz	180-mL c	227 g	
Instant	2-lb pkg	6-oz c	2-2½ lb	180-mL c	0.91-1.1 kg	
Coffee						
Urn grind	1 lb	6-oz c	1-1½ lb	180-mL c	454-680 g	
Instant	10-oz jar	6-oz c	3 oz	180-mL c	85 g	2 oz (57 g) freeze-dried
Juices, canned	46-oz can (1.36 L)	6 oz	7 cans	180 mL	7 cans	Size 195
Lemons for lemonade	doz	8 oz	3 doz	240 mL	3 doz	
Lemonade, frozen concentrate	32-oz can (950 mL)	8 oz	3-4 cans	240 mL	3-4 cans	Dilute 1:3 parts water
Orange juice						
Frozen	12-oz can (355 mL)	4 oz	4-5 cans	120 mL	4-5 cans	Dilute 1:3 parts water
Frozen	32-oz can (950 mL)	4 oz	1½-2 cans	120 mL	1½-2 cans	Dilute 1:3 parts water
Fresh	qt	4 oz	6¼ qt	120 mL	5.91 L	
Oranges, for juice	doz	6 oz	24-27 doz	180 mL	24-27 doz	Size 113
	doz	4 oz	16-18 doz	120 mL	16-18 doz	Size 113
Tea, hot, bulk	lb	6-oz cup	2 oz	180 mL	57 g	Amount will vary with quality of tea
Iced	1-oz bag	12-oz glass	6 bags	360-mL glass	170 g	6 1-oz (28-g) bags will make 3 gal (11.4 L) tea plus ice
Instant, iced	2-oz jar	12-oz glass	1-1½ oz	360-mL glass	28-43 g	

Table 1.1 AMOUNTS OF FOOD **AS PURCHASED** TO SERVE 50 (continued)

Food	U.S.			Metric		Miscellaneous Information
	Weight or Measure	Serving Portion	Amount to Serve 50	Serving Portion	Amount to Serve 50	
CEREALS AND CEREAL PRODUCTS						
Barley, for soup	lb		14 oz		397 g	For 3 gal (11.4 L) soup
Cream of wheat	lb	⅔ c	2 lb	160 mL	908 g	
Hominy grits	lb	⅔ c	2 lb	160 mL	908 g	Yield varies with quality of macaroni
Macaroni	lb	½-¾ c	3-4 lb	120-180 mL	1.36-1.81 kg	
Noodles, medium	lb	½-¾ c	3-4 lb	120-180 mL	1.36-1.81 kg	
Pettijohns	lb	⅔ c	3 lb	160 mL	1.36 kg	Yield varies with type of rice
Rice	lb	½ c	3-4 lb	120 mL	1.36-1.81 kg	
Rolled oats	lb	⅔ c	2 lb	160 mL	908 g	Yield varies with quality
Spaghetti	lb	½-¾ c	3-4 lb	120-180 mL	1.36-1.81 kg	
Cereal, ready to eat						
All Bran	1-lb pkg	½ c	3 pkg	120 mL	1.36 kg	16 servings per lb (454 g)
Cornflakes	1-lb pkg	¾ c	2¾ pkg	180 mL	1.25 kg	18 servings per lb (454 g)
Puffed Rice	8-oz pkg	¾ c	4 pkg	180 mL	908 g	12 servings per pkg
Rice Krispies	9½-oz pkg	⅔ c	4 pkg	160 mL	1.08 kg	20 servings per lb (454 g)
Shredded Wheat	12-oz pkg	1 large or 2 small	6¾ pkg	1 large or 2 small	2.29 kg	10 servings per lb (454 g)
Wheaties	12-oz pkg	¾ c	4 pkg	180 mL	1.36 kg	16 servings per lb (454 g)

CONVENIENCE FOODS

Food	Unit	Portion per serving	Amount for 50	Portion per serving (metric)	Amount for 50 (metric)	Remarks
Bread mixes						
Biscuits	5-lb bag	1-1¼ oz	2½ lb	28-35 g	1.14 kg	
Muffins, plain	5-lb bag	1-1½ oz	3½ lb	28-43 g	1.59 kg	
Rolls	5-lb bag	1-1¼ oz	2⅔ lb	28-35 g	1.25 kg	
Pancakes	5-lb bag	2 pancakes	6 lb	12 pancakes	2.72 kg	
Cake mixes						
Angel food	1-lb box	12-14 cuts per cake	4 boxes	12-14 cuts per cake	1.81 kg	Weight of box will vary with brand
Chocolate, yellow, white	18½-oz box	2-in. pieces	5 boxes	2-in. pieces	3.02 kg	Weight of box will vary with brand
	5-lb pkg	16 cuts per 9-in. layer	1 pkg	16 cuts per 9-in. layer	2.27 kg	3½ 2-layer cakes
Soup bases, beef, chicken, paste	1-lb jar		8 oz		227 g	3 gal (11.4 L) soup
Dehydrated	1 lb		1½ lb		680 g	3 gal (11.4 L) soup
Soup, concentrated	No. 10 can		2 cans		2 cans	3 gal (11.4 L) soup
Pudding	lb	4 oz (½ c)	3½ lb	114 g	1.59 kg	

DAIRY PRODUCTS AND EGGS

Food	Unit	Portion per serving	Amount for 50	Portion per serving (metric)	Amount for 50 (metric)	Remarks
Butter or margarine						
For sandwiches	lb		1 lb		454 g	
For table	lb	1-2 pats	1-1½ lb	1-2 pats	454-680 g	72 pats per lb (454 g). May be purchased in other sizes
For vegetables	lb	½-1 t	¼-½ lb	3-5 mL	114-227 g	
Cheddar cheese	lb	1¼-1½ oz	4-5 lb	35-43 g	1.81-2.27 kg	For sandwich or with cold cuts
Cottage cheese	1-lb carton	No. 20 dipper	6½ lb	No. 20 dipper	2.95 kg	For salad or side dish
Cream, coffee	qt		1-1½ qt		0.95-1.42 L	
Whipping	pt	1 T	1½ pt	15 mL	720 mL	For garnish

Table 1.1 AMOUNTS OF FOOD **AS PURCHASED** TO SERVE 50 (continued)

Food	Weight or Measure	U.S.		Metric		Miscellaneous Information
		Serving Portion	Amount to Serve 50	Serving Portion	Amount to Serve 50	
Cream cheese	2-lb pkg	½ oz	2 lb	14 g	908 g	For sandwich or salad garnish
Eggs, in shell	doz	1-2 eggs	4½-8½ doz	1-2 eggs	4½-8½ doz	
Ice cream, brick	qt	8 slices per brick	6½ bricks	8 slices per brick	6½ bricks	
Bulk	gal	No. 12 dipper	2 gal	No. 12 dipper	7.57 L	Dish of ice cream or sundae
Bulk	gal	No. 16 dipper	1½ gal	No. 16 dipper	5.68 L	With cake or cookie
Bulk	gal	No. 20 dipper	1¼ gal	No. 20 dipper	4.73 L	For à la mode
Milk, fluid	gal	8-oz glass	3 gal	240-mL glass	11.36 L	For dispenser
Instant nonfat	lb	8 oz	3 lb	240 mL	1.36 kg	3.5 oz (100 g) dry milk per qt of water. Amount may vary with brand
Sherbet	gal	No. 20 dipper	1¼ gal	No. 20 dipper	4.73 L	Meal accompaniment
FISH						
Fish fillets	lb	3 oz	14-16 lb	85 g	6.35-7.26 kg	1 lb (454 g) A.P.[a] = 0.64 lb (291 g) cooked fish
Whole, dressed	lb	3 oz	40 lb	85 g	18.14 kg	1 lb (454 g) A.P. = 0.27 lb (125 g) cooked fish

[a] A.P. denotes "as purchased."

Food	Unit	Amount per serving	Amount for 50	Amount per serving	Amount for 50	Remarks
Oysters	gal	3 oz	1½-2 gal	85 g	5.68-7.57 L	Amount will vary with method of preparation
Scallops, to fry	lb	3 oz	10-12 lb	85 g	4.54-5.44 kg	
Shrimp, raw, in shell	lb	2 oz	12½ lb	57 g	5.67 kg	1 lb (454 g) A.P. = 0.5 lb (227 g) cooked shrimp
	lb	3 oz	18-20 lb	85 g	8.16-9.08 kg	
Raw, peeled	lb	3 oz	16 lb	85 g	7.26 kg	1 lb (454 g) peeled = 9 oz (255 g) cooked
Cooked, peeled, and cleaned	lb	2 oz	6-6½ lb	57 g	2.72-2.95 kg	1 lb (454 g) A.P. = 1 lb (454 g) cooked
	lb	3 oz	10 lb	85 g	4.54 kg	
FRUITS						
Canned	No. 10 can	Varies	2-3 cans	Varies	2-3 cans	See table 1.15, p. 65
Dried						
Apricots	lb	3 oz	4½ lb	85 g	2.04 kg	
Dates, pitted	lb	5-6 each	3-4 lb	5-6 each	1.36-1.81 kg	
Prunes, with pits	lb	4-5 prunes	6 lb	4-5 prunes	2.72 kg	
Raisins, seedless	lb	1½-2½ oz	4½-7¾ lb	43-70 g	2.04-3.52 kg	
Fresh						
Avocado	lb (2 med)	8-9 per avocado	3 lb	8-9 per avocado	1.36 kg	For salad combinations
Apples, baking	box	1 apple	½ box	1 apple	½ box	Size 113
For pie	lb	6 cuts per pie	12 lb	6 cuts per pie	5.44 kg	8 8-in. pies
For sauce	lb	3-4 oz	12-15 lb	85-114 g	5.44-6.80 kg	
Bananas	lb	1 each	16 lb	1 each	7.26 kg	3 medium per lb (454 g)
For pie	lb	6 cuts per pie	5 lb	6 cuts per pie	2.27 kg	8 8-in. pies
For salad	lb	3 oz	10 lb	85 g	4.54 kg	
Blackberries, for pie	qt	6 cuts per pie	6-8 qt	6 cuts per pie	5.68-7.57 L	8 8-in. pies

Table 1.1 AMOUNTS OF FOOD **AS PURCHASED** TO SERVE 50 (continued)

Food	Weight or Measure	U.S.		Metric		Miscellaneous Information
		Serving Portion	Amount to Serve 50	Serving Portion	Amount to Serve 50	
Cherries, red, for pie	qt	6 cuts per pie	8-10 qt	6 cuts per pie	7.57-9.46 L	8 8-in. pies
Cranberries	lb	¼ c sauce	4 lb	60 mL sauce	1.81 kg	
Grapes, seedless	lb	¼ c	15 lb	60 mL	6.80 kg	
Lemons	Size 165	⅙ lemon	8-10 lemons	⅙ lemon	8-10 lemons	For tea or fish
Melon, sliced	lb	8-12-oz slice	30-40 lb	227-340 g	13.61-18.14 kg	
Pineapple	2 lb each	½ c diced	5 pineapples	120 mL diced	5 pineapples (4.54 kg)	
Strawberries						
For shortcake	qt	¾ c	8 qt	180 mL	7.57 L	
For sundaes	qt	½-⅔ c	6-7 qt	120-160 mL	5.68-6.62 L	
Frozen						
Apricots, apples	2½-lb pkg	3 oz	10 lb	85 g	4.54 kg	
Cherries, peaches	2½-lb pkg	3 oz	10 lb	85 g	4.54 kg	
Rhubarb, cut	2½-lb pkg	2¼ oz	7½ lb	64 g	3.4 kg	
Fruit for topping	2½-lb pkg	1½ oz	5 lb	43 g	2.27 kg	

MEATS
Beef

		Cooked weight[a]	A.P.[a]	Cooked weight[a]	A.P.	
Brisket, boneless	lb	3 oz	25-30 lb	85 g	11.3-13.6 kg	Yield varies with extent of trimming
Chuck, boneless, pot roast	lb	3 oz	18-20 lb	85 g	8.2-9.1 kg	1 lb (454 g) A.P. = 0.75 lb (340 g) cooked meat[b]
Corned beef	lb	3 oz	25-30 lb	85 g	11.3-13.6 kg	Yield varies with extent of trimming
Rib eye roast	lb	3 oz	20-22 lb	85 g	9.1-10 kg	Oven ready
Rib roast, standing	lb	6 oz	45-50 lb	170 g	20.4-22.7 kg	Bone in, oven prepared
Round, boneless	lb	3 oz	15-18 lb	85 g	6.8-8.2 kg	1 lb (454 g) A.P. = 0.76 lb (344 g) cooked meat
Rump roast, boneless	lb	3 oz	18-20 lb	85 g	8.2-9.1 kg	1 lb (454 g) A.P. = 0.73 lb (334 g) cooked meat
Sirloin, boneless roast, trimmed	lb	3 oz	15-18 lb	85 g	6.8-8.2 kg	1 lb (454 g) A.P. = 0.76 lb (344 g) cooked meat
Steaks						
Round, boneless cut 3 per lb	lb	3½ oz	16-18 lb	100 g	7.3-8.2 kg	1 lb (454 g) A.P. = 0.76 lb (344 g) cooked meat
Cubed, cut 4 per lb	lb	3 oz	13 lb	85 g	5.9 kg	

[a] A.P. (as purchased) weights given in table are estimated amounts to yield 50 portions of cooked weights as given in serving portion column. When calculating amounts for roasts or other meats to be sliced after cooking, a 10% slicing loss should be allowed.

[b] Yields of cooked meat from *Food Buying Guide for Type A School Lunches*, USDA PA-270, 1972.

Table 1.1 AMOUNTS OF FOOD **AS PURCHASED** TO SERVE 50 (continued)

Food	Weight or Measure	U.S.		Metric		Miscellaneous Information
		Serving Portion	Amount to Serve 50	Serving Portion	Amount to Serve 50	
Flank, cut 4 per lb	lb	3 oz	13 lb	85 g	5.9 kg	1 lb (454 g) A.P. = 0.67 lb (305 g) cooked meat
Loin, strip	lb	8 oz A.P.[a]	25 lb	227 g A.P.	11.3 kg	Short cut, bone in
Sirloin, boneless	lb	3½ oz	15-17 lb	100 g	6.8-7.7 kg	
Tenderloin, trimmed	lb	4 oz	17 lb	114 g	7.7 kg	
T-bone	lb	8 oz A.P.	25 lb	227 g A.P.	11.3 kg	
T-bone	lb	12 oz A.P.	36-38 lb	340 g A.P.	16.3-17.2 kg	
Short ribs, trimmed	lb	3 oz	35-40 lb	85 g	15.9-18.1 kg	1 lb (454 g) A.P. = 0.25 lb (114 g) cooked meat
Cubed (1-in.) meat for stew	lb	3 oz	12-15 lb	85 g	5.4-6.8 kg	1 lb (454 g) A.P. = 0.66 lb (298 g) cooked meat
Ground	lb	3 oz	13-15 lb	85 g	5.9-6.8 kg	1 lb (454 g) A.P. = 0.75 lb (332 g) cooked meat
Veal						
Chops, loin or rib	lb	4 oz	17 lb	114 g	7.7 kg	Cut 3 per lb (454 g) 1 lb A.P.[a] = 0.61 lb (276 g) cooked meat
Cutlets, leg, boneless, cut 3 per lb or 4 per lb	lb	3-3½ oz	12½-15 lb	85-100 g	5.7-6.8 kg	1 lb (454 g) A.P. = 0.78 lb (354 g) cooked meat
Ground	lb	3-4 oz	15 lb	85-114 g	6.8 kg	1 lb (454 g) A.P. = 0.73 lb (334 g) cooked meat

a A.P. denotes "as purchased."

Roast, leg, boneless	lb	3 oz	15-18 lb	85 g	6.8-8.2 kg	1 lb (454 g) A.P. = 0.69 lb (312 g) cooked meat
Pork, fresh						
Roast loin, boneless	lb	3 oz	16-20 lb	85 g	7.3-9.1 kg	1 lb (454 g) A.P. = 0.77 lb (347 g) cooked meat
Roast fresh ham, boneless	lb	3 oz	16-20 lb	85 g	7.3-9.1 kg	1 lb (454 g) A.P. = 0.68 lb (312 g) cooked meat
Whole with bone	lb	3 oz	25 lb	85 g	11.3 kg	1 lb (454 g) A.P. = 0.55 lb (255 g) cooked meat
Pork cutlets, cut 3 per lb or 4 per lb	lb	3-3½ oz	12½-15 lb	85-100 g	5.7-6.8 kg	1 lb (454 g) A.P. = 0.75 lb (340 g) cooked meat
Pork chops, loin						
Cut 3 per lb	lb	1 chop	17 lb	1 chop	7.7 kg	1 lb (454 g) A.P. = 0.54 lb (248 g) cooked meat
Cut 4 per lb	lb	1 chop	12½-13 lb	1 chop	5.7-5.9 kg	
Pork sausage, bulk	lb	2-oz cake	12½-15 lb	57 g	5.7-6.8 kg	1 lb (454 g) A.P. = 0.51 lb (234 g) cooked meat
Links	lb	2 links	7-8 lb	2 links	3.2-3.6 kg	12-16 links per lb (454 g)
	lb	4 links	13-17 lb	4 links	5.9-7.7 kg	
Spareribs	lb	8-12 oz A.P.[a]	25-40 lb	227-340 g A.P.	11.3-18 kg	1 lb (454 g) A.P. = 0.26 lb (120 g) cooked meat
Pork, smoked						
Bacon, sliced Hotel pack	lb	2 slices	4-4½ lb	2 slices	1.8-2.1 kg	24 slices per lb (454 g)
Sliced	lb	2 slices	5-5½ lb	2 slices	2.3-2.5 kg	17-20 slices per lb (454 g)
Canadian bacon	lb	2 oz	10 lb	57 g	4.54 kg	

[a] A.P. denotes "as purchased."

Table 1.1 AMOUNTS OF FOOD **AS PURCHASED** TO SERVE 50 (continued)

Food	Weight or Measure	U.S.		Metric		Miscellaneous Information
		Serving Portion	Amount to Serve 50	Serving Portion	Amount to Serve 50	
Ham, with bone	lb	3 oz	20-25 lb	85 g	9.3-11.34 kg	1 lb (454 g) A.P. = 0.56 lb (255 g) cooked slices; 0.67 lb (305 g) cooked slices and pieces
Boneless	lb	3 oz	15 lb	85 g	6.8 kg	1 lb (454 g) A.P.[a] = 0.64 lb (290 g) cooked slices; 0.77 lb (348 g) cooked slices and pieces
Slices	lb	2 oz	17 lb	57 g	7.7 kg	Served with eggs
Steak	lb	5 oz	19 lb	142 g	8.6 kg	Dinner meat
Pullman, canned	6-6½ lb can	3 oz	2 cans	85 g	5.4-5.9 kg	
Lamb						
Chops, rib, cut 4 per lb	lb	2 each	25 lb	2 each	11.3 kg	1 lb (454 g) A.P. = 0.54 lb (255 g) cooked meat
Leg, roast, bone in	lb	3 oz	18-20 lb	85 g	8.2-9.1 kg	1 lb (454 g) A.P. = 0.54 lb (255 g) cooked meat
Leg, roast, boneless	lb	3 oz	15 lb	85 g	6.8 kg	1 lb (454 g) A.P. = 0.7 lb (320 g) cooked meat
Variety and Luncheon Meats						
Bologna	lb	3 oz	10 lb	85 g	4.5 kg	Slice 16 per lb (454 g)

[a] A.P. denotes "as purchased."

		U.S. portion	U.S. amount for 50	Metric portion	Metric amount for 50	
Frankfurters						
8 per lb	lb	2 franks	12½ lb	2 franks	5.7 kg	
10 per lb	lb	1 frank	5 lb	1 frank	2.3 kg	
Heart	lb	3 oz	20-24 lb	85 g	9.1-10.9 kg	1 lb (454 g) A.P.[a] = 0.39 lb (178 g) cooked heart
Liver	lb	3 oz	12-13 lb	85 g	5.4-5.9 kg	1 lb (454 g) A.P. = 0.69 (320 g) cooked liver
Liverwurst	lb	2 oz	6½ lb	57 g	2.9 kg	
Salami, cooked	lb	2 oz	6½ lb	57 g	2.9 kg	
Spiced ham	lb	2 oz	6½ lb	57 g	2.9 kg	
Tongue	lb	3 oz	18-20 lb	85 g	8.2-9.1 kg	1 lb (454 g) A.P. = 0.51 lb (234 g) cooked tongue
POULTRY						
Chicken, to fry	2½-2¾ lb	½ breast, 1 drumstick with wing or back; 1 thigh with wing or back; or 1 quarter	13 fryers 30-33 lb	see U.S. portion column	13 fryers 13.6-15.0 kg	
To barbecue	2-2½ lb	¼ chicken	13 fryers	¼ chicken	13 fryers	1 lb (454 g) A.P.[a] = 0.38 lb (170 g) cooked chicken exclusive of neck or giblets. Yield will vary with size
To broil	2-2½ lb	½ broiler	25 broilers	½ broiler	25 broilers	
To bake	5-6 lb	3 oz	40 lb	85 g	18.1 kg	
To stew	5-6 lb hen or 3-3½ lb fryer	2 oz cooked meat	20 lb	57 g	9.1 kg	

[a] A.P. denotes "as purchased."

Table 1.1   AMOUNTS OF FOOD **AS PURCHASED** TO SERVE 50 (continued)

Food	Weight or Measure	U.S. Serving Portion	U.S. Amount to Serve 50	Metric Serving Portion	Metric Amount to Serve 50	Miscellaneous Information
Turkey, ready to cook	lb	3 oz	35-40 lb	85 g	15.9-18.1 kg	1 lb (454 g) A.P. = 0.40 lb (170 g) cooked turkey meat exclusive of neck, giblets, and skin. For slicing use larger amount
Boneless turkey roast or roll	lb	3-4 oz	16-18 lb	85-114 g	7.3-8.2 kg	1 lb (454 g) A.P. = 0.70 lb (312 g) cooked turkey meat
Turkey roast or roll, cooked	lb	3-4 oz	12-15 lb	85-114 g	5.4-6.8 kg	1 lb (454 g) A.P. = 0.92 lb (425 g) turkey meat
VEGETABLES Canned	No. 10 can	2½-3 oz	2-3 cans	70-85 g	2-3 cans	
Dried Beans: kidney, lima, or navy	lb	4 oz	4-5 lb	114 g	1.81-2.27 kg	
Potatoes, sliced, dehydrated	lb	3-4 oz	2 lb	85-114 g	908 g	
Instant for mashing	lb	4 oz	2-2½ lb	114 g	0.91-1.14 kg	
Fresh[a] Asparagus	lb	3-4 oz	18-20 lb	85-114 g	8.16-9.08 kg	
Beans, green	lb	3 oz	10-12 lb	85 g	4.54-5.44 kg	

[a] As purchased amounts given should yield 50 portions cooked vegetables. To convert to ready-to-cook weight, see p. 67.

Food	Unit	Portion	Amount	Portion (metric)	Amount (metric)	Notes
Beans, lima	lb	3 oz	18-20 lb	85 g	8.16-9.08 kg	
Beets, topped	lb	3 oz	12-14 lb	85 g	5.44-6.35 kg	
Broccoli	lb	3 oz	16-20 lb	85 g	7.26-9.08 kg	
Brussels sprouts	lb	2½-3 oz	12-15 lb	70-85 g	5.44-6.80 kg	
Cabbage, wedges	lb	2½-3 oz	11-12 lb	70-85 g	4.99-5.44 kg	
Shredded for salad	lb	1-2 oz	5-8 lb	28-57 g	2.27-3.63 kg	
Carrots, topped	lb	3 oz	12½ lb	85 g	5.67 kg	
Carrot strips	lb	3 strips, 4 × ½-in.	2½ lb	3 strips	1.14 kg	
Cauliflower (cello pack)	lb	3 oz	18-20 lb	85 g	8.16-9.08 kg	
Celery, for relishes	lb	4 strips, 4 × ½-in.	4 lb	4 strips	1.81 kg	
Corn on cob	doz	1 ear	5 doz	1 ear	5 doz	Order 4-5 doz crate
Cucumber	lb	1½-2 oz	5-6 lb	43-57 g	2.27-2.72 kg	
Eggplant	lb	3 oz	12-15 lb	85 g	5.44-6.80 kg	
Lettuce, for wedges	head	1/6 head	8-10 heads	1/6 head	8-10 heads	
Head, garnish	head		4-5 heads		4-5 heads	
Leaf, garnish	lb	leaf	3-4 lb	leaf	1.36-1.81 kg	
Mushrooms, for sauce	lb	2 oz	3-4 lb	57 g	1.36-1.81 kg	
Onions, whole, to bake	lb	1 medium	12-15 lb	1 medium	5.44-6.80 kg	
Parsnips	lb	3-3½ oz	10-12 lb	85-100 g	4.54-5.44 kg	
Peas, green	lb	3 oz	20-25 lb	85 g	9.08-11.34 kg	
Potatoes, to bake	lb	1 potato	17-25 lb	1 potato	7.71-11.34 kg	2 or 3 per lb (454 g)
To mash	lb	4 oz	12-14 lb	114 g	5.44-6.35 kg	
To brown	lb	4 oz	15-20 lb	114 g	6.80-9.08 kg	

Table 1.1　AMOUNTS OF FOOD **AS PURCHASED** TO SERVE 50 (continued)

Food	Weight or Measure	U.S.		Metric		Miscellaneous Information
		Serving Portion	Amount to Serve 50	Serving Portion	Amount to Serve 50	
To cream or scallop	lb	5 oz	10 lb	142 g	4.54 kg	
Potato chips	lb	1 oz	3 lb	28 g	1.36 kg	
Potato, sweet, to bake	lb	4½-5 oz	20-25 lb	128-142 g	9.08-11.34 kg	
Radishes with tops	Bunch	2 each	10-12 bunches	2 each	10-12 bunches	
Spinach to cook, (cello bag)	lb	3 oz	10 lb	85 g	4.54 kg	
For salad	lb	1 oz	4-5 lb	28 g	1.81-2.27 kg	
Squash, to mash	lb	3 oz	18-20 lb	85 g	8.16-9.08 kg	
To bake	lb	4 oz	20-25 lb	114 g	9.08-11.34 kg	
Zucchini	lb	3 oz	8-10 lb	85 g	3.63-4.54 kg	
Tomato, to slice	lb	3 slices	10-12 lb	3 slices	4.54-5.44 kg	
Wedges	lb	3 oz	10 lb	85 g	4.54 kg	
Turnips, to dice or mash	lb	3 oz	15 lb	85 g	6.80 kg	Without tops
Frozen Asparagus, lima beans, Brussels sprouts, broccoli, cauliflower, or spinach	2½-lb pkg	3 oz	4 pkg (10 lb)	85 g	4.54 kg	

Green beans, corn, peas	2½-lb pkg	2½-3 oz	3-4 pkg (7½-10 lb)	70-85 g	3.40-4.54 kg	
Onions, chopped	12-oz pkg (340 g)					Contains approximately 3 c (720 mL) chopped onions
Potatoes, for French fried	2½-, 4½-, or 5-lb pkg	4 oz	12-13 lb	114 g	5.44-5.90 kg	6 5-lb (2.27 kg) pkg per case
MISCELLANEOUS						
Gelatin, flavored	24-oz pkg (680 g)	⅓ c	1 pkg	80 mL	1 pkg	1 pkg makes 1 pan 12 × 20 × 2 in., using 1 gal (3.79 L) liquid
Marshmallows	lb	3 (1¼ in.)	2-2½ lb	3	0.91-1.14 kg	
Nuts, mixed, for cups	lb	1½ T	1-1½ lb	23 mL	454-680 g	
Nondairy creamer	oz	1 t	3 oz	5 mL	85 g	3 oz (85 g) = 1½ c (360 mL)
Olives, green	qt	3-4 each	2 qt	3-4 each	1.89 L	88-90 per qt (0.95 L)
Olives, ripe	No. 1 tall	3 each	3 cans	3 each	3 cans	1½ qt (120-150 per qt)
Pecans, salted, for tea table	lb	1¼ T	1-1¼ lb	20 mL	454-567 g	
Pickles, dill	qt	1 pickle	2½ qt	1 pickle	2.37 L	
Sweet sliced	qt	1 oz	2¼ qt	28 g	2.13 L	
Pickle relish	qt	1 oz	2 qt	28 g	1.89 L	
Sweets						
Candies, small	lb	2 each	1 lb	2 each	454 g	
Honey	lb	2 T	5 lb	30 mL	2.27 kg	
Jam	lb	1 T	2¼ lb	15 mL	1.02 kg	
Jelly	lb	1-1½ T	2-3 lb	15-23 mL	0.91-1.36 kg	
Syrup	qt	¼ c	3 qt	60 mL	2.84 L	
Sugar, cubes	1-lb pkg	1-2 cubes	1½ lb	1-2 cubes	680 g	
Granulated	lb	1½ t	12 oz	8 mL	340 g	

Table 1.1 AMOUNTS OF FOOD **AS PURCHASED** TO SERVE 50 (continued)

Food	Weight or Measure	U.S. Serving Portion	Amount to Serve 50	Metric Serving Portion	Amount to Serve 50	Miscellaneous Information
Toppings for dessert	qt	2 T	1½ qt	30 mL	1.42 L	
Ice, for water glasses	lb	3-4 oz per glass	10-12 lb	85-114 g	4.54-5.44 kg	
For punch bowl	lb		10 lb		4.54 kg	

Table 1.2 AMOUNTS OF **PREPARED** FOODS TO SERVE 50 (AMOUNTS ARE APPROXIMATE)

Food	U.S.		Metric	
	Serving Unit	Quantity	Serving Unit	Quantity
BEVERAGES				
Cocoa, coffee, hot tea	6-oz teacup	2½ gal	180 mL	9.46 L
Lemonade	8-oz glass	2½-3 gal	240 mL	9.46-11.36 L
Iced tea	12-oz glass	3 gal	360 mL	11.36 L
Punch	3-, 4-, or 5-oz punch cup	1½-2½ gal[a]	90, 120, 150 mL	5.68-9.46 L
BREADS				
Bread, thin, for sandwiches	2 oz (2 slices)	7 lb bread	57 g	3.18 kg
Quick, loaf (brown, nut, orange)	2-3 slices	5 loaves 4 × 9 in.	2-3 slices	5 loaves
Rolls, breakfast	3 oz (1 roll)	4⅓-4½ doz	85 g	4⅓-4½ doz
Raised yeast	1½-2 rolls	6-9 doz	1½-2 rolls	6-9 doz
Coffee cake	2 oz (1 piece 2 × 2½ in.)	1 pan 12 × 20 in.	57 g	1 pan 12 × 20 in.
Corn bread	1 piece 2 × 2½ in.	1 pan 12 × 20 in.	57 g	1 pan 12 × 20 in.
Muffins	2 oz (2 muffins)	9 doz	57 g	9 doz
Biscuits	2-3 oz (2-3 biscuits)	9-12½ doz	57-85 g	9-12½ doz
Griddle cakes	3½ oz (2 cakes)	6½ qt batter	100 g	6.15 L batter
Waffles	3 oz (1 waffle)	6½ qt batter	85 g	6.15 L batter
Doughnuts, cake type	1½ oz (2 doughnuts)	9 doz	43 g	9 doz
Yeast type	1½ oz (2 doughnuts)	9 doz	43 g	9 doz
Toast, French	4 oz (2 slices)	7 lb bread	114 g	3.18 kg bread
Buttered or cinnamon	2 oz (2 slices)	7 lb bread	57 g	3.18 kg bread
CEREAL PRODUCTS, COOKED				
Farina, Cream of Wheat, hominy grits, macaroni, spaghetti, rolled oats, noodles, pettijohns, rice for cereal	5 oz (⅔ c)	2 gal	142 g (160 mL)	7.57 L

Table 1.2 AMOUNTS OF **PREPARED** FOODS TO SERVE 50
(AMOUNTS ARE APPROXIMATE) (continued)

Food	U.S.		Metric	
	Serving Unit	Quantity	Serving Unit	Quantity
Rice, as vegetable	4 oz (½ c)	6¼ qt	114 g (120 mL)	5.91 L
Corn meal	6 oz (¾ c)	2 gal	170 g (180 mL)	7.57 L
Bread stuffing	1–1½ oz	7¼ qt	28–43 g	6.86 L
DESSERTS				
Cake				
Layer, 2 (9 in.)	2½ oz	3 cakes	70 g	3–4 cakes
Pound or loaf	3 oz	4 loaves	85 g	4 loaves
Sheet cake	2½ oz	1 pan 12 × 20 in. (40-48 portions) 1 bun pan 18 × 26 in. (60 portions)	70 g	1 pan 12 × 20 in.
Fruit cake	2½ oz	8 lb (2 cakes)	70 g	3.63 kg
Cupcakes	1½ oz	4½ doz	43 g	4½ doz
Angel food cake, plain	1 oz	3–4 10-in. cakes	28 g	3–4 10-in. cakes
Cake frosting				
Layer cake, 2 (9 in.)	3 cakes	2¼–2½ qt	3 cakes	2.13–2.37 L
Sheet cake (12 × 20 in.)	1 cake	1–1½ qt	1 cake	0.95–1.42 L
Angel food (10 in.)	3 cakes	2–2½ qt	3 cakes	1.89–2.37 L
Cookies for tea	2–3	10–12 doz	2–3	10–12 doz
Fruit cup, fresh	3 oz (½ c)	6 qt	85 g	5.68 L
Pies (8 in.)	6 cuts per pie	8 pies	6 cuts per pie	8 pies
Filling for pies				
Fruit	3 c per pie	6 qt	720 mL per pie	5.68 L
Cream	3 c per pie	6 qt	720 mL per pie	5.68 L
Custard or pumpkin	3 c per pie	6 qt	720 mL per pie	5.68 L
Pastry for pies				
For 2-crust pie	9 oz per pie	4 lb 8 oz	255 g per pie	2.04 kg
For 1-crust pie	5 oz per pie	2 lb 8 oz	142 g per pie	1.14 kg

Food				
Meringue for pies	3 oz per pie	1½ lb	85 g per pie	680 g
Puddings				
Cornstarch or tapioca	½ c (No. 10 dipper)	6¼ qt	120 mL	5.91 L
Gelatin dessert	½ c	6¼ qt	120 mL	5.91 L
Whips, fruit	½ c	6¼ qt	120 mL	5.91 L
Steamed pudding	2½ oz (No. 16 dipper)	4½ qt	70 g	4.26 L
Baked pudding	3 oz	1 pan 12 × 20 in.	85 g	1 pan 12 × 20 in.
ENTREES				
Baked casseroles	½ c	2 pans 12 × 20 × 2 in.	120 mL	2 pans 12 × 20 × 2 in.
Chicken, cubed	1½-2 oz	5-6 lb (3¾-4½ qt)	43-57 g	2.27-2.72 kg
Chicken or ham, creamed	½-⅔ c	6½-8½ qt	120-160 mL	6.15-8.05 L
Chili	1 c	3¼ gal	240 mL	12.30 L
Creamed eggs and other foods	½ c	6½ qt	120 mL	6.15 L
Ham, boiled, sliced	3 oz	9½ lb	85 g	4.31 kg
Meat loaf	4 oz	5 loaves (4 × 9 in.)	114 g	5 loaves
Beef stew	⅔ c	3 gal	160 mL	11.36 L
Roast beef, boneless	3 oz	9 lb	85 g	4.08 kg
SALADS AND SALAD DRESSINGS				
Salads				
Bulky vegetable	½-⅔ c	2 gal	120-160 mL	7.57 L
Fish or meat	⅔ c	2 gal	160 mL	7.57 L
Fruit	⅓ c	4¼ qt	80 mL	4.02 L
Gelatin, liquid	½ c	6¼ qt	120 mL	5.91 L
Potato	½ c	6¼ qt	120 mL	5.91 L
Dressings mixed in salad				
French, thin	2 t	3 c	10 mL	720 mL
Mayonnaise	1 T	1 qt	15 mL	0.95 L
Dressings for self-service				
French, thin	2 t	1 qt	10 mL	0.95 L
Mayonnaise	1 T	1 qt	15 mL	0.95 L
Thousand Island or Roquefort	1 T	1-1¼ qt	15 mL	0.95-1.18 L

Table 1.2 AMOUNTS OF **PREPARED** FOODS TO SERVE 50 (AMOUNTS ARE APPROXIMATE) (continued)

| Food | U.S. | | Metric | |
	Serving Unit	Quantity	Serving Unit	Quantity
SAUCES				
Gravy	3-4 T	3-4 qt	45-60 mL	2.84-3.79 L
Sauce, meat accompaniment	2 T	2 qt	30 mL	1.89 L
Pudding sauce	2-3 T	2-3 qt	30-45 mL	1.89-2.84 L
Vegetable sauce	2-3 T	2-3 qt	30-45 mL	1.89-2.84 L
Frozen strawberries for sundaes	½-⅔ c	15 lb	120-160 mL	6.80 kg
Fresh strawberries for sundaes or shortcake	½-⅔ c	6-7 qt	120-160 mL	5.68-6.62 L
SOUPS				
Soup, first course	⅔ c	2 gal	160 mL	7.57 L
Soup, main course	1 c	3¼ gal	240 mL	12.30 L
VEGETABLES				
Buttered	½ c	6 qt	120 mL	5.68 L
Creamed, diced	½ c	6 qt	120 mL	5.68 L
Kidney and other dry beans	½-¾ c	6¼-9½ qt	120-180 mL	5.91-9.02 L
Potatoes, mashed	½ c	6¼ qt	120 mL	5.91 L
Creamed	½ c	6¼ qt	120 mL	5.91 L
Chips	¾-1 oz	2½-3 lb	21-28 g	1.14-1.36 kg
French fried	4-5 oz	12-15 lb	114-142 g	5.44-6.80 kg

[a] 1 gal yields 30-35 4-oz (½-c) servings. 2½ gal would provide 50 servings plus 30 refills.

Tables of Weights and Measures

Table 1.3   WEIGHTS, MEASURES, AND THEIR ABBREVIATIONS

Abbreviations		Equivalent
f.d.	few drops	
f.g.	few grains	
fl oz	fluid ounces	
t	teaspoon	5 mL = 1 t
T	tablespoon	3 t = 1 T
c	cup	16 T = 1 c = 8 fl oz
pt	pint	2 c = 1 pt = 16 fl oz
qt	quart	2 pt = 1 qt = 32 fl oz
gal	gallon	4 qt = 1 gal = 128 fl oz
oz	ounce	28.35 g = 1 oz (2 T fluid)
lb	pound	16 oz = 1 lb or 453.6 g
pk	peck	8 qt = 1 pk
bu	bushel	4 pk = 1 bu
mL	milliliter	
L	liter	1 L = 1000 mL or 1.06 qt
g	gram	
kg	kilogram	2.2 lb = 1 kg

Table 1.4 U.S. MEASURES OF WEIGHT AND METRIC
EQUIVALENTS[a]

Ounces	Grams[b]	Pounds + Ounces		Grams	Pounds + Ounces		Kilograms
1	28	1		454	2	4	1.02
1½	43	1	1	482	2	8	1.14
2	57	1	2	510	2	12	1.25
2½	70	1	3	539	3		1.36
3	85	1	4	567	3	4	1.47
3½	100	1	5	595	3	8	1.59
4 (¼ lb)	114	1	6	624	3	12	1.70
5	142	1	7	652	4		1.81
6	170	1	8	680	4	4	1.93
7	198	1	9	709	4	8	2.04
8 (½ lb)	227	1	10	737	4	12	2.15
9	255	1	11	765	5		2.27
10	284	1	12	794	6		2.72
11	312	1	13	822	7		3.18
12 (¾ lb)	340	1	14	851	8		3.63
13	369	1	15	879	9		4.08
14	397	2		908	10		4.54
15	425				11		4.99
16 (1 lb)	454				12		5.44

[a] Basic figures used to calculate metric weights are: 1 oz = 28.35 g;
1 lb = 453.59 g. Resulting figures were rounded to nearest gram and
to 2 decimals for kilograms.
[b] To change grams to kilograms, move decimal 3 places to left;
e.g., 28 g = 0.028 kg.

Table 1.5 U.S. MEASURES OF VOLUME AND METRIC EQUIVALENTS[a]

Cups		Quarts	Milliliters	Quarts	Gallons	Liters
	(1 t)		5	1	¼	0.95
	(1 T)		15	1¼		1.18
¼	(4 T)		60	1½		1.42
⅓			80	1¾		1.66
½	(8 T)		120	2	½	1.89
⅔			160	2¼		2.13
¾	(12 T)		180	2½		2.37
1	(16 T)	¼	240	2¾		2.60
1¼			300	3	¾	2.84
1⅓			320	3¼		3.07
1½			360	3½		3.31
1⅔			400	3¾		3.55
1¾			420	4	1	3.79
2		½	480	5	1¼	4.73
2¼			540	6	1½	5.68
2½			600	7	1¾	6.62
2¾			660	8	2	7.57
3			720	9	2¼	8.52
3¼			780	10	2½	9.46
3½			840	11	2¾	10.41
3¾			900	12	3	11.36
4		1	950			

[a] Basic figures used to calculate metric volume are: 1 T = 14.8 mL rounded to 15 mL; 1 c = 237 mL rounded to 240 mL; 1 qt = 0.95 L (4 × 237 mL divided by 1000).

Table 1.6 FOOD WEIGHTS AND APPROXIMATE EQUIVALENTS IN MEASURE

Food	U.S. Weight	U.S. Approximate Measure	Metric Weight	Metric Approximate Measure
Allspice	1 oz	4½ T.	28 g	68 mL
Almonds, blanched	1 lb	3 c	454 g	720 mL
Apples, A.P.[a]	1 lb	3-4 medium	454 g	3-4 medium
Apples, A.P.	1½ lb	1 qt sliced	680 g	0.95 L
Apples, diced, ½-in. cubes, peeled	1 lb	4½ c	454 g	1.08 L
Applesauce	1 lb	2 c	454 g	480 mL
Apples, canned, pie pack	1½ lb	1 qt	680 g	0.95 L
Apricots, dried, A.P.	1 lb	3 c	454 g	720 mL
Apricots, dried, cooked, no juice	1 lb	4½-5 c	454 g	1.08-1.18 L
Apricots, fresh	1 lb	5-8 apricots	454 g	5-8 apricots
Apricots, canned, halves, without juice	1 lb	2 c or 12-20 halves	454 g	480 mL
Apricots, pie pack	1 lb	1¾ c	454 g	420 mL
Asparagus, fresh	1 lb	16-20 stalks	454 g	16-20 stalks
Asparagus, canned tips, drained	1 lb	17-19 stalks	454 g	17-19 stalks
Asparagus, canned, cuts, drained	1 lb	2½ c	454 g	600 mL
Avocado	1 lb	2 medium	454 g	2 medium
Bacon, raw	1 lb	15-25 slices	454 g	15-25 slices
Bacon, cooked	1 lb	85-95 slices	454 g	85-95 slices
Baking powder	1 oz	2 T	28 g	30 mL
Baking powder	1 lb	2 c	454 g	480 mL
Bananas, A.P.	1 lb	3 medium	454 g	3 medium
Bananas, diced	1 lb	2-2½ c	454 g	480-600 mL
Barley, pearl	1 lb	2 c	454 g	480 mL
Beans, baked	1 lb	2 c	454 g	480 mL
Beans, dried, Lima, A.P.	1 lb	2½ c	454 g	600 mL
Beans, dried, Lima, 1 lb, A.P., after cooking	2 lb 9 oz	6 c	1.16 kg	1.42 L

[a] A.P. denotes "as purchased."

Beans, Lima, fresh or canned	1 lb	2 c	454 g	480 mL
Beans, kidney, A.P.	1 lb	2⅔ c	454 g	640 mL
Beans, kidney, 1 lb, A.P., after cooking	2 lb 6 oz	6-7 c	1.08 kg	1.42-1.66 L
Beans, navy, A.P.	1 lb	2⅓ c	454 g	560 mL
Beans, navy, 1 lb, A.P., after cooking	2 lb 3 oz	5½-6 c	992 g	1.32-1.42 L
Beans, snap, cut, cooked, without juice	1 lb	3½ c	454 g	840 mL
Bean sprouts	1 lb	1 qt	454 g	0.95 L
Beef, dried, solid pack	1 lb	1 qt	454 g	0.95 L
Beef, ground, raw	1 lb	2 c	454 g	480 mL
Beef, cooked, diced	1 lb	3 c	454 g	720 mL
Beets, medium	1 lb	3-4 beets	454 g	3-4 beets
Beets, cooked, diced	1 lb	2½-2¾ c	454 g	600-660 mL
Beets, cooked, sliced	1 lb	2½ c	454 g	600 mL
Blackberries, fresh	1 lb	2-2½ c	454 g	480-600 mL
Blackberries, pie pack	1 lb	2½ c	454 g	600 mL
Bran, dry	1 lb	2 qt	454 g	1.89 L
Bran, all bran	8 oz	1 qt	227 g	0.95 L
Bran, flakes	1 lb	3 qt	454 g	2.84 L
Bread, loaf	1 lb	18 slices, ½ in. each	454 g	18 slices
Bread, sandwich	2 lb	36-40 slices, thin	908 g	36-40 slices
Bread, soft, broken	1 lb	2½ qt	454 g	2.37 L
Bread, dry, broken	1 lb	8-9 c	454 g	1.89-2.13 L
Bread, fresh	2 lb	1 lb dry crumbs	908 g	454 g dry crumbs
Bread crumbs, dry, ground	1 lb	4 c	454 g	0.95 L
Bread crumbs, soft	1 lb	2 qt	454 g	1.89 L
Brussels sprouts, A.P. [a]	1 lb	1 qt	454 g	0.95 L
Butter	1 lb	2 c	454 g	480 mL
Cabbage, shredded, E.P. [b] (raw)	1 lb	1 qt lightly packed	454 g	0.95 L
Cabbage, A.P., shredded, cooked	1 lb	1½ c	454 g	360 mL
Cake crumbs, soft	1 lb	6 c	454 g	1.42 L

[a] A.P. denotes "as purchased."
[b] E.P. denotes "edible portion."

Table 1.6 FOOD WEIGHTS AND APPROXIMATE EQUIVALENTS IN MEASURE (continued)

Food	U.S. Weight	U.S. Approximate Measure	Weight	Metric Approximate Measure
Cantaloupe	18 oz	1 melon, 4½ in. diameter	510 g	1 melon 4½ in.
Carrots, diced	1 lb	3-3¼ c	454 g	720-780 mL
Carrots, ground, raw, E.P.	1 lb	3 c	454 g	720 mL
Carrots, diced, cooked	1 lb	3 c	454 g	720 mL
Carrots	1 lb	4-5 medium	454 g	4-5 medium
Cauliflower, head	12 oz	1 small	340 g	1 small
Celery cabbage, shredded	1 lb	6 c	454 g	1.42 L
Celery, diced, E.P.	1 lb	1 qt	454 g	0.95 L
Celery, diced (depending on size)	1-2 bunches	1 qt	1-2 bunches	0.95 L
Celery seed	1 oz	4 T	28 g	60 mL
Cheese, cottage	1 lb	2 c	454 g	480 mL
Cheese, grated or ground	1 lb	1 qt	454 g	0.95 L
Cheese, Philadelphia cream	1 lb	2 c	454 g	480 mL
Cherries, red, pie pack, without juice	1 lb	3 c (scant)	454 g	720 mL
Cherries, glacé	1 lb	96 cherries or 2½ c	454 g	600 mL
Cherries, Royal Anne, drained	1 lb	2¼ c	454 g	540 mL
Chicken, ready-to-cook	4-4½ lb	1 qt cooked, diced	1.81-2.04 kg	0.95 L
Chicken, cooked, cubed	1 lb	3 c	454 g	720 mL
Chili powder	1 oz	4 T	28 g	60 mL
Chili sauce	14 oz	1¼ c	397 g	300 mL
Chocolate	1 lb	16 squares	454 g	16 squares
Chocolate bits	6 oz	1 c	170 g	240 mL

Chocolate, grated	1 lb	3½ c	840 mL
Chocolate, melted	1 lb	2 c (scant)	480 mL
Chocolate wafers	8 oz	2 c crumbs	480 mL
Cinnamon, ground	1 oz	4 T	60 mL
Cinnamon, ground	1 lb	4 c	0.95 L
Cinnamon, stick	¾ oz	4 sticks, 5 in. long	4 sticks
Citron, dried, chopped	1 lb	2½ c	600 mL
Cloves, ground	1 oz	5 T	75 mL
Cloves, whole	3 oz	1 c	240 mL
Cocoa	1 lb	4 c	0.95 L
Coconut, prepared, shredded	1 lb	6-7 c	1.42-1.66 L
Coconut, moist, canned	1 lb	5⅓ c	1.27 L
Coffee, ground coarse	1 lb	5-5½ c	1.18-1.30 L
Coffee, instant	1 oz	½ c	120 mL
Coffee, pulverized	1 lb	5 c	1.18 L
Corn, canned	1 lb	1¾-2 c	420-480 mL
Cornflakes	1 lb	4 qt	3.79 L
Corn meal, coarse	1 lb	3 c	720 mL
Corn meal, after cooking	1 lb	3 qt	2.84 L
Corn syrup	1 lb	1⅓ c	320 mL
Cornstarch	1 oz	3½ T	53 mL
Cornstarch	1 lb	3½ c	840 mL
Crabmeat, flaked	1 lb	3½ c	840 mL
Crab in shell	2 lb	1 c cooked meat	240 mL
Crackers, graham	1 lb	58-66 crackers	58-66 crackers
Crackers, 2⅝ in. × 2⅝ in.	12 oz	50 crackers	50 crackers
Crackers, 2 × 2 in.	1 lb	140-150 crackers	140-150 crackers
Cracker crumbs, medium fine	1 lb	5-6 c	1.18-1.42 L
Cranberries, raw	1 lb	1 qt	0.95 L
Cranberries, cooked	1 lb	1 qt	0.95 L
Cranberries, sauce, jellied	1 lb	2 c	480 mL
Cranberries, dehydrated, sliced	1 lb	8½ c	2.01 L
Cream of tartar	1 oz	3 T	45 mL

Table 1.6 FOOD WEIGHTS AND APPROXIMATE EQUIVALENTS IN MEASURE (continued)

Food	U.S.		Metric	
	Weight	Approximate Measure	Weight	Approximate Measure
Cream of Wheat, A.P. [a]	1 lb	2⅔ c	454 g	640 mL
Cream, cultured sour	1 lb	2 c	454 g	480 mL
Cream, whipping [b]	1 pt	1 qt whipped	475 mL	0.95 L whipped
Cucumbers, diced, E.P. [c]	1 lb	3 c	454 g	720 mL
Currants, dried	1 lb	3 c	454 g	720 mL
Curry powder	1 oz	4 T	28 g	60 mL
Dates, pitted	1 lb	2½ c	454 g	600 mL
Eggplant	1 lb	8 slices 4 × ½ in.	454 g	8 slices
Eggs, whole, A.P.	1 lb	8-9 eggs	454 g	8-9 eggs
Eggs, whole, [d] fresh or frozen	1 lb	2 c (9-11 eggs)	454 g	480 mL
Eggs, whites, fresh or frozen	1 lb	2 c (17-20 eggs)	454 g	480 mL
Eggs, yolks, fresh or frozen	1 lb	2 c (19-22 eggs)	454 g	480 mL
Eggs, hard cooked, chopped	1½ lb	1 qt	680 g	0.95 L
Eggs, dried	1 lb	4 c	454 g	0.95 L
Eggs, frozen, whole	1 lb	2 c (10 eggs)	454 g	480 mL
Eggs, whites, dried	1 lb	5 c	454 g	1.18 L
Eggs, yolks, dried	1 lb	5⅔ c	454 g	1.34 L
Farina, cooked	6 oz	¾ c	170 g	180 mL
Farina, A.P.	1 lb	3 c	454 g	720 mL
Farina, 1 lb, A.P., after cooking	8 lb	3¾ qt	3.63 kg	3.55 L
Figs, dry, cut fine	1 lb	2½ c	454 g	600 mL
Flour, all-purpose	1 lb	4 c	454 g	0.95 L
Flour, white, bread, unsifted	1 lb	3½ c (scant)	454 g	840 mL

[a] A.P. denotes "as purchased."
[b] Volume approximately doubles when whipped.
[c] E.P. denotes "edible portion."
[d] One case (30 doz) eggs weighs approximately 41 to 43 lb (1.86 to 19.5 kg) and yields approximately 35 lb (15.9 kg) liquid whole eggs.

Flour, white, bread, sifted	1 lb	4 c	0.95 L
Flour, cake or pastry, sifted	1 lb	4¾ c	1.14 L
Flour, whole wheat	1 lb	3¾ c	900 mL
Flour, rye	1 lb	5 c	1.18 L
Flour, soya, low fat	1 lb	5 c	1.18 L
Gelatin, granulated	1 oz	4 T	60 mL
Gelatin, granulated	1 lb	3 c	720 mL
Gelatin, prepared, flavored	1 lb	2⅓ c	560 mL
Ginger, ground	1 oz	5 T	75 mL
Ginger, ground	1 lb	5 c	1.18 L
Ginger, candied	1 oz	1 piece 2 × 2 × ⅜ in.	1 piece 2 × 2 × ⅜ in.
Grapefruit, medium	1 lb	1 grapefruit, 10-12 sections	1 grapefruit
Grapefruit, medium		⅔ c juice	160 mL juice
Grapefruit sections, size 36		1 gal, 238 sections	3.79 L, 238 sections
Grapenuts	1 lb	4 c	0.95 L
Grapes, cut, seeded, E.P. [a]	1 lb	2¾ c	660 mL
Grapes, on stem	1 lb	1 qt	0.95 L
Ham, cooked, diced	1 lb	3 c (+)	720 mL
Ham, cooked, ground	1 lb	2 c	480 mL
Ham, 1 lb, A.P., [b] after cooking	8 oz	1 c cooked	240 mL cooked
Hominy, coarse	1 lb	2½ c	600 mL
Hominy grits, raw	1 lb	3 c	720 mL
Hominy grits, 1 lb (454 g), A.P., after cooking	6½ lb	3¼ qt	3.07 L
Honey	1 lb	1⅓ c	320 mL
Horseradish	1 oz	2 T	30 mL
Jam	1 lb	1⅓ c	320 mL
Jelly	1 lb	1½ c	360 mL
Krumbles	1 lb	16 c	3.79 L
Lard	1 lb	2 c	480 mL
Lemons, size 165	1 lb	4-5 lemons	4-5 lemons
Lemons, large		6 = 1 c juice	6 = 240 mL juice

[a] E.P. denotes "edible portion."
[b] A.P. denotes "as purchased."

Table 1.6 FOOD WEIGHTS AND APPROXIMATE EQUIVALENTS IN MEASURE (continued)

Food	U.S. Weight	U.S. Approximate Measure	Metric Weight	Metric Approximate Measure
Lemons, large		1 = 3 T grated peel		1 = 45 mL grated peel
Lemon juice	1 lb	2 c (8-10 lemons)	454 g	480 mL
Lettuce, average head	9 oz	1 head	255 g	1 head
Lettuce, shredded	1 lb	6-8 c	454 g	1.42-1.89 L
Lettuce, leaf	1 lb	25-30 salad garnishes	454 g	25-30 garnishes
Macaroni, 1-in. pieces, A.P.[a]	1 lb	4 c	454 g	0.95 L
Macaroni, 1 lb, after cooking	4 lb	2¼ qt	1.81 kg	2.13 L
Macaroni, cooked	1 lb	2½ c	454 g	600 mL
Margarine	1 lb	2 c	454 g	480 mL
Marshmallows (1¼ in.)	1 lb	80	454 g	80
Marshmallows, miniature	1 lb	9 c	454 g	2.13 L
10 miniature = 1 regular				
Mayonnaise	1 lb	2 c (scant)	454 g	480 mL (scant)
Meat, chopped, cooked	1 lb	2 c	454 g	480 mL
Milk, fluid, whole	1 lb 1 oz	2 c	482 g	480 mL
Milk, sweetened condensed	1 lb	1½ c	454 g	360 mL
Milk, evaporated	1 lb	1¾ c	454 g	420 mL
Milk, evaporated, tall can	14½ oz	1⅔ c	412 g	400 mL
Milk, nonfat, dry	1 lb	4 c	454 g	0.95 L
Milk, nonfat, dry	1 oz	4 T	28 g	60 mL
Mincemeat	1 lb	2 c	454 g	480 mL
Molasses	1 lb	1⅓ c	454 g	320 mL
Mushrooms, fresh	1 lb	6¾ c	454 g	1.60 L
Mushrooms, fresh, 1 lb, A.P., after sautéing		1½ c	454 g	360 mL
Mushrooms, canned	1 lb	2 c	454 g	480 mL
Mustard, ground, dry	1 lb	4½ c	454 g	1.08 L

[a] A.P. denotes "as purchased."

Item				
Mustard, prepared	1 oz	4 T	28 g	60 mL
Mustard seed	1 oz	2½ T	28 g	37 mL
Noodles, dry, A.P.	1 lb	6 c	454 g	1.42 L
Noodles, 1 lb, A.P., after cooking	3 lb	2¼ qt	1.36 kg	2.13 L
Nutmeats	1 lb	3½ c	454 g	840 mL
Nutmeg, ground	1 oz	3½ T	28 g	53 mL
Oats, rolled, A.P. (quick)	1 lb	6 c	454 g	1.42 L
Oats, rolled, 1 lb, A.P. (quick), after cooking	2½ lb	4 qt	1.14 kg	3.79 L
Oil, vegetable	1 lb	2-2⅛ c	454 g	480-510 mL
Olives, green, small size 180-200, 1 qt		109-116 olives		109-116 olives per L
Olives, ripe, small size 120-150, 1 qt		152 olives		152 olives per L
Olives, A.P. [a]	4½ lb	3 c chopped	2.04 kg	720 mL chopped
Onions, A.P.	1 lb	4-5 medium	454 g	4-5 medium
Onions, chopped	1 lb	2-3 c	454 g	480-720 mL
Onions, dehydrated, chopped	1 lb	7½ c	454 g	1.80 L
Onions, dehydrated, chopped, 1 lb, A.P., after cooking	4½-5 lb	7½-11 c[b]	2.04-2.27 kg	1.80-2.60 L
Onions, dehydrated, sliced	1 lb	12 c	454 g	2.84 L
Onions, dehydrated, sliced, 1 lb, A.P., after cooking	4 lb 6 oz-5 lb	12-18 c[b]	1.98-2.27 kg	2.84-4.26 L
Onions, dehydrated, 2 No. 10 cans	3½ lb	50 lb raw (equivalent)	1.59 kg	22.68 kg raw (equivalent)
Oranges, size 72	1 lb	2	454 g	2
Oranges, diced with juice (size 150)	3 lb	1 qt	1.36 kg	0.95 L
Oranges, medium		2-4 = 1 c juice 2 = 1 c bite-size pieces 1 = 10-11 sections 1 = 4 T grated peel		2-4 = 240 mL juice 2 = 240 mL bite-size pieces

[a] A.P. denotes "as purchased."

[b] Two-hr rehydration gives 10% more volume than 30 min; overnight rehydration, 10% more volume than 2 hr.

Table 1.6 FOOD WEIGHTS AND APPROXIMATE EQUIVALENTS IN MEASURE (continued)

Food	U.S. Weight	U.S. Approximate Measure	Metric Weight	Metric Approximate Measure
Orange juice, frozen	6 oz	2¼ c reconstituted	170 g	540 mL
Orange juice, frozen	32 oz	3 qt reconstituted	908 g	2.84 L
Oysters, 1 qt	2 lb	40 large, 60 small	908 g	40 large, 60 small
Paprika	1 oz	4 T	28 g	60 mL
Parsley, coarsely chopped	1 oz	1 c	28 g	240 mL
Parsnips, A.P.	1 lb	4	454 g	4
Peanuts, E.P. [b]	1 lb	3¼ c	454 g	780 mL
Peanut butter	1 lb	1¾ c	454 g	420 mL
Peaches, medium, A.P.	1 lb	4	454 g	4
Peaches, canned, sliced, drained	1 lb	2 c	454 g	480 mL
Peas, A.P., in pod	1 lb	1 c shelled	454 g	240 mL shelled
Peas, canned, drained	1¼ lb	2-2½ c	567 g	480-600 mL
Peas, dried, split	1 lb	2⅓ c	454 g	560 mL
Peas, 1 lb, dried, after cooking	2½ lb	5½ c	1.14 kg	1.32 L
Pears, fresh, A.P.	1 lb	3-4	454 g	3-4
Pears, canned, drained, diced	1 lb	2½ c	454 g	600 mL
Pears, halves, large, drained	1 lb 14 oz	1 qt (9 halves)	850 g	0.95 L (9 halves)
Pecans	1 lb E.P. [b]	3¾ c	454 g	900 mL
Peppers, green	1 lb	7-9 medium	454 g	7-9 medium
Peppers, green, chopped	1 lb	3 c	454 g	720 mL
Pepper, ground	1 oz	4 T	28 g	60 mL
Pepper, ground	1 lb	4 c	454 g	0.95 L
Pickles, chopped	1 lb	3 c	454 g	720 mL
Pickles, halves, 3 in.	1 lb	3 c or 36 halves	454 g	720 mL or 36 halves
Pimiento, chopped	1 lb	2½ c	454 g	600 mL
Pineapple, canned tidbits	1 lb	2 c	454 g	480 mL

[b] E.P. denotes "edible portion."

Pineapple, fresh	2 lb	1 pineapple, 2-3 c	908 g	480-720 mL
Pineapple, canned, slices, drained	1 lb	8-12 slices	454 g	8-12 slices
Poppy seed	5 oz	1 c	142 g	240 mL
Potatoes, white, medium, A.P.[a]	1 lb	3	454 g	3
Potatoes, 2 lb, A.P., after cooking (diced and creamed or mashed)		1 qt		0.95 L
Potatoes, sweet	1 lb	3 medium	454 g	3 medium
Potato chips	1 lb	4-5 qt	454 g	3.79-4.73 L
Potato chips	¾-1 oz	1 serving	21-28 g	1 serving
Prunes, dried, A.P., size 30 to 40	1 lb	2½ c	454 g	600 mL
Prunes, dried, 1 lb, A.P., after cooking	2 lb	3-4 c	908 g	720-950 mL
Prunes, cooked, pitted	1 lb	3¼ c	454 g	780 mL
Pumpkin, cooked	1 lb	2½ c	454 g	600 mL
Raisins, A.P.	1 lb	3 c	454 g	720 mL
Raisins, 1 lb, A.P., after cooking	1 lb 12 oz	1 qt	794 g	0.95 L
Raspberries, A.P.	1 lb	3⅜ c	454 g	810 mL
Rhubarb, raw, 1-in. pieces	1 lb	4 c	454 g	0.95 L
Rhubarb, 1 lb, E.P., after cooking	1 lb	2½ c	454 g	600 mL
Rice, A.P.	1 lb	2 c	454 g	480 mL
Rice, 1 lb, A.P., after cooking	4-4½ lb	2 qt	1.81-2.04 kg	1.89 L
Rice, puffed	1 oz	1⅔ c	28 g	400 mL
Rutabagas, raw, cubed, E.P.	1 lb	3⅓ c	454 g	800 mL
Sage, finely ground	1 lb	8 c	454 g	1.89 L
Sage, finely ground	1 oz	½ c	28 g	120 mL
Salad dressing, cooked	1 lb	2 c	454 g	480 mL
Salmon, canned	1 lb	2 c	454 g	480 mL
Salt	1 oz	1½ T	28 g	23 mL
Sardines, canned	1 lb	48, 3 in. long	454 g	48, 3 in. long

[a] A.P. denotes "as purchased."

Table 1.6 FOOD WEIGHTS AND APPROXIMATE EQUIVALENTS IN MEASURE (continued)

Food	U.S.		Metric	
	Weight	Approximate Measure	Weight	Approximate Measure
Sausage, link, small	1 lb	16-17	454 g	16-17
Sauerkraut	1 lb	3 c packed	454 g	720 mL
Sesame seed	1 oz	3 T	28 g	45 mL
Shortening, hydrogenated fats	1 lb	2¼ c	454 g	540 mL
Shrimp, small, cleaned	1 lb	3¼ c	454 g	780 mL
Soda	1 oz	2⅓ T	28 g	33 mL
Soybeans	1 lb	2¼ c	454 g	540 mL
Spaghetti, 2-in. pieces	1 lb	5 c	454 g	1.18 L
Spaghetti, 1 lb, A.P.,[a] cooked	4 lb	2½ qt	1.81 kg	2.37 L
Spinach, raw	1 lb	5 qt (lightly packed)	454 g	4.73 L
Spinach, 1 lb raw, E.P.,[b] after cooking	13 oz	2¾ c	369 g	660 mL
Spinach, canned	1 lb	2 c	454 g	480 mL
Squash, summer, A.P.	2 lb	1 squash, 5-in. diameter	908 g	1 squash, 5 in. diameter
Squash, Hubbard, cooked	1 lb	2 c	454 g	480 mL
Starch, waxy maize	1 oz	3 T	28 g	45 mL
Strawberries, A.P.	1 lb	2¼ c	454 g	540 mL
Suet, ground	1 lb	3¾ c	454 g	900 mL
Sugar, brown, light pack	1 lb	3 c	454 g	720 mL
Sugar, brown, solid pack	1 lb	2 c	454 g	480 mL
Sugar, cubes	1 lb	96 cubes	454 g	96 cubes
Sugar, granulated	1 lb	2-2⅛ c	454 g	480-510 mL
Sugar, powdered, XXXX sifted	1 lb	3 c	454 g	720 mL
Sweetbreads, 5 lb (2.27 kg), A.P.	1 lb	1¾ qt cooked	454 g	1.66 L

[a] A.P. denotes "as purchased."
[b] E.P. denotes "edible portion."

Tapioca, quick cooking	1 lb	3 c	454 g	720 mL
Tapioca, pearl	1 lb	2¾ c	454 g	660 mL
Tapioca, 1 lb (454 g), after cooking		7½ c		1.78 L
Tea	1 lb	6 c	454 g	1.42 L
Tea, instant	1 oz	½ c	28 g	120 mL
Tomatoes, canned	1 lb	2 c	454 g	480 mL
Tomatoes, fresh	1 lb	3-4 medium	454 g	3-4 medium
Tomatoes, fresh, diced	1 lb	2¼ c	454 g	540 mL
Tomatoes, dehydrated, flaked	1 lb	2¾ c	454 g	660 mL
Tomatoes, dehydrated, flaked, 1 lb (454 g) A.P.,[a] after reconstituting (1 gal/3.79 L)		11 c	454 g	2.60 L
Turkey, A.P., dressed weight	14 lb	11-12 c diced, cooked meat	6.35 kg	2.60-2.84 L cooked meat
Turnips, A.P.	1 lb	2-3	454 g	2-3
Tuna	1 lb	2 c	454 g	480 mL
Vanilla	½ oz	1 T	14 g	15 mL
Vinegar	1 lb	2 c	454 g	480 mL
Walnuts, English, 1 lb, E.P.[b]	1 lb	4 c	454 g	0.95 L
Watercress	1 lb	5 bunches	454 g	5 bunches
Watermelon	1 lb	1-in. slice, 6-in. diameter	454 g	1-in. slice, 6-in. diameter
Wheat, puffed	1 lb	32 c	454 g	7.57 L
Wheat, rolled	1 lb	4¾ c	454 g	1.14 L
Wheat, shredded	1 lb	15-16 biscuits	454 g	15-16 biscuits
Yeast, compressed	3/5 oz	1 cake	17 g	1 cake
Yeast, dry	¼ oz	1 envelope	7 g	1 envelope
Yeast, dry		1 oz = 2 oz compressed yeast		
Yeast, dry		1 small pkg = 1 pkg compressed yeast		

[a] A.P. denotes "as purchased."
[b] E.P. denotes "edible portion."

Table 1.7 WEIGHT (1-16 oz) AND MEASURE EQUIVALENTS FOR COMMONLY USED FOODS

Food Item	1 oz	2 oz	3 oz	4 oz	5 oz	6 oz	7 oz	8 oz
Baking powder	2 T	¼ c	⅓ c + 2 t	½ c	½ c + 2 T	¾ c	¾ c + 2 T	1 c
Bread crumbs, dry	¼ c	½ c	¾ c	1 c	1¼ c	1½ c	1¾ c	2 c
Butter or margarine	2 T	¼ c	⅓ c + 2 t	½ c	½ c + 2 T	¾ c	¾ c + 2 T	1 c
Celery, chopped	¼ c	½ c	¾ c	1 c	1¼ c	1½ c	1¾ c	2 c
Cornstarch	3½ T	⅓ c + 2 T	⅔ c	¾ c + 2 T	1 c + 2 T	1¼ c + 1 T	1½ c + 1 T	1¾ c
Eggs, whole, whites or yolks, fresh or frozen	2 T	¼ c	⅓ c + 2 t	½ c	½ c + 2 T	¾ c	¾ c + 2 T	1 c
Eggs, dried	¼ c	½ c	¾ c	1 c	1¼ c	1½ c	1¾ c	2 c
Flour, all purpose	¼ c	½ c	¾ c	1 c	1¼ c	1½ c	1¾ c	2 c
Flour, cake	¼ c + 1 T	½ c + 2 T	¾ c + 2 T	1 c + 3 T	1½ c	1¾ c + 1 T	2 c + 1 T	2½ c
Gelatin, granulated	3 T	⅓ c + 2 t	½ c + 1 T	¾ c	¾ c + 3 T	1 c + 2 T	1¼ c + 1 T	1½ c
Gelatin, flavored	2 T + 1 t	¼ c + 2 t	⅓ c + 2 T	½ c + 1 T	⅔ c + 1 T	¾ c + 2 T	1 c	1 c + 3 T
Milk, nonfat dry	¼ c	½ c	¾ c	1 c	1¼ c	1½ c	1¾ c	2 c
Onion, chopped	2 T	¼ c	⅓ c + 2 t	½ c	½ c + 2 T	¾ c	¾ c + 2 T	1 c
Nutmeats	3½ T	⅓ c + 2 T	⅔ c	¾ c + 2 T	1 c + 2 T	1¼ c + 1 T	1½ c + 1 T	1¾ c
Pepper, green, chopped	3 T	⅓ c + 2 t	½ c + 1 T	¾ c	¾ c + 3 T	1 c + 2 T	1¼ c + 1 T	1½ c
Salt	1½ T	3 T	¼ c + 1½ t	⅓ c + 2 t	⅓ c + 2 T	½ c + 1 T	⅔ c	¾ c
Shortening, hydrogenated fat	2 T + 1 t	¼ c + 2 t	⅓ c + 2 T	½ c + 1 T	⅔ c + 1 T	¾ c + 2 T	1 c	1 c + 2 T
Soda	2 T + 1 t	¼ c + 2 t	⅓ c + 2 T	½ c + 1 T	⅔ c + 1 T	¾ c + 2 T	1 c	1 c + 3 T

	9 oz	10 oz	11 oz	12 oz	13 oz	14 oz	15 oz	16 oz
Sugar, brown, light pack	3 T	⅓ c + 2 t	½ c + 1 T	¾ c	¾ c + 3 T	1 c + 2 T	1¼ c + 1 T	1½ c
Sugar, granulated	2 T	¼ c	⅓ c + 2 t	½ c	½ c + 2 T	¾ c	¾ c + 2 T	1 c
Sugar, powdered, sifted	3 T	⅓ c + 2 t	½ c + 1 t	¾ c	¾ c + 3 T	1 c + 2 T	1¼ c + 1 T	1½ c
Yeast, dry	¼ c	½ c	¾ c	1 c	1¼ c	1½ c	1¾ c	2 c
Baking powder	1 c + 2 T	1¼ c	1⅓ c + 1 T	1½ c	1½ c + 2 T	1¾ c	1¾ c + 2 T	2 c
Bread crumbs, dry	2¼ c	2½ c	2¾ c	3 c	3¼ c + 2 T	3½ c	3¾ c	4 c
Butter or margarine	1 c + 2 T	1¼ c	1⅓ c + 1 T	1½ c	1½ c + 2 T	1¾ c	1¾ c + 2 T	2 c
Celery, chopped	2¼ c	2½ c	2¾ c	3 c	3¼ c + 2 T	3½ c	3¾ c	4 c
Cornstarch	2 c	2 c + 3 T	2⅓ c + 2 T	2½ c + 2 T	2¾ c + 2 T	3 c + 1 T	3¼ c + 1½ t	3½ c
Eggs, whole, whites or yolks, fresh or frozen	1 c + 2 T	1¼ c	1⅓ c + 1 T	1½ c	1½ c + 2 T	1¾ c	1¾ c + 2 T	2 c
Eggs, dried	2¼ c	2½ c	2¾ c	3 c	3¼ c + 2 T	3½ c	3¾ c	4 c
Flour, all purpose	2¼ c	2½ c	2¾ c	3 c	3¼ c + 2 T	3½ c	3¾ c	4 c
Flour, cake	2¾ c	3 c	3¼ c	3½ c + 1 T	3¾ c + 2 T	4 c + 2 T	4⅓ c + 2 T	4¾ c
Gelatin, granulated	1⅔ c	1¾ c + 2 T	2 c + 1 T	2¼ c	2⅓ c + 2 T	2½ c + 2 T	2¾ c	3 c
Gelatin, flavored	1¼ c + 1 T	1⅓ c + 2 T	1½ c + 2 T	1¾ c	1¾ c + 2 T	2 c + 1 T	2 c + 3 T	2⅓ c
Milk, nonfat dry	2¼ c	2½ c	2¾ c	3 c	3¼ c + 2 T	3½ c	3¾ c	4 c
Onion, chopped	1 c + 2 T	1¼ c	1⅓ c + 1 T	1½ c	1½ c + 2 T	1¾ c	1¾ c + 2 T	2 c
Nutmeats	2 c	2 c + 3 T	2⅓ c + 2 T	2½ c + 2 T	2¾ c + 2 T	3 c + 1 T	3¼ c + 1½ t	3½ c
Pepper, green, chopped	1⅔ c	1¾ c + 2 T	2 c + 2 T	2¼ c	2⅓ c + 2 T	2½ c	2¾ c	3 c
Salt	¾ c + 2 T	¾ c + 3 T	1 c + 1 T	1 c + 2 T	1¼ c	1¼ c + 1 T	1⅓ c + 1 T	1½ c

Table 1.7 WEIGHT (1-16 oz) AND MEASURE EQUIVALENTS FOR COMMONLY USED FOODS (continued)

Food Item	9 oz	10 oz	11 oz	12 oz	13 oz	14 oz	15 oz	16 oz
Shortening, hydrogenated fat	1¼ c	1⅓ c + 1 T	1½ c + 1 T	1⅔ c	1¾ c + 1 T	2 c	2 c + 2 T	2¼ c
Soda	1¼ c + 1 T	1⅓ c + 2 T	1½ c + 2 T	1¾ c	1¾ c + 2 T	2 c + 2 t	2 c + 3 T	2⅓ c
Sugar, brown, light pack	1⅔ c	1¾ c + 2 T	2 c + 1 T	2¼ c	2⅓ c + 2 T	2½ c + 2 T	2¾ c + 1 T	3 c
Sugar, granulated	1 c + 2 T	1¼ c	1⅓ c + 1 T	1½ c	1½ c + 2 T	1¾ c	1¾ c + 2 T	2 c
Sugar, powdered, sifted	1⅔ c	1¾ c + 2 T	2 c + 1 T	2¼ c	2⅓ c + 2 T	2½ c + 2 T	2¾ c + 1 T	3 c
Yeast, dry	2¼ c	2½ c	2¾ c	3 c	3¼ c	3½ c	3¾ c	4 c

Table 1.8 OUNCES AND DECIMAL EQUIVALENTS OF A POUND[a]

Ounces	Decimal Part of a Pound	Ounces	Decimal Part of a Pound
¼	0.016	8¼	0.516
½	0.031	8½	0.531
¾	0.047	8¾	0.547
1	0.063	9	0.563
1¼	0.078	9¼	0.578
1½	0.094	9½	0.594
1¾	0.109	9¾	0.609
2	0.125	10	0.625
2¼	0.141	10¼	0.641
2½	0.156	10½	0.656
2¾	0.172	10¾	0.672
3	0.188	11	0.688
3¼	0.203	11¼	0.703
3½	0.219	11½	0.719
3¾	0.234	11¾	0.734
4	0.250	12	0.750
4¼	0.266	12¼	0.766
4½	0.281	12½	0.781
4¾	0.297	12¾	0.797
5	0.313	13	0.813
5¼	0.328	13¼	0.828
5½	0.344	13½	0.844
5¾	0.359	13¾	0.859
6	0.375	14	0.875
6¼	0.391	14¼	0.891
6½	0.406	14½	0.906
6¾	0.422	14¾	0.922
7	0.438	15	0.938
7¼	0.453	15¼	0.953
7½	0.469	15½	0.969
7¾	0.484	15¾	0.984
8	0.500	16	1.000

[a] Adapted from *Standardizing Recipes for Institutional Use*. The American Dietetic Association, 1967.

Note: When increasing or decreasing recipes, the division or multiplication of pounds and ounces is simplified when decimals are substituted for ounces. For example, when multiplying 1 lb 7 oz by 4, convert from ounces to the decimal part of a pound. Thus, 1.438 lb times 4 is 5.752.

For metric equivalents, see p. 28.

Instructions for Using Table 1.9 that Follows[a]

1. Locate column that corresponds to the original yield of the recipe you wish to adjust. For example, let us assume your original recipe for meat loaf yields 100 portions. Locate the 100 column.

2. Run your finger down this column until you come to the amount of the ingredient required (or closest to this figure) in the recipe you wish to adjust. Say that your original recipe for 100 portions of meat loaf requires 21 lb of ground beef. Run your finger down the column headed 100 until you come to 21 lb.

3. Next, run your finger across the page, in line with that amount, until you come to the column that is headed to correspond with the yield you desire. Suppose you want to make 75 portions of meat loaf. Starting with your finger under the 21 lb (in the 100 column), slide it across to the column headed 75 and read the figure. You see you need 15 lb 12 oz ground beef to make 75 portions with your recipe.

4. Record this figure as the amount of the ingredient required for the new yield of your recipe. Repeat Steps 1, 2, and 3 for each ingredient in your original recipe to obtain the adjusted ingredient weight needed of each for your new yield. You can increase or decrease yield in this manner.

5. If you need to combine two columns to obtain your desired yield, follow the above procedure and add together the amounts given in the two columns to get the amount required for your adjusted yield. For example, to find the amount of ground beef for 225 portions of meat loaf (using the same basic recipe for 100 we used above), locate the figures in columns headed 200 and 25 and add them. In this case they would be: 42 lb + 5 lb 4 oz, and the required total would be 47 lb 4 oz.

6. The figures in Table 1.9 are given in exact weights including fractional ounces. After you have made yield adjustments for every ingredient, refer to Table 1.12 for "rounding-off" fractional amounts that are not of sufficient proportion to change product quality. No rounding-off is required for amounts needed for adjusted ingredients in the examples we have used here.

Table 1.9 DIRECT-READING TABLE FOR ADJUSTING YIELD OF RECIPES WITH INGREDIENT AMOUNTS GIVEN IN **WEIGHTS.** (PORTION YIELDS DIVISIBLE BY 25)[b]

ABBREVIATIONS IN TABLE: oz = ounce # = pound BASIC INFORMATION: 1 pound = 16 ounces

25	50	75	100	200	300	400	500
(c)	(c)	(c)	¼ oz	½ oz	¾ oz	1 oz	1¼ oz
(c)	(c)	(c)	½ oz	1 oz	1½ oz	2 oz	2½ oz
(c)	(c)	(c)	¾ oz	1½ oz	2¼ oz	3 oz	3¾ oz
¼ oz	½ oz	¾ oz	1 oz	2 oz	3 oz	4 oz	5 oz
(c)	(c)	(c)	1¼ oz	2½ oz	3¾ oz	5 oz	6¼ oz
(c)	¾ oz	(c)	1½ oz	3 oz	4½ oz	6 oz	7½ oz
(c)	(c)	(c)	1¾ oz	3½ oz	5¼ oz	7 oz	8¾ oz
½ oz	1 oz	1½ oz	2 oz	4 oz	6 oz	8 oz	10 oz
(c)	(c)	1¾ oz	2¼ oz	4½ oz	6¾ oz	9 oz	11¼ oz
(c)	1¼ oz	2 oz	2½ oz	5 oz	7½ oz	10 oz	12½ oz
(c)	(c)	2 oz	2¾ oz	5½ oz	8¼ oz	11 oz	13¾ oz
¾ oz	1½ oz	2¼ oz	3 oz	6 oz	9 oz	12 oz	15 oz
(c)	(c)	2½ oz	3¼ oz	6½ oz	9¾ oz	13 oz	1# ¼ oz
(c)	1¾ oz	2¾ oz	3½ oz	7 oz	10½ oz	14 oz	1# 1½ oz
1 oz	2 oz	2¾ oz	3¾ oz	7½ oz	11¼ oz	15 oz	1# 2¾ oz
1 oz	2 oz	3 oz	4 oz	8 oz	12 oz	1#	1# 4 oz
1 oz	2¼ oz	3¼ oz	4¼ oz	8½ oz	12¾ oz	1# 1 oz	1# 5¼ oz
(c)	2½ oz	3½ oz	4½ oz	9 oz	13½ oz	1# 2 oz	1# 6½ oz
(c)	2½ oz	3½ oz	4¾ oz	9½ oz	14¼ oz	1# 3 oz	1# 7¾ oz
1¼ oz	2½ oz	3¾ oz	5 oz	10 oz	15 oz	1# 4 oz	1# 9 oz
(c)	2¾ oz	4¼ oz	5½ oz	11 oz	1# ½ oz	1# 6 oz	1# 11½ oz
1½ oz	3 oz	4½ oz	6 oz	12 oz	1# 2 oz	1# 8 oz	1# 14 oz
(c)	3¼ oz	4¾ oz	6½ oz	13 oz	1# 3½ oz	1# 10 oz	2# ½ oz
1¾ oz	3½ oz	5¼ oz	7 oz	14 oz	1# 5 oz	1# 12 oz	2# 3 oz
2 oz	3¾ oz	5¾ oz	7½ oz	15 oz	1# 6½ oz	1# 14 oz	2# 5½ oz

Table 1.9 DIRECT-READING TABLE FOR ADJUSTING YIELD OF RECIPES WITH INGREDIENT AMOUNTS GIVEN IN **WEIGHTS.** (PORTION YIELDS DIVISIBLE BY 25)[b] (continued)

ABBREVIATIONS IN TABLE: oz = ounce # = pound BASIC INFORMATION: 1 pound = 16 ounces

25	*50*	*75*	*100*	*200*	*300*	*400*	*500*
2 oz	4 oz	6 oz	8 oz	1#	1# 8 oz	2#	2# 8 oz
2¼ oz	4¼ oz	6½ oz	8½ oz	1# 1 oz	1# 9½ oz	2# 2 oz	2# 10½ oz
2¼ oz	4½ oz	6¾ oz	9 oz	1# 2 oz	1# 11 oz	2# 4 oz	2# 13 oz
2½ oz	4¾ oz	7¼ oz	9½ oz	1# 3 oz	1# 12½ oz	2# 6 oz	2# 15½ oz
2½ oz	5 oz	7½ oz	10 oz	1# 4 oz	1# 14 oz	2# 8 oz	3# 2 oz
2¾ oz	5½ oz	8¼ oz	11 oz	1# 6 oz	2# 1 oz	2# 12 oz	3# 7 oz
3 oz	6 oz	9 oz	12 oz	1# 8 oz	2# 4 oz	3#	3# 12 oz
3¼ oz	6½ oz	9¾ oz	13 oz	1# 10 oz	2# 7 oz	3# 4 oz	4# 1 oz
3½ oz	7 oz	10½ oz	14 oz	1# 12 oz	2# 10 oz	3# 8 oz	4# 6 oz
3¾ oz	7½ oz	11¼ oz	15 oz	1# 14 oz	2# 13 oz	3# 12 oz	4# 11 oz
4 oz	8 oz	12 oz	1#	2#	3#	4#	5#
4½ oz	9 oz	13½ oz	1# 2 oz	2# 4 oz	3# 6 oz	4# 8 oz	5# 10 oz
5 oz	10 oz	15 oz	1# 4 oz	2# 8 oz	3# 12 oz	5#	6# 4 oz
5½ oz	11 oz	1# ½ oz	1# 6 oz	2# 12 oz	4# 2 oz	5# 8 oz	6# 14 oz
6 oz	12 oz	1# 2 oz	1# 8 oz	3#	4# 8 oz	6#	7# 8 oz
6½ oz	13 oz	1# 3½ oz	1# 10 oz	3# 4 oz	4# 14 oz	6# 8 oz	8# 2 oz
7 oz	14 oz	1# 5 oz	1# 12 oz	3# 8 oz	5# 4 oz	7#	8# 12 oz
7½ oz	15 oz	1# 6½ oz	1# 14 oz	3# 12 oz	5# 10 oz	7# 8 oz	9# 6 oz
8 oz	1#	1# 8 oz	2#	4#	6#	8#	10#
8½ oz	1# 1 oz	1# 9½ oz	2# 2 oz	4# 4 oz	6# 6 oz	8# 8 oz	10# 10 oz
9 oz	1# 2 oz	1# 11 oz	2# 4 oz	4# 8 oz	6# 12 oz	9#	11# 4 oz
9½ oz	1# 3 oz	1# 12½ oz	2# 6 oz	4# 12 oz	7# 2 oz	9# 8 oz	11# 14 oz
10 oz	1# 4 oz	1# 14 oz	2# 8 oz	5#	7# 8 oz	10#	12# 8 oz
11 oz	1# 6 oz	2# 1 oz	2# 12 oz	5# 8 oz	8# 4 oz	11#	13# 12 oz

12 oz	1#	8 oz	2#	4 oz	3#		6#		9#		12#		15#	
13 oz	1#	10 oz	2#	7 oz	3#	4 oz	6#	8 oz	9#	12 oz	13#		16#	4 oz
14 oz	1#	12 oz	2#	10 oz	3#	8 oz	7#		10#	8 oz	14#		17#	8 oz
15 oz	1#	14 oz	2#	13 oz	3#	12 oz	7#	8 oz	11#	4 oz	15#		18#	12 oz
	2#		3#		4#		8#		12#		16#		20#	
1 oz	2#	2 oz	3#	3 oz	4#	4 oz	8#	8 oz	12#	12 oz	17#		21#	4 oz
2 oz	2#	4 oz	3#	6 oz	4#	8 oz	9#		13#	8 oz	18#		22#	8 oz
3 oz	2#	6 oz	3#	9 oz	4#	12 oz	9#	8 oz	14#	4 oz	19#		23#	12 oz
4 oz	2#	8 oz	3#	12 oz	5#		10#		15#		20#		25#	
5 oz	2#	10 oz	3#	15 oz	5#	4 oz	10#	8 oz	15#	12 oz	21#		26#	4 oz
6 oz	2#	12 oz	4#	2 oz	5#	8 oz	11#		16#	8 oz	22#		27#	8 oz
7 oz	2#	14 oz	4#	5 oz	5#	12 oz	11#	8 oz	17#	4 oz	23#		28#	12 oz
8 oz	3#		4#	8 oz	6#		12#		18#		24#		30#	
10 oz	3#	4 oz	4#	14 oz	6#	8 oz	13#		19#	8 oz	26#		32#	8 oz
12 oz	3#	8 oz	5#	4 oz	7#		14#		21#		28#		35#	
14 oz	3#	12 oz	5#	10 oz	7#	8 oz	15#		22#	8 oz	30#		37#	8 oz
	4#		6#		8#		16#		24#		32#		40#	
2 oz	4#	4 oz	6#	6 oz	8#	8 oz	17#		25#	8 oz	34#		42#	8 oz
4 oz	4#	8 oz	6#	12 oz	9#		18#		27#		36#		45#	
6 oz	4#	12 oz	7#	2 oz	9#	8 oz	19#		28#	8 oz	38#		47#	8 oz
8 oz	5#		7#	8 oz	10#		20#		30#		40#		50#	
12 oz	5#	8 oz	8#	4 oz	11#		22#		33#		44#		55#	
	6#		9#		12#		24#		36#		48#		60#	
4 oz	6#	8 oz	9#	12 oz	13#		26#		39#		52#		65#	
8 oz	7#		10#	8 oz	14#		28#		42#		56#		70#	
12 oz	7#	8 oz	11#	4 oz	15#		30#		45#		60#		75#	
	8#		12#		16#		32#		48#		64#		80#	
4 oz	8#	8 oz	12#	12 oz	17#		34#		51#		68#		85#	
8 oz	9#		13#	8 oz	18#		36#		54#		72#		90#	
12 oz	9#	8 oz	14#	4 oz	19#		38#		57#		76#		95#	

Table 1.9. DIRECT-READING TABLE FOR ADJUSTING YIELD OF RECIPES WITH INGREDIENT AMOUNTS GIVEN IN WEIGHTS. (PORTION YIELDS DIVISIBLE BY 25)[b] (continued)

ABBREVIATIONS IN TABLE: oz = ounce   # = pound   BASIC INFORMATION: 1 pound = 16 ounces

25	50	75	100	200	300	400	500
5#	10#	15#	20#	40#	60#	80#	100#
5# 4 oz	10# 8 oz	15# 12 oz	21#	42#	63#	84#	105#
5# 8 oz	11#	16# 8 oz	22#	44#	66#	88#	110#
5# 12 oz	11# 8 oz	17# 4 oz	23#	46#	69#	92#	115#
6#	12#	18#	24#	48#	72#	96#	120#
6# 4 oz	12# 8 oz	18# 12 oz	25#	50#	75#	100#	125#
7# 8 oz	15#	22# 8 oz	30#	60#	90#	120#	150#
8# 12 oz	17#	26# 4 oz	35#	70#	105#	140#	175#
10#	20#	30#	40#	80#	120#	160#	200#
11# 4 oz	22# 8 oz	33# 12 oz	45#	90#	135#	180#	225#
12# 8 oz	25#	37# 8 oz	50#	100#	150#	200#	250#

[a] This table was adapted from conversion charts developed by the Nutrition Services Division of the New York State Department of Mental Hygiene, Albany, New York.

[b] From *Standardizing Recipes for Institutional Use*. The American Dietetic Association, 1967.

[c] The amounts cannot be weighed accurately without introducing errors. Change to measurement by using Table 1.6.

Instructions for Using Table 1.10 that Follows[a]

1. Locate column that corresponds to the original yield of the recipe you wish to adjust. For example, let us assume your original sour cream cookie recipe yields 300 cookies. Locate the 300 column.
2. Run your finger down this column until you come to the amount of the ingredient required (or closest to this figure) in the recipe you wish to adjust. Say that your original recipe for 300 cookies required 2¼ c fat. Run your finger down the column headed 300 until you come to 2¼ c.
3. Next, run your finger across the page, in line with that amount, until you come to the column that is headed to correspond with the yield you desire. Suppose you want to make 75 cookies. Starting with your finger under the 2¼ c (in the 300 column), slide it across to the column headed 75 and read the figure. You see you need ½ c + 1 T fat to make 75 cookies from your recipe.
4. Record this figure as the amount of the ingredient required for the new yield of your recipe. Repeat Steps 1, 2, and 3 for each ingredient in your original recipe to obtain the adjusted measure needed of each for your new yield. You can increase or decrease yield in this manner.
5. If you need to combine two columns to obtain your desired yield, follow the above procedure and add together the amounts given in the two columns to get the amount required for your adjusted yield. For example, to find the amount of fat needed to make 550 cookies (using the same basic recipe as above) locate the figures in columns headed 500 and 50 and add them. In this case they would be 3¾ c + 6 T and the required total would be 1 qt + 2 T fat.
6. The figures in Table 1.10 are given in measurements that provide absolute accuracy. After you have made yield adjustments for each ingredient, refer to Table 1.12 for "rounding-off" odd fractions and complicated measurements. You can safely round-off to 1 qt, as shown in Table 1.12, for the amount of fat needed in the recipe for 550 cookies.

Table 1.10 DIRECT-READING TABLE FOR ADJUSTING YIELD WITH INGREDIENT AMOUNTS GIVEN IN **MEASUREMENT** (PORTION YIELDS DIVISIBLE BY 25)[a]

ABBREVIATIONS IN TABLE

t = teaspoon
T = tablespoon
c = cup
qt = quart
gal = gallon
(r) = slightly rounded
(s) = scant

BASIC INFORMATION

3 t = 1 T	12 T = 3/4 c
4 T = 1/4 c	16 T = 1 c
5 T + 1 t = 1/3 c	4 c = 1 qt
8 T = 1/2 c	4 qt = 1 gal
10 T + 2 t = 2/3 c	

Measuring spoons
1 T
1 t
1/2 t
1/4 t
for 3/4 t combine 1/2 t + 1/4 t
for 1/8 t use half of the 1/4 t

Equivalents

25	50	75	100	200	300	400	500
1/4 t	1/2 t	3/4 t	1 t	2 t	1 T	1 T + 1 t	1 T + 2 t
1/4 t(r)	1/2 t(r)	1 t(s)	1 1/4 t	2 1/2 t	1 T + 3/4 t	1 T + 2 t	2 T + 1/4 t
1/4 t + 1/8 t	3/4 t	1 t + 1/8 t	1 1/2 t	1 T	1 1/2 T	2 T	2 1/2 T
1/2 t(s)	3/4 t(r)	1 1/4 t(r)	1 3/4 t	1 T + 1/2 t	1 T + 2 1/4 t	2 T + 1 t	2 T + 2 3/4 t
1/2 t	1 t	1 1/2 t	2 t	1 T + 1 t	2 T	2 T + 2 t	3 T + 1 t
1/2 t(r)	1 t + 1/8 t	1 3/4 t(s)	2 1/4 t	1 1/2 T	2 T + 3/4 t	3 T	3 T + 2 1/4 t
1/2 t + 1/8 t	1 1/4 t	2 t(s)	2 1/2 t	1 T + 2 t	2 1/2 T	3 T + 1 t	4 T + 1/2 t
3/4 t(s)	1 1/4 t + 1/8 t	2 t(r)	2 3/4 t	1 T + 2 1/2 t	2 T + 2 1/4 t	3 T + 2 t	4 T + 1 3/4 t
3/4 t	1 1/2 t	2 1/4 t	1 T	2 T	3 T	1/4 c	5 T
1 t + 1/8 t	2 1/4 t	1 T + 1/4 t + 1/8 t	1 1/2 T	3 T	1/4 c + 1 1/2 t	1/3 c + 2 t	1/4 c + 3 1/2 t
1 1/2 t	1 T	1 1/2 T	2 T	1/4 c	1/4 c + 2 T	1/2 c	1/2 c + 2 T
1 3/4 t + 1/8 t	1 T + 3/4 t	1 T + 2 1/2 t + 1/8 t	2 1/2 T	1/4 c + 1 T	1/4 c + 3 1/2 T	1/2 c + 2 T	3/4 c + 1/2 T
2 1/4 t	1 1/2 T	2 T + 3/4 t	3 T	1/3 c + 2 t	1/2 c + 1 T	3/4 c	3/4 c + 3 T
2 1/4 t + 1/8 t	1 T + 2 1/4 t	2 T + 1 1/2 t + 1/8 t	3 1/2 T	1/4 c + 3 T	1/2 c + 2 1/2 T	3/4 c + 2 T	1 c + 1 1/2 T

1 T	2 T	3 T	1/4 c	1/2 c	3/4 c	1 c	1 1/4 c
1 T + 1 t	2 T + 2 t	1/4 c	1/3 c	2/3 c	1 c	1 1/3 c	1 2/3 c
2 T	1/4 c	1/4 c + 2 T	1/2 c	1 c	1 1/2 c	2 c	2 1/2 c
2 T + 2 t	1/3 c	1/2 c	2/3 c	1 1/3 c	2 c	2 2/3 c	3 1/3 c
3 T	6 T	1/2 c + 1 T	3/4 c	1 1/2 c	2 1/4 c	3 c	3 3/4 c
1/4 c	1/2 c	3/4 c	1 c	2 c	3 c	1 qt	1 1/4 qt
1/4 c + 1 T	1/2 c + 2 T	3/4 c + 3 T	1 1/4 c	2 1/2 c	3 3/4 c	1 1/4 qt	1 1/2 qt + 1/4 c
1/3 c	2/3 c	1 c	1 1/3 c	2 2/3 c	1 qt	1 1/4 qt + 1/3 c	1 1/2 qt + 2/3 c
1/3 c + 2 t	3/4 c	1 c + 2 T	1 1/2 c	3 c	1 qt + 1/2 c	1 1/2 qt	1 3/4 qt + 1/2 c
6 T + 2 t	3/4 c + 4 t	1 1/4 c	1 2/3 c	3 1/3 c	1 1/4 qt	1 1/2 qt + 2/3 c	2 qt + 1/3 c
1/4 c + 3 T	3/4 c + 2 T	1 1/4 c + 1 T	1 3/4 c	3 1/2 c	1 1/4 qt + 1/4 c	1 3/4 qt	2 qt + 3/4 c
1/2 c	1 c	1 1/2 c	2 c	1 qt	1 1/2 qt	2 qt	2 1/2 qt
1/2 c + 1 T	1 c + 2 T	1 1/2 c + 3 T	2 1/4 c	1 qt + 1/2 c	1 1/2 qt + 3/4 c	2 1/4 qt	2 3/4 qt + 1/4 c
1/2 c + 4 t	1 c + 2 T + 2 t	1 3/4 c	2 1/3 c	1 qt + 2/3 c	1 3/4 qt	2 1/4 qt + 1/3 c	2 3/4 qt + 2/3 c
1/2 c + 2 T	1 1/4 c	1 3/4 c + 2 T	2 1/2 c	1 1/4 qt	1 3/4 qt + 1/2 c	2 1/2 qt	3 qt + 1/2 c
2/3 c	1 1/3 c	2 c	2 2/3 c	1 1/4 qt + 1/3 c	2 qt	2 1/2 qt + 2/3 c	3 1/4 qt + 1/3 c
1/2 c + 3 T	1 1/4 c + 2 T	2 c + 1 T	2 3/4 c	1 1/4 qt + 1/2 c	2 qt + 1/4 c	2 3/4 qt	3 1/4 qt + 3/4 c
3/4 c	1 1/2 c	2 1/4 c	3 c	1 1/2 qt	2 1/4 qt	3 qt	3 3/4 qt
3/4 c + 1 T	1 1/2 c + 2 T	2 1/4 c + 3 T	3 1/4 c	1 1/2 qt + 1/2 c	2 1/4 qt + 3/4 c	3 1/4 qt	1 gal + 1/4 c
3/4 c + 4 t	1 2/3 c	2 1/2 c	3 1/3 c	1 1/2 qt + 2/3 c	2 1/2 qt	3 1/4 qt + 1/3 c	1 gal + 2/3 c
3/4 c + 2 T	1 3/4 c	2 1/2 c + 2 T	3 1/2 c	1 3/4 qt	2 1/2 qt + 1/2 c	3 1/2 qt	1 gal + 1 1/2 c
3/4 c + 2 T + 2 t	1 3/4 c + 4 t	2 3/4 c	3 2/3 c	1 3/4 qt + 1/3 c	2 3/4 qt	3 1/2 qt + 2/3 c	1 gal + 2 1/3 c
3/4 c + 3 T	1 3/4 c + 2 T	2 3/4 c + 1 T	3 3/4 c	1 3/4 qt + 1/2 c	2 3/4 qt + 1/4 c	3 3/4 qt	1 gal + 2 3/4 c
1 c	2 c	3 c	1 qt	2 qt	3 qt	1 gal	1 1/4 gal
1 1/4 c	2 1/2 c	3 3/4 c	1 1/4 qt	2 1/2 qt	3 3/4 qt	1 1/4 gal	1 1/2 gal + 1 c
1 1/2 c	3 c	1 qt + 1/2 c	1 1/2 qt	3 qt	1 gal + 2 c	1 1/2 gal	1 3/4 gal + 2 c
1 3/4 c	3 1/2 c	1 1/4 qt + 1/4 c	1 3/4 qt	3 1/2 qt	1 1/4 gal + 1 c	1 3/4 gal	2 gal + 3 c
2 c	1 qt	1 1/2 qt	2 qt	1 gal	1 1/2 gal	2 gal	2 1/2 gal
2 1/4 c	1 qt + 1/2 c	1 1/2 qt + 3/4 c	2 1/4 qt	1 gal + 2 c	1 1/2 gal + 3 c	2 1/4 gal	2 3/4 gal + 1 c
2 1/2 c	1 1/4 qt	1 3/4 qt + 1/2 c	2 1/2 qt	1 1/4 gal	1 3/4 gal + 2 c	2 1/2 gal	3 gal + 2 c
2 3/4 c	1 1/4 qt + 1/2 c	2 qt + 1/4 c	2 3/4 qt	1 1/4 gal + 2 c	2 gal + 1 c	2 3/4 gal	3 1/4 gal + 3 c

Table 1.10 DIRECT-READING TABLE FOR ADJUSTING YIELD WITH INGREDIENT AMOUNTS GIVEN IN **MEASUREMENT** (PORTION YIELDS DIVISIBLE BY 25)[a] (continued)

25	50	75	100	200	300	400	500
3 c	1½ qt	2¼ qt	3 qt	1½ gal	2¼ gal	3 gal	3¾ gal
3¼ c	1½ qt + ½ c	2¼ qt + ¾ c	3¼ qt	1½ gal + 2 c	2¼ gal + 3 c	3¼ gal	4 gal + 1 c
3½ c	1¾ qt	2½ qt + ½ c	3½ qt	1¾ gal	2½ gal + 2 c	3½ gal	4¼ gal + 2 c
3¾ c	1¾ qt + ½ c	2¾ qt + ¼ c	3¾ qt	1¾ gal + 2 c	2¾ gal + 1 c	3¾ gal	4½ gal + 3 c
1 qt	2 qt	3 qt	1 gal	2 gal	3 gal	4 gal	5 gal
1¼ qt	2½ qt	3¾ qt	1¼ gal	2½ gal	3¾ gal	5 gal	6¼ gal
1½ qt	3 qt	1 gal + 2 c	1½ gal	3 gal	4½ gal	6 gal	7½ gal
1¾ qt	3½ qt	1¼ gal + 1 c	1¾ gal	3½ gal	5¼ gal	7 gal	8¾ gal
2 qt	1 gal	1½ gal	2 gal	4 gal	6 gal	8 gal	10 gal
2¼ qt	1 gal + 2 c	1½ gal + 3 c	2¼ gal	4½ gal	6¾ gal	9 gal	11¼ gal
2½ qt	1¼ gal	1¾ gal + 2 c	2½ gal	5 gal	7½ gal	10 gal	12½ gal
2¾ qt	1¼ gal + 2 c	2 gal + 1 c	2¾ gal	5½ gal	8¼ gal	11 gal	13¾ gal
3 qt	1½ gal	2¼ gal	3 gal	6 gal	9 gal	12 gal	15 gal
3 qt + 1 c	1½ gal + 2 c	2¼ gal + 3 c	3¼ gal	6½ gal	9¾ gal	13 gal	16¼ gal
3½ qt	1¾ gal	2½ gal + 2 c	3½ gal	7 gal	10½ gal	14 gal	17½ gal
3½ qt + 1 c	1¾ gal + 2 c	2¾ gal + 1 c	3¾ gal	7½ gal	11¼ gal	15 gal	18¾ gal
1 gal	2 gal	3 gal	4 gal	8 gal	12 gal	16 gal	20 gal
1 gal + 1 c	2 gal + 2 c	3 gal + 3 c	4¼ gal	8½ gal	12¾ gal	17 gal	21¼ gal
1 gal + 2 c	2¼ gal	3¼ gal + 2 c	4½ gal	9 gal	13½ gal	18 gal	22½ gal
1 gal + 3 c	2¼ gal + 2 c	3½ gal + 1 c	4¾ gal	9½ gal	14¼ gal	19 gal	23¾ gal
1¼ gal	2½ gal	3¾ gal	5 gal	10 gal	15 gal	20 gal	25 gal
1¼ gal + 1 c	2½ gal + 2 c	3¾ gal + 3 c	5¼ gal	10½ gal	15¾ gal	21 gal	26¼ gal
1¼ gal + 2 c	2¾ gal	4 gal + 2 c	5½ gal	11 gal	16½ gal	22 gal	27½ gal
1¼ gal + 3 c	2¾ gal + 2 c	4¼ gal + 1 c	5¾ gal	11½ gal	17¼ gal	23 gal	28¾ gal

1½ gal	3 gal	4½ gal	6 gal	12 gal	18 gal	24 gal	30 gal
1½ gal + 1 c	3 gal + 2 c	4½ gal + 3 c	6¼ gal	12½ gal	18¾ gal	25 gal	31¼ gal
1½ gal + 2 c	3¼ gal	4¾ gal + 2 c	6½ gal	13 gal	19½ gal	26 gal	32½ gal
1½ gal + 3 c	3¼ gal + 2 c	5 gal + 1 c	6¾ gal	13½ gal	20¼ gal	27 gal	33¾ gal
1¾ gal	3½ gal	5¼ gal	7 gal	14 gal	21 gal	28 gal	35 gal

[a] From *Standardizing Recipes for Institutional Use*. The American Dietetic Association, 1967.

Instructions for Using Table 1.11 that Follows[a]

1. Locate column that corresponds to the original yield of the recipe you wish to adjust. For example, let us assume your original custard sauce recipe yields 24 portions. Locate the 24 column.

2. Run your finger down this column until you come to the amount of the ingredient required (or closest to this figure) in the recipe you wish to adjust. Say that your original recipe for 24 portions requires 1½ T cornstarch and 1¼ qt milk. Run your finger down the column headed 24 until you come to 1½ T (for cornstarch) and then 1¼ qt (for milk), etc.

3. Next, run your finger across the page, in line with that amount, until you come to the column that is headed to correspond with the yield you desire. Suppose you want to make 32 portions. Starting with your finger under the 1½ T (in the 24 column), slide it across to the column headed 32 and read the figure. You need 2 T cornstarch for 32 portions. Repeat the procedure starting with 1¼ qt in the 24 column; tracing across to the 32 column, you find you need 1½ qt + ⅔ c milk.

4. Record this figure as the amount of the ingredient required for the new yield of your recipe. Repeat Steps 1, 2, and 3 for each ingredient in your original recipe to obtain the adjusted measure needed of each for your new yield. You can increase or decrease yield in this manner.

5. Amounts for 8-48 portions are given on pp. 57-60. This part of the table is helpful when increasing home size recipes to quantities of 24 and 48 portions, logical steps in recipe enlargement. Adjustments between 56 and 96 servings may be made from information on pp. 60-62. However, if increasing from a number of portions in the first pages of the table to one in the last three pages, care should be taken to locate the corresponding lines in the two tables.

6. The figures in Table 1.11 are given in measurements that provide absolute accuracy. After you have made yield adjustments for all ingredients, refer to Table 1.12 for "rounding-off" awkward fractions and complicated measurements. In our example (increasing from 24-32 portions) you can round the adjusted amount of milk to 1¾ qt without upsetting proportions. The total amount of cornstarch in our example need not be rounded-off, since it can be measured easily (2 T).

Table 1.11 DIRECT-READING TABLE FOR ADJUSTING YIELD OF RECIPES WITH INGREDIENT AMOUNTS GIVEN IN **MEASUREMENT** (PORTION YIELDS DIVISIBLE BY 8)[a]

ABBREVIATIONS IN TABLE

t = teaspoon
T = tablespoon
c = cup
qt = quart
gal = gallon
(r) = slightly rounded
(s) = scant
(*b*) = too small for accurate measure; use caution

BASIC INFORMATION

Measuring Spoons	Equivalents	
1 T	3 t = 1 T	12 T = ¾ c
1 t	4 T = ¼ c	16 T = 1 c
½ t	5 T + 1 t = ⅓ c	4 c = 1 qt
¼ t	8 T = ½ c	4 qt = 1 gal
for ¾ t combine ½ t + ¼ t	10 T + 2 t = ⅔ c	
for ⅛ t use half of the ¼ t		

8	*16*	*20*	*24*	*32*	*40*	*48*
(*b*)	(*b*)	⅛ t(s)	⅛ t	⅛ t(r)	¼ t(s)	¼ t
(*b*)	⅛ t(r)	¼ t(s)	¼ t	¼ t(r)	½ t(s)	½ t
¼ t(s)	¼ t(r)	½ t(s)	½ t	¾ t(s)	¾ t(r)	1 t
¼ t	½ t	½ t(r)	¾ t	1 t	1¼ t	1½ t
¼ t(r)	¾ t(s)	¾ t(r)	1 t	1¼ t(r)	1¾ t(s)	2 t
½ t(s)	¾ t(r)	1 t	1¼ t	1¾ t(s)	2 t	2½ t
½ t	1 t	1¼ t	1½ t	2 t	2½ t	1 T
½ t(r)	1¼ t(s)	1½ t	1¾ t	2¼ t(r)	1 T(s)	1 T + ½ t
¾ t(s)	1¼ t(r)	1¾ t(s)	2 t	2¾ t(r)	1 T + ¼ t	1 T + 1 t
¾ t	1½ t	1¾ t(r)	2¼ t	1 T	1 T + ¾ t	1 T + 1½ t
¾ t(r)	1¾ t(s)	2 t	2½ t	1 T + ¼ t(r)	1 T + 1¼ t	1 T + 2 t
1 t(s)	1¾ t(r)	2¼ t(r)	2¾ t	1 T + ¾ t(s)	1 T + 1½ t	1 T + 2½ t
1 t	2 t	2½ t	1 T	1 T + 1 t	1 T + 2 t	2 T
1½ t	1 T	1 T + ¾ t	1½ T	2 T	2½ T	3 T

Table 1.11 DIRECT-READING TABLE FOR ADJUSTING YIELD OF RECIPES WITH INGREDIENT AMOUNTS GIVEN IN **MEASUREMENT** (PORTION YIELDS DIVISIBLE BY 8)[a] (continued)

8	*16*	*20*	*24*	*32*	*40*	*48*
2 t	1 T + 1 t	1 T + 2 t	2 T	2 T + 2 t	3 T + 1 t	¼ c
2½ t	1 T + 2 t	2 T + ¼ t	2½ T	3 T + 1 t	¼ c + ½ t	¼ c + 1 T
1 T	2 T	2½ T	3 T	¼ c	¼ c + 1 T	⅓ c + 2 t
1 T + ½ t	2 T + 1 t	2 T + 2 ¾ t	3½ T	¼ c + 2 t	⅓ c + ½ T	¼ c + 3 T
1 T + 1 t	2 T + 2 t	3 T + 1 t	¼ c	⅓ c	⅓ c + 4 t	½ c
1 T + 2¼ t	3 T + 2¾ t	¼ c + 1¼ t	⅓ c	¼ c + 3 T	½ c + 2½ t	⅔ c
2 T + 2 t	⅓ c	⅓ c + 2 T	½ c	⅔ c	¾ c + 4 t	1 c
3 T + 1¾ t	⅓ c + 5 t	½ c + 2¾ t	⅔ c	¾ c + 2 T	1 c + 5½ t	1⅓ c
¼ c	½ c	½ c + 2 T	¾ c	1 c	1¼ c	1½ c
⅓ c	⅔ c	¾ c + 2 t	1 c	1⅓ c	1⅔ c	2 c
⅓ c + 4 t	¾ c + 4 t	1 c + 2 t	1¼ c	1⅔ c	2 c + 4 t	2½ c
⅓ c + 5¼ t	⅔ c + 3½ T	1 c + 5¼ t	1⅓ c	1¾ c + 1¼ t	2 c + 3½ T	2⅔ c
½ c	1 c	1¼ c	1½ c	2 c	2½ c	3 c
½ c + 2¼ t	1 c + 5¼ t	1⅓ c	1⅔ c	2 c + 3½ T	2⅔ c	3⅓ c
½ c + 4 t	1 c + 3 T	1⅓ c + 2 T	1¾ c	2⅓ c	2¾ c + 1½ T	3½ c
⅔ c	1⅓ c	1⅔ c	2 c	2⅔ c	3⅓ c	1 qt
¾ c	1½ c	1¾ c + 2 T	2¼ c	3 c	3¾ c	1 qt + ½ c
¾ c + 1¼ t	1½ c + 2¾ t	1¾ c + 3 T	2⅓ c	3 c + 2 T	3¾ c + 2 T	1 qt + ⅔ c
¾ c + 4 t	1⅔ c	2 c + 4 t	2½ c	3⅓ c	1 qt + 2½ T	1¼ qt
⅔ c + 3½ T	1¾ c + 1¼ t	2 c + 3½ T	2⅔ c	3½ c + 1 T	4¼ c + 3 T	1¼ qt + ⅓ c
⅔ c + ¼ c	1¾ c + 4 t	2¼ c + 2 t	2¾ c	3⅔ c	4½ c + 4 t	1¼ qt + ½ c

1 c	2 c	2½ c	3 c	1 qt	1¼ qt	1½ qt
1 c + 4 t	2 c + 2½ T	2⅔ c + 2 t	3¼ c	1 qt + ⅓ c	5⅓ c + 4 t	1½ qt + ½ c
1 c + 5¼ t	2 c + 3½ T	2¾ c + ½ T	3⅓ c	4¼ c + 3 T	5½ c + 1 T	1½ qt + ⅔ c
1 c + 2 T + 2 t	2¼ c + 4 t	2¾ c + 2½ T	3½ c	1 qt + ⅔ c	5¾ c + 1 T	1¾ qt
1 c + 3½ T	2¼ c + 3 T	3 c + 1 T	3⅔ c	4¾ c + 2 T	1½ qt + 2 T	1¾ qt + ⅓ c
1¼ c	2½ c	3 c + 2 T	3¾ c	1¼ qt	1½ qt + ¼ c	1¾ qt + ½ c
1⅓ c	2⅔ c	3⅓ c	1 qt	1¼ qt + ⅓ c	1½ qt + ⅔ c	2 qt
1⅔ c	3⅓ c	1 qt + 2½ T	1¼ qt	1½ qt + ⅔ c	2 qt + ¼ c + 1 T	2½ qt
2 c	1 qt	1¼ qt	1½ qt	2 qt	2½ qt	3 qt
2⅓ c	1 qt + ⅔ c	5¾ c + 1½ T	1¾ qt	2¼ qt + ⅓ c	2¾ qt + ⅔ c	3½ qt
2⅔ c	1¼ qt + ⅓ c	1½ qt + ⅔ c	2 qt	2½ qt + ⅔ c	3¼ qt + ⅓ c	1 gal
3 c	1½ qt	1¾ qt + ½ c	2¼ qt	3 qt	3¾ qt	1 gal + 2 c
3⅓ c	1½ qt + ⅔ c	2 qt + ⅓ c	2½ qt	3¼ qt + ⅓ c	1 gal + ⅔ c	1¼ gal
3⅔ c	1¾ qt + ⅓ c	2¼ qt + 2½ T	2¾ qt	3½ qt + ⅔ c	1 gal + 2⅓ c	1¼ gal + 2 c
1 qt	2 qt	2½ qt	3 qt	1 gal	1¼ gal	1½ gal
1 qt + ⅓ c	2 qt + ⅔ c	2½ qt + ¾ c + 1½ T	3¼ qt	1 gal + 1⅓ c	1¼ gal + 1⅔ c	1½ gal + 2 c
1 qt + ⅔ c	2¼ qt + ⅓ c	2¾ qt + ⅔ c	3½ qt	1 gal + 2⅔ c	1¼ gal + 3⅓ c	1¾ gal
1¼ qt	2½ qt	3 qt + ½ c	3¾ qt	1¼ gal	1½ gal + 1 c	1¾ gal + 2 c

Table 1.11 DIRECT-READING TABLE FOR ADJUSTING YIELD OF RECIPES WITH INGREDIENT AMOUNTS GIVEN IN **MEASUREMENT** (PORTION YIELDS DIVISIBLE BY 8)[a] (continued)

8	16	20	24	32	40	48
1¼ qt + ⅓ c	2½ qt + ⅔ c	3 qt + 1⅓ c	1 gal	1¼ gal + 1⅓ c	1½ gal + 2⅔ c	2 gal
1½ qt + ⅔ c	3¼ qt + ⅓ c	1 gal + ⅔ c	1¼ gal	1½ gal + 2⅔ c	2 gal + 1⅓ c	2½ gal
2 qt	1 gal	1¼ gal	1½ gal	2 gal	2½ gal	3 gal

56	60	64	72	80	88	96
¼ t(r)	¼ t(r)	¼ t(r)	¼ t + ⅛ t	½ t(s)	½ t(s)	½ t
½ t(r)	½ t(r)	¾ t(s)	¾ t	¾ t(r)	1 t(s)	1 t
1¼ t(s)	1¼ t	1¼ t(r)	1½ t	1¾ t(s)	1¾ t(r)	2 t
1¾ t	1¾ t(r)	2 t	2¼ t	2½ t	2¾ t	1 T
2¼ t(r)	2½ t	2¾ t(s)	1 T	1 T + ¼ t	1 T + ¾ t	1 T + 1 t
1 T(s)	1 T + ⅛ t	1 T + ¼ t	1 T + ¾ t	1 T + 1¼ t	1½ T	1 T + 2 t
1 T + ½ t	1 T + ¾ t	1 T + 1 t	1½ T	1 T + 2 t	1 T + 2½ t	2 T
1 T + 1 t	1 T + 1¼ t + ⅛ t	1 T + 1¾ t	1 T + 2¼ t	1 T + 2¾ t	2 T + ½ t	2 T + 1 t
1 T + 1¾ t	1 T + 2 t	1 T + 2¼ t	2 T	2 T + ¾ t	2 T + ¼ t	2 T + 2 t
1 T + 2¼ t	1 T + 2½ t	2 T	2 T + ¾ t	2½ T	2 T + 2¼ t	3 T
1 T + 2¾ t (r)	2 T + ¼ t	2 T + ¾ t	2 T + 1½ t	2 T + 2¼ t	3 T	3 T + 1 t
2 T + ½ t	2 T + ¾ t	2 T + 1¼ t	2 T + 2¼ t	3 T	3 T + 1 t	3 T + 2 t
2 T + 1 t	2½ T	2 T + 2 t	3 T	3 T + 1 t	3 T + 2 t	¼ c
3½ T	3 T + 2¼ t	¼ c	¼ c + 1½ t	¼ c + 1 T	⅓ c + ½ t	⅓ c + 2 t
¼ c + 2 t	¼ c + 1 T	⅓ c	⅓ c + 2 t	⅓ c + 4 t	⅓ c + 2 T	½ c
⅓ c + ½ T	⅓ c + 2¾ t	⅓ c + 4 t	¼ c + 3½ T	½ c + 1 t	½ c + 3½ t	½ c + 2 T
¼ c + 3 T	¼ c + 3½ T	½ c	½ c + 1 T	½ c + 2 T	½ c + 3 T	¾ c
½ c + ½ t	½ c + 2¼ t	½ c + 4 t	½ c + 2½ T	⅔ c + 1 T	¾ c + 2½ t	¾ c + 2 T

½ c + 4 t	½ c + 2 T	⅔ c	¾ c	¾ c + 4 t	¾ c + 2½ T	1 c
¾ c + ½ T	¾ c + 4 t	¾ c + 2 T	1 c	1 c + 5 t	1 c + 3½ T	1⅓ c
1 c + 2½ T	1¼ c	1⅓ c	1½ c	1⅔ c	1¾ c + 4 t	2 c
1½ c + 1 T	1⅔ c	1¾ c	2 c	2 c + 3½ T	2¼ c + 3 T	2⅔ c
1¾ c	1¾ c + 2 T	2 c	2¼ c	2½ c	2¾ c	3 c
2⅓ c	2½ c	2⅔ c	3 c	3⅓ c	3⅔ c	1 qt
2¾ c + 2½ T	3 c + 2 T	3⅓ c	3¾ c	1 qt + 2½ T	4¼ c + 4 T	1¼ qt
3 c + 2 T	3⅓ c	3½ c + 2½ t	1 qt	4¼ c + 3 T	4¾ c + 2 T + 1 t	1¼ qt + ⅓ c
3½ c	3¾ c	1 qt	1 qt + ½ c	1¼ qt	1¼ qt + ½ c	1½ qt
3¾ c + 2 T	1 qt + 2½ T	4¼ c + 3 T	1¼ qt	1¼ qt + ⅓ c	1½ qt + 5 t	1½ qt + ⅔ c
1 qt + 4 t	1 qt + ¼ c + 2 T	1 qt + ⅔ c	1¼ qt + ¼ c	5½ c + 3 T	1½ qt + ¼ c + 2½ T	1¾ qt
1 qt + ⅔ c	1¼ qt	1¼ qt + ⅓ c	1½ qt	1½ qt + ⅔ c	1¾ qt + ⅓ c	2 qt
1¼ qt + ¼ c	1¼ qt + ⅔ c	1½ qt	1½ qt + ¾ c	1¾ qt + ½ c	2 qt + ¼ c	2¼ qt
5¼ c + 3 T	5¾ c + 1½ T	1½ qt + ¼ c	1¾ qt	1¾ qt + ¾ c	2 qt + ½ c + 1 T	2¼ qt + ⅓ c
5¾ c + 1 T	1½ qt + ¼ c	1½ qt + ⅔ c	1¾ qt + ½ c	2 qt + 5 T	2¼ qt + 3 T	2½ qt
1½ qt + ¼ c	1½ qt + ⅔ c	1¾ qt + 2 T	2 qt	2 qt + ¾ c + 2 T	2¼ qt + ¾ c + ½ T	2½ qt + ⅔ c
1½ qt + ¼ c + 3 T	1½ qt + ¾ c + 2 T	1¾ qt + ⅓ c	2 qt + ¼ c	2¼ qt + 2½ T	2½ qt + 1½ T	2¾ qt
1¾ qt	1¾ qt + ½ c	2 qt	2¼ qt	2½ qt	2¾ qt	3 qt
1¾ qt + ⅓ c + ¼ c	2 qt + 2 T	2 qt + ⅔ c	2¼ qt + ¾ c	2½ qt + ¾ c + 1½ T	2¾ qt + ¾ c + 3 T	3¼ qt
1¾ qt + ¾ c	2 qt + ⅓ c	2 qt + ¾ c + 2 T	2½ qt	2¾ qt + 2 T	3 qt + ¼ c	3¼ qt + ⅓ c
2 qt + 3 T	2 qt + ¾ c	2¼ qt + ⅓ c	2½ qt + ½ c	2¾ qt + ½ c + 2 T	3 qt + ¾ c + 1½ T	3½ qt
2 qt + ½ c + 1 T	2¼ qt + 2½ T	2¼ qt + ¾ c	2¾ qt	3 qt + ¼ c	3¼ qt + ¼ c + 3 T	3 qt + 2⅔ c
2 qt + ¾ c	2¼ qt + ¼ c + 2 T	2½ qt	2¾ qt + ¼ c	3 qt + ½ c	3 qt + 1¾ c	3 qt + 3 c

Table 1.11 DIRECT-READING TABLE FOR ADJUSTING YIELD OF RECIPES WITH INGREDIENT AMOUNTS GIVEN IN **MEASUREMENT** (PORTION YIELDS DIVISIBLE BY 8)[a] (continued)

56	60	64	72	80	88	96
2 qt + 1⅓ c	2½ qt	2¾ qt + ⅓ c	3 qt	3 qt + 1⅓ c	3 qt + 2⅔ c	1 gal
2¾ qt + ⅔ c	3 qt + ½ c	3¼ qt + ⅓ c	3¾ qt	1 gal + ⅔ c	1 gal + 2⅓ c	1¼ gal
3½ qt	3¾ qt	1 gal	1 gal + 2 c	1¼ gal	1¼ gal + 2 c	1½ gal
1 gal + ⅓ c	1 gal + 1½ c	1 gal + 2⅔ c	1¼ gal + 1 c	1¼ gal + 3⅓ c	1½ gal + 1⅔ c	1¾ gal
1 gal + 2⅔ c	1¼ gal	1¼ gal + 1⅓ c	1½ gal	1½ gal + 2⅔ c	1¾ gal + 1⅓ c	2 gal
1¼ gal + 1 c	1¼ gal + 2½ c	1½ gal	1½ gal + 3 c	1¾ gal + 2 c	2 gal + 1 c	2¼ gal
1¼ gal + 3⅓ c	1½ gal + 1 c	1½ gal + 2⅔ c	1¾ gal + 2 c	2 gal + 1⅓ c	2¼ gal + ⅔ c	2½ gal
1½ gal + 1⅔ c	1½ gal + 3½ c	1¾ gal + 1⅓ c	2 gal + 1 c	2¼ gal + ⅔ c	2½ gal + ⅓ c	2¾ gal
1¾ gal	1¾ gal + 2 c	2 gal	2¼ gal	2½ gal	2¾ gal	3 gal
1¾ gal + 2⅓ c	2 gal + ½ c	2 gal + 2⅔ c	2¼ gal + 3 c	2½ gal + 3⅓ c	2¾ gal + 3⅔ c	3¼ gal
2 gal + ⅔ c	2 gal + 3 c	2¼ gal + 1⅓ c	2½ gal + 2 c	2¾ gal + 2⅔ c	3 gal + 3⅓ c	3½ gal
2 gal + 3 c	2¼ gal + 1½ c	2½ gal	2¾ gal + 1 c	3 gal + 2 c	3¼ gal + 3c	3¾ gal
2¼ gal + 1⅓ c	2½ gal	2½ gal + 2⅔ c	3 gal	3¼ gal + 1⅓ c	3½ gal + 2⅔ c	4 gal
2¾ gal + 2⅔ c	3 gal + 2c	3¼ gal + 1⅓ c	3¾ gal	4 gal + 2⅔ c	4½ gal + 1⅓ c	5 gal
3½ gal	3¾ gal	4 gal	4½ gal	5 gal	5½ gal	6 gal

[a] From *Standardizing Recipes for Institutional Use*. The American Dietetic Association, 1967.

Table 1.12 GUIDE FOR ROUNDING OFF WEIGHTS
AND MEASURES[a]

Item	If the Total Amount of an Ingredient Is	Round it to
	WEIGHTS	
	less than 2 oz	measure unless weight is in ¼-, ½-, ¾-oz amounts
Various miscellaneous ingredients	2 oz–10 oz	closest ¼ oz or convert to measure
	more than 10 oz but less than 2 lb 8 oz	closest ½ oz
	2 lb 8 oz–5 lb	closest full ounce
	more than 5 lb	closest ¼ lb
	MEASURES	
Primarily spices, seasonings, flavorings, condiments, leavenings, and similar items	less than 1 T	closest ⅛ t
	more than 1 T but less than 3 T	closest ¼ t
	3 T–½ c	closest ½ t or convert to weight
	more than ½ c but less than ¾ c	closest full teaspoon or convert to weight
	more than ¾ c but less than 2 c	closest full tablespoon or convert to weight
	2 c–2 qt	nearest ¼ c
	more than 2 qt but less than 4 qt	nearest ½ c
Primarily milk, water, eggs, juice, oil, syrup, molasses, etc.	1 gal–2 gal	nearest full cup or ¼ qt
	more than 2 gal but less than 10 gal	nearest full quart
	more than 10 gal but less than 20 gal	closest ½ gal
	over 20 gal	closest full gallon

[a] From *Standardizing Recipes for Institutional Use*. The American
Dietetic Association, 1967.

Note: These values for rounding have been calculated to be within the
limits of error normally introduced in the handling of ingredients in
preparing foods. They are intended to aid in "rounding" fractions and
complex measurements and weights into amounts that are as simple as
possible to weigh or measure while maintaining the accuracy needed for
quality control in products.

Food Measures, Substitutions, and Proportions

Table 1.13 APPROXIMATE DIPPER EQUIVALENTS

Dipper Number[a]	U.S.		Metric		
	Measure	Weight	Measure	Weight	Suggested Use
100	Scant 2 t		10 mL		Tea cookies
70	Scant 1 T	⅜ oz	13 mL	10 g	Drop cookies
60	1 T	½ oz	15 mL	14 g	Small cookies, garnishes
50	1¼ T	⅝ oz	19 mL	17 g	Drop cookies
40	1½ T	¾ oz	23 mL	21 g	Drop cookies
30	2 T +	1-1½ oz	30 mL	28-43 g	Drop cookies
24	2⅔ T +	1½-1¾ oz	40 mL	43-50 g	Cream puffs
20	3 T +	1¾-2 oz	45 mL	50-57 g	Muffins, cup cakes, sauces
16	4 T (¼ c)	2-2¼ oz	60 mL	57-64 g	Muffins, desserts, croquettes
12	5 T + (⅓ c)	2½-3 oz	75 mL	70-85 g	Croquettes, vegetables, muffins, desserts, salads
10	6 T +	3-4 oz	90 mL	85-114 g	Desserts, meat patties, vegetables, hot cereals
8	8 T (½ c)	4-5 oz	120 mL	114-142 g	Luncheon dishes, creamed meats
6	10 T +	6 oz	150 mL	170 g	Luncheon salads

[a] Portions per quart.

Note: These measurements are based on level dippers. If a heaping dipper is used, the measure and weight are closer to that of the next larger dipper.

Table 1.14 APPROXIMATE LADLE EQUIVALENTS

U.S.		Metric		
Volume	Weight	Volume	Weight	Suggested Use
⅛ c	1 oz	30 mL	28 g	Sauces
¼ c	2 oz	60 mL	57 g	Gravies, some sauces
½ c	4 oz	120 mL	114 g	Stews, creamed dishes
¾ c	6 oz	180 mL	170 g	Stews, creamed dishes
1 c	8 oz	240 mL	227 g	Soup

Note: These measurements are based on level ladles. If a heaping ladle is used, the measure is closer to that of the next larger ladle.

Table 1.15 COMMON CONTAINER SIZES[a]

	Container			
	Consumer Description			
Industry Term	*Approximate Net Weight or Fluid Measure*	*Approximate Cups*	*Metric Equivalent*	*Principal Products*
6 oz	6 oz	¾	170 g (177 mL)	Frozen concentrated and single strength juices. 5 servings.
8 oz	8 oz	1	227 g	Fruits, vegetables, specialties[b] for small families. 2 servings.
Picnic	10½-12 oz	1¼	298-340 g	Mainly condensed soups. Some fruits, vegetables, meat, fish, specialties.[b] 2-3 servings.
12 oz	12 oz	1½	340 g (355 mL)	Frozen fruit juices. 10 servings; vacuum packed corn, 3-4 servings.
No. 300	14-16 oz	1¾	397-454 g	Pork and beans, baked beans, meat products, cranberry sauce, blueberries, specialties.[b] 3-4 servings.
No. 303	16-17 oz	2	454-482 g	Principal size for fruits and vegetables. Some meat products, ready-to-serve soups, specialties.[b] 4 servings.
No. 2	20 oz or 18 fl oz	2½	567 g 535 mL	Juices,[c] ready-to-serve soups, some specialties,[b] pineapple, apple slices. No longer in popular use for most fruits and vegetables. 5 servings.

*continued on next page

Table 1.15 COMMON CONTAINER SIZES[a] (continued)

	Container			
	Consumer Description			
Industry Term	Approximate Net Weight or Fluid Measure	Approximate Cups	Metric Equivalent	Principal Products
No. 2½	27-29 oz	3½	765-822 g	Fruits, some vegetables (pumpkin, sauerkraut, spinach, and other greens, tomatoes). 5-7 servings.
32 oz	32 oz	4	0.95 L	Frozen fruit juices. 25 servings.
No. 3 or	51 oz	5¾	1.45 kg	Fruit and vegetable juices,[c] pork and beans. Institutional size for condensed soups, some vegetables. 10-12 servings.
46 fl oz	46 fl oz		1.36 L	
No. 10	6½ lb-7 lb 5 oz	12-13	2.95-3.32 kg	Institutional size for fruits, vegetables, and some other foods. 25 servings.

[a] Adapted from *Canned Food Tables,* Home Economics—Consumer Services, National Canners Association, Washington, D.C.
[b] Specialties: Usually a food combination such as macaroni, spaghetti, Spanish-style rice, Mexican-type foods, Chinese foods, or tomato aspic.
[c] Juices are now being packed in a number of can sizes.

Notes:
1. Strained and homogenized foods for infants, and chopped junior foods, come in small jars and cans suitable for the smaller servings used. The weight is given on the label.
2. Meats, poultry, fish, and seafood are almost entirely advertised and sold under weight terminology.

Table. 1.16 SUBSTITUTING ONE CAN FOR ANOTHER SIZE[a]

	Approximate
1 No. 10 can =	7 No. 303 (1 lb) cans
1 No. 10 can =	5 No. 2 (1 lb 4 oz) cans
1 No. 10 can =	4 No. 2½ (1 lb 13 oz) cans
1 No. 10 can =	2 No. 3 (46 to 50 oz) cans

[a] Adapted from *Canned Food Tables,* Home Economics—Consumer Services, National Canners Association, Washington, D.C.

Table 1.17 APPROXIMATE YIELD IN THE PREPARATION OF FRESH FRUITS AND VEGETABLES[a]

Weight of Ready-to-Cook or Ready-to-Serve-Raw Food from 1 lb as Purchased			
	lb		*lb*
Apple	0.76	Lettuce, head	0.75
Asparagus	0.56	Lettuce, leaf	0.67
Avocado	0.72	Mushrooms	0.97
Banana	0.67	Okra	0.78
Beans, green or wax	0.88	Onions, mature	0.89
Beans, lima	0.39	Orange sections	0.56
Beets	0.76	Parsnips	0.85
Blueberries	0.86	Peaches	0.76
Broccoli	0.61	Pears	0.78
Brussels sprouts	0.74	Peas, green	0.38
Cabbage, green	0.79	Peppers, green	0.82
Cantaloupe, served without rind	0.50	Pineapple	0.52
Carrots	0.82	Plums	0.94
Cauliflower	0.55	Potatoes	0.81
Celery	0.75	Potatoes, sweet	0.80
Chard	0.77	Rhubarb, partly trimmed	0.86
Cherries, pitted	0.89	Radishes	0.63
Cranberries	0.97	Rutabagas	0.85
Cucumber, unpared	0.95	Spinach, untrimmed	0.74
pared	0.73	partly trimmed	0.92
Eggplant	0.81	Squash, Acorn	0.88
Endive, chicory, escarole	0.74	Squash, Hubbard	0.66
Grapefruit sections	0.47	Squash, Zucchini	0.98
Grapes, seedless	0.95	Strawberries	0.89
Honeydew melon, served		Tomatoes	0.91
without rind	0.57	Turnips	0.81
Kale	0.74	Watermelon	0.47
Lettuce, head	0.75		

[a] Adapted from *Food Buying Guide for Type A School Lunches*, U.S. Dept. Agriculture PA-270, Revised 1972.

HOW TO USE THIS TABLE

To determine the amount of fruits or vegetables to yield the amount stated in a recipe as E.P. or as ready-to-cook in the Timetable for Boiling or Steaming Fresh Vegetables, p. 501.

Divide the weight of ready-to-cook or E.P. desired by the figure given in this table. For example, the recipe for Mashed Potatoes, p. 516, calls for 12 lb (E.P.) potatoes. To change the 12 lb (E.P.) to A.P., divide 12 lb by 0.81, the ready-to-cook weight from 1 lb A.P.

12 lb E.P. ÷ 0.81 lb = 14.8 or 15 lb to purchase

To use with metric weights, divide E.P. weight by factor in above table.

5.4 kg E.P. ÷ 0.81 = 6.61 kg to purchase

Table 1.18 APPROXIMATE EQUIVALENT SUBSTITUTIONS

Ingredient	*Approximate Equivalent*
Thickening Agents	
1 oz flour	3½ whole eggs (5½ oz)
	7 egg yolks (5 oz)
	1⅓ oz quick-cooking tapioca
	⅔ oz cornstarch
	½ oz waxy maize
	¾ oz bread crumbs
1 T flour	½ T cornstarch
	½ T waxy maize
	2 t quick-cooking tapioca
Shortening Agents	
1 lb butter	1 lb margarine
	⅞ lb hydrogenated shortening plus 1 t salt
	⅞ lb lard plus 1 t salt
	⅞ lb oil (1⅜ c) plus 1 t salt
	⅞ lb chicken fat plus 1 t salt
Leavening Agents[a]	
1 t baking powder	¼ t soda plus ⅝ t cream of tartar
	¼ t soda plus ½ c sour milk
	¼ t soda plus ½ T vinegar used with 7½ T sweet milk
	¼ t soda plus ¼ to ½ c molasses
	2 egg whites
1 small pkg active dry yeast	1 cake compressed yeast
1 oz dry yeast	2 oz compressed yeast
Chocolate and Cocoa	
1 oz or 1 square chocolate	3 T cocoa plus 1 T fat
Milk	
1 c whole milk	¼ c (approximately) dry whole milk[a] plus 1 c water
	3 T instant nonfat dry milk powder[a] plus 1 c water and 3 T butter
	6 T nonfat dry milk crystals plus 1 c water and 3 T butter
	½ c evaporated milk plus ½ c water
1 c sour milk[b]	1 c sweet milk plus 1 T lemon juice or vinegar
Cream	
1 c cream, thin (18-20%)	⅞ c milk plus 3 T butter
1 c cream, heavy (36-40%)	¾ c milk plus ⅓ c butter

Table 1.18 APPROXIMATE EQUIVALENT SUBSTITUTIONS (continued)

Ingredient	*Approximate Equivalent*
Flour	
1 c all purpose flour	1 c plus 2 T cake flour ⅞ c corn meal 1 c graham flour 1 c rye flour 1¼ c bran 1½ c bread crumbs 1 c rolled oats
Seasoning 1 medium-size onion	1 T instant minced onion

[a] A general guide is to use 3.2 oz, by weight, of instant or regular spray process nonfat dry milk to make 1 qt of liquid milk; or 4.5 oz of dry whole milk per quart.

[b] To substitute sour milk or buttermilk for sweet milk, add ½ t soda and decrease baking powder by 2 t per cup of milk. To sour reconstituted dry milk, add 1 c cultured buttermilk to 1 gal reconstituted dry milk.

For metric equivalents, see Tables 1.4 and 1.5.

Table 1.19 EQUIVALENTS FOR FROZEN, DRIED, AND SHELL EGGS

	Amount of Product to Use		*Shell Egg*
Product	*U.S.*	*Metric*	*Equivalent*
Frozen (thawed)			
Whole	3 T	45 mL	1 egg
Whole	2¼ c	540 mL	12 eggs
Yolks	1⅓ T	20 mL	1 egg
Yolks	1 c	240 mL	12 eggs
Whites	2 T	30 mL	1 egg
Whites	1½ c	360 mL	12 eggs
Dried (sifted)			
Whole	2½ T + 2½ T water	37 mL + 37 mL water	1 egg
Whole	2 c pl 2 c water	480 mL + 480 mL water	12 eggs
Yolks	2 T + 2 t water	30 mL + 10 mL water	1 egg
Yolks	1½ c + ½ c water	360 mL + 120 mL water	12 eggs
Whites	2 t + 2 T water	10 mL + 30 mL water	1 egg
Whites	½ c + 1½ c water	120 mL + 360 mL water	12 eggs

Table 1.20 RELATIVE PROPORTIONS OF INGREDIENTS

Ingredient	Relative Proportion
Thickening Agents	
Eggs	4-6 whole eggs to 1 qt milk 8-12 egg yolks to 1 qt milk 8-12 egg whites to 1 qt milk
Flour[a]	½ oz to 1 qt liquid—very thin sauce (cream soups, starchy vegetables) 1 oz to 1 qt liquid—thin sauce (cream soups, nonstarchy vegetables) 2 oz to 1 qt liquid—medium sauce (creamed dishes, gravy) 3-4 oz to 1 qt liquid—thick sauce (soufflés) 4-5 oz to 1 qt liquid—very thick sauce (croquettes) 1 lb to 1 qt liquid—pour batter (popovers) 2 lb to 1 qt liquid—drop batter (cake muffins) 3 lb to 1 qt liquid—soft dough (biscuit, rolls) 4 lb to 1 qt liquid—stiff dough (pastry, cookies, noodles)
Gelatin	2 T to 1 qt liquid—plain jellies (gelatin and fruit juices) 2 T to 1 qt liquid—whips (gelatin and fruit juices whipped) 3 T to 1 qt liquid—fruit jellies (gelatin, fruit juices, and chopped fruit) 3 T to 1 qt liquid—vegetable jellies (gelatin, liquid, and chopped vegetables) 3 T to 1 qt liquid—sponges (gelatin, fruit juices, and beaten egg whites) 4 T to 1 qt liquid—Bavarian cream (gelatin, fruit juice, fruit pulp, and whipped cream)
Seasonings	
Salt	1-2 t to 1 lb flour 1¼ t to 1 lb meat 2 t to 1 qt water (cereal) 2½ t to 1 pt liquid (rolls)

Table 1.20 RELATIVE PROPORTIONS OF INGREDIENTS (continued)

Ingredient	Relative Proportion
Leavening Agents	
Baking powder, quick acting (tartrate or phosphate)	2-2⅔ T to 1 lb flour
Baking powder, slow acting (S.A.S. or combination)	1½-2 T to 1 lb flour
Baking soda	2 t to 1 qt sour milk or molasses
Yeast	½-1 compressed cake (3/10-3/5 oz) or ½-1 envelope dry (⅛-¼ oz) to 1 lb flour (varies with ingredients and time allowed)

[a] For thickening equivalents for flour, see p. 68.

For metric equivalents, see Tables 1.4 and 1.5.

Baking Temperatures

Table 1.21 TERMS FOR OVEN TEMPERATURES

	Temperature	
Term	°F	°C[a]
Very slow	250-275	121-135
Slow	300-325	150-165
Moderate	350-375	175-190
Hot	400-425	205-220
Very hot (quick)	450-475	230-245
Extremely hot	500-525	260-275

[a] Metric temperatures were obtained by using the following formula: 5/9 of °F after subtracting 32. Resulting figures were rounded to a functional temperature.

Table 1.22 TEMPERATURES AND TIMES USED IN BAKING

Type of Product	Approximate Time Required for Baking[a] (min)	Oven Temperature	
		°F	°C[b]
Bread			
Biscuits	10-15	425-450	220-230
Corn bread	30-40	400-425	205-220
Cream puffs	40-60	375	190
Muffins	20-25	400-425	205-220
Popovers	60	375	190
Quick loaf bread	60-75	350-375	175-190
Yeast bread	30-40	400	205
Yeast rolls: plain	15-25	400-425	205-220
sweet	20-30	375	190
Cakes, with fat			
Cup	15-25	350-375	175-190
Layer	20-35	350-375	175-190
Loaf	45-60	350	175
Cakes, without fat			
Angel food and sponge	30-45	350-375	175-190
Cookies			
Drop	8-15	350-400	175-205
Rolled	8-10	375	190
Egg, meat, milk, cheese dishes			
Cheese soufflé (baked in pan of hot water)	30-60	350	175
Custard, plain, corn, other (baked in pan of hot water)	30-60	350	175
Macaroni and cheese	25-30	350	175
Meat loaf	60-90	300	150
Meat pie	25-30	400	205
Rice pudding (raw rice)	120-180	300	150
Scalloped potatoes	60	350	175
Pastry			
1-crust pie (custard type)	30-40	400-425	205-220
Meringue on cooked filling in preheated shell	12-15 or	350	175
	4-4½	425	205
Shell only	10-12	450	230
2-crust pies and uncooked filling in prebaked shell	45-55	400-425	205-220
2-crust pies with cooked filling	30-45	425-450	220-230

[a] For convection ovens follow time and temperature recommendations of manufacturer.
[b] Metric temperatures were obtained by using the following formula: 5/9 of °F after subtracting 32. Resulting figures were rounded to a functional temperature.

Table 1.23 METRIC TEMPERATURE EQUIVALENTS[a]

°F	°C	°F	°C	°F	°C	°F	°C
32	0	200	95	300	150	400	205
100	38	212	100	310	155	425	220
105	40	220	105	320	160	450	230
110	43	225	107	324	162	475	245
115	46	230	110	325	165	500	260
120	49	234	112	330	166	525	275
125	52	238	114	335	168	550	290
130	55	240	115	338	170	575	300
140	60	244	118	340	171	600	315
150	65	248	120	350	175		
160	70	250	121	360	180		
170	75	260	125	365	182		
175	80	266	130	370	185		
180	82	270	132	375	190		
185	85	275	135	380	195		
190	88	290	143	390	200		
195	90						

[a] Temperatures in this edition of *Food for Fifty* are given in Fahrenheit and Celsius (Centigrade). To convert from °F to °C, the following formula was used: °F − 32 × 5/9 = °C. Some temperatures were rounded to numbers that would be functional in ovens and other equipment.

Sugar Syrups

Table 1.24 TEMPERATURES AND TESTS FOR SYRUPS AND CANDIES

Product	Temperature of Syrup at Sea Level (Indicating Concentration Desired)[a]		Test	Description of Test
	°F	°C		
Syrup	230-234	110-112	Thread	Syrup spins a 2-in. thread when dropped from fork or spoon.
Fondant Fudge Penoche	234-240	112-115	Soft ball	When dropped into very cold water, syrup forms a soft ball that flattens on removal from water.
Caramels	244-248	118-120	Firm ball	When dropped into very cold water, syrup forms a firm ball that does not flatten on removal from water.
Divinity Marshmallows Popcorn balls	250-266	121-130	Hard ball	When dropped into very cold water, syrup forms a ball that is hard enough to hold its shape, yet plastic.
Butterscotch Taffies	270-290	132-143	Soft crack	When dropped into very cold water, syrup separates into threads that are hard, but not brittle.
Brittle Glacé	300-310	150-155	Hard crack	When dropped into very cold water, syrup separates into threads that are hard and brittle.
Barley sugar	320	160	Clear liquid	Sugar liquefies.
Caramel	338	170	Brown liquid	Liquid becomes brown.

[a] Cook syrup about 1 °C lower than temperature at sea level for each increase of 900 ft in elevation, or 1 °F lower than temperature at sea level for each increase of 500 ft in elevation.

Sugar Syrup (Thin)

2 lb (908 g) sugar and 1 qt (0.95 L) water, boil together; for a thicker syrup increase sugar to 2½ lb (1.14 kg) and add 1 T (15 mL) corn syrup to prevent crystallization. May be kept on hand for use in beverages or where recipe specifies simple syrup.

Burnt Sugar Syrup or Caramel Flavoring

1 lb (454 g) sugar and 2 c (480 mL) boiling water. Put sugar in a pan and melt slowly, stirring constantly. Cook until light brown (caramelized), being careful not to scorch. Add boiling water. Cook slowly until a syrup is formed.

Caramelized Sugar

Melt sugar over moderate heat in heavy, shallow pan. Stir constantly. Cook until light brown.

Deep-Fat Frying

Methods of Preparing Food for Deep-Fat Frying

Light Coating

Dip prepared food in milk. Drain. Dredge with seasoned flour. Use 1 lb (454 g) flour, 2 T (30 mL) salt, and other seasonings as desired.

Egg and Crumb

Dip prepared food in flour (may omit), then in a mixture of egg and milk or water. Drain and roll in fine crumbs to cover. Use 3 eggs to 1 c (240 mL) milk or water for most products. In some cases 1 egg to 1 c (240 mL) milk may be satisfactory. For softer mixtures, such as Egg Cutlets, use 6 eggs to 1 c (240 mL) liquid. Allow 12 oz (340 g) crumbs for 50 servings of most items.

Batter

Dip prepared food in a batter made in the following proportions: 12 oz (340 g) flour, 1½ t (8 mL) salt, 2 t (10 mL) baking powder, 3 T (45 mL) fat, 2 c (480 mL) milk, and 6 well-beaten eggs. This quantity is sufficient for 50 servings of most items.

Care of Fat and Fryer

For best results, select a bland-flavored frying fat with a high smoking point. Use the amount of fat recommended for the fryer, which should be enough to cover the food entirely. Clarify the fat regularly, at least once a day when fryer is in constant use, to remove accumulated sediment. This may be done by straining the fat through cheesecloth or by following instructions provided by the fryer manufacturer. Thoroughly wash, rinse, and dry fryer before replacing strained fat, then add enough fresh fat to bring back the required weight or amount necessary for best use of the deep-fat frying equipment.

Proper care will prolong the life of the fat but, when undesirable flavors develop, fat should be discarded.

Table 1.25 DEEP-FAT FRYING TEMPERATURES

| Type of Product | Preparation | Temperature | | Frying Time[a] (min) |
		°F	°C	
Bananas	Skin and scrape. Cut in pieces 2 in. long. Sprinkle with powdered sugar and lemon juice. Let stand 30 min. Dip in batter.	375	190	1-3
Cauliflower, pre-cooked	See p. 496.	370	185	3-5
Cheese balls	See p. 201	360	180	2-3
Chicken, disjointed,				
1½-2 lb fryers	Light coating or egg and crumb[b]	325	165	10-12
2-2½ lb fryers	Light coating or egg and crumb	325	165	12-15
Chicken, half				
1½-2 lb fryers	Light coating or egg and crumb	325	165	12-15
Croquettes (all previously cooked foods)		360-375	180-190	2-5
Cutlets, ½ in. thick	Egg and crumb	325-350	165-175	5-8
Doughnuts	See p. 129	360-375	180-190	3-5
Eggplant	See p. 516	370	185	5-7
Fish fillets	Egg and crumb	375	190	4-6
Fritters	See p. 136	370-380	185-195	2-5
Onion rings	Batter	350	175	3-4
Oysters	Egg and crumb	375	190	2-4
Potatoes, ½ in.	See p. 497, 517			
Complete fry		365	182	6-8
Blanching		360	180	3-5
Browning		375	190	2-3
Frozen, fat blanched		375	190	2-3
Sandwiches	See p. 454	350-360	175-180	3-4
Scallops	Egg and crumb	360-375	180-190	3-4
Shrimp	Batter or egg and crumb	360-375	180-190	3-5
Timbale cases	See p. 135	350-365	175-182	2-3
Fish sticks	Egg and crumb	375	190	3-4
French toast	See p. 157	360	180	3-4

[a] The exact frying time will vary with the equipment used, size and temperature of the food pieces, and the amount of food placed in the fryer at one time. If the kettle is overloaded, foods may become grease-soaked. If food is frozen, use lower temperatures listed and allow additional cooking time.
[b] See p. 75 for directions for egg and crumb.

Note: At high altitudes, the lower boiling point of water in foods requires lowering of temperatures for deep-fat frying.

Spices and Seasonings

Table 1.26 USE OF SPICES AND SEASONINGS IN COOKING

Spice	Use
Allspice, whole	Pickling, gravies, consommé, boiled fish and meat, eggplant, tomatoes, baked beans
Allspice, ground	Baked products, puddings, relishes, some fruit preserves, gravies
Anise seed, whole or ground	Coffee cakes, sweet rolls, cookies, candies
Basil, whole or ground	Tomato juice, beef stew, chicken, tomatoes, Lima beans, peas, French dressing
Bay leaves (laurel)	Pickling, stews, soups, roast beef, beets, tomatoes, kidney beans, string beans, eggplant
Caraway seed, whole or ground	Rye bread, sprinkled over pork liver, or kidney before cooking
Cardamom (cardamum)	Pickling, flavoring in coffee cakes, Danish pastry, curries, and soups
Celery seed, whole or ground	Pickling, salads, fish, salad dressings, cream cheese spread, ham spread, beef stew, meat loaf, croquettes, cabbage, cauliflower, onions, cole slaw
Cayenne pepper	Lima beans, meats, fish, sauces, Mexican dishes
Chili powder	Chili con carne, tamales, shell fish and oyster cocktail, sauces, cooked eggs, kidney beans, Spanish rice, meat sauces, gravies
Cinnamon, ground	Puddings, pastry, rolls
Cinnamon stick and Cassibuds	Pickling, preserving, stewed fruits
Cloves, whole	Pickling, hams, fruits, string beans
Cloves, ground	Baked products, desserts, cranberry juice, tomato soup, Mulligatawny soup, pot roast, boiled beef, beets, onions, sweet potatoes, tomato sauce, tomato aspic
Coriander, whole or ground	Pickling, curries, baked products
Cumin (Cumino), whole	Mexican cookery, sausages, stews, soups (ingredient of curry and chili powder)
Curry powder	Mulligatawny soup, lamb, veal stew, chicken, rice dishes, fish
Dill seed, whole or ground	Pickling, sauerkraut, cabbage, cauliflower, turnips
Fennel seed	Italian and Swedish cookery
Ginger, whole	Pickling, beverages
Ginger, ground	Baked products, barbecue sauce, pear salad
Horseradish	Sauces, relishes
Mace, ground	Fish, fish sauces, pickling, preserving, baked products, pastries, tomato juice
Marjoram, leaf or ground	Soups, stews, sausage, lamb, tomatoes, Swiss chard, spinach, peas, cottage cheese, French dressing

Spices and Seasonings

Table 1.26 USE OF SPICES AND SEASONINGS IN COOKING (continued)

Spice	*Use*
Mint leaves	Peas, lamb, iced tea, sauces
Mustard seed, whole	Pickling, salad garnish
Mustard seed, ground	Salad dressing, sauces, baked beans, sandwich fillings
Nutmeg, ground	Sauces (dessert), chicken, sweet potatoes, spinach, cauliflower, baked products, puddings, eggnog
Oregano leaves (Mexican sage)	Pork, ingredient of chili powder
Paprika	Fish, salad dressing, garnishes, corn, stews
Peppercorn (white and black)	Pickling, soups, meats
Pepper, ground (white and black)	Meat, sauces, gravies, vegetables
Poppy seed	Cake, cookies, topping for breads
Rosemary leaves	Italian sausages, Italian dishes
Sage, leaf or ground	Stuffing, sausage, cheese, soup, sauces
Saffron	Baked products, special dishes
Savory leaves	Poultry, meat
Sesame seed	Rolls, breads
Thyme, leaf or ground	Stews, meat loaf, soups, stuffing
Tarragon leaves	Vinegar, dressing, pickles, sauces, mustard
Turmeric, ground	Ingredient of curry powder, coloring for condiments

Glossary of Food Terms

Cooking Processes and Methods

Baking

Cooking by dry heat, usually in an oven but occasionally on heated metals. This term is used interchangeably with **roasting** when applied to meats in uncovered containers.

Barbecuing

Roasting slowly, usually basting with a highly seasoned sauce.

Basting

Moistening meat or other food while cooking to add flavor and to prevent drying of the surface. Melted fat, meat drippings, water, or water and fat may be used for basting.

Beating

A brisk regular motion that lifts a mixture over and over and thereby introduces air or makes the mixture smooth.

Blanching

Preheating in boiling water or steam (1) to remove inactive enzymes and shrink food for canning, freezing, and drying, and (2) to aid in the removal of skins from nuts, fruits, and some vegetables.

Blending

Thoroughly mixing two or more ingredients.

Boiling

Cooking in water or a liquid, mostly water, in which the bubbles are breaking on the surface and steam is given off. The boiling temperature of water at sea level is 100 °C (212 °F.) but will be approximately 1 °C. less for every 1000-ft elevation. The boiling point will be increased by the solution of solids in the water.

Braising

Cooking slowly in a covered utensil in a small amount of liquid. Meat stock, water, milk, or cream may be used for the liquid. (Meat may or may not be browned in a small amount of fat before braising.)

Breading

Dipping a food into an egg-milk mixture and then into fine dry crumbs.

Broiling

Cooking by direct heat. This may be done by placing the food under or over a clear flame.

Candying

Cooking in heavy syrup until plump and transparent, then draining and drying.

Caramelizing

Heating sugar, or food containing a high percentage of sugar, until a brown color and a characteristic flavor develops.

Chopping

Cutting food into fairly fine pieces with a knife or other sharp tool.

Creaming

The working of one or more foods until soft and creamy. This term is ordinarily applied to the mixing of fat and sugar.

Crisping

Heating foods such as cereals or crackers to remove excessive moisture.

Cutting in

The combining of a solid fat with dry ingredients by a horizontal motion with knives or mixer. A fat is thus combined with dry ingredients with the least amount of blending.

Dicing

Cutting into cubes.

Dredging

Coating or sprinkling a food with flour or other fine substance.

Egging and Crumbing

Dipping a food into diluted, slightly beaten egg, and dredging with crumbs. This treatment is used to prevent soaking of the food with fat or to form a surface easily browned.

Folding

Combining ingredients by using two motions, cutting vertically through the mixture, and turning over and over by sliding the implement across the bottom of the mixing bowl with each turn.

Fricasseeing

Cooking by browning in a small amount of fat, then stewing or steaming. This method is most often applied to fowl or veal cut into pieces.

Frizzling

Cooking in a small amount of fat to produce a food that is crisp and brown with curled edges.

Frying

Cooking in hot fat. The food may be cooked in a small amount of fat (also called sautéing or pan frying), or in a deep layer of fat (also called deep-fat frying).

Glacéing

Coating with a thin sugar syrup cooked to the crack stage. It may also refer to a less concentrated mixture containing thickening, and used for coating certain types of rolls or pastries.

Grilling

Cooking by direct heat.

Grinding

Changing a food to small particles.

Kneading

Manipulation with a pressing motion accompanied by folding and stretching.

Larding

The insertion of small strips of fat (lardoons) into or on top of uncooked lean meat or fish, to give flavor or prevent dryness.

Marinating

Placing a food into a marinade (usually an oil-acid mixture, such as French dressing).

Melting

Liquefying by the application of heat.

Mincing

Cutting or chopping food into very small pieces—not so fine and regular as grinding, yet finer than those produced by chopping.

Mixing

Uniting two or more ingredients.

Panbroiling

Cooking, uncovered, on hot metal, such as a fry pan. The fat is removed as it accumulates. Liquid is never added.

Panfrying

Cooking in a small amount of fat. (See *Frying*.)

Parboiling

Partially cooking a food by boiling, the cooking being completed by another method.

Parching

Browning by the application of dry heat usually applied to grains of corn.

Paring

Cutting off the outside covering, usually with a knife.

Peeling

Stripping off the outside covering.

Planking

Cooking or serving a food, usually fish or steak, on a hot wooden board or plank made especially for this purpose.

Poaching

Cooking in a hot liquid, the original shape of the food being retained.

Pot-Roasting

Cooking large cuts of meat by braising.

Reconstituting

Restoring concentrated foods to their normal state, usually by adding water. Applied to foods such as dry milk (for fluid milk) or frozen orange juice (for liquid juice).

Rehydration

Cooking, soaking, or using other procedures with dehydrated foods to restore water lost during drying.

Roasting

Cooking uncovered by dry heat. The term is usually applied to meat.

Sautéing

Cooking in a small amount of fat. (See *Frying*.)

Scalding

Heating a liquid to a point just below boiling.

Scalloping

Baking food, usually cut into pieces and covered with a liquid or sauce and crumbs. The food and sauce may be mixed together or arranged in alternate layers in a baking dish, with or without crumbs. *Escalloped* is a synonymous term.

Scoring

Making shallow lengthwise and crosswise slits on the surface of meat.

Searing

Browning the surface of meat by the application of intense heat for a short time.

Simmering

Cooking in a liquid in which bubbles form slowly and break just below the surface. The temperatures range from 85 °C. (185 °F.) to a temperature just below the boiling point.

Steaming

Cooking in steam with or without pressure. Steam may be applied directly to the food, as in a steamer, or to the vessel, as in a double boiler.

Steeping

The process of extracting flavors, colors, or other qualities by adding boiling water and allowing the mixture to stand. The mixture is always just below the boiling point.

Stewing

Simmering in a small amount of liquid.

Stirring

Mixing food materials with a circular motion. Food materials are blended or made into a uniform consistency by this process.

Toasting

The application of direct heat until the surface of the food is browned.

Whipping

Rapid beating to increase volume by the incorporation of air.

Menu Terms

See pp. 594-607.

Part

RECIPES

Recipe Information

Yield

The recipes in this book provide servings for 50 people unless otherwise stated. It is recognized that many factors affect the probable yield; portioning is possibly one of the most important. Yield also will vary with the type of foodservice, the clientele, and the skill of the employee serving the food.

Dippers numbered according to yield per quart and ladles for different portion weights are helpful in serving. The yield of dippers and ladles, given on p. 64, is based on level portions, so there could be variations if the food is liquid or very thick and if the server rounds or heaps the food into the dipper. If serving spoons are used, guidelines should be marked on the food in the pan or a portion weighed or measured to determine the correct quantity to serve.

A pan 12 x 20 x 2 in. has been indicated for many recipes, because it is an accepted counter pan size. For some entrées, 2 12 x 20 x 2 in. pans were specified, especially for those having a crusty or crumb topping. For breads, gelatin salads, cakes, and other desserts that are to be cut into servings, the yield has been given as 48 rather than 50 for ease of cutting. In some institutions where larger portions are needed, a pan 12 x 20 x 2 in. may yield only 32 or 40 servings.

Bun pans 18 x 26 in. are often preferred for sheet cakes, rolls, jelly rolls, and cookies. A 9-in. round 2-layer cake is calculated to yield 14-16 servings, although an 8-in. pie will give only 6 servings. All recipe yields vary according to desired portion size, pan size, and the institutional policies of quality (i.e., whether broken or corner pieces are to be served).

Cooking Time and Temperature

The cooking time given in each recipe is based on the size of pan indicated and the amount of food in the pan. If a smaller or larger pan is used, the cooking time should be adjusted accordingly. The number of pans placed in the oven at one time also may affect the length of baking time; the larger the number of pans, the longer the cooking time.

Temperatures are given both in Fahrenheit (°F) and Celsius (°C). Celsius temperatures were determined by the conversion formula on p. 73, then rounded off to a functional conversion.

Variations and Notes

Variations and notes have been placed at the bottom of many recipes. A variation may have one or more ingredients replaced, added, or deleted from the basic recipe. A note will include explanations and alternate methods of preparation.

Ingredients Used in Standardizing Recipes

Flour

In flour mixtures, the exact ratio between the flour and liquid will vary with the kind of flour. Cake flour was used in cake recipes, and all purpose flour in other recipes.

Baking Powder

Sodium-aluminum-sulphate–type baking powder (double acting) was used in all recipes.

Eggs

Fresh shell eggs weighing approximately 2 oz (57 g) each were used in the preparation of recipes.

Fats

High ratio and/or hydrogenated fats were used in cake and pastry recipes. Butter or margarine was used in cookies and most sauce recipes. Solid fats, such as butter, margarine, and hydrogenated fats, were used interchangeably in recipes that specify only "fat." Unsaturated fat, including corn and vegetable oils, was used in recipes that specify salad oil.

Abbreviations Used in Recipes

A.P.	as purchased	f.d.	few drops
c	cup	f.g.	few grains
°C	degrees Celsius	fl oz	fluid ounce
doz	dozen	g	gram
E.P.	edible portion	gal	gallon
°F	degrees Fahrenheit	hr	hour

in.	inch		oz	ounce
kg	kilogram		psi	pounds per square inch
L	liter		pt	pint
lb	pound		qt	quart
min	minute		t	teaspoon
mL	milliliter		T	tablespoon

Weights and Measures

Quantities of most dry ingredients weighing more than 1 oz (28 g) are given by weight in ounces and pounds and in metric grams and kilograms. Weights given are for foods as purchased (A.P.) unless otherwise stated. If the weight is for edible portions, it is designated E.P. Metric weights are given in grams (g) up to 1000 g; 1000 g and over are in kilograms (kg). Some foodservices, in changing to the metric system, may prefer to use the kg and its decimal configurations for all weights. In that case, the grams as shown may be converted to kilograms by moving the decimal point three places to the left. For example, 1 oz is equivalent to 28.0 g or 0.028 kg.

All liquids are indicated by measure. Metric measures are in milliliters (mL) up to 950 mL and in liters (L) beyond that. Again, if the liter is to be the only measure used, milliliters would be changed to liters by moving the decimal point three places to the left. For example, 1 T is equal to 15.0 mL or 0.015 L.

Accurate weighing and measuring of ingredients are essential for a satisfactory product. Weighing ingredients, when possible, is recommended, since it is more accurate. Reliable scales are essential. A table model scale, 15-20-lb capacity, with ¼-½ oz gradations, or a 10-kg metric scale is suitable for weighing ingredients for 50 portions.

When measuring, use standard measuring equipment and make measurements level. Use the largest appropriate measure to reduce the possibility of error and to save time. For example, use a 1-gal measure once instead of a 1-qt measure four times. (Flour is the exception. Use measure no larger than 1 qt for flour.)

Adjusting Recipes

Converting from Weight to Measure

If accurate scales are not available or if scales do not have gradations for weighing small amounts, the weights of ingredients may need to be converted to measures. The following tables will be helpful.

Example: To convert ingredients in Plain Muffins (p. 117): Turn to Table 1.6, Food Weights and Approximate Equivalents in Measure (p. 30). Change 2 lb 8 oz (2½ lb) flour to measure by multiplying by 4 c. The resulting 10 c would be equivalent to 2½ qt (p. 52). By referring to Table 1.7 (p. 42) the 2 oz baking powder, 6 oz sugar, and 8 oz fat may be quickly converted by finding the amount in the appropriate columns. The same information is included in the longer table (pp. 30-41) but, for conversion of small amounts of commonly used foods, Table 1.7 is useful.

Converting from U.S. Weights and Measures to Metric

There are two approaches to the change from customary U.S. weights and measures to metric—soft conversion and hard conversion. *Soft* conversion refers to the conversion of existing measurements to exact metric equivalents using a mathematical formula. *Hard* conversion involves changing to standardized metric modules, which will require new measuring devices, possibly different pan sizes, and changes in the packaging of some foods. The soft conversion was used in this edition because of the uncertainty about standardization of measuring devices, particularly for measuring volume.

When using the metric weights and measures in this book, some quantities may need to be rounded off to a measurable amount or to the scale marking of the metric measure. For example, 1 qt in the recipes has been converted to 0.95 L, which would be difficult to measure. In some recipes this could be rounded to 1 L without affecting the final product; in some, the other ingredients would need changing also. Recipes in which quantities have been changed should be tested in 50 portions before enlarging.

Conversion tables for metric weights and measures are given on pp. 28-29. A *Handbook for Metric Usage,* published by the American Home Economics Association, 2010 Massachusetts Avenue N.W., Washington, D.C. 20036, contains useful information that would be helpful in converting to metric weights and measures.

Increasing and Decreasing
Recipes

It may be necessary to adapt the recipes in this book to meet the needs of individual situations. Recipes may be increased to batch sizes compatible with equipment to be used in preparation, such as mixers and steam-jacketed kettles, or consistent with pan sizes for foods to be cooked in counter or baking pans.

Using Ingredient WEIGHT as the Basis

A direct reading table (p. 47) provides information for adjusting yields when ingredients are given in weights. It requires a minimum of calculation, but its use is limited to desired yields that can be divided by 25.

If adjusting to a yield not divisible by 25, or if closer portion control is desired, the factor method[1] may be useful. To use this method:

1. Divide the desired yield by the known yield of the recipe being adjusted to obtain a basic FACTOR. For example, to increase a recipe that yields 50 portions to 125 portions, divide 125 by 50 for a FACTOR of 2.5.

2. Wherever possible, convert ingredients to weight. If amounts of some ingredients are too small to convert to weight, leave them in measure.

3. Multiply the amount of each ingredient in the original recipe by the FACTOR. To work with decimal parts of a pound instead of ounces for this multiplication, Table 1.8 will be helpful.

4. Multiply the original total weight of ingredients by the FACTOR. Multiply the pounds and ounces separately and then combine them.

5. Add together the new weights of all ingredients for the adjusted recipe. If the answers in Steps 4 and 5 are not the same, check the calculations.

6. Change weights of any ingredients that can be more easily measured than weighed to measure.

7. Check all amounts and use Table 1.12 for rounding off unnecessary fractions to simplify weights or measures as far as accuracy permits.

Using Ingredient MEASURE as the Basis

A direct reading measurement table on pp. 52-55 lists ingredients in measure when both the yield of the original recipe and of the adjusted recipe can be divided

---

[1] Adapted from *Standardizing Recipes for Institutional Use,* The American Dietetic Association, 1967.

by 25. In Table 1.11, yields are in amounts divisible by 8. These tables can be used together with Table 1.9 for recipes that include ingredients expressed in both weight and measurement.

Appetizers

Appetizers include hors d'oeuvres, canapés, cocktails, and soups, and are served at the beginning of a meal to stimulate the appetite. They should be attractive in appearance, pleasing in flavor, and well seasoned.

Hors d'Oeuvres

Hors d'oeuvres are relishes served at the beginning of the meal. They may be stuffed celery, radishes, or other crisp, fresh vegetables, pickles, olives, cheese, fish, sausages, deviled eggs, or a combination. Hors d'oeuvres may be arranged on individual plates and served as the first course, or a tray containing a variety of hors d'oeuvres may be passed prior to seating the guests. Items selected for an appetizer tray should provide variety in color, texture, form, and flavor.

Hors d'oeuvres Suggestions

Apple-Cheese.   Core and cut crisp tart red apples into wedges. Dip in fruit juice to prevent discoloration. Spread with a bit of Roquefort cheese softened with cream, and spear each wedge with a toothpick. Arrange sections close together in a circle around a whole red apple.

Carrot Curls.   See p. 395.

Cheese Cubes.   Cut cheddar, Swiss, Edam, or other hard or semihard cheese into cubes. Spear with a toothpick and arrange on a tray or in a grapefruit or fresh red apple.

Cherry Tomatoes.   Select uniform firm cherry tomatoes; wash, chill, and serve whole; or marinate in French dressing for several hours.

Cocktail Wieners.   Broil small cocktail-size wieners. Spear with cocktail picks and serve immediately.

Deviled Eggs.   Prepare deviled eggs (p. 214). Garnish with paprika, pimiento, or anchovy.

Ginger-Cheese Balls.   Combine 8-oz (227-g) package cream cheese, 2½ oz (70 g) crumbled Roquefort cheese, 2 T (30 mL) candied ginger, shredded, and 2-4 T (30-60 mL) cream. Mix well. Chill thoroughly. Make into small balls. Roll in chopped pecans.

Ham-Cheese Wedges.   Spread 6 thin Pullman slices of ham or luncheon meat with whipped cream cheese and stack. Chill, cut into small wedges. Spear with cocktail picks.

Hot Cheese Balls.   Prepare small cheese balls, using recipe on p. 201. Serve hot on cocktail picks with chilled tomato juice.

Melon Cubes.   Cut fresh honeydew, cantaloupe, or other melon into cubes. Dip in lemon juice and spear with cocktail picks.

Parsleyed Olives.   Use a smooth cheese spread to cover small pimiento-stuffed olives. Roll in minced parsley and spear with colored cocktail picks.

Party Cheese Ball.   Combine 3 oz (85 g) cream cheese, 4 oz (114 g) Blue cheese, 6 oz (170 g) sharp Cheddar cheese, 1 T (15 mL) onion juice, and f.d. Worcestershire sauce. Add 1 T (15 mL) finely cut candied ginger if desired. Mix until smooth. Shape into a ball. Cover with pecans and chill. Serve in center of plate surrounded by crisp assorted crackers. Cheese mixture also may be formed into a long roll, wrapped in waxed paper, and chilled several hours. Slice and serve on crackers.

Pineapple-Shrimp.   Spear a small, whole, cooked shrimp and a pineapple cube that have been chilled on a cocktail pick. Serve with a cheese dip.

Shrimp.   Marinate large, cooked shrimp in garlic dressing.

Strawberries.   Arrange whole, perfect strawberries, with stems, around a bowl of sour cream.

Stuffed Celery.   Cut prepared celery into 3-in. lengths and stuff with cream cheese and Roquefort dip or with pimiento cheese.

Stuffed Burr Gherkins.   Place a whole almond in a half burr gherkin to form an "acorn," or stuff gherkin with red cherry.

Stuffed Cucumber.   Pare cucumber and scoop out center. Fill with ham or shrimp mixture. Chill. Cut into ½-in. slices.

Stuffed Olives. Use ripe or green olives. Prepare thin carrot sticks about 3 in. long and pull 2 or 3 through center of each large pitted olive. Place in ice water to crisp.

Vegetable Relishes. Cut carrots, green pepper, zucchini, cucumber, turnips, or celery into sticks, circles or slices. Cauliflower separated into flowerets and radishes also is a popular relish. Crisp vegetable relishes may be served with a "dip" made with a sour cream or cream cheese base (p. 95).

Canapés

Canapés are made by spreading a well-seasoned mixture of eggs, cheese, fish, or meat on a canapé base and garnishing with a colorful food such as pimiento, sliced stuffed olive, parsley, or chopped hard-cooked egg. A well-seasoned canapé mixture, thinned to dipping consistency by the addition of salad dressing or cream, is often served in a bowl, accompanied by crisp crackers or chips. Guests "dip" into the mixture to make their own canapés.

Canapé bases may include bread slices, cut into squares, rectangles, crescents, or triangles or into various other shapes with cookie or sandwich cutters; thin slices of pan rolls, toasted; crisp thin crackers, wafers, corn or potato chips; bread sticks; tiny plain or cheese biscuits; or puff pastry shells. A combination of these makes interesting canapé bases and offers a wide variety for a tray of canapés or combined with assorted hors d'oeuvres.

Choice of bread need not be limited to white yeast bread. Whole wheat, rye, or oatmeal also make satisfactory canapé bases, as do fruit, nut, and other quick breads. The base and spread should be complementary in flavor and texture. Day-old bread provides needed firmness, and a thin coating of butter or margarine helps prevent excess absorption of moisture from the spread. Herbs or other seasonings may be added to the butter or margarine.

If canapés are to be refrigerated prior to service, they should be placed on waxed paper on a tray and covered with a plastic wrap or with waxed paper and a damp cloth. Puff shells (p. 386) may be made in advance and filled shortly before serving.

Some canapés may be frozen for later use, if they are well packaged and made of bread and fillings that freeze well. Closed sandwiches such as rolled, ribbon, or checkerboard freeze more satisfactorily, however, and may be made well in advance and frozen, then sliced and thawed as needed.

Suggested canapé spreads, fillings, and dips follow.

Spreads and Fillings

Anchovy. Combine and blend 4 T (60 mL) anchovy paste, 2 oz (57 g) cream cheese, 2 T (30 mL) minced chives, 1 t (5 mL) lemon juice, and 1 T (15 mL) soft butter. Spread on canapé bases. Garnish with watercress and/or riced yolk and egg white.

Avocado-Shrimp.   Mash 2 soft avocados; season with 1 T (15 mL) lemon juice, 1 T (15 mL) minced onion, and f.g. salt. Spread on crackers or canapé bases and top each with small whole shrimp.

Carrot.   Combine ½ c (120 mL) ground carrot with 1 grated hard-cooked egg, f.d. onion juice, ½ t lemon juice, and enough French dressing to moisten. Spread on canapé base. Garnish with thinly sliced stuffed olive or parsley.

Cheese, Hot.   Combine 4 oz (114 g) sharp grated Cheddar cheese, ⅛ t salt, and f.g. cayenne. Spread on toasted canapé base. Sprinkle with sesame seed. Toast and serve hot.

Cheese-Mushroom.   Sauté a 4-oz (114-g) can mushrooms, drained, in 4 T (60 mL) butter or margarine. Add ¼ c (60 mL) heavy cream, f.d. onion juice, salt, pepper, and ¾ c (180 mL) Cheddar cheese. Mash to a paste. Spread toasted bread rounds with creamed butter and then cheese-mushroom mixture. Garnish with grated cheese and thinly sliced ripe olives.

Cheese Puffs.   Prepare Cream Puffs (p. 386) and drop on baking sheet by level teaspoonful. Combine 8 oz (227 g) cream cheese, 4½-oz (128-g) can deviled ham, 1 t (5 mL) grated onion, 1 T (15 mL) horseradish, ½ t Worcestershire sauce, and ¼ t pepper. Blend until smooth. Fill each tiny puff with cheese mixture (5 doz).

Cheese Straws.   See p. 137.

Cheese Wafers.   Blend 4 oz (114 g) grated sharp Cheddar cheese and 8 oz (227 g) butter or margarine. Add ½ t Worcestershire sauce, 6 oz (170 g) flour, ½ t salt, and f.g. cayenne pepper, and mix thoroughly. Form into 1-in. roll. Wrap in waxed paper and chill for several hours. Slice in ¼-in. slices and bake on un-greased baking sheet for 12-15 min at 375 °F (190 °C).

Chicken or Fish Puffs.   Fill tiny cream puffs with chicken or fish salad.

Chicken or Ham.   Combine 2 c (480 mL) chicken or ham, finely chopped, with creamed butter seasoned with ½ t curry powder or chutney. Spread on canapé bases. Garnish with watercress and/or paprika.

Crab or Lobster.   Moisten crab or lobster meat with mayonnaise. Add finely cut celery, if desired. Pile on canapé base spread with butter or margarine.

Crabmeat or Lobster with Egg. Mash 1 6-oz (170-g) can crabmeat or lobster. Add 2 chopped hard-cooked eggs, ½ t prepared mustard, 2 T (30 mL) mayonnaise, 1 T (15 mL) lemon juice, ½ t curry powder. Blend. Spread on canapé base.

Crabmeat and Parmesan Cheese. Mix 1 c (240 mL) crabmeat, 1 T (15 mL) onion browned lightly in butter, ¼ c (60 mL) Parmesan cheese, and mayonnaise to moisten. Spread on canapé bases. Garnish with thin strips of red pepper or pimiento.

Deviled Ham. Blend 3-oz (85-g) can deviled ham and 1 T (15 mL) mayonnaise. Spread on canapé bases that have been toasted on one side. Garnish with parsley.

Dried Beef. Blend 3 oz (85 g) finely chopped dried beef with 8 oz (227 g) cream cheese. Season with prepared mustard, horseradish, and chives. Moisten with cream or salad dressing to spreading consistency. Spread on white or rye bread canapé bases.

Liver Pâté. Mash 8 oz (277 g) liverwurst; add 1 t (5 mL) lemon juice, ½ t Worcestershire sauce, and cream to moisten. Spread on canapé bases. Garnish with outside border of riced hard-cooked egg yolks mixed with mayonnaise to moisten and season, and an inside border of finely chopped hard-cooked egg whites. Sprinkle with chopped parsley.

Sardine. Bone and mash 3 oz (85 g) sardines. Add 2 T (30 mL) lemon juice and French dressing to moisten. Spread canapé bases with creamed butter or margarine and then with sardine mixture. Garnish with riced egg yolk in center and a border of chopped hard-cooked egg whites.

Dips

Avocado Dip. Mash 2 ripe avocados and blend with 1 c (240 mL) cultured sour cream, ¼ t salt, 1 t (5 mL) onion juice, and 2 T (30 mL) prepared horseradish. Serve with cooked chilled shrimp.

California Dip. Combine 2 c (480 mL) cultured sour cream with 1 1½-oz (43-g) package dry onion soup mix. Blend thoroughly. Serve with crackers, potato or corn chips.

Cheddar Cheese Dip. Blend 4 oz (114 g) sharp Cheddar cheese, grated, with 2 t (10 mL) minced green onion, ½ c (120 mL) mayonnaise, and ¼ t salt. Just before serving, add ¼ c (60 mL) chopped crisp bacon. Garnish with ¼ c (60 mL) chopped toasted almonds. Serve with crisp crackers.

Cheese Bowl.   Mix 2 c (480 mL) cottage cheese, 1 c (240 mL) grated sharp Cheddar cheese, 2 T (30 mL) horseradish, 3 finely chopped young green onions, f.g. cayenne, and 2 T (30 mL) mayonnaise. Serve in bowl with crisp salty crackers.

Clam Dip.   Combine 1 7-oz (198-g) can minced clams, 1 c (240 mL) cottage cheese, 1 8-oz (227-g) package cream cheese, 2½ oz (70 g) Blue cheese, 2 t (10 mL) lemon juice, 1½ t (8 mL) Worcestershire sauce, ½ t salt, and f.d. Tabasco sauce. Thin with clam juice or cream. Blend well. Serve with crisp crackers, potato or corn chips.

Cream Cheese Dip.   Blend 3 oz (85 g) cream cheese, 2 oz (57 g) crumbled Blue cheese, 1 t (5 mL) onion juice, ⅛ t salt, ⅛ t pepper, f.d. Tabasco sauce, and 2 T (30 mL) cream. ¼ c (60 mL) chopped pecans may be added. Serve with potato chips or pretzels.

Guacamole Dip.   Mash 2 ripe avocados; add 1 T (15 mL) lemon or lime juice, ½ t salt, 1 T (15 mL) finely grated onion, ½ t chili powder, and 1 ripe tomato, peeled and mashed. Mix well. Spread ¼ c (60 mL) mayonnaise over top of mixture in a thin layer to prevent discoloration. Serve with potato chips or Melba toast.

Roquefort Dip.   Blend 6 oz (170 g) cream cheese with 1 oz (28 g) Roquefort cheese; then fold in 1 c (240 mL) whipped cream or cultured sour cream. Serve in bowl, garnish with paprika.

Tuna-Pineapple Dip.   Blend 1 6½-oz (184-g) can tuna, 9 oz (255 g) drained crushed pineapple, 8 oz (227 g) cream cheese, and 3 T (45 mL) pineapple juice. Serve in bowl with potato chips.

Cocktails

Cocktails are made of pieces of fruit, fruit or vegetable juices, carbonated or alcoholic beverages, or a combination of these. They may also be made of seafood, such as oysters, shrimp, crab, or lobster, and served with a highly seasoned sauce.

Fruit Cup or Cocktail Suggestions[1]

Avocado.   Cut avocado into cubes. Serve in small glasses with sauce made of 1 part catsup, 2 parts orange juice, and f.d. onion juice.

[1] Ginger ale may be used as liquid in recipes designated as ''cups.''

Avocado-Fruit. Cut avocado into sections. Combine with pineapple chunks and grapefruit sections. Chill.

Cantaloupe-Berry. Combine melon balls with berries. Place in sherbet glasses and chill.

Cranberry-Ginger Ale. Add sugar to cranberry purée. Chill. Add an equal amount of chilled ginger ale. Serve in cocktail glasses. Garnish with a sprig of mint or paper-thin slices of orange.

Cranberry-Grapefruit. Arrange grapefruit sections in cocktail glasses. Cover with chilled cranberry juice.

Frosted Fruit Cup. Pineapple cubes, grapefruit and orange sections, or berries topped with lime ice.

Fruit Coconut. Combine diced orange sections, pineapple, and shredded coconut. Chill.

Grape-Melon. Mix seedless grapes, diced honeydew melon, cubed orange sections, lemon juice, and sugar. Chill. Serve in sherbet glasses.

Grapefruit, broiled. Cut grapefruit in halves and remove centers and seeds. Cut fruit from skin with a sharp knife. Add 1 t (5 mL) butter and 1 oz (28 g) sugar to each center. Broil in a hot oven until fruit turns a golden brown.

Honeydew. Combine chilled pineapple tidbits and juice with honeydew melon balls, seedless grapes, and a little grenadine syrup. Place a grape or ivy leaf under cocktail dishes.

Melon Cup. Cut small round balls from heart of ripe watermelon, cantaloupe, or honeydew melon, or use a combination of the three. Chill thoroughly. Cover with chilled ginger ale.

Mint Cup. Cubes of fresh or canned pineapple and pear with mint or lime ice.

Minted Pineapple. Just before serving, mix 2 No. 10 cans of pineapple tidbits and 1 lb (454 g) mints (white, soft). Garnish with a maraschino cherry.

Orange Cup. Orange sections with orange ice or orange sections sprinkled with powdered sugar, covered with pineapple and lemon juice, and garnished with mint leaf.

Papaya.   Add chopped papaya, salt, and sugar to fresh grapefruit juice. Chill. Serve in frappé glasses. Garnish with cherries.

Pineapple-Strawberry Cup.   Cubes of fresh pineapple and whole fresh strawberries.

Raspberry Cup.   Fresh raspberries topped with raspberry ice.

Red Raspberry or Strawberry.   Prepare fresh berries. Add sugar. Chill. Place in cocktail dishes. Add lime juice and garnish with mint leaves.

Rhubarb-Strawberry.   Cut rhubarb into pieces. Cook, sweeten. Chill. Combine with strawberries.

Sherbet.   Place No. 16 dipper of lime, pineapple, lemon, orange, or raspberry sherbet in a chilled sherbet dish. Pour 2 T (30 mL) orange juice or ginger ale over sherbet just before serving.

Strawberry.   Arrange a few green leaves on each plate. Form a mound of powdered sugar in the center. Around the sugar arrange 5 or 6 large unhulled strawberries.

Strawberry Cup.   Fresh strawberries topped with strawberry ice.

Seafood Cocktail Suggestions

Crab Meat.   Line cocktail glasses with lettuce. Fill with alternate layers of crabmeat, chopped celery, or diced avocado and cocktail sauce (p. 470).

Oyster.   Drain small oysters. Chill and serve in cocktail cups with cocktail sauce (p. 470) and wedges of lemon.

Shrimp.   Line cocktail glasses with lettuce. Add cooked shrimp, either whole or cut into pieces, depending on size. Serve with cocktail sauce (p. 470).

Shrimp-Avocado-Grapefruit.   Arrange avocado wedges, grapefruit sections, and shrimp in lettuce-lined cocktail glasses. Serve with cocktail sauce (p. 470).

Beverages

Beverages are served as accompaniments to a meal, with snacks, or as the focal point for a reception or tea. The consumer often judges a foodservice by the quality of its beverages, particularly its coffee. Temperature is important in the acceptance of beverages. Hot beverages should be served hot and iced beverages very cold.

Coffee

Coffee in an institutional foodservice generally is made in an urn or in some type of drip or vacuum coffee maker. The type of equipment will determine the method of preparation and the grind of coffee to be used. The urn is most often used when large quantities of coffee are needed, as on a rapidly moving cafeteria line. Where the service is spread over a longer period, coffee may be prepared in small batches in a drip or vacuum coffee maker. The equipment selected should be one that will make a clear, rich brew, that will hold the coffee at a consistent temperature, and that will provide the quantity needed at an appropriate speed with a minimum of labor. Regardless of the method used, certain precautions should be observed.

1. A blend of coffee should be selected that is well liked by the clientele. The grind should be suitable for the equipment to be used.

2. The coffee should be fresh. After coffee is ground, it deteriorates rapidly. Large amounts should not be accumulated. Coffee should be protected from exposure to heat, moisture, and air. Coffee not needed for immediate use may be refrigerated.

3. The proportion of water to coffee should be appropriate for a brew of the strength preferred by the clintele. A proportion of 2½ gal (9.46 L) of water per pound (454 g) of coffee makes a brew of commonly accepted strength. When a milder flavor is preferred, 3 gal (11.36 L) is used. See p. 101 for coffee recipes. Coffee should be accurately measured. The number of servings per pound of coffee will vary with the quality of the coffee bean, equipment used, and cup size. A pound (454 g) of high-quality coffee properly made should yield on the average 52 4½-oz (135-mL) servings, using a 6-oz (180 mL) cup; 47 5-oz (150-mL) servings, using a 6½-oz (195-mL) cup; or 39 6-oz (180-mL) servings, using an 8-oz (240-mL) cup. Many foodservices purchase coffee in premeasured packages.

4. The water should be freshly drawn, accurately measured, and freshly brought to a boiling temperature.

5. Coffee should be held at a temperature of 185-190 °F (85-88 °C) and never allowed to boil.

6. Care of equipment is of utmost importance for a satisfactory brew. The urn or other equipment should be cleaned immediately after each use, following instructions that come with the equipment.

Tea

Tea is made by the process of infusion, in which boiling water is poured over tea leaves or tea bags and the mixture is allowed to stand until the desired concentration is reached. A stainless steel or earthenware container is preferable for brewing tea. Freshly drawn cold water, heated just to the boiling point, should be used.

For iced tea, the brew must be stronger than for tea that is to be served hot to compensate for the melting ice that is added at serving time, and must be kept at room temperature. Cloudiness develops in tea that is refrigerated. See p. 102 for tea recipes.

Punch

Frozen and canned juices are used most often as the base for punch and for vegetable drinks prepared in institutional foodservices. Fruit juices, such as lemon, orange, pineapple, cranberry, and the several nectars, are combined in varying proportions to produce a drink of the desired flavor and concentration.

Lemonade (p. 104) or Foundation Fruit Punch (p. 105) may be used as a base for many other fruit drinks by the addition of fresh, frozen, canned, or powdered juices of the desired flavor. The amount of sugar needed will vary with the sugar concentration of the added juice and individual preference. A sugar syrup for sweetening punch is made from 2 lb (908 g) sugar and 1 qt (0.95 L) water, heated to the boiling point and cooled. If time does not permit making the syrup, the sugar may be added directly to the punch and stirred until sugar is dissolved.

Punch most often is served iced, but may be served hot if desired. Ingredients for making iced punch should be refrigerated and the chilled ingredients combined well in advance of serving time. If ginger ale or other carbonated beverage is to be used, it should be chilled and added just before serving. A block of ice placed in the punch bowl is a satisfactory way of icing the punch. However, ice cubes and ring molds of ice are often used because of their availability and the opportunity they offer for color effects. Ring molds made with lemonade will accent flavor of other juices and will not dilute the flavor of the punch.

Decorative ice cubes are easily made by filling an ice cube tray with pastel colored water or fruit juice. A red cherry added to each ice cube section before freezing will add color. Ice ring molds may be made by arranging alternate slices of orange, lemon, and unstemmed strawberries or cherries in the ring molds. Sprigs of mint may be added as a garnish. Water is added to fill the mold ¾ full and frozen. The ring is unmolded and placed upside down in the punch bowl.

The amount of punch or iced beverage to prepare will depend on the size of the punch cup or glass, on the number of guests to be served, and whether guests will be offered second servings. Service from a punch bowl will require slightly more punch than if it is to be poured from a pitcher for individual service. It is always desirable to have on hand unopened cans of the main punch ingredients to facilitate serving a larger crowd than anticipated.

Most recipes in this book were developed for 2-2½ gal (7.57-9.46 L) of punch. Each gallon (3.79 L) will yield 30-35 ½-c (120-mL) portions. Punch cups vary in size from 3 oz (75 mL) to 6 oz (180 mL), so it is important that the size be considered in determining the correct amount of punch to prepare.

Coffee Recipes

COFFEE   **Yield: 2½-3 gal (9.46-11.36 L)**

Amount			
Metric	*U.S.*	*Ingredient*	*Method*
454 g	1 lb	Coffee	Use proper blend and grind for coffee maker used.
9.46-11.36 L	2½-3 gal	Water	Use method recommended by manufacturer of coffee maker.

Variations:
1. **Iced Coffee.** Make double strength coffee. Pour over ice in glasses. Coffee may be cooled to room temperature but should not be refrigerated.

2. **Instant Coffee.** Use 3 oz (85 g) instant coffee or 2 oz (57 g) freeze-dried to 2½-3 gal (9.46-11.36 L) boiling water. Dissolve the coffee in a small amount of boiling water and add to the remaining hot water. Keep hot just below the boiling point.

STEEPED COFFEE   **Yield: 2½-3 gal (9.46-11.36 L)**

Amount			
Metric	*U.S.*	*Ingredient*	*Method*
454 g	1 lb	Coffee, regular grind	Tie coffee loosely in a cloth bag.
9.46-11.36 L	2½-3 gal	Water, cold	Immerse bag in water. Heat to boiling point.
			Boil 3 min. Test. When coffee is of desired strength, remove coffee bag.
			Cover and hold over low heat to keep at serving temperature.

Note: For an extra clear brew, beat an egg and 1 c of water together and stir into coffee until dampened. Then proceed as above.

Tea Recipes

HOT TEA

Yield: 2 gal (7.57 L)

Amount		Ingredient	Method
Metric	U.S.		
2 28-g	2 1-oz	Tea bags	Place tea bags in a stainless steel, enamel, or earthenware container.
7.57-9.46 L	2-2½ gal	Water, boiling	Add water. Steep for 3 min. Remove bags.

Notes:
1. If bulk tea is used, tie loosely in a bag.
2. The amount of tea to be used will vary with the quality.
3. ¾-1 oz (21-28 g) instant tea may be used in place of the tea bags. The exact amount will vary according to the strength desired.

ICED TEA

Yield: 3 gal (11.36 L)

Amount		Ingredient	Method
Metric	U.S.		
6 28-g	6 1-oz	Tea bags	Place tea bags in stainless steel, earthenware, or enamel container.
3.79 L	1 gal	Water, boiling	Add boiling water. Steep 4-6 min.
7.57 L	2 gal	Water, cold	Remove bags. Pour hot tea into cold water.
4.54-6.8 kg	10-15 lb	Ice, chipped or cubed	Fill 12-oz (360-mL) glasses with ice. Pour tea over ice just before serving.

Notes:
1. Always pour the hot tea concentrate into the cold water. Do not refrigerate or ice the tea prior to service. Cloudiness develops in tea that has been refrigerated.
2. 1-1½ oz (28-43 g) instant tea may be used in place of the tea bags.
3. 6-7 lemons may be cut in eighths to serve with the tea.

SPICED TEA   **Yield: 1½ gal (5.68 L)**

Metric	U.S.	Ingredient	Method
	Amount		
5.68 L	1½ gal	Water, boiling	Mix all ingredients except tea.
680 g	1 lb 8 oz	Sugar	Simmer 20 min.
60 mL	¼ c	Lemon juice and 1 rind, grated	Strain.
240 mL	1 c	Orange juice and 1 rind, grated	
20 mL	4 t	Cloves, whole	
8	8	Cinnamon sticks	
1 28-g	1 1-oz	Tea bag	Add tea bag and let steep 5 min. Remove tea bag. Serve hot.

Variation:

Russian Tea. Use only 1¼ gal (4.73 L) water. Add 1 qt (0.95 L) grape juice when adding other juice.

Cocoa and Chocolate Recipes

COCOA   **Yield: 2½ gal (9.46 L)**

Metric	U.S.	Ingredient	Method
	Amount		
680 g	1 lb 8 oz	Sugar	Mix dry ingredients.
227 g	8 oz	Cocoa	Add water and mix until smooth.
½ t	½ t	Salt	Boil approximately 3 min or to form a thin syrup.
0.95 L	1 qt	Water	
8.52 L	2¼ gal	Milk, hot	Add syrup to milk.
5 mL	1 t	Vanilla	Just before serving, add vanilla and beat well with a wire whip.

Notes:
1. A marshmallow or 1 t whipped cream may be added to each cup if desired.
2. Cocoa syrup may be made in amounts larger than this recipe and stored in the refrigerator. To serve, add 1 qt (0.95 L) cocoa syrup to each 2 gal (7.57 L) of hot milk.

Variations:
1. **Hot Chocolate.** Substitute 10 oz (284 g) of chocolate for cocoa.

2. **Instant Hot Cocoa.** Dissolve 2½ lb (1.14 kg) cocoa powder in 2 gal (7.57 L) boiling water.

FRENCH CHOCOLATE   **Yield: 3 gal (11.36 L)**

	Amount		
Metric	*U.S.*	*Ingredient*	*Method*
510 g	1 lb 2 oz	Chocolate	Combine chocolate and water.
720 mL	3 c	Water, cold	Cook over direct heat about 5 min, stirring constantly.
			Remove from heat. Beat with a rotary beater until smooth.
1.14 kg	2 lb 8 oz	Sugar	Add sugar and salt to chocolate mixture.
½ t	½ t	Salt	Return to heat. Cook over hot water 20-30 min or until thick. Chill.
840 mL	3½ c	Whipping cream	Whip cream. Fold into cold chocolate mixture.
9.46 L	2½ gal	Milk, hot	To serve, place 1 rounded T chocolate mixture in each serving cup.
			Add hot milk to fill cup. Stir well to blend. Serve immediately.

Notes:
1. The milk must be kept very hot during the serving period.
2. The chocolate mixture may be stored for a short time in the refrigerator.

Punch Recipes

LEMONADE   *Yield: 3 gal (11.36 L)*

	Amount		
Metric	*U.S.*	*Ingredient*	*Method*
1.18 L	1¼ qt	Lemon juice (approx. 30 lemons)	Mix lemon juice and sugar.
1.14 kg	2 lb 8 oz	Sugar	Add water. Stir until sugar is dissolved.
8.52 L	2¼ gal	Water, cold	Chill.

Notes:
1. Lemonade makes a good base for fruit punch.
2. Three 6-oz (177 mL) cans undiluted frozen lemon juice may be substituted for fresh lemon juice. Increase water to 2½ gal (9.46 L).

FOUNDATION FRUIT PUNCH   **Yield: 2½ gal (9.46 L)**

Amount			
Metric	U.S.	Ingredient	Method
1.14 kg	2 lb 8 oz	Sugar	Mix sugar and water. Bring to boil.
0.95 L	1 qt	Water	Cool.
3 c (2 355-mL cans)	3 c (2 12-oz cans)	Orange juice, frozen, undiluted	Combine juices and water.
3 c (2 355-mL cans)	3 c (2 12-oz cans)	Lemon juice, frozen, undiluted	Add sugar syrup. Chill.
5.68 L	1½ gal	Water, cold	

Notes:
1. If time does not permit making and cooling syrup, the sugar may be added to the cold punch and stirred until dissolved. Increase cold water to 1¾ gal (6.62 L).
2. Ginger ale may be substituted for part or all of water. Chill and add just before serving.

Variations:
1. **Golden Punch.** Reduce orange and lemon juice to 1 12-oz (355-mL) can each. Add 2 46-oz (1.36-L) cans pineapple juice.

2. **Raspberry Punch.** Reduce orange juice to 1 12-oz (355-mL) can. Add 2 12-oz (340-g) packages of frozen red raspberries.

3. **Sparkling Grape Punch.** Reduce orange and lemon juice to 1 12-oz (355-mL) can each. Add 2 12-oz (355-mL) cans frozen grape juice. Just before serving, add 2 20-oz (600-mL) bottles of ginger ale.

SPARKLING APRICOT-PINEAPPLE PUNCH   **Yield: 2½ gal (9.46 L)**

Amount			
Metric	U.S.	Ingredient	Method
2.84 L	3 qt	Apricot nectar	Combine juices and water.
2.84 L	3 qt	Pineapple juice, unsweetened	Chill.
360 mL	1½ c	Lemon or lime juice concentrate, frozen	
1.89 L	2 qt	Water	
1.89 L	2 qt	Ginger ale, chilled	Add ginger ale just before serving.

GINGER ALE FRUIT PUNCH

Yield: 3 gal (11.36 L)

Amount			
Metric	U.S.	Ingredient	Method
1.36 kg	3 lb	Sugar	Mix sugar and water. Bring to boil. Cool.
0.95 L	1 qt	Water	
1.42 L	1½ qt	Lemon juice	Combine juices and water.
1.42 L	1½ qt	Orange juice	Add sugar syrup.
0.95 L	1 qt	Pineapple juice	Chill.
3.79 L	1 gal	Water	
1.89 L	2 qt	Ginger ale, chilled	Add ginger ale just before serving.

Note: Lime, orange, or lemon ice may be added to the punch just before serving.

BANANA PUNCH

Yield: 2 gal (7.57 L)

Amount			
Metric	U.S.	Ingredient	Method
908 g	2 lb	Sugar	Boil sugar and water for 3 min.
1.42 L	1½ qt	Water, hot	Cool.
360 mL	1½ c (1 12-oz can)	Orange juice, frozen, undiluted	Combine juices, fruits, and water.
180 mL	¾ c (1 6-oz can)	Lemon juice, frozen, undiluted	Add chilled sugar syrup.
0.95 L	1 qt	Water, cold	
2.84 L	3 qt (1 No. 10 can)	Pineapple, crushed	
6	6 medium	Bananas, ripe, crushed	
0.95 L	1 qt	Ginger ale, chilled	Add ginger ale just before serving.

Notes:
1. Mixture may be frozen (before ginger ale is added) and held for use later.
2. 2 46-oz (1.36-L) cans of unsweetened pineapple juice and 1 12-oz (355-mL) can lemonade may be substituted for the crushed pineapple and lemon juice.

Variation:
Banana Slush Punch. Mix and freeze juices, syrup, and crushed bananas. To serve, fill glass about half full of partially frozen slush and add ginger ale.

ORANGE GINGER ALE PUNCH   Yield: 2 gal (7.57 L)

Amount		Ingredient	Method
Metric	*U.S.*	*Ingredient*	*Method*
2.84 L	3 qt	Orange sherbet	Place sherbet in large chunks in well-chilled punch bowl.
4.73 L	5 qt	Ginger ale, chilled	Pour very cold ginger ale over the sherbet just before serving. Garnish with mint leaves.

Note: Lime, lemon, raspberry, or other sherbet may be substituted for the orange sherbet.

RHUBARB PUNCH   Yield: 1½ gal (5.68 L)

Amount		Ingredient	Method
Metric	*U.S.*	*Ingredient*	*Method*
4.54 kg	10 lb	Rhubarb, pink	Cut rhubarb into 1-in. pieces.
3.79 L	1 gal	Water	Add water and sugar. Cook below the boiling point until soft.
1.81-2.27 kg	4-5 lb	Sugar	Strain. There should be 1¼ gal (4.73 L) juice. Chill.
480 mL	2 c	Pineapple juice	Add chilled pineapple juice and ginger ale just before serving.
830 mL	1 28-oz bottle	Ginger ale	

CRANBERRY PUNCH   Yield: 2½ gal (9.46 L)

Amount		Ingredient	Method
Metric	*U.S.*	*Ingredient*	*Method*
2.84 L	3 qts	Cranberry juice	Mix juices and water.
2.84 L	3 qts (2 46-oz cans)	Pineapple juice	Chill.
0.95 L	1 qt (1 32-oz can)	Lemonade, frozen, undiluted	
0.95 L	1 qt	Water, cold	
2.5 L	3 28-oz bottles	Ginger ale, chilled	Add ginger ale just before serving.

CHILLED TOMATO JUICE

Yield: 2¼ gal (8.52 L)

Metric	U.S.	Ingredient	Method
	Amount		
8.04 L	8½ qt (6 46-oz cans)	Tomato juice, chilled	Mix all ingredients. Chill.
180 mL	¾ c	Lemon juice, fresh	
45 mL	3 T	Worcestershire sauce	
3 mL	½ t	Tabasco sauce	
45 mL	3 T	Celery salt	

Variation:

Sauerkraut Juice Cocktail. Omit the seasonings and substitute 2 qt (1.89 L) sauerkraut juice for 2 qt (1.89 L) tomato juice.

HOT SPICED TOMATO JUICE

Yield: 2 gal (7.57 L)

Metric	U.S.	Ingredient	Method
	Amount		
4.02 L	4¼ qt (3 46-oz cans)	Tomato juice	Mix all ingredients but consommé.
227 g	8 oz	Onion, chopped	Boil gently about 15 min.
3	3	Bay leaves	Strain.
12	12	Cloves, whole	
30 mL	2 T	Salt	
15 mL	1 T	Mustard, dry	
6	6	Celery stalks, cut	
3.79 L	1 gal	Consommé	Add consommé and reheat. Serve hot.

Note: 2 50-oz (1.48-L) cans condensed beef or chicken consommé, diluted with 2 qt (1.89 L) water, may be used.

SPICED CIDER   **Yield: 2½ gal (9.46 L)**

Amount			
Metric	*U.S.*	*Ingredient*	*Method*
9.46 L	2½ gal	Cider	Add sugar and spices (tied loosely in a cloth bag) to the cider.
340 g	12 oz	Brown sugar	Bring slowly to the boiling point. Boil about 15 min.
10	10	Cinnamon sticks	Remove spices.
37 mL	2½ T	Cloves, whole	Serve hot or chilled.
37 mL	2½ T	Allspice	
3 mL	½ t	Mace	
5 mL	1 t	Salt	
f.g.	f.g.	Cayenne	

Variation:

Cider Punch. Omit spices; substitute 1 qt (0.95 L) reconstituted frozen
   orange juice and 1 qt (0.95 L) pineapple juice for an equal amount of
   cider. Garnish with thin slices of orange.

WASSAIL BOWL   **Yield: 2½ gal (9.46 L)**

Amount			
Metric	*U.S.*	*Ingredient*	*Method*
1.14 kg	2 lb 8 oz	Sugar	Mix sugar, water, and spices. Boil 10 min.
2.37 L	2½ qt	Water	
8 mL	1½ t	Cloves, whole	Cover and let stand 1 hr in a warm place.
10	10	Cinnamon sticks	
10	10	Allspice berries	Strain.
57 g	2 oz	Crystallized ginger, chopped	
1.89 L	2 qt	Orange juice, strained	When ready to serve add juice and cider. Heat quickly to boiling point.
1.18 L	1¼ qt	Lemon juice, strained	Pour over crabapples or small oranges studded with cloves, in a punch bowl. If using a glass bowl, temper by filling with warm water to prevent cracking when hot punch is poured in.
4.73 L	5 qt	Apple cider	

Breads

Basic ingredients in all breads are flour, a liquid, a leavening agent, flavorings, and often fat and eggs. The type and quantity of each of these ingredients and their interaction affect the characteristics of the finished product. Breads are classified by the type of leavening agent used as either quick breads or yeast breads. They may be further classified according to the proportion of flour to liquid as pour batters, drop batters, and soft doughs, as shown in Table 2.1.

Table 2.1   PROPORTION OF FLOUR TO LIQUID (BY MEASURE) IN BATTERS AND DOUGHS

Type of Mixture	Flour	Liquid	Example of Product
Pour batter	1 part	1 part	Griddle cakes, waffles, popovers, crepes
Drop batter	2 parts	1 part	Muffins, pan breads (such as coffee cakes and cornbread), loaf breads
Soft dough	3 parts	1 part	Biscuits, yeast breads

Quick Breads

Quick breads are leavened by baking powder, soda, or steam, which act quickly, thus enabling them to be baked at once. If a double action baking powder is used, quick breads may be mixed at one time, refrigerated, and then baked as needed during the serving period. A variety of quick breads may be made from basic biscuit and muffin recipes by the addition of fruits, nuts, and other flavorings. Quick bread mixes can be prepared by sifting together the dry ingredients, which generally include nonfat dry milk, and then cutting in the shortening. Such a mix may be made on days when the work load is light and stored for periods up to 6 weeks without refrigeration or longer in the refrigerator. Many foodservices use some type of commercial mix, and the decision to purchase these or to make their own depends on the amount of skilled labor available and on the cost and quality of the mix.

Ingredients for most quick breads are combined by the muffin or biscuit method, although the cake method is used for some loaf breads. Most quick bread ingredients should be mixed only to blend, with as little handling as possible.

The **muffin** method is used for muffins, griddle cakes, waffles, popovers, and some loaf breads. The dry ingredients are mixed, and the liquids (beaten eggs, milk, and melted or liquid fat) are combined and added all at once. If dry milk is used, it is added to the dry ingredients. Excess mixing is avoided by separately mixing dry ingredients and liquids, and combining them quickly and mixing just enough to dampen the dry ingredients. Excess mixing causes gluten to develop and carbon dioxide to be lost, resulting in the formation of long "tunnels" in the baked product. Effects of overmixing are less evident in rich muffins and loaf breads that contain a higher proportion of fat and sugar, or when batter is made with cake or pastry flour. Care must be taken in dipping the batter into pans to avoid additional mixing.

In the **biscuit** method, the dry ingredients are combined, and the fat is cut in until the mixture resembles coarse cornmeal. The liquid is added last. A good biscuit dough is soft, not stiff or dry. The dough is kneaded lightly 15-20 strokes to develop the gluten; this results in a biscuit that has good volume and a crumb that peels off in flakes. Overkneading, however, produces a biscuit that is compact and less tender.

The **conventional** or dough-batter cake methods, described on p. 157, may be used successfully for coffee cakes, loaf breads, and rich muffins.

Yeast Breads

Ingredients

An understanding of the functions of the main ingredients used in yeast-raised doughs is essential to the production of good bread and rolls.

Flour. The flour used for baking must contain enough protein to make an elastic framework of gluten that will stretch and hold the gas bubbles formed as the dough ferments. Bread flour, made from hard wheat, contains more proteins than other flour and is used by bakers who make large quantities of bread. All-purpose flour is milled from a blend of wheats, using both hard and soft, and contains enough protein to provide the gluten essential to make good rolls and the homemade yeast specialties of most foodservices. An all-purpose flour was used in testing these recipes. Whole wheat, graham, rye, and other specialty flours add variety to breads. They should be combined with white flour, since they do not have enough gluten to effect proper bread structure.

Yeast. Either compressed or active dry yeast may be used in yeast doughs. When substituting active dry for compressed yeast, only 50% by weight is required. Active dry yeast does not require refrigeration and remains active a reasonable length of time in cool dry storage. Compressed yeast is perishable and must be held under refrigeration (30–34 °F/−1 to 1 °C) and storage is limited to not more than two weeks. It may be frozen to extend its keeping time, but must be used immediately after defrosting.

Compressed yeast is softened in lukewarm water (95 °F/35 °C). Active dry yeast is softened in warm water (105-110 °F/40-43 °C) or may be mixed with the dry ingredients. In this method the yeast is blended with a portion of the flour, the sugar, salt, and dry milk solids if used. The liquid ingredients may be heated to very warm (120 °F/49 °C). The yeast can withstand the higher temperature because of protection provided by the flour particles. Yeast grows best between 80 and 85 °F (27 and 29 °C). Dough should be kept in this temperature range during fermentation and should be near 80 °F (27 °C) when mixing is completed. A moderate increase in the amount of yeast speeds up fermentation, but too much gives the bread a yeasty flavor.

Liquid. The liquid used for yeast breads generally is milk or water, although potato water and fruit juice also may be used. Milk improves the nutritive value and quality of the bread and tends to delay its staling. Liquid used for bread should be lukewarm (95 °F/35 °C) for compressed yeast, warm (105-110 °F/40-43 °C) if active dry yeast is used, or very warm (120 °F/49 °C) if the dry yeast is mixed with the flour and other dry ingredients. If fresh fluid milk is used, it is scalded to stop enzyme action that may produce undesirable flavors, then cooled to the desired temperature. Nonfat dry milk commonly is used in quantity baking and may be mixed with the dry ingredients or reconstituted and used in liquid form. The nutritive value of the bread may be increased by the addition of extra quantities of dry milk. Evaporated milk may also be used in breadmaking and generally is diluted with an equal amount of water.

Other Ingredients. Although used in small quantity, other ingredients influence the quality of the finished product. **Salt** is added mainly for flavor, but does help to control the rate of fermentation. **Sugar,** a ready source of food for the yeast, accelerates the action of the yeast. Although the addition of a small amount of sugar makes the dough rise faster, too much sugar tends to slow the action of the yeast. If the dough is to be refrigerated or frozen, the amount of sugar is increased slightly. Granulated sugar generally is used for breadmaking, but honey, corn syrup, brown sugar, or molasses also are used, especially in dark whole grain bread, sweet rolls, or coffee cake. **Fat** is added to improve flavor, tenderness, browning, and keeping quality. Fat in large amounts, or if added directly to the yeast, will slow its action. Eggs are added for flavor and also to help form a framework.

Mixing the Dough

Mixing and kneading are essential in developing a good gluten network. Kneading is accomplished by continuing the mixing process beyond the point of combining. In a mixer this is done with a dough hook or flat beater attachment. The mixing speed and exact length of time will be determined by the type of mixer, the mixer attachment used, and the amount of dough. The last part of the flour should be added gradually to determine if the full amount is needed. It may be necessary to use more or less flour than the recipe specifies. The dough should be soft but not sticky. Dough for rolls is softer than for plain bread. Soft dough makes a lighter and more tender product than a stiff dough. The dough should be mixed only until it leaves the sides and bottom of the bowl.

Fermentation of Dough

Fermentation begins when the dough is mixed and continues until the yeast is killed by the heat of the oven. The dough must be set in a warm place (80-85 °F/ 27-29 °C), free from drafts, to ferment. The length of the fermentation period depends on the amount of yeast added, the strength of the flour, the amount of sugar added, and the temperature. Temperatures above 140 °F (60 °C) will destroy the yeast. Usually 1½ hr are required for the dough to double its bulk the first time. After the dough has doubled, it is punched down to its original bulk by placing the hand in the center of the dough and folding edges to the center, then turning over the ball of dough. Punching forces out excess carbon dioxide and incorporates oxygen, which allows the yeast cells to grow more rapidly. The yeast cells also are more uniformly distributed, producing an even-textured product with a fine grain. After the dough has been punched down, it must be handled lightly to avoid breaking the small air cells that have been formed.

The dough may be retarded at any point during the fermentation process by chilling the dough, as in refrigerator rolls. The dough also may be allowed to rise first, scaled into rolls, and then refrigerated. The baking process may be halted at a time when the rising is complete and before browning occurs, as in brown-and-serve rolls.

Yeast doughs can be frozen up to 6 weeks either before or after shaping. Sugar and yeast usually are increased slightly in doughs to be retarded or frozen. If the dough is to be frozen before shaping, it can be divided into pieces, flattened on baking sheets for quick freezing and defrosting, covered, and frozen. Rolls may be shaped and placed on greased baking sheets or in muffin pans, covered, and frozen. When completely frozen, they may be removed from the pans and stored in freezer bags. Time must be allowed for thawing and rising (about 6 hr for bread and 2 hr for rolls).

Shaping and Baking

When the dough has doubled in bulk and been punched down, it is divided into 3-4 lb (1.36-1.81 kg) balls and allowed to rest for 10-15 min, then shaped into loaves or rolls of the desired size. (See pp. 138-156 for recipes and directions for shaping.)

Bread dough, if made with bread flour, usually is allowed to rise a second time, although if the dough has been made with all-purpose flour, the second rising may be omitted.

The panned bread or rolls are allowed to rise (proofed) at 90-100 °F (32-38 °C) until double in bulk. Dough that has not risen long enough makes a small, compact product. Dough that has risen too long tends to have an open, crumbly texture.

Bread is baked at 375-400 °F (190-205 °C). The bread is done when tapping the crust produces a hollow sound. Bread should be removed from the pans immediately and placed on a wire rack to prevent steaming and softening of the crust. The loaves are cooled uncovered, and the tops brushed with fat if a soft crust is desired. If time does not permit bread to rise fully, the temperature of the oven may be lower for a brief period to permit the dough to rise. The best volume is obtained if fully risen dough is put into a hot oven. The heat of the oven causes a rapid expansion of the gas in the dough. Long baking thickens the crust. Desirable yeast breads are golden brown and well shaped, with a thin, tender crust. The texture will be even, moist, light, and tender with a medium-fine grain.

Rolls from plain bread dough can be baked quickly in a 425°F- (220-°C) oven. Rich doughs are baked at lower temperatures (350-375 °F/175-190 °C) to prevent excessive browning of the crust. Roll doughs may be refrigerated and portions of the dough baked at intervals. Storage time should be limited to less than a week to prevent crust formation.

Quick Bread Recipes

BAKING POWDER BISCUITS
Bake: 15 min
Oven: 425 °F (220 °C)

Yield: 100 2½-in. biscuits
130 2-in. biscuits

Amount		Ingredient	Method
Metric	*U.S.*	*Ingredient*	*Method*
2.27 kg	5 lb	Flour	Mix dry ingredients (low speed).
142 g	5 oz	Baking powder	
30 mL	2 T	Salt	
567 g	1 lb 4 oz	Fat	Add fat. Mix (low speed) until crumbly.
1.66-1.89 L	1¾-2 qt	Milk	Add milk. Mix (low speed) to form a soft dough. Do not overmix. Dough should be as soft as can be handled. 1. Place one-half of dough on lightly floured board or table. Knead lightly 15-20 times. 2. Roll to ¾-in. thickness. Cut with a 2½-in. (or 2-in.) cutter; or cut into 2-in. squares with a knife. 3. Place on baking sheet ½ in. apart for crusty biscuits, just touching for softer biscuits. Repeat, using remaining dough. 4. Biscuits may be held several hours in the refrigerator until time to bake.

Note: 7 oz (198 g) nonfat dry milk and 1¾ qt (1.66 L) water may be substituted for fluid milk. Combine dry milk with flour, baking powder, and salt.

Variations:

1. **Buttermilk Biscuits.** Substitute cultured buttermilk (or 9 oz/255 g dried buttermilk and 1¾ qt/1.66 L water) for milk. Add 1 T (15 mL) baking soda to dry ingredients.

2. **Butterscotch Biscuits.** Divide dough into 8 parts. Roll each part into a rectangle ¼ in. thick. Spread with melted butter or margarine and brown sugar. Roll the dough as for jelly roll. Cut off slices ¾ in. thick. Bake 15 min at 375 °F (190 °C).

3. **Cheese Biscuits.** Reduce fat to 1 lb (454 g) and add 1 lb (454 g) dry grated cheese.

4. **Cinnamon Biscuits.** Proceed as for Butterscotch Biscuits. Spread with a mixture of 1 lb (454 g) sugar, 2 oz (57 g) cinnamon, and 1 lb (454 g) raisins.

5. **Cornmeal Biscuits.** Substitute 2 lb (908 g) cornmeal for 2 lb (908 g) white flour.

6. **Drop Biscuits.** Increase milk by 1 qt (0.95 L). Drop by spoon or No. 30 dipper onto greased baking sheet.

7. **Nut Biscuits.** Cut biscuit dough with fancy cutter; sprinkle with 2 c (480 mL) finely chopped nuts and 1 c (240 mL) sugar, mixed.

8. **Orange Biscuits.** Proceed as for Butterscotch Biscuits. Spread with orange marmalade.

9. **Raisin Biscuits.** Reduce fat to 14 oz (397 g) and use ½ c (120 mL) less milk; add 4 whole eggs, 3 T (45 mL) grated orange rind, 8 oz (227 g) sugar, and 8 oz (227 g) chopped raisins.

11. **Scotch Scones.** Add 10 oz (284 g) sugar and 7 oz (198 g) currants to dry ingredients; use the 1¾ qt (1.66 L) milk and add 5 eggs, beaten. Cut dough in squares and then cut diagonally to form triangles. Brush lightly with milk.

12. **Shortcake.** Incrcase fat to 1 lb 12 oz (794 g). Add 8 oz (227 g) sugar.

13. **Whole Wheat Biscuits.** Substitute 2 lb (908 g) whole wheat flour for 2 lb (908 g) white flour.

PLAIN MUFFINS
Bake: 25 min   **Yield: 5 doz**
Oven: 400 °F (205 °C)

Amount		Ingredient	Method
Metric	U.S.		
1.14 kg	2 lb 8 oz	Flour	Combine dry ingredients in mixer bowl.
57 g	2 oz	Baking powder	Blend, using flat beater, on low speed.
15 mL	1 T	Salt	
170 g	6 oz	Sugar	
4	4	Eggs, beaten	Combine eggs, milk, and fat.
1.42 L	1½ qt	Milk	Add to dry ingredients. Mix only to blend (low speed) about 15 sec. Batter still will be lumpy.
227 g	8 oz	Fat, melted, cooled	Measure with No. 20 dipper into well-greased muffin pans, about ⅔ full. Batter should be dipped all at once with as little handling as possible, but may be refrigerated a short time and baked as needed.

Notes:
1. No. 24 dipper will yield 6½ doz muffins.
2. 5 oz (142 g) nonfat dry milk and 1½ qt (1.42 L) water may be substituted for fluid milk. Combine dry milk with other dry ingredients. Increase fat to 9 oz (255 g).

Variations:
1. **Apricot Muffins.** Add 3 c (720 mL) drained, chopped, cooked apricots to the liquid ingredients.

2. **Bacon Muffins.** Substitute 10 oz (284 g) chopped bacon, slightly broiled, and bacon fat for the fat in recipe.

3. **Blueberry Muffins.** Carefully fold 1 lb (454 g) blueberries into the batter. Increase sugar to 10 oz (284 g).

4. **Cherry Muffins.** Add 2 c (480 mL) well-drained, cooked cherries to liquid.

5. **Cornmeal muffins.** Substitute 1 lb (454 g) white cornmeal for 1 lb (454 g) flour.

6. **Cranberry Muffins.** Sprinkle 4 oz (114 g) sugar over 1 lb (454 g) chopped raw cranberries. Fold into batter.

7. **Currant Muffins.** Add 8 oz (227 g) chopped currants.

8. **Date Muffins.** Add 1 lb (454 g) chopped dates.

9. **Graham Muffins.** Substitute 12 oz (340 g) graham flour for 12 oz (340 g) white flour. Add 4 T (60 mL) molasses.

10. **Jelly Muffins.** Drop ¼ to ½ t jelly on top of each muffin when placed in oven.

11. **Nut Muffins.** Add 10 oz (284 g) chopped nuts.

12. **Raisin-Nut Muffins.** Add 6 oz (170 g) chopped nuts and 6 oz (170 g) chopped raisins.

13. **Spiced Muffins.** Add 1½ t (8 mL) cloves, 1 t (5 mL) ginger, and 1 t (5 mL) allspice to dry ingredients.

MUFFINS (CAKE METHOD)
Bake: 25 min   **Yield: 6 doz**
Oven: 400 °F (205 °C)

Amount			
Metric	*U.S.*	*Ingredient*	*Method*
340 g	12 oz	Fat	Cream fat and sugar 3 min.
454 g	1 lb	Sugar	
6	6	Eggs	Add eggs. Cream (medium speed) 3 min.
1.14 kg	2 lb 8 oz	Flour	Combine dry ingredients.
57 g	2 oz	Baking powder	Add to creamed mixture.
15 mL	1 T	Salt	
142 g	5 oz	Nonfat dry milk	
1.42 L	1½ qt	Water	Add water. Mix (low speed) 10 sec; scrape bowl, mix 10 sec. Measure with No. 20 dipper into well-greased muffin pans, about ⅔ full. Bake.

Variations:
See Plain Muffins.

FRENCH BREAKFAST PUFFS
Bake: 20-25 min   **Yield: 5 doz**
Oven: 350 °F (175 °C)

Amount			
Metric	*U.S.*	*Ingredient*	*Method*
510 g	1 lb 2 oz	Butter or margarine	Cream butter or margarine and sugar until light and fluffy.
737 g	1 lb 10 oz	Sugar	
6	6	Eggs	Add eggs. Cream well.
1.14 kg	2 lb 8 oz	Flour	Combine dry ingredients.
47 g	1⅔ oz	Baking powder	
15 mL	1 T	Salt	
8 mL	1½ t	Nutmeg	
85 g	3 oz	Nonfat dry milk	
800 mL	3⅓ c	Water	Add dry ingredients and water alternately to creamed mixture. Measure into greased muffin pans with No. 20 dipper. Bake.
567 g	1 lb 4 oz	Butter or margarine, melted	When muffins are baked, remove from pans. Roll in butter, then in sugar-cinnamon mixture.
737 g	1 lb 10 oz	Sugar	
30 mL	2 T	Cinnamon	

Note: For special occasions, dip batter with No. 40 dipper into small
(1½-in.) muffin pans.

HONEY CORNFLAKE MUFFINS
Bake: 20 min   **Yield: 4 doz.**
Oven: 400 °F (205 °C)

Amount		Ingredient	Method
Metric	*U.S.*		
227 g	8 oz	Fat	Cream fat and honey (low speed).
312 g	11 oz	Honey	Add eggs. Mix (medium speed)
4	4	Eggs, well beaten	about 30 sec.
794 g	1 lb 12 oz	Flour	Combine dry ingredients.
70 g	2½ oz	Baking powder	
5 mL	1 t	Salt	
0.95 L	1 qt	Milk	Add dry ingredients alternately with the milk to creamed mixture. Mix only to blend (low speed) about 15 sec.
227 g	8 oz	Cornflakes	Add cornflakes all at once. Stir only enough to mix. Measure with No. 20 dipper into well-greased muffin pans. Bake.

ALL-BRAN MUFFINS
Bake: 20 min   **Yield: 5 doz**
Oven: 400 °F (205 °C)

Amount		Ingredient	Method
Metric	*U.S.*		
680 g	1 lb 8 oz	All-Bran	Combine All-Bran, milk, and molasses in mixer bowl.
2.13 L	2¼ qt	Milk	
720 mL	3 c	Molasses	Let stand 15 min.
6	6	Eggs, beaten	Add eggs and fat. Mix (medium speed) 30 sec.
80 mL	⅓ c	Fat, melted, or oil	
680 g	1 lb 8 oz	Flour	Mix dry ingredients and add all at once.
15 mL	1 T	Salt	
30 mL	2 T	Soda	Mix (low speed) only to blend, about 15 sec. Measure with No. 20 dipper into well-greased muffin pans. Bake.

Note: 1½ lb (680 g) chopped dates, raisins, or nuts may be added for variety.

OATMEAL MUFFINS
Bake: 15-20 min   **Yield: 5 doz**
Oven: 400 °F (205 °C)

Amount			
Metric	*U.S.*	*Ingredient*	*Method*
397 g	14 oz	Rolled oats	Combine rolled oats and sour milk
1.18 L	1¼ qt	Sour milk or	in mixer bowl.
		buttermilk	Let stand 1 hr.
5	5	Eggs, beaten	Combine eggs, sugar, and fat. Add
567 g	1 lb 4 oz	Brown sugar	to rolled oat mixture. Mix 30
454 g	1 lb	Fat, melted,	sec. Scrape down bowl.
		cooled	
567 g	1 lb 4 oz	Flour	Add combined dry ingredients.
25 mL	5 t	Baking powder	Mix (low speed) about 15 sec or
13 mL	2½ t	Salt	only until dry ingredients are
13 mL	2½ t	Soda	moistened.
			Measure with No. 20 dipper into
			well-greased muffin pans (⅔
			full). Bake.

Note: No. 24 dipper will yield 7 doz muffins.

GRIDDLE CAKES   **Yield: 100 cakes 4-in. diameter**

Metric	U.S.	Ingredient	Method
Metric	*U.S.*	*Ingredient*	*Method*
2.04 kg	4 lb 8 oz	Flour	Combine dry ingredients in mixer
114 g	4 oz	Baking powder	bowl.
30 mL	2 T	Salt	
340 g	12 oz	Sugar	
12	12	Eggs, beaten until light	Combine eggs, milk, and fat. Add to dry ingredients.
3.31 L	3½ qt	Milk	Mix (low speed) 30 sec.
340 g	12 oz	Fat, melted and cooled, or oil	If batter is thicker than desired, thin with milk. Use No. 16 dipper to place batter on hot griddle. Bake until surface of cake is full of bubbles. Turn and finish baking.

(Amount spans Metric and U.S. columns)

Variations:

1. **Buttermilk Griddle Cakes.** Add 9 oz (255 g) dry buttermilk and 1 T (15 mL) soda to dry ingredients. Substitute 3½ qt (3.31 L) water for milk.

2. **Blueberry Griddle Cakes.** Add 1 lb (454 g) well-drained blueberries to batter after cakes are mixed. Handle carefully to avoid mashing berries.

GRIDDLE CAKE MIX   **Yield: 12 lb (5.44 kg) mix**

Metric	U.S.	Ingredient	Method
Metric	*U.S.*	*Ingredient*	*Method*
4.08 kg	9 lb	Flour	Combine ingredients in mixer
227 g	8 oz	Baking powder	bowl. Blend well, using flat
60 mL	¼ c	Salt	beater or whip.
680 g	1 lb 8 oz	Sugar	Store in covered container.
680 g	1 lb 8 oz	Instant nonfat dry milk	

Note: To use mix, weigh appropriate amount as given in the following table. Add beaten eggs, water, and cooled melted fat. Stir only until mix is dampened. Place on hot griddle with No. 16 dipper. Bake until cake is full of bubbles. Turn and finish baking.

TABLE FOR USING GRIDDLE CAKE MIX

Ingredient	30 cakes	50 cakes	100 cakes	200 cakes
Mix	2 lb/908 g	3 lb/1.36 kg	6 lb/2.72 kg	12 lb/5.44 kg
Eggs, beaten	4	6	12	24
Water	1 qt/0.95 L	1½ qt/1.42 L	3 qt/2.84 L	1½ gal/5.68 L
Fat, melted or oil	4 oz/114 g	6 oz/170 g	12 oz/340 g	1 lb 8 oz/680 g

Variation:
Buttermilk Griddle Cake Mix. Substitute 1 lb 2 oz (510 g) dry buttermilk
for the instant nonfat dry milk and add 2 T (30 mL) soda.

CREPES

Yield: 100 crepes
Portion: 2 crepes

Metric	U.S.	Ingredient	Method
1.14 kg	2 lb 8 oz	Flour	Combine flour and salt in mixer bowl.
23 mL	1½ T	Salt	
24	24	Eggs	Beat eggs until fluffy.
2.37 L	2½ qt	Milk	Add milk and butter or margarine to eggs.
60 mL	¼ c	Butter or margarine, melted	Add to flour and mix until smooth. Batter will be thinner than griddle cake batter.
			Drop on lightly greased hot griddle, using about 1½ oz (43 g) batter.
			Brown lightly on both sides. Crepes will roll more easily if they are not overcooked.
			Stack, with layers of waxed paper between, until ready to use.
			Crepes may be folded or rolled around desired filling. (See recipe for Chicken Crepes. p. 347.)

Note: If used for dessert crepes, add 3 T (45 mL) sugar to dry
ingredients.

WAFFLES   **Yield: 6 qt (5.68 L) batter**
                                                                  50-60 waffles

Amount			
Metric	*U.S.*	*Ingredient*	*Method*
1.36 kg	3 lb	Flour	Combine dry ingredients in mixer
85 g	3 oz	Baking powder	bowl.
30 mL	2 T	Salt	
114 g	4 oz	Sugar	
18	18	Egg yolks	Combine egg yolks, milk, and fat.
2.13 L	2¼ qt	Milk	Add to dry ingredients.
454 g	1 lb	Fat, melted, cooled	Mix (low speed) just enough to moisten dry ingredients.
18	18	Egg whites	Beat egg whites until stiff but not dry. Fold into batter. Use No. 10 dipper to place batter on preheated waffle iron. Bake about 4 min.

Note: 7 oz (198 g) nonfat dry milk and 2¼ qt (2.13 L) water may be
substituted for fluid milk. Mix dry milk with dry ingredients. Increase fat
to 1 lb 2 oz (510 g).

Variations:

1. **Bacon Waffles.** Add 1 lb (454 g) chopped bacon slightly cooked, and
    substitute bacon fat for the fat in recipe.

2. **Cornmeal Waffles.** Substitute 12 oz (340 g) fine cornmeal for 8 oz (227
    g) flour.

3. **Pecan Waffles.** Add 6 oz (170 g) chopped pecans.

CORN BREAD

Bake: 35 min
Oven: 400 °F (205 °C)

Yield: 1 pan 12 × 20 × 2 in.
40 portions 2¼ × 2½ in.
48 portions 2 × 2½ in.

Amount		Ingredient	Method
Metric	U.S.		
567 g	1 lb 4 oz	Cornmeal	Combine dry ingredients in mixer
595 g	1 lb 5 oz	Flour	bowl.
170 g	6 oz	Sugar	
28 g	1 oz	Salt	
57 g	2 oz	Baking powder	
5	5	Eggs, beaten	Combine eggs, milk, and fat. Add
0.95 L	1 qt	Milk	to dry ingredients.
170 g	6 oz	Fat, melted, cooled	Mix (low speed) only until ingredients are moistened. Spread into greased baking pan. Bake.

Notes:
1. 4 oz (114 g) nonfat dry milk and 1¼ qt (1.18 L) water may be substituted for fluid milk. Mix dry milk with dry ingredients.
2. Batter may be baked in corn stick or muffin pans. Reduce baking time to 15-20 min.
3. For 18 × 26 × 1 in. pan, use 1½ times recipe. Cut 6 × 10 for 60 3 × 2½ in. pieces.

BISHOP'S BREAD
Bake: 25 min
Oven: 400 °F (205 °C)

Yield: 1 pan 18 × 26 × 1 in.
60 portions 3 × 2½ in.
48 portions 3 × 3 in.

Amount			
Metric	*U.S.*	*Ingredient*	*Method*
397 g	14 oz	Fat	Cream fat and sugar (medium
1.25 kg	2 lb 12 oz	Brown sugar	speed) 5 min.
1.14 kg	2 lb 8 oz	Flour	Mix flour, salt, and cinnamon.
10 mL	2 t	Salt	Add to creamed mixture. Blend.
15 mL	1 T	Cinnamon	Remove 2½ c (600 mL) of the
			mixture to sprinkle on top later.
454 g	1 lb	Flour	Mix flour, baking powder, and
20 mL	4 t	Baking powder	soda.
10 mL	2 t	Soda	
1.18 L	1¼ qt	Buttermilk or	Combine buttermilk and eggs. Add
		sour milk	alternately with flour, baking
4	4	Eggs, beaten	powder, and soda to creamed
			mixture. Scrape down bowl.
			Mix (low speed) about 30 sec.
			(Batter will not be smooth.)
			Spread into greased baking sheet.
			Sprinkle with the 2½ c (600 mL)
			mixture reserved from second
			step. Bake.

Note: 4½ oz (128 g) dry buttermilk and 1¼ qt (1.18 L) water may be substituted for sour milk.

COFFEE CAKE
Bake: 25 min
Oven: 400 °F (205 °C)

Yield: 1 pan 12 × 20 × 2 in.
40 portions 2¼ × 2½ in.
48 portions 2 × 2½ in.

Amount			
Metric	*U.S.*	*Ingredient*	*Method*
908 g	2 lb	Flour	Combine dry ingredients in mixer
40 mL	2⅔ T	Baking powder	bowl.
567 g	1 lb 4 oz	Sugar	
15 mL	1 T	Salt	
4	4	Eggs, beaten	Add eggs and milk, combined.
720 mL	3 c	Milk	Mix (low speed) until dry ingredients are just moistened.
454 g	1 lb	Fat, melted, cooled	Add fat and mix (low speed) for 1 min. Spread into well-greased baking pan.
227 g	8 oz	Butter or margarine	Mix until crumbly. Sprinkle over batter.
454 g	1 lb	Sugar	Bake. Serve warm.
70 g	2½ oz	Flour	
45 mL	3 T	Cinnamon	
5 mL	1 t	Salt	

Note: For 18 × 26 × 1 in. baking sheet, use 1½ times recipe. Cut 6 × 8 for 48 3 × 3 in. pieces.

BLUEBERRY COFFEE CAKE

Bake: 45 min

Oven: 375 °F (190 °C)

Yield: 1 pan 18 × 26 × 1 in.

48 portions 3 × 3 in.

Amount		Ingredient	Method
Metric	*U.S.*		
340 g	12 oz	Fat	Cream fat and sugar (medium
1.02 kg	2 lb 4 oz	Sugar	speed) about 10 min.
6	6	Eggs	Add eggs and continue mixing about 5 min.
1.36 kg	3 lb	Flour	Combine flour, baking powder,
57 g	2 oz	Baking powder	and salt.
15 mL	1 T	Salt	
720 mL	3 c	Milk	Add dry ingredients alternately with milk to creamed mixture. Mix (low speed) 3 min. Scrape down bowl. Mix (medium speed) 10 sec.
680 g	1 lb 8 oz	Blueberries, drained	Carefully fold in well-drained blueberries. Pour into greased baking sheet.
227 g	8 oz	Brown sugar	Combine sugars, flour, cinnamon,
114 g	4 oz	Granulated sugar	and butter. Mix to a coarse crumb consis-
114 g	4 oz	Flour	tency.
10 mL	2 t	Cinnamon	Crumble evenly over top of bat-
170 g	6 oz	Butter or margarine, soft	ter. Bake.

Note: After cake is baked, thin Powdered Sugar Glaze (p. 181) may be drizzled in a fine stream over the top to form an irregular design.

DOUGHNUTS
Fry: 3-4 min   **Yield: 4 doz**
Deep Fat Fryer: 350-375 °F (175-190 °C)

Amount			
Metric	*U.S.*	*Ingredient*	*Method*
3	3	Eggs, slightly beaten	Mix eggs, sugar, and fat (medium speed) about 10 min.
284 g	10 oz	Sugar	
43 g	1½ oz	Fat, melted and cooled	
737 g	1 lb 10 oz	Flour	Combine dry ingredients.
45 mL	3 T	Baking powder	
6 mL	1¼ t	Salt	
5 mL	1 t	Nutmeg	
⅛ t	⅛ t	Ginger	
10 mL	2 t	Orange rind, grated	
480 mL	2 c	Milk	Add dry ingredients and milk alternately to egg mixture. Mix to form a soft dough (add more flour if dough is too soft to handle). Chill, roll to ⅜ in. thickness on floured board or table. Cut with 2½-in. cutter. Fry in deep fat. Sprinkle with sugar when partly cool.

Variation:
Chocolate Doughnuts. Substitute 1 oz (28 g) cocoa for 1 oz (28 g) flour.

BOSTON BROWN BREAD

Steam: 1¼-1½ hr   **Yield: 8 round loaves**
Steam pressure: 5-7 lb   **Portion: 8 per loaf**

Amount		Ingredient	Method
Metric	*U.S.*		
454 g	1 lb	Cornmeal	Combine dry ingredients in mixer bowl (low speed).
340 g	12 oz	Flour, whole wheat	
340 g	12 oz	Flour, white	
23 mL	1½ T	Salt	
23 mL	1½ T	Soda	
1.42 L	1½ qt	Sour milk or buttermilk	Blend milk and molasses. Add all at once to dry ingredients.
540 mL	2¼ c	Molasses	Mix (low speed) only until ingredients are blended. Fill 8 greased cans 3¼ × 4½ in. ¾ full. Cover tightly with aluminum foil. Steam.

Notes:
1. May be baked as loaves. Add 3 T (45 mL) melted fat. Bake 1 hr at 375 °F (190 °C).
2. 12 oz (340 g) raisins may be added.

BAKED BROWN BREAD
Bake: 45 min
Oven: 375 °F (190 °C)

Yield: 7 loaves 4 × 9 in.
Portion: 12-14 per loaf

Amount			
Metric	*U.S.*	*Ingredient*	*Method*
680 g	1 lb 8 oz	Brown sugar	Mix sugar, eggs, and fat (medium
4	4	Eggs	speed) about 5 min.
170 g	6 oz	Fat, melted, cooled	
1.89 L	2 qt	Sour milk or buttermilk	Combine sour milk and molasses.
300 mL	1¼ c	Molasses	
1.81 kg	4 lb	Flour, whole-wheat	Mix dry ingredients and add alternately with milk and molasses
15 mL	1 T	Salt	to first mixture.
37 mL	2½ T	Soda	Mix (low speed) about 3 min. Divide batter into 7 greased loaf pans, approximately 1½ lb (680 g) per pan. Bake.

Variations:

1. **Pecan Brown Bread.** Add 8 oz (227 g) chopped pecans.

2. **Prune Brown Bread.** Add 12 oz (340 g) chopped, pitted prunes.

3. **Raisin Brown Bread.** Add 12 oz (340 g) raisins.

NUT BREAD

Bake: 1 hr
Oven: 375 °F (190 °C)

Yield: 5 loaves 4 × 9 in.
Portion: 14 per loaf

Amount		Ingredient	Method
Metric	*U.S.*	*Ingredient*	*Method*
1.36 kg	3 lb	Flour	Combine dry ingredients and nuts
28 g	1 oz	Baking powder	in mixer bowl (low speed).
15 mL	1 T	Salt	
680 g	1 lb 8 oz	Sugar	
454 g	1 lb	Nuts, chopped	
6	6	Eggs, beaten	Combine eggs, milk, and fat.
1.42 L	1½ qt	Milk	Add to dry ingredients.
114 g	4 oz	Fat, melted, cooled	Mix (low speed) only until blended.
			Divide batter into 5 greased loaf pans, approximately 1 lb 14 oz (851 g) per pan.
			Let stand 30 min before baking.

Note: 5 oz (142 g) nonfat dry milk and 1½ qt (1.42 L) water may be substituted for dry milk. Combine dry milk with dry ingredients. Increase fat to 6 oz (170 g).

BANANA BREAD
Bake: 50 min
Oven: 350 °F (175 °C)

Yield: 4 loaves 4 × 9 in.
Portion: 14 per loaf

Amount		Ingredient	Method
Metric	U.S.		
284 g	10 oz	Fat	Cream fat and sugar (medium speed) 5 min.
737 g	1 lb 10 oz	Sugar	
5	5	Eggs	Add eggs to creamed mixture. Beat 2 min.
737 g	1 lb 10 oz	Bananas, mashed	Add bananas and beat 1 min.
908 g	2 lb	Flour	Combine dry ingredients and nuts.
60 mL	4 T	Baking powder	
10 mL	2 t	Salt	
3 mL	½ t	Soda	
227 g	8 oz	Nuts, chopped	
180 mL	¾ c	Milk	Add dry ingredients and milk to creamed mixture. Mix (low speed) 1 min. Divide batter into 4 greased loaf pans, approximately 1 lb 10 oz (737 g) per pan. Let stand 30 min before baking.

CRANBERRY NUT BREAD
Bake: 1 hr

Oven: 350 °F (175 °C)

Yield: 5 loaves 4 × 9 in.

Portion: 14 per loaf

Amount		Ingredient	Method
Metric	*U.S.*		
1.14 kg	2 lb 8 oz	Flour	Combine dry ingredients in mixer bowl.
1.02 kg	2 lb 4 oz	Sugar	
28 g	1 oz	Baking powder	
10 mL	2 t	Salt	
10 mL	2 t	Soda	
5	5	Eggs, beaten	Combine and add to dry ingredients.
360 mL	1½ c	Orange juice	
900 mL	3¾ c	Water	Mix (low speed) only until dry ingredients are moistened.
120 mL	½ c	Salad oil	
454 g	1 lb	Nuts, chopped	Add nuts, rind, and cranberries.
198 g	7 oz	Orange rind, ground	Mix (low speed) until blended. (Batter still may be lumpy.)
567 g	1 lb 4 oz	Cranberries, raw, coarsely ground	Divide batter into 5 greased loaf pans, approximately 2 lb (908 g) per pan. Bake. Cool before slicing.

DATE-NUT BREAD
Bake: 1 hr

Oven: 350 °F (175 °C)

Yield: 4 loaves 4 × 9 in.

Portion: 14 per loaf

Amount		Ingredient	Method
Metric	*U.S.*		
680 g	1 lb 8 oz	Dates, chopped	Add water and soda to dates. Let stand 20 min.
23 mL	1½ T	Soda	
780 mL	3¼ c	Water, boiling	
85 g	3 oz	Fat	Cream fat and sugar (medium speed) 5 min.
794 g	1 lb 12 oz	Sugar	
4	4	Eggs	Add eggs and vanilla. Mix 2 min (medium speed).
23 mL	1½ T	Vanilla	
908 g	2 lb	Flour	Combine flour and salt. Add alternately with dates to creamed mixture.
8 mL	1½ t	Salt	
227 g	8 oz	Nuts, chopped	Add nuts. Divide batter into 4 greased loaf pans, approximately 1 lb 12 oz (794 g) per pan.

PUMPKIN BREAD

Bake: 1 hr   **Yield: 4 loaves 4 × 9 in.**
Oven: 350 °F (175 °C)   **Portion: 14 per loaf**

Amount		Ingredient	Method
Metric	U.S.		
1.08 kg	2 lb 6 oz	Sugar	Cream sugar and fat (medium
397 g	14 oz	Fat	speed) for 5 min.
6	6	Eggs	Add eggs and pumpkin to creamed
737 g	1 lb 10 oz	Pumpkin	mixture. Mix (medium speed) for 8 min. Scrape down bowl.
624 g	1 lb 6 oz	Flour	Combine dry ingredients and add
10 mL	2 t	Salt	to pumpkin mixture. Mix 3 min
5 mL	1 t	Baking powder	(low speed); scrape down bowl,
10 mL	2 t	Soda	mix 3 min.
10 mL	2 t	Nutmeg	Divide batter into 4 greased loaf
10 mL	2 t	Cloves	pans, approximately 1 lb 12 oz
10 mL	2 t	Cinnamon	(794 g) per pan. Bake.
10 mL	2 t	Allspice	

SWEDISH TIMBALE CASES

Fry: 2-3 min   **Yield: 50**
Deep fat fryer: 350-365 °F (175-182 °C)

Amount		Ingredient	Method
Metric	U.S.		
3	3	Eggs, beaten	Mix eggs, milk, and fat.
360 mL	1½ c	Milk	
8 mL	1½ t	Oil or melted fat	
170 g	6 oz	Flour	Add combined dry ingredients.
5 mL	1 t	Salt	Stir until smooth.
8 mL	1½ t	Sugar	Let stand until air bubbles have come to top. Dip hot timbale iron into batter and fry in deep fat until brown.

Notes:
This recipe may be used for either timbale cases or rosettes.
1. Serve timbale cases filled with creamed chicken or creamed peas.
2. Serve rosettes sprinkled with powdered sugar, heaped with fresh or preserved fruits and garnished with whipped or ice cream; or use the same as timbale cases.

FRITTERS

Fry: 4-6 min   **Yield: 100**
Deep fat fryer: 375 °F (190 °C)   **Portion: 2 fritters**

Amount		Ingredient	Method
Metric	U.S.		
1.81 kg	4 lb	Flour	Mix dry ingredients.
15 mL	1 T	Salt	
114 g	4 oz	Baking powder	
57 g	2 oz	Sugar	
12	12	Eggs, beaten	Combine eggs, milk, and fat. Add
1.89 L	2 qt	Milk	to dry ingredients. Mix only
170 g	6 oz	Fat, melted	enough to moisten dry ingredients.
			Measure with No. 30 dipper into hot deep fat.
			Serve with syrup.

Variations:

1. **Apple Fritters.** Add 1 lb (454 g) raw apple, peeled and finely chopped.

2. **Corn Fritters.** Add 2 qt (1.89 L) whole kernel corn, drained.

3. **Fruit Fritters.** Add 1 qt (0.95 L) fruit: banana, drained peach, or pineapple.

4. **Banana Fritters.** Reduce flour to 2 lb (908 g). Dip quartered bananas into batter. Fry.

DUMPLINGS

Steam: 12-15 min under pressure   **Yield: 100**
                                                       Portion: 2 dumplings

Amount		Ingredient	Method
Metric	U.S.		
1.14 kg	2 lb 8 oz	Flour	Mix flour, baking powder, and
85 g	3 oz (6 T)	Baking powder	salt.
30 mL	2 T	Salt	
6	6	Eggs, beaten	Combine eggs and milk. Add to
1.32 L	5½ c	Milk	flour mixture. Mix only until blended.
			Use No. 24 dipper to drop on trays. Do not cover trays.
			Steam.
			Serve with meat stew.

Note: Mixture may be dropped onto hot meat or meat mixture in counter pans and steamed.

CHEESE STRAWS
Bake: 10-15 min   **Yield: 6 doz 4 × 1 in. straws**
Oven: 350 °F (175 °C)

Amount		Ingredient	Method
Metric	*U.S.*		
170 g	6 oz	Butter or margarine	Cream butter or margarine (medium speed) until soft.
227 g	8 oz	Cheese, sharp, grated	Add grated cheese and the combined dry ingredients (low speed).
227 g	8 oz	Flour	
10 mL	2 t	Baking powder	
5 mL	1 t	Salt	
¼ t	¼ t	Cayenne	
3	3	Eggs, beaten	Add eggs and water, combined. Mix (low speed) to form a stiff dough. Chill. Roll ¼ in. thick and cut into strips 4 in. long and 1 in. wide. Place on ungreased baking sheet. Bake.
30 mL	2 T	Water	

Variation:
Caraway Cheese Straws. Add 2 t (10 mL) caraway seeds to flour before mixing.

Yeast Bread Recipes

PLAIN ROLLS
Bake: 15-25 min   **Yield: 6 doz**
Oven: 400-425 °F (205-220 °C)

Amount			
Metric	*U.S.*	*Ingredient*	*Method*
114 g	4 oz	Sugar	Place sugar, salt, and fat in mixer
45 mL	3 T	Salt	bowl.
170 g	6 oz	Fat	
1.18 L	1¼ qt	Milk, scalded	Add hot milk. Mix (low speed) to blend. Cool to lukewarm.
43 g	1½ oz	Yeast, active dry	Soften yeast in warm water.
240 mL	1 c	Water, warm (110 °F/43 °C)	
4	4	Eggs, beaten	Add softened yeast and eggs to milk mixture.
2.15 kg	4 lb 12 oz (variable)	Flour	Add flour to make a moderately soft dough. Mix (low speed) until smooth and satiny.

1. Turn into lightly greased bowl, turn over to grease top. Cover. Let rise in warm place (80 °F/27 °C) until double in bulk.
2. Punch down. Divide into thirds for ease in handling. Shape into 1½-oz (43-g) rolls.
3. Let rise until double in bulk.
4. Bake.

Notes:
1. For compressed yeast, use 3 oz (85 g) softened in lukewarm (95 °F/35 °C) water.
2. 3-4 hr are required for mixing and rising. For a quicker rising dough, increase yeast to 2 oz (57 g) dry, 4 oz (114 g) compressed.
3. Dry yeast may be mixed with dry ingredients. (See p. 144.)
4. 5 oz (142 g) nonfat dry milk plus 1¼ qt (1.18 L) water may be substituted for milk. Combine dry milk powder with sugar and salt.

Variations:
1. **Bowknots.** Roll 1½-oz (43-g) portions of dough into strips 9 in. long. Tie loosely into a single knot. (See Fig. 2.1.)

2. **Braids.** Roll dough ¼ in. thick and cut in strips 6 in. long and ½ in. wide. Cross 3 strips in the middle and braid from center to end. Press ends together and fold under.

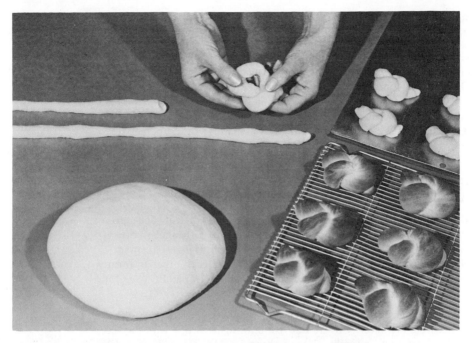

Figure 2.1   Bowknots. (Courtesy of the Wheat Flour Institute.)

Figure 2.2   Cloverleaf Rolls. (Courtesy of the Wheat Flour Institute.)

3. **Butterhorns.** Proceed as for crescents, but do not form a crescent shape.

4. **Caramel Crowns.** Scale dough into balls 1½ oz (43 g) each. Roll in melted butter or margarine, then in a sugar and cinnamon mixture. Drop 18 balls into each of 5 greased angel food cake pans. Sprinkle with nuts (and raisins if desired). The pan should be about ⅓ full. Let rise until double in bulk. Bake for 35-40 min at 350-375 °F (175-190 °C). Immediately loosen from pan with a spatula. Invert pan. After removing crowns from pan, place whole maraschino or glacé cherries on top.

5. **Cloverleaf Rolls.** Pinch off small balls of dough. Fit into greased muffin pans, allowing 3 balls for each roll (See Fig. 2.2.)

6. **Crescents.** Weigh dough into 12-oz (340-g) portions. Roll each into a circle ⅛ in. thick and 8 in. in diameter. Cut into 12 triangles, brush top with melted fat. Beginning at base, roll each triangle, keeping point in middle of roll and bringing ends toward each other to form a crescent shape. Place on greased baking sheet 1½ in. apart. (See Fig. 2.3.)

7. **Dinner or Pan Rolls.** Shape dough into small balls; place on well-greased baking sheet. Cover. Let rise until light. Brush with mixture made of egg yolk and milk—1 egg yolk to 1 T (15 mL) milk. (See Fig. 2.4.)

Figure 2.3 Crescents. (Courtesy of the Wheat Flour Institute.)

Figure 2.4 Dinner or Pan Rolls. (Courtesy of the Wheat Flour Institute.)

8. **Fan Tan or Butterflake Rolls.** Weigh dough into 12-oz (340-g) pieces. Roll out into very thin rectangular sheet. Brush with melted butter. Cut in strips about 1 in. wide. Pile six or seven strips together. Cut 1½-in. pieces and place on end in greased muffin pans. (See Fig. 2.5.)

9. **Finger or Wiener Rolls.** Divide dough into 2 portions. Roll each piece of dough into a strip 1½ in. in diameter. Cut strips of dough into pieces approximately 1 oz (28 g) each for Finger Rolls, 1½ oz (43 g) each for Wiener Rolls. Round pieces of dough; roll into pieces approximately 4½ in. long. Place in rows on greased baking sheet ½ in. apart.

10. **Half-and Half Rolls.** Proceed as for Twin Rolls. Use 1 round plain dough and 1 round whole wheat dough for each roll (p. 144).

11. **Hot Cross Buns.** Divide dough into thirds. Roll ½ in. thick. Cut rounds 3 in. in diameter. Brush top with beaten egg. Score top of bun to make cross before baking or, after baking, make a cross on top with frosting. (See Fig. 2.6).

12. **Parkerhouse Rolls.** Divide dough into thirds. Roll to ⅓-in. thickness. Cut rounds 2-2½ in. in diameter or form 1½-oz (43-g) balls. Allow balls to stand for 10 min, then elongate with rolling pin. Crease middle of each roll with dull edge of knife. Brush with melted butter

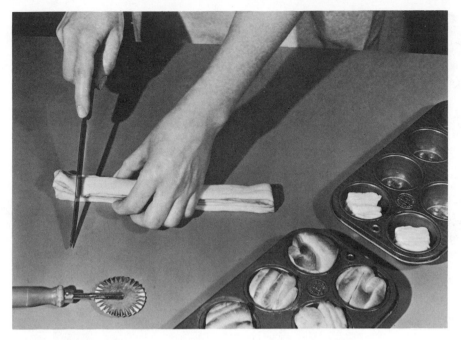

Figure 2.5 Fan Tan or Butterflakes. (Courtesy of the Wheat Flour Institute.)

Figure 2.6 Hot Cross Buns. (Courtesy of the Wheat Flour Institute.)

or margarine, fold over, and press together with palm of hand. (See Fig. 2.7.)

13. **Poppy Seed Rolls.** (*a*) Proceed as for Twists. Substitute poppy seeds for sugar and cinnamon. (*b*) Proceed as for Cinnamon Rolls. Substitute poppy seed for sugar, cinnamon, and raisins.

14. **Ribbon Rolls.** Weigh dough into 12-oz (340-g) pieces. Roll ¼ in. thick. Spread with melted butter or margarine. Place on top of this a layer of whole wheat dough rolled to the same thickness. Repeat, using the contrasting dough until 5 layers thick. Cut with a 1½-in. cutter. Place in greased muffin pans with cut surface down.

15. **Rosettes.** Follow directions for Bowknots. After tying, bring one end through center and the other over the side.

16. **Sandwich Buns.** Divide dough into 2 portions. Roll each piece of dough into a strip 1½-in. in diameter. Cut strips into pieces approximately 2 oz (57 g) each. Round the pieces into balls. Place balls in rows on greased baking sheet 1½-2 in. apart. Let stand 10-15 min; flatten to desired thickness with fingers, rolling pin, or another baking sheet.

17. **Sesame Rolls.** Proceed as for Twin Rolls. Brush tops with melted fat and sprinkle with sesame seeds.

Figure 2.7 Parkerhouse Rolls. (Courtesy of the Wheat Flour Institute.)

18. **Twin Rolls.** Weigh dough into 12-oz (340-g) pieces. Roll ⅝ in. thick. Cut rounds 1 in. in diameter. Brush with melted butter or margarine. Place on end in well-greased muffin pans, allowing 2 rounds for each roll.

19. **Twists.** Weigh dough into 12-oz (340-g) pieces. Roll ⅓ in. thick, spread with melted butter or margarine, sugar, and cinnamon. Cut into strips ⅓ × 8 in., bring both ends together, and twist dough.

20. **Whole Wheat Rolls.** Substitute 2 lb 6 oz (1.08 kg) whole wheat flour for 2 lb 6 oz (1.08 kg) white flour. Proceed as for Plain Rolls.

QUICK ROLL DOUGH
Bake: 15-20 min   **Yield: 10 doz**
Oven: 400-425 °F (205-220 °C)

Amount		Ingredient	Method
Metric	U.S.		
57 g	2 oz	Yeast, active dry	Soften yeast in warm water.
1.89 L	2 qt	Water, warm (110 °F/43 °C)	
12	12	Eggs, beaten	Add eggs and fat. Mix.
227 g	8 oz	Fat, melted	
3.29 kg	7 lb 4 oz	Flour (amount variable)	Add dry ingredients. Mix (low speed) until dough is smooth and elastic and leaves sides of bowl, 15-20 min.
198 g	7 oz	Nonfat dry milk	
227 g	8 oz	Sugar	
45 mL	3 T	Salt	Divide dough into 12 equal portions (approximately 1½ lb/680 g each). Let rest 10 min. Work with 1 portion at a time. This will be a rather soft dough. Shape and place rolls on greased baking sheets and let rise. Bake.

Notes:
1. For compressed yeast, use 4 oz (114 g) softened in lukewarm (95 °F/35 °C) water.
2. Mixing may be simplified by combining dry yeast with sugar, salt, dry milk, and 2 lb (908 g) of the flour. Add to beaten eggs, warm water (120 °F/49 ° C), and melted fat. Mix. Add remaining flour gradually, mixing until a smooth, elastic dough is formed.

Variations:
See variations for Plain Rolls, pp. 138-144.

REFRIGERATOR ROLLS
Bake: 15-20 min   **Yield: 6 doz**
Oven: 425 °F (220 °C)

Amount			
Metric	U.S.	Ingredient	Method
340 g	12 oz	Sugar	Place sugar, fat, salt, and potatoes
340 g	12 oz	Fat	in mixer bowl.
57 g	2 oz	Salt	
360 mL	1½ c	Mashed potatoes, hot	
1.18 L	1¼ qt	Milk, scalded	Add milk. Mix to blend. Cool to lukewarm.
28 g	1 oz	Yeast, active dry	Soften yeast in warm water.
240 mL	1 c	Water, warm (110 °F/43 °C)	
8 mL	1½ t	Soda	Add softened yeast, soda, and
15 mL	1 T	Baking powder	baking powder to milk mixture.
1.81 kg	4 lb	Flour	Add just enough of the flour to make a stiff batter. Let rise 15 min. Add remaining flour or enough to make a stiff dough. Mix until dough is smooth. Place in a greased container. Grease top. Cover and place in the refrigerator for 24 hr. Remove dough from refrigerator and shape into rolls. Let rise 1-1½ hr or until light. Bake.

Notes:
1. 2 oz (57 g) compressed yeast may be substituted for the dry yeast. Soften in lukewarm water (95 °F/35 °C).
2. 4 oz (114 g) nonfat dry milk and 1¼ qt (1.18 L) water may be substituted for fluid milk. Mix dry milk powder with soda, baking powder, and part of flour.

Variations:
See variations for Plain Rolls, pp. 138-144.

BASIC SWEET ROLL DOUGH
Bake: 20-25 min   **Yield: 8 doz**
Oven: 375 °F (190 °C)

Metric	U.S.	Ingredient	Method
	Amount		
Metric	*U.S.*	*Ingredient*	*Method*
720 mL	3 c	Milk, scalded	Combine milk, sugar, fat, and salt
454 g	1 lb	Sugar	in mixer bowl.
454 g	1 lb	Fat	Mix to blend.
57 g	2 oz	Salt	Cool to lukewarm.
9	9	Eggs, beaten	Add eggs. Mix.
57 g	2 oz	Yeast, active dry	Soften yeast in warm water. Add to milk mixture. Mix (medium speed) until blended.
360 mL	1½ c	Water, warm (110 °F/43 °C)	
2.27-2.72 kg (variable)	5-6 lb	Flour	Add flour gradually (low speed). Mix (medium speed) to a smooth dough (5-6 min). Do not overmix. Dough should be moderately soft. 1. The dough temperature just after mixing should be 78-82 °F (26-28 °C). 2. Place in lightly greased bowl. Grease top of dough, cover, and let rise in warm place until double in bulk, about 2 hr. 3. Punch down and let rise again, about 1 hr. 4. Punch down and divide into portions for rolls. Let rest 10 min. 5. Scale about 2 oz (57 g) per roll. Shape and let rise until rolls are almost double in bulk. 6. Bake.

Notes:
1. 4 oz (114 g) nonfat dry milk and 1 qt (0.95 L) water may be substituted for the fluid milk. Combine dry milk with part of the flour.
2. 4 oz (114 g) compressed yeast may be substituted for the dry yeast. Soften in lukewarm water (95 °F/35 °C).
3. For a quicker rising dough, increase yeast to 3 oz (85 g) dry or 6 oz (170 g) compressed.

4. Mixing may be simplified by combining dry yeast with sugar, salt, dry milk if used, and 2 lb (908 g) of the flour. In mixer bowl, blend beaten eggs, 1 qt (0.95 L) very warm water (120 °F/49 °C), and melted fat. Add yeast-flour mixture (low speed). Add remaining flour gradually, mixing until a smooth, elastic dough is formed.

Variations:

1. **Cherry-Nut Rolls.** Add 1 t (5 mL) nutmeg, 1 t (5 mL) lemon extract, 1 lb (454 g) chopped glacé cherries, and 1 lb (454 g) chopped pecans to dough. Shape into 1-oz (28-g) balls. When baked, cover with glaze made of orange juice and powdered sugar.

2. **Coffee Cake.** Scale 4 lb (1.81 kg) dough, roll out to size of sheet pan. Cover top of dough with melted butter or margarine and topping. *Butter Crunch Topping:* Blend 1 lb (454 g) sugar, 1 lb (454 g) butter or margarine, ½ t salt, 3 oz (85 g) honey, and 2 lb (908 g) flour together to form a crumbly mixture. *Butter Cinnamon Topping:* Cream 8 oz (227 g) butter or margarine, 1 lb (454 g) sugar, 3 T (45 mL) cinnamon, and ½ t salt. Add 4 beaten eggs and 3 oz (85 g) flour and blend. Fruit fillings may also be used.

3. **Crullers.** Roll dough ⅓ in. thick. Cut into strips ⅓ × 8 in. Bring 2 ends together and twist dough. Fry in deep fat after proofing. Frost with Powered Sugar Glaze (p. 181) or dip in fine granulated sugar.

4. **Danish Pastry.** Roll a 4- or 5-lb (1.81- or 2.27-kg) piece of dough into a rectangular shape about ¼ in. thick. Start at one edge and cover completely ⅔ of dough with small pieces of hard butter, margarine, or special Danish Pastry shortening. The latter is stable at bake shop temperature and is easier to use than butter or margarine. Use 2-5 oz (57-142 g) per lb (454 g) of dough. Fold the unbuttered ⅓ portion of dough over an equal portion of buttered dough. Fold the remaining ⅓ buttered dough over the top to make 3 layers of dough separated by a layer of fat. Roll out dough ¼ in. thick. This completes the first roll. Repeat folding and rolling two or more times. Do not allow fat to become soft while working with the dough. Let dough rest 45 min. Make into desired shapes.

5. **Hot Cross Buns.** Add to dough 8 oz (227 g) chopped glacé cherries, 8 oz (227 g) raisins, 2 T (30 mL) cinnamon, ¼ t cloves, and ¼ t nutmeg. Shape into round buns, 1 oz (28 g) per bun. When baked, make a cross on top with powdered sugar frosting. (See Fig. 2.6.)

6. **Kolaches.** Add 2 T (30 mL) grated lemon peel to dough. Shape dough into 1 oz (28 g) balls. Place on lightly greased baking sheet. Let rise until light. Press down center to make cavity and fill with 1 t (5 mL) filling. Brush with melted butter or margarine and sprinkle with chopped nuts. Suggested fillings: Chopped cooked prunes and dried apricots with sugar and cinnamon, poppy seed mixed with sugar and milk, apricot or peach marmalade.

7. **Long Johns.** Roll out dough to a thickness of ½ in. Cut dough into rectangular pieces ½ × 4 in. Let rise until double in bulk. Fry in deep fat.

8. **Swedish Braids.** Add to dough 1 lb (454 g) chopped candied fruit cake mix, 8 oz (227 g) pecans, and ½ t cardamon seed. Weigh dough into 1¾ lb (794 g) portions and braid. Place on greased sheet pans, 4 per pan. When baked, brush with Powered Sugar Glaze (p. 181) made with milk in place of water.

CINNAMON ROLLS

Bake: 20-25 min   **Yield: 7-8 doz**
Oven: 375 °F (190 °C)

Amount			
Metric	U.S.	Ingredient	Method
4.54 kg (1 recipe)	10 lb	Plain Roll Dough (p. 138) or Basic Sweet Roll Dough (p. 146) (raised and ready for shaping)	Divide dough into 8 portions about 1 lb 4 oz (567 g) each. Roll each portion into rectangular strip 9 × 14 × ⅓ in.
340 g	12 oz	Butter or margarine, melted	Spread each strip with butter, then sprinkle with 6 oz (170 g) of the mixed sugar and cinnamon.
908 g	2 lb	Sugar	Roll as for Jelly Roll (p. 173). Cut into 1-in. slices.
45 mL	3 T	Cinnamon	Place cut side down on greased baking sheets (2 doz rolls, 1½ oz/43 g each, per 18 × 26 × 1-in. pan) or in muffin pans. See Fig. 2.8. Let rise until doubled in bulk, about 45 min. Bake. After removing from oven, spread tops with Powdered Sugar Glaze (p. 181) made with milk in place of water.

Variations:
1. **Butterfly Rolls.** Cut rolled dough into 2-in. slices. Press each roll across center parallel to the cut side, with the back of a large knife handle. Press or flatten out the folds of each end. Place on greased baking sheet 1½ in. apart. (See Fig. 2.9.)

Figure 2.8   Cinnamon Rolls. (Courtesy of the Wheat Flour Institute.)

2. **Butterscotch Rolls.** Use brown sugar and omit cinnamon, if desired. Cream 8 oz (227 g) butter or margarine, 1½ lb (680 g) brown sugar, and 1 t (5 mL) salt. Gradually add 1 c (240 mL) water, blending thoroughly. Spread 1 T (15 mL) mixture into each greased muffin pan cup. Place rolls cut side down in pans.

3. **Cinnamon-Raisin Rolls.** Use brown sugar in place of granulated sugar and add 8 oz (227 g) raisins to filling.

4. **Double Cinnamon Buns.** Proceed as for Butterfly Rolls. Roll sheet of dough from both sides to form a double roll.

5. **Glazed Marmalade Rolls.** Omit cinnamon. Dip cut slice in additional melted butter and sugar. When baked, glaze with orange marmalade mixed with powdered sugar until of a consistency to spread. Apricot marmalade, strawberry jam, or other preserves may be used for the glaze.

6. **Honey Rolls.** Substitute honey filling for sugar and cinnamon. Whip 1 lb (454 g) butter or margarine and 1 lb (454 g) honey until light and fluffy.

7. **Orange Rolls.** Omit cinnamon. Spread with mixture of 1½ lb (680 g) sugar and 1 c (240 mL) grated orange rind. When baked, brush with glaze made of powdered sugar and orange juice. If desired, use a

Figure 2.9 Cinnamon Butterfly Rolls. (Courtesy of the Wheat Flour Institute.)

Figure 2.10 Pecan Rolls. (Courtesy of the Wheat Flour Institute.)

filling made by cooking 1½ lb (680 g) sugar and 1½ qt (1.42 L) ground whole oranges (about 9 medium-sized ones) until thickened. Cool. Spread on roll dough. A quick filling may be made by combining 12 oz (340 g) frozen orange juice and 1½ lb (680 g) sugar.

8. **Pecan Rolls.** Proceed as for Butterscotch Rolls. Add 12 oz (340 g) pecans to mixture placed in muffin pans. (See Fig. 2.10.)

9. **Sugared Snails.** Proceed as for Butterfly Rolls, rolling dough thinner before adding sugar filling. Cut rolled dough into slices ¾ in. thick. Dip cut surface of each roll in granulated sugar. Place on greased baking sheet ½ in. apart, with sugared side up. Allow to stand 10-15 min, then flatten before baking.

FRUIT COFFEE RINGS
Bake: 25-30 min   **Yield: 8 rings**
Oven: 375 °F (190 °C)

	Amount		
Metric	U.S.	Ingredient	Method
4.54 kg	10 lb (1 recipe)	Plain Roll Dough (p. 138) or Basic Sweet Roll Dough (p. 146) (raised and ready for shaping)	Divide dough into 1½-lb (680-g) portions. Roll out each portion into a rectangular strip 9 × 14 × ⅓ in.
1.89 L	2 qt	Filling (see below)	Spread each strip with 1 c (240 mL) filling. Roll as for cinnamon rolls. Arrange in ring mold or 10-in. tube pan. Cut slashes in dough with scissors about 1 in. apart. Let rise. Bake.

Suggested Fillings:

1. **Apricot Ring.** Use 2 qt (1.89 L) Apricot Filling (p. 187).

2. **Cranberry Ring** Use 2 qt (1.89 L) Cranberry Filling (p. 185).

3. **Fig Ring.** Use 2 qt (1.89 L) Fig Filling (p. 186).

4. **Honey Ring.** Whip 1 lb (454 g) butter or margarine and 1 lb (454 g) honey until light and fluffy.

5. **Orange Ring.** Use 2 qt (1.89 L) orange marmalade.

6. **Prune-Date Ring.** Use 2 qt (1.89 L) Prune-Date Filling (p. 187).

BRAN ROLLS

Bake: 15 min   **Yield: 8 doz**
Oven: 425 °F (220 °C)

Amount			
Metric	*U.S.*	*Ingredient*	*Method*
454 g	1 lb	Fat	Combine fat, sugar, salt, All-Bran,
340 g	12 oz	Sugar	and water in mixer bowl. Stir
15 mL	1 T	Salt	until fat is melted.
114 g	4 oz	All-Bran	Let stand until mixture is luke-
480 mL	2 c	Water, boiling	warm.
28 g	1 oz	Yeast, active dry	Soften yeast in warm water.
480 mL	2 c	Water, warm (110 °F/43 °C)	
4	4	Eggs, beaten	Add softened yeast and eggs to bran mixture.
			Mix (medium speed) until blended.
1.36 kg	3 lb (variable)	Flour	Add flour (low speed).
			Mix until soft dough is formed.
			1. Place in lightly greased bowl.
			2. Cover and place in refrigerator until chilled. (Dough may be held overnight in refrigerator.)
			3. Remove from refrigerator, form balls of dough to half fill greased muffin pans.
			4. Let rise 2 hr. Bake.

Note: 2 oz (57 g) compressed yeast may be substituted for the dry yeast.
Soften in lukewarm water (95 °F/35 °C).

RAISED MUFFINS
Bake: 20 min   **Yield: 8 doz**
Oven: 350 °F (175 °C)

Amount		Ingredient	Method
Metric	*U.S.*		
255 g	9 oz	Fat	Place fat, sugar, and salt in mixer
340 g	12 oz	Sugar	bowl.
57 g	2 oz	Salt	
1.42 L	1½ qt	Milk, scalded	Add milk. Mix (low speed). Cool to lukewarm.
43 g	1½ oz	Yeast, active	Soften yeast in warm water.
360 mL	1½ c	Water, warm (110 °F/43 °C)	
12	12	Eggs, beaten	Add softened yeast and eggs to milk mixture.
908 g	2 lb	Flour	Add flour. Beat (medium speed) 10 min. Let rise in warm place for 1½ hr.
1.25 kg	2 lb 12 oz (variable)	Flour	Add remaining flour. Beat until batter is smooth. Use No. 20 dipper to fill greased muffin pans. Let rise until double in bulk (about 1 hr).

Notes:
1. 3 oz (85 g) compressed yeast may be substituted for the dry yeast.
    Soften in lukewarm water (95 °F/35 °C).
2. 5 oz (142 g) nonfat dry milk and 1½ qt (1.42 L) water may be
    substituted for the fluid milk. Combine dry milk powder with the first
    portion of flour.

WHITE BREAD

Bake: 30-40 min
Oven: 400 °F (205 °C)

Yield: 16 1½-lb (680-g) loaves

Amount		Ingredient	Method
Metric	U.S.		
57-70 g	2-2½ oz	Yeast, active dry	Soften yeast in warm water. Let stand 10 min.
720 mL	3 c	Water, warm (110 °F/43 °C)	
284 g	10 oz	Sugar	Combine sugar, salt, dry milk, water, and fat.
142 g	5 oz	Salt	
397 g	14 oz	Nonfat dry milk	Add softened yeast. Mix (medium speed) until blended.
3.79 L	1 gal	Water, luke-warm	
340 g	12 oz	Fat, melted	
6.80 kg	15 lb	Flour	Add flour. Mix (low speed) about 10 min. or until dough is smooth and elastic.
			1. Let rise in a warm place (80 °F/ 27 °C) approximately 2 hr, or until double in bulk. Knead.
			2. Let rise approximately 1 hr. Knead and divide dough into 16 loaves. (26½ oz/752 g raw dough will yield 1½-lb/680-g loaf.)
			3. Let rise approximately 1½ hr, or until double in bulk.
			4. Bake.

Notes:
1. 4-5 oz (114-142 g) compressed yeast may be substituted for active dry yeast. Soften in lukewarm water (95 °F/35 °C).
2. The dough temperature should be about 80 °F (27 °C) when mixed.
3. Fat may be increased to 1 lb (454 g) and sugar to 2 oz (57 g) if a richer dough is desired.
3. 1¼ gal (4.73 L) fresh milk may be substituted for the water and dry milk.

Variations:
1. **Cinnamon Bread.** After dough has been divided and scaled into loaves, roll into a rectangular sheet. Brush with melted fat; sprinkle generously with cinnamon and sugar. Roll as for Jelly Roll (p. 173).

Seal edge of dough and place in greased baking pan sealed edge down. Sprinkle top with cinnamon and sugar.

2.   **Raisin Bread.** Add 3 lb (1.36 kg) raisins to dough after mixing.

3.   **Whole Wheat Bread.** Substitute whole wheat flour for ½ of white flour.

4.   **Butter Slices.** Divide dough into thirds. Roll ⅓ in. thick. Cut with 3-in. biscuit cutter. Dip in melted butter or margarine and stand pieces on edge in 4 × 9 in. loaf pans (8 pieces per pan). Let rise and bake. Dough may be shaped into long roll and cut into slices.

BUTTER BUNS
Bake: 15-20 min
Oven: 400 °F (205 °C)

Yield: 9-10 doz

Amount			
Metric	*U.S.*	*Ingredient*	*Method*
680 g	1 lb 8 oz	Butter or margarine	Place butter, sugar, and salt in mixer bowl.
454 g	1 lb	Sugar	
28 g	1 oz	Salt	
720 mL	3 c	Milk, scalded	Add milk. Mix (low speed). Cool to lukewarm.
57 g	2 oz	Yeast, active dry	Soften yeast in warm water.
240 mL	1 c	Water, warm (110 °F/43 °C)	
12	12	Eggs, beaten	Add eggs, lemon extract, and yeast to milk mixture.
16	16	Egg yolks, beaten	
20 mL	4 t	Lemon extract	
2.04 kg	4 lb 8 oz	Flour	Add flour. Mix thoroughly. Let rise until double in bulk. Use a No. 30 dipper to fill greased muffin pans. Let rise 1 hr. Bake.

Note: 4 oz (114 g) compressed yeast may be substituted for the dry yeast. Soften in lukewarm water (95 °F/35 °C).

NORWEGIAN CHRISTMAS BREAD

Bake: 40 min
Oven: 350 °F (175 °C)

Yield: 6 loaves 4× 9 in.
Portion: 12-14 per loaf

Amount			
Metric	*U.S.*	*Ingredient*	*Method*
0.95 L	1 qt	Milk	Scald milk. Add sugar, salt, and
454 g	1 lb	Sugar	cardamom seed.
10 mL	2 t	Salt	Cool to lukewarm.
5 mL	1 t	Cardamom seed, crushed	
43 g	1½ oz	Yeast, active dry	Soften yeast in water and add to milk.
240 mL	1 c	Water, warm (110 °F/43 °C)	
680 g	1 lb 8 oz	Flour	Add flour and butter. Mix to form
454 g	1 lb	Butter or margarine, soft	a batter. Let stand 15 min.
794 g	1 lb 12 oz (or more)	Flour	Slice cherries and dust with flour. Add cherries, pecans, and re-
340 g	12 oz	Candied cherries (red and green)	mainder of flour to batter. Mix until a smooth dough is formed. Cover and let rise until double in
170 g	6 oz	Pecans, chopped fine	bulk. Punch down gently. Turn onto lightly floured board. Divide into 6 loaves and shape. Let rise until almost double in bulk (about 40 min.). Bake.

Notes:
1. 3 oz (85 g) compressed yeast may be substituted for the dry yeast.
   Soften in lukewarm water (95 °F/35 °C).
2. 3.5 oz (100 g) nonfat dry milk and 1 qt (0.95 L) water may be
   substituted for fluid milk. Add dry milk powder to first portion of flour.
3. Candied mixed fruits may be substituted for candied cherries.

FRENCH TOAST   **Yield: 50 slices**

Metric	U.S.	Ingredient	Method
Amount			
18-24	18-24	Eggs	Beat eggs.
1.42 L	1½ qt	Milk	Combine with other ingredients.
15 mL	1 T	Salt	
120 mL	½ c	Sugar	
50	50	Bread slices	Dip bread into egg mixture. Do not let bread soak in the egg mixture. Fry in deep fat at 360 °F (180 °C) or on a well-greased griddle until golden brown. Sprinkle with powdered sugar to serve.

Notes:
1. The bread should be at least 2 days old.
2. Unsliced bread may be sliced double thickness, cut into triangles, or left whole, dipped in egg mixture or in thin batter (p. 75), and fried in deep fat.

Cakes, Frostings, and Fillings

Cakes

Cakes are classified as butter cakes and sponge cakes. Butter cakes are usually leavened with baking powder or soda and an acid and are mixed by the conventional, dough-batter, or muffin method. The **conventional** cake method consists of creaming the fat and sugar, adding the beaten eggs, and then adding the combined flour, leavening, and seasonings alternately with the liquid. In the **dough-batter** method, the flour, baking powder, and fat are creamed, then a mixture of the sugar, salt, and half of the milk is blended in, followed by the egg and the remaining milk. This method requires less time and fewer utensils than the conventional method and yields a highly desirable product. (See p. 164 for Plain Cake made by dough-batter method.) The **muffin** method, described on p. 110 may be used for making cakes, but is most successful if the cake is to be used soon after baking. Butter cakes are most often baked as sheet cakes, in layers, or as individual cup cakes, but they are occasionally baked in tube or bundt pans.

True sponge cakes are leavened chiefly by air incorporated in beaten eggs, although modified sponge cakes may have baking powder added. They are baked in tube pans or sheets.

Prepared cake mixes offer the foodservice a wide variety of products that can be produced with fewer and less-skilled employees than cakes prepared "from scratch." However, care should be given to the selection of the mix and the instructions for preparation should be carefully followed to assure high-quality products. The formulas in commercial mixes are balanced, and any deviation, such as the substitution of milk for water or the addition of eggs, can change the finished product. Mixes may be prepared in the institution kitchen by combining the dry ingredients, including dry milk, and cutting in the fat. Liquid ingredients and flavorings are added prior to baking. The recipe for a master cake mix is given on p. 162.

A properly balanced formula, correct temperature of ingredients, accurate measurements, controlled mixing of ingredients, proper relationship of batter to pan, and correct oven temperature and baking time are essential to good cake making. Cake flour yields better volume and texture than all-purpose flour and was used in testing recipes in this section.

Frostings and Fillings

The presentation of cakes may be varied by the use of different fillings and frostings. The amount to use will depend on the kind of cake to be frosted and the individual preferences of the patrons. The following may serve as a guide.

1½ qt (1.42 L) for a 12 × 20 in. sheet cake.

2½ qt (2.37 L) for an 18 × 26 in. sheet cake.

2½ qt (2.37 L) for 3 2-layer cakes.

2½ qt (2.37 L) for 3 10-in. angel food cakes.

Cake Recipes

ANGEL FOOD CAKE
Bake: 50-55 min at 325 °F (165 °C)
or 35 min at 400 °F (205 °C)

Yield: 3 10-in. cakes
Portion: 12-14 per cake

Amount		Ingredient	Method
Metric	*U.S.*		
1.14 kg	2 lb 8 oz (5 c)	Egg whites	Beat egg whites (high speed) 1 min.
5 mL	1 t	Salt	Add salt and cream of tartar.
30 mL	2 T	Cream of tartar	Continue beating until egg whites are just stiff enough to hold shape.
680 g	1 lb 8 oz	Sugar	Add sugar slowly (medium speed).
15 mL	1 T	Vanilla	Add vanilla. Continue beating
5 mL	1 t	Almond extract (optional)	(high speed) for 2 min or until mixture will stand in stiff peaks.
340 g	12 oz	Sugar	Mix sugar and flour. Gradually
340 g	12 oz	Cake flour	add to egg whites (low speed).[a] Continue mixing 2 min after last addition. Pour into 3 ungreased tube cake pans. Bake. Immediately upon removal from oven, invert cake to cool.

[a] To mix by hand, remove bowl from machine and fold sugar-flour mixture into meringue with wire whip or spatula, adding 1 c (240 mL) at a time. Mix about 5 strokes after each addition.

Note: Either frozen or fresh egg whites may be used. The frozen egg whites should be approximately 70 °F (21 °C) when whipped.

Variations:

1. **Chocolate Angel Food Cake.** Substitute 1½ oz (43 g) cocoa for 1½ oz (43 g) flour.

2. **Tutti Frutti Angel Food Cake.** Add chopped candied fruits, dates, and nuts to cake batter.

3. **Orange-Filled Angel Food Cake.** Cut cake into 3 slices. Spread Orange Filling (p. 186) between layers, and frost top and sides with Orange Frosting (p. 183).

4. **Gelatin-Filled Angel Food Cake.** Cut a slice from top of cake. Remove some from inside, leaving a ¾-in. wall. Fill case with any gelatin mixture. Replace top of cake, cover with icing or whipped cream, and garnish with almonds and cherries.

5. **Frozen Filled Angel Food Cake.** Cut cake into 3 slices. Spread softened strawberry ice cream on first layer and cover with cake slice. Spread second slice with softened pistachio ice cream. Top with remaining slice. Frost top and sides with sweetened whipped cream and toasted coconut. Freeze. Other ice cream or sherbet variations may be used as filling.

YELLOW ANGEL FOOD (EGG YOLK SPONGE CAKE)

Bake: 30-45 min
Oven: 350 °F (175°C)

Yield: 3 10-in. cakes
Portion: 12-14 per cake

Amount		Ingredient	Method
Metric	U.S.		
720 mL	3 c	Egg yolks	Beat egg yolks.
480 mL	2 c	Water, boiling	Add water. Beat (high speed) until light, approximately 5 min.
454 g	1 lb	Sugar, sifted	Add sugar gradually, beating (high speed) while adding.
340 g	12 oz	Cake flour	Add combined flour and sugar (low speed).
340 g	12 oz	Sugar	
284 g	10 oz	Cake flour	Mix flour, baking powder, and salt.
22 mL	4½ t	Baking powder	
5 mL	1 t	Salt	
45 mL	3 T	Lemon juice	Gradually add (low speed) dry ingredients alternately with lemon juice and rind to egg mixture.
15 mL	1 T	Lemon rind, grated	
15 mL	1 T	Vanilla	Add flavoring and continue mixing (low speed) 2 min. Pour into 3 ungreased tube cake pans. Bake. Immediately on removal from oven, invert cakes to cool.
8 mL	1½ t	Lemon extract	

ORANGE CHIFFON CAKE

Bake: 45-50 min
Oven: 350 °F (175 °C)

Yield: 3 10-in. cakes
Portion: 12-14 per cake

Metric	U.S.	Ingredient	Method
Amount			
680 g	1 lb 8 oz	Cake flour	Combine dry ingredients (low
43 g	1½ oz (3 T)	Baking powder	speed) in mixer bowl.
10 mL	2 t	Salt	
539 g	1 lb 3 oz	Sugar	
360 mL	1½ c	Salad oil	Add oil, yolks, and water.
454 g	1 lb (2 c)	Egg yolks, beaten	Mix (medium speed) until smooth.
360 mL	1½ c	Water	
240 mL	1 c	Orange juice	Add orange juice and rind gradu-
30 mL	2 T	Orange rind, grated	ally. Mix well after each addi- tion, but avoid overmixing.
567 g	1 lb 4 oz (2½ c)	Egg whites	Whip egg whites until foamy. Add cream of tartar; continue
10 mL	2 t	Cream of tartar	beating until egg whites form
510 g	1 lb 2 oz	Sugar	soft peaks. Add sugar gradually and continue beating until very stiff. Fold gently into the batter. Pour into 3 ungreased tube cake pans. Bake.

Note: Turn cake upside down as soon as removed from oven. When cake has cooled, remove from pans and frost with Orange Frosting (p. 183).

Variations:

1. **Cocoa Chiffon Cake.** Omit orange juice and rind. Add 5 oz (142 g) cocoa to dry ingredients. Increase water to 2⅓ c (560 mL). Add 1 T (15 mL) vanilla.

2. **Walnut Chiffon Cake.** Omit orange juice and rind. Increase water to 2⅓ c (560 mL). Add 2 T (30 mL) vanilla and 12 oz (340 g) finely chopped walnuts. Frost with Burnt Butter Frosting (p. 183).

MASTER CAKE MIX

Yield: 30 lb (13.61 kg) mix
7 12 × 20 × 2 in. cakes

Amount			
Metric	U.S.	Ingredient	Method
4.76 kg	10 lb 8 oz	Cake flour	Mix flour, dry milk, baking pow-
794 g	1 lb 12 oz	Nonfat dry milk	der, salt, and sugar (low speed)
227 g	8 oz	Baking powder, double acting	1 min.
57 g	2 oz	Salt	
2.38 kg	5 lb 4 oz	Sugar	
2.72 kg	6 lb	Sugar	Divide sugar into 2 lb (908 g) por-
2.21 kg	4 lb 14 oz	Shortening, hydrogenated, emulsified	tions.
			Cream shortening (medium speed) using flat beater 3 min. Scrape down bowl and beater.
			Add 2 lb (908 g) sugar. Cream (medium speed) 1 min. Repeat until all sugar is added. Scrape bowl and beater.
			Add 4 qt (3.79 L) blended dry ingredients. Mix (low speed) 1 min. Repeat once more.
			Lower bowl, add remaining dry ingredients. Blend (low speed) 1 min. while slowly raising mixer bowl. Mix should resemble cornmeal in consistency.
			Store in tightly covered container.

PLAIN CAKE (USING MASTER CAKE MIX)
Bake: 45 min   **Yield: 1 12 × 20 × 2 in. cake**
Oven: 350 °F (175 °C)

Amount			
Metric	*U.S.*	*Ingredient*	*Method*
1.93 kg	4 lb 4 oz	Master Cake Mix (p. 162)	Place mix in bowl. Add eggs, vanilla, and ½ of the water.
340 g	12 oz	Eggs, whole, frozen or fresh	Mix (low speed) 2 min. Scrape down bowl.
15 mL	1 T	Vanilla	Mix (medium speed) 3 min. Scrape bowl and beater.
600 mL	2½ c	Water	Add remaining water gradually, mixing (low speed) 2 min. Scrape down bowl and mix (medium speed) 1 min.
			Scale 5 lb (2.27 kg) batter in a slightly greased and lined pan. Bake.

Variations:

1. **Spice Cake.** Blend 1½ T (23 mL) cinnamon, 1 T (15 mL) nutmeg, 2½ T (37 mL) cloves, and 1½ t (8 mL) allspice with cake mix.

2. **Chocolate Cake.** Blend 4 oz (114 g) cocoa and 1¾ t (9 mL) baking soda with mix.

See p. 164 for additional variations.

PLAIN CAKE
Bake: 40-45 min
Oven: 350 °F (175 °C)

Yield: 1 pan 12 × 20 × 2 in.
40 portions 2¼ × 2½ in.
48 portions 2 × 2½ in.

Amount		Ingredient	Method
Metric	U.S.		
709 g	1 lb 9 oz	Cake flour	Mix flour, baking powder, and fat
37 mL	2½ T	Baking powder	(low speed) 2 min.
284 g	10 oz	Fat	Scrape down bowl; mix 3 min more.
850 g	1 lb 14 oz	Sugar	Add combined sugar, salt, and
8 mL	1½ t	Salt	milk. Mix (low speed) 2 min.
300 mL	1¼ c	Milk	Scrape down bowl; mix 3 min more.
5	5	Eggs	Add half of combined egg, milk,
400 mL	1⅔ c	Milk	and vanilla. Mix (low speed) 30
15 mL	1 T	Vanilla	sec.
			Scrape down bowl; mix 1 min.
			Add remaining egg mixture. Mix 1 min. Scrape down bowl; mix 2½ min.
			Pour into greased baking pan. Bake.

Notes:
1. Use 1½ recipe for 6 9-in. layer pans or for 18 × 26 in. baking sheet. For layer cake, scale 1 lb 8 oz (680 g) batter into each pan.
2. For cupcakes, measure into muffin pans with No. 30 dipper; yield 6 doz.

Variations:
1. **Boston Cream Pie.** Bake plain cake in sheet pan or in layer pans. Spread with Custard Filling (p. 185). Sprinkle with chopped nuts and serve with whipped cream.

2. **Chocolate Cake.** Omit 6 oz (170 g) flour and add 6 oz (170 g) cocoa to the flour and fat.

3. **Cottage Pudding.** Cut cake into squares and serve with No. 20 dipper of fruit sauce or other sauce.

4. **Dutch Apple Cake.** After the cake batter is poured into baking pan, arrange 2½ lb (1.14 kg) pared sliced apples in rows. Sprinkle over the top ½ c (120 mL) sugar and 1 t (5 mL) cinnamon, mixed.

5. **Lazy Daisy Cake.** Mix 9 oz (255 g) butter, melted, 1 lb (454 g) brown sugar, 1 lb (454 g) coconut, and ¾ c (180 mL) cream, or enough to moisten to consistency for spreading. Spread over Plain Cake (baked) and brown under broiler or in oven.

6. **Marble Cake.** Divide batter into 2 portions after mixing. To 1 portion add 1 T (15 mL) cocoa, 1 t (5 mL) cinnamon, ½ t cloves, and ½ t nutmeg. Place spoonsful of batters alternately in cake pans; mix slightly.

7. **Praline Cake.** Substitute chopped pecans for coconut in Lazy Daisy Cake.

8. **Spice Cake.** Add 1 T (15 mL) cocoa, 2 t (10 mL) cinnamon, ½ t cloves, and 1 t (5 mL) nutmeg.

9. **Upside-Down Cake.** Place 1 No. 10 can crushed pineapple (or tidbits), drained, 1 lb (454 g) butter or margarine, 1½ lb (680 g) brown sugar, and 8 oz (227 g) chopped nutmeats in bottom of the cake pan. Pour plain cake batter over mixture. (2½ lb/1.14 kg A.P. cooked dried apricots may be substituted for pineapple.)

5. **Washington Cream Pie.** Double the basic recipe and bake in 12 9-in. layers. Put the layers together with cream or chocolate filling. Sift powdered sugar on top of pie or cover with a thin Chocolate Frosting (p. 180).

WHITE CAKE

Bake: 40-45 min
Oven: 350 °F (175 °C)

Yield: 1 pan 12 × 20 × 2 in.
40 portions 2¼ × 2½ in.
48 portions 2 × 2½ in.

Amount			
Metric	*U.S.*	*Ingredient*	*Method*
680 g	1 lb 8 oz	Cake flour	Mix flour, baking powder, and fat
28 g	1 oz	Baking powder	(low speed) 2 min.
340 g	12 oz	Fat	Scrape down bowl; mix 3 min more.
680 g	1 lb 8 oz	Sugar	Add combined sugar, salt, and
8 mL	1½ t	Salt	milk. Mix (low speed) 2 min.
240 mL	1 c	Milk	Scrape down bowl; mix 3 min more.
8	8	Egg whites	Add half of combined egg whites,
300 mL	1¼ c	Milk	milk, and vanilla. Mix (low
15 mL	1 T	Vanilla	speed) 30 sec.
			Scrape down bowl; mix 1 min.
			Add remaining egg-milk mixture. Mix (low speed) 1 min.
			Scrape down bowl; mix 2½ min.
			Pour into greased baking pan. Bake.

Note: For 6 9-in. layer pans, use 1½ recipe; scale 1 lb 6 oz (624 g) per pan.

Variations:

1. **Chocolate Chip Cake.** Add 4 oz (114 g) chocolate chips.

2. **Coconut Lime Cake.** Use 1½ recipe. Scale into 6 9-in layer pans, 1 lb 6 oz (624 g) per pan. When baked, cool, then spread Lime Filling (p. 186) between layers. Frost with Fluffy Frosting (p. 178). Sprinkle with ½ c (120 mL) toasted flaked coconut.

3. **Cup Cakes.** Increase flour to 1 lb 14 oz (850 g). Use No. 20 dipper to portion into muffin pans or paper baking cups.

4. **Poppy Seed Cake.** Add 4 oz (114 g) poppy seeds. Frost with Chocolate Frosting (p. 180).

BANANA CAKE
Bake: 25-30 min
Oven: 350 °F (175 °C)

Yield: 3 2-layer cakes (9 in.)
Portion: 14-18 per cake

Amount		Ingredient	Method
Metric	*U.S.*		
340 g	12 oz	Fat	Cream fat, sugar, and vanilla (medium speed) 10 min.
680 g	1 lb 8 oz	Sugar	
15 mL	1 T	Vanilla	
720 mL	3 c	Bananas, mashed	Add bananas and eggs. Mix (medium speed) 5 min.
6	6	Eggs	
680 g	1 lb 8 oz	Cake flour	Combine flour, salt, baking powder, and soda.
5 mL	1 t	Salt	
37 mL	2½ T	Baking powder	
8 mL	½ T	Soda	
180 mL	¾ c	Buttermilk or sour milk	Add dry ingredients alternately with buttermilk (low speed). Mix (medium speed) 2-3 min. Scale into 6 greased layer cake pans, 1 lb 1 oz (482 g) per pan. Bake.

Note: May be baked in 12 × 20 × 2 in. pan.

APPLESAUCE CAKE

Bake: 40-45 min
Oven: 350 °F (175 °C)

Yield: 1 pan 12 × 20 × 2 in.
40 portions 2¼ × 2½ in.
48 portions 2 × 2½ in.

Amount		Ingredient	Method
Metric	*U.S.*	*Ingredient*	*Method*
340 g	12 oz	Fat	Cream fat and sugar (medium
680 g	1 lb 8 oz	Sugar	speed) 10 min.
6	6	Eggs	Add eggs to creamed mixture. Mix (medium speed) 5 min.
624 g	1 lb 6 oz	Cake flour	Combine dry ingredients.
30 mL	2 T	Baking powder	
8 mL	1½ t	Salt	
3 mL	½ t	Soda	
10 mL	2 t	Cinnamon	
10 mL	2 t	Cloves	
5 mL	1 t	Nutmeg	
480 mL	2 c	Water	Add dry ingredients alternately with water (low speed) to creamed mixture.
480 mL	2 c	Applesauce	Add remaining ingredients. Mix
454 g	1 lb	Raisins	(low speed) only to blend.
227 g	8 oz	Nuts, chopped	Pour into greased baking pan. Bake.

Notes:
1. This cake is too tender to bake in layers.
2. Suggested frostings: Caramel Frosting (p. 178); Ice Cream Frosting (p. 179).

FUDGE CAKE
Bake: 25-30 min
Oven: 350 °F (175 °C)

Yield: 3 2-layer cakes (9 in.)
Portion: 14-18 per cake

Amount			
Metric	*U.S.*	*Ingredient*	*Method*
340 g	12 oz	Fat	Cream fat, sugar, and vanilla (medium speed) 10 min.
908 g	2 lb	Sugar	
15 mL	1 T	Vanilla	
6	6	Eggs	Add eggs and mix (medium speed) 5 min.
142 g	5 oz	Cocoa	Mix cocoa and hot water.
360 mL	1½ c	Water, hot	
794 g	1 lb 12 oz	Cake flour	Combine flour, salt, and soda.
5 mL	1 t	Salt	
23 mL	1½ T	Soda	
720 mL	3 c	Buttermilk or sour milk	Add dry ingredients alternately with buttermilk and cocoa to creamed mixture (low speed). Scrape down bowl. Continue mixing until smooth and ingredients are mixed. Scale into 6 greased 9-in. layer pans, 1 lb 4 oz (567 g) per pan.

Note: Suggested Frostings: Chocolate Butter Cream Frosting (p. 180); Ice Cream Frosting (p. 179).

Variations:

1. **Chocolate Sheet Cake.** Bake cake on a baking sheet 18 × 26 × 1 in. If serving with ice cream, cut into 96 servings. Use ¾ recipe for 12 × 20 × 2 in. pan.

2. **Chocolate Cup Cakes.** Portion with No. 20 dipper into muffin pans; yield 5 doz.

GERMAN SWEET-CHOCOLATE CAKE
Bake: 35-40 min
Oven: 350 °F (175 °C)

Yield: 3 2-layer cakes (9 in.)
Portion: 14-18 per cake

Metric	U.S.	Ingredient	Method
	Amount		
454 g	1 lb	Fat	Cream fat and sugar (medium
908 g	2 lb	Sugar	speed) 10 min.
8	8	Egg yolks	Add yolks one at a time. Beat well after each addition.
227 g	8 oz	German sweet chocolate	Melt chocolate in water. Cool. Add vanilla.
240 mL	1 c	Water, boiling	Add to creamed mixture.
10 mL	2 t	Vanilla	
567 g	1 lb 4 oz	Cake flour	Combine flour, salt, and soda.
5 mL	1 t	Salt	
10 mL	2 t	Soda	
480 mL	2 c	Buttermilk	Add dry ingredients alternately with buttermilk (low speed) to creamed mixture.
8	8	Egg whites	Beat egg whites until stiff peaks form. Fold into batter (low speed). Scale into 6 greased layer pans, 1 lb 2 oz (510 g) per pan. Bake. When cool, cover with Coconut Pecan Frosting (p. 182).

Note: May be baked in 12 × 20 × 2 in. pan.

PINEAPPLE CASHEW CAKE
Bake: 25-30 min
Oven: 350 °F (175 °C)

Yield: 3 2-layer cakes (9 in.)
Portion: 14-18 per cake

Amount		Ingredient	Method
Metric	*U.S.*		
510 g	1 lb 2 oz	Butter or margarine	Cream butter or margarine, sugar, and vanilla (medium speed) 8 min.
850 g	1 lb 14 oz	Sugar	
15 mL	1 T	Vanilla	Add egg yolks in 3 portions, while creaming. Mix 2 min.
10	10	Egg yolks	
850 g	1 lb 14 oz	Cake flour	Combine flour, baking powder, and salt.
43 g	1½ oz	Baking powder	
8 mL	1½ t	Salt	
540 mL	2¼ c	Milk	Add dry ingredients alternately with milk (low speed) to creamed mixture.
454 g	1 lb	Pineapple, crushed, drained	Add pineapple. Mix (low speed) only to blend.
10	10	Egg whites	Beat egg whites until stiff but not dry (high speed). Fold into batter (low speed). Scale into 6 greased layer cake pans, 1 lb 4 oz (567 g) per pan. Bake.
227 g	8 oz	Cashew nuts, toasted, chopped	When cool, cover with Pineapple Butter Frosting (p. 181) and sprinkle with toasted cashews.

BURNT SUGAR CAKE

Bake: 25-30 min
Oven: 375 °F (190 °C)

Yield: 3 2-layer cakes (9 in.)
Portion: 14-18 per cake

Amount		Ingredient	Method
Metric	*U.S.*		
340 g	12 oz	Fat	Cream fat and sugar (medium
908 g	2 lb	Sugar	speed) 10 min.
6	6	Egg yolks	Add yolks and mix 5 min.
360 mL	1½ c	Milk	Combine liquids.
360 mL	1½ c	Water	
120 mL	½ c	Burnt Sugar Syrup (p. 75)	
15 mL	1 T	Vanilla	
737 g	1 lb 10 oz	Cake flour	Combine dry ingredients. Add to
30 mL	2 T	Baking powder	creamed mixture alternately
5 mL	1 t	Salt	with liquids (low speed).
			Scrape down bowl. Mix 2 min.
6	6	Egg whites	Beat egg whites until they form soft peaks.
			Fold into batter (low speed).
			Pour into 6 greased layer pans. Bake.

JELLY ROLL
Bake: 12 min
Oven: 375 °F (190 °C)

Yield: 3 rolls (3 pans 12 × 20 in.)
Portion: 15-20 per roll

Amount			
Metric	*U.S.*	*Ingredient*	*Method*
15	15	Eggs	Beat eggs (high speed) 1-2 min.
680 g	1 lb 8 oz	Sugar	Add sugar. Beat 10-15 min.
340 g	12 oz	Cake flour	Mix dry ingredients.
15 mL	1 T	Cream of tartar	Fold (low speed) into egg-sugar
30 mL	2 T	Baking powder	mixture.
8 mL	1½ t	Salt	
10 mL	2 t	Lemon juice	Add lemon juice. Mix only to blend, 1 min.
			Pour into 3 12 × 20 in. pans lined with waxed paper.
			When baked, turn onto a cloth or heavy paper covered with powdered sugar. Quickly remove waxed paper. Trim edges if hard. Immediately roll cake (tightly). When cooled but not cold, unroll, spread with a thin layer of jelly or Custard Filling (p. 185). Roll firmly and wrap with wax paper until serving time. Sprinkle top with powdered sugar.
			Slice to serve.

Variation:

Apricot Rolls. Cover with Apricot Filling (p. 187) and roll. Cover outside with sweetened whipped cream or whipped topping and toasted coconut.

CHOCOLATE ROLL

Bake: 20 min   **Yield: 4 rolls (2 pans 18 × 26 in.)**
Oven: 325 °F (165 °C)   **Portion: 13 per roll**

Amount		Ingredient	Method
Metric	U.S.		
24	24	Egg yolks	Beat yolks (high speed).
1.02 kg	2 lb 4 oz	Sugar	Add sugar and continue beating until mixture is lemon colored, thick, and fluffy.
340 g	12 oz	Chocolate, melted	Add chocolate and vanilla. Blend (low speed).
30 mL	2 T	Vanilla	
255 g	9 oz	Cake flour	Add combined dry ingredients (low speed).
15 mL	1 T	Baking powder	
8 mL	1½ t	Salt	
24	24	Egg whites	Beat egg whites (high speed) until they will form rounded peaks. Fold into cake mixture (low speed). Spread into 2 greased pans 18 × 26 in. lined with heavy waxed paper. When baked, cut each cake in half crosswise. Quickly remove waxed paper and trim edges if hard. Roll and let stand a few minutes. Unroll and spread with Custard Filling (p. 185) or Fluffy Frosting (p. 178) or whipped cream, plain or flavored with peppermint. Roll up securely. Cover with a thin layer of Chocolate Frosting (p. 180).

Variation:
Ice Cream Roll. Spread with a thick layer of vanilla ice cream, soft enough
to spread. Roll up securely and wrap in waxed paper. Place in freezer
for several hours before serving.

GINGERBREAD
Bake: 40 min
Oven: 350 °F (175 °C)

Yield: 1 pan 12 × 20 × 2 in.
40 portions 2¼ × 2½ in.
48 portions 2 × 2½ in.

Amount		Ingredient	Method
Metric	*U.S.*	*Ingredient*	*Method*
284 g	10 oz	Fat	Cream fat and sugar (medium speed) 10 min.
284 g	10 oz	Sugar	
600 mL	2½ c	Sorghum	Add sorghum and blend (low speed).
737 g	1 lb 10 oz	Cake flour	Combine dry ingredients.
13 mL	2½ t	Cinnamon	
13 mL	2½ t	Cloves	
13 mL	2½ t	Ginger	
23 mL	1½ T	Soda	
5 mL	1 t	Salt	
660 mL	2¾ c	Water, hot	Add alternately with dry ingredients to creamed mixture.
5	5	Eggs, beaten	Add eggs and mix (low speed) 2 min. Pour into greased baking pan. Bake.

Note: Sprinkle with powdered sugar and serve warm.

Variations:

1. **Almond Meringue Gingerbread.** Cover baked gingerbread with meringue (p. 312). Sprinkle with almonds and brown in a 375°F (190 °C) oven.

2. **Praline Gingerbread.** Spread baked gingerbread with topping of 9 oz (255 g) butter or margarine, melted, 1 lb (454 g) brown sugar, 1 lb (454 g) chopped pecans, and ¾-1 c (180-240 mL) cream. Brown under broiler, or return to oven and heat until topping is slightly browned.

3. **Ginger Muffins.** Measure into well-greased muffin pans with No. 24 dipper. Yield 5½ doz.

ORANGE CUPCAKES

Bake: 20-25 min
Oven: 375 °F (190 °C)

Yield: 4 doz

Amount		Ingredient	Method
Metric	*U.S.*	*Ingredient*	*Method*
284 g	10 oz	Fat	Cream fat and sugar (medium
482 g	1 lb 1 oz	Sugar	speed) 10 min.
15 mL	1 T	Vanilla	Add vanilla and eggs; mix (me-
5	5	Eggs	dium speed) until well blended.
198 g	7 oz	Raisins, ground	Add raisins and grated rind. Blend
3	3	Orange rinds, grated	(low speed).
680 g	1 lb 8 oz	Cake flour	Mix dry ingredients.
12 mL	¾ T	Soda	
43 g	1½ oz	Baking powder	
4 mL	¾ t	Salt	
420 mL	1¾ c	Milk, sour or buttermilk	Add dry ingredients alternately with sour milk (low speed) to creamed mixture. Mix only until smooth. Measure with No. 30 dipper into greased muffin pans. Bake.
170 g	6 oz	Sugar	While cakes are hot, brush with sugar and orange juice mixture, or frost with Orange Frosting (p. 183).
180 mL	¾ c	Orange juice	

Note: May be baked in loaves.

FRUIT CAKE
Bake: 2½ hr
Oven: 300 °F (150 °C)

Yield: 4 2-lb (908-g) cakes (4 × 9 in.)
Portion: 12-14 per cake

Amount		Ingredient	Method
Metric	*U.S.*	*Ingredient*	*Method*
227 g	8 oz	Fat	Cream fat and sugar (medium
454 g	1 lb	Sugar	speed) 8 min.
4	4	Eggs	Add eggs. Mix 5 min.
227 g	8 oz	Jelly	Add ingredients in the order listed.
10 mL	2 t	Cinnamon	Mix (low speed) only until fruit is
10 mL	2 t	Cloves	coated with flour mixture.
908 g	2 lb	Raisins	
454 g	1 lb	Currants	
454 g	1 lb	Dates, chopped	
227 g	8 oz	Nuts, chopped	
567 g	1 lb 4 oz	Cake flour	
10 mL	2 t	Soda	Dissolve soda in cold coffee; add
360 mL	1½ c	Coffee infusion, cold	to other ingredients. Mix until blended.
			Pour into 4 loaf pans lined with 2 layers of heavy waxed paper. Bake.

Notes:
1. May be steamed for 4 hr.
2. Store in a container with a tight cover. Most fruit cakes improve in flavor if kept about 2 weeks before using.

Frosting Recipes

BOILED FROSTING
Yield: 4½ qt (4.26 L)

Amount			
Metric	U.S.	Ingredient	Method
1.81 kg	4 lb	Sugar	Combine sugar and water. Stir
600 mL	2½ c	Water, hot	until sugar is dissolved.
			Boil without stirring to soft ball stage (238 °F, 114 °C)
8	8	Egg whites	Beat egg whites until stiff but not dry.
30 mL	2 T	Vanilla	Gradually pour syrup over egg whites while beating. Continue beating until frosting is of consistency to spread.
			Add vanilla.
			Spread on cake at once.

Variations:
See Variations of Ice Cream Frosting, p. 179.

FLUFFY FROSTING
Yield: 4¼ qt (4.02 L)

Amount			
Metric	U.S.	Ingredient	Method
1.14 kg	2 lb 8 oz	Sugar	Boil sugar, water, syrup and salt
360 mL	1½ c	Water	until mixture reaches the soft
75 mL	5 T	Corn syrup, white	ball stage (238 °F/114 °C).
¼ t	¼ t	Salt	
10	10	Egg whites	Beat egg whites (high speed) until stiff but not dry.
15 mL	1 T	Vanilla	Gradually add ½ hot syrup to egg whites, beating constantly.
			Cook remaining half of syrup until it forms a hard ball (250 °F/121 °C).
			Gradually add to first mixture.
			Beat (high speed) until it holds its shape.
			Add vanilla.

Variation:
Fluffy Brown Sugar Frosting. Substitute brown sugar for granulated sugar.

ICE CREAM FROSTING   **Yield: 2½ qt (2.37 L)**

Amount			
Metric	*U.S.*	*Ingredient*	*Method*
680 g	1 lb 8 oz	Granulated sugar	Combine sugar and water. Boil without stirring to soft ball stage (238 °F/114 °C).
240 mL	1 c	Water, hot	
9	9	Egg whites	Beat egg whites until frothy.
85 g	3 oz	Powdered sugar, sifted	Add powdered sugar and beat (high speed) to consistency of meringue. Add hot syrup slowly and continue beating until mixture is thick and creamy.
227 g	8 oz	Powdered sugar, sifted	Add powdered sugar and vanilla. Beat until smooth. Add more sugar if necessary to make frosting hold its shape when spread.
15 mL	1 T	Vanilla	

Note: This frosting can be kept several days in a covered container in refrigerator.

Variations:

1. **Bittersweet Frosting.** Melt 8 oz (227 g) bitter chocolate over water, gradually stir in 3 T (45 mL) butter; when slightly cool, pour over white frosting to form a design.

2. **Candied Fruit Frosting.** Add 8 oz (227 g) chopped candied fruit.

3. **Chocolate Frosting.** Add 8 oz (227 g) melted chocolate.

4. **Coconut Frosting.** Frost cake, sprinkle with 4 oz (114 g) dry shredded coconut.

5. **Lady Baltimore Frosting.** Use 1¾ qt (1.66 L) Ice Cream Frosting or Boiled Frosting. Add 1 t (5 mL) orange juice, 4½ oz (128 g) macaroon crumbs, 5 oz (142 g) chopped almonds, and 1 c (240 mL) chopped raisins.

6. **Maple Nut Frosting.** Flavor with maple flavoring; add 6 oz (170 g) chopped nuts.

7. **Maraschino Frosting.** Add 8 oz (227 g) chopped maraschino cherries.

8. **Peppermint Frosting.** Add 8 oz (227 g) finely crushed peppermint candy.

CREAMY FROSTING   **Yield: 1½ qt (1.42 L)**

	Amount		
Metric	*U.S.*	*Ingredient*	*Method*
340 g	12 oz	Butter or margarine	Cream butter or margarine (medium speed) 1 min or until soft.
120 mL	½ c	Evaporated milk	Add remaining ingredients gradually.
15 mL	1 T	Vanilla	
1.14 kg	2 lb 8 oz	Powdered sugar	Whip (medium speed) until mixture is smooth and creamy.
10 mL	2 t	Salt	

Note: Milk or cream may be substituted for evaporated milk.

Variations:

1. **Cocoa Frosting.** Increase liquid to 1¼ c (300 mL); add 6 oz (170 g) cocoa sifted with sugar.

2. **Lemon Butter Frosting.** Substitute ¼ c (60 mL) lemon juice for an equal amount of milk, and 1½ T (23 mL) grated lemon rind for the vanilla.

3. **Mocha Frosting.** Substitute cold coffee for liquid. Add 6 oz (170 g) cocoa sifted with sugar.

4. **Orange Butter Frosting.** Substitute ½ c (120 mL) orange juice for an equal amount of milk, and 1½ T (23 mL) grated orange rind for the vanilla.

CHOCOLATE BUTTER CREAM FROSTING   **Yield: 3 qt (2.84 L)**

	Amount		
Metric	*U.S.*	*Ingredient*	*Method*
908 g	2 lb	Butter or margarine, soft	Cream butter (medium speed). Add milk. Blend.
160 mL	⅔ c	Evaporated milk	Add sugar gradually. Mix until smooth (medium speed).
908 g	2 lb	Powdered sugar	
227 g	8 oz	Chocolate, unsweetened, melted	Add chocolate and vanilla. Beat (high speed) until light and fluffy.
5 mL	1 t	Vanilla	

POWDERED SUGAR GLAZE

Yield: 1 qt (0.95 L)

Amount		Ingredient	Method
Metric	*U.S.*	*Ingredient*	*Method*
908 g	2 lb	Powdered sugar	Gradually add water to sugar. Beat
180 mL	¾ c	Boiling water	until smooth.
10 mL	2 t	Vanilla	Add vanilla and blend. Thin, if necessary, to spread.

Note: Use for frosting baked rolls or products requiring a thin frosting.

BUTTER CREAM FROSTING

Yield: 1 qt (0.95 L)

Amount		Ingredient	Method
Metric	*U.S.*	*Ingredient*	*Method*
454 g	1 lb	Powdered sugar	Combine sugar and eggs. Cook over low heat and beat until lukewarm.
5	5	Eggs, beaten	Remove from heat.
454 g	1 lb	Butter, unsalted, soft	Add butter. Mix (high speed) until fluffy. Refrigerate several hours before using.

PINEAPPLE BUTTER FROSTING

Yield: 2½ qt (2.37 L)

Amount		Ingredient	Method
Metric	*U.S.*	*Ingredient*	*Method*
680 g	1 lb 8 oz	Butter or margarine	Mix butter or margarine, sugar, and salt (medium speed) until creamy.
1.36 kg	3 lb	Powdered sugar	
3 mL	½ t	Salt	
3	3	Egg yolks	Add egg yolks. Whip (high speed) until light and fluffy.
454 g	1 lb	Drained, crushed pineapple	Add pineapple and blend (low speed). Keep under refrigeration until ready to use.

COCONUT-PECAN FROSTING   **Yield: 2 qt (1.89 L)**

	Amount		
Metric	*U.S.*	*Ingredient*	*Method*
480 mL	2 c	Evaporated milk	Combine milk, yolks, sugar, and
6	6	Egg yolks	butter in double boiler. Cook
454 g	1 lb	Sugar	until thickened.
227 g	8 oz	Butter	
340 g	12 oz	Pecans, finely chopped	Add pecans, coconut, and vanilla. Cool, then beat well until thick
340 g	12 oz	Coconut, flaked	enough to spread.
10 mL	2 t	Vanilla	

MOCHA FROSTING   **Yield: 1 qt (0.95 L)**

	Amount		
Metric	*U.S.*	*Ingredient*	*Method*
240 mL	1 c	Hot coffee, strong	Add coffee to butter or margarine and cocoa.
57 g	2 oz	Butter or margarine, soft	Mix (medium speed) until blended.
85 g	3 oz	Cocoa	
908 g	2 lb	Powdered sugar	Add sugar, salt, and vanilla. Mix
3 mL	½ t	Salt	until smooth.
3 mL	½ t	Vanilla	Add more sugar if necessary to make frosting hold its shape when spread.

Note: Instant coffee, 1½ T (23 mL) dissolved in 1 c (240 mL) hot water, may be used in place of brewed coffee.

CREAM CHEESE FROSTING

Yield: 4½ c (1.08 L)

Amount			
Metric	*U.S.*	*Ingredient*	*Method*
2 227-g pkg	2 8-oz pkg	Cream cheese	Blend cream cheese and cream
60 mL	¼ c	Cream or milk	until smooth (medium speed).
794 g	1 lb 12 oz	Powdered sugar, sifted	Add sugar gradually. Whip (high speed) until smooth.
15 mL	1 T	Vanilla	Add vanilla and blend.

Note: This frosting is especially good on Gingerbread (p. 175) and Spice Cake (p. 165).

Variation:
Orange Cheese Frosting. Substitute 1 T (15 mL) orange juice and 1 T (15 mL) grated orange rind for vanilla.

ORANGE FROSTING

Yield: 1¼ qt (1.18 L)

Amount			
Metric	*U.S.*	*Ingredient*	*Method*
227 g	8 oz	Butter or margarine	Cream butter or margarine. Add sugar gradually (medium speed).
1.14 kg	2 lb 8 oz	Powdered sugar, sifted	Mix until creamy.
30 mL	2 T	Vanilla	Add remaining ingredients. Blend until smooth.
3 mL	½ t	Salt	
60 mL	¼ c	Orange juice	
60 mL	¼ c	Lemon juice	
5 mL	1 t	Orange rind, grated	

BURNT BUTTER FROSTING

Yield: 5 c (1.18 L) (Frosting for 8-doz 2½-in. cookies)

Amount			
Metric	*U.S.*	*Ingredient*	*Method*
255 g	9 oz	Butter	Heat butter until golden brown.
680 g	1 lb 8 oz	Powdered sugar	Blend in sugar.
15 mL	1 T	Vanilla	Add vanilla and water. Beat until right consistency to spread. Add more water if necessary.
120 mL	½ c	Water, hot	

ORNAMENTAL FROSTING   **Yield: 1 qt (0.95 L)**

Metric	U.S.	Ingredient	Method
	Amount		
Metric	*U.S.*	*Ingredient*	*Method*
8	8	Egg whites	Beat egg whites until stiff but not dry.
680 g	1 lb 8 oz	Powdered sugar	Add sugar (low speed). Beat (high speed) to consistency of heavy cream if used for frosting. If used for decorating with a pastry tube, beat until it will retain its shape when drawn to a point.

Notes:
1. This frosting dries quickly when exposed to the air and should be covered with a damp cloth.
2. A teaspoon of lemon juice or vanilla may be added for flavoring if desired.

Filling Recipes

CHOCOLATE CREAM FILLING   **Yield: 3 qt (2.84 L)**

Metric	U.S.	Ingredient	Method
	Amount		
Metric	*U.S.*	*Ingredient*	*Method*
1.02 kg (3 340-g pkg)	2 lb 4 oz (3 12-oz pkg)	Chocolate chips	Combine chocolate, orange juice, and sugar. Melt over hot water. Cool.
240 mL	1 c	Orange juice or water	
227 g	8 oz	Sugar	
1.42 L	1½ qt	Whipping cream	Whip cream and fold into chocolate mixture.

Note: Use as filling for Orange Cream Puffs (p. 386).

Variation:
Chocolate Mousse. Whip 10 egg whites to a soft peak and fold into chocolate-whipped cream mixture. Freeze.

CUSTARD FILLING   **Yield: 3 qt (2.84 L)**

Amount		Ingredient	Method
Metric	*U.S.*	*Ingredient*	*Method*
170 g	6 oz	Cornstarch	Combine dry ingredients.
454 g	1 lb	Sugar	Add cold milk and stir until
3 mL	½ t	Salt	smooth.
480 mL	2 c	Milk, cold	
2.37 L	2½ qt	Milk, hot	Add cold mixture to hot milk, stirring constantly. Cook over hot water until thick.
10	10	Eggs, beaten	Add eggs gradually to thickened mixture. Cook 7 min.
10 mL	2 t	Vanilla	Remove from heat. Add vanilla. Cool. Spread between layers of cake, 1½ c (360 mL) per cake.

Notes:
1. Use as a filling for Cream Puff (p. 386), Washington Cream Pie (p. 165), Chocolate Roll (p. 174), and Eclairs (p. 386).
2. To fill 3 9-in. layer cakes, use ⅓ recipe.

CRANBERRY FILLING   **Yield: 2 qt (1.89 L)**

Amount		Ingredient	Method
Metric	*U.S.*	*Ingredient*	*Method*
680 g	1 lb 8 oz	Cranberry relish (p. 430)	Cook all ingredients except butter until thick.
1 No. 2 can	1 No. 2 can	Crushed pine-apple	Add butter. Use as filling for Cranberry Ring (p. 151).
340 g	12 oz	Apples, ground	
227 g	8 oz	Sugar	
60 mL	¼ c	Flour	
28 g	1 oz	Butter	

LEMON FILLING   Yield: 1 qt (0.95 L)

	Amount		
Metric	U.S.	Ingredient	Method
454 g	1 lb	Sugar	Heat sugar and water to boiling
720 mL	3 c	Water	point.
70 g	2½ oz	Cornstarch	Gradually add cornstarch blended
180 mL	¾ c	Cold water	with cold water. Cook until thickened and clear, stirring constantly.
4	4	Egg yolks, beaten	Blend in egg yolks. Cook 5-8 min while stirring.
4 mL	¾ t	Salt	Add remaining ingredients. Stir to
10 mL	2 t	Lemon rind, grated	blend. Cool.
120 mL	½ c	Lemon juice	Spread between layers of cake,
30 mL	2 T	Butter or margarine	1½ c (360 mL) per cake.

Variations:

1. **Lime Filling.** Substitute fresh lime juice for lemon juice and grated lime rind for lemon rind. Add a few drops of green food coloring.

2. **Orange Filling.** Substitute orange juice for water and orange rind for lemon rind. Reduce lemon juice to 3 T (45 mL).

FIG FILLING   Yield: 2 qt (1.89 L)

	Amount		
Metric	U.S.	Ingredient	Method
908 g	2 lb	Figs	Chop figs and soak in water, then
480 mL	2 c	Water	cook together.
454 g	1 lb	Sugar	Add sugar, flour, salt, and lemon
114 g	4 oz	Flour	juice. Cook to a paste.
3 mL	½ t	Salt	Add butter.
240 mL	1 c	Lemon juice	
454 mL	1 lb	Butter	

PRUNE FILLING   **Yield: 1 qt (0.95 L)**

	Amount		
Metric	*U.S.*	*Ingredient*	*Method*
480 mL	2 c	Prunes, cooked, pitted, chopped	Add cream, butter, and eggs to prunes. Heat over hot water.
240 mL	1 c	Cultured sour cream	
57 g	2 oz	Butter or margarine	
4	4	Eggs, beaten	
454 g	1 lb	Sugar	Add mixed dry ingredients.
3 mL	½ t	Salt	Cook and stir over hot water until thick.
28 g (60 mL)	1 oz (¼ c)	Flour	Cool. Spread between layers of cake, 1½ c (360 mL) per cake.

Note: 8 oz (227 g) chopped nuts may be added.

Variation:
1. **Apricot Filling.** Substitute dried apricots for prunes.

PRUNE DATE FILLING   **Yield: 1 qt (0.95 L)**

	Amount		
Metric	*U.S.*	*Ingredient*	*Method*
240 mL	1 c	Prunes, cooked, pitted, and chopped	Combine all ingredients. Cook until thick, stirring constantly.
240 mL	1 c	Dates, chopped	
240 mL	1 c	Water and prune juice	
60 mL	¼ c	Lemon juice	
170 g	6 oz	Sugar	
80 mL	⅓ c	Flour	
28 g	1 oz	Butter	

DATE FILLING   **Yield: 1½ qt (1.42 L)**

Amount			
Metric	*U.S.*	*Ingredient*	*Method*
908 g	2 lb	Pitted dates, chopped	Combine dates, water, and sugar. Cook until mixture is thick.
540 mL	2¼ c	Water	Cool.
340 g	12 oz	Sugar	Use as cake or cookie filling.

Note: 6 oz (170 g) jelly or ¼ c (60 mL) orange juice may be used in place of ¼ c (60 mL) of the water.

Cereals and Cereal Products

The cooking of cereals and of macaroni, spaghetti, noodles, and other pasta is similar. Water and heat are applied, and cooking is continued until swelling of the starch granules is completed.

Breakfast cereals may be whole, cracked, flaked or rolled, or granular. The amount of water used for cooking determines largely the volume of the finished product. Cereal swells to the extent of water used until the limit of the grain is reached. As a rule, granular cereals absorb more water than whole or flaked. The fineness of the grind of cereal and the amount of bran or cellulose are factors that determine the length of time a cereal needs to be cooked.

Cereals and pasta in quantity usually are cooked in a steam-jacketed kettle or steamer, but they may be prepared in a heavy kettle on top of the range. Directions for cooking breakfast cereals are given on p. 189, for rice on p. 190, and for macaroni, spaghetti, and noodles on p. 191.

Cereal Recipes

COOKING BREAKFAST CEREALS

Yield: 2 gal (7.57 L)
Portion: ⅔ c (160 mL)

Amount		Ingredient	Method
Metric	*U.S.*		
7.57-8.52 L	2-2¼ gal	Water	Measure water into steam-jacketed kettle or heavy stock pot. Add salt and bring to a rolling boil.
45 mL	3 T	Salt	
908 g	2 lb	Cereal, flaked, granular, or cracked	Stir dry cereal gradually into boiling water, using wire whip. Each starch granule must come in contact with the liquid so that swelling is uniform.
			Granular cereals may be mixed with cold water to separate particles and prevent the formation of lumps.
			Stir until some thickening is apparent. Do not stir excessively; overstirring or overcooking produces a sticky, gummy product.
			Reduce heat and cook until cereal reaches desired consistency and raw starch taste has disappeared. Cereal should be thick and creamy but not sticky.
			Prepare as close to serving time as possible and keep covered until it is served. This will prevent the cereal from drying.

COOKING RICE

Yield: 6 qt (5.68 L) cooked rice
Portion: 4 oz (114 g)

Amount			
Metric	*U.S.*	*Ingredient*	*Method*
3.55 L	3¾ qt	Water, boiling	Top of range or steam-jacketed
30 mL	2 T	Salt	kettle
1.36 kg	3 lb	Rice, converted	Add salt and rice to boiling water. Stir. Cover tightly.
			Cook on low heat until rice is tender and all water is absorbed, about 15 min.
			Remove from heat and let stand covered 5-10 min.
			Steamer or oven
			Place rice in baking pan 12 × 20 × 2 in.
			Add salt to boiling water and pour over rice.
			Stir and cover pans tightly.
			Bake at 350 °F (175 °C) or steam at 5 lb pressure for 30-35 min.
			Remove from oven or steamer and let stand covered 5 min.

Notes:
1. 2 T (30 mL) oil may be added to the water. It tends to prevent foaming and boiling over.
2. 1 lb (454 g) uncooked rice yields 2 qt (1.89 L) cooked rice.
3. If using regular white rice in place of converted rice, the cooking time may need to be reduced.

Variations:
1. **Curried Rice.** Cook 8 oz (227 g) minced onion in 8 oz (227 g) butter or margarine. Add 3 lb (1.36 kg) rice and stir until fat is absorbed. Add 3 T (45 mL) curry powder, 1½ T (23 mL) salt, and 3 qt (2.84 L) boiling water. Boil 10 min. Add 2 qt (1.89 L) hot milk and cook over water until rice is tender. Serve with Veal Fricassee (p. 293), Creamed Chicken (p. 345), Creamed Eggs (p. 213), or Creamed Tuna (p. 249).

2. **Fried Rice with Almonds.** Cook together for 5 min 4 oz (114 g) chopped onion and 4 oz (114 g) chopped green pepper in 1 c (240 mL) salad oil. Add 6 qt (5.68 L) cooked rice (3 lb/1.36 kg before cooking), 1 T (15 mL) pepper, 1 t (5 mL) garlic salt, salt to taste, ½ c (120 mL) soy sauce, and 2 lb (908 g) blanched slivered almonds. Mix and bake until thoroughly heated.

3. **Green Rice.** Cook 3 lb (1.36 kg) rice. Add 6 lb (2.72 kg) finely chopped raw or frozen spinach, 3 T (45 mL) onion juice, and 2 qt (1.89 L) Medium White Sauce (p.458). Bake 30-40 min at 325 °F (160 °C).

4. **Rice Pilaff.** Brown 2 lb (908 g) rice in 1 lb (454 g) butter or margarine. Add 1 gal (3.79 L) water and 1½ T (23 mL) salt. Cook for 30 min in steamer. Add 1 lb (454 g) green pepper, 10 oz (284 g) onion, and 8 oz (227 g) pimiento, chopped. **Bake at 350 °F (175 °C) for 15 min.**

COOKING MACARONI, SPAGHETTI, OR NOODLES Approximate yield: 2¼ gal (8.52 L)
Portion: 5 oz (142 g)

Amount		Ingredient	Method
Metric	U.S.		
1.81 kg	4 lb	Macaroni, spaghetti, or noodles	Top of range or steam-jacketed kettle
			Add macaroni, spaghetti, or
11.36 L	3 gal	Water, boiling	noodles to boiling salted
60 mL	¼ c	Salt	water. Stir.
60 mL	¼ c	Oil or fat (optional)	Reheat to boiling temperature. Cook until tender, about 15 min.
			Drain. Rinse with hot water to remove excess starch.
			Steamer
			Divide macaroni, spaghetti, or noodles into 2 steamer pans.
			Add 1½ gal (5.68 L) boiling water, 2 T (30 mL) salt, and 2 T (30 mL) oil to each.
			Steam for 12-15 min at 5-lb pressure.
			Drain and rinse.

Note: Addition of oil is optional. It tends to prevent foaming.

RICE CROQUETTES
Fry: 3-4 min
Deep-fat fryer: 375 °F (190 °C)

Yield: 50 portions
Portion: 1 croquette

Metric	U.S.	Ingredient	Method
Amount			
1.36 kg	3 lb	Rice	Add rice to salted hot liquid. Cook
2.84 L	3 qt	Milk, hot	until tender (p. 190).
1.89 L	2 qt	Water, hot	
57 g	2 oz (3 T)	Salt	
18	18	Eggs, beaten	Add eggs and fat to hot rice.
57 g	2 oz	Fat, melted	Cook until eggs are done (10-15 min).
			Measure with No. 10 dipper onto a greased sheet pan. Chill 2 hr.
3	3	Eggs, beaten	Shape croquettes and dip in egg
240 mL	1 c	Milk or water	and milk mixture.
340 g	12 oz	Bread crumbs	Roll in crumbs. Chill.
			Fry in deep fat.

Note: Serve with Cheese Sauce (p. 459), or Creamed Chicken (p. 345).

SPANISH RICE
Bake: 1 hr
Oven: 350 °F (175 °C)

Yield: 2 pans 12 × 20 × 2 in.
Portion: 5 oz (142 g)

Amount		Ingredient	Method
Metric	*U.S.*		
1.14 kg	2 lb 8 oz	Rice	Cook rice (p. 190).
2.84 L	3 qt	Water, boiling	
23 mL	1½ T	Salt	
23 mL	1½ T	Fat or oil	
3.79 L	1 gal	Tomatoes	Add tomatoes and seasonings. to
567 g	1 lb 4 oz	Green pepper, chopped	cooked rice. Mix.
70 g	2½ oz	Pimiento, chopped	
45 mL	3 T	Salt	
680 g	1 lb 8 oz	Bacon, chopped	Sauté bacon and onions together.
454 g	1 lb	Onion, chopped	Add to rice mixture. Mix carefully. Pour into 2 greased baking pans. Bake.

Notes:
1. The bacon may be omitted and 5 lb (2.27 kg) ground beef added.
2. 2 qt (1.89 L) tomato purée, diluted with 2 qt (1.89 L) water, may be used in place of the tomatoes.

NOODLE RING

Bake: 30 min
Oven: 350 °F (175 °C)

**Yield: 4 large rings molds or
2 baking pans 12 × 20 × 2 in.**

Metric	U.S.	Ingredient	Method
	Amount		
794 g	1 lb 12 oz	Noodles	Cook noodles (p. 191).
5.68 L	6 qt	Water or broth	Drain.
30 mL	2 T	Salt	
227 g	8 oz	Bread crumbs, soft	Add remaining ingredients and mix lightly.
114 g	4 oz	Onion, finely chopped	Pour into 4 large greased ring molds or 2 greased baking pans
57 g	2 oz	Green pepper, finely chopped	12 × 20 × 2 in. Place molds in pan of hot water. Bake.
85 g	3 oz	Pimiento, finely chopped	Serve with Creamed Chicken (p. 345), Creamed Ham, (p. 301), or Creamed Tuna (p. 249).
10 mL	2 t	Parsley	
12	12	Eggs, beaten	
0.95 L	1 qt	Milk	
5 mL	1 t	Paprika	

Variations:

1. **Rice Ring.** Substitute 1 lb (454 g) of rice for noodles.

2. **Noodle Casserole.** Cook noodles in chicken stock (p. 479). Add 5 lb (2.27 kg) large-curd cottage cheese, 4 oz (114 g) grated onion, ⅓ c (80 mL) Worcestershire sauce, 2½ c (600 mL) dry bread crumbs, 1 T (15 mL) salt, and 1½ qt (1.42 L) cultured sour cream. Place in greased pan, cover with 2½ c (600 mL) grated Parmesan cheese, and bake 30-35 min at 350 °F (175 °C).

3. **Poppy Seed Noodles.** To 4 lb (1.81 kg) noodles, cooked, add 12 oz (340 g) butter or margarine, melted, ⅓ c (80 mL) poppy seeds, and 12 oz (340 g) chopped toasted almonds. Mix lightly.

4. **Noodles Romanoff.** Cook 3 lb (1.36 kg) noodles (p. 191). Drain. Make sauce of 10 oz (284 g) butter or margarine, 4 oz (114 g) flour, and 1¼ qt (1.18 L) milk. Season with 1½ T (23 mL) salt, 4 oz (114 g) finely chopped onion or ½ T (8 mL) onion juice, and ½ t (3 mL) garlic juice. Cool slightly and add 1½ c (360 mL) Parmesan cheese, 2½ lb (1.14 kg) cottage cheese, 2½ c (600 mL) cultured sour cream, and 1 T (15 mL) paprika. Combine with noodles and place in baking pans. Sprinkle 4 oz (114 g) grated Cheddar cheese over top of each pan. Cover with aluminum foil. Bake 30-35 min at 350 °F (175 °C).

SPOON BREAD
Bake: 1 hr   **Yield: 2 pans 12 × 20 × 2 in.**
Oven: 350 °F (175 °C)   **Portion: 4 oz (114 g)**

Amount		Ingredient	Method
Metric	U.S.		
5.44 L	5¾ qt	Milk	Scald milk.
794 g	1 lb 12 oz	Cornmeal	Add cornmeal and salt, stirring
45 mL	3 T	Salt	briskly with a wire whip. Cook 10 min, or until thick.
25	25	Eggs, beaten	Add eggs slowly while stirring.
170 g	6 oz	Fat, melted	Add fat and baking powder. Stir
57 g	2 oz	Baking powder	to blend. Pour into 2 greased pans 12 × 20 × 2 in. or 8 casseroles (1 lb 12 oz/794 g to each). Place in pans of hot water. Bake.

Note: Serve with crisp bacon, Creamed Chicken (p. 345), or Creamed Ham (p. 301).

Cheese, Eggs, and Milk

Cheese, eggs, and milk are basic ingredients in many quantity recipes, and their cookery requires carefully controlled temperatures and cooking times.

Cheese

Cheese used in cooking should be appropriate in flavor and texture to the item being prepared and should blend well with other ingredients. Aged natural cheese or process cheese blends more readily than green or unripened cheese. Process cheese is a blend of fresh and aged natural cheeses that have been melted, pasteurized, and mixed with an emulsifier. It has no rind or waste, is easy to slice, and melts readily but, during processing, it loses some of the characteristic flavor of natural cheese. For this reason, a natural cheese with a more pronounced flavor may be preferred for cheese sauce and as an addition to other cooked foods where a distinctive cheese flavor is desired.

Cheese to be combined with other ingredients usually is ground, shredded, or diced to expedite melting and blending. Cheese melts at 325 °F (162 °C), and baked dishes containing cheese should be cooked at a temperature no higher than 350 °F (175 °C). Excessive temperature and prolonged cooking cause cheese to toughen and become stringy and the fat to separate. When making cheese sauce, the cheese should be added after the white sauce is completely cooked and the mixture heated only enough to melt the cheese. When cheese is used as a topping, a thin layer of buttered bread crumbs will protect it from the heat and from becoming stringy.

Cheddar cheese, often called American cheese, leads all other types in amounts used in quantity food preparation. It is available in many forms and ranges in flavor from mild to very sharp. Other types of cheese are used for appetizers, sandwiches, salads, and with crackers and fruit for dessert. Table 2.2 lists some of the cheeses most often used in institution foodservices.

Table 2.2 GUIDE TO NATURAL CHEESES[a]

Type	Characteristics	Uses
Blue	Tangy, piquant flavor; semisoft, pasty sometimes crumbly texture; white interior marbled or streaked with blue veins of mold; resembles Roquefort	Appetizers, salads and salad dressings, desserts
Brick	Mild to moderately sharp flavor, semisoft to medium firm, elastic texture; creamy white-to-yellow interior; brownish exterior	Appetizers, sandwiches, desserts
Brie	Mild to pungent flavor; soft, smooth texture; creamy yellow interior; edible thin brown and white crust	Appetizers, sandwiches, desserts
Camembert	Distinctive mild to tangy flavor; soft, smooth texture, almost fluid when fully ripened; creamy yellow interior; edible thin white or gray-white crust	Appetizers, desserts
Cheddar	Mild to very sharp flavor, smooth texture, firm to crumbly; light cream to orange	Appetizers, main dishes, sauces, soups, sandwiches, salads, desserts
Colby	Mild to mellow flavor, similar to Cheddar; softer body and more open texture than Cheddar; light cream to orange	Sandwiches
Cottage	Mild, slightly acid flavor; soft open texture with tender curds of varying size; white to creamy white	Appetizers, salads, used in some cheese cakes
Cream	Delicate, slightly acid flavor; soft, smooth texture; white	Appetizers, salads, sandwiches, desserts

Table 2.2 GUIDE TO NATURAL CHEESES[a] (continued)

Type	Characteristics	Uses
Edam	Mellow, nutlike, sometimes salty flavor; rather firm, rubbery texture; creamy yellow or medium yellow-orange interior; surface coated with red wax; usually shaped like a flattened ball	Appetizers, salads, sandwiches, sauces, desserts
Gorgonzola	Tangy, rich, spicy flavor; semisoft, pasty, sometimes crumbly texture; creamy white interior, mottled or streaked with blue-green veins of mold; clay-colored surface	Appetizers, salads, desserts
Gouda	Mellow, nutlike, often slightly acid flavor; semisoft to firm, smooth texture, often containing small holes; creamy yellow or medium yellow-orange interior; usually has a red wax coating; usually shaped like a flattened ball	Appetizers, salads, sandwiches, sauces, desserts
Gruyere	Nutlike, salty flavor, similar to Swiss but sharper; firm, smooth texture with small holes or eyes; light yellow	Appetizers, desserts
Limburger	Highly pungent; very strong flavor and aroma; soft, smooth texture that usually contains small irregular openings; creamy white interior; reddish yellow surface	Appetizers, desserts
Mozzarella	Delicate, mild flavor; slightly firm, plastic texture; creamy white	Main dishes, such as lasagna, sandwiches
Muenster	Mild to mellow flavor; semisoft texture with numerous small openings; creamy white interior; yellowish tan surface	Appetizers, sandwiches, desserts
Neufchatel	Mild, acid flavor; soft, smooth texture similar to cream cheese but lower in fat; white	Salads, sandwiches, desserts
Parmesan	Sharp, distinctive flavor, very hard, granular texture; yellowish white	Grated for seasoning
Port du Salut	Mellow to robust flavor similar to Gouda; semisoft, smooth elastic texture; creamy white or yellow	Appetizers, desserts
Provolone	Mellow to sharp flavor, smoky and salty; firm, smooth texture; cuts without crumbling; light creamy yellow; light brown or golden yellow surface	Appetizers, main dishes, sandwiches, desserts

Table 2.2 GUIDE TO NATURAL CHEESES[a] (continued)

Type	Characteristics	Uses
Ricotta	Mild, sweet, nutlike flavor; soft, moist texture with loose curds (fresh Ricotta) or dry and suitable for grating	Salads, main dishes such as lasagna and ravioli, desserts
Romano	Very sharp, piquant flavor; very hard, granular texture; yellowish white interior; greenish black surface	Seasoning and general table use; when cured a year, it is suitable for grating
Roquefort (imported)	Sharp, peppery, piquant flavor; semisoft pasty, sometimes crumbly texture; white interior streaked with blue-green veins of mold	Appetizers, salads and salad dressings, desserts
Stilton	Piquant flavor, milder than Gorgonzola or Roquefort; open, flaky texture; creamy white interior streaked with blue-green veins of mold; wrinkled, melonlike rind	Appetizers, salads, desserts
Swiss	Mild, sweet, nutlike flavor; firm, smooth, elastic body with large round eyes; light yellow	Sandwiches, salads

[a] From U.S. Department of Agriculture, *Cheese in Family Meals,* Home and Garden Bulletin No. 112.

Eggs

Eggs may be purchased fresh, frozen, and dried. Fresh eggs deteriorate rapidly at room temperature and should be refrigerated and stored away from foods with strong odors. Although fresh shell eggs are used extensively for table service, processed eggs are convenient to use in quantity food preparation and eliminate the time-consuming task of breaking eggs.

Egg Cookery

Egg mixtures should be carefully protected against exposure to high temperatures. Poached, soft- or hard-cooked, and scrambled eggs should be prepared as close to serving time as possible by batch cooking or cooking to order. If eggs must be held on a hot counter, they should be undercooked slightly to compensate for the additional heating that will occur. Directions for cooking eggs are given on p. 207.

The surface of the yolks of hard-cooked eggs sometimes appears dark green. The greenish color is more likely to occur when eggs have been over-cooked or allowed to cool slowly in the cooking water. Cooking the eggs for the minimum length of time required to make them hard and cooling them in cold running water help to prevent this color formation.

Processed Eggs[1]

Whole eggs, whites, yolks, and various blends are processed and are available in liquid, frozen, and dried forms. Only those egg products that bear the USDA inspection mark should be purchased. This stamp indicates that the products were prepared from wholesome eggs, pasteurized, cooled, and packaged under sanitary conditions in accordance with the USDA regulations that govern the trading and inspection of egg products.

Thawed frozen eggs and reconstituted dried eggs are highly perishable, and careful handling by the user is essential to prevent contamination. To insure such safety, the guides that follow should be observed.

Frozen Eggs.   Store in freezer at 0 °F (-18°C) or below. Thaw only the amount needed at one time. Thaw in refrigerator or, to speed thawing, place container in cold running water without submerging it. Use thawed eggs immediately, or refrigerate promptly in an airtight container and use within 24 hr.

Dried Eggs.   Store unopened packages in cool, dry place where temperature is not more than 50 °F (10 °C), preferably in refrigerator. After opening, refrigerate any unused portion in container with a close-fitting lid. Reconstitute only the amount needed at one time. Reconstitute by blending with water, or combine with other dry ingredients in recipe and add amount of water needed to reconstitute. Use reconstituted eggs immediately, or refrigerate promptly in an airtight container and use within 1 hr.

A guide for substituting processed eggs for shell eggs is given in Table 2.3.

Table 2.3   EQUIVALENTS OF SHELL EGGS AND EGG PRODUCTS

Product	Whole Eggs per lb	Egg Yolks per lb	Egg Whites per lb
Frozen	10	26	16
Dried	32	54	100

[1] Adapted from U.S. Department of Agriculture, *Egg Products Inspection,* PA-886, July 1968.

Milk

Milk Cookery

Milk should be heated or cooked at a low temperature. At high temperatures the protein in milk coagulates into a film on top and a coating on the sides of the kettle that tends to scorch when milk is heated over direct heat. To prevent formation of this coating, milk should be heated over water, in a steamer, or in a steam-jacketed kettle. Whipping the milk to form a foam or tightly covering the pan and heating the milk below boiling temperature helps to prevent formation of a top scum.

Curdling may be caused by holding the milk at high temperature or by the addition of foods containing acids and tannins. For example, the tannins in potatoes often cause curdling of the milk used in scalloped potatoes. Milk in combination with ham or with certain vegetables, such as asparagus, green beans, carrots, peas, or tomatoes, may curdle. Curdling may be lessened by limiting the salt used, adding the milk in the form of a white sauce, keeping the temperature below boiling, and shortening the cooking time. Danger of curdling in tomato soup may be lessened by adding the tomato to the milk, having both the milk and tomato hot when they are combined, or thickening either the milk or tomato juice before they are combined.

Dry Milk Solids

Dry milk is substituted extensively for fluid milk in institution foodservices because of the comparatively low cost of dry milk and its ease in handling and storage. It is available as whole, nonfat, and buttermilk. Nonfat dry milk is pure fresh milk from which only the fat and water have been removed. It has better keeping qualities than dry whole milk, although both should be kept dry and cool. There are on the market different types and kinds of nonfat dry milk of equal nutritional food value. Instant nonfat milk is the type that is readily reconstituted in liquid form. Whatever the type, it may be used in dry form or reconstituted as fluid milk. Once it has been reconstituted, it should be refrigerated immediately.

When dry milk is used in recipes that contain a large proportion of dry ingredients, such as bread, biscuits, and cakes, the only change in method would be to mix the unsifted dry milk with the other dry ingredients and use water in place of fluid milk. For best results, dry milk should be weighed, not measured. Package directions for reconstituting dry milk solids should be followed. A general guide is to use 3.5 oz (100 g) by weight, of instant or regular spray process nonfat dry milk to make 1 qt of liquid milk; or 4.5 oz (128 g) of dry whole milk per quart. For some foods, additional fat (1.2 oz/35 g per quart/0.95

L of liquid) should be added when nonfat dry milk is used. Additional amounts of nonfat dry milk may be added to some foods to supplement their nutritional value, although excessive amounts that affect palatability should not be used.

Cheese Recipes

CHEESE BALLS
Fry: 2-3 min   **Yield: 150 balls**
Deep-fat fryer: 360 °F (180 °C)   **Portion: 3 balls**

Amount			
Metric	*U.S.*	*Ingredient*	*Method*
2.04 kg	4 lb 8 oz	Cheddar cheese, grated	Mix cheese, flour, salt, and cayenne.
114 g	4 oz	Flour	
15 mL	1 T	Salt	
f.g.	f.g.	Cayenne	
24	24	Egg whites	Beat egg whites until stiff. Fold into cheese mixture. Shape into balls 1-1¼ in. diameter or dip with No. 30 dipper onto trays or baking sheets. Chill.
3	3	Eggs	Combine eggs and milk. Dip cheese balls in egg mixture, then roll in crumbs. Chill for several hours. Fry in deep fat.
240 mL	1 c	Milk	
340 g	12 oz	Bread crumbs	

Notes:
1. Serve 3 balls in center of hot buttered pineapple ring.
2. For serving as first-course accompaniment, use half the recipe and shape into balls ½-¾ in. in diameter. Yield: 150 balls.
3. For 2 balls per portion, use No. 24 dipper; yield: 40 portions.

CHEESE CROQUETTES

Fry: 3-4 min
Deep-fat fryer: 360 °F (180 °C)

Yield: 50 croquettes
Portion: 3 oz (85 g)

Amount		Ingredient	Method
Metric	U.S.		
227 g	8 oz	Butter or margarine	Make into Thick White Sauce (p. 458).
227 g	8 oz	Flour	
1.89 L	2 qt	Milk	
32	32	Egg yolks, beaten	Add eggs, cheese, and seasonings. Stir until cheese is melted.
908 g	2 lb	Cheddar cheese, diced	Measure with No. 16 dipper onto greased pans. Chill.
23 mL	1½ T	Salt	Shape. Chill several hours.
15 mL	1 T	Paprika	
16	16	Egg whites	Beat egg whites and water slightly.
120 mL	½ c	Water	Dip each croquette in egg mixture and roll in crumbs. Chill.
454 g	1 lb	Bread crumbs	Fry in deep fat.

CHEESE FONDUE

Bake: 50-60 min
Oven: 350°F (175 °C)

Yield: 3 pans 10 × 12 in.
Portion: 4 oz (114 g)

Amount		Ingredient	Method
Metric	U.S.		
4.26 L	4½ qt	Milk, scalded	Add butter and seasonings to milk.
114 g	4 oz	Butter or margarine, melted	
8 mL	1½ t	Mustard	
15 mL	1 T	Salt	
f.g.	f.g.	Cayenne	
1.59 kg	3 lb 8 oz	Bread cubes, soft	Pour milk mixture over bread. Cool slightly.
2.04 kg	4 lb 8 oz	Cheddar cheese, shredded	Add cheese and egg yolks. Mix until blended.
24	24	Egg yolks, beaten	
24	24	Egg whites	Beat egg whites until stiff. Fold into cheese mixture. Pour into 3 greased pans 10 × 12 in. Set pans in hot water. Bake.

CHEESE SOUFFLÉ

Bake: 50 min   **Yield: 3 pans 10 × 12 in.**
Oven: 350 °F (175 °C)   **Portion: 2½ oz (71 g)**

Metric	U.S.	Ingredient	Method
	Amount		
Metric	*U.S.*	*Ingredient*	*Method*
2.37 L	2½ qt	Milk, hot	Add tapioca and salt to milk, stirring constantly.
284 g	10 oz	Tapioca, minute	
30 mL	2 T	Salt	Cook 15 min. Stir frequently during first 5 min.
1.36 kg	3 lb	Cheddar cheese, ground	Add cheese and egg yolks. Stir until cheese is melted.
24	24	Egg yolks, beaten	
24	24	Egg whites	Beat egg whites until stiff but not dry. Fold into cheese mixture. Pour into 3 greased pans 12 × 12 in. Set pans in hot water. Bake. Serve with Spanish Sauce (p. 466), Shrimp Sauce (p. 459), or Creamed Ham (p. 301).

Variation:

Mushroom Soufflé. Add 1 lb (454 g) chopped mushrooms and 5 oz (142 g) chopped green peppers to uncooked mixture. Serve with Bechamel Sauce (p. 461).

MACARONI AND CHEESE

Bake: 35 min   **Yield: 2 pans 12 × 20 × 2 in.**
Oven: 350 °F (175 °C)   **Portion: 5 oz (142 g)**

Metric	U.S.	Ingredient	Method
Amount			
1.14 kg	2 lb 8 oz	Macaroni	Cook macaroni (p. 191). Drain.
7.57 L	2 gal	Water, boiling	Pour into 2 baking pans.
30 mL	2 T	Salt	
227 g	8 oz	Butter or margarine	Make into Medium White Sauce (p. 458)
170 g	6 oz	Flour	
30 mL	2 T	Salt	
2.84 L	3 qt	Milk, hot	
1.36 kg	3 lb	Cheddar cheese, sharp, shredded	Add cheese to sauce. Pour over macaroni.
340 g	12 oz	Bread crumbs	Sprinkle with buttered crumbs. Bake.
114 g	4 oz	Butter or margarine, melted	

Notes:
1. Cheese may be mixed with macaroni, then covered with white sauce.
2. Fresh tomato sections, slivers of green pepper, or pimiento may be added for variety.

CHEESE SOUFFLÉ (WITH WHITE SAUCE BASE)

Bake: 1 hr
Oven: 300 °F (150 °C)

Yield: 2 pans 12 × 20 × 2 in.
Cut 6 × 4

Amount		Ingredient	Method
Metric	U.S.		
454 g	1 lb	Butter or margarine	Make into Thick White Sauce (p. 458).
227 g	8 oz	Flour	
2.37 L	2½ qt	Milk	
5 mL	1 t	Salt	
32	32	Egg yolks	Add egg yolks to white sauce. Stir and cook.
567 g	1 lb 4 oz	Cheddar cheese, shredded	Add cheese and stir until smooth. Remove from heat.
32	32	Egg whites	Add cream of tartar to egg whites.
8 mL	1½ t	Cream of tartar	Beat until stiff, but not dry. Fold into cheese mixture. Pour into 2 greased pans. Bake. Serve with Cheese Sauce (p. 459) or Shrimp Sauce (p. 459).

WELSH RAREBIT

Yield: 6½ qt (6.15 L)
Portion: ½ c (120 mL)

Amount		Ingredient	Method
Metric	U.S.		
284 g	10 oz	Butter or margarine	Make into White Sauce (p. 458).
227 g	8 oz	Flour	
3.79 L	1 gal	Milk	
28 g	1 oz	Salt	
2.27 kg	5 lb	Cheddar cheese, grated or ground	Add cheese and seasonings. Cook over hot water until cheese is melted.
30 mL	2 T	Mustard, dry	Serve on toasted buns.
30 mL	2 T	Worcestershire sauce	
3 mL	½ t	White pepper	

CORN RAREBIT

Yield: 6½ qt (6.15 L)
Portion: ½ c (120 mL)

Amount		Ingredient	Method
Metric	U.S.		
114 g	4 oz	Onion, chopped	Sauté onion in butter or margarine.
170 g	6 oz	Butter or margarine	
0.95 L	1 qt	Milk	Add milk to onion. Heat to boiling point.
480 mL	2 c	Milk, cold	Blend flour and seasonings with cold milk.
170 g	6 oz	Flour	
30 mL	2 T	Salt	Add gradually to hot mixture, stirring constantly.
f.g.	f.g.	Cayenne pepper	
680 g	1 lb 8 oz	Cheddar cheese, sharp, shredded	Add cheese and green pepper. Cook over hot water until cheese is melted.
85 g	3 oz	Green pepper, chopped	
1 No. 10 can	1 No. 10 can	Corn, whole kernel	Heat corn; drain. Add to cheese mixture. Serve immediately with No. 8 dipper on split toasted buns.

Variation:

Hot Corn Sandwich. Substitute 1 qt (0.95 L) tomato purée for milk and
pimiento for green pepper. To hot cheese-corn mixture, add 2 c (480
mL) beaten egg yolks. Continue cooking, stirring constantly, until yolks
are cooked. Serve immediately on split toasted buns.

Egg Recipes

DIRECTIONS FOR COOKING EGGS

Method	Directions	Cooking Time
Hard-cooked:		
Steamer I	Place eggs in solid steamer pan or counter pan. Cover with cold water. Steam at 5-lb pressure. Plunge at once into cold water.	25-30 min
Steamer II	Place eggs in shallow perforated pans. Steam at 5-lb pressure. Plunge at once into cold water.	15-18 min
Steamer III	Break eggs into lightly greased pan. Eggs should be thick enough in pan so whites come up to level of yolks. For 4-doz eggs, use pan 12 × 20 × 2 in.; for 1-doz, use pan 5 × 12 × 2 in. This method is suitable when eggs are to be chopped.	13-15 min
Kettle	Place eggs in wire baskets. Lower into kettles of boiling water. Simmer.	30 min
Soft-cooked:		
Kettle	Place eggs in kettle, cover with cold water. Bring to full rolling boil. Remove eggs from boiling water. Run cold water over eggs for a few seconds.	
Poached:		
Steamer	Break eggs into water in shallow counter pans. Steam at 5-lb pressure.	3-5 min
Top of range	Break eggs one at a time into sauce dishes. Line up dishes on trays. Carefully slide eggs into boiling water in skillets or shallow pans. Keep water at simmering temperature. Remove eggs with slotted spoon or turner.	5-7 min
Fried:		
Top of range	Break eggs into sauce dishes. Slide carefully into hot fat in skillets or on griddle. Cook over low heat, carefully basting eggs until of desired hardness. If eggs are to be served on hot counter, drain well before removing to counter pans.	
Oven	Heat fat in counter pans or skillets. Carefully slide eggs into fat. Bake at 400 °F (205 °C).	5-7 min, or until of desired hardness

SCRAMBLED EGGS

Yield: 50 portions
Portion: 3 oz (85 g)

Amount		Ingredient	Method
Metric	*U.S.*	*Ingredient*	*Method*
75	75	Eggs	Break eggs into mixer bowl. Beat
1.42 L	1½ qt	Milk, hot	slightly (medium speed).
30 mL	2 T	Salt	Add hot milk and salt. Beat until blended.
227 g	8 oz	Butter or margarine	Melt butter or margarine in skillet or steam-jacketed kettle. Pour in egg mixture. Cook over low heat, stirring occasionally, until of desired consistency. Serve with No. 10 dipper.

Notes:
1. *Steamer Method*. Melt 4 oz (114 g) butter or margarine in each of two steamer or counter pans. Pour egg mixture into pans. Steam for 6-8 min at 5-lb pressure until desired degree of hardness.
2. *Oven Method*. Melt 4 oz (114 g) butter or margarine in each of 2 counter or baking pans. Pour egg mixture into pans. Bake approximately 20 min at 350 °F (175 °C), stirring once after 10 min of baking.
3. For frozen eggs, use 7 lb 8 oz (3.40 kg) or 3¾ qt (3.55 L).

Variations:
1. **Scrambled Eggs and Cheese.** Add 1 lb (454 g) grated Cheddar cheese.

2. **Scrambled Eggs and Ham.** Add 1 lb 4 oz (567 g) chopped cooked ham. Salt may need to be reduced.

3. **Scrambled Eggs and Chipped Beef.** Add 1 lb (454 g) chopped chipped beef. Salt may need to be reduced.

OMELET
Bake: 45 min
Oven: 325 °F (165 °C)

Yield: 2 pans 12 × 20 × 2 in.
Portion: 3 oz (85 g)

Amount			
Metric	*U.S.*	*Ingredient*	*Method*
340 g	12 oz	Butter or mar-garine	Make into Thick White Sauce (p. 458).
227 g	8 oz	Flour	
30 mL	2 T	Salt	
3 mL	½ t	Pepper, white	
2.84 L	3 qt	Milk	
24	24	Eggs yolks, beaten	Add egg yolks and mix well with a wire whip.
24	24	Egg whites	Beat egg whites until they form rounded peaks. Fold into egg yolk mixture. Pour into 2 greased baking pans. Set pans in hot water. Bake.

Variations:

1. **Bacon Omelet.** Fry 1½ lb (680 g) diced bacon; substitute bacon fat for butter in white sauce. Add diced bacon to the egg mixture.

2. **Cheese Omelet.** Add 12 oz (340 g) grated cheese before placing pans in oven.

3. **Ham Omelet.** Add 3 lb (1.36 kg) finely diced cooked ham. Salt may need to be reduced.

4. **Jelly Omelet.** Spread 2 c (480 mL) tart jelly over cooked omelet.

5. **Spanish Omelet.** Serve with Spanish Sauce (p. 466).

CHINESE OMELET

Bake 45 min   Yield: 2 pans 12 × 20 × 2 in.
Oven: 325 °F (165 °C)   Portion: 4 oz (114 g)

Amount			
Metric	U.S.	Ingredient	Method
114 g	4 oz	Butter or mar-garine	Make into Medium White Sauce (p. 458).
57 g	2 oz	Flour	
5 mL	1 t	Salt	
0.95 L	1 qt	Milk	
454 g	1 lb	Cheddar cheese, sharp, shred-ded	Add cheese to white sauce. Blend.
24	24	Egg yolks	Beat egg yolks until light and fluffy. Add seasonings.
5 mL	1 t	Mustard	
30 mL	2 T	Salt	Add to cheese sauce. Stir until smooth.
5 mL	1 t	Paprika	
908 g	2 lb (A.P.)	Rice	Cook rice (p. 190).
2.37 L	2½ qt	Water	Add to sauce.
20 mL	4 t	Salt	
20 mL	4 t	Fat or oil	
24	24	Egg whites	Beat egg whites until they form a soft peak. Fold into rice mixture. Pour into 2 greased pans. Bake. Serve with Cheese Sauce (p. 459) or Tomato Sauce (p. 466).

POTATO OMELET

Bake: 1 hr
Oven: 325 °F (165 °C)

Yield: 2 pans 12 × 20 × 2 in.
Portion: 5 oz (142 g)

Metric	*U.S.*	*Ingredient*	*Method*
Amount			
50	50	Bacon slices	Arrange bacon, slightly overlapping, in baking pan. Cook in oven until crisp. Remove from pans.
4.08 kg	9 lb (E.P.)	Potatoes, cooked, diced	Brown potatoes slightly in bacon fat. Remove to 2 greased baking pans.
36	36	Eggs, beaten	Combine eggs, milk, and seasonings.
45 mL	3 T	Salt	
5 mL	1 t	Pepper	Pour over potatoes. Bake.
f.g.	f.g.	Cayenne	Serve as soon as removed from oven with a slice of crisp bacon on top of each serving.
2.84 L	3 qt	Milk, hot	

Variation:

Potato-Ham Omelet. Omit bacon. Add 4 lb (1.81 kg) diced cooked ham to potatoes. Reduce salt to 1 T (15 mL).

EGG FOO YUNG

Yield: 50
Portion: Egg Foo Yung, 4 oz (114 g), Sauce, 2 oz (57 g)

Amount			
Metric	U.S.	Ingredient	Method
454 g	1 lb	Mushrooms, shredded	Drain mushrooms and bean sprouts. Save juice.
1 No. 10 can	1 No. 10 can	Bean sprouts, chopped	Fry vegetables 2 min in fat.
680 g	1 lb 8 oz	Onions, shredded	
227 g	8 oz	Green peppers, shredded	
227 g	8 oz	Fat	
454 g	1 lb	Ham, cooked, shredded	Combine ham and eggs. Add to vegetables. Mix.
40	40	Egg, beaten	Use No. 10 dipper to place mixture on hot grill or frying pan. Brown well on 1 side, fold in half. Serve with following sauce.
57 g	2 oz	Cornstarch	Combine cornstarch and soy sauce into a smooth paste.
360 mL	1½ c	Soy sauce	
1.89 L	2 qt	Vegetable juice, hot	Add to vegetable juice, stirring with wire whip. Cook until thickened.

Note: Roast pork, chicken, or bacon may be used in place of ham; green onions in place of shredded onions; and bamboo shoots and shredded water chestnuts in place of bean sprouts.

CREAMED EGGS

Yield: 50 portions
Portion: 5 oz (142 g)

Amount			
Metric	U.S.	Ingredient	Method
454 g	1 lb	Butter or margarine	Make into Medium White Sauce (p. 458).
227 g	8 oz	Flour	
3.79 L	1 gal	Milk	
23 mL	1½ T	Salt	
¼ t	¼ t	White pepper	
75	75	Eggs, hard-cooked (p. 207)	Slice or quarter eggs. When ready to serve, pour hot sauce over eggs. Mix carefully. Reheat.

Variations:

1. **Curried Eggs.** Substitute chicken broth for milk and add 2 T (30 mL) curry powder. May be served with steamed rice or chow mein noodles.

2. **Eggs à la King.** Substitute chicken stock (p. 479) for milk and add 1 lb (454 g) mushrooms that have been sautéed, 12 oz (340 g) chopped green peppers, and 8 oz (227 g) chopped pimiento.

3. **Goldenrod Eggs.** Reserve 25 egg yolks to mash or rice, and sprinkle over top of creamed eggs.

4. **Scotch Woodcock.** Add 1 lb (454 g) sharp Cheddar cheese to White Sauce (p. 458) and blend. Cut eggs in half lengthwise and place in pans. Pour sauce over eggs. Cover with buttered crumbs. Bake until heated through and crumbs are brown.

EGG CUTLETS

Fry: 3 min   **Yield: 50 cutlets**
Deep-fat fryer: 375 °F (190 °C)   **Portion: 3 oz (85 g)**

Amount			
Metric	U.S.	Ingredient	Method
340 g	12 oz	Butter or mar-garine	Make into Very Thick White Sauce (p. 458).
284 g	10 oz	Flour	
45 mL	3 T	Salt	
1.89 L	2 qt	Milk	
48	48	Eggs, hard-cooked, (p. 207)	Peel eggs. Chop or grind coarsely. Add sauce. Mix. Portion with No. 12 dipper onto a greased sheet pan. Chill. Shape into cutlets. Chill.
6	6	Eggs, beaten	Combine eggs and milk.
240 mL	1 c	Milk	Dip cutlets in egg mixture and roll in crumbs.
340 g	12 oz	Bread crumbs	Chill 2 hr. Fry in deep fat.

DEVILED EGGS

                                                            Yield: 50 portions
                                                            Portion: 2 halves

Amount			
Metric	U.S.	Ingredient	Method
50	50	Eggs, hard-cooked (p. 207)	Peel eggs. Cut in half lengthwise. Remove yolks to mixing bowl. Arrange whites in rows on a tray.
120 mL	½ c	Milk, hot	Mash yolks. Add milk and mix until blended.
360 mL	1½ c	Mayonnaise or cooked salad dressing	Add remaining ingredients and mix until smooth.
15 mL	1 T	Salt	Refill whites with mashed yolks, using approximately 1½ T (23 mL) for each half egg white.
10 mL	2 t	Mustard, dry	
120 mL	½ c	Vinegar	

Notes:
1. Pastry bag may be used to fill egg whites. Yolk mixture should be smooth and creamy. Use plain or rose tube.
2. 6 oz (70 g) finely chopped pimientos may be added to yolk mixture.

HOT STUFFED EGGS
Bake: 30 min   **Yield: 50 eggs**
Oven: 325 °F (165 °C)   **Portion: 2 halves**

Amount			
Metric	U.S.	Ingredient	Method
50	50	Eggs, hard-cooked (p. 207)	Peel eggs. Cut in half lengthwise. Remove yolks to mixing bowl. Arrange whites in 2 baking pans 12 × 20 × 2.
85 g	3 oz	Butter or margarine, melted	Mash yolks. Add butter, seasonings, and ham.
10 mL	2 t	Salt	Refill whites.
⅛ t	⅛ t	Cayenne	
15 mL	1 T	Prepared mustard	
454 g	1 lb	Ham, minced	
340 g	12 oz	Butter or margarine	Make into Medium White Sauce (p. 458).
227 g	8 oz	Flour	Pour over eggs. Bake.
23 mL	1½ T	Salt	
3.79 L	1 gal	Milk	
60 mL	¼ c	Parsley, chopped	Sprinkle parsley over the eggs just before serving.

Note: Tuna may be substituted for the ham.

BAKED EGG AND BACON RING
Bake: 25 min or until firm   **Yield: 50 portions**
Oven: 350 °F (175 °C)   **Portion: 1 egg, 1 slice bacon**

Amount			
Metric	U.S.	Ingredient	Method
50 (1.14 kg)	50 (2½ lb)	Bacon slices	Arrange bacon around inside of 50 baking cups (or muffin pans), fat side up.
50	50	Eggs	Place in hot oven until fat is clear. Remove from oven.
			Break 1 egg into each cup. Return to oven. Bake until eggs are firm.

Variation:
Eggs Benedict. For each portion, place on toasted and buttered English muffin 1 slice cooked Canadian bacon and 1 poached egg. Serve with Hollandaise Sauce (p. 469).

BAKED EGGS WITH CHEESE

Bake: 25 min or until firm
Oven: 350 °F (175 °C)

Yield: 50 portions
Portion: 1 egg

Amount		Ingredient	Method
Metric	*U.S.*		
50	50	Eggs	Break eggs into greased custard cups or muffin pans.
85 g	3 oz	Butter or margarine	Make into Thin White Sauce (p. 458).
43 g	1½ oz	Flour	
1.42 L	1½ qt	Milk	
8 mL	1½ t	Salt	
20 mL	4 t	Salt	On top of each egg, place: sprinkle of salt, 2 T (30 mL) cheese, 2 T (30 mL) white sauce, and buttered crumbs.
680 g	1 lb 8 oz	Cheddar cheese, grated	
227 g	8 oz	Buttered crumbs	
			Set cups in pan of hot water. Bake.

Note: For variety, place a thin slice of raw tomato in the bottom of each cup.

EGG AND SAUSAGE BAKE

Bake: 1 hr
Oven: 325 °F (165 °C)

Yield: 2 pans 12 × 20 × 2 in.
Portion: 6 oz (170 g)

Amount		Ingredient	Method
Metric	*U.S.*		
1.36 kg	3 lb	Bread, sliced	Remove crusts from bread. Cut in cubes. Cover bottoms of 2 greased baking pans with bread cubes. Pans should be well covered.
4.08 kg	9 lb	Sausage, bulk	Brown sausage. Drain.
1.14 kg	2 lb 8 oz	Cheddar cheese, grated	Spread cheese and sausage over bread cubes.
42	42	Eggs	Beat eggs. Add milk and seasonings.
2.84 L	3 qt	Milk	
23 mL	1½ T	Mustard, dry	Pour over mixture in pans.
15 mL	1 T	Salt	Cover and refrigerate for 12 hr.
5 mL	1 t	Pepper	Bake uncovered 1 hr or until set. Cut in squares.

QUICHE

| Bake: 25-30 min | | | Yield: 12 8-in pies |
| Oven: 375 °F (190 °C) | | | Portion: ¼ pie (6 oz/170 g) |

Amount			
Metric	*U.S.*	*Ingredient*	*Method*
1.7 kg	3 lb 12 oz	Pastry (p. 310)	Line 12 8-in pie pans with pastry, 5 oz (142 g) per pie. Partially bake shells, about 10 min at 375 °F (190 °C).
30	30	Eggs	Beat eggs.
1.89 L	2 qt	Cream or half and half	Add cream, milk, and seasonings.
1.89 L	2 qt	Milk	
30 mL	2 T	Salt	
3 mL	½ t	Pepper, white	
1.14 kg	2 lb 4 oz	Swiss cheese, grated	Add cheese to egg mixture.
227 g	8 oz	Parmesan cheese, grated	
454 g	1 lb	Bacon, chopped, cooked, and drained OR Ham, finely diced	Sprinkle partially baked shells with bacon or ham. Pour egg mixture into shells, 3 c (720 mL) per pie. Bake until custard is set and lightly browned.

Note: ¼ pie makes a generous serving and needs only a salad to complete a meal. For 6 servings per pie, make ¾ recipe.

Variations:

1. **Mushroom Quiche.** Delete bacon or ham and Parmesan cheese. Sprinkle 2 lb (908 g) sliced fresh mushrooms and 8 oz (227 g) finely chopped onions sautéed in butter or margarine over bottoms of shells.

2. **Crab and Mushroom Quiche.** Use 3 lb (1.36 kg) crab meat, flaked, 1 lb (454 g) sliced fresh mushrooms, and 12 oz (340 g) finely chopped onions sautéed in butter or margarine. Substitute 1 lb 8 oz (680 g) shredded Mozarella cheese for Swiss and Parmesan cheeses.

Cookies

Cookies may be classified as drop and bar cookies, made from a soft dough; and as rolled, refrigerator, pressed, and molded cookies, made from a stiff dough. Almost all cookie doughs may be made in large amounts and stored in the refrigerator or freezer and used as needed.

For drop cookies, use a No. 40, 50, or 60 dipper, depending on the desired size. A No. 40 would make a large cookie. A No. 60 might be used for 2 cookies per serving. For a smaller, tea-size cookie, drop dough from the end of a teaspoon or use a No. 100 dipper, if available. Icebox cookies may be sliced with a meat slicer if they have been well chilled.

Bar cookies usually are baked on 18 × 26 in. baking sheets or 12 × 20 in. pans. The 12 × 20 in. pans yield 48 2 × 2½ in. bars by cutting 6 × 8. The 18 × 26 in. pans may be cut to yield 60 3½ × 2 in., 96 2 × 2 in., or 128 1 × 3 in. cookies.

Avoid overbaking cookies, and always remove from baking sheet onto cooling racks immediately after taking pans out of oven.

Drop Cookie Recipes

BUTTERSCOTCH PECAN COOKIES
Bake: 10-12 min   **Yield: 6 doz**
Oven: 375 °F (190 °C)

Metric	U.S.	Ingredient	Method
	Amount		
227 g	8 oz	Butter or margarine	Cream butter or margarine and sugar (medium speed) 5 min.
454 g	1 lb	Brown sugar	
2	2	Eggs	Add eggs and vanilla. Mix (medium speed) until well blended.
10 mL	2 t	Vanilla	
340 g	12 oz	Flour	Add flour and pecans. Mix (low speed).
227 g	8 oz	Pecans, chopped	Drop onto greased baking sheet with No. 50 dipper, ⅔ oz (19 g) per cookie.

BUTTERSCOTCH DROP COOKIES

Bake: 10-15 min   **Yield: 8 doz**
Oven: 400 °F (205 °C)

Amount			
Metric	*U.S.*	*Ingredient*	*Method*
227 g	8 oz	Butter or margarine	Cream butter or margarine and brown sugar (medium speed) 5 min.
454 g	1 lb	Brown sugar	
4	4	Eggs	Add eggs and vanilla. Mix (medium speed) until well blended.
10 mL	2 t	Vanilla	
567 g	1 lb 4 oz	Flour	Combine dry ingredients.
5 mL	1 t	Baking powder	
10 mL	2 t	Soda	
5 mL	1 t	Salt	
480 mL	2 c	Cultured sour cream	Add dry ingredients alternately with sour cream. Mix (low speed).
227 g	8 oz	Walnuts, chopped	Add nuts. Mix until blended. Chill dough until firm. Drop on greased baking sheet with No. 60 dipper, ½ oz (14 g) per cookie. Bake. Cover with Burnt Butter Frosting (p. 183) while still warm.

Variations:

1. **Butterscotch Squares.** Spread batter in 12 × 20 in. pan. Bake 25 min at 325 °F (165 °C).

2. **Chocolate Drop Cookies.** Add 4 oz (114 g) chocolate, melted, to creamed mixture.

OATMEAL DROP COOKIES
Bake: 12-15 min   **Yield: 6 doz**
Oven: 375 °F (190 °C)

Amount		Ingredient	Method
Metric	*U.S.*	*Ingredient*	*Method*
170 g	6 oz	Fat	Cream fat and sugar (medium
227 g	8 oz	Brown sugar	speed) 5 min.
2	2	Eggs	Add eggs and vanilla. Continue to
5 mL	1 t	Vanilla	cream until well mixed.
198 g	7 oz	Rolled oats, quick, un-cooked	Add oats. Mix (low speed) to blend.
227 g	8 oz	Flour	Combine dry ingredients.
10 mL	2 t	Baking powder	
5 mL	1 t	Salt	
3 mL	½ t	Soda	
75 mL	5 T	Milk	Add alternately with milk. Mix (low speed) until blended.
170 g	6 oz	Raisins, cooked, chopped	Add raisins. Mix only to blend. Drop on greased baking sheet with No. 50 dipper, ⅔ oz (19 g) per cookie. Bake.

CORNFLAKE KISSES
Bake: 15 min   **Yield: 6 doz**
Oven: 325 °F (165 °C)

Amount		Ingredient	Method
Metric	*U.S.*	*Ingredient*	*Method*
4	4	Egg whites	Beat egg whites (high speed) until frothy.
454 g	1 lb	Sugar, sifted	Gradually add sugar. Beat until sugar is dissolved.
114 g	4 oz	Cornflakes	Carefully fold in remaining ingre-dients.
227 g	8 oz	Nuts, chopped	
85 g	3 oz	Coconut, shred-ded	Drop on greased baking sheet with No. 60 dipper, ½ oz per cookie.
5 mL	1 t	Vanilla	Bake.

CHOCOLATE CHIP COOKIES
Bake: 10-12 min   **Yield: 8 doz**
Oven: 375 °F (190 °C)

Amount		Ingredient	Method
Metric	*U.S.*		
170 g	6 oz	Fat	Cream fat and sugars (medium
114 g	4 oz	Granulated sugar	speed) 5 min.
114 g	4 oz	Brown sugar	
2	2	Eggs	Add eggs and vanilla. Mix until
5 mL	1 t	Vanilla	well blended.
284 g	10 oz	Flour	Add combined dry ingredients
5 mL	1 t	Salt	(low speed).
5 mL	1 t	Soda	
227 g	8 oz	Nuts, chopped	Add nuts and chocolate chips.
340 g	12 oz	Chocolate chips	Mix until blended. Drop on greased baking sheet with No. 60 dipper, ½ oz (14 g) per cookie. Bake.

COCONUT MACAROONS
Bake: 15 min   **Yield: 8 doz**
Oven: 325 °F (165 °C)

Amount		Ingredient	Method
Metric	*U.S.*		
8	8	Egg whites	Beat egg whites and salt (high
⅛ t	⅛ t	Salt	speed) until foamy.
340 g	12 oz	Granulated sugar	Add sugars gradually. Add vanilla.
340 g	12 oz	Powdered sugar	Continue beating (high speed) un-
10 mL	2 t	Vanilla	til stiff.
624 g	1 lb 6 oz	Coconut, shredded	Carefully fold in coconut (low speed). Drop on greased baking sheet with No. 50 dipper, ⅔ oz (19 g) each. Bake.

COCONUT DROP COOKIES
Bake: 15-18 min
Oven: 325 °F (165 °C)

Yield: 4 doz

	Amount		
Metric	*U.S.*	*Ingredient*	*Method*
360 mL	1½ c	Condensed milk, sweetened	Combine all ingredients. Drop on greased baking sheet with No. 60 dipper, ½ oz (14 g) per cookie. Bake.
454 g	1 lb	Coconut, flaked	
15 mL	1 T	Vanilla	
227 g	8 oz	Nuts, chopped	

Bar Cookie Recipes

BROWNIES
Bake: 25-30 min
Oven: 325 °F (165 °C)

Yield: 1 pan 12 × 20 × 2 in.
48 portions 2 × 2½ in.

	Amount		
Metric	*U.S.*	*Ingredient*	*Method*
12	12	Eggs	Beat eggs (high speed).
908 g	2 lb	Sugar	Add sugar, fat, and vanilla. Mix (medium speed) 5 min.
454 g	1 lb	Fat, melted	
60 mL	¼ c	Vanilla	
340 g	12 oz	Cake flour	Add combined dry ingredients. Mix (low speed) about 5 min.
227 g	8 oz	Cocoa	
20 mL	4 t	Baking powder	
10 mL	2 t	Salt	
340 g	12 oz	Nuts, chopped	Add nuts. Mix to blend. Spread mixture ½ in. thick in pan. Bake. Should be soft to the touch when done. Do not over-bake. While warm sprinkle with powdered sugar or cover with a thin layer of mocha or chocolate frosting if desired.

Notes:
1. 3 oz (85 g) unsweetened chocolate may be substituted for the cocoa.
    Add to fat-sugar-egg mixture.
2. 2 lb (908 g) chopped dates may be added.
3. For 18 × 26 in. bun pan, use 1½ times the recipe.

OATMEAL DATE BARS

Bake: 45 min
Oven: 325 °F (165 °C)

Yield: 1 pan 12 × 20 in.
48 bars 2 × 2¼ in.

Amount		Ingredient	Method
Metric	U.S.		
369 g	13 oz	Fat	Cream fat and sugar (medium
624 g	1 lb 6 oz	Brown sugar	speed) 10 min.
454 g	1 lb	Flour	Add combined dry ingredients.
340 g	12 oz	Rolled oats, quick un-cooked	Mix (low speed) until crumbly.
20 mL	4 t	Soda	
1.42 L	1½ qt	Date Filling (p. 188)	Spread ⅔ of dough on greased baking pan. Pat down by hand to an even layer. Spread date filling evenly over entire surface. Cover with remainder of dough and pat down. Bake. Cut into bars.

Notes:
1. Crushed pineapple or cooked dried apricots may be used in place of dates in the filling.
2. For a thinner bar, mixture may be spread in a bun pan 18 × 26 in. Use 1½ times filling recipe.

MARSHMALLOW SQUARES

Yield: 1 pan 12 × 20 in.
48 2 × 2½ in.

Amount		Ingredient	Method
Metric	U.S.		
170 g	6 oz	Butter or margarine	Melt butter or margarine and marshmallows over hot water.
454 g	1 lb	Marshmallows	Add vanilla.
5 mL	1 t	Vanilla	
312 g	11 oz	Rice Krispies	Pour marshmallow mixture over Rice Krispies. Mix well. Press ½-in. layer into greased baking pan. Cool and cut into squares.

Variation:
Chocolate Marshmallow Squares. Cover squares with a thin, rich, chocolate frosting.

BUTTERSCOTCH SQUARES
Bake: 25 min
Oven: 325 °F (165 °C)

Yield: 1 pan 12 × 20 × 2 in.
48 squares 2 × 2½ in.

Metric	U.S.	Ingredient	Method
	Amount		
Metric	*U.S.*	*Ingredient*	*Method*
227 g	8 oz	Butter or mar- garine	Cream butter or margarine and sugar (medium speed) 5 min.
567 g	1 lb 4 oz	Brown sugar	
5	5	Eggs	Add eggs, one at a time, and va- nilla. Mix (low speed) until blended.
10 mL	2 t	Vanilla	
340 g	12 oz	Flour	Add combined dry ingredients. Mix (low speed) until blended.
15 mL	1 T	Baking powder	
3 mL	½ t	Salt	
170 g	6 oz	Nuts, chopped (optional)	Add nuts. Spread mixture evenly in a greased baking pan. Bake.

Note: Use twice as much for an 18 × 26 in. pan.

DATE BARS
Bake: 25-30 min
Oven: 350 °F (175 °C)

Yield: 1 pan 18 × 26 in.
96 bars 2 × 2 in.
128 bars 1 × 3 in.

Metric	U.S.	Ingredient	Method
	Amount		
Metric	*U.S.*	*Ingredient*	*Method*
12	12	Egg yolks	Beat yolks (high speed) until lemon colored. Add sugar gradually and continue beating after each addition.
908 g	2 lb	Sugar	
454 g	1 lb	Flour	Mix flour, salt, and baking pow- der.
3 mL	½ t	Salt	
23 mL	1½ T	Baking powder	Add dates and nuts.
1.36 kg	3 lb	Dates, chopped	Combine with egg-sugar mixture.
454 g	1 lb	Nuts, chopped	
12	12	Egg whites	Beat egg whites (high speed) until they form a soft peak. Fold into batter. Spread evenly in a greased bun pan. Bake. Cut into bars while warm and roll in powdered sugar.

COCONUT PECAN BARS
Bake: 30-35 min
Oven: 350 °F (175 °C)

Amount		Ingredient	Method
Metric	*U.S.*		
680 g	1 lb 8 oz	Butter or margarine	Blend butter or margarine, brown sugar, and flour (low speed) until mixture resembles coarse meal.
340 g	12 oz	Brown sugar	
567 g	1 lb 4 oz	Flour	
			Press even layer of mixture into bun pan.
			Bake until light brown, 15-20 min.
8	8	Eggs, beaten	Combine remaining ingredients to form topping.
114 g	4 oz	Flour	
15 mL	1 T	Baking powder	Spread over baked crust.
10 mL	2 t	Salt	Bake 20-25 min.
227 g	8 oz	Coconut, shredded or flaked	Frost with Orange Frosting (p. 183) if desired.
1.14 kg	2 lb 8 oz	Brown sugar	
15 mL	1 T	Vanilla	
340 g	12 oz	Pecans, chopped	

Rolled, Pressed, and Molded Cookie Recipes

SUGAR COOKIES
Bake: 7 min   **Yield: 7 doz 2-in. cookies**
Oven: 400 °F (205 °C)

Amount		Ingredient	Method
Metric	*U.S.*		
227 g	8 oz	Butter or margarine	Cream butter or margarine and sugar (medium speed) 5 min.
227 g	8 oz	Sugar	
2	2	Eggs	Add eggs and vanilla. Blend (medium speed) 2 min.
10 mL	2 t	Vanilla	
340 g	12 oz	Flour	Add combined dry ingredients. Mix (low speed).
5 mL	1 t	Salt	
5 mL	1 t	Baking powder	Roll dough ⅛ in. thick on board lightly dusted with a mixture of 1 c (240 mL) flour and ½ c (120 mL) sugar. Cut into desired shapes.
			Place on ungreased cookie sheets. Bake.

Note: Cookies also may be shaped with cookie press or may be measured with No. 60 dipper onto baking sheet about 1½ in. apart and flattened to ¼-in. thickness with small can dipped in sugar.

Variations:
1. **Coconut Cookies.** Cut rolled dough with a round cookie cutter. Brush each cookie with melted fat and sprinkle with shredded coconut.

2. **Filled Cookies.** Cut dough with a round cutter. Cover half with Fig or Date Filling (pp. 186, 188). Brush edges with milk, cover with remaining cookies. Press edges together with tines of a fork.

3. **Pinwheel Cookies.** Use half of Sugar Cookie recipe. Divide dough into 2 portions. Add 1 square melted chocolate to 1 portion. Roll each into ⅛-in. sheets the same size. Place the chocolate dough over the white dough and press together. Roll as for Jelly Roll. Chill thoroughly. Cut into thin slices.

4. **Ribbon Cookies.** Cut chocolate and plain dough into long strips 1¾ in. wide. Arrange chocolate and plain strips alternately, until 1¼ in. high. Press together. Chill thoroughly. Cut into thin slices.

5. **Wreath Cookies.** Cut rolled dough with a doughnut cutter. Brush with beaten egg and sprinkle with chopped nuts. For Christmas cookies, decorate with candied cherry rings and pieces of citron arranged to represent holly.

SANDIES
Bake: 20 min   **Yield: 8 doz**
Oven: 325 °F (165 °C)

Amount			
Metric	U.S.	Ingredient	Method
340 g	12 oz	Butter or mar-garine	Cream butter or margarine, sugar, and vanilla (medium speed) 5 min.
85 g	3 oz	Sugar	
5 mL	1 t	Vanilla	
510 g	1 lb 2 oz	Flour	Add flour and salt. Mix (low speed).
5 mL	1 t	Salt	
15 mL	1 T	Water	Add water and pecans.
227 g	8 oz	Pecans, chopped	Chill dough. Shape into small balls ¾ in. in diameter or into bars about 1½ in. long and ½ in. thick. If mixture crumbles so it will not stick together, add a small amount of melted butter or margarine. Place on lightly greased baking sheet. Bake until lightly browned. Roll in powdered sugar while still hot.

CHOCOLATE TEA COOKIES
Bake: 6-10 min   **Yield: 50-75**
Oven: 375 °F (190 °C)

Amount			
Metric	U.S.	Ingredient	Method
227 g	8 oz	Butter or mar-garine	Cream butter or margarine and sugar (medium speed) 5 min.
170 g	6 oz	Sugar	
1	1	Egg	Add egg and vanilla. Blend (medium speed).
10 mL	2 t	Vanilla	
255 g	9 oz	Flour	Add combined dry ingredients. Mix (low speed).
⅛ t	⅛ t	Salt	
½ t	½ t	Baking powder	Chill dough.
30 mL	2 T	Cocoa	Shape with cookie press onto ungreased baking pan. Bake.

BUTTER TEA COOKIES
Bake: 10-12 min   **Yield: 50-75**
Oven: 400 °F (205 °C)

	Amount		
Metric	U.S.	Ingredient	Method
227 g	8 oz	Butter	Cream butter and sugar (medium
128 g	4½ oz	Sugar	speed) 5 min.
3	3	Egg yolks	Add egg yolks and vanilla. Mix
3 mL	½ t	Vanilla	(medium speed) until blended.
284 g	10 oz	Flour	Add flour and mix (low speed). Chill dough. Shape with cookie press onto un-greased baking pan. Bake.

Variation:
Thimble Cookies. Roll dough into 1-in. balls. Dip in egg white and roll in
finely chopped pecans. Bake 3 min at 325 °F (150 °C), then make
indentation in center of cookies and fill with jelly. Bake 10-12 min
longer.

FUDGE BALLS
Bake: 8-10 min   **Yield: 6 doz**
Oven: 350 °F (175 °C)

	Amount		
Metric	U.S.	Ingredient	Method
340 g	12 oz	Flour	Combine flour, sugar, and salt in
454 g	1 lb	Sugar	mixer bowl.
5 mL	1 t	Salt	
340 g	12 oz	Fat, soft	Add fat, chocolate, and coffee.
114 g	4 oz	Chocolate, melted	Mix (medium speed) until smooth.
120 mL	½ c	Coffee, cold	
227 g	8 oz	Rolled oats, quick, un-cooked	Add rolled oats. Mix (low speed) until blended.
170 g	6 oz	Nuts, chopped	Shape dough into balls 1 in. in diameter. Roll in nuts. Place on ungreased baking sheet. Chill before baking.

PEANUT BUTTER COOKIES
Bake: 8 min
Oven: 375 °F (190 °C)

Yield: 5 doz

Amount		Ingredient	Method
Metric	U.S.		
227 g	8 oz	Fat	Cream fat and sugars (medium
227 g	8 oz	Sugar	speed) 5 min.
142 g	5 oz	Brown sugar	
2	2	Eggs	Add eggs and vanilla. Continue
5 mL	1 t	Vanilla	beating until blended.
255 g	9 oz	Peanut butter	Add peanut butter. Blend (low speed).
227 g	8 oz	Flour	Add combined dry ingredients.
5 mL	1 t	Soda	Mix (low speed) until well
3 mL	½ t	Salt	blended.
			Form into balls with No. 50 dipper, ⅔ oz (19 g) each.
			Flatten with tines of a fork or with a glass with damp cloth held over it. Bake.

CRISP GINGER COOKIES
Bake: 8-10 min
Oven: 375 °F (190 °C)

Yield: 8 doz

Amount		Ingredient	Method
Metric	U.S.		
240 mL	1 c	Molasses	Combine molasses and sugar. Boil
227 g	8 oz	Sugar	1 min.
			Cool.
227 g	8 oz	Fat	Add fat and blend (medium speed).
2	2	Eggs	Add eggs and mix well.
794 g	1 lb 12 oz (or more)	Flour	Add combined dry ingredients. Mix (low speed) until well
3 mL	½ t	Salt	blended.
5 mL	1 t	Soda	Form dough into a roll 2 in. in
10 mL	2 t	Ginger	diameter.
			Chill thoroughly and slice. (Dough also may be rolled and cut.)
			Place on greased baking sheet. Bake.

SNICKERDOODLES

Bake: 8-10 min   **Yield: 5 doz**
Oven: 400 °F (205 °C)

Amount		Ingredient	Method
Metric	*U.S.*	*Ingredient*	*Method*
227 g	8 oz	Butter or margarine	Cream butter or margarine and sugar.
340 g	12 oz	Sugar	
2	2	Eggs	Add eggs. Mix well.
312 g	11 oz	Flour	Mix flour, cream of tartar, soda, and salt.
10 mL	2 t	Cream of tartar	
5 mL	1 t	Soda	Add to creamed mixture. Mix.
¼ t	¼ t	Salt	
114 g	4 oz	Sugar	Roll dough into 1-in. balls.
37 g	2½ T	Cinnamon	Roll in mixture of sugar and cinnamon.
			Place 2 in. apart on ungreased baking sheet. Bake until lightly browned but still soft. These cookies puff up at first, then flatten out.

BUTTERSCOTCH ICE BOX COOKIES
Bake: 8-10 min   **Yield: 8 doz**
Oven: 400 °F (205 °C)

Amount		Ingredient	Method
Metric	**U.S.**		
227 g	8 oz	Butter or mar-garine	Cream fats and sugars (medium speed) 5 min.
227 g	8 oz	Fat	
340 g	12 oz	Granulated sugar	
454 g	1 lb	Brown sugar	
4	4	Eggs	Add eggs and vanilla. Mix (medium speed) 5 min.
10 mL	2 t	Vanilla	
908 g	2 lb	Flour	Add combined dry ingredients, dates, and nuts. Mix (low speed) until well blended.
10 mL	2 t	Cream of tartar	
10 mL	2 t	Soda	
227 g	8 oz	Dates, finely chopped	Place dough on waxed paper. Form into 3 2-lb (908-g) rolls. Wrap.
227 g	8 oz	Nuts, chopped	Chill several hours. Slice cookies ⅛ in. thick. Place on ungreased baking pan. Bake.

OATMEAL CRISPIES
Bake: 12-15 min
Oven: 350 °F (175 °C)   **Yield: 8 doz**

Amount			
Metric	U.S.	Ingredient	Method
340 g	12 oz	Flour	Combine flour, salt, and soda in
10 mL	2 t	Salt	mixer bowl.
10 mL	2 t	Soda	
454 g	1 lb	Fat	Add fat, sugars, eggs, and vanilla.
454 g	1 lb	Brown sugar	Mix (low speed) about 5 min.
454 g	1 lb	Granulated sugar	
4	4	Eggs	
10 mL	2 t	Vanilla	
454 g	1 lb	Rolled oats, quick, un-cooked	Add rolled oats and nuts. Mix (low speed) to blend.
227 g	8 oz	Nuts, chopped	Shape dough into rolls 2 in. in diameter. Wrap in waxed paper. Chill overnight. Cut into slices ¼ in. thick. Place 2 in. apart on ungreased baking pan. Bake.

Note: For smaller cookies, form into 1½-in. roll and slice ⅛ in. thick.
Yield: Approximately 25 doz.

Variation:
Oatmeal Coconut Crispies. Add 1 c (240 mL) flaked coconut.

Fish

The number of species of fresh seafood in the local market varies considerably with the location and the season, but it is now possible to buy a wide variety of frozen fish and shellfish the year round. Table 2.4 lists some of the types of fish most used in institution foodservice.

Although inspection for wholesomeness of fresh fish products is not mandatory, as it is for meat and poultry, the U.S. Department of Commerce has developed a voluntary fish inspection program. Fishery products certified under this program carry the USDC inspection stamp, certifying that it was packed under federal inspection, and the Grade A Shield, denoting top quality.

Seafood is perishable and should be handled with great care during storage, thawing, preparation, cooking, and serving. Fresh fish and shellfish should be delivered packed in crushed ice and stored in the refrigerator at 35-40 °F (1-4 °C). Frozen seafood should be delivered hard frozen and stored in the freezer at 0 °F (−18 °C) or below until it is removed for thawing and cooking. Neither fresh nor thawed fish or shellfish should be held longer than 1 day before cooking.

Fresh and Frozen Fish

Market Forms

Fish may be purchased fresh or frozen in many market forms. The most common are: *whole* or *round*, marketed just as they come from the water; *drawn*, entrails only removed; *dressed* or *pan-dressed*, scaled and eviscerated; *steaks*, cross-section slices of the larger types of dressed fish; *fillets*, boneless sides of fish cut lengthwise; *butterfly fillets*, two sides of fish corresponding to two single fillets held together by uncut flesh; *fish sticks*, pieces of fish from fillet blocks cut into uniform sticks weighing up to 1½ oz (43 g); and *portions*, cut from frozen fish blocks into uniform portions weighing between 1½ and 6 oz (43 and 170 g). Many kinds of fish are available in breaded ready-to-cook and precooked forms.

The cost per edible pound in terms of both convenience and waste should be considered when deciding which form of fish to buy. Whole or round fish yield about 50% edible flesh after being eviscerated, scaled, and the head, tail, and fins removed; dressed fish yield 70%; steaks 90%; and fillets, sticks, and portions 100%. *Breaded* fish should contain at least 50% fish, *lightly breaded*, 65% fish.

Thawing Frozen Fish

Frozen fish should be thawed in the refrigerator just prior to cooking. The thawing time will vary with the size and shape of the fish or package. Thawing time may be shortened by placing the wrapped packages under cold running water. Fish portions and fish sticks should *not* be thawed before cooking. Frozen fillets and steaks may be cooked without thawing if additional cooking time is allowed. Fillets or steaks to be breaded or stuffed should be thawed.

Cooking Methods

Fish by nature is tender and free of tough fibers that need to be softened by cooking and should be cooked only until the fish flakes easily when tested with a fork. Fish may be cooked in many ways, but the best method is determined by size, fat content, and flavor. Baking and broiling are suitable for fat fish, such as salmon, trout, and mackerel. Their natural fat content keeps them from becoming dry when cooked. If lean fish is baked or broiled, fat is added to prevent dryness, and it often is baked in a sauce. Lean fish are less likely to fall apart when poached or steamed than are fat fish. Fish cooked in moist heat requires very little cooking time and usually is served with a sauce. Frying is suitable for all types, but those with firm flesh that will not break apart easily are best for deep-fat frying. Table 2.4 suggests cooking methods for specific types of fish. Table 2.5 lists cooking times and temperatures.

Baking.   Dip fish steaks or fillets in melted fat, then in flour. Season with salt and pepper. Place a thin slice of lemon on each piece. Bake at 450 °F (230 °C) until lightly brown and tender, 20-25 min. Sprinkle with paprika or chopped parsley before serving.

Broiling.   Wipe fish fillets or steaks as dry as possible. Brush both sides with oil or melted butter or margarine. Season with salt and pepper and sprinkle with paprika. Lay fish on a pan covered with aluminum foil. Thick pieces of fish should be placed further from the flame than thinner pieces. Broil, turning skin side up just long enough to crisp and brown. Serve with lemon, melted butter, and chopped parsley.

Frying.   Use small whole fish, fillets, or steaks. To panfry, season with salt and pepper, roll in flour or cornmeal or a combination of both, and cook in a small amount of fat. Dip in egg and crumbs (p. 75) if fish is to be fried in deep fat. Fry 4-6 min at 375°F (190 °C). Fried fish should be served at once, while crisp. If it must be held, arrange fish in counter pans and place uncovered in 250 °F (121 °C) oven until serving time. To oven fry, dip fish fillets, steaks, or small pan-dressed fish in salted milk, drain, and coat with fine dry bread crumbs. Place in shallow well-greased pans. Pour melted fat or oil over fish. Bake at 500 °F (260 °C) 10-15 min.

Poaching or Steaming.   Place fillets or thick slices of fish in a flat baking pan and cover with liquid. This may be acidulated water, court bouillon, fish stock, milk, or milk and water. Cover with parchment or oiled paper. Cook in a moderate oven (350 °F/175 °C) or in a steamer until fish loses its transparent appearance or until bones may be removed easily. Drain. Allow about 10 min per pound for cooking whole fish or 10 min for cooking fillets cut 4 to the pound. Avoid overcooking. Serve with a sauce.

ACIDULATED WATER
Use 1 T (15 mL) salt and 3 T (45 mL) lemon juice or vinegar for each quart (0.95 L) of water.

COURT BOUILLON
Add to 1 gal (3.79 L) of water ¾ c (180 mL) each of chopped carrots, chopped onions, and chopped celery; 3 T (45 mL) salt, ½ c (120 mL) vinegar, 2 or 3 bay leaves, 6 peppercorns, 9 cloves, and 3 T (45 mL) butter or margarine. Boil gently for 20-30 min. Strain to remove spices and vegetables.

Table 2.4 FISH BUYING AND COOKING GUIDE[a]

Species	Fat or Lean	Usual Market Forms	Cooking Methods
Bass, sea	Lean	Fillets, steaks; whole pan-dressed	Fry, broil, bake
Butterfish	Fat	Whole, dressed, pan-dressed	Bake, poach, steam
Catfish	Lean	Whole, dressed; fillets	Fry
Cod	Lean	Fillets, steaks; breaded and precooked sticks, portions, sandwich squares	Bake, fry, broil
Flounder	Lean	Whole, pan-dressed; fillets; breaded and precooked portions	Fry, bake, broil
Grouper	Lean	Whole, steaks, fillets	Fry, bake, steam
Haddock	Lean	Whole, steaks, fillets; breaded and precooked sticks and portions	Bake, fry, steam
Halibut	Lean	Drawn, dressed, steaks	Broil, bake, fry
Mackerel	Fat	Whole, drawn; fillets	Broil, bake, poach, fry
Pike	Lean	Whole, dressed; fillets	Fry, bake
Perch	Lean	Whole, pan-dressed; fillets; breaded fillets and portions	Panfry, bake, deep-fat fry
Pollack	Lean	Fillets; breaded and precooked sticks and portions	Fry, broil, bake
Rockfish	Lean	Whole, dressed; fillets	Fry, broil, bake
Salmon	Fat	Dressed, steaks, fillets	Bake, poach, broil, panfry
Shad	Fat	Whole, drawn, fillets	Bake, poach, broil, fry
Smelt	Lean	Whole, dressed; breaded and precooked	Panfry, bake
Snapper, Red	Lean	Dressed, fillets, portions	Bake, fry, broil
Sole	Lean	Whole, fillets	Bake, fry, broil, poach
Swordfish	Lean	Dressed, steaks	Broil, bake, poach
Trout, lake	Fat	Whole, drawn, fillets	Bake, poach, panfry
Trout, Rainbow	Lean	Whole, dressed; boned and breaded fillets	Panfry, oven fry, broil, bake
Whitefish	Fat	Whole, drawn, dressed, fillets	Bake, broil, poach
Whiting	Lean	Drawn, skinned; breaded and precooked portions and fillets	Deep-fat fry, broil, sauté, steam

[a] From National Marine Fisheries Services, U.S. Department of Commerce.

Table 2.5 SUGGESTED METHODS OF COOKING FISH AND SHELLFISH[a]

Species	Approximate Weight[b] or Thickness	Baking Temperature[c]	Baking Min	Broiling Distance from Heat	Broiling Min	Boiling, Poaching or Steaming Method	Boiling, Poaching or Steaming Min	Deep-Fat Frying Temperature	Deep-Fat Frying Min	Panfrying Temperature	Panfrying Min
Fish											
Dressed	3–4 lb	350 °F	40–60			Poach	10 per lb	325–350 °F	4–6		
Pan-dressed	½–1 lb	350 °F	25–30	3 in.	10–15	Poach	10	350–375 °F	2–4	Moderate	10–15
Steaks	½–1¼ in.	350 °F	25–35	3 in.	10–15	Poach	10	350–375 °F	2–4	Moderate	10–15
Fillets		350 °F	25–35	3 in.	8–15	Poach	10	350–375 °F	2–4	Moderate	8–10
Portions	1–6 oz	350 °F	30–40					350 °F	4	Moderate	8–10
Sticks	¾–1¼ oz	400 °F	15–20					350 °F	3	Moderate	8–10
Shellfish											
Clams—live, shucked		450 °F	12–15	4 in.	5–8	Steam	5–10	350 °F	2–3	Moderate	4–5
Crabs—live, soft-shell				4 in.	8–10	Boil	10–15	375 °F	2–4	Moderate	8–10
Lobsters—live	¾–1 lb	400 °F	15–20	4 in.	12–15	Boil	15–20	350 °F	2–4	Moderate	8–10
Spiny lobster tails—frozen	¼–½ lb	450 °F	20–30	4 in.	8–12	Boil	10–15	350 °F	3–5	Moderate	8–10
Oysters—live, shucked		450 °F	12–15	4 in.	5–8	Steam	5–10	350 °F	2–3	Moderate	4–5
Scallops—shucked		350 °F	25–30	3 in.	6–8	Boil	3–4	350 °F	2–3	Moderate	4–6
Shrimp—											
Headless, raw						Boil	3–5				
Headless, raw, peeled		350 °F	20–25	3 in.	8–10	Boil	3–5	350 °F	2–3	Moderate	8–10

[a] From *How to Eye and Buy Seafood*, National Marine Fisheries Service, U.S. Department of Commerce, 1970.
[b] Metric weight equivalents: see p. 28.
[c] Metric temperature equivalents: see p. 73.

Shellfish

Among the common varieties of shellfish used as food are clams, oysters and scallops, and the crustaceans, crab, lobsters, and shrimp. These may be purchased fresh, frozen, and canned, in various forms (Table 2.6). Shrimp and crab are now freeze-dried.

Clams

Clams may be purchased alive in the shell, shucked, and canned. Shucked clams are marketed fresh or frozen in gallons and in No. 10 cans as whole, minced, or made into chowder. Frozen fresh clam strips are available for deep-fat frying.

Crabs

Crabs may be purchased alive, cooked in the shell, or as chilled, frozen, canned, or freeze-dried crab meat. Soft-shelled crab usually are parboiled, dipped in egg and crumbs (p. 75), panfried or cooked in deep fat. Cooked hard-shelled crabs are chilled, the shells broken apart, and the meat removed to be used in cooked dishes or salads. One 2-lb (908-g) crab yields about ¾ lb (340 g) cooked body and leg meat.

Lobsters

Lobsters may be purchased alive in the shell; frozen; fresh-cooked, chilled, canned, and frozen lobster meat; and frozen lobster tails. To prepare frozen lobster tails, follow instructions on the package. Lobster meat, frozen or canned, may be used for salads and in cooked dishes. Live lobsters only are broiled or boiled.

Oysters

Oysters are available in many markets in the shell, fresh and frozen, shucked, and canned. Shucked oysters are in far greater demand in institution foodservices than those in the shell. Eastern oysters are designated as small, selects, extra selects, and counts, according to the number of meats to the gallon. Because oysters are grown in water that may easily be contaminated and because they frequently are eaten raw, they are subject to strict sanitary inspection by the Public Health Service. After they are purchased, they should be held at freezing temperatures no longer than 10 days before use.

Oysters are not ordinarily washed before using. If washing seems necessary, care should be taken to remove the oysters from the water quickly, so that they do not become soaked or waterlogged. They should be inspected and any bits of shell removed. When making oyster stew (p. 492), add butter to oysters and heat only until edges begin to curl, then add to hot milk. Serve at once. To fry, dip oysters in egg and crumbs (p. 75) before frying.

Table 2.6 GUIDE TO PURCHASING SHELLFISH[a]

Fish	Count or Weight per Unit of Measure	Usual Market Form	Purchase Unit
Clams, hard-shell	80 per bushel	In shell, live	Per 100 or bu
	100-125 per gal	Shucked, fresh or frozen	Per gal or lb
Clams, soft-shell	45 per bushel	In shell, live	Per 100 or bu
	350-500 per gal	Shucked	Per 100 or bu
Crabs, all kinds	4 oz-20 lb (varies with kind)	Live, frozen, or fresh-cooked	Per lb or doz
Crabmeat, cooked, E.P.			
Blue	1-lb tins	Fresh or frozen	Per lb
Dungeness	5-lb tins	Fresh or frozen	Per lb
King	1- and 5-lb cartons	Frozen	Per lb
Lobster	1¼-2 lb each	Whole, live	Per lb
Lobster tails, Australian or South African	5-24 oz each	In shell Frozen raw	Per lb
Oysters (Eastern)			
Counts	160 or less per gal	Shucked, fresh or frozen	Per gal
Extra select	161-210 per gal		
Select	211-300 per gal		
Standard	301-500 per gal		
Shell oysters			
Half shell	800-900 per barrel	Live	Per 100 or barrel
Contuit	600-700 per barrel		
Scallops, bay	150-200 per gal	Fresh or frozen	Per lb or gal
Deep-sea	18-25 per gal (8 lb per gal)		
Shrimp, in shell, headless	Under 15 per lb	Frozen raw	Per lb
Jumbo	15-20 per lb		
Large	21-25 per lb		
Large-medium	26-30 per lb		
Medium	31-42 per lb		
Shrimp, peeled and deveined			
Jumbo	15-20 per lb	Frozen raw	Per lb
Large	21-25 per lb		
Large-medium	26-30 per lb		
Medium	30-50 per lb		

Table 2.6 GUIDE TO PURCHASING SHELLFISH[a] (continued)

Fish	Count or Weight per Unit of Measure	Usual Market Form	Purchase Unit
Shrimp, cooked, peeled, and deveined			
Jumbo	35-40 per lb	Fresh or frozen	Per lb
Large	40-50 per lb		
Medium	50-60 per lb		
Shrimp, breaded	15-20 per lb	Frozen raw	Per lb
Fantail or round	21-25 per lb		

[a] Adapted from *Fresh and Frozen Fish Buying Manual,* Fish and Wildlife Service, Circular No. 20, United States Department of the Interior, Washington, D.C.

Scallops

The adductor muscle or "eye" that holds together the shells of the scallop is removed, cut into pieces, and marketed fresh or frozen in gallon containers. The large, deep-sea scallops weigh 8 lb to a gallon and have a count of 110 to 170. Scallops also may be purchased breaded and ready-to-cook. To prepare fresh scallops, wash and remove any particles of shell. Drain. Dip in egg and crumbs (p. 75). Fry in deep fat at 350 °F (175 °C) 2-3 min.

Shrimp

Shrimp are marketed headless; peeled and deveined; cooked in the shell; cooked, peeled, and deveined; and breaded; they are available fresh, frozen, canned, and freeze-dried. They are graded according to the number per pound and usually are designated as jumbo, large, medium, or small. Shrimp also are marketed as broken, imperfect pieces for use in salads or mixed dishes where shape is unimportant. Two pounds (908 g) of raw shrimp in the shells will yield about 1 lb (454 g) cooked, shelled, and deveined meat; about 1¼ lb (567 g) cooked shrimp in the shells are needed to yield 1 lb (454 g) of shelled meat. One No. 10 can of freeze-dried shrimp weighs 13¼ oz (370 g) and is the equivalent of 7 lb (3.18 kg) of raw, green, headless shrimp.

Raw or green shrimp should be washed carefully. Cover with water and bring to a boil. Let simmer 3 min in water to which has been added 1½ t salt to each quart, 2 bay leaves, and mixed spice. Drain. Remove shell and dark vein from the center back of each shrimp. To fry, dip peeled and cleaned raw or cooked shrimp in batter, or egg and crumb (p. 75). Fry in deep fat 3-5 min at 350-365 °F (175-182 °C). Breaded frozen shrimp may be cooked from their hard-frozen state.

Fish Recipes

BAKED FISH FLLETS

Bake: 30 min
Oven: 350 °F (175 °C)

Yield: 50 portions
Portion: 5 oz (142 g)

Amount		Ingredient	Method
Metric	U.S.		
7.26 kg	16 lb	Fish fillets	Cut fish into 50 portions.
454 g	1 lb	Butter or margarine, melted	Dip fillets in butter or margarine.
794 g	1 lb 12 oz	Bread crumbs	Combine bread crumbs, flour, and
284 g	10 oz	Flour	seasonings.
15 mL	1 T	Salt	Dredge fish with mixture and place
23 mL	1½ T	Paprika	on greased baking sheets or
15 mL	1 T	Seasoned salt	counter pans.
5 mL	1 t	Marjoram	Bake.
5 mL	1 t	Lemon peel	

Note: Fish portions or steaks may be substituted for fish fillets.

LEMON BAKED FISH

Bake: 25 min
Oven: 350 °F (175 °C)

Yield: 50 portions
Portion: 5 oz (142 g)

Amount		Ingredient	Method
Metric	U.S.		
50	50	Fish fillets or steaks, cut 3 per lb	Mix fat, salt, pepper, and lemon juice.
454 g	1 lb	Fat, melted	Dip each portion into seasoned fat.
15 mL	1 T	Salt	
5 mL	1 t	Pepper, white	
120 mL	½ c	Lemon juice	
397 g	14 oz	Flour	Dredge fish with flour. Place close together in single layer in greased baking pans.
57 g	2 oz	Butter or margarine, melted	Mix butter or margarine and milk and pour over fish. Bake.
180 mL	¾ c	Milk	

FILLET OF SOLE AMANDINE

Bake: 15-20 min
Oven: 350 °F (175 °C)

Yield: 50 portions
Portion: 5 oz (142 g)

Amount		Ingredient	Method
Metric	*U.S.*	*Ingredient*	*Method*
7.71 kg	17 lb	Fillet of sole, unbreaded	Cut fish into 50 portions.
227 g	8 oz	Flour	Dredge fish in combined flour,
15 mL	1 T	Salt	salt, and pepper.
5 mL	1 t	Pepper	Place in greased counter pans.
680 g	1 lb 8 oz	Butter or margarine	Sauté onion and garlic in butter or margarine.
114 g	4 oz	Onion, finely chopped	
1	1	Garlic clove, minced	
480 mL	2 c	Water	Combine water, lemon juice, salt,
360 mL	1½ c	Lemon juice	and pepper.
15 mL	1 T	Salt	Add onion and garlic.
5 mL	1 t	Pepper	Heat. Do not boil.
			Just before baking, pour sauce over fish, 1 c (240 mL) per pan.
227 g	8 oz	Almonds, slivered	Sprinkle almonds over fish. Bake.

DEVILED CRAB

Bake: 15 min
Oven: 400 °F (205 °C)

Yield: 50 portions
Portion: 3 oz (85 g)

Metric	U.S.	Ingredient	Method
2.27-2.72 kg	5-6 lb	Crab meat	Separate crab meat into flakes.
60 mL	4 T	Lemon juice	Combine lemon juice, eggs, and seasonings.
23 mL	1½ T	Salt	Add to crab meat. Mix lightly.
10 mL	2 t	Pepper	
f.g.	f.g.	Cayenne	
5	5	Eggs, beaten	
15 mL	1 T	Worcestershire sauce	
30 mL	2 T	Onion juice (optional)	
340 g	12 oz	Butter or margarine	Make Thick White Sauce (p. 458) of butter, flour, and milk.
227 g	8 oz	Flour	Add mustard.
1.89 L	2 qt	Milk	Combine sauce and crab mixture. Mix lightly.
8 mL	1½ t	Mustard, prepared	Fill individual casseroles or shells.
227 g	8 oz	Bread crumbs	Sprinkle with buttered crumbs. Bake.
114 g	4 oz	Butter or margarine, melted	

Note: Croquettes may be made from this mixture.

CREOLE SHRIMP WITH RICE

Yield: 50 portions
Portion: 3 oz (85 g) Creole shrimp
4 oz (114 g) rice

Metric	U.S.	Ingredient	Method
85 g	3 oz	Fat	Brown onion and celery in fat.
170 g	6 oz	Onion, chopped fine	
340 g	12 oz	Celery, chopped fine	
45 mL	3 T	Flour	Add flour, salt, and water. Mix until smooth.
23 mL	1½ T	Salt	
480 mL	2 c	Water	Cook 15 min.
1.42 L	1½ qt	Tomatoes	Add tomatoes, vinegar, and sugar.
90 mL	6 T	Vinegar	
30 mL	2 T	Sugar	
2.27-2.72 g	5-6 lb (E.P.)	Shrimp, cooked, peeled, and deveined	Add shrimp to sauce. Heat to serving temperature.
2.04 kg	4 lb 8 oz	Rice	Cook rice (p. 190).
5.44 L	5¾ qt	Water, boiling	Serve shrimp with No. 12 dipper, over No. 8-dipper rice.
45 mL	3 T	Salt	
45 mL	3 T	Fat or oil	

Note: If raw shrimp are used, purchase 12-14 lb (5.44-6.35 kg). Cook as directed on p. 239.

SCALLOPED OYSTERS

Bake: 30 min　　　　　　　　　　　　　　　　**Yield: 2 pans 12 × 20 × 2 in.**
Oven: 400 °F (205 °C)　　　　　　　　　　　　　　　　**Portion: 5 oz (142 g)**

Amount		Ingredient	Method
Metric	U.S.		
5.68 L	6 qt	Oysters	Drain oysters, saving liquor. Remove any bits of shell.
2.84 L	3 qt	Cracker crumbs	Mix crumbs, butter, and seasonings.
454 g	1 lb	Butter or margarine, melted	
23 mL	1½ T	Salt	Spread a third over bottoms of 2 greased baking pans.
3 mL	½ t	Paprika	Cover with half of the oysters; repeat with crumbs and oysters.
3 mL	½ t	Pepper	
0.95 L	1 qt	Milk or cream	Mix milk or cream and oyster liquor. Pour over top of oysters.
720 mL	3 c	Oyster liquor (or milk)	Cover with remaining crumbs. Bake.

Note: 2 c (480 mL) finely chopped, partially cooked celery may be added.

SALMON LOAF

Bake: 1¼ hr　　　　　　　　　　　　　　　　**Yield: 5 loaves 4 × 9 in.**
Oven: 325 °F (165 °C)　　　　　　　　　　　　　　　　**Portion: 3½ oz (100 g)**

Amount		Ingredient	Method
Metric	U.S.		
720 mL	3 c	Milk, scalded	Mix milk and bread cubes.
454 g	1 lb	Bread cubes, soft	
3.63 kg	8 lb	Salmon, flaked	Add salmon and other ingredients.
23 mL	1½ T	Salt	
5 mL	1 t	Paprika	Mix lightly.
2	2	Lemon rinds, grated	Place in 5 greased loaf pans. Set pans in hot water to bake.
120 mL	½ c	Lemon juice	
15	15	Eggs, beaten	

Note: For a lighter-textured product, beat egg whites separately and fold into salmon mixture.

SALMON CROQUETTES
Fry: 4 min   **Yield: 100**
Deep-fat fryer: 375 °F (190 °C)   Portion: 2 2½-oz (70-g) croquettes

Amount		Ingredient	Method
Metric	*U.S.*	*Ingredient*	*Method*
340 g	12 oz	Butter or mar- garine	Make into Thick White Sauce (p. 458).
255 g	9 oz	Flour	Cool.
5 mL	1 t	Salt	
1.42 L	1½ qt	Milk	
3.63 kg	8 lb	Salmon	Remove skin and bones from salmon. Flake and add to white sauce.
170 g	6 oz	Cornflakes	Add cornflakes, onion juice, and pimiento to salmon mixture.
45 mL	3 T	Onion juice	Mix carefully.
198 g	7 oz	Pimiento, chopped	Measure with No. 30 dipper onto a greased baking sheet. Chill. Shape croquettes cylindrically.
8	8	Eggs, beaten	Dip croquettes in egg and milk mixture. Roll in crumbs.
480 mL	2 c	Milk or water	Fry in deep fat.
680 g	1 lb 8 oz	Bread crumbs	Serve with Egg Sauce (p. 459).

Note: The croquettes may be baked about 30 min in a 400 °F (205 °C) oven.

Variation:
Salmon Patties. Measure with No. 16 dipper and shape into 50 patties. Bake or panfry in a small amount of fat.

SCALLOPED SALMON

Bake: 25 min
Oven: 375 °F (190 °C)

Yield: 2 pans 12 × 20 × 2 in.
Portion: 4 oz (114 g)

Amount		Ingredient	Method
Metric	U.S.		
454 g	1 lb	Butter or margarine	Make into Medium White Sauce (p. 458).
340 g	12 oz	Flour	
23 mL	1½ T	Salt	
3 mL	½ t	Pepper	
3.79 L	1 gal	Milk	
60 mL	¼ c	Parsley, chopped	Add parsley, onion juice, and celery salt.
10 mL	2 t	Onion juice	
5 mL	1 t	Celery salt	
4.54 kg	10 lb	Salmon, flaked	Arrange salmon, sauce, and crumbs in layers in 2 baking pans.
227 g	8 oz	Bread crumbs	
114 g	4 oz	Crumbs	Sprinkle buttered crumbs over top. Bake.
114 g	4 oz	Butter or margarine, melted	Serve with No. 10 dipper.

Note: Diced hard-cooked eggs and frozen peas are good additions.

Variation:
Scalloped Tuna. Substitute tuna for salmon.

TANGY TOPPED SALMON
Bake: 30 min, 10 min
Oven: 350 °F (175 °C)

Yield: 2 pans 12 × 20 × 2 in.
Portion: 6 oz (170 g)

Amount		Ingredient	Method
Metric	*U.S.*	*Ingredient*	*Method*
720 mL	3 c	Cultured sour cream	Place sour cream, milk, and eggs in mixer bowl.
0.95 L	1 qt	Milk	Beat (medium speed) until combined.
15	15	Eggs	
454 g	1 lb	Croutons, herb seasoned	Add croutons to sour cream mixture. Let stand 10 min until croutons are softened. Beat again until mixture is smooth.
3.63 kg	8 lb	Salmon, red, canned	Drain salmon; remove skin and bones.
170 g	6 oz	Onions, finely chopped	Add salmon, onions, lemon juice, salt, and pepper to crouton mixture.
227 g	8 oz	Celery, finely chopped	Portion into 2 greased baking pans.
120 mL	½ c	Lemon juice	Bake 20 min, or until knife inserted in center comes out clean.
30 mL	2 T	Salt	
5 mL	1 t	Pepper	
1.89 L	2 qt	Mayonnaise	While salmon mixture bakes, mix mayonnaise and mustard.
120 mL	½ c	Prepared mustard	
240 mL	1 c	Egg whites	Beat egg whites until stiff. Fold in mayonnaise mixture. Spread on salmon. Return to oven and continue baking for 10-15 min, or until topping is slightly browned.
240 mL	1 c	Parsley flakes	Sprinkle with parsley. Cut into squares.

SALMON AND POTATO CHIP CASSEROLE

Bake: 20 min
Oven: 375 °F (190 °C)

Yield: 2 pans 12 × 20 × 2 in.
or 50 casseroles
Portion: 5 oz (142 g)

Amount		Ingredient	Method
Metric	U.S.		
227 g	8 oz	Butter or margarine	Melt butter or margarine, add flour, and stir until blended.
142 g	5 oz	Flour	Add soup and cook until mixture
2 1.42-kg cans)	2 50-oz cans	Cream of mushroom soup	is thickened.
3.63 kg	8 lb	Salmon, flaked	Arrange salmon, potato chips, and
1.14 kg	2 lb 8 oz	Potato chips, coarsely crushed	sauce in layers in casseroles or in 2 baking pans. Bake.

Variation:

Tuna and Potato Chip Casserole. Substitute tuna for salmon.

TUNA AND NOODLES

Bake: 45 min
Oven: 350 °F (175 °C)

Yield: 2 pans 12 × 20 × 2 in.
Portion: 5 oz (142 g)

Amount		Ingredient	Method
Metric	U.S.		
908 g	2 lb	Noodles	Cook noodles until tender (p. 191).
5.68 L	1½ gal	Water, boiling	Drain.
30 mL	2 T	Salt	
30 mL	2 T	Oil (optional)	
2.27 kg	5 lb	Tuna	Flake tuna and add to noodles.
227 g	8 oz	Butter or margarine	Make into Medium White Sauce (p. 458).
114 g	4 oz	Flour	Add to tuna and noodles.
23 mL	1½ T	Salt	Divide into 2 greased baking pans.
1.89 L	2 qt	Milk	Bake 30 min.
454 g	1 lb	Cheese, grated	Sprinkle cheese over the noodles. Bake 15 min longer.

Variation:

Tuna and Rice. Substitute rice for the noodles.

CREAMED TUNA

Yield: 7½ qt (7.10 L)
Portion: 4 oz (114 g)

Amount		Ingredient	Method
Metric	*U.S.*		
340 g	12 oz	Butter or margarine	Make into Medium White Sauce (p. 458).
170 g	6 oz	Flour	
3.79 L	1 gal	Milk	
90 mL	6 T	Worcestershire sauce (optional)	Add remaining ingredients. Mix.
¼ t	¼ t	Cayenne	
15 mL	1 T	Salt	
9	9	Eggs, hard-cooked, chopped	
170 g	6 oz	Green pepper, chopped	
170 g	6 oz	Pimiento, chopped	
2.27 kg	5 lb	Tuna, flaked	When ready to serve, add flaked tuna to the sauce and reheat. Serve with 4-oz ladle on toast or biscuits.

Note: Other cooked fish may be substituted for tuna.

Variations:

1. **Creamed Tuna and Celery.** Substitute 1 lb (454 g) diced cooked celery for an equal amount of tuna.

2. **Tuna Rarebit.** Use 4 lb (1.81 kg) tuna; add 1½ lb (680 g) shredded cheese.

3. **Creamed Salmon.** Substitute salmon for tuna.

4. **Creamed Tuna and Peas.** Add 3 lb (1.36 kg) frozen peas, cooked until just tender and drained.

TUNA-CASHEW CASSEROLE

Bake: 30-40 min
Oven: 350 °F (175 °C)

Yield: 2 pans 12 × 20 × 2 in.
Portion: 5 oz (142 g)

Amount		Ingredient	Method
Metric	*U.S.*		
3.63 kg	8 lb	Tuna, flaked	Arrange ingredients in layers in 2
170 g	6 oz	Onion, finely chopped	greased baking pans, with noodles as top layer. Bake.
227 g	8 oz	Celery, diced	
680 g	1 lb 8 oz	Cashews	
2 1.42-kg cans)	2 50-oz cans	Cream of mushroom soup	
1 No. 10 can	1 No. 10 can	Chinese noodles	

Variation:
Chicken-Cashew Casserole. Substitute diced cooked chicken for tuna.

Garnishes for Fish

1. Parsley, chopped or sprig.

2. Lemon wedges, plain or with edges dipped in paprika or chopped parsley.

3. Thin slices of lemon or orange, plain or notched.

4. Small lettuce cup filled with cole slaw or cranberry sauce.

5. Small green pepper cups with tartar sauce.

6. Black, green, or stuffed olives and a bit of salad green.

7. Celery hearts or celery curls and radish roses.

8. Carrot curls or strips, onion ring, green onions, or pickled onions.

9. Tomato slices, wedges, or small whole cherry tomato and parsley sprig.

10. Cucumber slices, peeled and fluted, or unpeeled and accented with pimiento strips.

11. Slices of hard-cooked egg, chopped egg, riced egg yolk, or ½ stuffed egg.

12. Latticed pickled beets.

13. Lemon butter balls. Mint leaves.

14. Sautéed button mushrooms.

15. Toasted croutons.

16. Spiced whole apricot or crabapple.

17. Shredded toasted almonds.

18. Sprig of frosted white grapes or sprigs of green or red grapes.

19. Tartar Sauce (p. 471).

Meat

The quality of cooked meat will depend on the quality purchased, the storage and handling of meat after delivery, and cooking methods. All meats marketed in interstate commerce must meet federal inspection standards for wholesomeness. This includes all processed meat products and fresh and frozen meats. Meat slaughtered, processed, and sold within a given state may not necessarily be federally inspected, but would be subject to state inspection.

Federal grading is on a voluntary basis. Federal and packer brand grades of meat are based on quality of the flesh and the degree of marbling and fat cover. Beef and lamb, when federally graded, also must be given a yield grade that measures the amount of lean meat that can be cut from a carcass.

Purchasing and Storing Meat

Meat for institutional foodservice is available in carcass, wholesale cuts, fabricated roasts, and portion-ready items. The form in which meat is purchased depends on the policies and size of the institution, the type of service it offers, and its storage and meat-cutting facilities. Fabricated and portion-ready cuts require less storage space, eliminate skilled labor for cutting, and do away with waste. Costs are easily controlled, since the weight and price of each portion are predetermined and only the amount needed is ordered.

Fresh meat may be stored unwrapped or loosely covered with wax paper on trays or hung on hooks at a temperature of 35-40 °F (1-4 °C), with relative humidity 80-90%. It should be used as soon after purchase as possible. The temperature should not fall below freezing, unless frozen meat is being stored.

Frozen meat requires a uniform holding temperature of 0 °F (−18 °C) or below. It should be well-wrapped to exclude air and to prevent drying. If the meat is to be frozen on the premises, the temperature should be even lower, with some air movement. If possible, meat should be frozen in a blast freezer set at −20 to −40 °F (−29 to −40 °C) with forced air convection.

Frozen meat should not be unwrapped before defrosting in the refrigerator at 30 to 35 °F (−1 to 1 °C). It is not necessary to defrost meat cuts before cooking, with the exception of steaks and chops that are to be coated for frying or baking.

Meat should be cooked soon after defrosting. Once thawed, it should not be refrozen unless in an emergency and then there will be some sacrifice in juiciness. Cooked meat may be frozen provided it is frozen immediately after cooking and cooling.

Cured, and cured and smoked, meats such as ham and bacon, sausages, and dried beef require refrigerator storage. The limited keeping qualities of ham cannot be overemphasized. The two principal types of ham used in institution food-services are:

1. **Cook-before-eating ham.** Partially cooked in processing and must be kept under refrigeration.

2. **Fully cooked ham.** Cooked sufficiently so that it may be served without further cooking or may be heated just enough to serve hot. Fully cooked hams require storage at refrigerator temperature before and after heating. Most canned hams, which are also fully cooked, require refrigeration.

Commercially processed hams indicate on the label which type they are or to what degree they have been cooked. Although ham, bacon, and other cured meats can be frozen, it should be only for short periods, since undesirable flavor changes occur because of the salt and spices in them.

Cooking Methods

Meat is cooked either by dry or moist heat. The method used will depend on the grade and location of the cut. Tender cuts of high-grade meat are usually cooked by dry heat (roasted, broiled, or fried). Moist heat (braised or cooked in liquid) is used for less tender cuts from the upper grades and for all lower-grade cuts. There are exceptions to this rule, however. Veal, lamb, and pork, all tender meats, are often cooked with moist heat to develop their flavor and to provide variety in menu items. Veal, because of its delicate flavor and low fat content, combines well with sauces and other foods. Dry-heat cookery does not improve tenderness and, under some conditions, it reduces it. Cooking with moist heat tends to make meat tender. A low temperature, regardless of the method, is desirable. The degree of doneness affects losses. The percentage loss is smaller in rare meat than in medium- or well-done meat, provided other factors are the same.

Roasting

In roasting, which is a dry-heat method, meat is cooked in an oven, in an open pan, with no moisture added. Meat cuts must be tender to be roasted. In beef these are the less-used muscles, or those attached to the backbone. In veal, pork, and lamb practically any cut may be cooked by this method.

Meats may be completely or partially defrosted or frozen at the time the cooking process is begun. Research has shown that meat roasted from the frozen state will yield as much meat as roasts partially or completely thawed before cooking. However, when time is a factor, as it is in a foodservice, defrosting meat before cooking is usually the accepted method. The additional cooking time required for frozen roasts is from ⅓ to ½ again the amount of time recommended for cooking a similar cut from the chilled state. Steps in roasting are:

1. Place the meat, fat side up, on a rack, in an open roasting pan.

2. Insert a meat thermometer in the roast so that the bulb rests in the center of the cut, but not in contact with bone or pocket of fat. If the meat is frozen, the thermometer is inserted toward the end of the cooking period after the meat has thawed.

3. Season the roast with salt and pepper or other spices if desired. Salt penetrates less than an inch during cooking, so it may make little difference whether the roast is seasoned at the beginning, during, or end of cooking.

4. Do not add water and do not cover. If water is added to the pan, the cooking will be by moist heat.

5. Roast at a constant low oven temperature, 250-350 °F (121-175 °C), depending on the kind of meat and the size of the roast. If cooking in a convection oven, the temperature should be reduced by 50 °F (10 °C) to minimize drying of the surface of the roast by moving air. Searing the roast initially at a high temperature does not hold in meat juices and may increase cooking losses. A constant low temperature reduces shrinkage and produces a more evenly done roast that is easier to carve and more attractive to serve.

6. Roast to the desired degree of doneness. The length of the cooking period depends on several factors: oven temperature, size and shape of roast, style of cut (boned or bone in), oven load, quality of meat, and degree of doneness desired. Approximate cooking times and temperatures are given in Tables 2.7, 2.8, and 2.9. Although approximate total cooking time can be used as a general guide, the interior temperature of the meat as measured by a meat thermometer is a more reliable indicator of doneness. Roasts will continue cooking for a period of time after removal from the oven, and the internal temperature of the roast may rise as much as 5 °F.

The roast should be allowed to set in a warm place for 15-20 min before it is sliced. The roast becomes more firm, retains more of its juices, and is easier to slice. Refrigerating the roast for an extended period of time prior to slicing and service, however, results in loss of flavor. To insure the highest quality, roasts should be served as soon as possible after cooking and slicing.

Table 2.7 TIMETABLE FOR ROASTING BEEF[a]

Cut	Approximate Weight of Single Roast (lb)[b]	Number of Roasts in Oven	Approximate Total Weight of Roasts (lb)	Oven Temperature[c]	Interior Temperature of Roast when Removed from Oven[c]	Minutes per Pound Based on One Roast	Minutes per Pound Based on Total Weight of Roasts in Oven	Approximate Total Cooking Time
Rib (7-rib)	20-25			250 °F	130 °F (rare) 140 °F (medium) 150 °F (well)	13-15 15-17 17-19		4½-5 hr 5-6 hr 6-6½ hr
Rib (7-rib)	20-25			300 °F	130 °F (rare) 140 °F (medium) 150 °F (well)	10-12 12-14 14-16		4-4½ hr 4½-5 hr 5-5½ hr
Rib (7-rib)		2	56	300 °F	130 °F (rare) 140 °F (medium) 150 °F (well)		5 to 6 6 7 to 8	5-5½ hr 6 hr 6-7 hr
Rib eye	4-6			350 °F	140 °F (rare) 160 °F (medium) 170 °F (well)	18-20 20-22 22-24		1⅓-1⅔ hr 1½-2 hr 1⅔-2¼ hr
Tenderloin, whole	4-6			425 °F	140 °F (rare)			45-60 min
Top loin (boneless)	10-12			325 °F	140 °F (rare)	10		1½-2 hr
Top sirloin butt	8			300 °F	140 °F (rare)	25		3½ hr
Rump	5-7			300 °F	150 °F to 170 °F	25-30		2-3 hr
Top round	10			300 °F	140 °F (rare) 150 °F (medium)	18-19 22-23		3-3¼ hr 3½-4 hr

Table 2.7 TIMETABLE FOR ROASTING BEEF[a] (continued)

Cut	Approximate Weight of Single Roast (lb)[b]	Number of Roasts in Oven	Approximate Total Weight of Roasts (lb)	Oven Temperature[c]	Interior Temperature of Roast when Removed from Oven[c]	Minutes per Pound Based on One Roast	Minutes per Pound Based on Total Weight of Roasts in Oven	Approximate Total Cooking Time
Top round	15			300 °F	140 °F (rare) 150 °F (medium)	15 17		3½-4 hr 4-4½ hr
Round (rump and shank off)	50			250 °F	140 °F (medium) 155 °F (well)	12 14		10 hr 11-12 hr

[a] From *Meat in the Foodservice Industry*, National Live Stock and Meat Board, Chicago, Illinois, p. 62, 1977.
[b] Metric weight equivalents: see p. 28.
[c] Metric temperature equivalents: see p. 73.

Table 2.8 TIMETABLE FOR ROASTING LAMB AND VEAL[a]

Cut	Approx. Weight (lb)[b]	Oven Temperature[c]	Interior Temperature of Roast when Removed from Oven	Minutes per pound Based on One Roast	Approximate Total Cooking Time
LAMB					
Leg	5-9	325 °F	140 °F (rare)	20-25	2-3 hr
			160 °F (medium)	25-30	2½-3¾ hr
			170 °F-180 °F (well)	30-35	3-4½ hr
Leg, boneless	4-7	325 °F	140 °F (rare)	25-30	2-3 hr
			160 °F (medium)	30-35	2¼-3½ hr
			170 °F-180 °F (well)	35-40	2½-4 hr
Crown roast	2½-4	325 °F	140 °F (rare)	30-35	1½-2 hr
			160 °F (medium)	35-40	1¾-2¼ hr
			170 °F-180 °F (well)	40-45	2-2¾ hr
Shoulder, boneless	3½-5	325 °F	140 °F (rare)	30-35	2-2½ hr
			160 °F (medium)	35-40	2¼-3 hr
			170 °F-180 °F (well)	40-45	2½-3½ hr
Rib	1½-2	375 °F	140 °F (rare)	30-35	¾-1 hr
			160 °F (medium)	35-40	1-1¼ hr
			160 °F-180 °F (well)	40-45	1-1½ hr
Rib	2-3	375 °F	140 °F (rare)	25-30	1-1¼ hr
			160 °F (medium)	30-35	1¼-1½ hr
			170 °F-180 °F (well)	35-40	1½-1¾ hr

Table 2.8 TIMETABLE FOR ROASTING LAMB AND VEAL [a] (continued)

Cut	Approx. Weight (lb)[b]	Oven Temperature[c]	Interior Temperature of Roast when Removed from Oven	Minutes per pound Based on One Roast	Approximate Total Cooking Time
VEAL					
Leg, rump and shank off	5-8	325 °F	170 °F	25-35	3-3½ hr
Leg, rump and shank off, boneless	3½-7	325 °F	170 °F	25-30	2-3 hr
Loin	4-6	325 °F	170 °F	30-35	2½-3 hr
Rib (rack)	3-5	325 °F	170 °F	30-35	1½-2½ hr
Shoulder, boneless	4-6	325 °F	170 °F	40-45	3-3½ hr

[a] From *Meat in the Foodservice Industry*, National Live Stock and Meat Board, Chicago, Illinois, p. 63, 1977.

[b] Metric weight equivalents: see p. 28.

[c] Metric temperature equivalents: see p. 73.

Table 2.9 TIMETABLE FOR ROASTING FRESH AND CURED PORK[a]

Cut	Approx. Weight (lb)[b]	Oven Temperature [c]	Interior Temperature of Roast when Removed from Oven[c]	Minutes per Pound Based on One Roast	Approximate Total Cooking Time
FRESH PORK					
Loin, boneless, tied	8-10	325 °F	170 °F	30-35	4½-5½ hr
Center loin	3-5	325 °F	170 °F	30-35	1¾-2½ hr
Picnic (shoulder)	5-8	325 °F	170 °F	30-35	3-4 hr
Picnic shoulder, boneless	4-6	325 °F	170 °F	35-40	3-3½ hr
Boston shoulder, boneless	4-6	325 °F	170 °F	40-45	3-4 hr
Ham (leg)	12-16	325 °F	170 ° F	22-26	5-6 hr
Ham (leg) boneless, tied	10-14	325 °F	170 °F	24-28	4½-5½ hr
Spareribs	2-3	325 °F	Cooked well done		1½-2½ hr
CURED PORK[d]					
Whole ham[e]	10-14	325 °F	160 °F	18-20	3-4 hr
Half ham[e]	5-7	325 °F	160 °F	22-25	2-3 hr
Loin	3-5	325 °F	160 °F	25-30	1½-2½ hr
Shoulder roll (butt)	2-4	325 °F	170 °F	35-40	1-2 hr
Arm picnic shoulder	5-8	325 °F	170 °F	30-35	3-4 hr
Canadian-style bacon	2-4	325 °F	160 °F	35-40	1-1¾ hr

[a] From *Meat in the Foodservice Industry*, National Live Stock and Meat Board, Chicago, Illinois, pp. 62, 63, 1977.
[b] Metric weight equivalents: see p. 28.
[c] Metric temperature equivalents: see p. 73.
[d] Cooking times for cook-before-eating products.
[e] Heat "fully cooked" hams to 140 °F allowing 15-18 min per pound for whole ham, 18-24 min per pound for half ham.

Broiling

Broiling is a dry-heat cookery method using direct or radiant heat. It is used for small individualized cuts such as steaks, chops, and patties. Broiling is most successful for cuts 1-2 in. thick. Veal should not be broiled unless it is fairly mature and well-marbled with fat, and then only loin chops or steaks. Recent research has shown that broiling is an acceptable cookery method for pork chops, but because pork should be cooked to an internal temperature of 170 °F (75 °C), the temperature should be moderate so the chop does not become charred by the time it is cooked well done.

Frozen cuts may be successfully broiled, especially those 1½ in. thick or less. They should be broiled at a greater distance from the heat or at a lower temperature than unfrozen cuts to provide more uniform doneness. Although cooking times will vary, a general guideline is that frozen steaks will take nearly twice as long as unfrozen steaks.

Meat may be broiled in an oven broiler or other type of heat-from-above gas or electric broiler, or on an open hearth, which is heated from below. In pan-broiling or griddle broiling, the heat is transferred from the pan or grill to the meat being cooked.

Ovenbroiling

1. Preheat the broiler.

2. Place meat on the broiler rack or grid 3-5 in. from the heat, depending on the thickness of the meat, the type and size of the equipment, the source of heat, and whether the meat is frozen.

3. Broil on one side until meat is browned and approximately half done. Season browned side, then turn and brown on the opposite side and cook to the desired degree of doneness. (See Table 2.10 for time.) Season second side. The meat should be turned only once.

Table 2.10 TIMETABLE FOR BROILING MEAT[a]

		Approximate Total Cooking Time		
Cut	Approximate Thickness	Rare, min	Medium, min	Well done, min
Rib, club, top loin, T-bone,	1 in.	15	20	
Porterhouse, tenderloin, or	1½ in.	25	35	
individual servings of beef sirloin steak	2 in.	35	50	
Beef sirloin steak	1 in.	20-25	30-35	
	1½ in.	30-35	40-45	
Ground beef patties	1 in. (4 oz)	15	20	
Pork chops (rib or loin)	¾-1 in.			20-25
Pork shoulder steaks	½-¾ in.			20-22
Smoked pork chops (rib or loin)	½-¾ in.			15-20
Lamb shoulder, rib, loin, and	1 in.		12-16	
sirloin chops or leg chops	1½ in.		17-20	
(steaks)	2 in.		20-25	
Ground lamb patties	1 in. (4 oz)		18-20	
Smoked ham slice (cook-before	½ in.			10-12
eating)[b]	1 in.			16-20
Bacon				4-5

[a] From *Meat in the Foodservice Industry,* National Live Stock and Meat Board, Chicago, Illinois, p. 66, 1977.
[b] Allow 8-10 min for broiling ½-in. thick "fully cooked" ham slice and 14-16 min for 1-in. thick "fully cooked" ham slice.

Panbroiling and Griddle Broiling

1. Place meat on a preheated ungreased griddle or heavy frying pan.

2. Cook slowly, turning as necessary. Since the meat is in contact with the hot metal of the pan or griddle, turning more than once may be necessary for even cooking. If the steak is a thick one, reduce the temperature after browning. Griddle broiling requires more attention than true broiling, but is more rapid than cooking in some types of broilers.

3. Care should be taken not to puncture the meat with a fork while cooking. Long-handled tongs or a spatula are better than a fork for turning the meat.

4. Neither water nor fat should be added. Excess fat should be scraped from the griddle as it accumulates.

5. Cook the meat to the desired degree of doneness. See Table 2.11 for approximate cooking times.

Table 2.11 TIMETABLE FOR GRIDDLE BROILING MEAT[a]

Cut	Approximate Thickness	Approximate Total Cooking Time		
		Rare, min	Medium, min	Well done, min
Beef steaks	¾ in.	4	8	12
	1 in.	6	10	15
	1½ in.	10-12	15-18	20
Ground beef patties	¾ in.	4-5	8-10	12
	1 in. (4 oz)	6-8	10-12	15
Lamb chops	1 in.		10	15
	1½ in.		15	20-25
Ground lamb patties	¾ in.		10	12-15
	1 in. (4 oz)		10-15	15-20
Smoked ham slice	½ in.			6-10
Bacon				2-3

[a] From *Meat in the Foodservice Industry,* National Live Stock and Meat Board, Chicago, Illinois, p. 68, 1977.

Frying

Frying is cooking in fat and may be accomplished by panfrying or griddle frying in a small amount of fat or by deep-fat frying, which uses a large amount of fat.

Meat for frying generally is cut thinner than that for broiling and may be breaded or tenderized by scoring, cubing, or grinding. Cuts lacking fat, such as veal cutlets and liver or other variety meats, usually are fried.

Procedures for panfrying or griddle frying are similar to pan- or griddle broiling, but the meat may be dredged with seasoned flour, and a small amount of fat is used for cooking.

Procedures for deep-fat frying follow:[1]

1. Coat or bread meat (see p. 75 for methods of preparing food for deep-fat frying). Portioned, prebreaded items may be cooked from a frozen state in the deep-fat fryer.

2. Heat the fat to approximately 350 °F (175 °C).

3. Place pieces of meat in the wire basket and carefully lower into the fryer. Do not fill the basket while holding over the fat, because crumbs could fall into the fat.

[1] Adapted from *Meat in the Foodservice Industry,* National Live Stock and Meat Board, Chicago, Illinois, p. 68, 1977.

4. Do not overload the basket or the fryer. An overload drastically reduces the temperature of the fat, thereby increasing fat absorption and inhibiting browning. This is especially true when the product is frozen. A ratio of about 5 to 1 by weight of fat to product is the maximum effective load.

5. Continue cooking until the outside of the product is browned and crisp and the meat reaches the desired doneness.

6. Remove meat from the fat and let drain. Do not shake the basket over the fat if the product is coated; this will cause particles and crumbs to fall into the fat. The product should not be salted over the fat, either, because salt shortens the life of the fat.

Braising

Braising is a moist-cookery method adapted to the less-tender cuts of meat, particularly the much used muscles and low grades of beef. Certain cuts of veal and thin cuts of pork, such as chops and steaks, are better if braised, although they are tender. The terms pot roasting or fricasseeing also are applied to this method of cooking.

Steps in braising are:

1. Season meat with salt (¼ t per pound of meat) and pepper if desired. Meat may be dredged with flour to increase browning.

2. Brown meat in a small amount of fat in a heavy kettle, roasting pan, tilting frypan, or steam-jacketed kettle.

3. Add small amount of water or other liquid; use additional liquid as needed during the cooking. Braising or pot roasting in a steam-jacketed kettle will require more water than pot roasting in the oven. Other liquid, such as meat stock, tomato juice, or cultured sour cream, may be used.

4. Cover; simmer until tender or bake at 325 °F (165 °C). See Table 2.12 for approximate cooking times.

Table 2.12 TIMETABLE FOR BRAISING MEAT[a]

Cut	Average Weight or Thickness	Approximate Total Cooking Time
Pot-roast	4-6 lb	3-4 hr
Swiss steak	1-2½ in.	2-3 hr
Round steak	½ in. (pounded)	45 min-1 hr
Short ribs	pieces 2 × 2 × 2 in.	1½-2 hr
Lamb shanks	½ lb each	1-1½ hr
Lamb neck slices	½-¾ in.	1-1½ hr
Lamb riblets	¾ × 2½ × 3 in.	1½-2½ hr
Pork chops or steaks	¾-1 in.	45 min-1 hr
Spareribs	2-3 lb	1½ hr
Veal cutlets	½ × 3 × 5½ in.	45 min-1 hr
Veal steaks or chops	½-¾ in.	45 min-1 hr

[a] From *Meat in the Foodservice Industry,* National Live Stock and Meat Board, Chicago, Illinois, p. 73, 1977.

Cooking in Liquid

This method of moist cookery involves cooking meat covered with water or other liquid and is sometimes referred to as simmering, boiling, or stewing. This method is suitable for the least tender cuts, such as shank, neck, and brisket, and for variety meats such as heart and tongue.

1. Brown meat if desired and cover with water.

2. Season with salt and pepper. Herbs and spices, used wisely, add to the variety and flavor of stewed meats. Suggested seasonings are carrots, celery, onions, bay leaves, thyme, marjoram, and parsley.

3. Cook below boiling point until tender in a steam-jacketed kettle, tilting frypan, or in a tightly covered heavy utensil on top of the range. See Table 2.13 for approximate cooking times.

Table 2.13 TIMETABLE FOR COOKING MEAT IN LIQUID (LARGE CUTS AND STEWS)[a]

	Average Size or Average Weight	*Approximate Cooking Time*	
Cut		*Min per lb*	*Total hr*
Fresh beef	4-8 lb	40-50	3-4
Corned beef	6-8 lb	40-50	4-6
Beef shank cross-cuts	¾-1 lb		2½-3½
Lamb or veal for stew	1-2 in. cubes		1½-2½
Beef for stew	1-2 in. cubes		2-3

[a] From *Meat in the Foodservice Industry,* National Live Stock and Meat Board, Chicago, Illinois, p. 75, 1977.

Meat Recipes

Beef

SWISS STEAK
Bake: 2-2½ hr
Oven: 350 °F (175 °C)

Yield: 50 portions
Portion: 5 oz (142 g)

Amount		Ingredient	Method
Metric	*U.S.*		
7.71 kg	17 lb	Beef round, sliced ¾ in. thick	Cut meat into portions, 3 per lb (454 g)
454 g	1 lb	Flour	Mix flour, salt, and pepper. Pound into meat.
85 g	3 oz	Salt	
10 mL	2 t	Pepper	
680 g	1 lb 8 oz	Fat, hot	Brown meat in fat. Place, slightly overlapping, in 2 baking or counter pans.
170 g	6 oz	Fat (meat drippings) hot	Make gravy (p. 463). Add 1½ qt (1.42 L) to each pan.
170 g	6 oz	Flour	Cover pans tightly with aluminum foil.
10 mL	2 t	Salt	
4 mL	¾ t	Pepper	Bake.
2.84 L	3 qt	Water or meat stock	

Notes:
1. If portioned steaks are used, order boneless beef round, cut 3 per pound (454 g), scored twice. This will tenderize steaks but, if scored more than twice, steaks may fall apart when cooked. Dredge steak with flour mixture and brown. Proceed as above.
2. 1 No. 10 can tomatoes may be substituted for the gravy. Add 4 oz (114 g) chopped onion.

Variations:
1. **Spanish Steak.** Substitute Spanish Sauce (p. 466) for gravy.

2. **Country Fried Steak.** Use beef round cut ⅜ in. thick. Proceed as for Swiss Steak except for adding gravy. Place steaks on racks in roaster or counter pans. Cover bottom of pan with water, 2 c (480 mL) per pan. Cover with aluminum foil and bake. Make Cream Gravy (p. 463) to serve with steaks.

3. **Smothered Steak with Onions.** Proceed as for Swiss Steak. Add 3 lb (1.36 kg) sliced onions lightly browned.

PEPPER STEAK

Yield: 50 portions
Portion: 4 oz (114 g)

Amount		Ingredient	Method
Metric	U.S.		
5.9 kg	13 lb	Beef round or sirloin, cut into thin strips	Cook meat in fat until lightly browned.
227 g	8 oz	Fat	
2.84 L	3 qt	Beef stock	Add stock, tomatoes, and seasonings to meat.
2 No. 10 cans	2 No. 10 cans	Tomatoes	Simmer until tender, 1-1½ hr.
454 g	1 lb	Onions, chopped	
3	3	Garlic cloves, cut in half	
30 mL	2 T	Salt	
12	12	Green peppers, thinly sliced in rings	Add green pepper and cook until tender but firm.
114 g	4 oz	Cornstarch	Combine cornstarch, water, and soy sauce into a smooth paste.
600 mL	2½ c	Water, cold	Add to meat-vegetable mixture.
160 mL	⅔ c	Soy sauce	Cook 5 min.

Note: If beef sirloin is used, the cooking time can be reduced. Sauté meat in fat until tender, then add rest of ingredients and simmer until they are cooked.

POT ROAST OF BEEF

Bake: 4-5 hr
Oven: 300 °F (150 °C)

Yield: 50 portions
Portion: 3 oz (85 g)

Metric	U.S.	Ingredient	Method
	Amount		
Metric	*U.S.*	*Ingredient*	*Method*
9.08 kg	20 lb	Beef, boneless chuck, round, or rump	Season meat with salt and pepper. Place in roasting pan and brown in 450 °F (230 °C) oven.
28 g	1 oz	Salt	
3 mL	½ t	Pepper	
1.89 L	2 qt	Water	When meat is browned, add water. Reduce heat to 300 °F (150 °C). Cover. Cook slowly until tender (3-5 hr). Add water as necessary. When meat is done, remove from pan. Let stand ½ hr before slicing.
184 g	6½ oz	Flour	Thicken the drippings in the pan with the flour that has been mixed with the cold water. Remove excess fat if necessary and add water to make 1 gal (3.79 L) gravy.
360 mL	1½ c	Water, cold	
28 g	1 oz	Salt	
3 mL	½ t	Pepper	
		Water as necessary	

Note: Meat may be cooked in a steam-jacketed kettle. Brown in a small amount of fat. Add water, salt, and pepper. Cover kettle and cook until tender. Add water as necessary.

Variations:

1. **Beef à la Mode.** About 1½ hr before serving add: 5 lb (2.27 kg) carrot halves, 8 oz (227 g) onion, chopped; 4 oz (114 g) green pepper, chopped; and 3 lb (1.36 kg) celery cut into 2-in. strips. Serve a slice of meat with vegetables and a spoonful of gravy on top.

2. **Yankee Pot Roast.** Add 1½ qt (1.42 L) tomato purée and 1 bay leaf to the water used in cooking pot roast.

3. **Savory Pot Roast.** Place roast on heavy aluminum foil in baking pan. Sprinkle with 5 oz (142 g) dry onion soup mix. Close foil tightly. Bake at 300 °F (150 °C) 4-5 hr. Open foil and bake ½ hr longer. Use juice for gravy.

4. **Beef Brisket.** Cook fresh beef brisket as for Savory Pot Roast. The meat may be brushed with Cooked Barbecue Sauce (p. 465) for the last half hour of cooking.

BEEF STEW

Amount		Ingredient	Method
Metric	*U.S.*	*Ingredient*	*Method*
5.67 kg	12 lb 8 oz	Beef, 1-in. cubes	Brown beef in kettle or oven.
2.84 L	3 qt	Water	Add water and seasonings to meat.
28 g	1 oz	Salt	Cover and simmer 2 hr. Add
5 mL	1 t	Pepper	more water as necessary.
908 g	2 lb	Potatoes, cubed	Cook vegetables in steamer or in
908 g	2 lb	Carrots, sliced	small amount of water in kettle
		or cubed	or oven.
454 g	1 lb	Onion, cubed	
680 g	1 lb 8 oz	Celery, diced	
28 g	1 oz	Salt	
5 mL	1 t	Pepper	
142 g	5 oz	Flour	Mix flour and water until smooth.
300 mL	1¼ c	Water	Add to meat and cook until
			thickened.
			Add vegetables.

Notes:
1. If a higher ratio of meat is desired, use 15 lb (6.80 kg) cubed beef;
    reduce vegetables to 4 lb (1.81 kg). A total of 3 gal (11.36 L) stew is
    needed to serve 50 6-oz (170-g) portions.
2. Veal may be substituted for beef.

Variations:
1. **Beef Pot Pie.** Omit potatoes and add 1 40-oz (1.14-kg) pkg frozen
    peas. Place cooked stew in 2 greased baking pans or in casseroles.
    Cover with Pastry (p. 310) or Batter Crust (p. 351). Bake 20-25 min at
    450 °F (230 °C).

2. **Beef Stew with Biscuits.** Place cooked stew in 2 baking pans just
    before serving. Completely cover with hot Baking Powder Biscuits
    (p. 115).

3. **Beef Stew with Dumplings.** Drop Dumplings (p. 136) on meat mixture
    and steam 15-18 min.

CORNED BEEF AND CABBAGE

Yield: 50 portions
Portion: 3 oz (85 g) cooked meat

Metric	U.S.	Ingredient	Method
	Amount		
11.34-13.61 kg	25-30 lb	Corned beef brisket	Cover meat with water and simmer until tender, 4-5 hr. When done, remove from liquid. Allow to stand 20-30 min before slicing.
5.44 kg	12 lb	Cabbage, cut into wedges	Cook cabbage (p. 510) in corned beef stock. Serve 1 wedge with 3 oz (85 g) sliced meat.

HUNGARIAN GOULASH
Time: 2½-3 hr

Yield: 50 8-oz (227-g) portions
Portion: 4 oz (114 g) goulash,
4 oz (114 g) noodles

Metric	U.S.	Ingredient	Method
	Amount		
4.54 kg	10 lb	Beef, cubed	Brown beef and vegetables in fat.
680 g	1 lb 8 oz	Onion, chopped	
1 clove	1 clove	Garlic, finely chopped	
227 g	8 oz	Fat	
142 g	5 oz	Brown sugar	Combine seasonings and water. Add to browned meat.
15 mL	1 T	Mustard, dry	
60 mL	¼ c	Paprika	Cover container and simmer 2½-3 hr or until meat is tender.
⅛ t	⅛ t	Cayenne pepper	
60 mL	¼ c	Salt	
360 mL	1½ c	Worcestershire sauce	
30 mL	2 T	Vinegar	
0.95 L	1 qt	Catsup	
2.84 L	3 qt	Water	
567 g	1 lb 4 oz	Flour	Mix flour and water until smooth. Add to hot mixture and cook until thickened.
0.95 L	1 qt	Water, cold	
1.81 kg	4 lb	Noodles	Cook noodles (p. 191).
11.36 L	3 gal	Water, boiling	Serve 4-oz (114-g) ladle goulash over 4 oz (114 g) noodles.
60 mL	¼ c	Salt	
60 mL	¼ c	Oil (optional)	

Note: Beef may be browned in a roasting pan in 450 °F (230 °C) oven.

BEEF STROGANOFF

Yield: 50 portions
Portion: 5 oz (142 g) Stroganoff
4 oz (114 g) noodles

Amount		Ingredient	Method
Metric	*U.S.*	*Ingredient*	*Method*
4.54 kg	10 lb	Beef round, cut in ¼-in. strips	Brown meat in fat. Add onion and seasonings.
227 g	8 oz	Fat	
567 g	1 lb 4 oz	Onion, chopped	
30 mL	2 T	Salt	
5 mL	1 t	Pepper	
2.37 L	2½ qt	Beef stock, hot (p. 477)	Add stock. Simmer 35-40 min or until meat is tender.
1.14 kg	2 lb 8 oz	Mushrooms, fresh, sliced	Sauté mushrooms in fat. Add to meat.
114 g	4 oz	Fat	
1.89 L	2 qt	Cultured sour cream	Blend sour cream with flour. Just before serving, add to meat mixture, stirring constantly. Stir until thickened.
227 g	8 oz	Flour	
1.81 kg	4 lb	Noodles	Cook noodles (p. 191)
11.36 L	3 gal	Water	Serve 5 oz (142 g) Stroganoff over 4 oz (114 g) noodles.
60 mL	¼ c	Salt	
60 mL	¼ c	Oil (optional)	

Notes:
1. 3 oz (85 g) beef soup base and 2½ qt (2.37 L) water may be substituted for beef stock.
2. May be served over rice. Cook 3 lb (1.36 kg) rice in 3¾ qt (3.55 L) water, 2 T (30 mL) salt, and 2 T (30 mL) fat or oil. (See p. 190)

Variation:
Hamburger Stroganoff. Substitute ground beef for beef round. Add 1½ lb (680 g) chopped celery, ¼ c (60 mL) paprika, ¼ c (60 mL) Worcestershire sauce, and 2 t (10 mL) dry mustard.

CHOP SUEY

Yield: 6¼ qt (5.91 L)
Portion: 4 oz (114 g) chop suey
4 oz (114 g) rice

Amount			
Metric	*U.S.*	*Ingredient*	*Method*
2.27 kg	5 lb	Beef or veal, ½-in. cubes	Brown meat in steam-jacketed kettle or roasting pan.
2.27 kg	5 lb	Pork, ½-in. cubes	
60 mL	¼ c	Salt	Add salt and water to meat.
3.79 L	1 gal	Water	Simmer until tender.
114 g	4 oz	Green peppers, chopped (optional)	Add vegetables. Cook 10-15 min. Vegetables should still be crisp.
227 g	8 oz	Onion, chopped	
2.27 kg	5 lb	Celery, sliced	
170 g	6 oz	Cornstarch	Mix cornstarch and water to a smooth paste. Add to hot mixture while stirring.
480 mL	2 c	Water	
3 No. 2 cans	3 No. 2 cans	Bean sprouts or Chinese vegetables	Add vegetables and soy sauce.
240-360 mL	1-1½ c	Soy sauce	
1.36 kg	3 lb	Rice	Cook rice (p. 190).
3.55 L	3¾ qt	Water, boiling	
30 mL	2 T	Salt	
30 mL	2 T	Oil (optional)	
3 No. 2½ cans	3 No. 2½ cans	Chinese noodles	Serve No. 10 dipper of meat on No. 8 dipper of rice. Garnish with Chinese noodles.

Variations:

1. **Chicken Chow Mein.** Substitute cubed, cooked chicken or turkey for beef.

2. **Tuna Chow Mein.** Omit beef and pork. Add 8 lb (3.63 kg) tuna, coarsely flaked, and 2 lb (908 g) water chestnuts, sliced.

MEAT LOAF

Bake: 1½ hr
Oven: 325 °F (165 °C)

Yield: 5 loaves
Portion: 4 oz (114 g)

Amount		Ingredient	Method
Metric	U.S.		
3.63 kg	8 lb	Ground beef	Mix all ingredients (low speed)
908 g	2 lb	Ground pork	until blended. **DO NOT OVER-**
284 g	10 oz	Bread crumbs, soft	**MIX.**
1.89 L	2 qt	Milk	Press mixture into 5 loaf pans 4 × 9 in., 3 lb 4 oz (1.47 kg) per pan.
12	12	Eggs, beaten	Meat loaf also may be made in 12
60 mL	¼ c	Salt	× 20 × 4 in. counter pan. Press
57 g	2 oz	Onion, finely chopped	mixture into pan. Divide into 4 loaves. Bake 2 hr at 300 °F (150
5 mL	1 t	Pepper	°C).
f.g.	f.g.	Cayenne	

Variations:

1. **Vegetable Meat Loaf.** Add 2 c (480 mL) catsup, 8 oz (227 g) each raw carrots, onions, and celery, and 4 oz (114 g) green peppers. Grind vegetables. Pour a small amount of tomato juice over loaf before baking.

2. **Sour Cream Meat Loaf.** Add 1 qt (0.95 L) chopped stuffed olives to meat mixture. Cover the unbaked loaves with cultured sour cream, 1 qt (0.95 L) divided among the 5 loaves (1 c/240 L per loaf).

3. **Meatballs.** Measure with No. 8 dipper and shape into balls. Proceed as for Swedish Meatballs (p. 274) or Meatballs and Spaghetti (p. 276).

4. **Barbecued Meatballs.** Measure with No. 8 dipper. Shape into balls. Cover with 1 gal (3.79 L) Barbecue Sauce (p. 464).

SWEDISH MEATBALLS

Bake: 1 hr
Oven: 300 °F (150 °C)

Yield: 50 portions
Portion: 2 2½-oz (70-g) meatballs

Amount		Ingredient	Method
Metric	U.S.		
1.14 kg	2 lb 8 oz	Bread	Soak bread in milk 1 hr.
1.42 L	1½ qt	Milk	
1.36 kg	3 lb	Ground beef	Combine meat, potato, and seasonings in mixer bowl.
1.14 kg	2 lb 8 oz	Ground veal	Add bread. Mix to blend. Do not overmix.
1.14 kg	2 lb 8 oz	Ground pork	
567 g	1 lb 4 oz	Potato, raw, grated	Dip with No. 16 dipper. Shape into balls. Place in baking pan.
340 g	12 oz	Onion, minced	Brown in hot oven (400 °F/205 °C).
45 mL	3 T	Salt	Transfer to 2 12 × 20 in. counter pans.
10 mL	2 t	Pepper	
170 g	6 oz	Meat drippings	Make Cream Gravy (p. 463) from meat drippings.
170 g	6 oz	Flour	Pour over meatballs. Bake.
2.84 L	3 qt	Milk	
10 mL	2 t	Salt	
4 mL	¾ t	Pepper	

Note: Beef may be substituted for veal and pork.

SPANISH MEATBALLS
Bake: 2½ hr   **Yield: 50 portions**
Oven: 325 °F (165 °C)   **Portion: 1 4-oz (114-g) meatball**

Amount			
Metric	*U.S.*	*Ingredient*	*Method*
5.44 kg	12 lb	Ground beef	Mix all ingredients except tomato
12	12	Eggs, beaten	and water.
57 g	2 oz	Onion, grated	Measure with No. 8 dipper and
30 mL	2 T	Salt	form into balls.
510 g	1 lb 2 oz	Rice, partially	Place in 2 baking pans 12 × 20 ×
		cooked	2 in.
454 g	1 lb	Potatoes,	
		mashed	
114 g	4 oz	Green peppers,	
		chopped	
2.84 L	3 qt	Tomato purée	Mix purée and water. Pour over
1.89 L	2 qt	Water	meatballs.
			Cover tightly and bake. Add more
			liquid if necessary.

Notes:
1.   For 2 balls per serving use No. 16 dipper.
2.   Spanish Sauce, p. 466, may be substituted for tomato purée.

MEATBALLS AND SPAGHETTI
Brown: 20 min, 400 °F (205 °C)
Bake in Sauce: 30 min, 375 °F (190 °C)

Yield: 50 portions
Portion: 3 meatballs
5 oz (142 g) spaghetti

Amount		Ingredient	Method
Metric	*U.S.*	*Ingredient*	*Method*
3.63 kg	8 lb	Ground beef	Mix meat, bread, milk, and sea-
1.81 kg	4 lb	Ground pork	sonings (low speed). **DO NOT**
6 slices	6 slices	Bread, crumbled	**OVERMIX.**
480 mL	2 c	Milk	Dip with No. 24 dipper onto baking sheet.
30 mL	2 T	Salt	Brown in 400 °F (205 °C) oven.
10 mL	2 t	Pepper	Remove to deep counter pan or roasting pan.
2.84 L	3 qt (2 50-oz cans)	Tomato soup	Make sauce of all ingredients and simmer 1½-2 hr.
1.18 L	1¼ qt (1 46-oz can)	Tomato paste	Pour over browned meatballs.
3.31 L	3½ qt	Water, boiling	Cover and cook in 375 °F (190 °C) oven about 30 min.
30 mL	2 T	Mustard, prepared	
30 mL	2 T	Paprika	
120 mL	½ c	Worcestershire sauce	
30 mL	2 T	Sugar	
4 cloves	4 cloves	Garlic	
227 g	8 oz	Onion, chopped	
1.81 kg	4 lb	Spaghetti	Cook spaghetti (p. 191).
11.36 L	3 gal	Water, boiling	Serve 3 meatballs and sauce over
60 mL	¼ c	Salt	5 oz (142 g) spaghetti.
60 mL	¼ c	Oil (optional)	

Note: If desired mix the cooked spaghetti with the tomato sauce. Place in 2 counter pans, arrange meatballs over top, and bake 20-30 min at 375 °F (190 °C).

SPAGHETTI WITH MEAT SAUCE

Yield: 50 portions
Portion: 6 oz (170 g) sauce
5 oz (142 g) spaghetti

Metric	U.S.	Ingredient	Method
Amount			
Metric	*U.S.*	*Ingredient*	*Method*
3.63 kg	8 lb	Ground beef	Brown beef. Pour off excess fat.
4.73 L	5 qt	Tomato purée (or tomatoes)	Add remaining sauce ingredients to cooked beef.
0.95 L	1 qt	Water	Cook slowly, stirring frequently,
1.66 L	1¾ qt	Catsup	until thickened, approximately
454 g	1 lb	Onions, chopped	½ hr.
2	2	Bay leaves	
5 mL	1 t	Thyme	
1 clove	1 clove	Garlic	
60 mL	¼ c	Worcestershire sauce	
10 mL	2 t	Cayenne pepper	
23 mL	1½ T	Salt	
1.81 kg	4 lb	Spaghetti	Cook spaghetti (p. 191). Drain.
11.36 L	3 gal	Water, boiling	Serve 6 oz (170 g) sauce over 5 oz
60 mL	¼ c	Salt	(142 g) spaghetti.
60 mL	¼ c	Salad oil (optional)	

CREOLE SPAGHETTI

Bake: 45 min
Oven: 325 °F (165 °C)

Yield: 2 pans 12 × 20 × 2 in.
Portion: 6 oz (170 g)

Amount		Ingredient	Method
Metric	U.S.		
3.63 kg	8 lb	Ground beef	Brown beef, onion, and green pepper. Add salt.
170 g	6 oz	Onion, finely chopped	Drain off excess fat.
454 g	1 lb	Green pepper, chopped	
28 g	1 oz	Salt	
2.84 L	3 qt	Tomato purée (or tomatoes)	Add tomato to meat.
1.36 kg	3 lb	Spaghetti	Cook spaghetti (p. 191). Drain.
7.57 L	2 gal	Water, boiling	
57 g	2 oz	Salt	
45 mL	3 T	Salad oil (optional)	
680 g	1 lb 8 oz	Cheddar cheese, ground	Combine sauce and cooked spaghetti.
			Pour into 2 baking pans. Sprinkle cheese over top. Bake.

LASAGNE
Bake: 40-45 min
Oven: 350°F (175 °C)

Yield: 2 pans 12 × 20 × 2 in.
Portion: 6 oz (170 g)

Amount		*Ingredient*	*Method*
Metric	*U.S.*		
2.27 kg	5 lb	Ground beef	Cook ground beef, onion, and
340 g	12 oz	Onion, finely chopped	garlic until pink color has disappeared.
5 cloves	5 cloves	Garlic, chopped	Drain off excess fat.
2.84 L	3 qt	Tomato sauce	Add tomato sauce, tomato paste,
0.95 L	1 qt	Tomato paste	and spices to meat. Continue
5 mL	1 t	Pepper	cooking, about 30 min, stirring
5 mL	1 t	Basil, crumbled	occasionally.
15 mL	1 T	Oregano, crumbled	
1.14 kg	2 lb 8 oz	Noodles, lasagne	Cook noodles (p. 191). Hold in cold water to keep noodles from
7.57 L	2 gal	Water, boiling	sticking together.
30 mL	2 T	Salt	Drain when ready to use.
30 mL	2 T	Oil	
1.14 kg	2 lb 8 oz	Swiss or mozzarella cheese, grated	Combine cheeses. Arrange in 2 counter pans in layers in the following order:
170 g	6 oz	Parmesan cheese, grated	Meat sauce (1 qt/0.95 L) Noodles, overlapping (1 lb 12
1.14 kg	2 lb 8 oz	Cottage cheese, dry or drained	oz/794 g) Cheeses (1 lb 4 oz/567 g) Repeat sauce, noodles, and cheeses. Spoon remainder of meat sauce on top. Bake.

Variations:

1. **Meatless Cheese Lasagne.** Omit beef. Add 2 lb (908 g) slicd American cheese, arranged in layers over noodles. Increase cottage cheese to 4 lb (1.81 kg).

2. **Spinach Lasagne.** Omit beef. Increase cottage cheese (or ricotta cheese) to 5 lb (2.27 kg). Defrost 6 lb (2.72 kg) frozen chopped spinach. Drain and squeeze out excess liquid. Combine with cottage cheese and Parmesan cheese. Arrange noodles and spinach-cheese mixture in layers. Pour tomato mixture over and sprinkle with mozzarella cheese.

PIZZA

| Bake: 10-15 min | | | Yield: 2 pans 18 × 26 in. |
| Oven: 450 °F (230 °C) | | | Portion: 5 oz (142 g) |

Amount			
Metric	U.S.	Ingredient	Method
1.64 kg	3 lb 10 oz	Flour	Place flour, salt, and sugar in mixer bowl.
8 mL	1½ t	Salt	
45 mL	3 T	Sugar	Using dough hook, mix thoroughly (low speed).
14 g	½ oz	Yeast, active dry	Soften yeast in warm water.
640 mL	2⅔ c	Water, warm (110 °F/43 °C)	
57 g	2 oz	Fat, soft	Add softened yeast and fat to dry ingredients. Mix (low speed) to form dough.
			Knead until smooth and elastic. Cover and let rise until double in bulk, about 2 hr.
			Punch down and let rest 45 min.
			Divide into 2 portions. Roll out as thin as possible, stretching to desired size to fit 18 × 26 in. bun pans.
			Fit dough into 2 greased pans, allowing ¼ in. to extend up onto sides of pan. Trim and seal edges.
TOPPING			
0.95 L	1 qt	Tomato paste	Mix tomato and seasonings.
0.95 L	1 qt	Tomato purée	Spread over dough, 1 qt (0.95 L) per pan.
10 mL	2 t	Thyme or oregano	
15 mL	1 T	Salt	
3 mL	½ t	Cumin, ground	
1	1	Garlic clove, crushed	
30 mL	2 T	Chili powder	
1.14 kg	2 lb 8 oz	Sausage	Partially cook sausage and beef. Drain off excess fat.
1.14 kg	2 lb 8 oz	Ground beef	Sprinkle evenly over tomato sauce.

| 1.14 kg | 2 lb 8 oz | Mozzarella cheese, sliced or shredded | Top with cheese. Bake. |

Notes:
1. 1 oz (28 g) compressed yeast may be substituted for the active dry yeast. Soften in lukewarm water (95 °F/35 °C).
2. Active dry yeast may be mixed with dry ingredients; add water at 120 °F (49 °C).
3. Processed Cheddar cheese may be substituted for Mozzarella. Sweet basil may be sprinkled over top.

CHEESEBURGER PIE
Bake: Crust 10 min at 450 °F (230 °C)
Pie 1 hr at 350 °F (175 °C)

Yield: 2 pans 12 × 20 × 2 in.
Portion: 6 oz (170 g)

Amount			
Metric	*U.S.*	*Ingredient*	*Method*
680 g	1 lb 8 oz	Flour	Make pastry (p. 310)
510 g	1 lb 2 oz	Fat	Divide dough in half. Roll to cover
240-300 mL	1-1¼ c	Water, cold	bottom and sides of 2 12 × 20
15 mL	1 T	Salt	in. baking pans (1½ lb/680 g each). Bake 10 min at 450 °F (230 °C).
4.54 kg	10 lb	Ground beef	Brown beef; drain excess fat.
85 g	3 oz (¼ c)	Salt	Add seasonings and crumbs to
15 mL	1 T	Pepper	ground beef.
30 mL	2 T	Oregano	Spread mixture over baked crusts.
454 g	1 lb	Green pepper, chopped	
737 g	1 lb 10 oz	Bread crumbs	
12	12	Eggs, beaten	Combine eggs and milk. Add seasonings and cheese.
800 mL	3⅓ c	Milk	
1.36 kg	3 lb	Cheese, shredded	Spread evenly over meat mixture.
30 mL	2 T	Salt	
30 mL	2 T	Mustard, dry	
30 mL	2 T	Worcestershire sauce	
720 mL	3 c	Tomato sauce	Distribute 1½ c (360 mL) sauce unevenly over cheese mixture in each pan. Bake 1 hr at 350 °F (175 °C).

BEEF AND PORK CASSEROLE

Bake: 30 min   **Yield: 2 pans 12 × 20 × 2 in.**
Oven: 300 °F (150 °C)   **Portion: 5 oz (142 g)**

Amount			
Metric	*U.S.*	*Ingredient*	*Method*
1.81 kg	4 lb	Ground beef	Brown meat and onion. Drain excess fat.
1.81 kg	4 lb	Ground pork	
454 g	1 lb	Onion, finely chopped	
1.42 L	1½ qt	Tomato soup	Mix soup, water, and seasonings. Add to meat.
1.42 L	1½ qt	Water	
15 mL	1 T	Salt	
5 mL	1 t	Pepper	
794 g	1 lb 12 oz	Noodles	Cook noodles (p. 191).
4.73 L	1¼ gal	Water, boiling	Drain.
30 mL	2 T	Salt	
30 mL	2 T	Oil (optional)	
908 g	2 lb	Cheddar cheese	Grate or grind cheese. Combine noodles, meat mixture, and cheese. Place in 2 baking pans.
510 g	1 lb 2 oz	Bread crumbs	Combine crumbs and butter or margarine. Sprinkle over meat and noodle mixture. Bake.
142 g	5 oz	Butter or margarine, melted	

STUFFED PEPPERS

Bake: 45-60 min
Oven: 350 °F (175 °C)

Yield: 50 peppers
Portion: 5 oz (142 g)

Amount		Ingredient	Method
Metric	U.S.		
25	25	Green peppers, large	Wash peppers and remove stem end. Cut in halves lengthwise. Remove seeds and tough white portions. Reserve pepper trimmings for filling. Place in baking pans and steam or parboil for 3-5 min.
114 g	4 oz	Onion, chopped	Sauté onion and green pepper trimmings in the fat about 3 min.
114 g	4 oz	Fat	
		Green pepper trimmings	
4.08 kg	9 lb	Cooked meat, ground	Add to meat.
6	6	Eggs, beaten	Combine eggs, salt, and milk. Add to meat. Mix.
23 mL	1½ T	Salt	
5 mL	1 t	Pepper	
480 mL	2 c	Milk	
170 g	6 oz	Bread crumbs	Using No. 10 dipper, fill each pepper half with meat mixture. Mix crumbs and fat. Sprinkle over tops of peppers.
114 g	4 oz	Fat, melted	

Notes:
1. Corn, rice, or spaghetti may be substituted for part of the meat.
2. Fresh ground beef, cooked; Corned Beef Hash (p. 285); or Salmon Loaf mixture (p. 244) may be used for stuffing.
3. 2 qt (1.89 L) tomato juice may be poured around peppers before baking; or peppers may be served with Tomato Sauce (p. 466).

MEAT CROQUETTES

Fry: 3-4 min

Yield: 50 croquettes

Temp. 350-375 °F (175-190 °C)

Portion: 3½ oz (100 g)

Amount		Ingredient	Method
Metric	U.S.		
114 g	4 oz	Butter or margarine	Make Thick White Sauce (p. 458).
114 g	4 oz	Flour	
0.95 L	1 qt	Milk	
5 mL	1 t	Salt	
4.54 kg	10 lb	Meat, cooked, ground	Combine meat, onion, white sauce, and salt.
57 g	2 oz	Onion, finely chopped	Dip with No. 12 dipper onto a crumb-covered sheet pan. Chill.
15 mL	1 T	Salt	Shape into cylindrical croquettes.
3	3	Eggs	Dip croquettes into egg and milk mixture. Drain.
240 mL	1 c	Milk	
340 g	12 oz	Bread crumbs, fine	Roll in crumbs. Chill 2 hr before frying. Fry in deep fat.
			Serve with Mushroom Sauce (p. 463) or Tomato Sauce (p. 466).

Note: If desired, croquettes may be placed on a well-greased sheet pan and baked 1 hr at 375 °F (190 °C).

BAKED HASH
Bake: 1-1¼ hr   **Yield: 2 pans 12 × 20 × 2 in.**
Oven: 350 °F (175 °C)   **Portion: 6 oz (170 g)**

Amount			
Metric	*U.S.*	*Ingredient*	*Method*
4.54 kg	10 lb	Beef, cooked	Chop or grind meat and vegeta-
3.63 kg	8 lb	Potatoes, cooked	bles coarsely.
454 g	1 lb	Onions	
5 mL	1 t	Pepper	Add seasonings and liquid. Mix to
60 mL	¼ c	Salt	blend.
1.89 L	2 qt	Meat stock, gravy, or water	Pour into 2 baking pans. Bake. Serve with No. 6 dipper.

Note: Raw potatoes, well chopped, or hashed brown potatoes may be used in place of cooked potatoes. Increase baking time to 1¼-1½ hr.

Variations:

1. **Corned Beef Hash.** Substitute cooked corned beef for the cooked beef and decrease salt to 2 T (30 mL).

2. **Saucy Beef Hash.** Substitute 2 qt (1.89 L) condensed cream of celery soup for meat stock. Add 2 T (30 mL) Worcestershire sauce.

MEAT ROLL

Bake: 15 min   **Yield: 50 portions**
Oven: 450 °F (230 °C)   **Portion: 5 oz (142 g)**

Amount			
Metric	*U.S.*	*Ingredient*	*Method*
1.14 kg	2 lb 8 oz	Flour	Mix ingredients as for Baking
57 g	2 oz	Baking powder	Powder Biscuits (p. 115).
23 mL	1½ T	Salt	Divide dough into 4 portions. Roll
70 g	2½ oz	Fat	each portion ¼ in. thick.
0.95 L	1 qt	Milk	
3.18 kg	7 lb	Beef or other meat, cooked	Grind meat. Add gravy and seasoning, as
720 mL	3 c	Gravy, cold	needed. Mix well. Spread 2 lb (908 g) meat mixture over each dough portion. Roll as for jelly roll. Slice each roll into pieces 1 in. thick. Place on greased baking sheet. Bake.
2.84 L	3 qt	Brown Gravy or Mushroom Sauce	Serve with Brown Gravy (p. 463) or Mushroom Sauce (p. 463)

Variations:

1. **Ham Biscuit Roll.** Use ground cooked ham. Serve with Mushroom Sauce (p. 463).

2. **Tuna or Salmon Biscuit Roll.** Substitute tuna or salmon for meat and combine with Thick White Sauce (p. 458). Serve with Cheese Sauce (p. 459).

3. **Chicken or Turkey Biscuit Roll.** Substitute cooked poultry for meat. Serve with Mushroom Sauce (p. 463).

CREAMED BEEF

Yield: 6¼ qt (5.91 L)
Portion: ½ c (120 mL)

Amount		Ingredient	Method
Metric	U.S.		
4.54 kg	10 lb	Ground beef	Brown beef and onion.
120 mL	½ c	Onions, chopped	Drain excess fat. Use for making sauce.
340 g	12 oz	Fat	Make into Medium White Sauce (p. 458).
170 g	6 oz	Flour	
1.42 L	1½ qt	Meat stock	Add to browned meat.
1.42 L	1½ qt	Milk	Serve with 4-oz (114-g) ladle over toast, biscuits, or baked potato.
45 mL	3 T	Salt	
5 mL	1 t	Pepper	

Note: 1½ oz (43 g) beef soup base added to 1½ qt (1.42 L) water may be substituted for meat stock.

CREAMED CHIPPED BEEF

Yield: 6¼ qt (5.91 L)
Portion: ½ c (120 mL)

Amount		Ingredient	Method
Metric	U.S.		
1.14 kg	2 lb 8 oz	Chipped beef	Chop beef coarsely.
454 g	1 lb	Fat	Brown lightly in fat.
567 g	1 lb 4 oz	Butter or margarine	Make into Medium White Sauce (p. 458).
284 g	10 oz	Flour	Add chipped beef.
4.73 L	5 qt	Milk	Add salt and pepper to taste. Serve with 4-oz (114-g) ladle on toast or with baked potato.

Variations:

1. **Creamed Chipped Beef and Peas.** Reduce beef to 2 lb (908 g) and add 1 40-oz (114-kg) package frozen peas, cooked until just done, just before serving.

2. **Chipped Beef and Noodles.** Add 2 lb (908 g) ground Cheddar cheese to white sauce. Combine with 2 lb (908 g) noodles, cooked. Top with buttered crumbs. Bake 30 min at 350 °F (175 °C).

3. **Chipped Beef and Eggs.** Add 2 doz hard-cooked eggs, sliced or coarsely chopped. Reduce white sauce to 1 gal (3.79 L).

CHILI CON CARNE

Yield: 3 gal (11.36 L)
Portion: 1 c (240 mL)

Amount			
Metric	U.S.	Ingredient	Method
1.36 kg	3 lb	Pinto, kidney, or red beans	Wash beans. Add boiling water. Cover and let soak 1 hr or longer.
3.79 L	1 gal	Water, boiling	Cook until tender, approximately 1½ hr.
4.08 kg	9 lb	Ground beef	Brown beef and onions in steam-jacketed kettle.
227 g	8 oz	Onions, chopped	
1.42 L	1½ qt	Tomato purée	Mix tomato and seasonings.
57 g	2 oz	Chili powder	Add to beef. Cook until blended.
85 g	3 oz	Cumin seed, ground	
45 mL	3 T	Salt	
57 g	2 oz	Sugar	
		Water to make total volume of 3 gal. (11.36 L)	Add beans and water. Simmer 1½-2 hr.

Notes:
1. If desired, thicken chili by mixing 5 oz (142 g) flour and 2 c (480 mL) cold water. Add to chili mixture and heat until flour is cooked.
2. If canned beans are used, substitute 1½ No. 10 cans.

Variation:
Chili Spaghetti. Use only 6 lb (2.72 kg) ground beef. Proceed as for Chili Con Carne. Cook 1½ lb (680 g) spaghetti and add to chili mixture just before serving. Macaroni may be substituted for spaghetti.

Veal

BREADED VEAL

Bake: 1½ hr
Oven: 300 °F (150 °C)

Yield: 50 portions
Portion: 5 oz (142 g) A.P.

Amount		Ingredient	Method
Metric	*U.S.*		
6.80 kg	15 lb	Veal round, sliced ¼ in. thick	Cut meat into 5-oz (142 g) portions. Dredge in flour and salt.
227 g	8 oz	Flour	
45 mL	3 T	Salt	
3	3	Eggs, beaten	Dip veal in mixture of egg and milk. Drain.
240 mL	1 c	Milk	
340 g	12 oz	Bread crumbs	Roll in fine bread crumbs.
908 g	2 lb	Fat	Brown meat in hot fat. Place, slightly overlapping, in 2 baking pans 12 × 20 × 2 in. Add about 2 c (480 mL) of water to each pan. Cover with aluminum foil. Bake.

Note: Veal cutlets, 4 or 5 oz (114 or 142 g) each, may be used.

Variations:

1. **Veal Parmesan.** Add 8 oz (227 g) grated Parmesan cheese to bread crumbs. After cutlets are browned and arranged in baking pans, pour 2 qt (1.89 L) Tomato Sauce (p. 466) over them. Bake 1 hr.

2. **Veal Scallopini.** Dredge cutlets in seasoned flour and sauté in hot fat. Arrange in baking pans. Sauté 3 lb (1.36 kg) fresh mushrooms, sliced, and 1 lb (454 g) chopped onion in 8 oz (227 g) butter or margarine. Add 2 qt (1.89 L) chicken stock (p. 479), 1½ c (360 mL) lemon juice or vinegar, and 1 t (5 mL) each of parsley, rosemary, and oregano or marjoram. Pour over cutlets. Bake 1 hr.

VEAL IN SOUR CREAM

Bake: 2 hr
Oven: 300 °F (150 °C)

Yield: 50 chops
Portion: 5 oz (142 g) A.P.

Amount		Ingredient	Method
Metric	*U.S.*	*Ingredient*	*Method*
7.71 kg	17 lb (50 chops cut 3 per lb)	Veal chops	Mix flour and seasonings. Dredge chops in flour mixture.
227 g	8 oz	Flour	
45 mL	3 T	Salt	
5 mL	1 t	Pepper	
680 g	1 lb 8 oz	Fat	Brown chops in hot fat. Place, slightly overlapping, in 2 baking pans.
1.89 L	2 qt	Cultured sour cream	Mix cream and water. Pour over chops.
1.89 L	2 qt	Water	Cover with aluminum foil. Bake.

Note: Veal cutlets, 3 or 4 per lb (454 g) may be used in place of veal chops.

VEAL BIRDS
Bake: 2 hr
Oven: 300 °F (150 °C)

Yield: 50 portions
Portion: 4 oz (114 g)

Amount			
Metric	*U.S.*	*Ingredient*	*Method*
5.67 kg	12 lb 8 oz	Veal round, ¼ in. thick	Cut veal into 4-oz (114 g) servings.
170 g	6 oz	Fat	Sauté onion and celery in the fat.
60 mL	¼ c	Onions, finely chopped	
240 mL	1 c	Celery, finely chopped	
1.36 kg	3 lb	Bread, dry, cubed	Combine bread, onion, seasonings, and stock.
10 mL	2 t	Salt	Place No. 16 dipper of bread mixture on each piece of meat. Roll and fasten with a toothpick.
3 mL	½ t	Pepper	
30 mL	2 T	Sage	
1.18 L	1¼ qt (variable)	Beef or chicken stock (p. 479) or water.	
227 g	8 oz	Flour	Roll each bird in flour and salt mixture. Brown in hot fat.
45 mL	3 T	Salt	
1.14 kg	2 lb 8 oz	Fat	Place in 2 baking pans. Add 2 c (480 mL) water to each pan. Cover with aluminum foil. Bake.

Note: Veal cutlets (4 oz/114 g) may be substituted for the veal round.

Variations:
1. **Beef Birds.** Make with beef cubed steaks.
2. **Pork Birds.** Make with pork cutlets.

MOCK DRUMSTICKS
Bake: 2 hr   **Yield: 50**
Oven: 350 °F (175 °C)   **Portion: 4 oz (114 g)**

Amount		Ingredient	Method
Metric	*U.S.*		
4.54 kg	10 lb	Veal, 1-in. or beef, 1-in. cubes	Place meat on skewers, alternating veal and pork pieces. Use 2 pork and 3 veal on each skewer.
3.18 kg	7 lb	Pork, 1-in. cubes	
50	50	Skewers	
227 g	8 oz	Flour	Dredge each drumstick in flour and salt.
45 mL	3 T	Salt	
3	3	Eggs, beaten	Dip in combined eggs and water. Drain.
240 mL	1 c	Water or milk	
340 g	12 oz	Crumbs, fine	Roll in crumbs to cover.
454 g	1 lb	Fat	Brown drumsticks in hot fat. Place in 2 baking pans. Add 2 c (480 mL) water to each pan. Cover with aluminum foil. Bake.

Note: 1 fresh mushroom may be placed at each end of skewer before cooking.

Variation:
Barbecued Kabobs. Arrange meat on skewers as above. Dredge in flour and brown in hot fat. Cover with Barbecue Sauce (p. 464). Bake 2 hr at 350 °F (175 °C).

VEAL FRICASSEE

Yield: 50 portions
Portion: 5 oz (142 g)

Amount			
Metric	*U.S.*	*Ingredient*	*Method*
6.80 kg	15 lb	Veal, 1-in. cubes	Dredge veal in flour. Brown in hot fat.
227 g	8 oz	Flour	
454 g	1 lb	Fat	
3.79 L	1 gal	Water	Add water and salt. Simmer 2 hr or until meat is tender.
45 mL	3 T	Salt	

Variations:

1. **Curried Veal.** Add 2 oz (57 g) curry powder when water is added.

2. **Veal Paprika with Rice.** Add ½ c (120 mL) paprika to flour. Cook 12 oz (340 g) minced onions with veal. Add 2 qt (1.89 L) cultured sour cream the last few minutes of cooking. Serve with hot rice.

VEAL PATTIES
Bake: 25-30 min
Oven: 375 °F (190 °C)

Yield: 50 patties
Portion: 5 oz (142 g)

Amount			
Metric	*U.S.*	*Ingredient*	*Method*
5.44 kg	12 lb	Veal, ground	Combine all ingredients carefully. Do not overmix.
908 g	2 lb	Salt pork, ground	Measure with No. 8 dipper. Form into patties. Place on sheet pan.
227 g	8 oz	Bread crumbs	
12	12	Eggs, beaten	Bake.
45 mL	3 T	Salt	
10 mL	2 t	Pepper	
28 g	1 oz	Onion, grated	
360 mL	1½ c	Milk	

Note: Wrap with a strip of bacon and fasten with a toothpick if desired.

Variations:

1. **Lamb Patties.** Substitute 14 lb (6.35 kg) ground lamb for veal and salt pork. Wrap each pattie with a strip of bacon. Bake approximately 30 min.

2. **Stuffed Meat Cakes.** Place thin slice of onion and tomato between 2 thin meat patties. Press edges together and fasten with a toothpick. Bake approximately 30 min.

Pork

DEVILED PORK CHOPS
Bake: 1½ hr   **Yield: 50 chops**
Oven: 350 °F (175 °C)   **Portion: 5 oz (142 g) A.P.**

Amount		Ingredient	Method
Metric	*U.S.*		
7.71 kg	17 lb	Pork chops, cut 3 per lb	Combine chili sauce, water, and seasonings into a sauce.
1.42 L	1½ qt	Chili sauce	Dip each chop in sauce. Place on
720 mL	3 c	Water	baking pan. Bake.
5 mL	1 t	Mustard, dry	
45 mL	3 T	Worcestershire sauce	
45 mL	3 T	Lemon juice	
10 mL	2 t	Onion, grated	

Note: Chops also may be placed on edge, close together, with fat side up.
Bake 2-2½ hr.

Variations:
1. **Barbecued Pork Chops.** Pour Barbecue Sauce (p. 464) over chops.
   Bake.

2. **Pork Chops Supreme.** Arrange chops on baking pans. Sprinkle with
   salt. Place on each chop: 1 thin slice lemon, 1 thin slice onion, 1 T (15
   mL) brown sugar, and 1 T (15 mL) catsup. Cover and bake 45 min;
   uncover and bake 30 min longer. Baste just before serving.

PORK CHOPS WITH DRESSING
Bake: 1½ hr
Oven: 350 °F (175 °C)

Yield: 50 chops
Portion: 5 oz (142 g)

Amount		Ingredient	Method
Metric	*U.S.*		
7.71 kg	17 lb	Pork chops, cut 3 per lb	Brown chops. Arrange in 2 12 × 20 × 2 in. baking or counter pans.
57 g	2 oz	Salt	Sprinkle with salt.
⅔ recipe	⅔ recipe	Bread Dressing (p. 362)	Place 2 oz (57 g) dressing (No. 16 dipper) on each chop.
2.84 L	3 qt	Milk	Pour milk over chops. Bake. Baste frequently with milk.

Note: Dressing may be spread in pan and pork chops placed on top.

Variations:

1. **Baked Pork Chops.** Dredge chops in 8 oz (227 g) flour, 2 oz (57 g) fat, and 2 oz (57 g) salt, mixed. Place on well-greased sheet pans. Bake until thoroughly cooked and browned (approximately 1¼ hr at 350 °F/ 175 °C).

2. **Breaded Pork Chops.** Dip chops in mixture of 3 eggs and 1 c (240 mL) water. Roll in bread crumbs (approximately 1 lb/454 g). Place on greased sheet pans. Pour about 8 oz (227 g) melted fat over top of chops. Bake at 400 °F (205 °C) until browned—about 20 min. Remove from oven and arrange in partially overlapping rows in 2 counter pans. Add 2 c (480 mL) water to each counter pan and return to oven. Cook slowly until well done, approximately 1 hr at 325 °F (165 °C).

3. **Stuffed Pork Chops.** Use 6-oz (170-g) pork chops. Cut pocket in each chop. Fill with dressing and proceed as above. Use ½ Bread Dressing recipe or Apple Stuffing recipe (p. 362).

BARBECUED SPARERIBS
Bake: 2 hr
Oven: 350 °C (175 °C)

Yield: 50 portions
Portion: 8 oz (227 g) A.P.

	Amount			
Metric	*U.S.*	*Ingredient*	*Method*	
11.34 kg	25 lb	Pork spareribs or loin back ribs	Separate ribs into 8-oz (227-g) portions. Place in roasting pans. Brown uncovered in oven. Pour off excess fat.	
2.84 L	3 qt	Barbecue Sauce (p. 464)	Pour Barbecue Sauce over ribs. Cover. Bake until meat is tender. Uncover and bake an additional 20-30 min.	

Note: For more generous portions, use 40 lb (18.14 kg) spareribs and 1 gal (3.79 L) Barbecue Sauce.

Variations:

1. **Barbecued Lamb.** Substitute lamb shanks for spareribs.

2. **Barbecued Shortribs.** Substitute beef or veal shortribs for spareribs.

3. **Sweet-Sour Spareribs.** Brown spareribs for 30 min in 400 °F (205 °C) oven, or simmer in water 1 hr. Drain and cover with Sweet-Sour Sauce (p. 467). Bake in 350 °F (175 °C) oven until meat is done. Serve with Steamed Rice or Fried Rice with Almonds (p. 190).

SWEET AND SOUR PORK

Yield: 50 portions
Portion: 6 oz (170 g) pork,
4 oz (114 g) rice

Amount		Ingredient	Method
Metric	*U.S.*		
4.54 kg	10 lb	Pork, lean, 1-in. cubes	Pour soy sauce over meat. Mix lightly. Let stand at least 1 hr.
240 mL	1 c	Soy sauce	
340 g	12 oz	Fat	Drain soy sauce; save. Brown meat in hot fat. Drain excess fat.
1.42 L	1½ qt	Stock, chicken or meat	Add broth and drained soy sauce to meat. Simmer until meat is tender, approximately 1 hr
284 g	10 oz	Brown sugar	Combine sugar, cornstarch, and salt.
85 g	3 oz	Cornstarch	
8 mL	1½ t	Salt	Add pineapple juice, vinegar, and soy sauce. Mix until smooth.
360 mL	1½ c	Pineapple juice	
480 mL	2 c	Vinegar	Add to meat mixture while stirring. Cook slowly until thickened.
180 mL	¾ c	Soy sauce	
454 g	1 lb	Green pepper strips	15 min before serving, add green peppers and onions and cook gently.
908 g	2 lb	Onions, medium, cut into eighths	Just before serving, add tomato wedges and pineapple chunks.
1.36 kg	3 lb	Tomatoes, medium, cut into wedges	Heat.
1 No. 10 can	1 No. 10 can	Pineapple chunks, well drained	
1.36 kg	3 lb	Rice	Cook rice (p. 190)
3.55 L	3¾ qt	Water, boiling	Serve pork over rice.
30 mL	2 T	Salt	
30 mL	2 T	Oil (optional)	

Note: 1½ oz (43 g) chicken soup base added to 1½ qt (1.42 L) water may be substituted for stock.

Variation:
Sweet and Sour Chicken. Substitute cooked chicken or turkey for the pork.
   Do not brown.

GLAZED BAKED HAM

Bake: 4½ hr at 300 °F (150 °C)
then ½ hr at 400 °F (205 °C)

Yield: 50 portions
Portion: 3 oz (85 g)

Amount		Ingredient	Method
Metric	*U.S.*		
9.08 kg	20 lb	Ham, whole, cured	Trim excess fat from ham if necessary. Place fat side up on a rack in roasting pan. Do not cover. Bake about 4½ hr at 300 °F (150 °C). (See timetable p. 259.) If ready-to-eat ham is used, shorten baking time.
45 mL	3 T	Whole cloves	Remove ham from oven about ½ hr before it is done. Drain off drippings and trim thin layer of browned fat from entire surface. Score ham fat ¼ in. deep in diamond pattern. Stud with whole cloves. Cover with glaze.
HAM GLAZE			
227 g	8 oz	Brown sugar	Combine ingredients for glaze. Spoon over ham. Repeat if a heavier glaze is desired. Return ham to hot oven (400 °F/ 205 °C) and complete baking.
30 mL	2 T	Cornstarch	
60 mL	¼ c	Corn syrup	
30 mL	2 T	Pineapple juice	

Notes:
1. Ham may be simmered in kettle for 3-4 hr, then trimmed, glazed, and the cooking completed in oven.
2. 15 lb (6.80 kg) boneless, fully cooked ham may be used. Bake 15-18 min per lb or until internal temperature reaches 140 °F (60 °C). Add glaze during last half hour of cooking.

Variations:
1. **Apricot Glaze.** 1 c (240 mL) apricot jam and ¼ c (60 mL) fruit juice or enough to cover ham.

2. **Brown Sugar Glaze.** 1 c (240 mL) brown sugar, 1½ t (8 mL) dry mustard (or 3 T/45 mL prepared mustard), and ¼ c (60 mL) vinegar.

3. **Cranberry Glaze.** 1¼ c (300 mL) strained cranberry sauce, or enough to cover.

4. **Honey Glaze.** 1 c (240 mL) honey, ½ c (120 mL) brown sugar, and ¼ c (60 mL) fruit juice. Baste with fruit juice or ginger ale.

5. **Orange Glaze.** 1 c (240 mL) orange marmalade and ¼ c (60 mL) spiced peach juice or orange juice.

BAKED HAM SLICES
Bake: 1½-2 hr
Oven: 325 °F (165 °C)

Yield: 50 portions
Portion: 2½ oz (85 g) cooked meat

Amount		*Ingredient*	*Method*
Metric	*U.S.*		
8.16 kg	18 lb	Ham, cured, center cut, ½ in. thick	Cut ham into 5-oz (142-g) portions.
397 g	14 oz	Brown sugar	Combine sugar and mustard. Rub over surface of ham slices. Place in 2 baking pans 12 × 20 × 2 in.
45 mL	3 T	Mustard, dry	
1.89 L	2 qt	Water	Pour combined liquids over ham slices. Cover with aluminum foil. Bake.
240 mL	1 c	Pineapple or spiced fruit juice	

Notes:
1. If fully cooked ham is used, reduce cooking time to 30-45 min.
2. Milk may be substituted for fruit juice.

Variations:
1. **Baked Ham Slices with Pineapple Rings.** When ham is tender, cover with pineapple rings, bake until pineapple is browned.

2. **Baked Ham Slices with Orange Sauce.** Arrange ham slices in counter pan and cover with Orange Sauce (p. 474). Cover with aluminum foil and bake.

HAM LOAF

Bake: 1-1½ hr
Oven: 350 °F (175 °C)

Yield: 5 pans 4 × 9 in.
Portion: 5 oz (142 g)

Amount		Ingredient	Method
Metric	U.S.		
1.81 kg	4 lb	Ground cured ham	Combine all ingredients.
1.81 kg	4 lb	Ground veal or beef	Mix (low speed) only until ingredients are blended. **DO NOT OVERMIX.**
1.81 kg	4 lb	Ground fresh pork	Press mixture into 5 loaf pans, about 3 lb (1.36 kg) per pan.
0.95 L	1 qt	Milk	(Meat may be baked in 12 × 20 × 4 in. baking or counter pan.
12	12	Eggs, beaten	Press mixture into pan and divide into 4 loaves. Increase
5 mL	1 t	Pepper	baking time to 1½-2 hr.
454 g	1 lb	Bread crumbs	Cover top of loaves with glaze during last 30 min of cooking if desired.

Notes:
1. Ground cooked ham may be used.
2. Veal or beef may be omitted, using 8 lb (3.63 kg) ground cooked ham and 4 lb (1.81 kg) fresh pork.

Variations:
1. **Glazed Ham Loaf.** Cover top of loaves with a mixture of 1½ lb (680 g) brown sugar, 1 c (240 mL) vinegar, and 1½ T (23 mL) dry mustard.

2. **Glazed Ham Balls.** Measure with No. 8 dipper and shape into balls. Place on baking pans. Brush with glaze and bake.

3. **Ham Patties with Pineapple.** Measure with No. 8 dipper and shape into patties. Top with slice of pineapple and clove. Pour pineapple juice over patties and bake.

4. **Ham Patties with Cranberries.** Spread pan with Cranberry Sauce (p. 431). Place ham patties on sauce and bake.

HAM AND EGG SCALLOP

Bake: 30-40 min
Oven: 400 °F (205 °C)

Yield: 2 pans 12 × 20 × 2 in.
Portion: 5 oz (142 g)

Amount		Ingredient	Method
Metric	U.S.		
454 g	1 lb	Butter or margarine	Make into Medium White Sauce (p. 458).
227 g	8 oz	Flour	
15 mL	1 T	Salt	
3.55 L	3¾ qt	Milk	
1.81 kg	4 lb	Ham, chopped	Fill 2 greased baking pans with alternate layers of ham, eggs, and white sauce.
36	36	Eggs, hard cooked, sliced	
340 g	12 oz	Bread crumbs	Sprinkle buttered crumbs over top of ham and egg mixture. Bake.
85 g	3 oz	Butter or margarine, melted	

Variation:
Ham and Sweetbread Casserole. Cut ham into cubes. Substitute 4 lb
(1.81 kg) sweetbreads, cooked and cubed, for eggs.

CREAMED HAM

Yield: 6¼ qt (5.91 L)
Portion: ½ c (120 mL)

Amount		Ingredient	Method
Metric	U.S.		
454 g	1 lb	Butter or margarine	Make into Medium White Sauce (p. 458).
170 g	6 oz	Flour	
3.79 L	1 gal	Milk	
2.72 kg	6 lb	Ham, cooked, cubed	Add ham and heat slowly for approximately 20 min.
To taste	To taste	Salt	Salt to taste. Serve with 4-oz (114-g) ladle over biscuits, toast, spoon bread, corn bread, or cheese soufflé.

Note: 1 lb (454 g) chopped celery, sliced mushrooms, or chopped hard-cooked eggs may be added. Reduce ham to 5 lb (2.27 kg).

Variation:
Plantation Shortcake. Substitute 3 lb (1.36 kg) cooked turkey for 3 lb (1.36 kg) cooked ham. Add 1 lb (454 g) grated Cheddar cheese to sauce. Serve over hot corn bread.

HAM-CHEESE CASSEROLE

Bake: 1 hr
Oven: 325 °F (165 °C)

Yield: 2 pans 12 × 20 × 2 in.
Portion: 6 oz (170 g)

Amount		Ingredient	Method
Metric	*U.S.*		
794 g	1 lb 12 oz	Noodles, fine	Cook noodles (p. 191).
5.68 L	1½ gal	Water, boiling	Drain.
23 mL	1½ T	Salt	
23 mL	1½ T	Oil (optional)	
567 g	1 lb 4 oz	Butter or margarine	Make Medium White Sauce (p. 458).
454 g	1 lb	Flour	
3.79 L	1 gal	Milk	
28 g	1 oz	Salt	
5 mL	1 t	Pepper	
3.63 kg	8 lb	Ham, coarsely ground	Arrange in alternate layers in 2 greased baking pans half the noodles, ham, and cheese.
1.36 kg	3 lb	Cheddar cheese, grated	Cover with half the white sauce. Repeat layers; pour remaining white sauce over top.
454 g	1 lb	Bread crumbs	Sprinkle with buttered crumbs.
114 g	4 oz	Butter or margarine, melted	Bake.

CREAMY NOODLES WITH HAM

Bake: 1 hr
Oven: 325 °F (165 °C)

Yield: 2 pans 12 × 20 × 2 in.
Portion: 6 oz (170 g)

Amount		*Ingredient*	*Method*
Metric	*U.S.*		
908 g	2 lb	Noodles	Cook noodles (p. 191). Drain.
568 L	1½ gal	Water, boiling	
30 mL	2 T	Salt	
30 mL	2 T	Oil (optional)	
3.18 kg	7 lb	Ham, coarsely ground	Combine and add to cooked noodles; mix lightly.
2.27 kg	5 lb	Cottage cheese	Place in 2 greased baking pans.
1.42 L	1½ qt	Cultured sour cream	
340 g	12 oz	Onion, minced fine	
60 mL	¼ c	Worcestershire Sauce	
30 mL	2 T	Garlic salt	
30 mL	2 T	Salt	
2 dashes	2 dashes	Tabasco sauce	
340 g	12 oz	Parmesan cheese	
114 g	4 oz	Parmesan cheese	Sprinkle cheese over top. Bake.

OVEN-FRIED BACON

Bake: 6-8 min
Temp. 375 °F (190 °C)

Yield: 50 portions
Portion: 2 slices

Amount			
Metric	*U.S.*	*Ingredient*	*Method*
50 slices (2.27-2.72 kg)	50 slices (5-6 lb)	Bacon (17-20 slices per lb)	Arrange bacon slices on sheet pans. Bake without turning until crisp. Pour off accumulating fat if necessary. Drain on paper towels or place in perforated pans for serving.

CHEESE-STUFFED WIENERS

Bake: 30 min
Oven: 350 °F (175 °C)

Yield: 100 wieners
Portion: 2 wieners

Amount			
Metric	*U.S.*	*Ingredient*	*Method*
3.74 kg	8 lb 4 oz	Weiners, 12 per lb	Split wieners lengthwise, but do not cut completely through.
1.36 kg 0.95 L	3 lb 1 qt	Cheddar cheese Pickle relish	Cut cheese into strips about 3½ in. long. Place a strip of cheese and about ½ T relish in each wiener.
100 slices (1.93 kg)	100 slices (4 lb 4 oz)	Bacon, 24-26 slices per lb	Wrap a slice of bacon around each wiener. Secure with a tooth-pick. Bake.

Note: 1 slice of bacon may be wrapped around 2 wieners.

Variations:

1. **Barbecued Wieners.** Leave wieners whole. Place in counter pans. Cover with Barbecue Sauce (p. 464) and bake about 30 min at 400 °F (205 °C). Add more sauce as necessary.

2. **Wieners and Sauerkraut.** Steam wieners or cook in boiling water. Serve with sauerkraut (2 No. 10 cans).

SAUSAGE ROLLS

Bake: 20 min
Oven: 400 °F (205 °C)

Yield: 50 rolls
Portion: 1 roll, ¼ c (60 mL) gravy

Amount		Ingredient	Method
Metric	U.S.		
5.67 kg	12 lb 8 oz	Sausages, link	Partially cook sausages. Save fat for gravy.
1.14 g	2 lb 8 oz	Flour	Make into biscuit dough (p. 115).
85 g	3 oz	Baking powder	Divide dough into 2 portions. Roll
28 g	1 oz	Salt	each portion to ½-in. thickness
454 g	1 lb	Fat	and cut into 3 × 4 in. rectan-
0.95 L	1 qt	Milk	gles.
			Place 2 sausages in the center of each piece of dough and fold over. Bake.
170 g	6 oz	Sausage fat	Make into gravy (p. 463).
170 g	6 oz	Flour	Serve 2-oz (57-g) ladle of gravy
10 mL	2 t	Salt	over each sausage roll.
3 mL	½ t	Pepper	
2.84 L	3 qt	Water or meat stock	

Variation:

Pigs in Blankets. Substitute wieners for link sausages. Serve with Cheese Sauce (p. 459).

POTATO FRANKFURTER CASSEROLE

Bake: 45 min
Oven: 350 °F (175 °C)

Yield: 2 pans 12 × 20 × 2 in.
Portion: 6 oz (170 g)

Metric	U.S.	Ingredient	Method
	Amount		
Metric	*U.S.*	*Ingredient*	*Method*
2.27 kg	5 lb	Frankfurters	Cut each frankfurter into 4 or 5 pieces
1.42 L	1½ qt	Green beans, cut	Drain beans, reserving liquid. Measure and add enough milk to make 3 qt (2.84 L).
227 g	8 oz	Butter or margarine	Melt butter or margarine. Sauté onion and green pepper until tender.
567 g	1 lb 4 oz	Onion, chopped	
142 g	5 oz	Green pepper, chopped	
227 g	8 oz	Flour	Add flour to onion and green pepper. Mix well.
15 mL	1 T	Salt	
2.84 L	3 qt	Milk and liquid from green beans	Gradually stir in liquid. Cook until sauce thickens.
4.54 kg	10 lb	Potatoes, frozen hash brown	Combine potatoes and green beans. Place in 2 greased baking pans. Pour sauce evenly over vegetables. Arrange frankfurter pieces over top.
454 g	1 lb	Cheddar cheese, grated	Sprinkle with cheese. Bake.

SCRAPPLE

Amount		Ingredient	Method
Metric	*U.S.*		
3.63 kg	8 lb	Pork, fresh	Boil pork, water, and salt until
5.68 L	6 qt	Water	meat falls to pieces. Add water
60 mL	¼ c	Salt	as necessary.
			When done, remove meat and bones from liquid. Remove bones and gristle from meat.
			Finely chop meat and return to liquid (about 1¼ gal/4.73 L).
1.36 kg	3 lb	Cornmeal, yellow	Add corn meal slowly, while stirring constantly.
			Boil 5 min, place in steamer and cook 3 hr.
			Turn into 5 loaf pans to mold.
			Cut into ½-in. slices. Dip in flour. Fry until brown and crisp on both sides.

Note: 8 lb (3.63 kg) pork sausage may be substituted for fresh pork. Cook in 1½ gal (5.68 L) water, skim excess fat, then add corn meal and cook until thick.

Variety Meats

LIVER WITH SPANISH SAUCE
Bake: 1 hr   **Yield: 50 portions**
Oven: 350 °F (175 °C)   **Portion: 3½ oz (100 g)**

Amount			
Metric	*U.S.*	*Ingredient*	*Method*
4.54 kg	10 lb	Liver, sliced, cut 5 per lb	Dredge liver in seasoned flour. Brown in hot fat.
227 g	8 oz	Flour	
45 mL	3 T	Salt	
10 mL	2 t	Pepper	
680 g	1 lb 8 oz	Fat	
1 recipe	1 recipe	Spanish Sauce (p. 466)	Place liver in 2 baking pans. Pour Spanish Sauce over liver. Cover with aluminum foil. Bake until tender.

Note: Soaking liver in milk before cooking improves the flavor.

Variations:
1. **Liver and Onions.** Cover browned liver with 4 lb (1.81 kg) onion, sliced, and 2 qt (1.89 L) water. Bake until tender.

2. **Liver and Bacon.** Dredge liver with flour and fry in bacon fat. Top each serving with 1 slice crisp bacon.

3. **Braised Liver.** Brown liver. Cover with sauce made of: 10 oz (284 g) fat, 5 oz (142 g) flour, 3 qt (2.84 L) meat stock, 2 oz (57 g) salt, and 2 t (10 mL) pepper.

BAKED HEART WITH DRESSING
Bake: 1 hr   **Yield: 50 portions**
Oven: 300 °F (150 °C)   **Portion: 3 oz (85 g) heart,**
                                                                          3 oz (85 g) dressing

Amount			
Metric	*U.S.*	*Ingredient*	*Method*
9.08 kg	20 lb	Heart, beef	Wash, split hearts. Cut away arteries and gristle.
7.57 L	2 gal	Water	
227 g	8 oz	Onion	Add water, onion, and spices.
60 mL	4 T	Peppercorns	Simmer until almost tender (about
6	6	Bay leaves	3 hr). Drain. Reserve broth for gravy.

⅔ recipe	⅔ recipe	Bread Dressing (p. 362)	Slice heart into 3-oz (85-g) portions. Place in 2 12 × 20 × 2 in. baking or counter pans. To serve, place 3-oz (85-g) portion sliced heart over No. 10 dipper of dressing. Cover with gravy made from broth. Use cornstarch for thickening for a clear gravy.

Pies and Pastry

A good pie should have a tender, flaky crust and a filling that will just hold its shape. The type of crust produced is partially determined by the method of combining the fat and flour. A flaky crust results when fat and flour are mixed until small lumps are formed throughout the mixture. A mealy crust results when fat and flour are mixed thoroughly.

Tenderness depends largely on the kind of flour and amount of fat and water used. Excess fat increases tenderness and excess water gives a tough product. Overmixing after water has been added or use of too much flour when rolling toughens pastry also.

To make a 1-crust pie:

1. Weigh 5 oz (142 g) dough for each 8-in. crust.

2. Roll into circle 2 in. larger than pie pan.

3. Fit crust loosely into pan so that there are no air spaces between the crust and the pan.

4. Trim, allowing ½ in. extra to build up edge.

5. For custard-type pie, crimp edge, add filling and bake.

6. For cream or chiffon pies, fit pie crust over inside or outsde of pie pans. Crimp edge and prick crust with fork. Bake in a hot oven (425 °F/220 °C) 10 min or until light brown. Cool and fill. A second pan may be placed over the crust for the first part of baking, then removed and crust allowed to brown. The second pan helps to keep the crust in shape.

To make a 2-crust pie:

1. Scale 5 oz (142 g) for bottom crust and 4 oz (114 g) for top crust for each 8-in. pie.

2. Roll pastry into circle. Place bottom crust in pan and trim. If desired, leave ½ in. extra crust around edge and fold over to make a pocket of pastry to prevent fruit juices from running out.

3. Add fruit filling and brush edge of bottom crust with water.

4. Cover with top crust, in which slits or vents have been cut to allow steam to escape.

5. Trim, flute, and seal by pressing the two crusts together with the fingertips. Brush top crust with milk. Bake.

Pie Recipes

PASTRY I

Yield: 4½ lb (2.04 kg)
Pastry for 8 8-in., 2-crust pies

Amount		Ingredient	Method
Metric	*U.S.*	*Ingredient*	*Method*
908 g	2 lb	Flour	Mix flour and fat (low speed) 1
680 g	1 lb 8 oz	Fat	min.
360-420 mL	1½-1¾ c	Water, cold	Add water and salt.
23 mL	1½ T	Salt	Mix (low speed) only until a dough is formed, about 40 sec.
			Portion into 5-oz (142-g) balls for bottom crust and 4-oz (114-g) balls for top crust.
			Let stand 10 min in refrigerator before rolling.
			See p. 309 for directions for rolling.

PASTRY II[a]   **Yield: 50 lb (22.68 kg)**

| Amount | | | |
Metric	U.S.	Ingredient	Method
11.34 kg 8.16 kg	25 lb 18 lb	Flour Fat	Mix flour and fat (low speed) until blended.
3.55 L 340 g	3¾ qt 12 oz	Water, cold Salt	Add water and salt. Mix (low speed) only until dough will hold together.

[a] Similar to recipe for Pastry I except for quantity.

Notes:
1. Pastry should be mixed several hours before it is to be used. It may be stored (covered) in refrigerator for several days.
2. Hydrogenated fat was used in this recipe. If lard is used, reduce the amount by ⅛.
3. Use approximately 5 oz (142 g) for bottom crust and 4 oz (114 g) for top crust for 8-in. pie.
4. See p. 309 for directions for rolling.

GRAHAM CRACKER CRUST
Bake: 5 min   **Yield: 8 8-in. pie shells**
Oven: 375 °F (190 °C)

| Amount | | | |
Metric	U.S.	Ingredient	Method
595 g	1 lb 5 oz	Graham cracker crumbs	Mix all ingredients. Pat about 5 oz (142 g) of crumb mixture evenly into each pie
284 g	10 oz	Sugar	pan.
284 g	10 oz	Butter or margarine, melted	Bake. Fill shells with Cream Pie Filling (p. 321) or Chiffon Pie Filling (p. 326, 327).

Notes:
1. Crusts may be refrigerated several hours instead of baking.
2. Vanilla wafer crumbs may be substituted for graham cracker crumbs.
3. For 9-in. shells, 8 oz (227 g) per shell, make 1½ times the recipe.

MERINGUE FOR PIES
Bake: 12 min
Oven: 375 °F (190 °C)   **Yield: Meringue for 8 8-in. pies**

	Amount		
Metric	U.S.	Ingredient	Method
480 mL	16 (2c)	Egg whites	Add salt to egg whites. Whip past frothy stage (high speed), approximately 1½ min.
3 mL	½ t	Salt	
454 g	1 lb	Sugar	Add sugar gradually while beating. Beat until sugar has dissolved. The meringue should be stiff enough to hold peaks but not dry.
			Spread meringue on filling while it is hot. It should touch all edges of the crust. Brown in oven.

RHUBARB CUSTARD PIE
Bake: 30-35 min
Oven: 375 °F (190 °C)   **Yield: 8 8-in. pies**
                                             Portion: 6 per pie

	Amount		
Metric	U.S.	Ingredient	Method
1.81 kg	4 lb	Sugar	Mix dry ingredients.
227 g	8 oz	Flour	
5 mL	1 t	Salt	
4	4	Lemon rinds, grated	
12	12	Eggs, beaten	Combine eggs and rhubarb.
3.40 kg	7 lb 8 oz	Rhubarb, fresh, cut fine	Add dry ingredients and mix.
1.14 kg	2 lb 8 oz	Pastry (p. 310)	Make pastry. Line 8 8-in. pie pans, 5 oz (142 g) per pan. Flute edges.
			Portion 3 c (720 mL) filling into each unbaked crust. Bake.

Notes:
1.   May be topped with meringue (p. 312).
2.   Unbaked pie may be covered with a top crust or a latticed top made of ⅜-in. pastry strips.

PIES MADE WITH CANNED FRUIT
Bake: 30 min   **Yield: 8 8-in. pies**
Oven: 400 °F (205 °C)   **Portion: 6 per pie**

Amount		Ingredient	Method
Metric	*U.S.*		
1½ No. 10 cans	1½ No. 10 cans	Fruit, water pack	Drain fruit. Measure liquid and add water to make 1½ qt (1.42 L).
170 g	6 oz	Cornstarch	Bring 1 qt (0.95 L) of the liquid to boiling.
			Mix remaining 2 c (480 mL) liquid with cornstarch, then add gradually while stirring to hot liquid.
			Cook until thick and clear.
1.36 kg	3 lb	Sugar	While still hot, add sugar and salt.
15 mL	1 T	Salt	Mix thoroughly and bring to boiling point.
			Add drained fruit and mix carefully.
			Cool slightly.
2.04 kg	4 lb 8 oz	Pastry (p. 310)	Divide pastry into 5-oz (142-g) balls for bottom crust, 4-oz (114-g) balls for top crusts.
			Roll and place bottom crusts in pans.
			Measure 3 c (720 mL) filling into each unbaked pie shell. Moisten edge of bottom crust with water. Cover with perforated top crust. Seal edge, trim, and flute edges.
			Bake.

Notes:
1. May be used for all canned fruit fillings, such as apricot, blackberry, cherry, gooseberry, peach, or raspberry (sugar variable).
2. For pies made with frozen fruit, see Table 2.14.
3. For 9-in. pies, use 2 No. 10 cans fruit, 3½ lb (1.59 kg) sugar (variable), 8 oz (227 g) cornstarch, and 1 oz (28 g) salt. Use 3½ c (840 mL) filling per pie.
4. Other thickening agents may be used, such as waxy maize (4½ oz/128 g) or tapioca (7½ oz/213 g). Cold water starches also are available on the market.

PIES MADE WITH FROZEN FRUIT

BAKE: 30-40 min   **Yield: 8 8-in. pies**

Oven: 400 °F (205 °C)   **Portion: 6 per pie**

Amount			
Metric	*U.S.*	*Ingredient*	*Method*
4.54 kg	10 lb	Fruit, frozen	Thaw fruit in the unopened original container.
See Table 2.14 See Table 2.14		Sugar Cornstarch or waxy maize[a]	Measure juice. If necessary, add water to bring total liquid to 1½-2 qt (1.42-1.89 L), according to consistency desired. Heat to boiling point. Add combined sugar and starch, stirring constantly with wire whip. Add seasonings. Pour over fruit.
2.04 kg	4 lb 8 oz	Pastry (p. 310)	Divide pastry into 5-oz (142-g) balls for bottom crust, 4-oz (114-g) balls for top crust. Roll and place bottom crusts in pans. Measure 3 c (720 mL) filling into each unbaked pie shell. Moisten edge of bottom crust with water. Cover with perforated top crust. Seal edge, trim, and flute edges. Bake.

[a] Allow 2-3 oz (57-85 g) cornstarch or 2-2½ oz (57-70 g) waxy maize per qt (0.95 L) of liquid. Use of waxy maize or other waxy starch products results in a translucent soft gel through which the fruit shows clearly. The color is brighter and the gel is less opaque and less rigid. These properties make it ideal for thickening fruit fillings. It is especially important to use a waxy starch if the pies are to be frozen.

STRAWBERRY PIE

Yield: 8 8-in. pies
Portion: 6 per pie

Amount			
Metric	*U.S.*	*Ingredient*	*Method*
1.14 kg	2 lb 8 oz	Pastry (p. 310)	Make pastry. Line 8 8-in. pie pans, 5 oz (142 g) per pan. Flute edges and prick crust with fork. Bake at 425 °F (220 °C) 10 min or until light brown.
11.36 L	3 gal	Strawberries, fresh	Wash and hull berries. Set aside half of the best berries and mash the rest.
1.7 kg	3 lb 12 oz	Sugar	Mix sugar and cornstarch. Add to mashed berries.
213 g	7½ oz	Cornstarch	Cook 5-6 min or until thick and clear. Add lemon juice. Cool.
180 mL	¾ c	Lemon juice	Add reserved berries, whole or cut. Pour into baked pie shells, 3 c (720 mL) per pie.
0.95 L	1 qt	Whipping cream	Whip cream and add sugar. Top each pie with 1 c (240 mL) whipped cream.
60 mL	¼ c	Sugar	

Variation:
Strawberry-Cream Cheese Pie. Line baked crust with cream cheese (2 lb/ 908 g cream cheese, whipped with ½ c/120 mL lemon juice, ½ c/120 mL sugar, and ½ c/120 mL cream). Proceed as above. May be made in tart shells for individual servings.

Table 2.14 GUIDE FOR USING FROZEN FRUIT IN PIES OR
COBBLERS (8 8-in. pies)

Fruit *10 lb (4.54 kg)*	*Sugar*[a]	*Thickening*		*Seasonings*[b]
		Cornstarch[a]	*Waxy Maize*[a]	
Apples	1 lb 12 oz (794 g)	3 oz (85 g)	2½ oz (70 g)	Salt, 1 t, nutmeg, 1 t, cinnamon, 1 T, butter, 2 oz (57 g)
Apricots	2-2½ lb (0.91-1.14 kg)	5½ oz (156 g)	4 oz (114 g)	Cinnamon, 2 t
Berries	2½-3½ lb (1.14-1.59 kg)	6½ oz (184 g)	5 oz (142 g)	Lemon juice, 2 T Salt, 1 t
Blueberries	3 lb (1.36 kg)	8 oz (227 g)	6 oz (170 g)	Salt, 1 t, butter 2 oz (57 g), lemon juice, 1½ c, cinnamon, 1 t
Blue plums	2-2½ lb (0.91-1.14 kg)	5½ oz (156 g)	4 oz (114 g)	Salt, 1 t, butter, 2 oz (57 g)
Cherries	2 lb (908 g)	7 oz (198 g)	5 oz (142 g)	Salt, 1 t
Gooseberries	6 lb (2.72 kg)	14 oz (397 g)	10 oz (284 g)	Salt, ½ t
Peaches	1 lb 6 oz (624 g)	5½ oz (156 g)	4 oz (114 g)	Butter, 1 oz, salt, 1 t, almond extract, ¼ t
Pineapple	2-2½ lb (0.91-1.14 kg)	5½ oz (156 g)	4 oz (114 g)	Salt, 1 t
Rhubarb	2 lb (908 g)	7 oz (198 g)	5 oz (142 g)	Salt, 1 t
Strawberries	2 lb (908 g)	12 oz (340 g)	8½ oz (240 g)	Lemon juice, ¾ c, red color, ¾ t

[a] The amount of sugar and cornstarch or waxy maize added to the fruit
will vary according to the pack of the fruit and individual preferences of
flavor and consistency. Frozen fruits packed without the addition of sugar
are known as "dry pack." When sugar is added during the freezing
process, the ratio is usually 3, 4, or 5 parts by weight of fruit to 1 part by
weight of sugar. Use less thickening for cobblers.
[b] Metric equivalents: 1 t (5 mL), 1 T (15 mL), ¾ c (180 mL), 1½ c (360
mL).

FRESH APPLE PIE
Bake: 45 min or until
apples are done
Oven: 400 °F (205 °C)

Yield: 8 8-in. pies
Portion: 6 per pie

Amount		Ingredient	Method
Metric	*U.S.*		
5.44 kg	12 lb (E.P.)	Apples, tart, peeled and sliced	Combine sugar, flour, and nutmeg. Add to apples and mix carefully.
1.47 kg	3 lb 4 oz	Sugar	
114 g	4 oz	Flour	
10 mL	2 t	Nutmeg	
2.04 kg	4 lb 8 oz	Pastry (p. 310)	Make pastry. Line 8 8-in. pie pans, 5 oz (142 g) per pan.
227 g	8 oz	Butter or margarine, melted	Portion 2 lb (908 g) filling into each unbaked crust. Add 1 oz (28 g) butter or margarine to each pie. Moisten edge of bottom crust. Cover with perforated top crust (4 oz/114 g). Seal edge, trim excess dough, and flute edges. Bake.

Variation:
Apple Crumb Pie. Omit top crust. Sprinkle apples with Streusel Topping:
Mix 1 lb (454 g) flour, 1 lb 10 oz (737 g) sugar, 2 oz (57 g) nonfat dry milk,
and 1 t (5 mL) salt. Cut in 10 oz (284 g) butter or margarine and add 6 oz
(170 g) chopped pecans. Use 1 c (240 mL) per pie. Bake until apples are
done and topping is brown.

RAISIN PIE

Bake: 30 min
Oven: 400 °F (205 °C)

Yield: 8 8-in. pies
Portion: 6 per pie

Amount			
Metric	*U.S.*	*Ingredient*	*Method*
1.81 kg 4.26 L	4 lb 4½ qt	Raisins, washed Water, hot	Simmer raisins until plump.
1.02 kg 170 g 10 mL	2 lb 4 oz 6 oz 2 t	Sugar Cornstarch Salt	Add combined sugar, cornstarch, and salt. Cook until thickened. Remove from heat.

90 mL
85 g
	6 T
	3 oz
		Lemon juice
		Butter or mar-
		  garine
			Add juice and butter or margar-
			  ine.
			Cool slightly.

2.04 kg	4 lb 8 oz	Pastry (p. 310)	Make pastry. Line 8 8-in. pie pans,
			  5 oz (142 g) per pan.
			Portion 3 c (720 mL) filling into
			  each unbaked crust.
			Moisten edge of bottom crust.
			Cover with perforated top crust (4
			  oz/114 g). Seal edge, trim ex-
			  cess dough, and flute edges.
			Bake.

Note: A superior product is obtained if 3 qt (2.84 L) cream is substituted
for 3 qt (2.84 L) water.

DRIED APRICOT PIE
Bake: 30 min
Oven: 400 °F (205 °C)

Yield: 8 8-in pies
Portion: 6 per pie

Amount			
Metric	*U.S.*	*Ingredient*	*Method*
2.27 kg	5 lb	Apricots, dried	Wash and drain apricots. Cover with hot water; let stand 1 hr. Cook slowly without stirring until tender.
1.81 kg 70 g 120 mL	4 lb 2½ oz ½ c	Sugar Cornstarch Water	Combine sugar and cornstarch. Mix with water. Add to apricots a few minutes before done. Continue cooking until juice is clear.
2.04 kg	4 lb 8 oz	Pastry (p. 310)	Make pastry. Line 8 8-in. pie pans, 5 oz (142 g) per pan. Portion 3 c (720 mL) filling into each unbaked crust. Moisten edge of bottom crust. Cover with perforated top crust (4 oz/114 g). Seal edge, trim excess dough, and flute edges. Bake.

FRESH RHUBARB PIE

Bake: 35 min
Oven: 400 °F (205°C)

Yield: 8 8-in. pies
Portion: 6 per pie

Amount			
Metric	*U.S.*	*Ingredient*	*Method*
4.54 kg	10 lb	Rhubarb, ½-in. pieces	Combine all ingredients. Let stand 30 min.
170 g	6 oz	Tapioca	
2.5 kg	5 lb 8 oz	Sugar	
10 mL	2 t	Salt	
45 mL	3 T	Orange rind, grated	
142 g	5 oz	Butter or margarine, melted	
2.04 kg	4 lb 8 oz	Pastry (p. 310)	Make pastry. Line 8 8-in. pie pans, 5 oz (142 g) per pan. Portion 3 c (720 mL) filling into each unbaked crust. Moisten edges with cold water. Cover with top crust or pastry strips. Press edges together. Bake.

Note: 8 oz (227 g) cornstarch or 5 oz (142 g) waxy maize may be substituted for tapioca.

CREAM PIE
Bake: 12 min   **Yield: 8 8-in. pies**
Oven: 375 °F (190 °C)   **Portion: 6 per pie**

Amount			
Metric	*U.S.*	*Ingredient*	*Method*
1.14 kg	2 lb 8 oz	Pastry (p. 310)	Make pastry. Line 8 8-in. pie pans, 5 oz (142 g) per pan. Flute edges and prick crust with fork. Bake at 425 °F (220 °C) 10 min or until light brown.
2.84 L	3 qt	Milk	Heat milk to boiling point.
312 g	11 oz	Cornstarch	Mix dry ingredients. Add cold milk and stir until smooth.
1.02 kg	2 lb 4 oz	Sugar	Add to hot milk gradually, stirring
10 mL	2 t	Salt	briskly with a wire whip. Cook
0.95 L	1 qt	Milk, cold	over hot water until smooth and thick, approximately 10 min.
16	16	Egg yolks, beaten	Add while stirring a small amount of hot mixture to the beaten egg yolks. Combine all ingredients stirring constantly. Stir slowly and cook 5-10 min. Remove from heat.
114 g	4 oz	Butter or margarine	Add butter or margarine and vanilla.
30 mL	2 T	Vanilla	Pour 3 c (720 mL) filling into each baked pie shell. Cover with meringue (p. 312). Brown.

Variations:

1.   **Banana Cream Pie.** Slice 1 large banana in each pie shell before adding cream filling.

2.   **Chocolate Cream Pie.** Add 6 oz (170 g) cocoa and 3 oz (85 g) sugar. Omit 1 oz (28 g) cornstarch.

3.   **Coconut Cream Pie.** Add 10 oz (284 g) toasted coconut to filling and sprinkle 2 oz (57 g) coconut over meringue.

4.   **Date Cream Pie.** Add 3 lb (1.36 kg) chopped, pitted dates to cooked filling.

5.   **Fruit Glazed Pie.** Use frozen blueberries, strawberries, or cherries. Thaw 6 lb (2.72 kg) frozen fruit and drain. Measure 1 qt (0.95 L) fruit

syrup, adding water if needed to make that amount. Add slowly to a mixture of 4 oz (114 g) cornstarch, 6 oz (170 g) sugar, and ¾ c (180 mL) lemon juice. Cook until thick and clear. Cool slightly. Add drained fruit. Spread over cream pies.

6. **Fruit Tarts.** Substitute 2 qt (1.89 L) cream for equal quantity of milk. Fill baked individual pastry shells ⅓ full of cream pie filling; add fresh, canned, or frozen fruits. Cover with whipped cream.

7. **Nut Cream Pie.** Add ½ c (120 mL) chopped pecans or other nuts.

8. **Pineapple Cream Pie.** Add 3½ c (840 mL) crushed pineapple, drained, to cooked filling.

LEMON PIE

BAKE: 12 min　　　　　　　　　　　　　　　　　　Yield: 8 8-in. pies
Oven: 375 °F (190 °C)　　　　　　　　　　　　　　Portion: 6 per pie

Amount			
Metric	*U.S.*	*Ingredient*	*Method*
1.14 kg	2 lb 8 oz	Pastry (p. 310)	Make pastry. Line 8 8-in. pie pans, 5 oz (142 g) per pan. Flute edges and prick crust with fork. Bake at 425 °F (220 °C) 10 min or until light brown.
2.13 L	2¼ qt	Water	Heat water, salt, and grated rind to boiling point.
10 mL	2 t	Salt	
3	3	Lemon rinds, grated	
340 g	12 oz	Cornstarch	Mix cornstarch and cold water.
720 mL	3 c	Water, cold	Add slowly to boiling water, stirring constantly. Cook until thickened and clear.
1.59 kg	3 lb 8 oz	Sugar	Add sugar. Remove from heat.
360 mL	1½ c	Whole eggs or 16 yolks, well beaten	Add eggs slowly to hot mixture, stirring constantly. Return to heat. Cook about 5 min. Remove from heat.
85 g	3 oz	Butter or margarine	Add butter or margarine and lemon juice. Blend.
360 mL	1½ c	Lemon juice	Pour into baked pie shells. Cover with Meringue (p. 312). Brown.

BUTTERSCOTCH CREAM PIE
Bake: 12 min   **Yield: 8 8-in. pies**
Oven: 375 °F (190 °C)   **Portion: 6 per pie**

Amount			
Metric	*U.S.*	*Ingredient*	*Method*
1.14 kg	2 lb 8 oz	Pastry (p. 310)	Make pastry. Line 8 8-in. pie pans, 5 oz (142 g) per pan. Flute edges and prick crust with fork. Bake at 425 °F (220 °C) 10 min or until light brown.
454 g	1 lb	Butter or margarine	Melt butter or margarine; add sugar and mix thoroughly.
1.14 kg	2 lb 8 oz	Brown sugar	Cook over low heat to 220 °F (105 °C), stirring occasionally.
2.84 L	3 qt	Milk	Add milk slowly, while stirring. Stir until all sugar is dissolved. Heat mixture to boiling point.
170 g	6 oz	Cornstarch	Combine cornstarch, flour, and salt.
170 g	6 oz	Flour	Add milk and eggs and mix thoroughly.
15 mL	1 T	Salt	Add to the hot mixture while stirring. Cook until thick.
0.95 L	1 qt	Milk, warm	Remove from heat.
5	5	Eggs, whole	
10	10	Egg yolks	
30 mL	2 T	Vanilla	Add vanilla and butter or margarine.
114 g	4 oz	Butter or margarine	Partially cool. Fill baked pie shells. Cover with meringue (p. 312). Brown.

Note: Recipe may also be used for pudding. Omit flour, increase
cornstarch to 8 oz (227 g).

CUSTARD PIE

| Bake: 15 min 450 °F (230 °C) | Yield: 8 8-in. pies |
| 20 min 350 °F (175 °C) | Portions: 6 per pie |

Amount			
Metric	U.S.	Ingredient	Method
1.14 kg	2 lb 8 oz	Pastry (p. 310)	Make pastry. Line 8 8-in. pie pans, 5 oz (142 g) per pan. Flute edges.
24	24	Eggs	Beat eggs slightly.
680 g	1 lb 8 oz	Sugar	Add sugar, salt, and vanilla. Mix.
5 mL	1 t	Salt	
30 mL	2 T	Vanilla	
3.79 L	1 gal	Milk, scalded	Add hot milk, slowly at first, then more rapidly. Pour into unbaked pie shells.
10 mL	2 t	Nutmeg	Sprinkle nutmeg over top. Bake. The custard filling is done when a knife inserted half way between the edge and center comes out clean.

Variation:
Coconut Custard Pie. Add 1 lb (454 g) flaked coconut. Omit nutmeg.

PUMPKIN PIE
Bake: 15 min 450 °F (230 °C)   **Yield: 8 8-in. pies**
25 min 350 °F (175 °C)   **Portion: 6 per pie**

Amount			
Metric	*U.S.*	*Ingredient*	*Method*
1.14 kg	2 lb 8 oz	Pastry (p. 310)	Make pastry. Line 8 8-in. pie pans, 5 oz (142 g) per pan. Flute edges.
14 2.37 L	14 2½ qt (3 No. 2½ cans)	Eggs, beaten Pumpkin	Combine eggs and pumpkin in mixer bowl.
794 g 284 g 8 mL 23 mL 15 mL	1 lb 12 oz 10 oz ½ T 1½ T 1 T	Granulated sugar Brown sugar Ginger Cinnamon Salt	Combine and add to pumpkin-egg mixture.
2.6 L	2¾ qt	Milk, hot	Add milk. Mix. Pour into unbaked pie shells. Bake. The filling is done when a knife inserted halfway between the edge and center comes out clean.

Notes:
1. Undiluted evaporated milk may be used in place of fresh milk.
2. 1 lb (454 g) chopped pecans may be sprinkled over tops of pies after 15 min of baking. Continue baking.

Variation:
Praline Pumpkin Pie. Mix 12 oz (340 g) finely chopped pecans, 14 oz (397 g) brown sugar, and 8 oz (227 g) butter or margarine. Pat into unbaked pie shells before pouring in filling.

LEMON CHIFFON PIE

Yield: 8 8-in pies
Portion: 6 per pie

Metric	U.S.	Ingredient	Method
	Amount		
1.14 kg	2 lb 8 oz	Pastry (p. 310)	Make pastry. Line 8 8-in. pie pans, 5 oz (142 g) per pan. Flute edges and prick crust with fork. Bake at 425 °F (220 °C) 10 min or until light brown.
43 g 420 mL	1½ oz 1¾ c	Gelatin Water, cold	Sprinkle gelatin over water. Let stand 10 min.
21 680 g 10 mL 600 mL 30 mL	21 1 lb 8 oz 2 t 2½ c 2 T	Egg yolks Sugar Salt Lemon juice Lemon rind, grated	Beat egg yolks. Add sugar, salt, and lemon juice. Cook over hot water until consistency of custard. Remove from heat. Add softened gelatin. Stir until dissolved. Add lemon rind. Chill until mixture begins to congeal.
21 510 g	21 1 lb 2 oz	Egg whites Sugar	Beat egg whites until frothy. Gradually add sugar and beat until meringue will form soft peaks. Fold into lemon mixture. Pour into baked pie shells. Chill.
0.95 L 60 mL	1 qt ¼ c	Whipping cream Sugar	Just before serving, whip cream, add sugar. Spread 1 c (240 mL) of the whipped cream over each pie.

Variations:

1. **Frozen Lemon Pie.** Increase sugar in custard to 2 lb (908 g). Delete sugar from meringue. Beat egg whites, fold into 2 qt (1.89 L) cream, whipped. Fold into chilled lemon mixture. Pour into Graham Cracker Pie Shells (p. 311). Freeze. Serve frozen.

2. **Lemon Refrigerator Dessert.** Crush 3 lb 8 oz (1.59 kg) vanilla wafers. Spread half of crumbs in bottom of 12 × 20 in. pan. Pour chiffon pie mixture over crumbs and cover with remaining crumbs.

3. **Orange Chiffon Pie.** Substitute 2 c (480 mL) orange juice for 2 c (480 mL) lemon juice. Substitute grated orange rind for lemon rind.

CHOCOLATE CHIFFON PIE

Amount			
Metric	U.S.	Ingredient	Method
1.14 kg	2 lb 8 oz	Pastry (p. 310)	Make pastry. Line 8 8-in. pie pans, 5 oz (142 g) per pan. Flute edges and prick crust with fork. Bake at 425 °F (220 °C) 10 min or until light brown.
43 g 360 mL	1½ oz 1½ c	Gelatin Water, cold	Sprinkle gelatin over water. Let stand 10 min.
227 g 720 mL	8 oz 3 c	Chocolate, un-sweetened Water, boiling	Melt chocolate. Add hot water slowly. Stir until mixed. Add gelatin and stir until dissolved.
24 680 g 8 mL 30 mL	24 1 lb 8 oz 1½ t 2 T	Egg yolks, beaten Sugar Salt Vanilla	Combine egg yolks, sugar, and salt. Cook until mixture begins to thicken. Add vanilla and chocolate mixture. Chill until mixture begins to congeal.
24 680 g	24 1 lb 8 oz	Egg whites Sugar	Beat egg whites until frothy. Gradually add sugar and beat (high speed) until meringue will form soft peaks. Fold into chocolate mixture. Pour into baked pie shells and chill.
0.95 L 60 mL	1 qt ¼ c	Whipping cream Sugar	Just before serving, whip cream. Add sugar. Spread 1 c (240 mL) of the whipped cream over each pie.

Variations:
1. **Chocolate Peppermint Chiffon Pie.** Cover pie with whipped cream to which 1 lb (454 g) crushed peppermint candy sticks has been added.

2. **Chocolate Refrigerator Dessert.** Use ⅔ Chocolate Chiffon Pie recipe. Spread 1 lb 12 oz (794 g) vanilla wafer crumbs over bottom of 12 × 20 in. pan. Pour in chocolate chiffon mixture and cover with 1 lb 12 oz (794 g) crumbs.

3. **Frozen Chocolate Chiffon Pie.** Fold in 3 c (720 mL) cream, whipped. Pile into pastry or graham cracker crust. Spread over tops of pies 1½ c (360 mL) cream, whipped, sweetened with 3 T (45 mL) sugar. Freeze. Serve frozen.

CHOCOLATE SUNDAE PIE

Yield: 8 8-in. pies
Portion: 6 per pie

Metric	U.S.	Ingredient	Method
	Amount		
1.14 kg	2 lb 8 oz	Pastry (p. 310)	Make pastry. Line 8 8-in. pie pans, 5 oz (142 g) per pan. Flute edges and prick crust with fork. Bake at 425 °F (220 °C) 10 min or until light brown.
57 g	2 oz	Gelatin	Sprinkle gelatin over water. Let stand 10 min.
360 mL	1½ c	Water, cold	
454 g	1 lb	Sugar	Combine dry ingredients.
28 g	1 oz	Cornstarch	Add slowly to milk while stirring.
3 mL	½ t	Salt	Cook 5 min.
2.84 L	3 qt	Milk, scalded	
22	22	Egg yolks, beaten slightly	Add egg yolks slowly. Cook 10 min while gently stirring. Remove from heat. Add softened gelatin. Stir until dissolved. Chill until mixture begins to congeal.
15 mL	1 T	Vanilla	Add flavorings.
10 mL	2 t	Almond extract	Carefully fold in egg whites and sugar that have been combined to form a meringue (p. 312). Pour into baked pie shells. Chill until set.
22	22	Egg whites	
340 g	12 oz	Sugar	
0.95 L	1 qt	Whipping cream	Just before serving, whip cream. Add sugar. Spread 1 c (240 mL) of the whipped cream over each pie. Sprinkle with grated chocolate.
60 mL	¼ c	Sugar	
227 g	8 oz	Chocolate, grated	

Variation:

Black Bottom Pie. Add 8 oz (227 g) melted chocolate to 3 qt (2.84 L) custard. Pour 1½ c (360 mL) into each baked pie shell. Fold beaten egg whites into partially congealed remaining custard. Pour 2½ c (600 mL) of this mixture over chocolate layer in crusts.

FROZEN MOCHA ALMOND PIE

Yield: 8 8-in. pies
Portion: 6 per pie

Amount			
Metric	*U.S.*	*Ingredient*	*Method*
1 recipe	1 recipe	Graham Cracker Crusts (p. 311)	Prepare 8 8-in. graham cracker crusts.
90 mL 360 mL	6 T 1½ c	Gelatin Water, cold	Sprinkle gelatin over water. Let stand 10 min.
18 680 g 15 mL 1.78 L	18 1 lb 8 oz 1 T 7½ c	Egg yolks Sugar Salt Coffee, hot	Beat egg yolks. Add sugar, salt, and coffee. Cook over hot water until mixture coats spoon. Remove from heat. Add softened gelatin. Stir until dissolved. Chill until mixture is consistency of unbeaten egg whites.
18 8 mL 680 g	18 1½ t 1 lb 8 oz	Egg whites Cream of tartar Sugar	Add cream of tartar to egg whites. Beat until frothy. Add sugar gradually and beat (high speed) until consistency of meringue. Fold into gelatin mixture.
720 mL 720 mL 30 mL	3 c 3 c 2 T	Whipping cream Almonds, toasted, chopped Vanilla	Whip cream. Fold cream, almonds, and vanilla into mixture. Pour into prepared crusts.
360 mL 45 mL	1½ c 3 T	Whipping cream Sugar	Whip cream, add sugar, and cover top of pies. Freeze. Serve frozen.

ICE CREAM PIE

Brown: 2-3 min

Oven: 500 °F (260 °C)

Yield: 8 8-in. pies

Portion: 6 per pie

Amount			
Metric	*U.S.*	*Ingredient*	*Method*
1 recipe	1 recipe	Graham Cracker Crusts (p. 311)	Prepare 8 8-in. crusts.
7.57 L	2 gal	Vanilla ice cream	Soften ice cream. Dip into prepared crusts, using 1 qt (0.95 L) per pie. Freeze several hours.
24 4 mL 680 g 8 mL	24 ¾ t 1 lb 8 oz 1½ t	Egg whites Salt Sugar Vanilla	Add salt to egg whites. Beat until frothy. Add sugar gradually, beating constantly, until sugar has dissolved. Add vanilla. Cover pies with meringue. Brown in oven. Return to freezer if not served immediately.
1.42 L	1½ qt	Chocolate Sauce (p. 471)	Serve with Chocolate Sauce.

Notes:
1. Pastry crust, baked, may be used in place of graham cracker crust.
2. Other flavors of ice cream may be used.

Variation:

Raspberry Alaska Pie. Thicken 3 40-oz (1.14-kg) packages frozen raspberries with 6 T (90 mL) cornstarch. Make thin layers of thickened berries and ice cream in graham cracker crusts, using about half of the berries. Proceed as for Ice Cream Pie. Spoon remaining berries over individual servings of pie.

SOUR CREAM RAISIN PIE
Bake: 12 min   **Yield: 8 8-in. pies**
Oven: 375 °F (190 °C)   **Portion: 6 per pie**

Amount		Ingredient	Method
Metric	*U.S.*		
1.14 kg	2 lb 8 oz	Pastry (p. 310)	Make pastry. Line 8 8-in. pie pans, 5 oz (142 g) per pan. Flute edges and prick crust with fork. Bake at 425 °F (220 °C) 10 min or until light brown.
2.37 L	2½ qt	Cultured sour cream	Mix all ingredients except raisins. Cook until thick.
1.25 kg	2 lb 12 oz	Sugar	
170 g	6 oz	Flour	
45 mL	3 T	Cinnamon	
23 mL	1½ T	Cloves	
30 mL	2 T	Nutmeg	
21	21	Egg yolks, beaten	
1.59 kg	3 lb 8 oz	Raisins, cooked	Add raisins. Pour into baked pie shells.
21	21	Egg whites	Prepare meringue (p. 312). Spread on pies. Brown.
567 g	1 lb 4 oz	Sugar	
4 mL	¾ t	Salt	

PECAN PIE
Bake: 40 min
Oven: 350 °F (175 °C)

Yield: 8 8-in. pies
Portion: 6 per pie

Metric	*U.S.*	*Ingredient*	*Method*
	Amount		
1.14 kg	2 lb 8 oz	Pastry (p. 310)	Make pastry. Line 8 8-in. pie pans, 5 oz (142 g) per pan.
1.81 kg	4 lb	Sugar	Cream sugar, butter, and salt (medium speed) until fluffy.
114 g	4 oz	Butter	
15 mL	1 T	Salt	
24	24	Eggs, beaten	Add eggs and mix well.
0.95 L	1 qt	Corn syrup, white	Add corn syrup and vanilla. Mix well.
37 mL	2½ T	Vanilla	
680 g	1 lb 8 oz	Pecans	Place 3 oz (85 g) pecans in each unbaked pie shell. Pour egg-sugar mixture over pecans. Bake.

Poultry

Purchasing and Storing Poultry

Poultry for institution foodservices usually is purchased in the ready-to-cook state. Whether it is cut up or whole, chilled or frozen, will depend on the class of poultry concerned and the preferences of the buyer. Frozen birds may be of the same high quality as unfrozen. Freezing does not change the original quality, but maintains it under proper processing and storage conditions. In young birds and broilers, the freezing temperature may darken the bones; other than appearance, there are no detrimental effects as a result of freezing. The purchase of fresh or frozen poultry depends on the preference of the buyer, the facilities of the institution, and the availability of poultry in local markets.

All poultry must be inspected for wholesomeness either under U.S. government supervision in officially approved processing plants or through an adequate state system. Most of the poultry in market channels is graded, and all classes are available in U.S. Grades A, B, and C. Grade A birds present the best appearance, but the grade to purchase will depend on the use and price differential. The grade does not indicate tenderness—the age (class) is the determining factor. Age is identified by terms such as fryer, broiler, roaster, young, or mature. Most types of ready-to-cook poultry are available as parts and in whole, halved, and quartered forms. Some kinds, usually turkeys, also are available as boneless roasts. The ready-to-cook birds require no further processing. There is a trend toward purchasing custom-cut, ready-for-the-pan chicken parts, such as whole or half breasts, legs, or thighs. Many institutions find it advantageous to purchase chicken parts, although there is some price differential between custom-cut pieces and whole poultry. Each portion in the package is of identical weight; there is no waste, and the cost of each portion is easily determined. Such a method of purchase makes it possible to order only the amount needed.

Whole ready-to-cook turkeys range in size from 4-24 lb (1.81-10.9 kg), and some even higher. The larger birds yield more meat in proportion to bone weight than smaller ones, but their use may not be feasible because of equipment capacity and cooking time required. Many foodservice managers prefer to buy halves, quarters, or parts for ease of cooking and handling. Boneless turkey roasts and rolls, available as all white meat, all dark meat, or a combination are used extensively in foodservice. They may be purchased in cooked or ready-to-cook form, and their weight ranges from 3-10 lb (1.36-4.54 kg).

Many other convenience products are on the market today, such as frozen breaded chicken breast fillets, turkey steaks, and chicken patties. Canned boned chicken and quick-frozen diced chicken or turkey may be used satisfactorily in casseroles, salads, sandwiches, and soups. Chicken soup base added to water may be used in recipes specifying chicken stock or broth. Stewing chickens or hens, formerly purchased for this purpose, are no longer readily available on the market, and the time required for cooking, boning, and dicing may be prohibitive in some foodservices. However, if freshly cooked chicken and broth are preferred, large fryers (3-3½ lb/1.36-1.59 kg) may be satisfactorily used.

All poultry is highly perishable, and extreme caution regarding cleanliness should be exercised in preparing, cooking, cooling, storing, and serving poultry products. Fresh-chilled poultry should be used within 1-2 days, and frozen poultry should be kept hard-frozen at 0°F (-18 °C) until it is removed from storage for thawing and cooking.

Whenever possible, poultry should be defrosted in a refrigerator. Place wrapped birds on trays to catch any drippings and space on refrigerator shelves so that air can circulate around them. Allow time as follows:

Chicken, whole or cut up	12-16 hr
Turkey, whole	
18 lb (8.16 kg)	2-3 days
Under 18 lb (8.16 kg)	1-2 days
Turkey parts	8-9 hr
Boneless turkey roasts	12-18 hr

If faster thawing is necessary, partially thaw in the original wrapper in the refrigerator and then place in cold water until completely thawed. *Change cold water often. Do not thaw in warm water.* Once thawed, poultry may be kept safely no longer than 24 hr at 38 °F (3 °C) before cooking. It should never be refrozen.

Cooking Methods

Most frozen poultry, except prebreaded and precooked convenience products, is thawed prior to cooking. If cooking is started from the frozen state it will take approximately 1½ times the total allowance for thawed poultry.

Poultry should be cooked at moderate heat (325-350 °F/165-175 °C) for optimum tenderness and juiciness, and the cookery method chosen should be appropriate for the age of the bird. Dry-heat methods (broiling, frying, or roasting) are used for young, tender birds. Moist-heat methods (stewing, steaming, and braising or fricasseeing) are suitable for the older, more mature birds. Recommended cooking methods for various classes of poultry are given in Table 2.15.

Table 2.15 COOKING METHODS FOR POULTRY

Kind of Poultry	Class	Average Ready-to-Cook Weight		Cookery Method	Per Capita Allowance Ready-to-Cook Weight	
		lb	kg		oz	g
Chicken	Broiler-fryer	2-3	0.9-1.4	Barbecue, fry, or broil	¼-½ bird	¼-½ bird
	Roaster	3-5	1.4-2.3	Roast	12-16	340-454
	Fowl or hen	3-5	1.4-2.3	Stew or fricassee	8-12	227-340
Turkey	Whole	8-24	3.6-10.9	Roast	12-16	340-454
	Roast, boned and tied	12	5.4	Roast	4-5	114-142
	Roast, cooked	8-10	3.6-4.5	Slice and heat in broth or heat in an uncovered pan	2½-3	70-85
	Roll, ready to cook	3-6	1.4-2.7	Roast	4-5	114-142
Duck		4-6	1.8-2.7	Roast	12-16	340-454
Goose		6-8	2.7-3.6	Roast	12-16	340-454

Note: For cooked yields for chicken and turkey, see p. 337.

Broiling

Only young tender chickens, 2½ lb (1.14 kg) or under, or 3-5 lb (1.36-2.27 kg) ready-to-cook turkeys should be broiled. Split each bird in half lengthwise or into quarters, depending on size. Fold wing tip back onto cut side with the thick part around the shoulder joint. Brush with melted fat. Season each piece with salt and pepper, and place, skin side down, on broiler. Place broiler 7 in. below source of heat; chicken and turkey should broil slowly. Turn and brush with fat while broiling in order to brown and cook evenly. The time required to cook chicken varies from 50-60 min, and 1-1¼ hr for turkey.

Deep-Fat Frying

Cut 1¾-2 lb (794-908 g) broiler-fryers into pieces of desired serving size. Roll chicken in seasoned flour; or dredge in flour, dip in egg and water mixture, then roll in crumbs; or, dip in batter. Fry in deep fat 12-15 min at no more than 330 °F (166 °C). (See recipe, p. 339.)

Panfrying

Cut 13 2-2½ lb (0.908-1.14 kg) broiler-fryers into pieces. Roll chicken in seasoned flour (see recipe, p. 339) and brown in a skillet containing ½ in. of hot fat. Reduce heat and cook slowly until tender—usually about 45-60 min. Cooking time depends on size of pieces. Turn as necessary to assure even browning and doneness.

Ovenfrying

Cut 13 2-2½ lb (0.908-1.14 kg) broiler-fryers into pieces. Dredge in seasoned flour, roll in melted fat, place on sheet pans, and bake 1-1½ hr at 350 °F (175 °C). This method should result in browning with no turning. (See recipe, p. 340.)

Stewing or Simmering

Cover fowl with water and add 2 t (10 mL) salt for each 4-5 lb (1.81-2.27 kg) bird. Cover kettle closely and simmer fowl until tender, approximately 2½ hr. Do not boil. When meat is to be used in jellied loaves, salads, or creamed dishes, add to cooking water for additional flavor 1 carrot, 1 medium onion, 1 stalk of celery, 2 or 3 cloves, and 2 whole peppercorns for each bird. For cooking in a steamer, place whole or parts of birds in a solid steamer pan. Cook until tender, following instructions of the manufacturer.

If cooked fowl is to be held, it must be cooled immediately. Remove from broth and place on sheet pans. When poultry is cool enough to handle, remove meat from bones, place in shallow pans, and store in refrigerator at 38 °F (3 °C) or below. Cool broth rapidly, stirring frequently to hasten cooling, by placing container in cold, running water or ice water. When broth is completely cooled, cover container and refrigerate. Cooked poultry should be used no later than the second day after it is cooked.

Roasting

For large-quantity cookery, it usually is recommended that poultry be roasted unstuffed and that dressing be baked separately. If turkey is to be stuffed, *mix the stuffing just before it is needed*. Do not prepare dressing or stuff the bird in advance. Follow this order of procedure in preparing a roaster.

1. Prepare bird. Remove pin feathers if necessary. Wash well inside and out.

2. Salt inside and outside of bird.

3. Brush with soft fat or oil.

4. Place bird on a rack in a shallow baking pan, breast up.

5. Baste with fat and hot water (4 oz/114 g fat to 1 qt/0.95 L hot water) if desired. Drippings also may be used for basting.

6. Roast at 325 °F (165 °C) to an internal temperature of 180 °F (82 °C). Insert meat thermometer in center of inside thigh muscle. Allow approximately 15-18 min per lb (454 g) for a 20-lb (9.08-kg) unstuffed turkey. Allow approximately 30 min per lb (454 g) for a 5-lb (2.27-kg) chicken. (See Table 2.16 for roasting guide.) If thermometer is not available, test doneness by moving drumstick. It moves easily at the thigh joint when done.

7. To roast turkey halves or quarters, place skin side up in an open pan. Roast at 325 °F (165 °C) for 2-3 hr.

8. To roast a boneless turkey roast or roll, place on rack in an open pan. Roast at 325 °F (165 °C) until a meat thermometer inserted in the center registers 170-175 °F (75-80 °C), or follow cooking directions on package.

The yield of cooked meat from poultry is influenced by the size of the bird, the amount of bone, the method of preparation and service, and the size portions desired. Whole ready-to-cook turkey will yield approximately 40-42% edible cooked meat; turkey roast or roll will yield 70%. Ready-to-cook chickens (large fryers or hens) will yield approximately 30-35% usable cooked meat for combination dishes.

Table 2.16 ROASTING GUIDE FOR POULTRY[a]

Kind	Ready-to-Cook Weight		Approximate Total Roasting Time at 325 °F (165 °C) (hr)	Internal Temperature of Poultry When Done[b]	
	lb	*kg*		*°F*	*°C*
Chicken, whole					
Roasters	2½-4½	1.1-2.0	2-3½		
Ducks	4-6	1.8-2.7	2-3		
Geese	6-8	2.7-3.6	3-3½		
	8-12	3.6-5.4	3½-4½		
Turkeys					
Whole	6-8	2.7-3.6	3-3½	180-185	82-85
	8-12	3.6-5.4	3½-4½	180-185	82-85
	12-16	5.4-7.3	4½-5½	180-185	82-85
	16-20	7.3-9.1	5½-6½	180-185	82-85
	20-24	9.1-10.9	6½-7	180-185	82-85
Halves, quarters, and pieces	3-8	1.4-3.6	2-3		
	8-12	3.6-5.4	3-4		
Boneless turkey roasts	3-10	1.4-4.5	3-4	170-175	75-80

[a] Adapted from *Poultry in Family Meals,* U.S. Department of Agriculture, Home and Garden Bulletin No. 110, 1976.
[b] Thermometer inserted in thigh of whole turkeys, in center of turkey roasts.

Poultry Recipes

PAN-FRIED CHICKEN

Yield: 50 portions
Portion: 8-12 oz (227-340 g) A.P.

Amount			
Metric	*U.S.*	*Ingredient*	*Method*
13	13	Fryers, 2-3 lb (0.9-1.4 kg)	Cut chickens into pieces of desired serving size.
454 g	1 lb	Flour	Roll chicken pieces in seasoned flour.
30 mL	2 T	Salt	
15 mL	1 T	Paprika or poultry seasoning	
454 g	1 lb	Fat	Brown chicken in hot fat ½ in. deep in pan. Reduce heat and cook slowly until tender, usually 45-60 min. Turn as necessary to assure even browning and doneness.

Notes:
1. Purchase of chicken portions (quarters, thighs, or breasts) simplifies preparation and service.
2. Chicken may be browned in a skillet, then placed in counter insets or baking pans and finished in the oven at 325 °F (165 °C) for 20-30 min.

Variation:
Deep-Fat Fried Chicken. Use 1¾-2 lb (794-908 g) broiler-fryers. Dredge in seasoned flour as above; or dredge in flour, dip in egg and water mixture (3 eggs to 1 c/240 mL water), and roll in crumbs (12 oz/340 g); or dip in batter (p. 75). Fry in deep fat 12-15 min at 325 °F (165 °C). Larger fryers may be browned in deep fat, then placed in baking pans and finished in the oven at 325 °F (165 °C) for 20-30 min.

OVEN-FRIED CHICKEN
Bake: 1-1½ hr
Oven: 350 °F (175 °C)

Yield: 50 portions
Portion: 1 chicken quarter
or 2 pieces

Amount			
Metric	*U.S.*	*Ingredient*	*Method*
50 *or* 100	50 *or* 100	Chicken quarters *or* Chicken breasts and thighs	Dredge chicken with seasoned flour.
454 g	1 lb	Flour	
227 g	8 oz	Nonfat dry milk	
30 mL	2 T	Salt	
15 mL	1 T	Paprika	
454 g	1 lb	Fat	Melt fat in baking pans. Place chicken pieces in 1 layer in pans; turn pieces to coat both sides with fat, ending with skin side up. Bake 1-1½ hr or until tender.

Note: Chicken may be placed on pan lined with silicone-coated paper and brushed with melted fat or margarine before baking.

Variation:

Oven Crusty Chicken. Dredge chicken in seasoned flour (omit nonfat dry milk). Dip in 1 qt (0.95 L) evaporated milk. Roll in cornflake crumbs to coat (2½ lb/1.14 kg). Place on well-greased baking pans. Pour melted margarine or fat (2 c/480 mL) over chicken. Bake 1½ hr or until tender. It may be necessary to baste the chicken with melted fat once or twice during cooking.

CHICKEN À LA MARYLAND
Bake: 2½-3 hr   **Yield: 50 portions**
Oven: 325 °F (165 °C)   **Portion: 3 oz (85 g) cooked meat**

Amount			
Metric	*U.S.*	*Ingredient*	*Method*
15.88 kg (A.P.)[a]	35 lb (A.P.)[a]	Chicken	Cut chicken into desired pieces. Roll in flour and salt.
340 g	12 oz	Flour	Brown in hot fat.
30 mL	2 T	Salt	
454 g	1 lb	Fat	
2.84 L	3 qt	Cream, thin	Arrange pieces of chicken close together in baking pans. Cover with cream. Bake.

[a] 13 2½-3 lb (1.14-1.36 kg) fryers.

Variation:
Paprika Chicken. Omit cream. Add 2 large onions, diced and browned in hot fat, 1 qt (0.95 L) water or chicken stock, 4 egg yolks mixed with 1 qt (0.95 L) cultured sour cream, and ¼ c (60 mL) paprika. Bake.

BARBECUED CHICKEN
Bake: 1½-2 hr   **Yield: 52 portions**
Oven: 325 °F (165 °C)   **Portion: ¼ fryer**

Amount			
Metric	*U.S.*	*Ingredient*	*Method*
15.88 kg (A.P.)[a]	35 lb (A.P.)[a]	Chicken	Cut fryers into quarters or pieces as desired.
30 mL	2 T	Salt	Season with salt.
454 g	1 lb	Fat, melted	Roll chicken in melted fat and place on bun pans. Brown in oven.
1 recipe	1 recipe	Cooked Barbe-cue Sauce (p. 465)	Pour sauce over chicken. Bake 1 hr.

[a] 13 2½-3 lb (1.14-1.36 kg) fryers.

Variation:
Chicken Cacciatore. Brown chicken. Cover with sauce made of: 1 No. 10 can tomatoes, 2 lb (908 g) green peppers, cut into strips, 2 t (10 mL) black pepper, 2 t (10 mL) oregano, and 2 garlic cloves, minced. Bake 35-40 min.

FRICASSEE OF CHICKEN

Bake: 1½-2 hr
Oven: 325 °F (165 °C)

Yield: 50 portions
Portion: 3 oz (85 g) cooked meat

Amount		Ingredient	Method
Metric	U.S.		
15.88 kg (A.P.)[a]	35 lb (A.P.)[a]	Chicken	Cut chicken into desired pieces. Dip each piece in seasoned flour.
340 g	12 oz	Flour	Brown in hot fat.
30 mL	2 T	Salt	Remove to roasting pan (or steam
5 mL	1 t	Pepper	kettle) and cover with boiling
454 g	1 lb	Fat	water. Cook slowly, adding more water if necessary.
284 g	10 oz	Fat	When tender, remove chicken
170 g	6 oz	Flour	from stock.
3.31 L	3½ qt	Chicken broth	Make gravy, using liquid in which chicken was cooked. Serve over chicken.

[a] 13 2½-3 lb (1.14-1.36 kg) fryers.

Variations:

1. **White Fricassee of Chicken.** Do not brown chicken. Stew until tender. Remove from liquid. Boil liquid until concentrated. Add milk or cream to make 1½ gal (5.68 L), thicken to make a Medium White Sauce (p. 458). Beat constantly while pouring sauce gradually over 10 beaten egg yolks. Season to taste. Add chicken.

2. **Chicken with Black Olive Sauce.** Brown floured chicken. Place in baking pans. Cover with chicken gravy. Bake 1-1½ hr. Prior to serving, sprinkle with sliced ripe olives and sauteed fresh mushrooms.

CHICKEN TAHITIAN
Brown 30 min, bake 35-40 min
Oven: 350 °F (175 °C)

Yield: 52 portions
Portion: ¼ fryer

Amount		Ingredient	Method
Metric	*U.S.*		
15.88 kg (A.P.)[a]	35 lb (A.P.)[a]	Chicken, cut into quarters	Melt fat in baking pan. Arrange chicken in pans in single layer.
340 g	12 oz	Fat	Brown in oven.
4 177-mL cans	4 6-oz cans	Frozen orange juice, undiluted	Combine juice, butter or margarine, ginger, and soy sauce. Brush chicken with orange mixture.
454 g	1 lb	Butter or margarine	Bake. Baste with orange mixture until chicken is glazed.
30 mL	2 T	Ginger	Serve with Steamed Rice (p. 190) and garnish with slivered almonds and avocado wedges.
30 mL	2 T	Soy sauce	

[a] 13 2½-3 lb (1.14-1.36 kg) fryers.

Variation:

Chicken Cantonese. Flour chicken and brown as in Pan-Fried Chicken (p. 339). Place in 12 × 20 in. inset pans. Cover with aluminum foil. Bake approximately 1 hr at 350 °F (175 °C). Before serving cover with sauce made of 3 qt (2.84 L) pineapple juice, 3 qt (2.84 L) orange juice, ¾ lb (340 g) flour, 3 lb (1.36 kg) pineapple cubes, 12 oranges peeled and diced, 1¼ lb (567 g) almonds slivered and browned, 2 t (10 mL) nutmeg, and 2 t (10 mL) salt. Combine juice with flour; cook until thickened. Add seasonings, fruit, and almonds. Pour over chicken. Bake uncovered about 10 min. Serve with Cooked Rice (p. 190).

CHICKEN CUTLETS
Fry: 3-4 min
Deep-fat fryer: 360 °F (180 °C)

Yield: 50 cutlets
Portion: 3 oz (85 g)

Metric	U.S.	Ingredient	Method
Amount			
Metric	*U.S.*	*Ingredient*	*Method*
2.72 kg	6 lb	Cooked chicken	Finely chop chicken.
340 g	12 oz	Chicken fat or butter	Make as Thick White Sauce (p. 458).
170 g	6 oz	Flour	
28 g	1 oz	Salt	
480 mL	2 c	Milk, cold	
0.95 L	1 qt	Chicken stock, hot (p. 479)	
8	8	Eggs, beaten	When sauce is thickened, add eggs. Stir to blend. Cook 10 min. Add chicken. Mix lightly. Measure with No. 12 dipper onto lightly greased sheet pan. Chill.
4	4	Eggs, beaten	Flatten chicken mixture into oval or kidney-shaped cutlets.
240 mL	1 c	Milk	Combine eggs and milk. Dip cutlets in egg mixture and roll in crumbs. Chill not less than 2 hr before frying. Fry in deep fat.
340 g	12 oz	Bread crumbs	

Note: 18-20 lb (8.16-9.08 kg) chickens A.P. will yield approximately 6 lb (2.72 kg) cooked meat.

Variation:
Sweetbread Cutlets. Substitute 12 lb (5.44 kg) A.P. sweetbreads for the cooked chicken. Simmer sweetbreads in 1½ qt (1.42 L) water, 1 oz (28 g) salt, and 1 t (5 mL) vinegar for 20-30 min. Drain. Plunge into cold water. Remove connective membrane. Chop coarsely. Proceed as for chicken cutlets. Add ¼ c (60 mL) lemon juice, ½ t nutmeg, and 8 oz (227 g) chopped mushrooms to the mixture.

CHICKEN TURNOVERS

Bake: 25-30 min
Oven: 400 °F (205 °C)

Metric	U.S.	Ingredient	Method
	Amount		
Metric	*U.S.*	*Ingredient*	*Method*
2.72 kg	6 lb	Cooked chicken	Dice or coarsely chop chicken.
170 g	6 oz	Chicken fat or butter	Make as Thick White Sauce (p. 458).
114 g	4 oz	Flour	When thick, add chicken.
28 g	1 oz	Salt	
0.95 L	1 qt	Chicken stock (p. 479)	
2.27 kg	5 lb (50 rounds)	Pastry (p. 310), cut with 6-in. cutter	Place No. 20 dipper of chicken mixture on each pastry round. Fold rounds over and seal by pressing edges together with a fork. Bake. Serve with chicken gravy or mushroom sauce (1 gal/3.79 L).

Note: 18-20 lb (8.16-9.08 kg) chickens A.P. will yield approximately 6 lb (2.72 kg) cooked meat.

CREAMED CHICKEN

Metric	U.S.	Ingredient	Method
	Amount		
Metric	*U.S.*	*Ingredient*	*Method*
2.72 kg	6 lb	Cooked chicken	Dice chicken.
794 g	1 lb 12 oz	Chicken fat or butter	Make into Medium White Sauce (p. 458).
567 g	1 lb 4 oz	Flour	Add chicken. Cook until chicken is thoroughly heated.
2.84 L	3 qt	Chicken stock (p. 479)	
2.13 L	2¼ qt	Milk	
28 g	1 oz	Salt	

Note: 18-20 lb (8.16-9.08 kg) chickens A.P. will yield approximately 6 lb (2.72 kg) cooked meat.

Variation:
Chicken à la King. Add 12 chopped, hard-cooked eggs, 8 oz (227 g) shredded pimiento, and 1 lb (454 g) chopped sautéed mushrooms.

SCALLOPED CHICKEN

Bake: 30-40 min

Oven: 350 °F (175 °C)

Yield: 2 pans 12 × 20 × 2 in.

Portion: 6 oz (170 g)

Amount		Ingredient	Method
Metric	U.S.		
2.72 kg	6 lb	Cooked chicken	Dice chicken.
454 g	1 lb	Chicken fat or butter	Make as Medium White Sauce (p. 458).
227 g	8 oz	Flour	
3.79 L	1 gal	Chicken stock (p. 479)	
28 g	1 oz	Salt	
12	12	Eggs, beaten	When thick and smooth, add eggs, stirring constantly.
⅔ recipe	⅔ recipe	Bread Dressing (p. 362)	Place layer of dressing in 2 baking pans, layer of sauce, layer of chicken, another layer of sauce.
170 g	6 oz	Cracker crumbs, coarse	Cover with buttered crumbs. Bake.
85 g	3 oz	Butter or margarine, melted	

Note: 18-20 lb (8.16-9.08 kg) chickens A.P. will yield approximately 6 lb (2.72 kg) cooked meat.

CHICKEN CREPES
Heat: 10 min   **Yield: 50 portions**
Oven: 325 °F (165 °C)   **Portion: 2 crepes**

Amount			
Metric	*U.S.*	*Ingredient*	*Method*
680 g	1 lb 8 oz	Chicken fat or margarine	Melt fat; add flour and salt. Blend. Gradually add chicken stock, while stirring.
340 g	12 oz	Flour	
30 mL	2 T	Salt	
5.68 L	1½ gal	Chicken stock	
4.54 kg	10 lb	Cooked chicken, diced	Combine chicken, mushrooms, and seasonings.
2 227-g cans	2 8-oz cans	Mushrooms, chopped	Add enough sauce to hold chicken together. Reserve remaining sauce to pour over crepes.
30 mL	2 T	Worcestershire sauce	
30 mL	2 T	Curry powder Salt to taste	
1 recipe	1 recipe	Crepes (p. 123)	Make batter. Fry on lightly greased griddle, using about 1½ oz (43 g) batter. Brown lightly on one side. Turn and cook to set batter. Portion No. 20 dipper of chicken mixture onto each crepe; roll and place on baking sheets. Heat in 325 °F (165 °C) oven for 10 min. Serve with remaining sauce.

Variations:
1. **Spinach Crepes.** Omit chicken. Fill crepes with Spinach Souffle (p. 527). Serve with Cheese Sauce (p. 459).

2. **Fruit-Cheese Crepes.** Fill crepes with 1½ T (23 mL) of the following mixture: 2 lb (908 g) cream cheese, whipped and combined with 2 c (480 mL) cultured sour cream. Serve with frozen strawberries or raspberries, thickened slightly, or with prepared fruit pie filling, heated.

HOT CHICKEN SALAD
Bake: 25-30 min
Oven: 350 °F (175 °C)

Yield: 2 pans 12 × 20 × 2 in.
or 50 individual casseroles
Portion: 5 oz (142 g)

Amount		*Ingredient*	*Method*
Metric	*U.S.*		
2.72 kg	6 lb	Cooked chicken	Dice chicken.
1.81 kg	4 lb	Celery, diced	Combine with chicken. Mix
85 g	3 oz	Onion, chopped	lightly.
454 g	1 lb	Almonds, browned and chopped	Place in 2 pans (or in individual casseroles, using No. 8 dipper).
180 mL	¾ c	Lemon juice	
45 mL	3 T	Lemon rind, grated	
5 mL	1 t	Pepper, white	
15 mL	1 T	Salt	
1.42 L	1½ qt	Mayonnaise	
1.36 kg	3 lb	Cheddar cheese, grated	Sprinkle cheese, then potato chips over top of salad mixture.
340 g	12 oz	Potato chips, crushed	Bake.

Note: 18-20 lb (8.16-9.08 kg) chickens A.P. will yield approximately 6 lb (2.72 kg) cooked meat.

Variation:

Hot Turkey Salad. Substitute cooked turkey for chicken. 16-18 lb (7.26-8.16 kg) turkey A.P. will yield approximately 6 lb (2.72 kg) cooked meat.

CHICKEN LOAF
Bake: 1½ hr
Oven: 325 °F (165 °C)

Yield: 5 loaves 4 × 9 in.
Portion: 5 oz (142 g)

Amount			
Metric	*U.S.*	*Ingredient*	*Method*
454 g	1 lb	Rice	Cook rice (p. 190).
1.18 L	1¼ qt	Water, boiling	
10 mL	2 t	Salt	
10 mL	2 t	Salad oil (optional)	
3.18 kg	7 lb	Cooked chicken	Dice chicken.
170 g	6 oz	Pimiento, chopped	Combine chicken, cooked rice, pimiento, and onion. Mix lightly.
57 g	2 oz	Onion grated	
16	16	Eggs beaten	Add remaining ingredients. Mix only until blended.
28 g	1 oz	Salt	Divide into 5 greased loaf pans or 12 × 20 × 4 in. baking pan. Bake.
5 mL	1 t	Pepper	
1.89 L	2 qt	Chicken stock	
0.95 L	1 qt	Milk	
454 g	1 lb	Bread crumbs, soft	Serve with Chicken Gravy (p. 463) or Mushroom Sauce (p. 463).

Notes:
1. 22-25 lb (9.98-11.34 kg) chickens A.P. will yield approximately 7 lb (3.18 kg) cooked meat.
2. Turkey or tuna may be used in place of chicken.

CHICKEN PIE
Bake: 12-15 min
Oven: 450 °F (230 °C)

Yield: 50 individual casseroles or
2 pans 12 × 20 × 2 in.
Portion: 8 oz (227 g)

Amount			
Metric	*U.S.*	*Ingredient*	*Method*
2.72 kg	6 lb	Cooked chicken, diced	Place in each of 50 8-oz (227-g) baking dishes: 2 oz (57 g) chicken, 1 oz (28 g) potato, 1 T (15 mL) peas, and ⅓ c (80 mL) chicken gravy.
1.59 kg	3 lb 8 oz (E.P.)	Potatoes, cubed, partially cooked	
908 g	2 lb	Peas, frozen	
3.79 L	1 gal	Chicken gravy (p. 463)	
1 recipe	1 recipe	Batter Crust (p. 351)	Cover each casserole with ½ c (120 mL) batter crust. Bake.

Notes:

1. 18-20 lb (8.16-9.08 kg) chickens A.P. will yield approximately 6 lb (2.72 kg) cooked meat.
2. Chicken pie may be made in 2 12 × 20 × 2 in. baking or counter pans. Combine 3 lb (1.36 kg) chicken, 1 lb 12 oz (794 g) potatoes, 1 lb (454 g) peas, and 2 qt (1.89 L) gravy for each pan. Cover with biscuits, pastry, or batter crust.
3. Pastry rounds or biscuits may be used in place of batter crust for individual casseroles.

BATTER CRUST FOR CHICKEN OR MEAT POT PIES

Bake: 12-15 min
Oven: 450 °F (230 °C)

Yield: 6 qt (5.68 L)
Portion: ½ c (120 mL) per pie

Amount		Ingredient	Method
Metric	U.S.		
1.02 kg	2 lb 4 oz	Flour	Combine dry ingredients.
43 g	1½ oz	Baking powder	
15 mL	1 T	Salt	
57 g	2 oz	Sugar	
1.89 L	2 qt	Milk	Combine milk, egg yolks, and butter or margarine.
18	18	Egg yolks, beaten	Add to dry ingredients. Stir only enough to mix.
114 g	4 oz	Butter or margarine	
18	18	Egg whites	Beat egg whites until stiff. Fold into batter.
			Pour ½ c (120 mL) batter over contents of each individual casserole. Pour around edges and then in center to form a thin covering over meat or chicken mixture.
			If using for 12 × 20 × 2 in. pans, pour 3 qt (2.84 L) batter over each pan.

Note: Batter may be refrigerated until needed. Thin mixture with cold milk if too thick.

BRUNSWICK STEW

Yield: 3 gal (11.36 L)
Portion: 1 cup (240 mL)

Amount			
Metric	*U.S.*	*Ingredient*	*Method*
6.8 kg	15 lb (A.P.)	Chicken (hens or large fryers)	Simmer chicken until done. Remove meat from bones. Dice.
1.59 kg	3 lb 8 oz	Pork, diced	Brown pork. Drain off excess fat.
1.14 kg	2 lb 8 oz	Celery, diced	Cook vegetables until partially done.
1.59 kg	3 lb 8 oz	Carrots, diced	
1.36 kg	3 lb	Potatoes, diced	
454 g	1 lb	Onions, finely chopped	
340 g	12 oz	Butter or margarine, melted	Make roux of butter or margarine and flour; add stock gradually, while stirring.
340 g	12 oz	Flour	
4.73 L	1¼ gal	Chicken stock	Cook until thickened. Add chicken, pork, and vegetables.
454 g	1 lb	Peas, frozen	Add peas. Simmer until vegetables are done. Do not overcook at this point. Stew should be fairly thick.

CHICKEN SOUFFLÉ
Bake: 1 hr or until set
Oven: 325 °F (165 °C)

Yield: 2 pans 12 × 20 × 2 in.
Portion: 5 oz (142 g)

Amount		Ingredient	Method
Metric	*U.S.*		
2.72 kg	6 lb	Cooked chicken	Dice chicken.
454 g	1 lb	Butter or chicken fat	Make as Thin White Sauce (p. 458).
114 g	4 oz	Flour	
28 g	1 oz	Salt	
5 mL	1 t	Pepper	
600 mL	2½ c	Chicken stock, cold	
3.55 L	3¾ qt	Milk	
454 g	1 lb	Bread crumbs	Add crumbs and egg yolks. Mix well after each addition.
24	24	Egg yolks, beaten	Add chicken. Mix lightly.
24	24	Egg whites	Beat egg whites until they form a rounded peak. Fold into chicken mixture. Pour into 2 pans 12 × 20 in. Bake. Serve with Bechamel Sauce (p. 461) or Mushroom Sauce (p. 463).

Notes:
1. 18-20 lb (8.16-9.08 kg) chickens A.P. will yield approximately 6 lb (2.72 kg) cooked meat.
2. Ham, turkey, or tuna may be substituted for the chicken.

CHICKEN TIMBALES

Bake: 30 min or until firm
Oven: 350 °F (175 °C)

Yield: 50 timbales
Portion: 5 oz (142 g)

Metric	U.S.	Ingredient	Method
	Amount		
2.72 kg	6 lb	Cooked chicken	Chop or grind chicken.
454 g	1 lb	Butter or margarine	Melt butter or margarine. Add bread crumbs and milk.
340 g	12 oz	Bread crumbs, dry	Cook 5 min, stirring constantly.
2.37 L	2½ qt	Milk	
32	32	Eggs	Beat eggs slightly.
28 g	1 oz	Salt	Add to crumb mixture.
5 mL	1 t	Pepper, white	Add chicken and seasonings. Stir until mixed. Pour into 50 custard cups. Bake as custard in pans of hot water. Serve with Bechamel Sauce (p. 461). Garnish with riced egg yolk.

Note: 18-20 lb (8.16-9.08 kg) chickens A.P. will yield approximately 6 lb (2.72 kg) cooked meat.

Variations:

1. **Ham Timbales.** Substitute ham for chicken; reduce salt to 1 T (15 mL).

2. **Vegetable Timbales.** Substitute 3 qt (2.84 L) finely chopped or puréed vegetables for chicken. Serve with Cheese Sauce (p. 459).

CHICKEN CROQUETTES
Fry: 3-4 min
Deep-fat fryer: 375 °F (190 °C)

Yield: 50 croquettes
Portion: 3 oz (85 g)

Amount		Ingredient	Method
Metric	U.S.		
2.72 kg	6 lb	Cooked chicken	Chop chicken finely.
680 g	1 lb 8 oz	Rice	Cook rice in chicken stock.
2.84 L	3 qt	Chicken stock	
57 g	2 oz	Salt	Add seasonings to rice and mix lightly.
5 mL	1 t	Celery salt	
15 mL	1 T	Lemon juice	
30 mL	2 T	Onion juice	
170 g	6 oz	Flour	Make a smooth paste of flour and cold chicken stock.
480 mL	2 c	Chcken stock, cold	
480 mL	2 c	Chicken stock, hot	Add to boiling stock. Stir and cook until thick. Add sauce and chicken to rice. Mix well. Measure with No. 12 dipper onto greased sheet pan. Chill.
3	3	Eggs, beaten	Shape chicken mixture into croquettes.
240 mL	1 c	Milk or water	Dip in egg mixture and roll in crumbs. Chill at least 2 hr before frying. Fry in deep fat.
340 g	12 oz	Bread crumbs	

Notes:
1. 18-20 lb (8.16-9.08 kg) chickens A.P. will yield approximately 6 lb (2.72 kg) cooked meat.
2. Croquettes may be baked about 30 min in 400 °F (205 °C) oven.

Variation:
Ham Croquettes. Substitute ground cooked ham for chicken. Reduce salt to 1 oz (28 g).

CHICKEN AND NOODLES

Bake: 30 min
Oven: 350 °F (175 °C)

Yield: 2 pans 12 × 20 × 2 in.
Portion: 4 oz (114 g)

Amount			
Metric	U.S.	Ingredient	Method
2.72 kg	6 lb	Cooked chicken	Dice chicken.
1.14 kg	2 lb 8 oz	Noodles	Heat chicken stock to boiling.
7.57 L	2 gal	Chicken stock (p. 479)	Add noodles and reheat to boiling. Cook approximately 20 min or until tender. Remove from stock and place in 2 greased baking pans. Add diced chicken.
284 g	10 oz	Chicken fat or butter	Make as Medium White Sauce (p. 4.8).
170 g	6 oz	Flour	Pour over chicken and noodles.
2.84 L	3 qt	Chicken stock or milk	Mix. Bake.
15 mL	1 T	Salt	

Note: 18-20 lb (8.16-9.08 kg) chickens A.P. will yield approximately 6 lb (2.72 kg) cooked meat.

Variations:

1. **Turkey and Noodle Casserole.** Substitute cooked turkey for chicken (cook 18 lb/8.16 kg turkey). If using frozen or canned diced turkey, cook noodles in water. Use 3 oz (85 g) chicken soup base and 3 qt (2.84 L) water for stock for the sauce.

2. **Pork and Noodle Casserole.** Substitute 10-lb (4.54-kg) pork shoulder, diced and cooked, for chicken.

CHICKEN TETRAZZINI
Bake: 30 min
Oven: 375 °F (190 °C)

Yield: 2 pans 12 × 20 × 2 in.
Portion: 6 oz (170 g)

Amount		Ingredient	Method
Metric	*U.S.*		
2.72 kg	6 lb	Cooked chicken	Dice chicken.
170 g	6 oz	Pimiento, chopped	Add pimiento and parsley.
30 mL	2 T	Parsley, chopped	
908 g	2 lb	Spaghetti	Cook spaghetti (p. 191). Drain.
5.68 L	1½ gal	Water, boiling	
28 g	1 oz	Salt	
30 mL	2 T	Salad oil (optional)	
340 g	12 oz	Butter or margarine	Sauté onions and mushrooms in butter or margarine.
170 g	6 oz	Onion, finely chopped	
454 g	1 lb	Mushrooms, sliced	
170 g	6 oz	Flour	Blend in flour and salt.
28 g	1 oz	Salt	Add milk and stock; cook and stir until smooth and thick.
1.89 L	2 qt	Milk	
0.95 L	1 qt	Chicken stock (p. 479)	
340 g	12 oz	Cheddar cheese, shredded	Combine cooked spaghetti, chicken, and sauce. Place in 2 baking pans. Sprinkle 6 oz (170 g) cheese over top of each pan. Bake.

Note: 18-20 lb (8.16-9.08 kg) chickens A.P. will yield approximately 6 lb (2.72 kg) cooked meat.

Variations:
  1. **Turkey Tetrazzini.** Substitute turkey for chicken.

  2. **Tuna Tetrazzini.** Substitute tuna for chicken.

TURKEY CASSEROLE

Bake: 25-30 min
Oven: 350 °F (175 °C)

Yield: 50 portions
Portion: 6 oz (170 g)

Amount			
Metric	*U.S.*	*Ingredient*	*Method*
2.72 kg	6 lb	Cooked turkey	Dice turkey.
454 g	1 lb	Butter or turkey fat	Make sauce of fat, flour, and turkey stock.
680 g	1 lb 8 oz	Flour	Add soup and blend.
2.84 L	3 qt	Turkey stock (p. 479)	
2 1.42-kg cans	2 50-oz cans	Cream of mushroom soup	
170 g	6 oz	Onion, chopped	Cook onion and celery for 3 min.
1.81 kg	4 lb (E.P.)	Celery, chopped	Add to sauce.
1.36 kg	3 lb	Cashews, toasted	Combine turkey, sauce, and cashews. Portion into individual casseroles or into 2 pans 12 × 20 × 2 in. Bake.
1 No. 10 can	1 No. 10 can	Mandarin oranges	To serve, garnish with mandarin oranges.

Note: A 16-18 lb (7.26-8.16 kg) turkey will yield approximately 6 lb (2.72 kg) cooked meat.

Variation:

Chicken Casserole. Combine 6 lb (2.72 kg) cooked chicken, 1 lb (454 g) chopped onions, and 1 lb 4 oz (567 g) chopped celery sautéed in 8 oz (227 g) butter or margarine, and 12 oz (340 g) grated Cheddar cheese. Place layers of chicken mixture, 3 qt (2.84 L) buttered bread cubes, and 1 gal (3.79 L) chicken gravy or cream of chicken soup (2 50-oz cans) thinned slightly with chicken broth. Bake at 300 °F (150 °C) 1-1½ hr.

CHICKEN AND RICE CASSEROLE
Bake: 1 hr   **Yield: 2 pans 12 × 20 × 2 in.**
Oven: 350 °F (175 °C)   **Portion: 6 oz (170 g)**

Metric	U.S.	Ingredient	Method
	Amount		
2.72 kg	6 lb	Cooked chicken	Dice chicken.
1.81 kg	4 lb	Rice	Cook rice (p. 190).
4.73 L	5 qt	Water, boiling	
57 g	2 oz	Salt	
227 g	8 oz	Chicken fat or butter	Make into Medium White Sauce (p. 458).
114 g	4 oz	Flour	
2.37 L	2½ qt	Milk	
1.89 L	2 qt	Chicken stock (p. 479)	
28 g	1 oz	Salt	
794 g	1 lb 12 oz	Mushrooms, sliced	When sauce is thickened, add mushrooms, almonds, and pimiento.
227 g	8 oz	Almonds, shredded	
114 g	4 oz	Pimiento, chopped	
340 g	12 oz	Bread crumbs	Arrange rice, chicken, and sauce in layers in 2 lightly greased baking pans. Sprinkle with buttered crumbs. Bake.
114 g	4 oz	Butter or margarine	

Note: 18-20 lb (8.16-9.08 kg) chickens A.P. will yield approximately 6 lb (2.72 kg) cooked meat.

TURKEY DIVAN
Bake: 12-15 min
Oven: 400 °F (205 °C)

Yield: 50 5-oz (142-g) portions
Portion: 3 oz (85 g) broccoli
2 oz (57 g) turkey

Amount		Ingredient	Method
Metric	**U.S.**		
4.54 kg	10 lb (E.P.)	Broccoli spears, fresh or frozen	Cook broccoli (p. 498). Drain well. Arrange in 3-oz (85-g) servings in 2 12 × 20 × 2 in. counter pans.
227 g	8 oz	Butter or margarine, melted	Pour butter or margarine over broccoli.
28 g	1 oz	Salt	Sprinkle with salt, pepper, and cheese.
3 mL	½ t	Pepper	
255 g	9 oz	Parmesan cheese, grated	
3.18 kg	7 lb	Turkey roll, cooked (p. 335)	Slice turkey in 2-oz (57-g) portions. Arrange turkey slices over broccoli. Serving will be easier if edges of turkey slices are tucked under the broccoli portions.
340 g	12 oz	Butter or margarine	Melt butter or margarine. Add flour and salt. Cook until blended.
170 g	6 oz	Flour	
28 g	1 oz	Salt	Add milk. Cook until thickened.
2.84 L	3 qt	Milk	Add egg yolks. Stir until blended.
240 mL	1 c	Egg yolks, slightly beaten	Pour sauce over turkey and broccoli. Bake.

Note: Turkey or chicken stock may be substituted for part of milk in sauce; salt may then be reduced.

CURRIED CHICKEN (FOR SINGAPORE CURRY)

Yield: 50 portions
Portion: 6 oz (170 g) curry
6 oz (170 g) rice

Amount		Ingredient	Method
Metric	*U.S.*	*Ingredient*	*Method*
16-18 kg	35-40 lb	Stewing chickens or large fryers	Simmer chickens until tender (p. 336). Remove meat from bones and cut into bite-size pieces. There should be about 10 lb (4.54 kg) cooked meat.
454 g	1 lb	Butter or chicken fat	Make sauce of fat, flour, and chicken broth. Add salt and pepper to taste. Add curry powder.
567 g	1 lb 4 oz	Flour	
4.73 L	5 qt	Chicken broth	
57 g	2 oz	Curry powder	Add chicken and stir gently. Let set to blend flavors. Taste and add more seasonings, as the chicken takes up the curry flavor. It should be quite yellow and have a distinct curry flavor.
2.27 kg	5 lb	Rice	Cook rice (p. 190). This will allow very generous servings of rice.
85 g	3 oz	Salt	
5.91 L	6¼ qt	Water, boiling	
50 servings	50 servings	French fried onion rings	Serve curried chicken over rice, with accompaniments. (See directions for serving below.)
4.54 kg	10 lb	Tomatoes, sliced	
6.80 kg	15 lb	Bananas, sliced or cut in chunks	
2 No. 10 cans	2 No. 10 cans	Pineapple chunks, drained	
908 g	2 lb	Coconut	
454 g	1 lb	Salted peanuts	
2 454-g jars	2 1-lb jars	Chutney	

Notes:
1. Shrimp, veal, lamb, or a combination of chicken and pork may be used.
2. For a Singapore Curry dinner, arrange foods on buffet table in the following order: rice, curried chicken or other meat, and accompaniments in order listed in recipe. Each guest serves rice in the center of the plate, dips a generous serving of curried meat over the rice, then adds accompaniments as desired.

BREAD DRESSING (OR STUFFING)

Bake: 30-45 min
Oven: 350 °F (175 °C)

Yield: 2 pans 12 × 20 × 2 in.
Portion: 4 oz (114 g)

Metric	U.S.	Ingredient	Method
	Amount		
2.72 kg	6 lb	Dry bread, cubed	Add seasonings to bread.
28 g	1 oz	Salt	
5 mL	1 t	Pepper	
28 g	1 oz	Sage or poultry seasoning	
114 g	4 oz	Onion, minced	Sauté onion and celery in butter
227 g	8 oz	Celery, chopped (optional)	or margarine until tender. Add to bread mixture. Mix lightly.
454 g	1 lb	Butter or margarine	
2.37 L	2½ qt	Chicken stock (p. 479)	Add stock and eggs to bread mixture. Toss lightly. Avoid over-
6	6	Eggs, beaten	mixing, which causes dressing to be soggy and solid. Place in 2 greased baking pans 12 × 20 × 2 in. Bake.

Notes:
1. The amount of liquid (water, stock, or milk) will depend on the dryness of the bread.
2. Stock may be made of 3 oz (85 g) chicken soup base and 2½ qt (2.37 L) water.
3. Approximately 5 lb (2.27 kg) stuffing is required for a 20 lb (9.08 kg) turkey.
4. This dressing may be used for fish, veal, or pork or as a stuffing for veal birds.

Variations:
1. **Apple stuffing.** Add 1 lb (454 g) finely chopped apples. Reduce bread cubes to 5 lb 8 oz (2.50 kg). Add 4 oz (114 g) chopped celery.

2. **Chestnut Stuffing.** Add 1¼ lb (567 g) cooked chestnuts, chopped, and 8 oz (227 g) chopped celery. Reduce bread to 5 lb 8 oz (2.50 kg). Substitute milk for stock.

3. **Corn Bread Stuffing.** Substitute 4½ lb (2.04 kg) corn bread crumbs for 4½ lb (2.04 kg) bread cubes. Add 6 oz (170 g) minced onion, 12 oz (340 g) chopped celery. Omit sage. 6 hard-cooked eggs, chopped, may be added.

4. **Mushroom Stuffing.** Substitute 2 lb (908 g) mushrooms sautéed in butter for 6 oz (170 g) bread cubes. Omit sage.

5. **Nut Stuffing.** Add 2 c (480 mL) chopped almonds or pecans that have been browned lightly in 4 oz (114 g) melted fat. Substitute 2 c (480 mL) milk for 2 c (480 mL) of other liquid.

6. **Oyster Stuffing.** Substitute 1½ lb (680 g) oysters for 6 oz (170 g) bread cubes. Add 1 lb (454 g) cooked ham, minced, and ½ bay leaf, minced.

7. **Raisin Stuffing.** Add 1 lb (454 g) washed seedless raisins.

8. **Sausage Stuffing.** Substitute 2 lb (908 g) sausage for 8 oz (227 g) bread cubes. Add 1 lb (454 g) tart apples, chopped, and 3 oz (85 g) green pepper, minced.

Puddings and Other Desserts

Recipes in this section include custards and other puddings made with milk and eggs, fruit desserts, gelatin desserts, refrigerator desserts, and steamed puddings. All are used extensively in foodservices.

Custards are made with eggs, while most puddings use flour, cornstarch, or other starch for thickening. These desserts require sweetening, usually sugar. Too much sugar interferes with the thickening of the eggs and the starch, so it is important to use a properly balanced formula. Custards, which coagulate at about 185 °F (85 °C), should be cooked in a water bath to avoid curdling.

Soft puddings should be creamy and smooth. A product that is too thick, too thin, or lumpy will lose its appeal. Milk for cream puddings should be heated to 180 °F (82 °C) (not boiling) to prevent scorching. When increasing a recipe for cream puddings or pie fillings, it may be necessary to increase slightly the proportion of flour to milk.

In the preparation of gelatin desserts, a firm but delicate product is desired. The use of too much gelatin will produce a tough, rubbery product, while too little will not allow the dessert to set.

Pudding and Dessert Recipes

BAKED CUSTARD
Bake: 45 min   **Yield: 50 custards**
Oven: 325 °F (165 °C)   **Portion: 4 oz (114 g)**

	Amount		
Metric	*U.S.*	*Ingredient*	*Method*
20	20	Eggs	Beat eggs slightly.
567 g	1 lb 4 oz	Sugar	Add sugar, salt, and cold milk.
3 mL	½ t	Salt	Mix (low speed) only until
0.95 L	1 qt	Milk, cold	blended.
3.79 L	1 gal	Milk, scalded	Add scalded milk and vanilla.
30 mL	2 T	Vanilla	Pour into custard cups that have
10 mL	2 t	Nutmeg	been arranged in baking pans.
			Sprinkle nutmeg over top.
			Pour hot water around cups. Bake.
			Custard is done when a knife in-
			serted in custard comes out
			clean.

Variations:

1. **Caramel Custard.** Add 1 c (240 mL) Caramelized Sugar (p. 75)
   slowly to scalded milk and stir carefully until melted.

2. **Rice Custard.** Use ½ of custard recipe, adding 1 lb (454 g) A.P. rice,
   cooked, 1 lb (454 g) raisins, and 3 oz (85 g) melted butter or
   margarine.

3. **Bread Pudding.** Pour liquid mixture over 1 lb (454 g) dry bread cubes
   and let stand until bread is softened. Add 1 lb (454 g) raisins if
   desired. Bake.

FLOATING ISLAND

Yield: 6 qt (5.68 L)
Portion: ½ c (120 mL)

Amount			
Metric	*U.S.*	*Ingredient*	*Method*
4.26 L	4½ qt	Milk	Heat milk to boiling point.
454 g 114 g 3 mL	1 lb 4 oz ½ t	Sugar Cornstarch Salt	Combine sugar, cornstarch, and salt. Add gradually to hot milk, stirring briskly with wire whip. Cook over hot water or in heat-controlled kettle until slightly thickened.
24	24	Egg yolks, beaten	Gradually stir in egg yolks. Continue cooking until thickened, about 5 min.
30 mL	2 T	Vanilla	Add vanilla and blend.
24 340 g	24 12 oz	Egg whites Sugar	Beat egg whites (high speed) past frothy stage, approximately 1½ min. Add sugar gradually, while beating. Beat until sugar has dissolved. Drop meringue by spoonsful onto hot water and bake at 375 °F (190 °C) until set.
			Cool custard slightly and pour into sherbet dishes, or dip, using a No. 10 dipper. Lift meringues from the water with a fork and place on top of portioned custard. Add a dash of nutmeg. Chill before serving.

VANILLA CREAM PUDDING

Yield: 6 qt (5.68 L)
Portion: ½ c (120 mL)

Metric	U.S.	Ingredient	Method
	Amount		
4.26 L	4½ qt	Milk	Heat milk to boiling point.
680 g	1 lb 8 oz	Sugar	Mix sugar, flour, and salt. Add
227 g	8 oz	Flour	cold milk and stir until smooth.
10 mL	2 t	Salt	Add to the hot milk gradually,
720 mL	3 c	Milk, cold	stirring briskly with a wire whip. Cook over hot water until smooth and thick, approximately 10 min.
12	12	Eggs, beaten	Add, while stirring, a small amount of hot mixture to the beaten eggs. Combine all ingredients, stirring constantly. Stir slowly and cook about 5 min. Remove from heat.
30 mL	2 T	Vanilla	Add vanilla and butter. Cover and
114 g	4 oz	Butter or margarine	cool. Serve with No. 10 dipper.

Note: 5 oz (142 g) cornstarch may be substituted for flour.

Variations:
1. **Banana Cream Pudding.** Use only ¾ of recipe. Add 12 bananas, sliced, to cold pudding.

2. **Chocolate Cream Pudding.** Add 6 oz (170 g) sugar and 8 oz (227 g) cocoa.

3. **Coconut Cream Pudding.** Add 8 oz (227 g) shredded coconut just before serving.

4. **Pineapple Cream Pudding.** Add 1 qt (0.95 L) crushed pineapple, well drained.

TAPIOCA CREAM

Yield: 6 qt (5.68 L)
Portion: ½ c (120 mL)

Amount			
Metric	*U.S.*	*Ingredient*	*Method*
3.79 L	1 gal	Milk	Heat milk to boiling point.
255 g	9 oz	Tapioca	Add tapioca gradually. Cook until clear, stirring frequently.
10	10	Egg yolks, beaten	Mix egg yolks, sugar, and salt. Add slowly to hot mixture, while stirring. Cook about 10 min. Remove from heat.
454 g	1 lb	Sugar	
10 mL	2 t	Salt	
10	10	Egg whites	Beat egg whites until frothy. Add sugar and beat (high speed) to form a meringue. Fold egg whites and vanilla into the tapioca mixture. Serve with No. 10 dipper.
114 g	4 oz	Sugar	
30 mL	2 T	Vanilla	

Note: 1 lb (454 g) instant dry milk and 1 gal (3.79 L) water may be substituted for fluid milk.

Variation:
Fruit Tapioca Cream. Add 1 qt (0.95 L) chopped canned peaches or crushed pineapple, drained. Add ½ t (3 mL) almond extract for peach tapioca.

CHOCOLATE CREAM PUDDING

Yield: 6 qt (5.68 L)
Portion: ½ c (120 mL)

Amount			
Metric	*U.S.*	*Ingredient*	*Method*
3.79 L	1 gal	Milk	Heat milk to boiling point.
1.08 kg	2 lb 6 oz	Sugar	Mix dry ingredients. Add to hot milk gradually, while stirring briskly with a wire whip. Cook until thickened (about 10 min), stirring occasionally. Remove from heat.
170 g	6 oz	Flour	
85 g	3 oz	Cornstarch	
5 mL	1 t	Salt	
227 g	8 oz	Cocoa	
227 g	8 oz	Butter or margarine	Add butter and vanilla. Blend. Cover while cooling to prevent formation of scum. Serve with No. 10 dipper.
30 mL	2 T	Vanilla	

BUTTERSCOTCH PUDDING

Yield: 7 qt (6.62 L)
Portion: ½ c (120 mL)

Metric	U.S.	Ingredient	Method
	Amount		
Metric	*U.S.*	*Ingredient*	*Method*
2.84 L	3 qt	Milk	Heat milk to boiling point.
510 g	1 lb 2 oz	Flour	Mix flour, sugar, and cold milk
1.14 kg	2 lb 8 oz	Brown sugar	until smooth.
1.42 L	1½ qt	Milk, cold	Add gradually to hot milk. Cook and stir with wire whip until thickened.
18	18	Eggs, beaten	Add eggs and salt gradually to hot
8 mL	1½ t	Salt	mixture, while stirring. Cook about 10 min. Remove from heat.
15 mL	1 T	Vanilla	Add vanilla and butter or margar-
340 g	12 oz	Butter or mar-garine	ine. Chill. Serve with No. 10 dipper.

LEMON SNOW

Yield: 1 pan 12 × 20 × 2 in.
Cut 6 × 8
Portion: 2 × 2½ in.

Metric	U.S.	Ingredient	Method
	Amount		
Metric	*U.S.*	*Ingredient*	*Method*
680 g	1 lb 8 oz	Sugar	Mix sugar, cornstarch and salt.
227 g	8 oz	Cornstarch	
3 mL	½ t	Salt	
1.89 L	2 qt	Water, boiling	Add boiling water gradually, while stirring with a wire whip. Cook until thickened.
16	16	Egg whites	Beat egg whites until frothy.
170 g	6 oz	Sugar	Gradually add sugar and beat until rounded peaks will form. Add hot cornstarch mixture slowly, beating constantly.
240 mL	1 c	Lemon juice	Add lemon juice and rind. Blend.
30 mL	2 T	Lemon rind, grated	Pour into pan. Chill. Cut and serve with chilled Custard Sauce (p. 474).

DATE PUDDING

Bake: 45 min
Oven: 350 °F (175 °C)

Yield: 1 pan 12 × 20 × 2 in.
Portion: 3 oz (85 g)

Amount			
Metric	*U.S.*	*Ingredient*	*Method*
908 g	2 lb	Sugar	Mix dry ingredients, dates, and
454 g	1 lb	Flour	nuts.
43 g	1½ oz	Baking powder	
8 mL	1½ t	Salt	
340 g	12 oz	Nuts, chopped	
1.02 kg	2 lb 4 oz	Dates, chopped	
540 mL	2¼ c	Milk	Add milk and blend. Pour into a well-greased baking pan.
850 g	1 lb 14 oz	Brown sugar	Mix sugar, butter or margarine, and water.
57 g	2 oz	Butter or margarine	Pour over cake mixture. Bake.
2.13 L	2¼ qt	Water, boiling	

RUSSIAN CREAM

Yield: 6 qt (5.68 L)
Portion: ½ c (120 mL)

Amount			
Metric	*U.S.*	*Ingredient*	*Method*
75 mL	5 T	Gelatin	Sprinkle gelatin over cold water.
1.18 L	1¼ qt	Water, cold	Let stand 10 min.
1.42 L	1½ qt	Half and half or light cream	Combine cream and sugar. Heat until warm in steam-jacketed kettle or over hot water.
908 g	2 lb	Sugar	Add softened gelatin. Stir until dissolved. Cool.
1.18 L	1¼ qt	Cultured sour cream	When mixture begins to thicken, fold in sour cream and vanilla, which have been beaten until smooth.
37 mL	2½ T	Vanilla	Chill.
2.27 kg	5 lb	Raspberries, strawberries, or boysenberries, frozen	Dip pudding with No. 12 dipper. Serve with No. 30 dipper of partially defrosted fruit.

APRICOT WHIP

Yield: Approximately 4 qt (3.79 L)
Portion: ⅓ c (80 mL)

Amount			
Metric	*U.S.*	*Ingredient*	*Method*
43 g	1½ oz	Gelatin	Sprinkle gelatin over water. Let
360 mL	1½ c	Water, cold	stand about 10 min.
240 mL	1 c	Water or apricot juice, boiling	Add hot liquid to gelatine. Stir until dissolved.
454 g	1 lb	Sugar	Add sugar, lemon juice, and purée. Mix. Chill.
60 mL	¼ c	Lemon juice	
0.95 L	1 qt	Apricot purée	When mixture begins to congeal, beat (high speed) until light.
12	12	Egg whites	Beat egg whites until foamy. Add sugar and beat (high speed) to form a meringue. Fold into apricot mixture.
340 g	12 oz	Sugar	
			Portion into sherbet dishes with No. 12 dipper. Chill.
			Garnish with whipped cream or whipped topping.

Note: Raspberries, frozen strawberries, or prune purée may be substituted for apricot purée.

Variation:
Apricot Chiffon Pie. Pour Apricot Whip into graham cracker crusts.
   Reserve 2 c (480 mL) crumb mixture to sprinkle over top.

ROYAL RICE PUDDING   **Yield: 6 qt (5.68 L)**
                                                               Portion: 4 oz (114 g)

Amount		Ingredient	Method
Metric	*U.S.*		
454 g	1 lb	Rice	Cook rice (p. 190).
1.18 L	1¼ qt	Water, boiling	Chill.
10 mL	2 t	Salt	
0.95 L	1 qt	Pineapple, crushed, drained	Combine remaining ingredients except cream, and add to cooked rice.
227 g	8 oz	Marshmallows, miniature	Mix lightly.
227 g	8 oz	Nuts, chopped	
794 g	1 lb 12 oz	Powdered sugar	
10 mL	2 t	Salt	
240 mL	1 c	Maraschino cherries, chopped	
0.95 L	1 qt	Whipping cream	Just before serving, whip cream and fold into rice mixture. Portion into serving dishes, using No. 12 dipper.

FUDGE PUDDING
Bake: 45 min   **Yield: 1 pan 12 × 20 × 2 in.**
Oven: 350 °F (175 °C)   **Portion: 3 oz (85 g)**

Amount		Ingredient	Method
Metric	*U.S.*		
510 g	1 lb 2 oz	Flour	Mix dry ingredients (low speed).
35 g	1¼ oz	Baking powder	
794 g	1 lb 12 oz	Sugar	
5 mL	1 t	Salt	
57 g	2 oz	Cocoa	
480 mL	2 c	Milk	Add milk, vanilla, and butter or margarine. Mix until smooth.
30 mL	2 T	Vanilla	
255 g	9 oz	Butter or margarine, melted	Add nuts. Spread batter ¾-1 in. thick in pan.
454 g	1 lb	Nuts, chopped	
1.02 kg	2 lb 4 oz	Brown sugar	Mix sugar, cocoa, and hot water.
85 g	3 oz	Cocoa	Pour over batter. Bake.
1.89 L	2 qt	Water, hot	

LEMON CAKE PUDDING

Bake: 45 min
Oven: 350 °F (175 °C)

Yield: 1 pan 12 × 20 × 2 in.
Cut 6 × 8
Portion: 2 × 2½ in.

Amount		Ingredient	Method
Metric	U.S.		
1.36 kg	3 lb	Sugar	Cream sugar and butter (medium
170 g	6 oz	Butter or margarine	speed) 10 min.
85 g	3 oz	Flour	Add flour, salt, juice, and rind.
10 mL	2 t	Salt	Blend.
480 mL	2 c	Lemon juice	
75 mL	5 T	Lemon rind, grated	
18	18	Egg yolks, beaten	Add combined egg yolks and milk.
2.84 L	3 qt	Milk	
18	18	Egg whites	Fold in egg whites that have been beaten until they form rounded peaks. Pour into greased pan. Place in pan of hot water. Bake.

DATE ROLL

Yield: 4 rolls
Portion: 2½ oz (70 g)

Amount			
Metric	U.S.	Ingredient	Method
908 g	2 lb	Dates, chopped fine	Combine all ingredients except milk.
908 g	2 lb	Marshmallows, miniature	Mix lightly.
1.14 kg	2 lb 8 oz	Graham crackers, ground	
227 g	8 oz	Nuts, chopped	
170 g	6 oz	Maraschino cherries, chopped	
480 mL	2 c	Milk	Add milk. Mix only until ingredients are combined. Form into 4 rolls; roll in powdered sugar. Place in refrigerator for 24 hr. Cut each roll into 12 or 13 slices. Serve with Hard Sauce (p. 475) or whipped cream.

CHEESE CAKE

Bake: 35 min, 10 min   **Yield: 6 8-in. cakes**
Oven: 350 °F (175 °C)   **Portion: 8 per cake**

Metric	U.S.	Ingredient	Method
	Amount		
Metric	*U.S.*	*Ingredient*	*Method*
680 g	1 lb 8 oz	Graham cracker crumbs	Combine crumbs, sugar, and melted butter or margarine.
340 g	12 oz	Sugar	Place 1 c (240 mL) crumb mixture
340 g	12 oz	Butter or margarine, melted	into each of 6 8-in. pie pans or 6 6 × 6 in. square cake pans. Press crumbs to sides and bottom of pans.
2.04 kg	4 lb 8 oz	Cream cheese	Let cheese stand until it reaches room temperature.
11	11	Eggs	Cream until smooth. Add eggs slowly, while beating.
510 g	1 lb 2 oz	Sugar	Add sugar and vanilla. Beat (high speed) about 5 min.
30 mL	2 T	Vanilla	Place about 3 c (720 mL) filling in each shell. Bake 30-35 min. Do not overbake.
1.18 L	1¼ qt	Cultured sour cream	Mix sour cream, sugar, and vanilla.
114 g	4 oz	Sugar	Spread 1 c (240 mL) topping on each cake.
8 mL	1½ t	Vanilla	
114 g	4 oz	Graham cracker crumbs	Sprinkle with a few graham cracker crumbs. Bake 10 min.

Variation:

Cheese Cake with Fruit Glaze. Cover baked cheese cake with the following glaze. Thaw and drain 6 lb (2.72 kg) frozen strawberries, raspberries, or cherries. Measure 1 qt (0.95 L) fruit syrup, adding water if needed to make that amount. Add slowly to a mixture of 4 oz (114 g) cornstarch, 6 oz (170 g) sugar, and ¾ c (180 mL) lemon juice. Cook until thick and clear. Cool slightly. Add drained fruit. Spread over cheese cakes.

FRUIT COBBLER
Bake: 30 min
Oven: 425 °F (220 °C)

Yield: 1 pan 12 × 20 × 2 in.
Cut 6 × 8
Portion: 2 × 2½ in.

Amount		Ingredient	Method
Metric	*U.S.*	*Ingredient*	*Method*
2.37 L	2½ qt	Fruit juice	Heat juice to boiling point.
170 g 480 mL	6 oz 2 c	Cornstarch Water, cold	Mix cornstarch and water until smooth. Add to hot juice while stirring briskly with a wire whip. Cook until thickened.
1.14 kg 15 mL	2 lb 8 oz 1 T	Sugar Salt	Add sugar and salt. Bring to boiling point.
4.54 kg	10 lb	Fruit, drained, unsweetened or pie pack	Add cooked, drained fruit. Mix carefully. Cool. Pour into baking pan.
908 g	2 lb	Pastry (p. 310)	Roll pastry to fit pan. Place on top of fruit. Seal edges to sides of pan. Perforate top. Bake.

Notes:
1. The amount of sugar will vary with the tartness of the fruit.
2. Use cherries, berries, peaches, apricots, apples, plums, or other fruits.
3. For frozen fruit, see p. 316.

Variations:
1. **Fruit Slices.** Use 2¾ lb (1.25 kg) pastry. Line an 18 × 26 in. baking sheet with 1½ lb (680 g) of the pastry. Add fruit filling prepared as for cobbler. Moisten edges of dough and cover with crust made of remaining pastry. Trim and seal edges and perforate top. Bake 1-1¼ hr at 400 °F (205 °C).

2. **Peach Cobbler with Hard Sauce.** Use 10 lb (4.54 kg) frozen sliced peaches, thawed, mixed with 1 lb (454 g) sugar, 1 t (5 mL) nutmeg, 4 oz (114 g) flour, and 6 oz (170 g) butter or margarine, melted. Top with pastry crust and bake. Serve warm with hard sauce made with 8 oz (227 g) butter, whipped until fluffy with 1 lb (454 g) powdered sugar and ¼ c (60 mL) lemon juice.

OLD-FASHIONED STRAWBERRY SHORTCAKE

Bake: 15 min   **Yield: 50 individual shortcakes.**
Oven: 450 °F (230 °C)   **Portion: 1 shortcake**
                                    ½ c (120 mL) strawberries

Amount		Ingredient	Method
Metric	U.S.		
1.36 kg	3 lb	Flour	Mix dry ingredients.
114 g	4 oz	Baking powder	Cut in butter or margarine.
20 mL	4 t	Salt	
454 g	1 lb	Sugar	
680 g	1 lb 8 oz	Butter or margarine	
720 mL	3 c	Heavy cream	Mix cream and water. Stir quickly into flour mixture.
360 mL	1½ c	Water	Drop dough with No. 20 dipper onto ungreased cookie sheets. Place about 2 in. apart to allow for spreading. Bake.
7.57 L	8 qt	Strawberries Sugar to taste	Slice or mash strawberries. Sweeten to taste. Pour over shortcakes, or split cakes and serve berries between layers and over the top. Serve with cream.

APPLE DUMPLINGS
Bake: 40-45 min
Oven: 400 °F (205 °C)

Yield: 50 portions
Portion: 1 dumpling

Amount			
Metric	*U.S.*	*Ingredient*	*Method*
2.27 kg	5 lb	Pastry (p. 310)	Roll to ⅛ in. thickness and cut into 5-in. squares.
5.44 kg	12 lb	Sliced apples, frozen	Place No. 16 dipper of apples in center of each pastry square. Fold corners to center on top of fruit and seal edges together. Place in lightly greased baking pans. Prick top of dumplings.
1.81 kg	4 lb	Sugar	Make syrup of sugar, hot water, butter, and spices. Pour around dumplings. Bake.
1.89 L	2 qt	Water, hot	
454 g	1 lb	Butter or margarine	
10mL	2 t	Cinnamon	
10 mL	2 t	Nutmeg	

Notes:
1. Fresh or canned fruit may be used. The amount of sugar will vary with the type of fruit.
2. Pineapple juice may be substituted for part or all of the water.
3. Whole peeled, cored apples may be used. Wrap pastry around apple. Seal corners. Increase syrup to 6 qt (5.68 L). Serve ½ c (120 mL) syrup over each dumpling.

Variation:
Peach Dumplings. Substitute peaches for apples.

BAKED APPLES

Bake: 45 min
Oven: 375 °F (190 °C)   **Yield: 50 apples**

Amount			
Metric	U.S.	Ingredient	Method
50	50	Apples	Wash and core apples. Pare down about ¼ of the way from top. Place in baking pan, pared side up.
1.36 kg	3 lb	Sugar	Mix sugar, water, salt, and cinnamon.
720 mL	3 c	Water, hot	
5 mL	1 t	Salt	Pour over apples.
15 mL	1 T	Cinnamon	Baste occasionally while cooking to glaze. Bake until tender when tested with a pointed knife.

Notes:
1. Use apples of uniform size, suitable for baking, such as Rome Beauty or Jonathan.
2. Amount of sugar will vary with tartness of apples.
3. ½ c (120 mL) red cinnamon candies may be substituted for cinnamon.
4. Apple centers may be filled with chopped dates, raisins, nuts, or mincemeat.
5. 3 oz (85 g) butter may be added to the syrup for flavor if desired.

APPLESAUCE

Yield: 50 portions
Portion: 3 oz (85 g)

Amount			
Metric	*U.S.*	*Ingredient*	*Method*
6.8 kg	15 lb (A.P.)	Apples, tart	Pare and core apples. Cut into
0.95 L	1 qt	Water	quarters. Add water.
			Cook slowly until soft.
1.81 kg	4 lb	Sugar	Add sugar. Stir until sugar is dis-
			solved.
			Serve with No. 16 dipper.

Notes:
1. Thin slices of lemon, lemon juice, or 1 t (5 mL) cinnamon may be added.
2. Peaches or pears may be substituted for apples.
3. Apples may be cooked unpared.
4. Amount of sugar will vary with tartness of apples.

Variation:
Apple Compote. Combine sugar and water and heat to boiling point. Add apples and cook until transparent.

APPLE BROWN BETTY

Bake: 1 hr (or longer)
Oven: 350 °F (175 °C)

Yield: 1 pan 12 × 20 × 2 in.
Cut 6 × 8
Portion: 2 × 2½ in.

Amount			
Metric	*U.S.*	*Ingredient*	*Method*
5.44 kg	12 lb (A.P.)	Apples, fresh	Pare, core, and slice apples.
908 g	2 lb	Cake (or bread) crumbs	Arrange apples and crumbs in layers in greased baking pan.
680 g	1 lb 8 oz	Brown sugar	Mix sugar, spices, water, and juice.
5 mL	1 t	Cinnamon	
3 mL	½ t	Nutmeg	Pour a small portion over each layer.
1.89 L	2 qt (or less)	Water or fruit juice	
30 mL	2 T	Lemon juice	
227 g	8 oz	Butter or margarine, melted	Pour melted butter or margarine over top. Bake. Serve hot with Lemon Sauce (p. 474) or cold with whipped cream.

Notes:
1. 10 lb (4.54 kg) canned or frozen apples may be used.
2. The amount of water will vary according to the dryness of the crumbs used.
3. Graham cracker crumbs may be substituted for cake crumbs. 8 oz (227 g) nutmeats may be added.
4. Peaches, apricots, or rhubarb may be substituted for the apples.

APPLE CRISP
Bake: 45-50 min
Oven: 350 °F (175 °C)

Yield: 1 pan 12 × 20 × 2 in.
Cut 6 × 8
Portion: 2 × 2½ in.

Amount		Ingredient	Method
Metric	*U.S.*		
4.54 kg	10 lb (E.P.)	Apples, sliced	Mix sugar and lemon juice with
227 g	8 oz	Sugar	apples.
60 mL	¼ c	Lemon juice	Arrange in greased pan.
567 g	1 lb 4 oz	Butter or margarine, soft	Combine remaining ingredients and mix until crumbly.
340 g	12 oz	Flour	Spread evenly over apples.
340 g	12 oz	Rolled oats, quick, uncooked	Bake. Serve with whipped cream, ice cream, or cheese.
908 g	2 lb	Brown sugar	

Note: Fresh, frozen, or canned apples may be used.

Variations:

1. **Cherry Crisp.** Substitute frozen pie cherries for apples.

2. **Peach Crisp.** Substitute sliced peaches for apples.

3. **Cheese Apple Crisp.** Add 8 oz (227 g) grated cheese to topping mixture.

4. **Fresh Fruit Crisp.** Combine 2 lb (908 g) sugar, 8 oz (227 g) flour, 1 T (15 mL) nutmeg, and 1 T (15 mL) cinnamon. Add to 10 lb (4.54 kg) fresh fruit, pared and sliced. Top with mixture of 2 lb 6 oz (1.08 kg) butter or margarine, 2 lb 8 oz (1.14 kg) brown sugar, and 2 lb 6 oz (1.08 kg) flour. Cream butter, add brown sugar and flour, and mix until of dough consistency. Spread over fruit. Bake. Serve warm with cream.

PINEAPPLE BAVARIAN CREAM

Yield: 1 pan 12 × 20 × 2 in.
Cut 6 × 8
Portion: 2 × 2½ in.

Amount		Ingredient	Method
Metric	*U.S.*		
85 g	3 oz	Gelatin	Sprinkle gelatin over water. Let
0.95 L	1 qt	Water, cold	stand 10 min.
1 No. 10 can	1 No. 10 can	Pineapple, crushed	Heat pineapple and sugar to boiling point.
794 g	1 lb 12 oz	Sugar	
60 mL	¼ c	Lemon juice	Add gelatin to pineapple and sugar. Stir until dissolved. Add lemon juice. Chill until mixture begins to congeal.
0.95 L	1 qt	Whipping cream	Whip cream and fold into pineapple mixture. Pour into 50 individual molds or 12 × 20 × 2 in. pan.

Note: May be used for pie filling.

Variations:

1. **Apricot Bavarian Cream.** Substitute 3 lb (1.36 kg) cooked dried apricots (A.P.) or 6 lb (2.72 kg) canned apricots, sieved, for crushed pineapple. Fold 6 beaten egg whites into the whipped cream.

2. **Strawberry Bavarian Cream.** Substitute 6 lb (2.72 kg) fresh or frozen sliced strawberries for pineapple.

PINEAPPLE REFRIGERATOR DESSERT

Yield: 1 pan 12 × 20 × 2 in.
Cut 6 × 8
Portion: 2 × 2½ in.

Amount		Ingredient	Method
Metric	*U.S.*		
1.59 kg	3 lb 8 oz	Sugar	Cream sugar and butter or margarine (medium speed) 5 min.
340 g	12 oz	Butter or margarine	
18	18	Egg yolks	Add egg yolks. Continue creaming until well blended.
1.42 L	1½ qt	Pineapple, crushed	Add pineapple and cream. Cook over hot water until thick. Cool.
240 mL	1 c	Cream	
114 g	4 oz	Nuts, chopped	Add nuts and cherries.
85 g	3 oz	Maraschino cherries, chopped	
1.59 kg	3 lb 8 oz	Vanilla wafers, crushed	Place a thin layer of crushed wafers in bottom of pan. Fill pan with alternate thin layers of fruit mixture and crushed wafers. Store overnight in refrigerator. Serve with whipped cream or whipped topping.

Note: Dry cake crumbs or sliced cake may be substituted for the wafers.

ENGLISH TOFFEE DESSERT

Yield: 1 pan 12 × 20 × 2 in.
Cut 6 × 8
Portion: 2 × 2½ in.

Amount		Ingredient	Method
Metric	U.S.		
680 g	1 lb 8 oz	Vanilla wafers, finely crushed	Mix crumbs, nuts, and butter. Cover bottom of pan with approximately ⅔ of mixture. (Save remaining crumbs for top.)
454 g	1 lb	Nuts, finely chopped	
340 g	12 oz	Butter or margarine, melted	
567 g	1 lb 4 oz	Butter or margarine, soft	Combine remaining ingredients except egg whites.
1.36 kg	3 lb	Powdered sugar	Mix (medium speed) until smooth and fluffy.
227 g	8 oz	Nonfat dry milk	
16	16	Egg yolks	
227 g	8 oz	Chocolate, melted	
45 mL	3 T	Vanilla	
16	16	Egg whites	Add egg whites, beaten stiffly. Pour over crumbs in pan. Sprinkle remaining crumbs on top of filling. Place in refrigerator for several hours. Garnish with whipped cream if desired.

Notes:
1. Graham cracker crumbs may be used in place of vanilla wafers.
2. May be made in 8 8-in. pie pans.

JELLIED FRUIT CUP

Yield: 1 pan 12 × 20 × 2 in.
Cut 6 × 8
Portion: 2 × 2½ in.

Amount			
Metric	*U.S.*	*Ingredient*	*Method*
680 g	1 lb 8 oz	Gelatin, fla-vored	Pour boiling water over gelatin. Stir until dissolved.
1.89 L	2 qt	Water, boiling	Add cold juice or water. Chill.
1.89 L	2 qt	Fruit juice or water	
1.81-2.27 kg	4-5 lb	Fruit, drained	Arrange fruit in counter pan, individual molds, or serving dishes. When gelatin begins to congeal, pour over fruit. Refrigerate.

Note: For detailed instructions on preparation of gelatin, see p. 415.

Suggested Combinations
1. Orange gelatin, 2 lb (908 g) orange sections, 1½ lb (680 g) pineapple chunks, 1½ lb (680 g) banana cubes.
2. Raspberry gelatin, 2 lb (908 g) frozen raspberries, 2 lb (908 g) sliced bananas.
3. Strawberry gelatin, 2 lb (908 g) frozen strawberries, 1 lb (454 g) sliced bananas, 1 lb (454 g) pineapple chunks.
4. Lemon gelatin, 2 lb (908 g) sliced peaches, 2 lb (908 g) mandarin oranges, 8 oz (227 g) maraschino cherries.
5. Lime gelatin, 2 lb (908 g) canned pear pieces, 2 lb (908 g) canned pineapple chunks.

CREAM PUFFS
Bake: 15 min at 425 °F (220 °C)   **Yield: 50 portions**
then 30 min at 325 °F (165 °C)   **Portion: 1 large puff**

Amount		*Ingredient*	*Method*
Metric	*U.S.*		
454 g	1 lb	Butter or margarine	Melt butter or margarine in boiling water.
0.95 L	1 qt	Water, boiling	
539 g	1 lb 3 oz	Flour	Add flour and salt all at once.
5 mL	1 t	Salt	Beat vigorously.
			Remove from heat as soon as mixture leaves sides of pan.
			Transfer to mixer bowl.
			Cool slightly.
16	16	Eggs	Add eggs one at a time, beating (high speed) after each addition.
			Drop batter with No. 24 dipper onto greased baking sheet.
			Bake.
			When ready to use, make cut in top of each puff with a sharp knife.
			Fill with Custard Filling (p. 185), using a No. 16 dipper. Top with Chocolate Sauce (p. 471) if desired.

Variations:

1. **Butterscotch Cream Puffs.** Fill cream puffs with Butterscotch Pudding (p. 368). Top with Butterscotch Sauce (p. 472) if desired.

2. **Eclairs.** Shape cream puff mixture with pastry tube into 4½-in. strips. Bake. Split lengthwise. Proceed as in directions for Cream Puffs.

3. **Ice Cream Puffs.** Fill with vanilla ice cream and serve with Chocolate Sauce (p. 471).

4. **Orange Cream Puffs with Chocolate Filling.** Add ½ c (120 mL) grated orange rind and 2 c (480 mL) chopped almonds to cream puff mixture. Bake. Fill with Chocolate Cream Pudding (p. 367) or Chocolate Cream Filling (p. 184).

5. **Puff Shells.** Make bite-size shells with pastry tube. Fill with chicken, fish, or ham salad. Yield: Approximately 200 puffs.

CHRISTMAS PUDDING
Steam: 45 min to 1 hr
under pressure (5-6 lb)

Yield: 50 portions
Portion: 3 oz (85 g)

Amount		Ingredient	Method
Metric	U.S.		
567 g	1 lb 4 oz	Carrots, raw, grated	Mix ingredients (low speed) until blended.
765 g	1 lb 11 oz	Potatoes, raw, grated	
567 g	1 lb 4 oz	Raisins	
567 g	1 lb 4 oz	Dates, chopped	
908 g	2 lb	Sugar	
454 g	1 lb	Butter or margarine	
340 g	12 oz	Nuts, chopped	
454 g	1 lb	Flour	Add combined dry ingredients. Mix (low speed).
20 mL	4 t	Soda	
15 mL	1 T	Cinnamon	Measure with No. 16 dipper into
15 mL	1 T	Cloves	greased muffin pans. Cover each
15 mL	1 T	Nutmeg	filled pan with an empty muffin
¼ t	¼ t	Salt	pan. Steam. Serve with Vanilla Sauce (p. 474) or Hard Sauce (p. 475).

Variation:
Flaming Pudding. Dip sugar cube in lemon extract. Place on hot pudding and light just before serving.

STEAMED PUDDING
Steam: 1 hr under pressure (5-6 lb)

Yield: 50 portions
Portion: 2½ oz (70 g)

Amount			
Metric	*U.S.*	*Ingredient*	*Method*
70 g	2½ oz	Butter or margarine	Cream butter or margarine, sugar, eggs, and molasses (medium speed) until light.
539 g	1 lb 3 oz	Sugar	
5	5	Eggs	
560 mL	2⅓ c	Molasses	
128 g	4½ oz	Flour	Combine flour, soda, spices, and bread crumbs.
15 mL	1 T	Soda	
15 mL	1 T	Cloves	
23 mL	1½ T	Cinnamon	
850 g	1 lb 14 oz	Bread crumbs, dry	
600 mL	2½ c	Sour milk or buttermilk	Add dry ingredients and milk alternately to creamed mixture. Mix (low speed) only until blended.
340 g	12 oz	Raisins	Add raisins and nuts.
227 g	8 oz	Nuts, chopped	Measure with No. 16 dipper into greased muffin pans. Cover with empty muffin pans. Steam. Serve puddings hot with Vanilla Sauce (p. 474) or Hard Sauce (p. 475).

MERINGUE SHELLS
Bake: 1 hr
Oven: 275 °F (135 °C)

Yield: 50 shells
Portion: 3 oz (85 g)

Metric	U.S.	Ingredient	Method
Amount			
28 (720 mL)	28 (3 c)	Egg whites	Add salt and cream of tartar to egg whites.
5 mL	1 t	Salt	
5 mL	1 t	Cream of tartar	Beat (high speed) until frothy.
1.36 kg	3 lb	Sugar	Add sugar ½ c (120 mL) at a time, beating (high speed) between each addition until sugar is dissolved and mixture will hold its shape (approximately 20-30 min).
			Using No. 10 dipper, place on well-greased and floured baking sheets.
			Shape into nests with spoon or use pastry tube to form nests. Bake. Watch carefully the last 15-20 min to avoid overcooking. Meringues should be white, not brown. If overcooked, they will be too brittle.
			Serve ice cream or fruit in center; or crush baked meringue and serve on ice cream.

Variations:
1. **Meringue Sticks.** Force mixture through pastry tube to form sticks. Sprinkle with nuts. Bake.

2. **Angel Pie.** Place meringue in well-greased and floured pie pan, about 1¼ qt (1.18 L) per pan. Use spoon and form a nest. After baking, fill each shell with 3 c (720 mL) of Cream Pie filling (p. 321), Lemon Pie Filling (p. 322), or Chocolate Pie Filling (p. 321). Then top with a thin layer of whipped cream.

Salads and Salad Dressings

Salads usually consist of cold foods, cooked or uncooked, served with a dressing. They may be served as:

1. A first course in a dinner menu: fruit or sea food.

2. A main course of a luncheon: meat, fish, poultry, cheese. For suggested accompaniments, see p. 396.

3. An accompaniment to the main course of a dinner or luncheon: salad greens with vegetables, fruit, or combination.

4. A second course in a dinner menu: fruit or vegetable.

Cafeterias may offer a variety of salads, including a choice of tossed greens, a fruit salad, a protein salad, and one or more gelatin salads. Many foodservices now have a salad bar, where the choice consists of salad greens, with a number of accompaniments and dressings. Croutons, garbanzo beans, tomatoes, cucumbers, onions, chopped hard-cooked egg, crumbled bacon, and Parmesan cheese are examples of accompaniments that add variety to the salad bar.

Although lettuce is the most commonly used of the salad greens, other types are available for garnish or as a basic ingredient in a salad. Lettuce is available in several varieties, including iceberg, leaf, romaine, bibb, and Boston or butterhead. Spinach, endive, chicory, escarole, parsley, and watercress add interest in flavor and texture to salads. Other vegetables often used in salads are red and green cabbage, celery, carrots, celery cabbage, and green and red pepper.

Greens should be clean, crisp, chilled, and well drained. It may be necessary to separate leaves for thorough washing. Wash in a spray of water or in a large container of water. Shake off excess water, drain thoroughly, and refrigerate. Draining in a colander or on a rack placed on a sheet pan will keep the greens from standing in water while chilling. Cover with a clean damp cloth or plastic to prevent dehydration. Directions for preparation of specific greens and other salad ingredients are given on pp. (391-395).

Salad Arrangement

1. Use only clean, cold, and crisp salad greens, broken or cut. If a salad cutter is used, care should be taken not to chop too fine.

2. Cut fruits and vegetables into generous wedges, slices, or cubes for an attractive salad. Each piece should retain its identity.

3. Drain fruit or any ingredients surrounded by liquid.

4. When desired, marinate each ingredient separately with a well-seasoned French dressing, p. 438).

5. Drain and toss ingredients together lightly, if a mixed salad. Add tomato sections or juicy fruits just before serving to avoid wilting salad greens.

6. Set up salads as follows:
a. Arrange chilled plates on large trays or in rows on the table. Select china, if possible, that will add to the attractiveness of the salad.
b. Place salad green on plates. Place a lettuce cup so that the frilly edge is at the back and top of the salad. The leaf should not extend over the edge of the plate.
c. Build from the back to the front, with the salad green as a base. To give height, chopped lettuce may be placed in the lettuce cup under salad ingredients such as fruit or vegetables slices, asparagus tips, or gelatin ring molds.
d. Top salad lightly with some material that will give accent in color and flavor, if desired.
e. Select a dressing that will enhance the flavor of the salad ingredients. Add salad dressing just before serving (sprinkle, do not pour), or pass for individual service. Sogginess and wilting can be avoided by using only enough dressing to moisten the vegetables or fruits. For a green salad, 2-3 c (480-720 mL) is ample allowance for 50 servings.

Preparation of Salad Ingredients

Salad Greens

Chicory. See Endive.

Endive. Wash, remove objectionable portions. Drain, place in plastic bag, and refrigerate.

Escarole. See Endive.

Head Lettuce. Remove ragged and objectionable leaves from head. For a garnish, cut out stem end or core. Hold inverted head under running cold water until the leaves are loosened. Do not soak. Turn heads right side up to drain. Separate the leaves, and stack 6 or 7 leaves in a nest. Invert the nest and pack in a covered container or plastic bag. Place in refrigerator 2 hr or more to complete crisping.

Leaf Lettuce. Wash, drain, place in plastic bag, and refrigerate.

Romaine.   See Leaf Lettuce.

Spinach.   Remove tough stems. Examine leaves and discard all dry, yellow, wilted, or slimy leaves. Wash first in warm, then in cold water, as many times as necessary to remove sand. Crisp and use as a salad green.

Watercress.   See Endive.

Fresh Fruit

Apples.   Wash, pare, core, remove bruises and spots. If the skins are tender and the desired color, do not pare.

To dice, cut into rings and dice with sectional cutter. Drop diced pieces into salad dressing, lemon, pineapple, or other acid fruit juice to prevent discoloration. If diced apple is placed in fruit juice, drain before using in a salad.

To section, cut into uniform pieces, so the widest part of the section is not more than ½ in. thick. Remove core from each section. If the peeling has not been removed, score it in several places to facilitate cutting when it is served. Prevent discoloration by the same method as for diced apples, only do not use salad dressing.

Apricots.   Cut into halves or sections and remove seed. Remove skins if desired.

Avocados.   If hard, ripen at room temperature. Peel shortly before serving, cut into halves or quarters, and remove seed. Slice, dice, or cut into balls. Dip into French dressing or lemon juice to prevent discoloration.

Bananas.   Remove skins and soft or discolored parts. Cut into strips, sections, wedges, or slices. Dip each piece into pineapple, other acid fruit juice, or salad dressing to prevent discoloration.

Cantaloupes and Other Melons.   Pare, dice, and cut into balls, or cut into uniform wedges or strips.

Cherries and Grapes.   Wash, drain, halve, and remove seeds. To frost, brush with slightly beaten egg white. Sprinkle with sugar. Let dry before using.

Grapefruit.   For sections select large grapefruit, wash and dry. Cut off a thick layer of skin from the top and bottom. Place grapefruit on cutting board, start at the top, and cut toward the board. Always cut with a downward stroke and deeply enough to remove all the white membrane. Turn grapefruit with the left hand. When paring is completed and pulp is exposed, remove sections by cutting along the membrane of one section to the center of the fruit. Turn the knife and force the blade along the membrane of the next section to the exterior of the fruit. Repeat for each section.

Oranges. Pare, section as grapefruit, or slice or dice.

Peaches. Remove skins only a short time before using. Peel or submerge in boiling water for a few seconds and remove skins. Chill. Cut into halves, wedges, or slices. Drop into acid fruit juice to prevent discoloration.

Pears. Pare and remove core and seeds a short time before serving. Cut into halves, wedges, or slices. Dipping in lemon or other acid fruit juice will prevent discoloration.

Pineapple. Twist out top. Cut into 5-7 slices, crosswise. Pare each slice and cut out eyes. Remove hard center and cut each slice into cubes. If sugar is added, let stand several hours before serving.

Pomegranate. Cut open and remove seeds. Discard peeling and white membrane.

Canned Fruit

Select whole pieces uniform in size and shape and with a firm appearance. Drain. If cubes or sections are desired, cut into pieces uniform in size and shape with well-defined edges. Pieces should not be too small.

Dried Fruit

Prunes. Size 20-30. Wash in warm water. Add boiling water to prunes. Cover tightly and let stand about 12 hr. Do not drain. Add sugar and cook slowly without stirring for about 30 min or until tender and glazed. Pour into a shallow pan to cool.

Raisins. Add hot water and let stand until cool. Wash, drain well. Add to salad ingredients or dressing.

Meat, Fish, Chicken, Eggs, Cheese, and Nuts

Meat. Cut cooked meat into ⅓-in. cubes. Marinate. Mix just before serving.

Fish. Cook, remove skin and bones. Flake. Marinate if desired. Mix with dressing just before serving. See p. 237 for preparation of crab, lobster, and shrimp.

Chicken. Cook, remove skin, gristle, and bone. Cut into ⅓-in. cubes. Marinate if desired. Mix with dressing and other ingredients just before serving.

Eggs. Hard-cook (p. 207). Use whole, halved, sliced, or sectioned. Slice or mince whites. Force yolks through ricer.

Cheese. Grate, cut in tiny cubes, or put through a ricer or pastry tube.

Nuts. Heat in hot oven to freshen if desired. Use whole, shredded, or chopped.

Blanched Almonds. To blanch almonds, cover with boiling water and let stand until skins will slip. Drain. Cover with cold water and rub off skins. Place skinned almonds between dry clean towels to remove water.

Toasted Almonds. Spread blanched almonds in a shallow pan in a thin layer. Heat at 250 °F (121 °C), stirring occasionally until nuts are light brown in color.

Vegetables

Whether used raw or cooked, strive to preserve shape, color, flavor, and crispness of vegetables. To marinate, see p. 391.

Asparagus. Cook and marinate tips.

Beans, dry. Cook, keeping beans whole (p. 500).

Beans, green. Leave whole or cut lengthwise. Wash, cook, and marinate.

Beets. Wash, cook, peel, remove any blemishes. Cut into desired shape and marinate.

Cabbage. Remove outer leaves. Wash heads, cut into 4-6 pieces. Remove center stalk. Shred remaining portions as desired with a long sharp knife or shredder. Crisp in ice water 15-30 min.

Carrots. Pare and remove blemishes. Cut into wedges, rounds, or strips. Grind, shred, or cook; then cut into desired shapes and marinate. For carrot curls, see Relishes, p. 395.

Cauliflower. Remove all leaves and cut away dark spots. Separate into flowerets, leaving 1-in stem. Soak in salt water [1 oz (28 g) salt or ⅓ c (80 mL) vinegar per gal]. Cauliflower may be cooked and marinated, or it may be marinated and served raw.

Celery. Separate outer stalks from heart. (Outer stalks may be used for soup.) Wash, trim, and remove strings, bruised, and blemished parts. If necessary to sanitize, add 1 T (15 mL) household bleach to each gal (3.79 L) water. Submerge celery for 30 seconds. Rinse well. Air dry. Use within 8 hr. To dice, cut lengthwise. Several stalks may be cut at one time. Place on a board and cut crosswise with a French knife. For celery curls, see p. 396.

Celery Cabbage. Remove outer leaves and wash. Shred as lettuce or cut into 1-2 in. slices.

Chives. Remove roots and any objectionable portions. Wash. Drain. Cut leaves crosswise with a sharp knife or scissors.

Cucumbers. Wash and pare, or score lengthwise with a fork. Crisp and let stand in salted ice water 15 min. Cut into slices or wedges.

Green peppers. Wash, remove seeds and stems. Cut into rings or strips; dice or chop.

Onions. Pour water over onions to cover. Under water, remove wilted leaves, outer layer of the bulb, firm root end, and all bruised or decayed parts. Cut as desired.

Potatoes. Pare. Remove eyes and bruised parts. Cut into ½-in. cubes and cook; or wash, cook with skins on, peel, and dice. Marinate 2 hr before using.

Tomatoes. Wash and peel. If skins are difficult to remove, place in a wire basket and dip in boiling water until the skins begin to loosen. Dip in cold water and remove skins. Chill.

Turnips. Remove tops, wash, pare by hand. Shred or cut into fine strips.

Relishes

Carrot Curls. Cut long, paper-thin slices. Roll each strip around finger, fasten with toothpick, and chill in ice water for several hours.

Carrot Sticks.   Cut carrots into thin strips. Chill in ice water for several hours.

Celery Curls or Fans.   Cut celery into 2½-in. lengths. Make lengthwise cuts ⅛ in. apart and about 1 in. in length on one or both ends of celery strips. Place in ice water about 2 hr before serving.

Celery Rings.   Cut celery into 2-in. lengths and then into pieces ⅛ in. thick. Place in ice water for several hours. Each strip of celery will form a ring.

Green Pepper Rings.   Remove stem and seeds. Cut into thin slices.

Green Pepper Sticks.   Cut pepper lengthwise into narrow strips.

Radish Roses.   Cut off root end of radish with sharp knife. Leave an inch or two of the green stem. Cut 4 or 5 petal-shaped slices around the radish from cut tip to center. Place radishes in ice water, and petals will open.

Radish Accordions.   Cut long radishes not quite through into 10-12 narrow slices. Place in ice water. Slices will fan out accordion-style.

Accompaniments for Salads Used as a Separate Course

Breads

Hot breads, buttered: biscuits, rolls, muffins.

Crisp breads: bread sticks, crackers, Melba toast, hard rolls.

Sandwiches (small): rolled, ribbon, or open face; banana, date, nut, or orange bread.

Cheese

Cream cheese balls, plain or rolled in nuts or parsley.

Toasted cheese crackers, cheese straws.

Miscellaneous Crisp Materials

Celery curls, celery hearts, stuffed celery, or radish roses.

Olives, plain, stuffed, or ripe.

Pickles, sweet, sour, dill, burr gherkins, fans, rounds.

Potatoes, chips or latticed, shoestring.

Salted nuts.

Fruit Salad Recipes

APPLE CELERY SALAD

Yield: 5 qt (4.73 L)
Portion: ⅓ c (80 mL)

Amount		Ingredient	Method
Metric	*U.S.*	*Ingredient*	*Method*
480 mL	2 c	Mayonnaise or Cooked Salad Dressing (pp. 434, 437)	Combine mayonnaise and whipped cream.
120 mL	½ c	Cream, whipped (optional)	
3.63 kg	8 lb (E.P.)	Apples, tart (peeled or un-peeled)	Dice apples. Add to dressing as soon as diced to prevent apples turning dark.
908 g	2 lb (E.P.)	Celery, chopped	Add celery, salt, sugar, and marshmallows.
23 mL	1½ T	Salt	
170 g	6 oz	Sugar (optional)	Mix lightly until all ingredients are coated with dressing.
227 g	8 oz	Marshmallows, cut (optional)	Serve with No. 12 dipper.

Variations:

1. **Waldorf Salad.** Add 8 oz (227 g) chopped walnuts just before serving.

2. **Apple-Fruit Salad.** Use 3 lb (1.36 kg) cubed pineapple, 2 lb (908 g) cubed oranges, sliced peaches, or grapes, and 5 lb (2.27 kg) apples.

3. **Apple-Date Salad.** Substitute 2 lb (908 g) cut dates for celery.

4. **Apple-Carrot Salad.** Use 6 lb (2.72 kg) diced apples, 3 lb (1.36 kg) shredded carrots, and only 1 lb (454 g) chopped celery.

5. **Apple-Cabbage Salad.** Use 6 lb (2.72 kg) diced apples and 4 lb (1.81 kg) crisp shredded cabbage. Omit celery.

SPICED APPLE SALAD

Yield: 50 portions
Portion: 1 apple

Amount		Ingredient	Method
Metric	*U.S.*		
50 (approximately 5.44 kg)	50 (approximately 12 lb)	Apples	Core and peel apples. Leave whole unless apples are large; then cut in half crosswise. Place apples in a flat pan.
2.72 kg	6 lb	Sugar	Combine sugar, water, and seasonings. Boil about 5 min to form a thin syrup.
1.89 L	2 qt	Water	
240 mL	1 c	Vinegar	
3 mL	½ t	Red coloring	Pour over apples.
28 g	1 oz	Stick cinnamon or a few drops of oil of cinnamon	Cook on top of range or in oven until tender. Turn while cooking. Cool.
28 g	1 oz	Whole cloves	
227 g	8 oz	Celery, chopped	Fill centers of apples with celery-nut mixture.
114 g	4 oz	Nuts, chopped	
180 mL	¾ c	Mayonnaise	
3 mL	½ t	Salt	

Note: Select apples that will hold their shape when cooked.

FRUIT SALAD

Yield: 4¼ qt (4.02 L)
Portion: ⅓ c (80 mL)

Amount		Ingredient	Method
Metric	*U.S.*		
2.72 kg	6 lb	Pineapple, cubed	Drain fruit. Combine carefully.
908 g	2 lb	Cherries, Royal Anne or Bing, seeded	Serve with No. 12 dipper. Dip onto lettuce leaf. Serve with Fruit Salad Dressing
2.72 kg	6 lb	Peaches, cubed	(p. 441) or Sweet-Sour Cream
12	12	Oranges, peeled and diced	Dressing (p. 440).

Note: Other fruit combinations may be used (see p. 402).

Variation:
24-Hour Salad. Add ½ lb (227 g) miniature marshmallows and 6 lb (2.72 kg) sliced bananas. Reduce pineapple and peaches to 4 lb (1.81 kg) each. Combine with Fruit Salad Dressing (p. 441). Chill for several hours.

GRAPEFRUIT-ORANGE SALAD

Yield: 50 portions
Portion: 2 orange, 3 grapefruit sections

Metric	Amount U.S.	Ingredient	Method
16	16 (size 40)	Grapefruit	Pare and section fruit (p. 392).
17	17 (size 56)	Oranges	For each salad use 2 sections of orange and 3 sections of grapefruit. Arrange alternately on garnish. Serve with Celery Seed Fruit Dressing (p. 440) or Honey French Dressing (p. 441).

Note: For other citrus fruit combinations, see p. 403.

Variations:

1. **Citrus-Pomegranate Salad.** Arrange grapefruit and orange sections on curly endive. Sprinkle pomegranate seeds over fruit (see p. 393).

2. **Fresh Fruit Salad Bowl.** Place chopped lettuce or other salad greens in individual salad bowls (2 oz/57 g per bowl). Arrange wedges of cantaloupe, honeydew melon, and avocado, and orange or grapefruit sections on lettuce. Garnish with green grapes or bing cherries. Fresh pineapple, peaches, or apricots are also good in this salad. Serve with Celery Seed Fruit Dressing (p. 440).

3. **Grapefruit-Orange-Avocado Salad.** Place avocado sections between grapefruit and orange sections.

FROZEN FRUIT SALAD

Yield: 4¼ qt (4.02 L)
Portion: 4 oz (114 g)

Metric	U.S.	Ingredient	Method
Amount			
28 g	1 oz	Plain gelatin	Sprinkle gelatin over water. Soak
120 mL	½ c	Water, cold	10 min.
420 mL	1¾ c	Orange juice	Combine juices and heat to boiling point.
420 mL	1¾ c	Pineapple juice	Add gelatin. Stir to dissolve. Cool until slightly congealed.
240 mL	1 c	Mayonnaise	Combine whipped cream and mayonnaise.
480 mL	2 c	Cream, whipped	Fold into the slightly congealed gelatin mixture.
794 g	1 lb 12 oz	Pineapple, diced, drained	Fold in fruit. Pour into molds and freeze.
680 g	1 lb 8 oz	Orange sections, cut in halves	
680 g	1 lb 8 oz	Peaches, sliced, drained	
908 g	2 lb	Bananas, diced	
340 g	12 oz	Pecans, chopped	
227 g	8 oz	Maraschino cherries	
227 g	8 oz	Marshmallows, diced	

Notes:
1. Frozen nondairy topping may be used in place of whipped cream.
2. Salad may be frozen in counter pans and cut in squares.
3. Other combinations of fruit (a total of 5-6 qt/4.73-5.68 L) may be used.

Fruit Salad Combinations[1]

Apple

1.   Apples, celery, Malaga grapes. Chantilly Dressing.

2.   Apples, grapes, bananas, pineapple. Fruit Dressing.

3.   Apples, bananas, pineapple. Mayonnaise.

4.   Apples, celery, dates. Combination Dressing.

5.   Apples, pineapple, Tokay grapes. Chantilly Dressing.

6.   Apples, grapes, bananas, pineapple, oranges, lemon juice. Chantilly Dressing.

7.   Apples, oranges, dates, marshmallows. Combination Dressing.

8.   Apples, celery, grapefruit. Mayonnaise.

9.   Apple, orange, and pear sections. French Dressing.

10.   Apple, orange, and pear mixed with Mayonnaise.

11.   Avocado half, filled with Waldorf Salad (p. 397), Tomato Aspic (p. 421), Chicken Salad (p. 423), or fish salad (Shrimp or Lobster, pp. 424, 426).

12.   Red apple wedges, grapefruit or orange sections, and avocado on leaf lettuce. Thick French Dressing.

13.   Waldorf salad served on a slice of pineapple, garnished with maraschino cherry and sprig of parsley.

Banana

1.   Bananas, grapes, pineapple chunks, marshmallows. Fruit Dressing.

2.   Diced banana, pineapple chunks, pear, and peach. Whipped Cream Dressing.

3.   Banana sliced lengthwise, orange, and grapefruit sections. Celery Seed Dressing.

4.   Banana and orange sections arranged alternately on Bibb lettuce. French Dressing.

[1]See pp. 434-441 for salad dressing recipes.

5. Banana cut in thirds crosswise and lengthwise, rolled in thin cooked dressing and chopped nuts or cornflakes. Arrange with thin slices of orange.

Grapefruit

1. Grapefruit sections arranged alternately with orange or apple sections. French Dressing.

2. Grapefruit sections with tomato sections and ½ slice pineapple. French Dressing.

3. Grapefruit, fresh pear, and orange sections arranged on lettuce, radiating from center; cream cheese in center, topped with cherry. French Dressing.

4. Five grapefruit sections arranged on endive and garnished with pomegranate seeds. Celery Seed Dressing.

5. Three sections of grapefruit and orange placed on a lettuce leaf, garnished with avocado. Poppy Seed Dressing.

6. Grapefruit sections and avocado wedges, garnished with fresh strawberries. French Dressing.

Melon

1. Honeydew melon wedges garnished with watermelon balls. Honey Fruit Dressing.

2. Melon spear, orange slices, garnished with small cluster of grapes. French Dressing.

Orange

1. Orange slices, Bermuda onion rings, cream cheese balls rolled in chopped nuts. French Dressing.

2. Orange and avocado sections, halves of Ribier grapes. French Dressing.

Peach

1. Peach half stuffed with cream cheese balls, cottage cheese, chopped dates, stuffed prunes, Waldorf Salad, or toasted slivered almonds.

2. Peach half filled with blueberries, garnished with mint sprig. French Dressing.

Pear

1. Pear half stuffed with cream cheese, cottage cheese, or shredded Cheddar cheese.

2. Pear half, with frosted blueberries in center, fresh plum-slice garnish.

3. Pear half sprinkled with colored flavored gelatin.

Pineapple

1. Diced pineapple, marshmallows, white grapes, and nuts. Fruit Dressing.

2. Diced pineapple, celery, white grapes. Whipped Cream Dressing.

3. Pineapple slice with cream cheese ball in center. French Dressing.

4. Pineapple slice, orange slice, and apricot half arranged in pyramid style, garnished with maraschino cherry. Celery Seed Dressing.

5. Fresh pineapple, honeydew, and cantaloupe wedges, garnished with whole fresh strawberries. Celery Seed Dressing.

Prune

1. Large cooked prunes stuffed with cream cheese or orange sections. Mayonnaise or Celery Seed Dressing.

Vegetable Salad Recipes

TOSSED GREEN SALAD **Yield: 9 lb (4.08 kg)**
Portion: 1 c (240 mL)

Metric	U.S.	Ingredient	Method
Amount			
Metric	*U.S.*	*Ingredient*	*Method*
2.72 kg	6 lb	Head lettuce	Break or cut lettuce and other
1.36 kg	3 lb	Leaf lettuce, Bibb lettuce, or Romaine	greens into pieces.
1.18 L	1¼ qt	French Dressing	Just before serving, toss lightly with French Dressing (p. 438).

Note: Any combination of salad greens may be used. Serve in individual salad bowls.

Variations:

1. **Green Salad Bowl.** To 7 lb (3.18 kg) Tossed Green Salad, add 4 sliced cucumbers and 3 bunches sliced radishes. Garnish with 6 lb (2.72 kg) tomato wedges, 2 wedges per salad. Serve with French, Roquefort, or Thousand Island Dressing.

2. **Combination Fresh Vegetable Salad.** To 5 lb (2.27 kg) Tossed Green Salad, add 1 lb (454 g) cauliflowerets, 3 bunches radishes and 2 cucumbers, sliced, and 2 lb (908 g) red cabbage, coarsely chopped. Serve with French, Roquefort, or Thousand Island Dressing.

3. **Salad Greens with Grapefruit.** Serve 8 lb (3.63 kg) Tossed Green Salad in individual bowls. Garnish each with 3 sections pink grapefruit. Serve with Poppy Seed or French Dressing.

4. **Hawaiian Tossed Salad.** To 7 lb (3.18 kg) Tossed Green Salad, add sections from 8 grapefruit, 8 oranges, 4 avocados, and 1 fresh pineapple, cubed. Serve with Honey-Orange Dressing.

5. **Chef's Salad Bowl.** Place 6 lb (2.72 kg) mixed salad greens in bowls. Arrange 6 lb (2.72 kg) meat (turkey, ham, roast beef, or pork) cut in slivers and 3 lb (1.36 kg) Cheddar cheese, cut Julienne or in cubes, over top of salad. Garnish with green pepper ring, carrot curl, and tomato wedges. Serve with French, Thousand Island, or Roquefort Dressing.

6. **Russian Salad.** Mix 5 lb (2.27 kg) head lettuce, 2 bunches radishes, sliced, and 1 lb (454 g) crisp spinach leaves broken into pieces. Fill individual salad bowls ⅔ full. Top each salad with 1 oz (28 g) ham or luncheon meat, 2 oz (57 g) turkey, and 1 oz (28 g) Cheddar cheese,

cut into strips. Garnish with quarters of hard-cooked egg and tomato wedges. Serve with Thousand Island Dressing.

7. **Bacon and Chicken Salad.** To 6 lb (2.72 kg) mixed salad greens, add 5 lb (2.27 kg) cooked chicken or turkey cut in strips. Mix lightly and portion into salad bowls. Sprinkle 4 lb (1.81 kg) chopped, crisply cooked bacon over top of salads. Serve with choice of dressing.

8. **Spinach-Mushroom Salad.** Use 4 lb (1.81 kg) lettuce, 3 lb (1.36 kg) fresh spinach, and 2 lb (908 g) fresh mushrooms, sliced. Toss with French Dressing.

9. **Spinach-Egg Salad.** Use 3 lb (1.36 kg) lettuce, 4 lb (1.81 kg) fresh spinach, 1 bunch green onions, sliced, 12 eggs, hard-cooked and sliced, and 2 lb (908 g) bacon, diced, cooked until crisp, and drained. Toss lightly with French Dressing.

10. **Seafood Chef Salad.** Place 6 lb (2.72 kg) mixed salad greens in bowls (2 oz/57 g) per bowl. Arrange on each 1 oz (28 g) tuna, drained and broken into small chunks, 1 oz (28 g) cheese, cut into Julienne strips, 1 oz (28 g) shrimp pieces or 2 whole shrimp, 2 halves hard-cooked egg, 2 tomato wedges, and 1 dill pickle wedge or 1 ripe olive. Serve with Thousand Island or French Dressing.

SAUERKRAUT SALAD

Yield: 50 portions
Portion: ⅓ c (80 mL)

Metric	U.S.	Ingredient	Method
	Amount		
1 No. 10 can	1 No. 10 can	Sauerkraut	Combine all ingredients. Refrigerate for at least 12 hr.
454 g	1 lb	Carrots, grated	
340 g	12 oz	Celery, diced	
227 g	8 oz	Onion, chopped	
454 g	1 lb	Green pepper, chopped	
680 g	1 lb 8 oz	Sugar	

Note: Sauerkraut may be cut with scissors before combining with other ingredients.

CABBAGE SALAD

Yield: 4¼ qt (4.02 L)
Portion: ⅓ c (80 mL)

Amount		Ingredient	Method
Metric	U.S.		
3.18 kg	7 lb	Cabbage, shredded	Add salad dressing to shredded cabbage. Mix lightly. If dressing is too thick, add cream to thin.
0.95 L	1 qt	Cooked Salad Dressing (p. 437)	
28 g	1 oz	Salt	Mix just before serving so cabbage does not lose its crispness. Serve with No. 12 dipper.

Variations:

1. **Cabbage-Apple Salad.** Use 4 lb (1.81 kg) shredded cabbage. Add 3 lb (1.36 kg) diced unpeeled red apples.

2. **Cabbage-Carrot Salad.** Substitute 2 lb (908 g) shredded carrots for 2 lb (908 g) shredded cabbage.

3. **Cabbage-Pineapple-Marshmallow Salad.** Add 2 lb (908 g) diced pineapple, 1 lb (454 g) miniature marshmallows, 2 c (480 mL) cream, whipped, and 2 c (480 mL) mayonnaise. Omit Cooked Salad Dressing.

4. **Cole Slaw.** Add 1½ lb (680 g) sugar and 3 c (720 mL) vinegar, mixed. Omit Cooked Salad Dressing. 1 T (15 mL) celery seed may be added.

5. **Creamy Cole Slaw.** Use 2 c (480 mL) mayonnaise, 2 c (480 L) sweet or sour cream, ½ c (120 mL) vinegar, and ½ c (120 mL) sugar.

6. **Red Cabbage-Celery Salad.** Use 3 lb (1.36 kg) shredded green cabbage and 3 lb (1.36 kg) red cabbage. Add 1 lb (454 g) diced celery and approximately 1 qt (0.95 L) Sour Cream Dressing (p. 440). Omit Cooked Salad Dressing.

CARROT RAISIN SALAD

Yield: 4¼ qt (4.02 L)

Portion: ⅓ c (80 mL)

Amount		Ingredient	Method
Metric	**U.S.**		
2.95 kg	6 lb 8 oz	Carrots, raw, coarsely ground or shredded	Mix all ingredients lightly. Serve with No. 12 dipper.
227 g	8 oz	Raisins	
15 mL	1 T	Salt	
480 mL	2 c	Mayonnaise	
480 mL	2 c	Cooked Salad Dressing (p. 437)	

Variations:

1. **Carrifruit Salad.** Omit raisins. Use 4 lb 8 oz (2.04 kg) shredded carrots. Add 2 lb 12 oz (1.25 kg) pineapple tidbits, drained, and 8 oz (227 g) flaked coconut.

2. **Carrot-Coconut Salad.** 1 lb (454 g) toasted coconut may be substituted for raisins.

3. **Carrot-Celery Salad.** Omit raisins. Use 5 lb (2.27 kg) ground carrots. Add 2 lb (908 g) chopped celery and 2 oz (57 g) sugar.

4. **Carrot-Celery-Apple Salad.** Substitute 3 lb (1.36 kg) diced apples for 2 lb (908 g) carrots.

5. **Carrot-Celery-Cucumber Salad.** Use 4½ lb (2.04 kg) shredded carrots, 1½ lb (680 g) chopped celery, and 1½ lb (680 g) chopped cucumber.

STUFFED TOMATO SALAD

Yield: 50 portions
Portion: 1 tomato

Amount		Ingredient	Method
Metric	*U.S.*	*Ingredient*	*Method*
50 (approximately 5.44 kg)	50 (approximately 12 lb)	Tomatoes	Peel tomatoes. Remove core and part of pulp from each.
454 g	1 lb	Cabbage, chopped fine	Combine tomato pulp with chopped cabbage, celery, and pickle.
454 g	1 lb	Celery, chopped fine	Add mayonnaise and salt. Mix lightly.
227 g	8 oz	Sweet pickle, chopped	
240 mL	1 c	Mayonnaise	
15 mL	1 T	Salt	
23 mL	1½ T	Salt	Sprinkle salt in tomato cavities. Stuff each tomato with approximately 2 T (No. 30 dipper) of the vegetable mixture.

Notes:
1. Tomatoes may be cut into fourths to within ½ in. of bottoms. Spread apart. Sprinkle with salt and fill with salad mixture.
2. Fish, egg, or chicken salad may be substituted for vegetable mixture.

Variations:
1. **Tomato-Shrimp Salad.** Fill tomato cups with Shrimp Salad (p. 424). Omit lettuce in Shrimp Salad recipe.

2. **Tomato-Cottage Cheese Salad.** Substitute 6 lb (2.72 kg) cottage cheese, seasoned, for vegetable mixture. Fill tomato cups, using No. 20 dipper.

SLICED CUCUMBER AND ONION IN SOUR CREAM

Yield: 4¼ qt (4.02 L)
Portion: ⅓ c (80 mL)

Amount			
Metric	*U.S.*	*Ingredient*	*Method*
1.93 kg	4 lb 4 oz	Cucumbers	Cut cucumbers and onions in thin
255 g	9 oz	Onions	slices.
720 mL	3 c	Cultured sour cream	Blend rest of ingredients to form a thin cream dressing.
720 mL	3 c	Mayonnaise	Pour over cucumbers and onions.
8 mL	1½ t	Salt	Mix lightly.
45 mL	3 T	Sugar	
180 mL	¾ c	Vinegar	

Note: This cream dressing also may be served as a dressing for lettuce.

POTATO SALAD

Yield: 6½ qt (6.15 L)
Portion: 4 oz (114 g)

Amount			
Metric	*U.S.*	*Ingredient*	*Method*
6.8 kg (E.P.)	15 lb (E.P.)	Potatoes, pared	Cook potatoes until tender. Dice.
480 mL	2 c	French dressing	Combine dressing, salt, and vinegar.
28 g	1 oz	Salt (or more)	
120 mL	½ c	Vinegar	Add to potatoes. Mix carefully while potatoes are still warm. Marinate until cold.
12	12	Eggs, hard-cooked, diced	Add eggs, peppers, pimiento, celery, onion, and pickle to marinated potatoes. Mix lightly.
114 g	4 oz	Green peppers, chopped	
170 g	6 oz	Pimiento, chopped	
454 g	1 lb	Celery, diced	
227 g	8 oz	Onion, finely chopped	
227 g	8 oz	Pickles, chopped	
480 mL	2 c	Mayonnaise	Add mayonnaise. Mix carefully to blend. Chill at least 1 hr before serving.

HOT POTATO SALAD

Yield: 50 portions
Portion: 6 oz (170 g)

Amount		Ingredient	Method
Metric	*U.S.*		
6.8 kg	15 lb	Potatoes	Wash potatoes and trim as necessary. Steam until just tender. Peel and dice.
16	16	Eggs, hard-cooked	Peel and dice eggs.
454 g	1 lb	Bacon	Dice bacon. Cook until crisp. Drain; reserve fat.
85 g	3 oz	Onion, chopped	Add bacon, onion, and green pepper to potatoes.
170 g	6 oz	Green pepper, chopped	Add mayonnaise and reheat to serving temperature.
1.42 L	1½ qt	Mayonnaise	Serve hot.

Notes:
1. Hot Vegetable Sauce (p. 465) may be substituted for Mayonnaise, or half Mayonnaise and half Cooked Salad Dressing (p. 437) may be used.
2. Bacon may be omitted.

BROWN BEAN SALAD

Yield: 4¼ qt (4.02 L)
Portion: ⅓ c (80 mL)

Amount		Ingredient	Method
Metric	*U.S.*		
2 No. 10 cans	2 No. 10 cans	Beans, brown or kidney, drained	Mix all ingredients. Allow to season at least 1 hr before serving.
18	18	Eggs, hard-cooked, diced	Serve with No. 12 dipper.
454 g	1 lb	Pickles, chopped (or pickle relish)	
114 g	4 oz	Onion, minced	
567 g	1 lb 4 oz	Celery, diced	
114 g	4 oz	Green pepper, chopped	
120 mL	½ c	Vinegar	
45 mL	3 T	Salt	
0.95 L	1 qt	Salad dressing	

Note: 4 lb (1.81 kg) dried beans, cooked, may be substituted for canned beans.

TRIPLE BEAN SALAD

Yield: 5 qt (4.73 L)
Portion: ⅓ c (80 mL)

Amount		Ingredient	Method
Metric	U.S.		
1 No. 10 can	1 No. 10 can	Green beans, French style or cut	Drain beans well.
2 No. 2½ cans	2 No. 2½ cans	Wax beans, cut	
2 No. 2½ cans	2 No. 2½ cans	Kidney beans	
680 g	1 lb 8 oz	Onion, thinly sliced	Combine vegetables and seasonings. Cover. Marinate overnight in refrigerator.
240 mL	1 c	Green pepper, diced	
720 mL	3 c	Vinegar	
680 g	1 lb 8 oz	Sugar	
60 mL	¼ c	Soy sauce	
60 mL	4 T	Celery salt	
10 mL	2 t	Salt	
10 mL	2 t	Pepper	
240 mL	1 c	Salad oil	Just before serving, drain vegetables well. Add oil and toss lightly. Serve with No. 12 dipper.

Vegetable Salad Combinations[1]

Asparagus

1. Three asparagus tips through a ring of green pepper placed on a slice of tomato. Bibb lettuce garnish. Mayonnaise.

2. Asparagus tips on shredded lettuce, garnished with sliced hard-cooked egg and pimiento strip. French Dressing.

Green Beans

1. Cooked green beans mixed with chopped small green onions and thinly sliced radishes. Thick French Dressing.

2. Marinated whole green beans, garnished with pimiento strips. French Dressing.

Beets

1. Sliced pickled beets and hard-cooked eggs arranged on lettuce. Mayonnaise.

2. Julienne beets and celery on endive. French Dressing.

3. Sliced cooked beets, Bermuda onion rings, quartered hard-cooked eggs, arranged on shredded lettuce. French Dressing.

Cucumbers

1. Thin slices of cucumber on slices of tomato, arranged on a lettuce leaf. Tarragon Dressing.

2. Thin slices of cucumber and Bermuda onion marinated. Vinaigrette Dressing.

Peas

1. Cooked peas, diced cheese, celery, pickle, and pimiento. Combination Dressing.

Spinach

1. Chopped raw spinach, combined with hard-cooked eggs, garnished with crumbled crisp bacon. Tarragon Dressing.

[1] See pp. 434-441 for salad dressing recipes.

Tomatoes

1. Tomato and avocado slices, arranged alternately on endive. French Dressing.

2. Tomato sections and marinated broccoli spears. French Dressing.

3. Tomato sections garnished with watercress. French Dressing.

Gelatin Salad Recipes

FRUIT GELATIN SALAD

Yield: 1 pan 12 × 20 × 2 in.
40 portions 2¼ × 2½ in.
48 portions 2 × 2½ in.

Amount		Ingredient	Method
Metric	*U.S.*		
680 g	1 lb 8 oz	Gelatin, fla-vored	Pour boiling water over gelatin. Stir until dissolved.
1.89 L	2 qt	Water, boiling	Add juice or cold water.
1.89 L	2 qt	Fruit juice or water, cold	Chill.
1.81-2.27 kg	4-5 lb	Fruit, drained	Place fruit in counter pan. When gelatin begins to congeal, pour over fruit. Place in refrigerator to congeal.

Notes:
1. For quick preparation, dissolve 24 oz (680 g) flavored gelatin dessert in 1½ qt (1.42 L) boiling water. Measure 2½ qt (2.37 L) chipped or finely crushed ice, then add enough cold water or fruit juice to cover ice. Add to gelatin and stir constantly until ice is melted. Gelatin will begin to congeal at once. Speed of congealing depends on proportion of ice to water and size of ice particles.
2. One or more canned, frozen, or fresh fruits, cut into desired shapes and sizes, may be used. Fresh or frozen pineapple must be cooked before adding to gelatin salad.
3. Fruit juice may be used for part or all of the liquid.
4. If unflavored granulated gelatin is used, soak 2½ oz (70 g) plain gelatin for 10 min in 2 c (480 mL) cold water. Add 3½ qt (3.31 L) boiling fruit juice and 1 lb (454 g) sugar.

Variations:
1. **Jellied Vegetable Salad.** Substitute vegetables for fruit. Add 1 t (5 mL) salt and substitute ½ c (120 mL) vinegar for ½ c (120 mL) fruit juice.

Use water or vegetable juice for remainder of liquid. If unflavored gelatin is used, add 1 T (15 mL) salt and 1 c (240 mL) vinegar or lemon juice.

2. **Applesauce Mold.** Add 24 oz (680 g) lime gelatin to 3 qt (2.84 L) boiling hot applesauce and stir until dissolved. Add 1 qt (0.95 L) ginger ale and pour into salad molds or 12 × 20 in. pan.

3. **Arabian Peach Salad.** Drain 1 No. 10 can sliced peaches, saving juice. Combine peach juice, 1½ c (360 mL) white vinegar, 1 lb 12 oz (794 g) sugar, 1 oz (28 g) stick cinnamon, and 2 t (10 mL) whole cloves. Simmer 10 min, strain, and add enough hot water to make 1 gal (3.79 L) liquid. Add to 24 oz (680 g) orange gelatin and stir until dissolved. When slightly thickened, add peaches.

4. **Autumn Salad.** Dissolve 24 oz (680 g) orange gelatin in 2 qt (1.89 L) hot water. Add 2 qt (1.89 L) cold liquid, 2½ lb (1.14 kg) sliced fresh peaches, and 2½ lb (1.14 kg) fresh pears.

5. **Blueberry Mold.** Make in two layers. First layer: 12 oz (340 g) raspberry gelatin dissolved in 1 qt (0.95 L) boiling water; add 1 qt (0.95 L) blueberry juice and 6 No. 303 cans blueberries, drained. Chill. Second layer: 12 oz (340 g) lemon gelatin, dissolved in 1 qt (0.95 L) hot pineapple juice; add 1 No. 10 can crushed pineapple and 1 qt (0.95 L) sour cream. Cool. Pour over first layer.

6. **Cabbage Parfait.** Dissolve 24 oz (680 g) lemon gelatin in 2 qt (1.89 L) hot water. Blend in 1 qt (0.95 L) mayonnaise, 1 qt (0.95 L) cold water, 1 c (240 mL) vinegar, and 2 t (10 mL) salt. Chill until mixture is partially congealed, then beat until fluffy. Add 2 qt (1.89 L) finely shredded cabbage, 1 qt (0.95 L) radish slices, 1 qt (0.95 L) diced celery, 1 c (240 mL) chopped green pepper, and ½ c (120 mL) minced onion.

7. **Cranberry Ring Mold.** Dissolve 24 oz (680 g) cherry or raspberry gelatin in 2 qt (1.89 L) hot water. Add 3 lb (1.36 kg) fresh or frozen cranberry relish, 1 lb (454 g) chopped apples, and 1 lb (454 g) crushed pineapple or 1 No. 10 can whole cranberry sauce and 6 oranges, ground. Pour into individual ring molds or 12 × 20 in. pan.

8. **Cucumber Soufflé Salad.** Dissolve 24 oz (680 g) lime or lemon gelatin in 1½ qt (1.42 L) hot water. Add 2 qt (1.89 L) ice and water. Chill until partially set. Whip until fluffy. Add 3 c (720 mL) mayonnaise and ⅓ c (80 mL) lemon juice. Fold in 1 gal (3.79 L) chopped cucumbers (10-12 cucumbers).

9. **Frosted Cherry Salad.** Dissolve 24 oz (680 g) cherry gelatin in 2 qt (1.89 L) hot water. Add 2 qt (1.89 L) cold fruit juice, 3 lb (1.36 kg) drained, pitted red cherries, and 2 lb (908 g) crushed pineapple. When congealed, frost with whipped cream cheese and chopped toasted almonds.

10. **Frosted Lime Mold.** Dissolve 24 oz (680 g) lime gelatin in 2 qt (1.89 L) hot water. Add 2 qt (1.89 L) cold fruit juice and, when mixture begins to congeal, add 2 qt (1.89 L) crushed pineapple, 2½ lb (1.14 kg) cottage cheese, 8 oz (227 g) diced celery, 4 oz (114 g) chopped pimiento, and 4 oz (114 g) nutmeats. When congealed, frost with mixture of 4 lb (1.81 kg) cream cheese blended with ½ c (120 mL) mayonnaise.

11. **Jellied Citrus Salad.** Dissolve 24 oz (680 g) lemon or orange gelatin in 2 qt (1.89 L) hot water. Add 2 qt (1.89 L) cold water, sections from 15 oranges and 8 grapefruit; or 4 No. 2 cans mandarin oranges and 3 lb (1.36 kg) frozen grapefruit sections.

12. **Jellied Waldorf Salad.** Dissolve 24 oz (680 g) raspberry or cherry gelatin in 2 qt (1.89 L) boiling water. Add 1 c (240 mL) red cinnamon candies and stir until dissolved. Add 2 qt (1.89 L) cold liquid. When mixture begins to congeal, add 2 qt (1.89 L) diced apple, 3 c (720 mL) finely diced celery, and 2 c (480 mL) chopped pecans.

13. **Molded Grapefruit Salad.** Dissolve 24 oz (680 g) lime gelatin in 2 qt (1.89 L) hot water. Add 2 qt (1.89 L) cold fruit juice, sections from 15 grapefruit, or 6 lb (2.72 kg) frozen grapefruit sections.

14. **Molded Pear Salad.** Dissolve 24 oz (680 g) lime gelatin in 2 qt (1.89 L) hot water. Add 2 qt (1.89 L) cold fruit juice and 50 pear halves.

15. **Molded Pineapple-Cheese Salad.** Dissolve 24 oz (680 g) lemon gelatin in 2 qt (1.89 L) hot liquid. Add 2 qt (1.89 L) cold fruit juice, 1 lb (454 g) grated Cheddar cheese, 3 lb (1.36 kg) drained crushed pineapple, 3 oz (85 g) chopped green pepper or pimiento, and 4 oz (114 g) finely chopped celery.

16. **Molded Pineapple-Cucumber Salad.** Dissolve 24 oz (680 g) lime gelatin in 2 qt (1.89 L) hot liquid. Add 2 qt (1.89 L) cold fruit juice, 3 lb (1.36 kg) drained crushed pineapple, 1½ lb (680 g) diced cucumber, and 4 oz (114 g) finely chopped pimiento.

17. **Molded Pineapple-Relish Salad.** Dissolve 24 oz (680 g) lemon gelatin in 2 qt (1.89 L) hot liquid. Add 2 qt (1.89 L) cold fruit juice, 4 lb (1.81 kg) pineapple tidbits, and 1½ c (360 mL) pickle relish.

18. **Molded Pineapple and Rhubarb Salad.** To 4 lb (1.81 kg) frozen rhubarb, add 2 lb (908 g) sugar and 1 qt (0.95 L) water. Cook 5 min. Add 4 lb (1.81 kg) pineapple tidbits and 24 oz (680 g) strawberry gelatin dissolved in juice from rhubarb and pineapple. Add enough water to make 1 gal (3.79 L).

19. **Raspberry Ring Mold.** Dissolve 24 oz (680 g) raspberry gelatin in 2 qt (1.89 L) hot liquid. Add 2 qt (1.89 L) cold raspberry juice, 3 lb (1.36 kg) frozen raspberries, and 2 lb (908 g) cantaloupe or watermelon balls. Pour into individual ring molds.

20. **Ribbon Gelatin Salad.** Dissolve 24 oz (680 g) raspberry gelatin in 1 gal (3.79 L) hot water. Divide into 3 equal parts. Pour ⅓ into 12 × 20 in. pan and chill. Add 1 lb (454 g) cream cheese to another third and whip to blend; pour on the first part when it is congealed. Return to the refrigerator until it, too, is congealed, then top with remaining portion.

21. **Spicy Apricot Mold.** To syrup drained from 2 No. 10 cans peeled apricot halves, add 1 c (240 mL) vinegar, 6 pieces stick cinnamon, and 1 T (15 mL) whole cloves. Simmer 10 min. Remove spices and add enough hot water to make 1 gal (3.79 L) liquid. Combine with 24 oz (680 g) orange gelatin and chill. When slightly thickened, add apricots.

22. **Strawberry-Rhubarb Salad.** To 4 lb (1.81 kg) frozen rhubarb, add 2 lb (908 g) sugar and 1 qt (0.95 L) water. Cook 5 min. Add 4 lb (1.81 kg) frozen sliced strawberries and 24 oz (680 g) strawberry gelatin dissolved in juice from rhubarb and strawberries. Add enough hot water to make 1 gal (3.79 L) liquid.

23. **Sunshine Salad.** Dissolve 24 oz (680 g) lemon gelatin in 2 qt (1.89 L) hot liquid. Add 2 qt (1.89 L) cold fruit juice, 3 lb (1.36 kg) drained crushed pineapple, and 8 oz (227 g) grated raw carrot.

24. **Swedish Green-Top Salad.** Dissolve 12 oz (340 g) lime gelatin in 2 qt (1.89 L) boiling water. Pour into 12 × 20 in. pan. Dissolve 12 oz (340 g) orange gelatin in 2 qt (1.89 L) boiling water and stir until dissolved. While mixture is still hot, add 1½ lb (680 g) marshmallows and stir until melted. When cool, add 12 oz (340 g) cream cheese, 1½ c (360 mL) mayonnaise, and ½ t (3 mL) salt, blended together. Fold in 1 pt (475 mL) cream, whipped. Pour over congealed lime gelatin and return to refrigerator to chill.

25. **Under-the-Sea Salad.** Dissolve 24 oz (680 g) lime gelatin in 1 gal (3.79 L) hot water. Divide into two parts. Pour one part into a pan and chill. When it begins to congeal, add 3 c (720 mL) sliced pears or drained crushed pineapple. To the remaining gelatin mixture, add 1 lb (454 g) cream cheese, whipping until smooth. Pour over first portion.

GINGER ALE FRUIT SALAD

Yield: 1 pan 12 × 20 × 2 in.
40 portions 2¼ × 2½ in.
48 portions 2 × 2½ in.

Amount		Ingredient	Method
Metric	*U.S.*		
680 g	1 lb 8 oz	Gelatin, lemon flavored	Pour boiling water over gelatin. Stir until gelatin is dissolved.
1.89 L	2 qt	Water, boiling	Cool.
1.89 L	2 qt	Ginger ale	Add ginger ale.
454 g	1 lb	Grapes (or white cherries)	When liquid begins to congeal, add remaining ingredients. Pour into counter pan or into individual molds. Place in refrigerator to congeal.
340 g	12 oz	Celery, chopped fine	
454 g	1 lb	Apples, cubed	
1 No. 10 can	1 No. 10 can	Pineapple, diced	
60 mL	¼ c	Lemon juice	

Note: Cider may be used in place of ginger ale.

JELLIED BEET SALAD

Yield: 1 pan 12 × 20 × 2 in.
40 portions 2¼ × 2½ in.
48 portions 2 × 2½ in.

Amount		Ingredient	Method
Metric	*U.S.*		
680 g	1 lb 8 oz	Gelatin, lemon flavored	Pour boiling water over gelatin. Stir until dissolved.
1.89 L	2 qt	Water, boiling	
0.95 L	1 qt	Beet juice (or water)	Add beet juice, vinegar, salt, and onion juice.
240 mL	1 c	Vinegar, mild	Chill.
30 mL	2 T	Salt	
45 mL	3 T	Onion juice	
90 mL	6 T	Horseradish	When mixture begins to congeal, add horseradish and vegetables. Pour into counter pan. Place in refrigerator to congeal.
1.14 kg	2 lb 8 oz	Celery, finely diced	
1.14 kg	2 lb 8 oz	Beets, diced or chopped	

BING CHERRY SALAD

Yield: 1 pan 12 × 20 × 2 in.
40 portions 2¼ × 2½ in.
48 portions 2 × 2½ in.

Amount			
Metric	*U.S.*	*Ingredient*	*Method*
680 g	1 lb 8 oz	Gelatin, raspberry or cherry flavored	Pour boiling water over gelatin. Stir until dissolved. Cool. Add water and juice.
0.95 L	1 qt	Water, boiling	Chill until mixture begins to congeal.
3.31 L	3½ qt	Water and cherry juice	
2 No. 2½ cans	2 No. 2½ cans	Bing cherries, pitted	Add cherries, pecans, and olives. Pour into counter pan or into 50 individual molds. Place in refrigerator to congeal.
227 g	8 oz	Pecans, chopped	
480 mL	2 c	Stuffed olives, sliced (optional)	

Notes:
1. 8 oz (227 g) cream cheese, rolled into small balls, may be added with cherries and pecans to gelatin mixture.
2. Omit stuffed olives. Add 1 No. 10 can crushed pineapple, drained.

TOMATO ASPIC

Yield: 1 pan 12 × 20 × 2 in.
40 portions 2¼ × 2½ in.
48 portions 2 × 2½ in.

Amount		Ingredient	Method
Metric	U.S.		
114 g	4 oz	Gelatin, plain	Sprinkle gelatin over water. Soak
0.95 L	1 qt	Water, cold	10 min.
3.79 L	4 qt	Tomato juice	Combine tomato juice and sea-
2	2	Onions, small	sonings. Boil 5 min. Strain.
1	1	Bay leaf	Add gelatin. Stir until dissolved.
4	4	Celery stalks	
8	8	Cloves, whole	
10 mL	2 t	Mustard, dry	
397 g	14 oz	Sugar	
15 mL	1 T	Salt	
480 mL	2 c	Vinegar or lemon juice	Add vinegar or lemon juice. Pour into counter pan or ring molds. Place in refrigerator to congeal.

Note: If ring molds are used, recipe will yield approximately 75 servings. Centers may be filled with cole slaw, cottage cheese, crab salad, or lobster salad.

PERFECTION SALAD

Yield: 1 pan 12 × 20 × 2 in.
40 portions 2¼ × 2½ in.
48 portions 2 × 2½ in.

Amount		Ingredient	Method
Metric	U.S.		
85 g	3 oz	Gelatin, plain	Sprinkle gelatin over cold water.
480 mL	2 c	Water, cold	Soak 10 min.
2.84 L	3 qt	Water, boiling	Add boiling water. Stir until gelatin is dissolved.
240 mL	1 c	Vinegar	Add vinegar, lemon juice, salt,
240 mL	1 c	Lemon juice	and sugar. Stir until sugar is
28 g	1 oz	Salt	dissolved. Chill.
454 g	1 lb	Sugar	
680 g (E.P.)	1 lb 8 oz (E.P.)	Cabbage, chopped	When liquid begins to congeal, add vegetables.
284 g	10 oz	Celery, chopped	Pour into counter pan. Place in
114 g	4 oz	Pimiento, chopped	refrigerator to congeal.
114 g	4 oz	Green pepper, chopped	
15 mL	1 T	Paprika	

Luncheon Salad Recipes

CHICKEN SALAD

Yield: 6¼ qt (5.91 L)
Portion: ½ c (120 mL)

Amount			
Metric	*U.S.*	*Ingredient*	*Method*
2.72 Kg	6 lb	Cooked chicken	Cut chicken meat into ½-in. cubes.
12	12	Eggs, hard-cooked, diced	Add remaining ingredients. Mix lightly. Chill.
1.36 kg	3 lb	Celery, diced	Serve with No. 10 dipper.
30 mL	2 T	Salt	
5 mL	1 t	Pepper, white	
720 mL	3 c	Mayonnaise	
20 mL	4 t	Lemon juice	

Notes:
1. 18-20 lb (8.16-9.08 kg) chickens A.P. will yield approximately 6 lb (2.72 kg) cooked meat.
2. The marinating of cubed chicken with ⅔ c (160 mL) French dressing (p. 438) for 2 hr will improve the flavor.
3. Just before serving, 8 oz (227 g) toasted almonds, white cherries, ripe olives, pineapple chunks, sweet pickle, or cucumbers may be added.
4. Turkey may be substituted for chicken.
5. Canned or frozen chicken or turkey may be used.

Variations:
1. **Chicken-Avocado-Orange Salad.** Delete eggs. Add 1 qt (0.95 L) diced orange segments, 2 c (480 mL) broken toasted almonds, and 1 c (240 mL) chopped pimiento. Just before serving, add 6 avocados, diced.

2. **Chicken Salad in Cranberry or Raspberry Mold.** Fill center of individual or raspberry ring molds (p. 417) with chicken salad.

SHRIMP SALAD   **Yield: 6¼ qt (5.91 L)**
                                                Portion: ½ c (120 mL)

Amount		Ingredient	Method
Metric	U.S.		
2.72 kg	6 lb	Cooked shrimp (p. 239)	Cut shrimp into ½-in. pieces. Place in bowl.
908 g	2 lb	Celery, diced	Add vegetables to shrimp.
454 g	1 lb	Cucumber, diced	
1 head	1 head	Lettuce, chopped (optional)	
720 mL	3 c	Mayonnaise	Combine mayonnaise and seasonings.
30 mL	2 T	Lemon juice	ings.
10 mL	2 t	Salt	Add to shrimp and vegetables.
5 mL	1 t	Paprika	Mix lightly. Chill.
10 mL	2 t	Mustard, prepared	Serve with No. 10 dipper in lettuce cup.

Notes:
1. If shrimp are small, they may be left whole.
2. 1 doz hard-cooked eggs, coarsely chopped, may be added; reduce shrimp to 5 lb (2.27 kg).
3. May be garnished with tomato wedges or served in a tomato cup.

SHRIMP-RICE SALAD

Yield: 50 portions
Portion: 5 oz (142 g)

Amount		Ingredient	Method
Metric	U.S.		
454 g	1 lb	Rice, long grain	Cook rice (p. 190).
1.18 L	1¼ qt	Water	Chill.
15 mL	1 T	Salt	
2.27 kg(E.P.)	5 lb (E.P.)	Cooked shrimp, chilled	Combine cooked rice, shrimp, celery, and green peppers.
680 g	1 lb 8 oz	Celery, sliced crosswise, thin	
454 g	1 lb	Green peppers, sliced in thin strips	
240 mL	1 c	Vinegar	Combine seasonings.
120 mL	½ c	Salad oil	Pour over shrimp-rice mixture.
30 mL	2 T	Worcestershire sauce	Marinate at least 3 hr.
			Just before serving, add pineapple
30 mL	2 T	Sugar	tidbits.
15 mL	1 T	Salt	Serve with No. 8 dipper on let-
10 mL	2 t	Curry powder	tuce leaf.
4 mL	¾ t	Ginger	
3 mL	½ t	Black pepper	
1.36 kg (3 No. 2½ cans)	3 lb (3 No. 2½ cans)	Pineapple tidbits, drained	

CRAB SALAD

Yield: 4¼ qt (4.02 L)
Portion: ⅓ c (80 mL)

Amount		Ingredient	Method
Metric	U.S.		
10 cans (or 1.81 kg fresh)	10 6½-oz cans (or 4 lb fresh or fro- zen)	Crab, coarsely flaked	Combine ingredients lightly. Chill. Serve with No. 10 dipper.
80 mL	⅓ c	Lemon juice	
30	30	Eggs, hard- cooked, chopped	
480 mL	2 c	Ripe olives, sliced	
454 g	1 lb	Almonds, blanched, slivered (op- tional)	
0.95 L	1 qt	Mayonnaise	

Notes:
1. Olives may be deleted and 1 lb (454 g) diced cucumbers added.
2. If desired, omit mayonnaise and marinate with French dressing (p. 438).

Variation:
Lobster Salad. Substitute lobster for crab.

MACARONI SALAD

Yield: 1 gal (3.79 L)
Portion: ⅓ c (80 mL)

Amount			
Metric	*U.S.*	*Ingredient*	*Method*
1.14 kg	2 lb 8 oz	Macaroni, el-bow	Cook macaroni (p. 191). Drain. Chill.
7.57 L	2 gal	Water, boiling	
45 mL	3 T	Salt	
45 mL	3 T	Salad oil	
908 g	2 lb	Cheddar cheese, diced or shredded	Add remaining ingredients. Mix lightly. Chill.
680 g	1 lb 8 oz	Sweet pickle, chopped (or pickle relish)	Serve with No. 12 dipper.
18	18	Eggs, hard-cooked, chopped	
908 g	2 lb	Celery, chopped fine	
57 g	2 oz	Onion, finely chopped	
114 g	4 oz	Pimiento, chopped	
23 mL	1½ T	Salt	
5 mL	1 t	Pepper	
0.95 L	1 qt	Mayonnaise	

Note: Spaghetti or shell macaroni may be substituted for elbow macaroni.

TUNA SALAD

Yield: 6¼ qt (5.91 L)
Portion: ½ c (120 mL)

Amount		Ingredient	Method
Metric	U.S.		
3.63 kg	8 lb	Tuna, flaked	Combine ingredients lightly.
680 g	1 lb 8 oz	Celery, chopped fine	Chill. Serve with No. 10 dipper.
680 g	1 lb 8 oz	Cucumber, diced	
12	12	Eggs, hard-cooked, chopped	
240 mL	1 c	Sweet pickle, chopped	
0.95 L	1 qt	Mayonnaise	

Variations:

1. **Tuna-Apple Salad.** Substitute tart, diced apples for cucumbers.

2. **Salmon Salad.** Substitute salmon for tuna.

COTTAGE CHEESE SALAD

Yield: 1 gal (3.79 L)
Portion: ⅓ c (80 mL)

Amount		Ingredient	Method
Metric	U.S.		
2.72 kg	6 lb	Cottage cheese, dry	Combine ingredients lightly. Chill.
1.36 kg	3 lb	Tomatoes, peeled, diced	Serve with No. 12 dipper.
114 g	4 oz	Green peppers, chopped	
454 g	1 lb	Celery, diced	
454 g	1 lb	Cucumber, diced	
227 g	8 oz	Radishes, diced	
45 mL	3 T	Salt	
720 mL	3 c	Mayonnaise (use less if cheese contains cream)	

Salad Plate Combinations

Fruit

1. Cranberry ring mold, cantaloupe and watermelon balls in center; 3 slices honeydew melon cut ¾ in. thick; cluster of white grapes; Honey French Dressing (p. 441); small rolled cinnamon bread sandwich; lettuce garnish.

2. Fiesta Fruit Plate: 3 pineapple chunks; ⅓ banana, cut in strips and rolled in cream dressing and chopped nuts; 4 grapefruit and 3 orange sections; ½ fresh pear. Garnish with avocado and lettuce. Fill fluted baking cup with No. 16 dipper of raspberry sherbet and place in center of plate as it is served. Serve with Ginger Muffins (p. 175).

3. Frozen Fruit Salad Mold (p. 401) in lettuce cup; pear half on thin slice of whole orange; peach half and large prune stuffed with cream cheese; finger (chicken) sandwich. Garnish with parsley or mint.

4. Two honeydew melon sections; small cluster of red grapes; peach half, rounded side up, ½ orange, thinly sliced; pineapple spears; ⅓ c (80 mL) fresh strawberries; raisin bread and cream cheese sandwich, cut into thirds; watercress garnish.

5. Cottage cheese, No. 12 dipper; peach half with Royal Cranberry Sauce (p. 431) in center; ½ banana with dressing and chopped nut garnish; 2 figs; pineapple ring; lettuce garnish; All-Bran Muffin (p. 120).

6. Cottage cheese, No. 12 dipper; grapefruit and orange sections; Apple Salad (p. 397), topped with ½ red maraschino cherry; Celery Seed Dressing (p. 439); Nut Bread Sandwiches (p. 132), 2-in. squares cut diagonally.

Meat, Fish, Poultry, and Eggs

1. Baked, pullman-style ham, 2 1½-in. slices rolled; 2 tomato slices in lettuce cup; ½ deviled egg, ripe olive garnish. Small hard roll.

2. Baked ham, 2 2½-oz (70 g) slices; potato salad, No. 12 dipper, in lettuce cup; green pepper ring, ½ hard-cooked egg; carrot and celery strips.

3. Baked ham, 2½-oz (70 g) slice; ½ cubed banana, dipped in Whipped Cream dressing (p. 437); peach half with cream cheese center; 1 Italian prune; lettuce and parsley garnish. Toasted English muffin.

4. Cold sliced turkey and baked ham sliced, 2½ oz (70 g) each; Bing Cherry Gelatin Mold (p. 420) in lettuce cup; cheese stuffed celery; carrot curls. Banana Nut Bread (p. 133) sandwich strips.

5. Cold roast pork, 2½-oz (70-g) slice; Applesauce Mold (p. 416); potato salad, No. 12 dipper; radish roses and lettuce garnish.

6. Cold roast beef, 2-oz (57-g) slice; Macaroni Salad (p. 427), No. 12 dipper, with green pepper ring; sliced tomatoes, 3 oz (85 g); cucumber slices, 1½ oz (43 g); lettuce garnish.

7. Cold cuts, 2 oz (57 g), American cheese, 1 oz (28 g); Triple Bean Salad (p. 413), No. 12 dipper; lettuce wedge, ⅛ head; cucumber slices, 1½ oz (43 g); lettuce garnish.

8. Tuna Salad (p. 428), No. 12 dipper, stuffed olive garnish; pineapple ring topped with a No. 16 dipper Waldorf Salad (p. 397), ½ maraschino cherry; potato chips, ¾ oz (21 g); lettuce and parsley garnish.

9. Deviled egg, 2 halves; chilled canned salmon, 2 oz (57 g); potato chips, ¾ oz (21 g); lemon wedge, curly endive garnish.

10. Egg Salad (p. 450), No. 12 dipper; 2 tomato wedges, 2 oz (57 g) each; ripe olive garnish; 3 asparagus spears; Cucumber Butter Sandwich strips (p. 446); lettuce garnish.

11. Avocado half filled with chicken or shrimp salad, No. 12 dipper; spiced peach, sliced tomatoes, lettuce garnish.

Relish Recipes

CRANBERRY RELISH (RAW)   Yield: 1 gal (3.79 L)
                                                    Portion: ¼ c (60 mL)

Amount			
Metric	U.S.	Ingredient	Method
4 (size 72)	4 (size 72)	Oranges, un-peeled	Wash and quarter oranges and apples.
1.81 kg	4 lb	Cranberries, raw	Sort and wash cranberries.
2.72 kg	6 lb	Apples, cored	Put fruit through chopper or grinder.
1.36 kg	3 lb	Sugar	Add sugar and blend. Chill 24 hr. Serve with No. 16 dipper as a relish or salad. If using as a salad, drain before serving.

Variation:
Cranberry-Orange Relish. Delete apples. Increase oranges to 8 and sugar to 4 lb (1.81 kg); add ½ c (120 mL) lemon juice.

CRANBERRY SAUCE

Yield: 1 gal (3.79 L)
Portion: ¼ c (60 mL)

Amount		Ingredient	Method
Metric	*U.S.*	*Ingredient*	*Method*
1.81 kg	4 lb	Cranberries	Wash cranberries. Discard soft
1.81 kg	4 lb	Sugar	berries.
0.95 L	1 qt	Water	Add sugar and water. Cover, boil gently until skins burst. Do not overcook. Serve with No. 16 dipper.

Note: Make sauce at least 24 hr before using. Cranberries may be puréed before adding sugar.

Variation:
Whole Cranberry Sauce. Make syrup of sugar and 2 qt (1.89 L) water. Boil
   10 min, add cranberries, cover, and boil until skins burst.

ROYAL CRANBERRY SAUCE

Yield: 1 gal (3.79 L)
Portion: 2½ T (37 mL)

Amount		Ingredient	Method
Metric	*U.S.*	*Ingredient*	*Method*
908 g	2 lb	Cranberries	Wash cranberries. Discard soft
908 g	2 lb	Sugar	berries.
480 mL	2 c	Water, hot	Add sugar and hot water to cranberries. Cover and simmer until tender. Cool.
2 (size 72)	2 (size 72)	Oranges, chopped	When cool, add remaining ingredients.
454 g	1 lb	Apples, tart, chopped	Serve with No. 24 dipper as a relish.
454 g	1 lb	White grapes, seeded	
454 g	1 lb	Pineapple, diced	
114 g	4 oz	Pecans, chopped	

Note: The sauce will keep for several weeks if placed in a covered jar in a refrigerator.

CABBAGE RELISH

Yield: 1 gal (3.79 L)
Portion: ⅓ c (80 mL)

Metric	U.S.	Ingredient	Method
	Amount		
2.72 kg	6 lb	Cabbage	Grind or shred vegetables.
255 g	9 oz	Green peppers	
794 g	1 lb 12 oz	Carrots	
0.95 L	1 qt	Cultured sour cream	Combine remaining ingredients. Add to vegetables and mix lightly.
30 mL	2 T	Salt	Serve with No. 12 dipper.
255 g	9 oz	Sugar	
240 mL	1 c	Vinegar	

Variation:

Cucumber Relish. Substitute 8 lb (3.63 kg) finely diced cucumber for cabbage, carrots, and peppers. Season with salt, pepper, and lemon juice. Fold in sour cream and chill. Serve in lettuce cup; garnish with thin slice of red radish or sprig of parsley.

BEET RELISH

Yield: 3 qt (2.84 L)
Portion: 1 T (15 mL)

Metric	U.S.	Ingredient	Method
	Amount		
0.95 L (2 No. 2½ cans)	1 qt (2 No. 2½ cans)	Beets, cooked, chopped	Combine beets and cabbage.
340 g	12 oz	Cabbage, raw, shredded	
454 g	1 lb	Sugar	Mix remaining ingredients and add to vegetables.
5 mL	1 t	Salt	
240 mL	1 c	Horseradish	Chill 24 hr.
114 g	4 oz	Onion, chopped fine	Serve with No. 60 dipper as a relish with meat.
480 mL	2 c	Vinegar	

PICKLED BEETS

Yield: 2 gal (7.57 L)
Portion: ⅓ c (80 mL)

Amount		Ingredient	Method
Metric	U.S.		
1.89 L	2 qt	Vinegar, mild	Mix vinegar, sugar, and spices.
454 g	1 lb	Brown sugar	Heat to boiling point. Boil 5 min.
227 g	8 oz	Sugar	
5 mL	1 t	Salt	
3 mL	½ t	Pepper	
5 mL	1 t	Cinnamon	
5 mL	1 t	Cloves	
5 mL	1 t	Allspice	
4.54 kg (E.P.) or 2 No. 10 cans	10 lb (E.P.) or 2 No. 10 cans	Beets, cooked, sliced	Pour hot, spiced vinegar over beets. Chill.

Note: Add onion rings if desired.

Salad Dressing Recipes

MAYONNAISE   **Yield: 1 gal (3.79 L)**

Amount		Ingredient	Method
Metric	*U.S.*	*Ingredient*	*Method*
8 (or 4 whole eggs)	8 (or 4 whole eggs)	Egg yolks	Place egg yolks, salt, paprika, and mustard in mixer bowl. Mix well.
45 mL	3 T	Salt	
10 mL	2 t	Paprika	
30 mL	2 T	Mustard, dry	
60 mL	¼ c	Vinegar	Add vinegar and blend.
1.89 L	2 qt	Salad oil	Add oil very slowly, beating steadily (high speed) until an emulsion is formed. Oil may then be added, ½ c (120 mL) at a time (and later 1 c/240 mL at a time), beating well after each addition.
60 mL	¼ c	Vinegar	Add vinegar after the 2 qt (1.89 L) of oil have been added. Beat well.
1.89 L	2 qt	Salad oil	Continue beating and adding oil until all oil has been added and emulsified.

Note: The addition of oil too rapidly or insufficient beating may cause the oil to separate from the other ingredients, resulting in a curdled appearance. Curdled, or broken mayonnaise, may be reformed by adding it (a small amount at a time and beating well after each addition) to 2 well-beaten eggs or egg yolks. It also may be reformed by adding it to a small portion of good mayonnaise.

Variations:

1. **Blue Cheese Dressing.** Mix 6 oz (170 g) blue cheese with 3 c (720 mL) Mayonnaise and ¼ c (60 mL) cream or milk. Add a few drops Tabasco sauce.

2. **Campus Dressing.** Combine 3 T (45 mL) chopped parsley, 2 T (30 mL) chopped green pepper, and ¼ c (60 mL) finely chopped celery with 1 qt (0.95 L) Mayonnaise.

3. **Chantilly Dressing.** Whip ¾ c (180 mL) heavy cream and fold in 3 c (720 mL) Mayonnaise.

4. **Combination Dressing.** Combine 2 c (480 mL) Mayonnaise and 2 c (480 mL) Cooked Salad Dressing (p. 437).

5. **Cranberry Dressing.** Blend 2½ c (600 mL) Mayonnaise and 2 c (480 mL) jellied cranberries, beaten until smooth. Fold in 1 c (240 mL) whipped cream just before serving.

6. **Egg Dressing.** Chop 4 hard-cooked eggs and combine with 1 qt (0.95 L) Mayonnaise.

7. **Egg and Green Pepper Dressing.** Combine 6 chopped, hard-cooked eggs, 2 T (30 mL) finely chopped green pepper, 1 T (15 mL) onion juice, and a few grains cayenne pepper with 3½ c (840 mL) Mayonnaise.

8. **Garden Dressing.** Add 1 qt (0.95 L) cultured sour cream, ¼ c (60 mL) sugar, 1 T (15 mL) salt, f.g. pepper, 1 c (240 mL) minced green onion, 1 c (240 mL) sliced radishes, 1 c (240 mL) chopped cucumber, and 1 c (240 mL) minced green peppers to 2 c (480 mL) Mayonnaise.

9. **Honey-Cream Dressing.** Blend 1 oz (28 g) cream cheese, ⅔ c (160 mL) strained honey, ½ c (60 mL) lemon or pineapple juice, and ¼ t salt. Fold in 3½ c (840 mL) Mayonnaise.

10. **Roquefort Dressing.** Add 1 c (240 mL) French Dressing, 4 oz (114 g) Roquefort cheese, crumbled, and 1 t (5 mL) Worcestershire sauce to 3 c (720 mL) Mayonnaise.

11. **Russian Dressing.** Add 1 c (240 mL) chili sauce, 1 T (15 mL) Worcestershire sauce, 1 t (5 mL) onion juice, and f.g. cayenne pepper to 1 qt (0.95 L) Mayonnaise.

12. **Sour Cream-Roquefort Dressing.** Add 1 c (240 mL) cultured sour cream, 2 T (30 mL) lemon juice, 2 t (10 mL) grated onion, ½ t salt, and 4 oz (114 g) Roquefort cheese, crumbled fine, to 2 c (480 mL) Mayonnaise.

13. **Thousand Island Dressing.** Add 1½ oz (43 g) minced onion, 3 oz (85 g) chopped pimiento, 1¾ c (420 mL) chili sauce, 10 chopped hard-cooked eggs, 1 t (5 mL) salt, ½ c (120 mL) chopped pickles or olives, and f.g. cayenne pepper to 1¾ qt (1.66 L) Mayonnaise.

MAYONNAISE WITH COOKED BASE   **Yield: 3 gal (11.36 L)**

Amount		Ingredient	Method
Metric	*U.S.*	*Ingredient*	*Method*
454 g	1 lb	Cornstarch	Mix cornstarch and water to a
480 mL	2 c	Water, cold	smooth paste.
1.89 L	2 qt	Water, boiling	Add boiling water, stirring vigorously with a wire whip. Cook until mixture is clear.
			Pour into mixer bowl. Beat until cool.
20 (or 12 whole eggs)	20 (or 12 whole eggs)	Egg yolks	Add eggs, ¼ at a time, while beating (high speed).
45 mL	3 T	Salt	Add seasonings. Mix well.
60 mL	¼ c	Mustard, dry	Add vinegar.
10 mL	2 t	Paprika	
480 mL	2 c	Vinegar	
3.79 L	1 gal	Salad oil	Gradually add oil, 1 c (240 mL) at a time. Beat well (high speed) after each addition. (See Mayonnaise recipe, p. 434).
480 mL	2 c	Vinegar	Add vinegar, then add oil slowly,
3.79 L	1 gal	Salad oil	beating constantly.

COOKED SALAD DRESSING   **Yield: 3 gal (11.36 L)**

Amount			
Metric	*U.S.*	*Ingredient*	*Method*
1.36 kg	3 lb	Sugar	Combine dry ingredients.
680 g	1 lb 8 oz	Flour	Add water and stir until a smooth
170 g	6 oz	Salt	paste is formed.
85 g	3 oz	Mustard, dry	
0.95 L	1 qt	Water	
3.79 L	1 gal	Milk, hot	Add hot milk and water, stirring
1.89 L	2 qt	Water, hot	continuously while adding.
			Cook 20 min, or until thickened.
454 g	1 lb	Butter or mar-garine	Add butter or margarine and vinegar.
2.84 L	3 qt	Vinegar, hot	
50 (1.25 kg)	50 (2 lb 12 oz)	Egg yolks, beaten	Add cooked mixture slowly to egg yolks, stirring briskly. Cook 7-10 min. Remove from heat and cool.

Note: 25 whole eggs may be substituted for egg yolks, and hot water for
hot milk.

Variations:

1. **Combination Dressing.** Combine 2 c (480 mL) Cooked Salad Dressing
    and 2 c (480 mL) Mayonnaise (p. 434).

2. **Egg Dressing.** Add 4 chopped hard-cooked eggs, ½ c (120 mL)
    chopped pimiento, and ¼ c (60 mL) chopped pickles to 1 qt (0.95 L)
    Cooked Salad Dressing.

3. **Whipped Cream Dressing.** Add 2 c (480 mL) cream, whipped, to 1 qt
    (0.95 L) Cooked Salad Dressing.

FRENCH DRESSING   Yield: 3 qt (2.84 L)

Amount			
Metric	U.S.	Ingredient	Method
45 mL	3 T	Salt	Combine dry ingredients in mixer
30 mL	2 T	Mustard, dry	bowl.
30 mL	2 T	Paprika	
15 mL	1 T	Pepper	
1.89 L	2 qt	Oil	Add oil, vinegar, and onion juice.
0.95 L	1 qt	Vinegar	Beat (high speed) until thick
20 mL	4 t	Onion juice	and blended.
			This is a temporary emulsion that separates rapidly. Beat well or pour into a jar and shake vigorously just before serving.

Note: An egg white beaten into each quart of dressing just before using will keep it from separating.

Variations:

1. **California Dressing.** Add 2 c (480 mL) mashed avocado, 2 T (30 mL) lemon juice, and 1 t (5 mL) salt to 3 c (720 mL) French Dressing.

2. **Catsup Dressing.** Blend 1 c (240 mL) catsup with 3 c (720 mL) French Dressing.

3. **Chiffonade Dressing.** Add 4 t (20 mL) chopped parsley, 1 oz (28 g) chopped onion, 1½ oz (43 g) chopped green pepper, 1 oz (28 g) chopped red pepper or pimiento, and 4 chopped hard-cooked eggs to 3 c (720 mL) French Dressing.

4. **Italian Dressing.** Delete paprika. Add 2 t (10 mL) oregano and 1 T (15 mL) garlic salt.

5. **Mexican Dressing.** Add 2½ oz (70 g) chopped green pepper, ¾ c (180 mL) chili sauce, and 1 oz (28 g) chopped onion to 3 c (720 mL) French Dressing.

6. **Piquante Dressing.** Add 2 t (10 mL) mustard, ½ t (3 mL) Worcestershire sauce, and 2 t (10 mL) onion juice to 1 qt (0.95 L) French Dressing.

7. **Roquefort Cheese Dressing.** Add slowly, 3 c (720 mL) French Dressing to 4 oz (114 g) Roquefort cheese, finely crumbled. Whip dressing slowly into cheese. 1 c (240 mL) heavy cream may be mixed with cheese before adding French Dressing.

8. **Tomato Dressing.** Add 4 oz (114 g) sugar, 1 t (5 mL) onion juice, and 1½ c (360 mL) tomato soup to 3 c (720 mL) French Dressing.

9. **Vinaigrette Dressing.** Add ¾ c (180 mL) chopped pickle, ½ c (120 mL) chopped green olives, 6 T (90 mL) chopped parsley, 1 t (5 mL) onion juice, and 2 T (30 mL) capers to 3 c (720 mL) French Dressing.

THICK FRENCH DRESSING   Yield: 1½ qt (1.42 L)

Metric	U.S.	Ingredient	Method
908 g	2 lb	Sugar	Combine sugar and seasonings in mixer bowl.
30 mL	2 T	Paprika	
20 mL	4 t	Mustard, dry	
30 mL	2 T	Salt	
8 mL	1½ t	Onion juice	
320 mL	1⅓ c	Vinegar	Add vinegar. Mix well.
0.95 L	1 qt	Salad oil	Gradually add oil in small amounts. Beat well after each addition.

Note: If a dressing of the usual consistency is desired, use only 8 oz (227 g) sugar.

Variations:
1. **Poppy Seed Dressing.** Add ½ c (120 mL) poppy seed.
2. **Celery Seed Dressing.** Add ½ c (120 mL) celery seed.

FRENCH DRESSING, SEMIPERMANENT   Yield: 1¼ qt (1.18 L)

Metric	U.S.	Ingredient	Method
20 mL	4 t	Gelatin, plain	Soften gelatin in cold water.
60 mL	4 T	Water, cold	Dissolve in boiling water.
120 mL	½ c	Water, boiling	Chill.
20 mL	4 t	Mustard, dry	Mix dry ingredients in mixer bowl.
20 mL	4 t	Paprika	
45 mL	3 T	Sugar	
f.g.	f.g.	Red pepper	
30 mL	2T	Salt	
0.95 L	1 qt	Salad oil	Add oil slowly while beating (high speed).
240 mL	1 c	Vinegar	Add vinegar slowly. Beat (high speed) 5 min. Add gelatin.

CELERY SEED FRUIT DRESSING   Yield: 2 qt (1.89 L)

Amount		Ingredient	Method
Metric	U.S.		
680 g	1 lb 8 oz	Sugar	Mix dry ingredients.
80 mL	⅓ c	Cornstarch	Add vinegar. Cook until thick-
30 mL	2 T	Mustard, dry	ened and clear.
30 mL	2 T	Salt	Cool to room temperature.
30 mL	2 T	Paprika	
480 mL	2 c	Vinegar	
5 mL	1 t	Onion juice	Add onion juice to cooked mix-
0.95 L	1 qt	Salad oil	ture.
			Add oil slowly while beating (high speed).
30 mL	2 T	Celery seed	Add celery seed.
			Serve with any fruit salad combination.

Variation:
Poppy Seed Dressing. Add poppy seed in place of celery seed.

SOUR CREAM DRESSING   Yield: 2 qt (1.89 L)

Amount		Ingredient	Method
Metric	U.S.		
16	16	Eggs, beaten	Mix eggs and sour cream.
0.95 L	1 qt	Cultured sour cream	
908 g	2 lb	Sugar	Mix sugar, flour, and water until
43 g	1½ oz	Flour	smooth.
240 mL	1 c	Water	Add to the cream and egg mixture.
480 mL	2 c	Vinegar	Add vinegar. Cook until thick. Stir as necessary.

Notes:
1. Dressing may be stored several days in refrigerator.
2. 1 pt (475 mL) cream, whipped, may be added before serving.

Variation:
Sweet-Sour Cream Dressing. Combine 1 qt (0.95 L) cultured sour cream, ½ c (120 mL) sugar, 2 t (10 mL) salt, and ½ c (120 mL) vinegar. May be combined with shredded cabbage or served over tomatoes, cucumbers, or any fruit combination.

FRUIT SALAD DRESSING   Yield: 5 qt (4.73 L)

Amount			
Metric	U.S.	Ingredient	Method
0.95 L	1 qt	Pineapple juice	Heat juices to boiling point.
720 mL	3 c	Orange juice	
480 mL	2 c	Lemon juice	
908 g	2 lb	Sugar	Mix sugar and cornstarch. Add to
142 g	5 oz	Cornstarch	hot mixture while stirring with a
16	16	Eggs, well beaten	wire whip. Add eggs. Cook until thickened. Chill.
480 mL	2 c	Whipping cream	Whip cream and fold in just before serving. Serve with fruit salads.

HONEY FRENCH DRESSING   Yield: 2 qt (1.89 L)

Amount			
Metric	U.S.	Ingredient	Method
20 mL	4 t	Dry mustard	Mix mustard, salt, and celery seed
5 mL	1 t	Salt	in large mixing bowl.
20 mL	4 t	Celery seed or poppy seed	
480 mL	2 c	Honey	While mixing, add remaining ingredients in given order.
300 mL	1¼ c	Vinegar	Pour into covered jar. Refrigerate.
60 mL	¼ c	Lemon juice	
15 mL	1 T	Grated lemon	
0.95 L	1 qt	Salad oil	

CHILEAN DRESSING   Yield: 1½ qt (1.42 L)

Amount			
Metric	U.S.	Ingredient	Method
480 mL	2 c	Salad oil	Combine all ingredients.
240 mL	1 c	Vinegar	Beat (low speed) until well
114 g	4 oz	Sugar	blended.
10 mL	2 t	Salt	Store in covered container. Shake
60 mL	4 T	Onion, chopped fine	or beat well before serving.
480 mL	2 c	Chili sauce	
240 mL	1 c	Catsup	

Sandwiches

Sandwiches may be hearty and substantial, approximating a meal, or light and dainty, as an accompaniment to tea, and may be served hot or cold. They are made of one or more slices of bread, spread with one or more kinds of filling. The closed sandwich is made by spreading one slice of bread with a filling and covering it with a second slice. The open-faced sandwich is made by spreading a slice of bread with filling and decorating it.

Sandwich Ingredients

Bread

Bread is used in sandwiches to provide a variety of color, flavor, texture, and shape. Cracked wheat, graham, whole wheat, white, rye, pumpernickel, French, Italian, or Boston Brown bread are most often used for the substantial type of sandwich. Hamburger, frankfurter, hard, and soft rolls, submarine, or Vienna buns also are popular for hearty sandwiches. Tea sandwiches are made from white or whole wheat bread, or from nut, orange, raisin, date, banana, or cranberry bread.

A Pullman or sandwich loaf is used for most sandwiches. The bread should be sliced ⅛-¼ in. thick, depending on the type of sandwich to be made.

Butter or Margarine

Butter or margarine should be softened or whipped for easy spreading. To **whip butter,** place in mixer bowl and allow to stand at room temperature until soft enough to mix. A half cup of milk or boiling water per pound of butter may be added gradually while whipping to increase the volume. Mix first on low speed and then whip on second and high speed until fluffy. A savory spread for meat and fish sandwiches may be made by adding minced cucumber, spices, onion, prepared mustard, chopped chives, parsley, or pimiento to the whipped butter. Butter or margarine need not always be used on sandwiches when a rich filling is used. However, butter helps to prevent fillings from soaking into the bread and improves the flavor. Eight ounces (227 g) butter or margarine or 1 c (240 ml) mayonnaise should spread one side of 50 sandwiches, using 1 t (5 mL) per slice.

Fillings

Sandwiches may be filled with sliced meat, poultry, or cheese; with fish, poultry, or meat patties; or with a spreadable mixture. A filling may be made of chopped meats, poultry, fish, cheese, vegetables, jellies, nuts, or fruits. One of these ingredients or a combination of them is usually mixed with mayonnaise, salad dressing, or cream. Use of leftovers should be avoided unless it is certain they have been protected from bacterial growth and that proper temperatures have been maintained.

Soft mixed fillings should be measured with a spoon or small dipper to insure a uniform amount in each sandwich. Using a No. 20 dipper, 2½ qt (2.37 L) filling is needed for 50 sandwiches.

If slices of meat or cheese are used for filling, the slices should be even in thickness and the same size as the bread on which they are to be placed. Very thinly sliced meat, 1-2 oz (28-57 g), gives greater volume and may be more tender than one thick slice.

Garnishes

The garnishes to be used depend on the type of sandwich. Lettuce, parsley, watercress, and other salad greens, olives, pickles, pimiento, green peppers, radishes, nuts, paprika, and cheese are often used as garnishes for various types of sandwiches.

See p. 446 for filling suggestions and pp. 446-456 for sandwich recipes.

Making Sandwiches

Closed Sandwiches

1. Have filling, garnish, and butter or margarine prepared.

2. Arrange fresh bread in rows, preferably 4 rows of 10 slices each.

3. Spread all bread slices out to the edges with softened butter or margarine.

4. Portion filling with dipper or spoon on alternate rows of bread and spread to the edges or arrange sliced filling to fit sandwich.

5. If lettuce is used, arrange leaves on filling. Omit lettuce if sandwiches are to be held for some time.

6. Place plain buttered slices of bread on the filled slices.

7. Stack several sandwiches together and cut with a sharp knife.

8. To keep sandwiches fresh, place in sandwich bags or waxed paper. Or place sandwiches in storage pans on damp towel covered with waxed paper and cover completely with more waxed paper and a damp towel.

9. Refrigerate until serving time. If freezing sandwiches for later use, see precautions on p. 445.

Simple sandwiches may be made more attractive by cutting into rounds, triangles, or small squares.

Grilled and Toasted Sandwiches

Many ingredients may be combined to make suitable fillings for toasted or grilled sandwiches. For a grilled sandwich, the filling is placed between 2 slices of bread, the outside is brushed with butter or margarine, and the sandwich is browned on the grill, in a hot oven, or under a broiler. Fillings for a grilled sandwich may include cheese, meat, fish, or poultry salads, or a combination of fillings, as in a Reuben sandwich (p. 452).

Bread for toasted sandwiches may be toasted before or after filling is added, although a crisp ingredient like lettuce is added after the sandwich is toasted. Toasted sandwiches may be either closed or open faced. A few suggestions for toasted sandwiches follow.

1. Thinly sliced tomato, broiled bacon, lettuce, and salad dressing.

2. Chicken livers, mashed, crisp bacon, and salad dressing.

3. Sliced cheese, sliced ham, and prepared mustard.

4. Sliced cheese, tomato, and mayonnaise.

5. Sliced corned beef, Swiss cheese, lettuce, on rye bread.

6. Meat, fish, or poultry salads.

Tea Sandwiches

Open Sandwiches.   Cut slices of bread ¼ in. thick into rounds, hearts, stars, diamonds, crescents, squares, or any desired shape. Spread with creamed butter, then with filling, and decorate. The filling may be ham and sliced cheese, chicken, tuna, shrimp, lobster, or crab salad, or other fillings (p. 446). Open sandwiches may be decorated with a variety of garnishes (p. 443) such as parsley, sliced olives, sliced radishes, pickles, nuts, and pimiento. A few suggestions for open sandwiches follow.

1. Place a thin slice of tomato on a round of buttered bread. Garnish with mayonnaise and a sprig of parsley, or butter the edges of the bread and roll in chopped parsley.

2. Spread bread cut into diamond shapes with butter and cream cheese. Garnish with pimiento or green peppers.

3. Spread bread cut in heartshapes with a mixture of chopped almonds, maraschino cherries, and whipped cream.

4. Mix chopped walnuts, candied ginger, and mayonnaise. Cut bread into tiny squares and garnish with a half walnut and bit of paprika.

5. Mix ground American cheese, butter, lemon juice, Worcestershire sauce, paprika, cayenne, and onion juice. Spread on rounds of rye bread. Garnish with stuffed olive slices.

For additional sandwich spreads, see pp. 446-449.

Ribbon Sandwiches. Make stacks of 5 slices of bread, alternating whole wheat and white and filling with one or more spreads. Firmly press together. Cut off crusts. Arrange stacks in shallow pan; cover with waxed paper and moist cloth. Chill for several hours. Cut each slice into thirds, halves, or triangles.

Checkerboard Sandwiches. Make stacks of ribbon sandwiches by alternating 2 slices white and 2 slices whole wheat bread and filling with desired spread. Trim, and cut each stack into ½-in. slices. Using butter or smooth spread as a filling, stack 3 slices together so that white and whole wheat squares alternate to give a checkerboard effect. Chill for several hours. Remove from refrigerator and, with sharp knife, slice into checkerboard slices, ½ in. thick.

Rolled Sandwiches. Remove crusts from 3 sides of unsliced bread. With crust at left, cut loaf into lengthwise slices, ⅛-¼ in. thick. Run rolling pin the length of each slice to make it easier to handle. Spread with softened butter or margarine, then with desired smooth spread. Olives, gherkins, frankfurters, or other foods may be placed across end. Starting at end with garnish, roll tightly, being careful to keep sides straight. Tight rolling makes for easier slicing. Wrap rolls individually in waxed paper or aluminum foil, twisting ends securely. Chill several hours or overnight. Rolls may be made ahead of time, then wrapped and frozen. Let thaw about 45 min before slicing. Cut chilled rolls into ¼-½ in. slices.

Freezing Sandwiches

When making sandwiches to be frozen for later use, certain precautions need to be taken. Bread should be spread with butter or margarine instead of mayonnaise or salad dressing. Fillings such as minced chicken, meat, egg yolks, fish, or peanut butter freeze well, but sliced cooked eggs and some vegetables, such as tomatoes and parsley, should not be frozen.

Wrap large closed sandwiches individually. Pack tea-sized closed sandwiches in layers in freezer boxes; or place in any suitable box and overwrap with moisture vapor-proof material. Place open-faced sandwiches on cardboard or trays, wrap as for closed sandwiches. Wrap ribbon, rolled or other loaf sandwiches, uncut.

Sandwiches will thaw in 1-2 hr, shorter for open-face. Outer wrapping should not be removed until sandwiches are partly thawed. If sandwiches are not served immediately after thawing, they should be held in the refrigerator until serving time.

Sandwich Filling Suggestions

1. Dates, figs, raisins, orange, ground.

2. Peanut butter and Cheddar cheese, mixed.

3. Hard-cooked eggs and olives, chopped, grated cheese and mayonnaise, mixed.

4. Sliced cold boiled tongue and mayonnaise.

5. Cucumber, chopped and mixed with creamed butter.

6. Dates, lemon juice, and nuts, minced.

7. Sliced tomato and mayonnaise.

8. Cream cheese, minced dried beef, mixed with mayonnaise and seasoned with horseradish, grated onion, and mustard.

9. Cream cheese and chopped chives.

10. Cream cheese, chopped preserved ginger, mixed.

11. Cabbage and carrot, chopped fine, mixed with salad dressing.

12. Grated carrots, chopped nuts, and mayonnaise, mixed.

13. Cottage cheese and chopped green onions on rye bread.

Sandwich Recipes

SANDWICH SPREAD

Amount			
Metric	U.S.	Ingredient	Method
454 g	1 lb	Butter or margarine	Whip butter or margarine (high speed) until fluffy.
120 mL	½ c	Light cream	Add cream.
15 mL	1 T	Mustard	Fold in remaining ingredients.
1.42 L	1½ qt	Mayonnaise	Use as a spread for a meat or
240 mL	1 c	Pickle relish	cheese sandwich.

CHICKEN SALAD SANDWICHES

Yield: 50 sandwiches

Amount			
Metric	*U.S.*	*Ingredient*	*Method*
1.81 kg	4 lb	Cooked chicken, chopped	Combine filling ingredients.
114 g	4 oz	Almonds, chopped, toasted	
10 mL	2 t	Salt	
227 g	8 oz	Celery, chopped fine	
60 mL	¼ c	Vinegar	
240 mL	1 c	Mayonnaise	
100 slices	100 slices	Bread	Portion filling with No. 24 dipper.
2-3 heads	2-3 heads	Lettuce	Assemble filling, bread, and lettuce (p. 443).

TUNA SALAD SANDWICHES

Yield: 50 sandwiches

Amount			
Metric	*U.S.*	*Ingredient*	*Method*
1.81 kg	4 lb	Tuna, flaked	Combine filling ingredients.
6	6	Eggs, hard-cooked, chopped	
60 mL	¼ c	Lemon juice	
5 mL	1 t	Onion juice	
240 mL	1 c	Mayonnaise	
240 mL	1 c	Cooked Salad Dressing (p. 437)	
100 slices	100 slices	Bread	Portion filling with No. 20 dipper.
2-3 heads	2-3 heads	Lettuce	Assemble filling, bread, and lettuce (p. 443).

Note: 1 c (240 mL) chopped pickle may be added.

MEAT SALAD SANDWICHES

Yield: 50 sandwiches

Amount			
Metric	*U.S.*	*Ingredient*	*Method*
1.81 kg	4 lb	Meat, cooked, finely chopped	Combine filling ingredients.
114 g	4 oz	Celery, chopped fine	
227 g	8 oz	Olives or pickles, chopped	
240 mL	1 c	Mayonnaise	
240 mL	1 c	Cooked Salad Dressing (p. 437)	
60 mL	¼ c	Vinegar	
5 mL	1 t	Salt	
100 slices	100 slices	Bread	Portion filling with No. 20 dipper.
2-3 heads	2-3 heads	Lettuce	Assemble filling, bread, and lettuce (p. 443).

HAM SALAD SANDWICHES

Yield: 50 sandwiches

Amount			
Metric	*U.S.*	*Ingredient*	*Method*
1.81 kg	4 lb	Ham, cooked, coarsely ground	Combine filling ingredients.
227 g	8 oz	Pickles, chopped	
57 g	2 oz	Pimiento, chopped	
240 mL	1 c	Mayonnaise	
240 mL	1 c	Cooked Salad Dressing (p. 437)	
100 slices	100 slices	Bread	Portion filling with No. 20 dipper.
2-3 heads	2-3 heads	Lettuce	Assemble filling, bread, and lettuce (p. 443).

Note: 6 hard-cooked eggs, chopped, may be added.

BACON AND TOMATO SANDWICHES

Yield: 50 sandwiches

Amount			
Metric	*U.S.*	*Ingredient*	*Method*
1.81 kg (100 slices)	4 lb (100 slices)	Bacon	Cook bacon (p. 304).
100 slices	100 slices	Bread	Spread 50 slices of bread with mayonnaise, place 2 cooked ba-
240 mL	1 c	Mayonnaise	con slices, 2 thin slices of to-
227 g	8 oz	Butter or mar- garine	mato, and a lettuce leaf on each. Top with remaining 50 slices of
3.18 kg	7 lb	Tomatoes, sliced	bread, which have been spread with whipped butter or margar-
2-3 heads	2-3 heads	Lettuce	ine.

SUBMARINE SANDWICHES

Yield: 50 sandwiches

Amount			
Metric	*U.S.*	*Ingredient*	*Method*
50	50	Submarine or Vienna buns	Split buns, leaving hinged.
227 g	8 oz	Butter or mar- garine	Whip butter until fluffy. Add cream.
60 mL	¼ c	Light cream	Lightly blend in remaining ingre-
720 mL	3 c	Mayonnaise	dients.
60 mL	¼ c	Mustard, pre- pared	Spread on open sides of buns.
120 mL	½ c	Pickle relish	
794 g	1 lb 12 oz	Salami, ½-oz slices	Arrange on each bun ½ oz each of 3 kinds of meat, 2½-oz (70 g)
794 g	1 lb 12 oz	Spiced ham, ½- oz slices	triangles of cheese, 2 slices of tomato, and 2 slices of dill
794 g	1 lb 12 oz	Ham, pullman, ½-oz slices	pickle.
1.42 kg	3 lb 2 oz	American cheese, 1-oz slices cut di- agonally	
2 doz me- dium	2 doz me- dium	Tomatoes, fresh, sliced	
0.95 L	1 qt	Dill pickle slices, well drained	

Note: Other meats, as turkey, ham, corned beef, or pork may be used.

EGG SALAD SANDWICHES

Yield: 50 sandwiches

Amount			
Metric	*U.S.*	*Ingredient*	*Method*
3 doz	3 doz	Eggs, hard-cooked, chopped	Combine filling ingredients.
480 mL	2 c	Mayonnaise	
480 mL	2 c	Pickle relish	
10 mL	2 t	Salt	
120 mL	½ c	Pimiento, chopped	
100 slices	100 slices	Bread	Portion filling with No. 24 dipper.
2-3 heads	2-3 heads	Lettuce	Assemble filling, bread, and lettuce (p. 443).

OVEN-BAKED HAMBURGERS

Bake: 15-20 min　　　　　　　　　　　　　　　　　　　**Yield: 50 portions**
Oven: 400 °F (205 °C)　　　　　　　　　　　　　　　**Portion: 4 oz (114 g)**

Amount			
Metric	*U.S.*	*Ingredient*	*Method*
5.44 kg	12 lb	Ground beef	Combine all ingredients.
3	3	Eggs, beaten	Measure with No. 10 dipper and
480 mL	2 c	Milk	flatten into patties.
480 mL	2 c	Bread crumbs, soft	Place on lightly greased baking sheet. Bake.
30 mL	2 T	Salt	
10 mL	2 t	Pepper	
114 g	4 oz	Onion, chopped	
50	50	Hamburger buns	Serve patties on hot buns.

Variation:

Barbecued Hamburgers. Place browned hamburgers in baking pans. Pour
Barbecue Sauce (p. 464) over patties. Cover with aluminum foil and
bake 20-25 min.

WESTERN SANDWICHES

Yield: 50 sandwiches
Portion: 4 oz (114 g)

Metric	U.S.	Ingredient	Method
	Amount		
4.54 kg	10 lb	Ground beef	Brown beef and onion.
227 g	8 oz	Onion, chopped	
0.95 L	1 qt	Tomato purée	Add remaining ingredients.
30 mL	2 T	Salt	Simmer 20-30 min.
10 mL	2 t	Paprika	
10 mL	2 t	Dry mustard	
30 mL	2 T	Worcestershire sauce	
10 mL	2 t	Chili powder	
50	50	Hamburger buns	Serve with No. 10 dipper on buns.

HOT ROAST BEEF SANDWICHES

Yield: 50 sandwiches
Portion: 2½ oz (70 g) meat
¼ c (60 mL) gravy

Metric	U.S.	Ingredient	Method
	Amount		
3.63 kg	8 lb	Roast beef	Cut meat into very thin slices.
50 slices	50 slices	Bread	Place 2½ oz (70 g) meat on each
2.84 L	3 qt	Gravy (p. 463)	slice of bread.
			Cover with gravy, using 2 oz ladle.

Note: Meat may be covered with additional slice of bread if desired. Then cover entire sandwich with gravy.

Variations:
1. **French Dip Sandwich.** Place thin sliced beef on Kaiser roll. Serve with hot seasoned beef broth for dipping.

2. **Hot Roast Pork Sandwich.** Substitute roast pork for beef.

3. **Hot Turkey Sandwich.** Substitute roast turkey or turkey roll for beef.

REUBEN SANDWICH

Yield: 50 sandwiches

Metric	U.S.	Ingredient	Method
Amount			
100 slices	100 slices	Rye bread	Spread No. 100 dipper (scant 2 t/
480 mL	2 c	Thousand Island Dressing, Mayonnaise, or Sandwich Spread (p. 446)	10 mL) dressing on bread.
1.81 kg (E.P.)	4 lb (E.P.)	Corned beef, cooked, sliced very thin	Place on bread, in order given: 1 oz (28 g) corned beef 2 T (30 mL) sauerkraut
1.42 L	1½ qt	Sauerkraut, well drained	1 oz (28 g) cheese Cover with top slice of bread.
1.42 kg	3 lb 2 oz	Swiss cheese, 1-oz (28-g) slices	
454 g	1 lb	Butter or margarine, melted	Brush sandwich with melted butter or margarine. Grill.

HOT CHIPPED BEEF AND CHEESE SANDWICHES

Bake: 3-5 min
Oven: 350 °F (175 °C)   **Yield: 50 sandwiches**

Metric	U.S.	Ingredient	Method
Amount			
340 g	12 oz	Butter or margarine	Make into Medium White Sauce, (p. 458).
28 g	1 oz	Flour	
480 mL	2 c	Milk	
908 g	2 lb	Beef, chipped, shredded	Add remaining ingredients. Cook 2 min.
60 mL	¼ c	Horseradish	
15 mL	1 T	Mustard	
50 slices	50 slices	Bread, toasted and buttered	Place No. 30 dip of mixture on bread.
1.42 kg	3 lb 2 oz	Cheddar cheese, sliced	Cover with 1 slice cheese. Bake.

HOT TUNA BUNS

Bake: 15-20 min
Oven: 350 °F (175 °C)   **Yield: 50 sandwiches**

Amount		Ingredient	Method
Metric	*U.S.*	*Ingredient*	*Method*
1.81 kg	4 lb	Tuna	Combine all ingredients.
680 g	1 lb 8 oz	Cheddar cheese, shredded	
18	18	Eggs, hard-cooked, chopped	
120 mL	½ c	Green pepper, chopped	
60 mL	¼ c	Onion, chopped	
180 mL	¾ c	Stuffed olives, chopped	
180 mL	¾ c	Sweet pickle, chopped	
720 mL	3 c	Mayonnaise	
50	50	Hamburger or coney buns	Fill buns using No. 16 dipper. Place in counter pan, cover with aluminum foil. Bake.

Variation:

Hot Luncheon Sandwiches. Substitute any ground prepared luncheon meat
for tuna, omitting green pepper and olives, and adding ½ c (120 mL)
prepared mustard.

GRILLED CHEESE SANDWICHES

Yield: 50 sandwiches

Metric	U.S.	Ingredient	Method
	Amount		
100 slices	100 slices	Bread	Make sandwiches.
1.42 kg	3 lb 2 oz	Cheese, 1-oz (28-g) slices	Brush both sides with butter or margarine.
454 g	1 lb	Butter or margarine, melted	Grill on hot griddle until golden brown on both sides.

Notes:
1. Cheese may be ground and the following ingredients added to make a spread: 2 T (30 mL) prepared mustard, ½ c (120 mL) chili sauce, 1 c (240 mL) mayonnaise.
2. Salad mixtures such as chicken, ham, tuna, and egg salad are satisfactory fillings for grilled sandwiches.

Variations:
1. **Toasted Cheese Sandwiches.** Assemble cheese sandwiches, place on greased baking sheet, and broil until brown. Invert on second greased baking sheet and broil on other side until brown.

2. **Oven-Baked Cheese Sandwiches.** Assemble cheese sandwiches and place on greased baking sheet. Cover with second greased baking sheet. Bake in 400 °F (205 °C) oven 10 min.

3. **French Fried Cheese Sandwiches.** Dip in batter (p. 75) and fry in deep fat 1-2 min at 375 °F (190 °C).

CHEESE SANDWICHES

Yield: 50 sandwiches

Metric	U.S.	Ingredient	Method
	Amount		
1.59 kg	3 lb 8 oz	Cheese, ground	Combine filling ingredients.
480 mL	2 c	Salad dressing or cream	
10 mL	2 t	Salt	
f.g.	f.g.	Cayenne	
114 g	4 oz	Butter or margarine	
100 slices	100 slices	Bread	Portion filling with No. 24 dipper. Assemble filling and bread (p. 443).

Variation:
Pimiento Cheese Sandwiches. Add 6 oz (170 g) chopped pimiento.

PEANUT SANDWICHES

Yield: 50 sandwiches

Amount		Ingredient	Method
Metric	U.S.		
908 g	2 lb	Shelled peanuts, ground	Mix peanuts and butter or margarine.
170 g	6 oz	Butter or margarine, soft	
240 mL	1 c	Cream, whipped	Fold whipped cream and salt into mayonnaise.
240 mL	1 c	Mayonnaise	Combine with peanuts.
15 mL	1 T	Salt	
100 slices	100 slices	Bread, cracked wheat	Portion filling with No. 24 dipper. Assemble filling, bread, and lettuce (p. 443).
2 heads	2 heads	Lettuce	

Variation:

Peanut Butter Sandwiches. Substitute 4 lb (1.81 kg) peanut butter for peanuts. Omit butter, cream, and salt.

HOT PICNIC BUNS

Bake: 20 min
Oven: 325 °F (165 °C)

Yield: 50 buns
Portion: 2¾ oz (78 g) filling

Amount		Ingredient	Method
Metric	U.S.		
1.36 kg	3 lb	Bologna, cubed or coarsely ground	Combine bologna and cheese.
908 g	2 lb	Cheese, grated	
480 mL	2 c	Pickle relish	Combine remaining ingredients. Mix lightly with bologna and cheese.
240 mL	1 c	Chili sauce	
240 mL	1 c	Mayonnaise	
120 mL	½ c	Mustard, prepared	
60 mL	¼ c	Onion, grated	
10 mL	2 t	Salt	
50	50	Sandwich buns	Fill split buns with mixture, using No. 16 dipper. Wrap each in foil (or place in 12 × 20 × 2 in. pan and cover securely with foil). Heat.

Note: Other lunch meat may be substituted for bologna.

RUNZA

Bake: 25-30 min
Oven: 400 °F (205 °C)

Yield: 56 sandwiches

Amount			
Metric	*U.S.*	*Ingredient*	*Method*
DOUGH:			
35 g	1¼ oz	Yeast, active dry	Sprinkle yeast over water. Let stand 5 min.
1.89 L	2 qt	Water, warm	
397 g	14 oz	Sugar	Add sugar, salt and flour.
28 g	1 oz (1½ T)	Salt	Beat (medium speed) until smooth.
1.08 kg	2 lb 6 oz	Flour	
8	8	Eggs	Add eggs and shortening. Continue beating.
142 g	5 oz	Shortening, melted	
2.5 kg	5 lb 8 oz	Flour	Add flour (low speed) to make a soft dough. Knead 5 min.
			Cover and let rise until double. Punch down. Divide dough in 4-5 portions.
			Roll out. Cut into 4 × 6 in. rectangles (3 oz/85 g dough).
			Place ⅔ c (160 mL) (No. 6 dipper) filling on dough.
			Fold lengthwise and pinch edges of dough securely to seal.
			Place on baking sheet with sealed edges down.
			Bake 10 min.
1	1	Egg yolk	Combine yolk and water.
30 mL	2 T	Water	Remove runzas from oven. Brush with glaze.
			Return to oven for 15-20 min.
FILLING:			
3.63 kg	8 lb	Ground beef	Brown and drain beef.
908 g	2 lb	Cabbage	Steam cabbage and onion until slightly underdone.
992 g	2 lb 3 oz	Onion, chopped	
60 mL	¼ c	Worcestershire sauce	Add seasonings and vegetables to ground beef. Mix lightly.
57 g	2 oz	Salt	
5 mL	1 t	Pepper	

5 mL	1 t	Savory
5 mL	1 t	Chili powder
10 mL	2 t	Seasoned salt

Sauces

A sauce is a dressing used to complement another food and may be served as a background or as an accompaniment. It also may be used as a binding agent to hold foods together, or as a topping to another food. Sauces may add color and form to foods and may enhance or offer contrast in flavor or color to the foods they accompany. Some sauces are served with meat, fish, poultry, eggs, and vegetables; others are used as dessert toppings.

Many meat and vegetable sauces are modifications of basic recipes, such as white sauce, bechamel sauce, and brown sauce. White sauce (p. 458), made with a roux of fat and flour and with milk as the liquid, has many uses in quantity food preparation, as a sauce with vegetables, eggs, and fish and as an ingredient in many casseroles. A white sauce mix (p. 460) in which flour, fat, and nonfat dry milk are combined may be made and stored in the refrigerator until needed. Water and seasonings are added when the mixture is to be used. Bechamel sauce (p. 461) and its variations use milk and chicken stock as the liquid and are usually served with poultry, seafood, eggs, or vegetables. Brown sauce (p. 462) is made with a well-browned roux and beef stock and is used mainly with meat. Other sauces may have a butter, tomato, or mayonnaise base. A broth made with a high-quality commercial soup base can be substituted for the chicken or beef stock called for in sauces, but the salt in the recipe may need to be adjusted if the soup base is highly seasoned.

Sauces made from concentrated canned soups are time-saving and may be used effectively in many casserole-type items. Undiluted canned cream soups such as chicken, mushroom, celery, cheese, and tomato may be used alone or in combination. If the soup is too thick, a small amount of milk or chicken or meat stock may be added. Two soups may be combined for a special flavor effect or pimiento, green pepper, almonds, curry powder, or other ingredients added for variety.

Marinades are used to flavor and tenderize meats and poultry. The less tender cuts of meat should be marinated at least 2 hr; pork, chicken, and the more tender cuts of beef often are basted before and during cooking but do not need to stand in the marinade.

Meat and Vegetable Sauce Recipes

WHITE SAUCE

	Ingredients				
Consistency	Milk[a]	Flour	Butter or Margarine	Salt	Uses
Very thin	4 qt (3.79 L)	2 oz (57 g)	8 oz (227 g)	1½ T (23 mL)	Cream soup made from starchy foods
Thin	4 qt (3.79 L)	4 oz (114 g)	8 oz (227 g)	1½ T (23 mL)	Cream soup made from nonstarchy foods
Medium	4 qt (3.79 L)	8 oz (227 g)	1 lb[b] (454 g)	1½ T (23 mL)	Creamed dishes, gravies
Thick	4 qt (3.79 L)	12-16 oz (340-454 g)	1 lb[b] (454 g)	1½ T (23 mL)	Soufflés
Very thick	4 qt (3.79 L)	1 lb 4 oz (567 g)	1 lb 4 oz (567 g)	1½ T (23 mL)	Croquettes

Method 1. Melt butter or margarine, remove from heat. Add flour; stir until smooth. Add salt, then hot milk gradually, stirring constantly. Cook and stir as necessary, until smooth and thick (15-20 min).

Method 2. Combine flour with ¼ milk. Add flour-milk paste to remainder of milk (hot). Cook to desired consistency, then add fat and salt.

Method 3. This method is used for making large quantities, more than 4 qt (3.79 L). Add ¼ milk to the fat-flour mixture; beat until smooth. Add mixture to remaining milk.

Method 4. This method uses a steamer. Make a paste of flour and butter or margarine. Add cold milk until mixture is the consistency of cream. Heat remaining milk; add flour and fat mixture, stirring constantly with wire whip. Place in steamer until flour is cooked; if necessary, stir once during cooking.

[a] 1 lb (454 g) nonfat dry milk and 3¾ qt (3.55 L) cool water may be substituted for fluid milk. Combine dry milk and water. Whip until smooth. Heat to scalding. Add roux made of butter and flour, while stirring. Cook on low heat, stirring as necessary, until thickened.

[b] Reduce butter or margarine to 8-10 oz (227-284 g) in medium, thick, and very thick White Sauce when using Method 2.

Variations:

1. **Sauce à la King.** Add 12 oz (340 g) chopped green pepper and 12 oz (340 g) sliced mushrooms, sautéed, and 1 lb (454 g) chopped pimiento to 1 gal (3.79 L) Medium White Sauce. Combine with cubed cooked chicken, meats, vegetables, or eggs.

2. **Bacon Sauce.** Add 1½ lb (680 g) cooked chopped bacon to 1 gal (3.79 L) Medium White Sauce. Use bacon fat in making the sauce. Combine with eggs or vegetables in scalloped dishes.

3. **Cheese Sauce.** Add 3 lb (1.36 kg) sharp Cheddar cheese (grated or ground), 2 T (30 mL) Worcestershire sauce, and f.g. cayenne pepper to 1 gal (3.79 L) Medium White Sauce. Serve on fish, egg dishes, soufflés, and vegetables.

4. **Egg Sauce.** Add 20 chopped hard-cooked eggs and 2 T (30 mL) prepared mustard to 1 gal (3.79 L) Medium White Sauce. Serve with cooked fish or croquettes.

5. **Golden Sauce.** Add 2 c (480 mL) slightly beaten egg yolks to 1 gal (3.79 L) Medium White Sauce. Serve on fish, chicken, or vegetables.

6. **Mushroom Sauce.** Add 1½ lb (680 g) sliced mushrooms and 4 oz (114 g) minced onion, sautéed in 4 oz (114 g) butter or margarine, to 1 gal (3.79 L) Medium White Sauce. Serve over egg, meat, or poultry dishes or vegetables.

7. **Pimiento Sauce.** Add 1¼ lb (567 g) finely chopped pimiento and 2 c (480 mL) finely chopped parsley to 1 gal (3.79 L) Medium White Sauce. Serve with poached fish, croquettes, or egg dishes.

8. **Shrimp Sauce.** Add 4 lb (1.81 kg) cooked shrimp, 2 T (30 mL) prepared mustard, and 2 T (30 mL) Worcestershire sauce to 1 gal (3.79 L) Medium White Sauce. Serve with fish, eggs, or cheese soufflé.

MEUNIERE SAUCE   Yield: 3 c (720 mL)

Metric	U.S.	Ingredient	Method
	Amount		
567 g	1 lb 4 oz	Butter or margarine	Heat butter until lightly browned. Add onion and brown slightly.
57 g	2 oz	Onion, minced	
120 mL	½ c	Lemon juice	Add juice and seasonings.
15 mL	1 T	Worcestershire sauce	Serve hot over broccoli, Brussels sprouts, green beans, spinach, or cabbage.
15 mL	1 T	Lemon rind, grated	
5 mL	1 t	Salt	

Note: ½ c (120 mL) toasted sliced almonds may be sprinkled over top of vegetable.

WHITE SAUCE MIX   **Yield: 21 lb (9.53 kg) mix**

Amount		Ingredient	Method
Metric	*U.S.*	*Ingredient*	*Method*
1.36 kg	3 lb	Flour	Blend flour and milk in large (60-
4.08 kg	9 lb	Milk, nonfat dry	qt) mixing bowl.
2.04 kg	4 lb 8 oz	Fat	Using pastry knife or flat beater,
2.04 kg	4 lb 8 oz	Butter or margarine	blend fats with dry ingredients until mixture is crumbly, scraping down bowl occasionally.
			Store in covered containers in refrigerator.

To prepare 1 gal white sauce

3.79 L	1 gal	Water	Heat water and salt to boiling
43 g	1½ oz	Salt	point.
	Thin:		
964 g	2 lb 2 oz	White sauce mix	Add mix for sauce of desired thickness.
	Medium:		
1.30 kg	2 lb 14 oz	White sauce mix	Stirring with French whip, continue cooking until thickened.
	Thick:		
1.59 kg	3 lb 8 oz	White sauce mix	

BECHAMEL SAUCE

Yield: 2 qt (1.89 L)

Amount		Ingredient	Method
Metric	U.S.		
1.42 L	1½ qt	Chicken stock (p. 479)	Cook stock and seasonings together 20 min. Strain.
4	4	Onion slices	Save liquid for preparation of
30 mL	2 T	Peppercorns	sauce. There should be 1 qt
85 g	3 oz	Carrots, chopped	(0.95 L) liquid.
1	1	Bay leaf	
227 g	8 oz	Butter or margarine	Melt butter or margarine. Add flour, stir until smooth.
114 g	4 oz	Flour	Add liquids gradually, stirring
0.95 L	1 qt	Seasoned stock (prepared above)	constantly. Cook until smooth and thickened. Add seasonings.
0.95 L	1 qt	Milk, hot	Serve with meat or chicken tim-
3 mL	½ t	Salt	bales or soufflés.
3 mL	½ t	White pepper	
f.g.	f.g.	Cayenne	

Note: Chicken soup base may be used to prepare chicken stock.

Variations:

1. **Mornay Sauce.** Add gradually to hot Bechamel Sauce f.g. cayenne pepper and 1 c (240 mL) each of grated Parmesan and Swiss cheese. Let sauce remain over hcat until cheese is melted, then remove and gradually beat in 8 oz (227 g) butter or margarine. Serve with fish and egg dishes.

2. **Velouté Sauce.** Substitute chicken stock for milk.

BROWN SAUCE

Yield: 1 gal (3.79 L)

Amount			
Metric	*U.S.*	*Ingredient*	*Method*
3.79 L	1 gal	Beef stock (p. 477)	Add onion and seasoning to meat stock.
227 g	8 oz	Onion thinly sliced	Simmer about 10 min. Strain.
23 mL	1½ T	Salt	
3 mL	½ t	Pepper	
454 g	1 lb	Fat	Heat fat and blend with flour.
284 g	10 oz	Flour	Cook until it becomes uniformly brown in color. Add hot stock while stirring. Cook until thickened.

Variations:

1. **Jelly Sauce.** Add 2 c (480 mL) currant jelly, beaten until melted, 2 T (30 mL) tarragon vinegar, and 4 oz (114 g) sautéed minced onions to 2 qt (1.89 L) Brown Sauce. Serve with lamb or game.

2. **Mushroom Sauce.** Add 1 lb (454 g) sliced mushrooms and 2 oz (57 g) minced onions, sautéed, to 2 qt (1.89 L) Brown Sauce. Serve with steak.

3. **Olive Sauce.** Add 1 c (240 mL) chopped stuffed olives to 2 qt (1.89 L) Brown Sauce. Serve with meat or duck.

4. **Piquante Sauce.** Add 2 oz (57 g) minced onions, 2 oz (57 g) capers, ½ c (120 mL) vinegar, ¼ c (60 mL) sugar, ¼ t salt, ¼ t paprika, and ½ c (120 mL) chili sauce or chopped sweet pickle to 2 qt (1.89 L) Brown Sauce. Serve with meats.

5. **Savory Mustard Sauce.** Add ½ c (120 mL) prepared mustard and ½ c (120 mL) horseradish to 2 qt (1.89 L) Brown Sauce. Serve with meats.

PAN GRAVY   **Yield: 1 gal (3.79 L)**

Amount		Ingredient	Method
Metric	U.S.		
227 g	8 oz	Fat (meat drippings), hot	Add flour to fat and blend. Add salt and pepper.
227 g	8 oz	Flour	Add water or stock gradually,
15 mL	1 T	Salt	stirring constantly.
5 mL	1 t	Pepper	Cook until smooth and thickened.
3.79 L	1 gal	Water or meat stock	

Variations:

1. **Brown Gravy.** Use 10 oz (284 g) flour and brown in the fat.

2. **Cream Gravy.** Substitute milk for water or stock.

3. **Giblet Gravy.** Use chicken drippings for fat and chicken stock for liquid. Add 1 qt (0.95 L) cooked giblets, chopped.

4. **Onion Gravy.** Lightly brown 1 lb (454 g) thinly sliced onions in fat before adding flour.

5. **Vegetable Gravy.** Add 1 lb (454 g) diced carrots, 4 oz (114 g) chopped celery, and 12 oz (340 g) chopped onion, cooked in water or meat stock.

MUSHROOM SAUCE   **Yield: 4½ qt (4.26 L)**

Amount		Ingredient	Method
Metric	U.S.		
1.81 kg	4 lb	Mushrooms, sliced	Sauté mushrooms in butter. Add flour and blend.
227 g	8 oz	Butter or margarine	Add chicken stock and cream while stirring.
114 g	4 oz	Flour	Stir and cook until thick.
1.89 L	2 qt	Chicken stock, hot	Add salt.
480 mL	2 c	Cream or milk Salt to taste	

Variations:

1. **Mushroom and Almond Sauce.** Add 1 lb (454 g) slivered almonds. Serve over rice as an entrée.

2. **Mushroom and Cheese Sauce.** Add 1 lb (454 g) grated Cheddar cheese. Serve over asparagus or broccoli.

DRAWN BUTTER SAUCE
Yield: 2 qt (1.89 L)

Amount		Ingredient	Method
Metric	U.S.		
57 g	2 oz	Butter or margarine	Melt butter or margarine. Add flour and blend.
114 g	4 oz	Flour	Gradually add hot water while
1.89 L	2 qt	Water, hot	stirring. Cook 5 min.
5 mL	1 t	Salt	When ready to serve, add salt and
170 g	6 oz	Butter, cut into pieces	butter. Beat until blended. Serve with green vegetables, fried or broiled fish, or egg dishes.

Variations:

1. **Almond Butter Sauce.** Add 4 T (60 mL) lemon juice and 1 c (240 mL) toasted slivered almonds just before serving.

2. **Lemon Butter Sauce.** Add 1 T (15 mL) grated lemon rind and 4 T (60 mL) lemon juice just before serving. Serve with fish, new potatoes, broccoli, or asparagus.

3. **Maitre d'Hotel Sauce.** Add 4 T (60 mL) lemon juice, 4 T (60 mL) chopped parsley, and 8 egg yolks, well beaten.

4. **Parsley Butter Sauce.** Add 1½ c (360 mL) minced parsley just before serving. Serve with fish, potatoes, or other vegetables.

UNCOOKED BARBECUE SAUCE
Yield: 1 gal (3.79 L)

Amount		Ingredient	Method
Metric	U.S.		
1 No. 10 can	1 No. 10 can	Catsup	Mix all ingredients. Pour over spareribs, shortribs,
720 mL	3 c	Vinegar	chops, or lamb shanks. Bake.
340 g	12 oz	Sugar	
114 g	4 oz	Salt	
114 g	4 oz	Onion, grated	

COOKED BARBECUE SAUCE

Yield: 1½ gal (5.68 L)

Metric	U.S.	Ingredient	Method
Amount			
Metric	*U.S.*	*Ingredient*	*Method*
1 No. 10 can	1 No. 10 can	Catsup	Combine all ingredients. Simmer 10 min.
2.84 L	3 qt	Water	Baste chicken or meat with sauce during cooking.
480 mL	2 c	Vinegar	
30 mL	2 T	Salt	
5 mL	1 t	Pepper	
120 mL	½ c	Sugar	
5 mL	1 t	Chili powder	
60 mL	¼ c	Worcestershire sauce	
15 mL	1 T	Tabasco sauce	
120 mL	½ c	Onion, grated	
2	2	Lemons, sliced	

Note: Sauce also may be used for barbecued hamburgers or to combine with beef, pork, or ham slices for barbecued sandwiches.

HOT VEGETABLE SAUCE

Yield: 2½ qt (2.37 L)

Metric	U.S.	Ingredient	Method
Amount			
Metric	*U.S.*	*Ingredient*	*Method*
454 g	1 lb	Bacon, cubed (or ½ lb butter or margarine)	Fry bacon until crisp. Add flour. Stir until smooth.
114 g	4 oz	Flour	
567 g	1 lb 4 oz	Sugar	Mix sugar, salt, vinegar, and water. Boil 1 min.
60 mL	¼ c	Salt	Add to fat-flour mixture gradually while stirring.
720 mL	3 c	Vinegar	Cook over hot water until slightly thickened.
720 mL	3 c	Water	Use to wilt lettuce or spinach; or with hot potato salad or shredded cabbage.

TOMATO SAUCE

Yield: 2 qt (1.89 L)

Metric	U.S.	Ingredient	Method
170 g	6 oz	Butter or margarine	Melt butter or margarine. Add flour and blend.
114 g	4 oz	Flour	
1.89 L	2 qt	Tomato juice	Combine tomato juice and seasonings. Simmer 20 min.
114 g	4 oz	Onion, finely chopped	Add gradually to blended butter and flour, while stirring.
30 mL	2 T	Sugar	Cook until thickened.
5 mL	1 t	Salt	
¼ t	¼ t	Pepper	
5 mL	1 t	Worcestershire sauce	

(column group header: Amount — Metric, U.S.)

SPANISH SAUCE

Yield: 2½ qt (2.37 L)

Metric	U.S.	Ingredient	Method
114 g	4 oz	Onion, chopped	Sauté onions in fat.
114 g	4 oz	Fat	
1.89 L	2 qt	Tomatoes, canned	Add remaining ingredients. Simmer until vegetables are tender.
454 g	1 lb	Celery, diced	
227 g	8 oz	Green pepper, chopped	Serve with meat, fish, or cheese dishes.
170 g	6 oz	Pimiento, chopped	
15 mL	1 T	Salt	
3 mL	½ t	Pepper	
f.g.	f.g.	Cayenne	

(column group header: Amount — Metric, U.S.)

RAISIN SAUCE

Yield: 1¼ qt (1.18 L)

Amount			
Metric	U.S.	Ingredient	Method
114 g	4 oz	Sugar	Heat sugar and water to boiling
480 mL	2 c	Water	point.
454 g	1 lb	Raisins, cooked	Add remaining ingredients.
80 mL	⅓ c	Vinegar	Simmer 5 min or until jelly is dis-
57 g	2 oz	Butter or mar-	solved.
		garine	Serve with baked ham.
15 mL	1 T	Worcestershire	
		sauce	
5 mL	1 t	Salt	
¼ t	¼ t	White pepper	
½ t	½ t	Cloves	
⅛ t	⅛ t	Mace	
454 g	1 lb	Currant jelly	
f.d.	f.d.	Red coloring,	
		(optional)	

SWEET-SOUR SAUCE

Yield: 5 qt (4.73 L)

Amount			
Metric	U.S.	Ingredient	Method
480 mL	2 c	Vinegar	Combine vinegar, water, sugar,
480 mL	2 c	Water	soy sauce, and salt.
227 g	8 oz	Sugar	Bring to boil.
60 mL	¼ c	Soy sauce	
15 mL	1 T	Salt	
114 g	4 oz	Cornstarch	Mix cornstarch and water into a
240 mL	1 c	Water, cold	smooth paste.
			Add to hot liquid. Cook until
			clear.
227 g	8 oz	Onion, chopped	Sauté vegetables in fat for 5 min.
170 g	6 oz	Celery, chopped	Add vegetables and pineapple to
170 g	6 oz	Green pepper,	sauce.
		chopped	Pour over spareribs or other pork
114 g	4 oz	Fat	cuts and bake.
1 No. 10 can	1 No. 10 can	Pineapple tid-bits	

MUSTARD SAUCE

Yield: 2½ c (600 mL)

Amount			
Metric	*U.S.*	*Ingredient*	*Method*
30 mL	2 T	Sugar	Mix dry ingredients.
3 mL	½ t	Salt	Add eggs, water, and vinegar.
10 mL	2 t	Mustard, dry	Cook over hot water until thick.
2	2	Eggs, beaten	
30 mL	2 T	Water	
60 mL	¼ c	Vinegar	
28 g	1 oz	Butter or margarine	Add butter. Stir until melted. Cool.
480 mL	2 c	Whipping cream	Whip cream and fold into cooked mixture. Serve cold with pork, beef, or ham roast.

HOT MUSTARD SAUCE

Yield: 2 qt (1.89 L)

Amount			
Metric	*U.S.*	*Ingredient*	*Method*
1.89 L	2 qt	Beef stock (p. 477)	Heat stock.
142 g	5 oz	Cornstarch	Blend dry ingredients with cold water.
30 mL	2 T	Sugar	
10 mL	2 t	Salt	Add gradually to hot broth.
3 mL	½ t	Pepper	Cook and stir until thickened.
120 mL	½ c	Water	
57 g	2 oz	Mustard, prepared	Add remaining ingredients. Stir until blended.
114 g	4 oz	Horseradish	Serve hot with boiled beef, fresh or cured ham, or fish.
30 mL	2 T	Vinegar	
28 g	1 oz	Butter or margarine	

HOLLANDAISE SAUCE

Yield: 12 portions
Portion: 1½ T (23 mL)

Metric	U.S.	Ingredient	Method
Amount			
Metric	*U.S.*	*Ingredient*	*Method*
57 g	2 oz	Butter	Place butter, lemon juice, and egg
23 mL	1½ T	Lemon juice	yolks over hot water (not boil-
3	3	Egg yolks	ing).
			Cook slowly, beating constantly.
57 g	2 oz	Butter	When first portion of butter is melted, add second portion and beat until mixture thickens.
57 g	2 oz	Butter	Add third portion of butter and
f.g.	f.g.	Salt	seasonings.
f.g.	f.g.	Cayenne	Beat until thickened.
			Serve immediately. Serve with fish or green vegetables such as asparagus or broccoli.

Notes:
1. If sauce tends to curdle, add hot water, a teaspoon at a time, stirring vigorously.
2. It is recommended that this sauce be made only in small quantity.

MOCK HOLLANDAISE SAUCE

Yield: 2 qt (1.89 L)

Metric	U.S.	Ingredient	Method
Amount			
Metric	*U.S.*	*Ingredient*	*Method*
170 g	6 oz	Butter	Melt butter or margarine.
85 g	3 oz	Flour	Add flour; stir until smooth.
1.42 L	1½ qt	Milk	Add milk gradually, stirring con-
5 mL	1 t	Salt	stantly.
3 mL	½ t	Pepper	Cook until smooth and thickened.
f.g.	f.g.	Cayenne	Add seasonings.
12	12	Egg yolks, unbeaten	Add 1 egg yolk at a time, a little butter, and a little lemon juice
454 g	1 lb	Butter	until all are added.
120 mL	½ c	Lemon juice	Beat well.

APPLE-HORSERADISH SAUCE

Yield: 3 c (720 mL)

Metric	U.S.	Ingredient	Method
	Amount		
240 mL	1 c	Applesauce, sieved	Fold applesauce and horseradish into mayonnaise.
240 mL	1 c	Horseradish	Serve with ham.
240 mL	1 c	Mayonnaise	

Note: Whipped cream may be substituted for mayonnaise if served at once.

COCKTAIL SAUCE

Yield: 2 qt (1.89 L)

Metric	U.S.	Ingredient	Method
	Amount		
0.95 L	1 qt	Chili sauce	Mix all ingredients.
480 mL	2 c	Catsup	Chill.
240 mL	1 c	Lemon juice	Serve over clam, crab, lobster,
30 mL	2 T	Onion juice	oyster, or shrimp.
600 mL	2½ c	Celery, chopped fine	
25 mL	5 t	Worcestershire sauce	
90 mL	6 T	Horseradish	
f.d.	f.d.	Tabasco sauce	

CUCUMBER SAUCE

Yield: 2¾ c (660 mL)

Metric	U.S.	Ingredient	Method
	Amount		
480 mL	2 c	Cucumber	Peel cucumbers; remove seeds. Grate or chop finely.
15 mL	1 T	Onion, grated	Combine remaining ingredients
15 mL	1 T	Vinegar	and add to cucumber.
23 mL	1½ T	Lemon juice	Serve cold with fish.
240 mL	1 c	Cultured sour cream	
3 mL	½ t	Salt	
Dash	Dash	Red pepper	

TARTAR SAUCE   **Yield: 1¾ qt (1.66 L)**

Amount			
Metric	*U.S.*	*Ingredient*	*Method*
0.95 L	1 qt	Mayonnaise	Mix all ingredients.
240 mL	1 c	Pickles, chopped	Serve with fish.
60 mL	¼ c	Green pepper, chopped	
60 mL	¼ c	Parsley, chopped	
240 mL	1 c	Green olives, chopped	
15 mL	1 T	Onion, minced	
60 mL	¼ c	Pimiento, chopped	
120 mL	½ c	Vinegar or lemon juice	
f.d.	f.d.	Worcestershire sauce	
f.d.	f.d.	Tabasco sauce	

Dessert Sauce Recipes

CHOCOLATE SAUCE   **Yield: 1½ qt (1.42 L)**

Amount			
Metric	*U.S.*	*Ingredient*	*Method*
340 g	12 oz	Sugar	Mix dry ingredients.
57 g	2 oz	Cornstarch	Add cold water gradually to form a smooth paste.
5 mL	1 t	Salt	
85 g	3 oz	Cocoa	
240 mL	1 c	Water, cold	
840 mL	3½ c	Water, boiling	Add boiling water slowly while stirring. Boil 5 min or until thickened. Remove from heat.
170 g	6 oz	Butter or margarine	Add butter or margarine. Stir to blend. Serve hot or cold on puddings, cake, or ice cream.

BUTTERSCOTCH SAUCE

Yield: 1¼ qt (1.18 L)

Amount			
Metric	*U.S.*	*Ingredient*	*Method*
454 g	1 lb	Brown sugar	Combine sugar, syrup, and water.
320 mL	1⅓ c	Corn syrup	Cook to soft ball stage (240 °F/115
160 mL	⅔ c	Water	°C).
			Remove from heat.
170 g	6 oz	Butter or margarine	Add butter or margarine and marshmallows. Stir until melted.
57 g	2 oz	Marshmallows	Cool.
320 mL	1⅓ c	Evaporated milk	When cool, add milk.

HOT FUDGE SAUCE

Yield: 1¼ qt (1.18 L)

Amount			
Metric	*U.S.*	*Ingredient*	*Method*
227 g	8 oz	Butter or margarine, soft	Combine butter or margarine, powdered sugar, and milk over hot water.
680 g	1 lb 8 oz	Powdered sugar	
300 mL	1¼ c	Evaporated milk	Stir and cook slowly 30 min.
227 g	8 oz	Chocolate, chipped or melted	Add chocolate. Stir until blended. Serve hot over ice cream, using 1-oz (28-g) ladle.

Note: This sauce may be stored in refrigerator. Heat over hot water before serving. If too thick or grainy, add evaporated milk before heating.

HOT MINCEMEAT SAUCE

Yield: 5 qt (4.73 L)

Amount			
Metric	*U.S.*	*Ingredient*	*Method*
1.42 L	1½ qt	Water	Combine water, sugar, and rind.
1.59 kg	3 lb 8 oz	Sugar	Cook to soft ball stage (240 °F/115
30 mL	2 T	Orange rind, grated	°C).
1 No. 10 can	1 No. 10 can	Mincemeat	Add mincemeat and orange juice. Boil about10 min.
120 mL	½ c	Orange juice	Serve hot over vanilla ice cream.

Note: Syrup may be omitted and hot mincemeat served on the ice cream.

ORIENTAL SAUCE   **Yield: 1 qt (0.95 L)**

Amount			
Metric	*U.S.*	*Ingredient*	*Method*
908 g	2 lb	Sugar	Dissolve sugar in hot water. Add
720 mL	3 c	Water, hot	juice and rinds cut into long,
30 mL	2 T	Lemon juice	thin strips.
60 mL	¼ c	Orange juice	Cook until rinds are clear.
1	1	Lemon rind	
1	1	Orange rind	
170 g	6 oz	Candied ginger	Cut ginger into thin strips and add to hot mixture. Cook to soft ball stage (234 °F/112 °C). Remove from heat.
114 g	4 oz	Almonds, blanched, slivered	Add almonds. Serve cold over vanilla ice cream.

MELBA SAUCE   **Yield: 2½ qt (2.37 L)**

Amount			
Metric	*U.S.*	*Ingredient*	*Method*
2.37 L	2½ qt	Red raspberries, frozen, and juice	Defrost berries. Add combined sugar and cornstarch.
60 mL	¼ c	Sugar	Cook until clear.
53 mL	3½ T	Cornstarch	
600 mL	2½ c	Currant jelly	Add jelly. Cool. Serve over vanilla ice cream or lime sherbet.

Variations:

1. **Peach Melba.** Pour 3 T (45 mL) Melba Sauce over a scoop of vanilla ice cream placed in the center of a canned or fresh peach half.

2. **Sherbet with Melba Sauce.** Spoon 3 T (45 mL) Melba Sauce over scoop of raspberry, orange, or lemon sherbet.

CUSTARD SAUCE

Yield: 5 qt (4.73 L)

	Amount		
Metric	U.S.	Ingredient	Method
397 g	14 oz	Sugar	Mix dry ingredients.
57 g	2 oz	Cornstarch	Add cold milk. Mix until smooth.
3 mL	½ t	Salt	
480 mL	2 c	Milk, cold	
2.84 L	3 qt	Milk, hot	Add cold mixture to hot milk gradually while stirring.
10	10	Egg yolks, beaten	Add egg yolks. Cook over hot water until thickened (about 5 min).
30 mL	2 T	Vanilla	Remove from heat and add vanilla. Cool.
			Serve over cake-type puddings or over cubed oranges or bananas.

LEMON SAUCE

Yield: 2 qt (1.89 L)

	Amount		
Metric	U.S.	Ingredient	Method
908 g	2 lb	Sugar	Mix dry ingredients.
85 g	3 oz	Cornstarch	Add boiling water.
3 mL	½ t	Salt	Cook until clear.
1.89 L	2 qt	Water, boiling	
142 g	5 oz	Lemon juice	Add lemon juice and butter or margarine.
30 mL	2 T	Butter or margarine	Serve hot with Steamed Pudding (p. 388), Bread Pudding (p. 364), or Rice Pudding (p. 364).

Variations:

1. **Vanilla Sauce.** Omit lemon juice and reduce sugar to 1¼ lb (567 g). Add 2 T (30 mL) vanilla.

2. **Nutmeg Sauce.** Omit lemon juice and reduce sugar to 1 lb (454 g). Add ¾ t (4 mL) nutmeg.

3. **Orange Sauce.** Substitute orange juice for lemon juice.

FOAMY SAUCE   **Yield: 3 qt (2.84 L)**

	Amount		
Metric	*U.S.*	*Ingredient*	*Method*
595 g	1 lb 5 oz	Butter or mar-garine	Melt butter or margarine. Gradually add sugar. Beat with
964 g	2 lb 2 oz	Powdered sugar	wire whip until like whipped cream.
10	10	Eggs, beaten	Add eggs slowly, beating constantly.
420 mL	1¾ c	Orange juice	Slowly blend in orange juice and rind.
23 mL	1½ T	Orange rind, grated	Heat 10-15 min. Beat again.

Note: This sauce is good served on bread pudding or chocolate souffle.

HARD SAUCE   **Yield: 3⅓ c (800 mL)**

	Amount		
Metric	*U.S.*	*Ingredient*	*Method*
227 g	8 oz	Butter	Cream butter (medium speed).
30 mL	2 T	Water, boiling	Add water and continue to cream.
539 g	1 lb 3 oz	Powdered sugar	Add sugar gradually. Blend.
3 mL	½ t	Lemon extract or lemon juice	Add lemon extract. Place in refrigerator to harden. Serve with Christmas Pudding (p. 387) or Steamed Pudding (p. 388).

Variations:
1. **Strawberry Hard Sauce.** Omit lemon extract and water. Add ¾ c (180 mL) fresh or frozen strawberries.

2. **Cherry Hard Sauce.** Add ½ c (120 mL) chopped maraschino cherries.

BROWN SUGAR HARD SAUCE

Yield: 1 qt (0.95 L)

Metric	U.S.	Ingredient	Method
	Amount		
340 g	12 oz	Butter	Cream butter (medium speed).
567 g	1 lb 4 oz	Light brown sugar, sifted	Add brown sugar gradually. Cream well.
180 mL	¾ c	Whipping cream	Whip cream. Fold cream and vanilla into creamed mixture. Chill. Serve with Christmas Pudding'(p. 387) or Steamed Pudding (p. 388).
10 mL	2 t	Vanilla	

BROWN SUGAR SYRUP

Yield: 2 gal (7.57 L)

Metric	U.S.	Ingredient	Method
	Amount		
2.27 kg	5 lb	Brown sugar	Combine all ingredients.
2.5 kg	5 lb 8 oz	Granulated sugar	Stir and heat until sugar is dissolved.
240 mL	1 c	Corn syrup	Serve hot or cold on griddle cakes, fritters, or waffles.
2.37 L	2½ qt	Water	
114 g	4 oz	Butter or margarine	

Soups

Soups may be clear and light or thick and hearty. Most soups are at their best piping hot; others are served chilled. *Stock,* the basic ingredient of many soups, is made by simmering meat, poultry, fish, and/or vegetables in water to extract their flavor. Brown stock, made from beef that has been browned before simmering, and white or light stock, made from veal and/or chicken, are the stocks used most often. Cooking of the meat or poultry is started in cold water, brought to the boiling point, and then simmered for 3-4 hr. The broth is strained and cooled, and the fat removed. The stock may be clarified after it has been chilled by adding egg whites and crushed egg shells and boiling, then straining (see p. 800). Stock in highly perishable. If it is not to be used immediately, it may be reduced in volume by boiling to ½ or ¼ its volume and frozen for later use. *Bouillon* is made from clarified beef broth, *consommé* from clarified white or light stock.

Cream soups are made with a thin white sauce and mashed or strained vegetables, meat, chicken, or fish. Some stock may be used in the sauce to enhance the flavor. *Bisque* is a mixture of chopped shellfish, stock, milk, and seasonings, usually thickened. *Purée* is a thick soup made by pressing cooked vegetables or fish through a sieve into their own stock. *Chowder* is an unstrained, heavy, thick soup prepared from meat, poultry, fish, and/or vegetables.

The preparation of soups, especially those made from stock, is time consuming, although many dietitians and foodservice managers believe the "home-cooked" flavor of the soups prepared from fresh ingredients is worth the preparation time required. However, acceptable soups can be made from high-quality beef, chicken, and other soup bases or from canned bouillon and consommé. A wide variety of soups is possible by combining two or more canned soups. Examples are cream of asparagus and cream of chicken, Cheddar cheese and tomato, and cream of mushroom with chicken and rice.

Soup Recipes

BEEF STOCK   **Yield: 3 gal (11.36 L)**

Metric	*U.S.*	*Ingredient*	*Method*
	Amount		
6.80 kg	15 lb	Beef shank, lean	Pour water over beef shanks.
18.93 L	5 gal	Water, cold	Bring to boiling point.
227 g	8 oz	Onion, chopped	Add vegetables and seasonings.
227 g	8 oz	Celery, chopped	Simmer until meat leaves bone
227 g	8 oz	Carrot, chopped	(about 4 hr).
15 mL	1 T	Peppercorns	Remove meat, strain, cool, and
2	2	Bay leaves	skim off fat.
85 g	3 oz	Salt	

Note: A quick beef stock may be made by adding concentrated beef soup base to water in amounts given in manufacturer's directions. When using this stock for sauces for casseroles, reduce salt by 1 T (15 mL) per gal (3.79 L) of sauce.

Variations:
1. **Brown Stock.** Allow 10 lb (4.54 kg) beef shank to stand 30 min in cold water. Heat slowly to boiling point. Simmer 2 hr. Add vegetables that have been browned with remaining meat. Add seasonings. Simmer 3 hr.

2. **Alphabet Soup.** To 3 gal (11.36 L) Beef Stock, add 2 T (30 mL) celery salt, ¼ t pepper, 4 oz (114 g) grated onions, 6 oz (170 g) grated carrots, and 10 oz (284 g) alphabet noodles. Cook until added ingredients are tender. Serving: 1 c (240 mL).

3. **Barley Soup.** To 3 gal (11.36 L) Beef Stock, add 1¾ lb (794 g) barley. Cook until barley is done. Serving: 1 c (240 mL).

4. **Beef Noodle Soup.** To 3 gal (11.36 L) Beef Stock, add 1½ lb (680 g) noodles (A.P.). Cook until noodles are tender. Serving: 1 c (240 mL).

5. **Beef Rice Soup.** To 3 gal (11.36 L) Beef Stock, add 1½ lb (680 g) rice (A.P.). Cook until rice is done. Serving: 1 c (240 mL).

6. **Beef Vegetable Soup.** To 3 gal (11.36 L) Beef Stock, add 3 lb (1.36 kg) freshly ground beef, 5 oz (142 g) chopped celery, 5 oz (142 g) chopped carrots, 3 oz (85 g) chopped onions, 12 oz (340 g) peas, and 8 oz (227 g) rice (if desired). Cook until ingredients are tender. Serving: 1 c (240 mL).

7. **Beef Vermicelli Soup.** To 3 gal (11.36 L) Beef Stock, add 1½ lb (680 g) spaghetti or vermicelli and cook until tender. Serving: 1 c (240 mL).

8. **Creole Soup.** To 2¼ gal (8.52 L) Beef Stock, add 1 No. 10 can tomatoes, 1 lb (454 g) shredded green peppers, 1 lb (454 g) chopped onions, 1 lb (454 g) cooked shell macaroni, 2 oz (57 g) salt (may vary), ¼ t pepper, and 4 bay leaves. Cook until ingredients are tender. Serving: 1 c (240 mL).

9. **French Onion Soup.** To 3 gal (11.36 L) Beef Stock, add 8 lb (3.63 kg) onions, thinly sliced and sautéed in 12 oz (340 g) fat, 3 oz (85 g) flour, blended with fat and onions, 3 T (45 mL) Worcestershire sauce, and salt and pepper to taste. Cook until onions are tender. Serving: 1 c (240 mL). To serve, pour over toasted bread cubes or strips and sprinkle with grated Parmesan cheese.

10. **Julienne Soup.** To 3 gal (11.36 L) Beef Stock, add 2 T (30 mL) celery salt, 1 lb (454 g) carrots, 1 lb (454 g) green beans, 12 oz (340 g) celery, cut long and thin, 2 oz (57 g) chopped onions, and 2 oz (57 g) salt (may vary). Cook until vegetables are tender. Serving: 1 c (240 mL).

11. **Minestrone Soup.** To 3 gal (11.36 L) Beef Stock, add 1 No. 2 can kidney or brown beans, 12 oz (340 g) spaghetti, 1 lb (454 g) chopped onions, 1 lb (454 g) shredded potatoes, 1¾ lb (794 g) carrot strips, and 1 oz (28 g) chopped parsley. Cook until ingredients are tender. Serving: 1 c (240 mL).

CHICKEN STOCK

Yield: 3 gal (11.36 L)

Metric	U.S.	Ingredient	Method
Amount			
Metric	*U.S.*	*Ingredient*	*Method*
9.08 kg	20 lb	Chicken	Cut up chicken. Add water and
18.93 L	5 gal	Water, cold	heat slowly to boiling point.
227 g	8 oz	Onion, chopped	Add vegetables and seasonings.
227 g	8 oz	Celery, chopped	Simmer until tender.
227 g	8 oz	Carrot, chopped	Remove chicken and strain broth.
85 g	3 oz	Salt	Refrigerate.
15 mL	1 T	Peppercorns	When cold, remove fat from broth.
2	2	Bay leaves	
10 mL	2 t	Marjoram	
3	3	Egg shells, crushed	Add egg shells and whites to clarify the broth.
3	3	Egg whites, beaten	Bring to boiling point. Simmer 15 min. Strain through cheesecloth or fine strainer.

Note: A quick chicken stock may be made by adding concentrated
chicken soup base to water in amounts given in manufacturer's directions.
When using this stock for sauces for casseroles, some adjustment in salt
may be necessary.

Variation:
White Stock. Substitute knuckle of veal for part of chicken.

BOUILLON

Yield: 3 gal (11.36 L)
Portion: 1 c (240 mL)

Amount			
Metric	*U.S.*	*Ingredient*	*Method*
3.63 kg	8 lb	Beef, lean	Sear beef. Add bone and water.
1.81 kg	4 lb	Bone, cracked	Let stand 1 hr.
15.14 L	4 gal	Water, cold	Simmer for 3-4 hr. Replace water as necessary.
227 g	8 oz	Carrots, diced	Add vegetables and seasonings.
227 g	8 oz	Celery, chopped	Cook 1 hr. Strain.
227 g	8 oz	Onion, chopped	Chill overnight.
1	1	Bay leaf	Remove fat.
15 mL	1 T	Peppercorns	
60 mL	¼ c	Salt	
3	3	Egg shells, crushed	Add egg shells and whites to clear the broth.
3	3	Egg whites, beaten	Bring slowly to boiling point, stirring constantly. Boil 15-20 min without stirring. Strain through a cloth.

Variations:

1. **Chicken Bouillon.** Substitute 20 lb (9.08 kg) chicken, cut up, for the beef and bone. Do not sear chicken.

2. **Tomato Bouillon.** To 1½ gal (5.68 L) bouillon, add 4 46-oz (1.36-L) cans tomato juice, 1 oz (28 g) chopped onion, 2 oz (57 g) sugar, 3 T (45 mL) salt (amount may vary), ½ t pepper, ½ t cloves, 2 bay leaves, ½ T peppercorns, and ½ t soda.

VEGETABLE-BEEF SOUP

Yield: 3 gal (11.36 L)
Portion: 1 c (240 mL)

Amount		Ingredient	Method
Metric	U.S.		
6.80 kg	15 lb	Beef shank, with meat	Add water and seasonings to beef shank.
15.14 L	4 gal	Water, cold	Bring to boiling point. Simmer 3-4 hr.
2	2	Bay leaves	
45 mL	3 T	Salt	Remove meat from bones and chop.
680 g	1 lb 8 oz	Carrots, cubed	Add vegetables to meat stock.
680 g	1 lb 8 oz	Celery, chopped	Cover and simmer about 1 hr. Replace water as necessary.
454 g	1 lb	Onion, chopped	
908 g	2 lb	Potatoes, cubed	Add salt, pepper, and chopped meat. Reheat.
60 mL	¼ c	Salt	
5 mL	1 t	Pepper	

TOMATO-RICE SOUP

Yield: 3 gal (11.36 L)
Portion: 1 c (240 mL)

Amount		Ingredient	Method
Metric	U.S.		
7.57 L	2 gal	Beef or chicken stock (p. 477)	Heat stock, purée, and salt to boiling point.
3.79 L	1 gal	Tomato purée	
23 mL	1½ T	Salt	
57 g	2 oz	Onion, chopped	Add vegetables and rice.
114 g	4 oz	Green pepper, chopped	Cook until rice is tender.
227 g	8 oz	Rice	
170 g	6 oz	Butter or margarine	Melt butter and add flour. Mix until smooth.
85 g	3 oz	Flour	Add to soup while stirring. Salt to taste.

Note: If soup base is used to make stock, salt may need to be reduced.

Variation:
Tomato-Barley Soup. Add 1 lb (454 g) barley in place of rice.

JELLIED MADRILENE

Yield: 3 gal (11.36 L)
Portion: 1 c (240 mL)

Metric	U.S.	Ingredient	Method
	Amount		
3.79 L	1 gal	Chicken stock (p. 479)	Combine stocks, tomato juice, and seasonings.
3.79 L	1 gal	Beef stock (p. 477)	Cover and simmer just below boiling for 1 hr.
3.79 L	1 gal	Tomato juice	
114 g	4 oz	Onions, chopped	
624 g	1 lb 6 oz	Carrots, sliced	
454 g	1 lb	Celery, diced	
3 mL	½ t	Cloves, whole	
3 mL	½ t	Peppercorns	
10 mL	2 t	Salt	
20 mL	4 t	Sugar	
160 mL	⅔ c	Gelatin	Soften gelatin in cold water.
0.95 L	1 qt	Water, cold	Add to hot soup. Stir until dissolved.
			Strain mixture into stainless steel container and refrigerate until firm.
			Beat slightly with a wire whip and serve in bouillon cups. Garnish with a thin lemon slice.

Note: The mixture may be poured into counter insets to 1 in. thickness.
When firm, cut in small squares and spoon into bouillon cups.

MULLIGATAWNY SOUP

Amount			
Metric	*U.S.*	*Ingredient*	*Method*
340 g	12 oz	Onions, finely chopped	Combine in steam-jacketed kettle or stockpot.
340 g	12 oz	Carrots, Julienne	Bring to a boil.
340 g	12 oz	Celery, thinly sliced	
454 g	1 lb	Green peppers, cut in thin strips	
3 sprigs	3 sprigs	Parsley	
908 g	2 lb	Apples, pared and ground	
7.57 L	2 gal	Chicken stock	
1 No. 10 can	1 No. 10 can	Tomatoes	
8	8	Whole cloves	
15 mL	1 T	Curry powder	
23 mL	1½ T	Salt	
1.36 kg	3 lb	Cooked chicken, diced	Add chicken. Simmer until vegetables are tender, about 50 min.
567 g	1 lb 4 oz	Flour	Combine flour and water to make a smooth paste.
0.95 l.	1 qt	Water, cold	Slowly add to soup, stirring constantly. Simmer 5 min. Remove parsley sprigs before serving.

PEPPER POT SOUP

Yield: 3 gal (11.36 L)
Portion: 1 c (240 mL)

Amount			
Metric	U.S.	Ingredient	Method
57 g	2 oz	Onion, chopped fine	Sauté vegetables in butter or margarine until lightly browned, about 15 min.
227 g	8 oz	Green peppers, chopped fine	
170 g	6 oz	Celery, chopped	
1.59 kg (E.P.)	3 lb 8 oz (E.P.)	Potatoes, diced	
340 g	12 oz	Butter or margarine	
142 g	5 oz	Flour	Add flour. Stir until well blended.
8.52 L	2¼ gal	Beef or chicken stock, hot (p. 477)	Combine stock, milk, and salt. Add to vegetable mixture, while stirring.
0.95 L	1 qt	Milk, hot	Add red pepper.
23 mL	1½ T	Salt	Keep just below boiling point 30 min.
30 mL	2 T	Red pepper, chopped	Serve with Spatzels (Egg Dumplings) (p. 494)

Note: If soup base is used to make stock, salt may need to be reduced.

RICE SOUP   **Yield: 3 gal (11.36 L)**
                                                            Portion: 1 c (240 mL)

Metric	U.S.	Ingredient	Method
Amount			
Metric	*U.S.*	*Ingredient*	*Method*
4.73 L	5 qt	Beef or chicken stock (p. 477)	
340 g	12 oz	Rice	Cook rice (p. 190). Add to hot
900 mL	3¾ c	Water, boiling	stock.
8 mL	1½ t	Salt	
3.79 L	1 gal	Milk, hot	Add milk and seasonings to stock
5 mL	1 t	Onion juice	and rice.
45 mL	3 T	Salt	To serve, garnish with toast rings
5 mL	1 t	Pepper	sprinkled with chopped parsley
60 mL	¼ c	Parsley, chopped	and Parmesan cheese.

Note: If soup base is used to make stock, salt may need to be reduced.

SPLIT PEA SOUP   **Yield: 3 gal (11.36 L)**
                                                            Portion: 1 c (240 mL)

Metric	U.S.	Ingredient	Method
Amount			
Metric	*U.S.*	*Ingredient*	*Method*
1.81 kg	4 lb	Split peas	Wash peas.
7.57 L	2 gal	Water, boiling	Add boiling water, cover, and soak 1 hr or longer.
1	1	Ham bone (or 2 lb sliced salt pork or bacon ends)	Add ham bone and onion to peas and water in which they were soaked.
114 g	4 oz	Onion, chopped	Cook 4-5 hr, or until peas are soft. Remove bone. Add water to make 2½ gal (9.46 L).
114 g	4 oz	Fat	Make into Thin White Sauce (p.
57 g	2 oz	Flour	458).
1.89 L	2 qt	Milk	Add to peas.
30 mL	2 T	Salt	
3 mL	½ t	Pepper	

Note: If soup becomes too thick, add hot milk to bring to desired
consistency. If a smoother soup is desired, purée peas.

NAVY BEAN SOUP

Yield: 3 gal (11.36 L)
Portion: 1 c (240 mL)

Amount			
Metric	*U.S.*	*Ingredient*	*Method*
1.36 kg	3 lb	Navy beans	Wash beans. Add boiling water.
5.68 L	1½ gal	Water, boiling	Cover and let stand 1 hr or longer.
2.27 kg	5 lb	Ham shanks	Add ham shanks. Simmer until beans are cooked. Remove ham from bones, chop, and add later.
114 g	4 oz	Onion, chopped	Add onion, celery, and water to make a total volume of 3¼ gal (12.30 L). Cook 30 min. Add chopped ham. Season to taste. Heat to serving temperature.
227 g	8 oz	Celery, diced	

CORN CHOWDER

Yield: 3 gal (11.36 L)
Portion: 1 c (240 mL)

Amount			
Metric	*U.S.*	*Ingredient*	*Method*
454 g	1 lb	Salt pork or bacon, cubed	Fry pork until crisp. Add onions and cook slowly 5 min.
340 g	12 oz	Onion, chopped	Remove pork and onions from fat.
114 g	4 oz	Fat, fried from pork	Add flour to pork fat. Blend. Add milk and salt, stirring constantly.
114 g	4 oz	Flour	
7.57 L	2 gal	Milk	
45 mL	3 T	Salt	
2.27 kg (E.P.)	5 lb (E.P.)	Potatoes, cubed, cooked	Add potatoes, corn, pork, and onions.
1 No. 10 can	1 No. 10 can	Corn, whole kernel	

Variation:
Potato Chowder. Omit corn and increase potatoes to 8 lb (3.63 kg).

SPANISH BEAN SOUP

Amount		Ingredient	Method
Metric	U.S.		
2.27 kg	5 lb	Beans, kidney or garbanzo	Wash beans. Add boiling water. Cover and let stand 1 hr or longer.
17.03 L	4½ gal	Water, boiling	
340 g	12 oz	Onion, chopped	Cook in same water until tender. Purée. Add water to make 1½ gal (5.68 L).
170 g	6 oz	Onion, chopped	Sauté vegetables in butter until slightly browned.
57 g	2 oz	Green pepper, chopped	
57 g	2 oz	Butter or bacon fat	
5.68 L	1½ gal	Tomato purée	Heat tomato purée and add with seasoning to bean purée.
60 mL	¼ c	Salt	
20 mL	1¼ T	Pepper	Cook 5 min to blend ingredients.

Notes:
1. Baked-bean purée may be substituted for kidney bean purée.
2. Ham stock may be used in place of tomato purée. 2 t (10 mL) saffron may be added if desired.

CREAM OF TOMATO SOUP

Amount		Ingredient	Method
Metric	U.S.		
5.68 L	1½ gal	Tomato juice	Add onion and bay leaf to tomato juice.
28 g	1 oz	Onion, chopped	
½	½	Bay leaf	Heat to boiling point.
15 mL	1 T	Soda	Add soda.
284 g	10 oz	Butter or margarine, melted	Make into a Very Thin White Sauce (p. 458).
85 g	3 oz	Flour	Just before serving, add tomato mixture gradually, while stirring.
45 mL	3 T	Salt	
5 mL	1 t	Pepper	
114 g	4 oz	Sugar	
5.68 L	1½ gal	Milk, hot	

Note: Chopped parsley and 1 t whipped cream may be used as a garnish for each serving.

GAZPACHO (SPANISH CHILLED SOUP)

Yield: 1¾ gal (6.62 L)
Portion: ½ c (120 mL)

Amount		Ingredient	Method
Metric	*U.S.*		
114 g	4 oz	Mushrooms, fresh, chopped	Sauté mushrooms in olive oil until light brown.
120 mL	½ c	Olive oil	
3 cloves	3 cloves	Garlic	Crush garlic in salt.
30 mL	2 T	Salt	
1.36 kg	3 lb	Tomatoes, fresh, finely chopped	Combine in a stainless steel or glass container.
			Add mushrooms and garlic.
567 g	1 lb 4 oz	Green peppers, finely chopped	If too thick, add additional tomato juice.
			Cover and chill.
340 g	12 oz	Celery, finely chopped	Serve with croutons, crackers, or specialty breads.
454 g	1 lb	Cucumbers, finely chopped	
680 g	1 lb 8 oz	Onion,, finely chopped	
30 mL	2 T	Chives, chopped	
45 mL	3 T	Parsley, chopped	
15 mL	1 T	Pepper	
15 mL	1 T	Worcestershire sauce	
360 mL	1½ c	Tarragon wine vinegar	
5 mL	1 t	Tabasco sauce	
2.37 L	2½ qt	Tomato juice	

BASIC SAUCE FOR CREAM SOUP

Yield: 2½ gal (9.46 L) Basic Sauce

Metric	U.S.	Ingredient	Method
	Amount		
Metric	*U.S.*	*Ingredient*	*Method*
340 g	12 oz	Butter or margarine	Make as Thin White Sauce (p. 458).
170 g	6 oz	Flour	Add vegetables and seasonings as suggested below to make a variety of cream soups.
45 mL	3 T	Salt	
3 mL	½ t	White pepper	
8.52 L	2¼ gal	Milk, hot	

Suggestions for Cream Soups:
To 2½ gal (9.46 L) (1 recipe) Basic Sauce for Cream Soup for 3 gal (11.36 L) soup (1 c/240 mL portions):

1. **Cream of Asparagus Soup.** Add 6½ lb (2.95 kg) cooked, chopped asparagus.

2. **Cream of Celery Soup.** Add 1½ lb (680 g) chopped celery, 8 oz (227 g) diced carrots, and 2½ oz (70 g) chopped onions cooked in 1 gal (3.79 L) water about 1 hr.

3. **Cream of Corn Soup.** Add 3 qt (2.84 L) corn, cream style, and 1 oz (28 g) chopped onions.

4. **Cream of Mushroom Soup.** Add 2 lb (908 g) mushrooms, sliced or chopped. Reduce flour to 4 oz (114 g). Chicken stock may be substituted for part of the milk.

5. **Cream of Pea Soup.** Add 3 qt (2.84 L) pea purée, 2 oz (57 g) minced onions, and 1 oz (28 g) sugar.

6. **Cream of Potato Soup.** Add 12 lb (5.44 kg) diced potatoes, 6 oz (170 g) chopped onions, and 8 oz (227 g) chopped celery that have been cooked in 3 qt (2.84 L) water until soft. Potatoes may be mashed or puréed if desired.

7. **Cream of Spinach Soup.** Add 3 qt (2.84 L) chopped, fresh, or frozen spinach and 2 oz (57 g) grated onion (optional).

8. **Cream of Vegetable Soup.** Add 1 lb (454 g) chopped celery, 4 oz (114 g) chopped onions, 1 lb (454 g) diced carrots, and 2 lb (908 g) diced potatoes, cooked in 1 gal (3.79 L) water, seasoned with 3 T (45 mL) salt, until soft.

9. **Vegetable Chowder.** Add 2 No. 2 cans whole kernel corn, 5 oz (142 g) green pepper, chopped, and 1 lb (454 g) diced cooked bacon or salt pork.

CREAM OF CHICKEN SOUP

Yield: 3 gal (11.36 L)
Portion: 1 c (240 mL)

Amount		Ingredient	Method
Metric	*U.S.*	*Ingredient*	*Method*
227 g	8 oz	Chicken fat (or butter)	Make into a Very Thin White Sauce (p. 458).
85 g	3 oz	Flour	
3.79 L	1 gal	Milk	
23 mL	1½ T	Salt	
7.57 L	2 gal	Chicken stock	Add stock, seasoning, and chopped chicken.
10 mL	2 t	Celery salt	
¼ t	¼ t	White pepper	
680 g	1 lb 8 oz	Chicken, cooked, chopped	

Notes:
1. Chicken bouillon or chicken soup base may be added to enhance flavor. Salt may need to be decreased.
2. 1 lb (454 g) cooked rice or noodles may be added.

Variation:
Chicken Velvet Soup. Substitute light cream or half and half for milk. Increase flour to 9 oz (255 g) and cooked chopped chicken to 2½ lb (1.14 kg).

CHEESE SOUP

Amount		Ingredient	Method
Metric	U.S.		
227 g	8 oz	Butter or margarine	Sauté onion in butter or margarine until lightly browned.
227 g	8 oz	Onion, chopped	Add flour and cornstarch. Blend.
114 g	4 oz	Flour	Cook 3-4 min.
57 g	2 oz	Cornstarch	
5 mL	1 t	Paprika	Add seasonings and blend.
30 mL	2 T	Salt	Add milk and stock slowly, while stirring.
5 mL	1 t	White pepper	
3.79 L	1 gal	Milk	Cook until thickened.
5.68 L	1½ gal	Chicken stock (p. 479)	
720 mL	3 c	Carrots, finely diced, cooked	Add carrots and celery.
720 mL	3 c	Celery, finely diced, cooked	
454 g	1 lb	Cheddar cheese, sharp, diced fine	Add cheese just before serving. Blend. Garnish with chopped parsley as served.

ORANGE SOUP (CH'EN TZU KENG)

Amount		Ingredient	Method
Metric	U.S.		
480 mL	2 c	Water	Combine water, sugar, and salt.
170 g	6 oz	Sugar	Heat to boiling point.
5 mL	1 t	Salt	
57 g	2 oz	Cornstarch	Add cornstarch and water, mixed to a smooth paste.
120 mL	½ c	Water, cold	Cook and stir until clear.
5.68 L	6 qt	Orange juice	When ready to serve, add orange juice and butter.
57 g	2 oz	Butter	Reheat and serve at once.

Variation:
Chilled Orange Soup. Omit butter. Add 1 qt (0.95 L) cut orange sections and 8 oz (227 g) slivered almonds. Serve chilled.

VICHYSSOISE (CHILLED POTATO SOUP)

Yield: 3 gal (11.36 L)
Portion: 1 c (240 mL)

Metric	U.S.	Ingredient	Method
3.79 L	1 gal	Chicken stock (p. 479)	Combine and cook until onions are tender. Strain.
1.36 kg	3 lb	Onions, chopped	
2.72 kg	6 lb	Potatoes, diced	Steam potatoes until done. Mash.
15 mL	1 T	Salt	Add seasonings and chicken stock to potatoes.
10 mL	2 t	Celery salt	
5 mL	1 t	Garlic salt	
3 mL	½ t	White pepper	
4.73 L	1¼ gal	Cream, half and half	Add cream. Chill thoroughly.
80 mL	⅓ c	Parsley, chives, or green onion tops, chopped	Garnish with chopped parsley, chives, or onion tops.

OYSTER STEW

Yield: 3 gal (11.36 L)
Portion: 1 c (240 mL)

Metric	U.S.	Ingredient	Method
9.46 L	2½ gal	Milk	Scald milk.
2.37 L	2½ qt	Oysters	Heat oysters and butter or margarine only until edges of oysters begin to curl.
227 g	8 oz	Butter or margarine	
45 mL	3 T	Salt	About 10 min before serving time, add oysters and oyster liquor and seasonings to scalded milk. Serve immediately to avoid curdling.
3 mL	½ t	Pepper	

NEW ENGLAND CLAM CHOWDER

Yield: 3 gal (11.36 L)
Portion: 1 c (240 mL)

Amount Metric	U.S.	Ingredient	Method
3.79 L	1 gal	Clams, fresh	Clean clams. Steam until tender. Drain and chop (save juice).
57 g	2 oz	Onion, chopped	Sauté onion and pork 5 min until lightly browned. Add to clams.
114 g	4 oz	Salt pork or bacon, finely cubed	
2.72 kg (E.P.)	6 lb (E.P.)	Potatoes, cubed	Cook potatoes until tender. Save liquid.
0.95 L	1 qt	Water	
15 mL	1 T	Salt	
227 g	8 oz	Butter or margarine	Melt butter or margarine. Add flour. Stir until smooth.
57 g	2 oz	Flour	Add milk gradually, while stirring. Cook until consistency of Very Thin White Sauce (p. 458).
7.57 L	2 gal	Milk	Add clams, onion, salt, pork, potaoes, potato water, and seasoning.
5 mL	1 t	Pepper	

Notes:
1. 4 15-oz (425-g) cans minced clams may be used in place of fresh clams.
2. Juice drained from clams may be substituted for an equal quantity of the milk. Heat and add just before serving.

Variation:
Manhattan Clam Chowder. Substitute 1 No. 10 can tomatoes and water or meat stock to make 2 gal (7.57 L) liquid for the milk. Add 12 oz (340 g) chopped celery and 6 oz (170 g) chopped carrot, cooked.

SPATZELS (EGG DUMPLINGS)

Amount			
Metric	*U.S.*	*Ingredient*	*Method*
567 g	1 lb 4 oz	Flour	Combine dry ingredients.
5 mL	1 t	Baking powder	
8 mL	1½ t	Salt	
720 mL	3 c	Milk	Add combined milk and eggs, all at once, to dry ingredients. Mix to form a soft dough. Drop small bits of dough or press through a colander into 3 gal (11.36 L) hot soup. Cook approximately 5 min.
6	6	Eggs, whole	

Note: Soup must be very hot in order to cook dumplings.

Garnishes for Soup

Cream Soups

Almonds, shredded, toasted.

Bacon, broiled, diced.

Cheese, grated.

Chives, chopped.

Croutons.

Fresh mint.

Hard-cooked egg white, finely chopped.

Hard-cooked egg yolk, riced.

Paprika.

Parsley, finely chopped.

Pimiento, minced, in whipped cream.

Stock Soups

Cheese, grated.

Lemon, thin slices.

Lime, thin slices.

Onion rings.

Parsley, finely chopped.

Popcorn.

Vegetables, diced or shredded.

Vegetables

Great care should be given to the preparation of fresh vegetables before cooking or serving raw. This procedure, as well as the cookery, influences the nutritive value, attractiveness, palatability, and color of the finished product. All leafy and stem vegetables should be washed thoroughly and crisped before they are cooked or used raw. Details of preparation of vegetables are given on p. 496.

Fresh or frozen vegetables may be cooked by boiling, steaming, baking, pan- or deep-fat frying. The method used will depend largely on the quality of the product, the amount to be cooked, and the equipment available. To insure a high-quality product, it is important that vegetables be cooked in as small an amount of water as is practicable and as quickly as possible. Water should be brought to a second boil immediately following the addition of vegetables. Add no soda to cooking water.

A small, steam-jacketed kettle, if time and pressure are carefully controlled, is highly satisfactory for cooking both fresh and frozen vegetables. It usually is large enough to prevent crowding; it will bring water to a boil quickly after vegetables are added; and it will cook a large or small amount equally well. A tilting frypan may successfully be used also.

Vegetables may be cooked with satisfactory results in a steamer under pressure if cooked in small quantities and arranged in thin layers in shallow pans. Here, too, the time and temperature must be carefully controlled. Quick cooking in a high-pressure steamer (12-15 psi) is especially successful. One advantage of steam cooking is that vegetables may be weighed and placed in hot food inset pans as they are prepared, then cooked and served from the same pans, thus minimizing the breakage that results from transferring vegetables.

When steam equipment is not available, top-of-range or oven cooking may be used. Whatever the method used, vegetables should be cooked only until tender. *Do not overcook.* Vegetables should be cooked in as small quantity at one time as is feasible for the type of service. The needs of most foodservices can be met by the continuous cooking of vegetables in small quantities. Vegetables should be served as soon as possible after cooking for optimum quality and should be handled carefully to prevent breaking or mashing. A variety of seasonings may be used to add interest to vegetables (see p. 532).

Fresh Vegetables

Preparation of Fresh Vegetables

Asparagus.   Cut off tough part of stems. Wash and thoroughly clean remaining portions. Asparagus spears may be tied in bundles of 1-2 lb each for boiling. For cuts, cut spears into 1-in. pieces.

Beans, green or wax.   Wash beans. Trim ends and remove strings. Cut or break beans into 1-in. pieces.

Beans, lima.   Shell beans. (Scald pods to make shelling easier.) Wash.

Beet greens.   Sort. Cut off tough stems. Wash greens at least 5 times, lifting them out of water after each washing.

Beets, whole.   Remove tops, leaving 2-in. stems on beets. Wash. Do not peel or remove root until beets are cooked.

Broccoli.   Cut off tough stalk and ends and wash. Soak in salted water for ½ hr if insects are present. Drain. Peel stalks. Cut broccoli lengthwise if thick to speed cooking.

Brussels sprouts.   Remove withered leaves and wash thoroughly.

Cabbage.   Remove wilted outside leaves. Wash, quarter, and core cabbage. Crisp in cold water, if wilted. Cut in wedges, or shred.

Carrots.   Wash, scrape, or pare. Trim ends. Cut as desired.

Cauliflower.   Remove outer leaves and stalks. Break into flowerets. Wash. Soak in salted water to draw out any insects present.

Celery.   Wash, trim, cut as desired.

Chard.   Sort. Cut off tough stems. Wash greens at least 5 times, lifting them out of water after each washing.

Collards.   Sort and trim. Strip leaves from coarse stems. Wash at least 5 times, lifting them out of water after each washing.

Corn on cob.   Husk. Remove silks. Wash. Do not allow to stand in water.

Eggplant.   Peel and cut into slices or pieces.

Kale.   Sort. Strip leaves from coarse stems. Wash at least 5 times, lifting out of water after each washing.

Mustard greens.   Sort. Cut off tough stems. Wash greens at least 5 times, lifting them out of water after each washing.

Okra.   Trim stem. Slice or leave whole.

Onions.   Peel and wash. Quarter if large, or cut as desired.

Parsnips.   Wash. Pare. Quarter lengthwise and cut as desired. Cut core from center if tough and woody.

Peas, green.   Shell. Rinse.

Potatoes.   Scrub. Cook in skins or pare and remove eyes. Cut into serving size. Cover with cold water until time for cooking to prevent darkening. Prolonged soaking causes loss of nutrients.

Pumpkin.   Wash. Cut in half; remove seeds, fiber, and peel. Cut pieces. (If peel is hard and tough, soften by steaming or boiling 10 min.)

Rutabagas.   Wash. Pare and cut as desired.

Spinach.   Sort and trim. Cut off coarse stems and roots. Wash leaves at least 5 times, lifting out of water after each washing.

Squash, summer.   Wash. Trim and cut as desired.

Squash, winter.   Wash. Cut in half; remove seeds, fiber, and peel. Cut into pieces. (If peel is hard and tough, soften by steaming or boiling 10 min.)

Squash, zucchini.   Wash. Cut off ends but do not peel. Slice or cut as desired.

Sweet potatoes.   Scrub.

Turnip greens.   Sort. Cut off tough stems. Wash greens at least 5 times, lifting them out of water after each washing.

Turnips.   Wash. Pare and cut as desired.

Cooking Fresh Vegetables

1. Prepare vegetables according to directions given on p. 496.

2. To determine amount to buy, convert ready-to-cook weight to As Purchased weight by using chart on preparation yields (p. 67). A 10-lb (4.54-kg) lot of ready-to-cook raw vegetables makes about 50 3-oz (85-g) portions when cooked, drained, and seasoned.

3. Schedule cooking of fresh vegetables so they will be served soon after they are cooked.

4. Cook in lots no larger than 10 lb (4.54 kg) of prepared raw vegetable. Cook until just tender, no longer than necessary to give a palatable product. For a given vegetable, cooking time will differ according to the method of cookery, variety and maturity of the vegetable, length of time and temperature at which it has been held since harvesting, and its size or the size pieces into which it is cut. See Table 2.17 for approximate cooking time (p. 501).

Directions for Boiling

1. Add prepared vegetables to boiling salted water in steam-jacketed kettle or stockpot. Use 1⅓ T (20 mL) salt to amount of water specified in Table 2.17, except for corn. Addition of salt or sugar to the cooking water will cause kernels to toughen and discolor. The amount of water used in cooking all vegetables is important for retention of nutrients. The less water used, the more nutrients retained. Older root vegetables that need longer cooking will require more water than young, tender vegetables. Spinach and other greens need only the water clinging to their leaves from washing.

2. Cover and bring water quickly back to boiling point. Green vegetables retain their color better if lid is removed just before boiling begins; strong flavored vegetables, such as cabbage, cauliflower, and Brussels sprouts, should be cooked uncovered to prevent development of unpleasant flavors.

3. Start timing when water returns to boiling point. Use Table 2.17 as a guide. Stir greens occasionally while boiling.

4. Drain cooked vegetables and place in serving pans. Add 4 oz (114 g) melted butter or margarine to each 50 portions.

5. Adjust seasonings.

Directions for Steaming

1. Place prepared vegetables in steamer pans or counter inset pans. Best results are obtained when tender vegetables are arranged in thin layers, not over

2 in. in depth, in shallow pans. This allows steam to circulate, so cooking is rapid and vegetables will not be crushed. *Do not add water.*

2. Steam in a compartment steamer using time indicated in Table 2.17 as a guide. Begin timing when steamer reaches proper cooking pressure.

3. Add 4 oz (114 g) melted butter or margarine and 1⅓ T (20 mL) salt to each 50 portions of cooked vegetables.

Frozen Vegetables

1. 10 lb (4.54 kg) frozen vegetables makes about 50 3-oz (85-g) portions.

2. Do not thaw vegetables before cooking except for solid pack frozen vegetables, which should be thawed only long enough to break apart easily.

3. Boil vegetables in lots no larger than 10-12 lb (4.54-5.44 kg). Steam vegetables in lots no larger than 5-6 lb (2.27-2.72 kg) per steamer pan.

4. Schedule cooking of frozen vegetables so they will be served soon after they are cooked.

Directions for Boiling

1. Add vegetables to boiling salted water (1⅓ T/20 mL) salt to amount of water specified in Table 2.18, except for corn, which is seasoned after cooking. Cook in steam-jacketed kettle or stockpot uncovered except starchy vegetables such as lima beans. Bring water quickly back to a boil.

2. Start timing when water returns to boil (see Table 2.18).

3. Drain cooked vegetables and place in serving pans. Add 4 oz (114 g) melted butter or margarine to each 10-12 lb (4.54-5.44 kg) of cooked vegetables.

4. For a creamed vegetable, add 2-3 qt (1.89-2.84 L) Thin or Medium White Sauce (p. 458).

Directions for Steaming

1. Place vegetables in steamer pans (5-6 lb/2.27-2.72 kg in each 12 × 20 × 2 in. pan). When cooking winter squash or sweet potatoes, cover with a lid or foil to prevent water from accumulating in pan.

2. Steam in compartment steamer using Table 2.18 as a guide. Begin timing when steamer reaches proper cooking pressure.

3. Add 2 oz (57 g) melted butter or margarine and 2 t (10 mL) salt to each 5-6 lb (2.27-2.72 kg) of drained cooked vegetables.

Canned Vegetables

1. Schedule heating of canned vegetables so they will be served soon after heating.

2. Prepare in lots of 2 No. 10 cans. This will make approximately 50 portions.

Directions for Heating in Stock Pot or in Steam-Jacketed Kettle

1. Drain off half the liquid; use for soups, gravies, and sauces.

2. Heat vegetables and remaining liquid in a stock pot or steam-jacketed kettle. Heat only long enough to bring to serving temperature.

3. Drain vegetables and place in serving pans. Add 4 oz (114 g) melted butter or margarine.

Directions for Heating in Steamer or Oven

1. Drain off half the liquid, use for soups, gravies, and sauces.

2. Transfer vegetables and remaining liquid to steamer pans and cover. (A 12 × 20 × 2 in. pan will hold contents of 2 No. 10 cans.)

3. Heat in steamer at 5-6 lb pressure for about 3 min, at 12-15 lb pressure for 1 min, or in a 350 °F (175 °C) oven until serving temperature is reached.

4. Drain vegetables and add 4 oz (114 g) melted butter or margarine for each lot of vegetables.

Dried Vegetables

To cook dried beans, peas, or lentils:

1. Sort and wash.

2. Heat 1½ gal (5.68 L) water to boiling in steam-jacketed kettle.

3. Add vegetable and boil for 2 min.

4. Turn off steam and allow to stand for 1 hr.

5. Add salt and cook slowly until vegetables are tender (1-1½ hr).

6. Vegetable may be covered with cold water and soaked overnight, then cooked.

Table 2.17 TIMETABLE FOR BOILING OR STEAMING FRESH
VEGETABLES (50 PORTIONS, ½ C/120 ML EACH)

Prepared Vegetable	Ready-to-Cook Weight[a]	Boiling Water[a]	Boiling Cooking Time (min)	Steaming Cooking Time (min) 5-6 lb pressure	12-15 lb pressure
Asparagus, spears	11 lb 4 oz	3 qt	10-25	7-10	5-7
cuts	7 lb 12 oz	3 qt	5-15	5-10	5
Beans, blackeye beans or peas	10 lb 8 oz	2½ qt	30-45	20-40	20
Beans, green or wax, 1-in. pieces	8 lb 4 oz	2½ qt	15-30	20-30	10-12
Beans, lima	9 lb 4 oz	2½ qt	15-25	15-20	10
Beet greens	11 lb 12 oz	Water clinging to leaves	15-25	15-25	10-15
Beets, whole (as purchased)	13 lb 8 oz	Water to cover	45-60	60-75	25-30
Broccoli, spears	9 lb 8 oz	3 qt	10-20	7-10	5
Brussels sprouts	8 lb 8 oz	1½ gal	10-20	5-12	5
Cabbage, shredded	8 lb 8 oz	2 qt	10-15	5-12	5
wedges	10 lb 4 oz	2 qt	15-20	12-20	7
Carrots, whole	9 lb 12 oz	2 qt	20-30	15-30	10
sliced	9 lb 12 oz	2 qt	10-20	15-30	10
Cauliflower, flowerets	7 lb 12 oz	1½ gal	15-20	8-12	4-6
Celery, 1-in. pieces	9 lb	1 gal	15-20	10-15	5-7
Chard	13 lb 12 oz	Water clinging to leaves	15-25	15-25	10-15
Collards	8 lb 4 oz	1 gal	20-40	15-30	10-15
Corn on cob	16 lb 12 oz (50 medium ears)	1¼ gal or to cover	5-15	8-10	5-7
Eggplant, pieces or slices	12 lb 8 oz	3 qt	15-20	10-15	5-8
Kale	7 lb	3 qt	25-45	15-35	10-15
Mustard greens	14 lb 4 oz	Water clinging to leaves	15-25	15-25	10-15
Okra, whole	8 lb 8 oz	2 qt	10-15	8-15	5-8

Table 2.17 TIMETABLE FOR BOILING OR STEAMING FRESH VEGETABLES (50 PORTIONS, ½ C/120 ML EACH)

Prepared Vegetable	Ready-to-Cook Weight[a]	Boiling		Steaming	
		Boiling Water[a]	Cooking Time (min)	Cooking Time (min) 5-6 lb pressure	12-15 lb pressure
Onions, mature, quartered if large	13 lb 12 oz	1½ gal	20-35	20-35	10-12
Parsnips, 3-in. pieces	11 lb	1¼ gal	20-30	15-20	10-12
Peas, green	9 lb 8 oz	2 qt	10-20	10-20	5-8
Potatoes, whole	12 lb 8 oz				
For dicing	8 lb 12 oz				
For slicing	8 lb	1¼ gal	30-40	30-45	25-30
For mashing	11 lb 12 oz				
Pumpkin, pieces	15 lb	1¼ gal	15-30	15-20	10-12
Rutabagas, 1-in. cubes	10 lb 4 oz	3 qt	20-30	15-30	10-20
for mashing	14 lb 8 oz				
Spinach	12 lb	Water clinging to leaves	10-20	4-8	3-5
Squash, summer, sliced	11 lb 12 oz	2 qt	10-20	8-20	5-10
Squash, winter (Hubbard or butternut) pieces					
For cubing	14 lb	1¼ gal	15-30	15-20	10-15
For mashing	15 lb 8 oz				
Sweet potatoes, whole					
For mashing	17 lb 8 oz	1¼ gal	30-45	20-40	12-20
For slicing	15 lb 8 oz				
Turnip greens	15 lb	Water clinging to leaves	15-25	15-25	10-15
Turnips, 1-inch cubes	11 lb 8 oz	3 qt	15-20	10-15	5-7
for mashing	14 lb 8 oz				

[a] For metric weight and measure equivalents, see pp. 28-29.

Table 2.18 TIMETABLE FOR BOILING OR STEAMING **FROZEN** VEGETABLES (FIGURES GIVEN ARE FOR *BOILING* 10-12 LB/4.54-5.44 KG BATCHES; FOR *STEAMING* 5-6 LB/2.27-2.72 KG BATCHES)

	Boiling		*Steaming Cooking Time (min)*	
Vegetable	*Boiling Water (qt)* [a]	*Cooking Time (min)*	*5-6 lb pressure*	*12-15 lb pressure*
Asparagus, cuts and tips	1½	7-10	5-10	5
Beans, blackeye beans or peas	2	25-30	15-25	10
Beans, green or wax	1	10-20	10-15	5
Beans, lima, baby	2	12-15	10-15	10
Fordhook	2	6-12	12-20	10
Broccoli, spears	1½	10-15	5-10	5
cut or chopped	1½	8-20	10-20	5-7
Brussels sprouts	1½	10-15	5-10	5
Carrots	1	8-10	3-5	3
Cauliflower	1½	10-12	4-5	4
Collards	1¾	30-40	20-40	15
Corn, whole kernel	1½	5-10	5-10	7-10
Kale	1¾	20-30	15-30	10
Mustard greens	1¾	20-30	15-20	10
Okra	1¼	3-5	3-5	2-3
Peas and carrots	1	8-10	3-5	3
Peas, green	1	5-10	3-5	3
Spinach	1	5-10	5-10	5-7
Squash, summer	1	5-10	5-10	5
Squash, winter				
(in double boiler)		30-40		
(cover with foil)			20-25	10-12
Succotash	2	6-15	12-20	7-10
Sweet potatoes (cover with foil)			15-20	10
Turnip greens	1¾	20-30	15-20	10
Vegetables, mixed	1	12-20	12-20	10

[a] For metric measure equivalents, see p. 29.

Vegetable Recipes

GREEN BEAN CASSEROLE
Bake: 40 min
Oven: 300 °F (150 °C)

Yield: 2 12 × 20 in. pans
Portion: 5 oz (142 g)

	Amount		
Metric	*U.S.*	*Ingredient*	*Method*
4.54 kg	10 lb	Green beans, French cut or cut, frozen	Cook green beans (p. 503).
454 g	1 lb	Mushrooms, fresh, sliced	Sauté mushrooms in butter or margarine.
114 g	4 oz	Butter or margarine	
1 can (1.45 kg)	1 can (51 oz)	Mushroom soup	Blend mushroom soup and milk.
720 mL	3 c	Milk	
2 340-g cans	2 12-oz cans	Water chestnuts	Drain water chestnuts. Slice. Combine soup, mushrooms, and water chestnuts. Add to green beans. Mix lightly. Pour into 2 12 × 20 in. pans.
114 g	4 oz	Cheddar cheese, grated	Sprinkle cheese over beans. Bake 30 min.
3 100-g cans	3 3½-oz cans	French fried onions, canned	Sprinkle onions over bean mixture. Bake 10 min.

Note: 2 No. 10 cans cut green beans may be substituted for frozen beans.

SPANISH GREEN BEANS

Yield: 50 portions
Portion: 3 oz (85 g)

Amount		Ingredient	Method
Metric	U.S.		
227 g	8 oz	Bacon, diced	Sauté bacon, onion, and green
170 g	6 oz	Onion, chopped	pepper until lightly browned.
114 g	4 oz	Green pepper, chopped	
114 g	4 oz	Flour	Add flour and stir until smooth.
1.89 L	2 qt	Tomatoes, hot	Add tomatoes and salt gradually.
15 mL	1 T	Salt	Stir and cook until thickened.
2 No. 10 can cans (or 4.54 kg fresh)	2 No. 10 cans (or 10 lb fresh)	Green beans, drained	Add tomato sauce to the green beans. Simmer approximately 30 min.

Variations:

1. **Creole Green Beans.** Omit bacon. Sauté onion, green pepper, and 8 oz (227 g) celery in 2 oz (57 g) butter or margarine. Add 2 oz (57 g) sugar to tomatoes.

2. **Southern-Style Green Beans.** Cut 1½ lb (680 g) bacon or salt pork into small pieces. Add 6 oz (170 g) chopped onion and sauté until onion is lightly browned. Add to hot, drained green beans. Serve with boiled ham and corn bread.

3. **Green Beans with Dill.** Delete bacon and onion. Sauté the green pepper in 5 oz (142 g) butter or margarine. Add 1 t (5 mL) pepper and 1 T (15 mL) dill seeds. Simmer slowly 10-15 min. Tomato may be increased to 1 No. 10 can.

BAKED LIMA BEANS
Bake: 2 hr
Oven: 350 °F (175 °C)

Yield: 2 pans 12 × 20 × 2 in.
Portion: 5 oz (142 g)

Amount		Ingredient	Method
Metric	U.S.		
2.72 kg	6 lb	Lima beans	Wash beans. Add boiling water.
3.79 L	1 gal	Water, boiling	Cover. Let stand 1 hr or longer. Cook beans in the same water until tender (about 1 hr).
114 g	4 oz	Pimiento, chopped	Add seasonings. Pour into 2 baking pans.
227 g	8 oz	Bacon fat	
23 mL	1½ T	Salt	
240 mL	1 c	Molasses	
680 g	1 lb 8 oz	Salt pork, sliced	Place salt pork on top of beans. Bake until top is brown (about 1 hr).

Variations:

1. **Baked Lima Beans with Sausage.** Omit salt pork and bacon fat. Place 6 lb (2.72 kg) link sausages on top of beans.

2. **Boiled Lima Beans and Ham.** Omit salt pork and seasonings. Add 5 lb (2.27 kg) cured ham, diced, to beans and simmer until tender.

BAKED BEANS
Bake: 5-6 hr   **Yield: 50 portions**
Oven: 350 °F (175 °C)   **Portion: 5 oz (142 g)**

	Amount		
Metric	*U.S.*	*Ingredient*	*Method*
2.27 kg (A.P.)	5 lb (A.P.)	Navy beans	Wash beans. Add boiling water. Cover. Let stand 1 hr or longer.
5.68 L	1½ gal	Water, boiling	Cook in same water until tender (about 1 hr). Add more water as necessary.
114 g	4 oz	Salt	Add all ingredients to the beans.
170 g	6 oz	Brown sugar	Blend.
5 mL	1 t	Mustard, dry	Pour beans into deep baking pan.
30 mL	2 T	Vinegar	Bake.
240 mL	1 c	Molasses	
600 mL	2½ c	Catsup (optional)	
454 g	1 lb	Salt pork, cubed	

Variation:
Boston Baked Beans. Omit catsup and bake in oven the entire cooking time.

HARVARD BEETS

Yield: 50 portions
Portion: 3 oz (85 g)

Amount		Ingredient	Method
Metric	*U.S.*		
1.42 L	1½ qt	Beet juice	Add bay leaf and cloves to beet
1	1	Bay leaf	juice. Heat to boiling point.
5 mL	1 t	Cloves, whole	
340 g	12 oz	Sugar	Add combined dry ingredients
28 g	1 oz	Salt	while stirring briskly. Cook un-
170 g	6 oz	Cornstarch	til thickened and clear.
114 g	4 oz	Butter or mar-garine	Add butter or margarine and vine-gar.
480 mL	2 c	Vinegar	Pour sauce over hot beets.
2 No. 10 cans	2 No. 10 cans	Beets, sliced, drained	

Note: 12 lb (5.44 kg) fresh beets, cooked, may be substituted for canned beets.

Variations:

1. **Beets with Orange Sauce.** Omit bay leaf, cloves, and vinegar; add 2 c (480 mL) orange juice and ½ c (120 mL) lemon juice.

2. **Hot Spiced Beets.** Drain juice from 2 No. 10 cans sliced beets and add 1 T (15 mL) cloves, 1½ T (23 mL) salt, ½ t (3 mL) cinnamon, 1 lb (454 g) brown sugar, 8 oz (227 g) granulated sugar, and 1 qt (0.95 L) vinegar. Cook 10 min. Pour sauce over beets and reheat.

RANCH STYLE BEANS
Bake: 6-8 hr   **Yield: 50 portions**
Oven: 300 °F (150 °C)   **Portion: 5 oz (142 g)**

Amount		Ingredient	Method
Metric	U.S.		
2.27 kg	5 lb	Beans, red or pinto	Soak beans overnight; drain off water.
5.68 L	1½ gal	Water	
1.14 kg	2 lb 8 oz	Salt pork, 1-in. cubes	Add salt pork to beans. Add cold water to cover.
		Water, cold	Cook slowly until tender.
3-4 pods	3-4 pods	Chili peppers	Soak chili peppers in warm water. Remove pulp from pods and add to beans.
1.89 L	2 qt	Tomatoes, cooked	
227 g	8 oz	Onion, sliced	Add tomatoes and other seasonings.
23 mL	1½ T	Salt	
15 mL	1 T	Pepper	Cook slowly in kettle an additional 5 hr or pour into 12 × 20 × 4 in. pan and bake 6-8 hr at 300 °F (175 °C).
f.g.	f.g.	Cayenne	
2 cloves	2 cloves	Garlic, chopped	

Note: If chili peppers are not available, 1 oz (28 g) chili powder may be used.

HOT SLAW
                                                                        Yield: 1 gal (3.79 L)
                                                                        Portion: 3 oz (85 g)

Amount		Ingredient	Method
Metric	U.S.		
595 g	1 lb 5 oz	Sugar	Mix dry ingredients.
23 mL	1½ T	Salt	
114 g	4 oz	Flour	
10 mL	2 t	Mustard, dry	
0.95 L	1 qt	Milk, hot	Add milk and water while stirring. Cook until thickened.
1.18 L	1¼ qt	Water, hot	
8	8	Eggs, beaten	Add eggs gradually while stirring briskly. Cook 2-3 min. Add vinegar.
640 mL	2⅔ c	Vinegar, hot	
5.44 kg (E.P.)	12 lb (E.P.)	Cabbage, raw, shredded	Pour hot sauce over cabbage just before serving.
20 mL	4 t	Celery seed	Add celery seed and mix lightly.

BUTTERED CABBAGE

Yield: 50 portions
Portions: 3 oz (85 g)

Amount			
Metric	U.S.	Ingredient	Method
6.80 kg (E.P.)	15 lb (E.P.)	Cabbage	Cut cabbage into wedges or shred coarsely.
15.14 L	4 gal	Water, boiling	Cook until tender (p. 501) 15-20 min for wedges, 5-8 min for shredded.
30 mL	2 T	Salt	Drain.
227 g	8 oz	Butter or margarine, melted	Add butter or margarine.

Notes:
1. Cabbage will cook in a shorter time if shredded and will yield a more desirable product.
2. Bacon fat may be used in place of butter. Add it to the water in which cabbage is to be cooked.

Variations:
1. **Cabbage Polonnaise.** Arrange 10 lb (4.54 kg) cabbage wedges, partially cooked, in baking pans. Cover with Medium White Sauce (3 qt/2.84 L) (p. 458). Sprinkle with buttered bread crumbs. Bake about 25 min at 350 °F (175 °C).

2. **Cabbage au Gratin.** Alternate layers of 7-min cooked coarsely shredded cabbage, Medium White Sauce (p. 458), and grated sharp cheese in a baking pan. Sprinkle with buttered crumbs. Use 10 lb (4.54 kg) cabbage, 3 qt (2.84 L) white sauce, 12 oz (340 g) cheese, 8 oz (227 g) crumbs, and 4 oz (114 g) butter or margarine. Bake about 25 min at 350 °F (175 °C).

3. **Creamed Cabbage.** Omit butter or margarine. Pour 2 qt (1.89 L) Medium White Sauce (p. 458) over shredded, cooked, drained cabbage.

4. **Scalloped Cabbage.** Omit butter or margarine. Pour 2 qt (1.89 L) Medium White Sauce (p. 458) over chopped, cooked, drained cabbage. Cover with buttered crumbs. Bake 15-20 min at 400 °F (205 °C). Shredded cheese may be added.

5. **Seven-Minute Cabbage.** Steam (12-15 psi) shredded cabbage in inset pans 7 min. Season.

CAULIFLOWER CASSEROLE

Bake: 40-45 min

Oven: 325 °F (165 °C)

Yield: 50 portions

Portion: 4 oz (114 g)

Amount		Ingredient	Method
Metric	*U.S.*		
5.44 kg (E.P.)	12 lb[a] (E.P.)	Cauliflower	Clean cauliflower and break into flowerets. Cook (p. 501) until just done. Do not overcook. Drain and place in 2 baking pans 12 × 20 × 2 in.
18	18	Eggs, beaten	Combine eggs, milk, cheese, and salt. Pour over cauliflower.
1.89 L	2 qt	Milk	
340 g	12 oz	Cheddar cheese, grated	Set in pans of hot water and bake. Serve with Tomato Sauce (p. 466).
15 mL	1 T	Salt	

[a] Approximately 20 lb (9.08 kg) cauliflower A.P.

Note: With crisp bacon, this casserole may be served as a luncheon dish.

Variations:

1. **Cauliflower with Almond Butter.** Season 12 lb (5.44 kg) freshly cooked cauliflower with 2 c (480 mL) slivered almonds that have been browned in 8 oz (227 g) butter or margarine.

2. **Cauliflower with Cheese Sauce.** Pour 3 qt (2.84 L) Cheese Sauce (p. 459) over 12 lb (5.44 kg) cooked fresh cauliflower.

PARSLEY BUTTERED CARROTS

Yield: 50 portions
Portion: 3 oz (85 g)

Metric	U.S.	Ingredient	Method
	Amount		
Metric	*U.S.*	*Ingredient*	*Method*
5.67 kg	12 lb 8 oz	Carrots	Pare and cut into desired shapes (slices, strips, or quarters). Steam or boil (p. 501) until just tender.
114-227 g	4-8 oz	Butter or margarine, melted	Pour melted butter or margarine over carrots.
28 g	1 oz	Parsley, chopped	Sprinkle with chopped parsley.

Variations:

1. **Candied Carrots.** Cut carrots into 1-in. pieces. Cook until tender but not soft. Melt 12 oz (340 g) butter or margarine. Add 9 oz (255 g) sugar and 1½ T (23 mL) salt. Add to carrots. Bake 15-20 min at 400 °F (205 °C). Turn frequently.

2. **Cranberry Carrots.** Add 3 c (720 mL) cranberry sauce to buttered carrots. Reheat to serving temperature.

3. **Lyonnaise Carrots.** Arrange 10 lb (4.54 kg) cooked carrot strips in baking pan. Add 3 lb (1.36 kg) chopped onion that has been cooked until soft in 4 oz (114 g) butter or margarine. Bake at 350 °F (175 °C) 10-15 min or until vegetables are lightly browned. Just before serving sprinkle with chopped parsley.

4. **Marinated Carrots.** Cut carrots into slices, not too thin. Cook until just done. Drain and cool. Add 4 medium onions, sliced, and 4 small green peppers, sliced. Toss lightly. Heat 1 51-oz (1.45-kg) can tomato soup, 2 c (240 mL) salad oil, 2½ lb (1.14 kg) sugar, 1 qt (0.95 L) vinegar, 2 T (30 mL) prepared mustard, 2 T (30 mL) Worcestershire sauce, 1½ T (23 mL) salt, and 1 T (15 mL) pepper. Pour over vegetables. Cover and marinate 12 hr or more in the refrigerator. Drain to serve.

5. **Mint-Glazed Carrots.** Cut carrots into quarters lengthwise. Cook until almost tender. Drain. Melt 8 oz (227 g) butter or margarine, 8 oz (227 g) sugar, 1½ T (23 mL) salt, and 1 c (240 mL) mint jelly. Blend. Add carrots and simmer 5-10 min.

6. **Savory Carrots.** Cook carrots in beef or chicken stock. When done, season with 4 oz (114 g) melted butter or margarine, salt and pepper, and ¼ c (60 mL) lemon juice. Sprinkle with chopped parsley.

7. **Sweet-Sour Carrots.** Add to cooked carrots sauce made of 1½ qt (1.42 L) vinegar, 2¼ lb (1.02 kg) sugar, 2 T (30 mL) salt, and 12 oz (340 g) melted butter or margarine. Bake 15-20 min at 350 °F (175 °C) or simmer until carrots and sauce are thoroughly heated.

CREOLE EGGPLANT
Bake: 30 min
Oven: 350 °F (175 °C)

Yield: 50 portions
Portion: 5 oz (142 g)

Amount		Ingredient	Method
Metric	*U.S.*		
3.63 kg (E.P.)[a]	8 lb (E.P.)[a]	Eggplant, pared, diced	Cook eggplant in boiling salted water for 5 min.
5.68 L	1½ gal	Water, boiling	
30 mL	2 T	Salt	
454 g	1 lb	Butter or margarine, melted	Cook until tender.
680 g	1 lb 8 oz	Onion, chopped	
340 g	12 oz	Green pepper, coarsely chopped	
454 g	1 lb	Celery, coarsely chopped	
1 No. 10 can	1 No. 10 can	Tomatoes	Combine with eggplant and other ingredients.
30 mL	2 T	Salt	Pour into 2 baking pans 12 × 20 × 2 in.
10 mL	2 t	Pepper	
30 mL	2 T	Sugar	
340 g	12 oz	Bread crumbs	Top with buttered crumbs. Bake.
227 g	8 oz	Butter or margarine, melted.	

[a] Approximately 10 lb (4.54 kg) A.P.

Variation:
Baked Eggplant. Pare and slice 10 lb (4.54 kg) eggplant into ½-in. slices. Soak in salt water (1 T/15 mL salt to 1 qt/0.95 L water) 30 min. Drain. Dip slices in flour, eggs, and crumbs (p. 75). Place on greased baking sheets. Sprinkle with melted butter or margarine. Bake at 375 °F (190 °C) for 30 min.

SCALLOPED CORN

Bake: 35-40 min

Oven: 350 °F (175 °C)

Yield: 50 portions

Portion: 4 oz (114 g)

Amount		Ingredient	Method
Metric	U.S.		
2 No. 10 cans	2 No. 10 cans	Corn, cream style	Mix corn, milk, and seasonings.
0.95 L	1 qt	Milk	
15 mL	1 T	Salt	
3 mL	½ t	Pepper	
397 g	14 oz	Cracker crumbs	Combine crumbs and butter or margarine.
340 g	12 oz	Butter or margarine, melted	Place alternate layers of buttered crumbs and corn mixture in greased baking pans.
			Bake.

Note: 6 oz (170 g) chopped green pepper and 6 oz (170 g) chopped pimiento may be added.

CORN PUDDING

Bake: 40-45 min

Oven: 325 °F (165 °C)

Yield: 50 portions

Portion: 5 oz (142 g)

Amount		Ingredient	Method
Metric	U.S.		
4.08 kg	9 lb	Corn, whole kernel, frozen	Thaw corn.
2.84 L	3 qt	Milk	Combine with all ingredients except egg whites.
170 g	6 oz	Butter or margarine, melted	
30 mL	2 T	Salt	
24	24	Egg yolks, beaten	
24	24	Egg whites	Beat egg whites until stiff but not dry. Fold into corn mixture. Pour into greased baking pans. Place in pan of hot water and bake.

Note: 1 No. 10 can cream style corn may be substituted for whole kernel corn.

BAKED ONIONS
Bake: 20-30 min
Oven: 400 °F (205 °C)

Yield: 50 portions
Portion: 1 4-oz (114-g) onion

Amount		Ingredient	Method
Metric	U.S.		
50	50	Onions, 4 oz (114 g)	Peel onions and steam (p. 502) until tender. Place in greased baking pans.
15 mL	1 T	Salt	Sprinkle with salt and buttered bread crumbs.
227 g	8 oz	Bread crumbs	
227 g	8 oz	Butter or margarine, melted	
0.95 L	1 qt	Beef or chicken stock	Pour stock over onions. Bake.

Notes:
1. Purchase approximately 15 lb (6.80 kg) Spanish or Bermuda onions.
2. Onions may be cut into thick slices.

Variations:
1. **Onion Casserole.** Combine 10 lb (4.54 kg) cooked tiny onions, 10 oz (284 g) chopped walnuts, 1 c (240 mL) pimiento strips, and 8 10½-oz cans cream of mushroom soup. Cover with 1½ c (360 mL) grated cheese. Bake approximately 30 min at 400 °F (205 °C).

2. **Stuffed Baked Onions.** Scoop out center of 50 large onions. Fill with mixture of 1½ qt (1.42 L) Medium White Sauce (p. 458), 8 oz (227 g) butter or margarine, 6 beaten egg yolks, and onion centers cooked and chopped. 12 oz (340 g) chopped toasted almonds may be added. Cover tops of onions with buttered crumbs. Bake.

FRENCH FRIED ONIONS

Fry: 3-4 min
Deep-fat fryer: 350 °F (175 °C)

Yield: 50 portions
Portion: 3 oz (85 g)

Amount		Ingredient	Method
Metric	*U.S.*		
3.63 kg (E.P.)	8 lb (E.P.)	Onions	Cut onions into ¼-in. slices. Separate into rings.
6	6	Eggs, beaten	Combine eggs and milk.
480 mL	2 c	Milk	Add dry ingredients and mix to make batter.
340 g	12 oz	Flour	make batter.
10 mL	2 t	Baking powder	Dip onion rings in batter and fry in deep fat. Drain.
8 mL	1½ t	Salt	in deep fat. Drain.

Variations:

1. **French Fried Cauliflower.** Dip 10 lb (4.54 kg) cold cooked cauliflower into batter and fry 3-4 min at 370 °F (185 °C).

2. **French Fried Eggplant.** Pare and cut into ¼-in. slices or cut in strips as for French Fried Potatoes (p. 517). Dip in batter and fry 5-7 min at 370 °F (185 °C). Eggplant discolors quickly, so it should be placed in cold water if not breaded immediately.

3. **French Fried Zucchini Sticks.** Cut unpared zucchini lengthwise into strips about ½ in. thick. Dip in batter. Fry 4-6 min at 370 °F (185 °C).

FRENCH FRIED POTATOES

Amount		Ingredient	Method
Metric	*U.S.*		
6.80 kg	15 lb	Potatoes	Pare and cut potatoes into uniform strips from ⅜-¼ in. thick. Cover with cold water to keep potatoes from darkening. Just before frying, drain well or dry with paper towels. Fill fryer basket about ⅓ full of potatoes. Fry according to method 1 or 2.

Method 1. Half fill fry kettle with fat. Preheat fat to 365 °F (182 °C). Fry potatoes for 6-8 min. Drain. Sprinkle with salt. Serve.

Method 2. Blanching. Heat fat to 360 °F (180 °C). Place drained potato strips in hot fat, using an 8 to 1 ratio of fat to potatoes, by weight, as a guide for filling fryer basket. Fry 3-5 min, depending on thickness of potato. (The potatoes should not brown.) Drain. Hold for later browning. *Browning*. Reheat fat to 375 °F (190 °C). Place about twice as many potato strips in kettle as for first-stage frying. Fry 2-3 min, or until golden brown. Drain; sprinkle with salt if desired. Serve immediately.

Notes:
1. Select a mealy type potato for French frying. For best results, use potatoes that have been stored at room temperature for 2 weeks.
2. To cook frozen French fried potatoes, use 12 lb (5.44 kg) for 50 3-oz (85-g) portions. Fry 2½-3 min at 375 °F (190 °C).

Variations:
1. **Shoestring Potatoes.** Cut potatoes into ⅛-in. strips. Fry 3-10 min at 325-335 °F (165-168 °C).

2. **Lattice Potatoes.** Cut potatoes with lattice slicer. Fry 3-10 min at 350-375 °F (175-190 °C).

3. **Potato Chips.** Cut potatoes into very thin slices. Fry 3-6 min at 325 °F (165 °C).

4. **Deep-Fat Browned Potatoes.** Partially cook whole or half potatoes. Fry in deep fat 5-7 min at 350 °F (175 °C).

BAKED POTATOES
Bake: 1-1½ hr
Oven: 400 °F (205 °C)

Yield: 50 portions
Portion: 1 potato

Amount		Ingredient	Method
Metric	*U.S.*		
50	50	Baking potatoes, uniform size	Scrub potatoes and remove blemishes. Rub or brush lightly with fat.
114 g	4 oz	Fat	Place on baking pans. Bake until soft.

Variations:

1. **Baked Potatoes with Sour Cream and Chives.** Serve with 1 oz (28 g) cultured sour cream and chives.

2. **Baked Potatoes with Cheese Sauce.** Make 3 qt (2.84 L) Cheese Sauce (p. 459). Serve 2 oz (57 g) sauce on each baked potato. Sprinkle with chopped green onion and/or crisp bacon bits.

3. **Stuffed Baked Potato.** Cut hot baked potatoes into halves lengthwise. If potatoes are small, cut a slice from one side. Scoop out contents. Mash, season with 2 T (30 mL) salt, 1 t (5 mL) white pepper, 8 oz (227 g) butter or margarine, melted, and 3-4 c(720-950 mL) hot milk. Beat until light and fluffy. Pile lightly into shells, leaving tops rough. Sprinkle with paprika or parmesan cheese, if desired. Bake at 425 °F (220 °C) until potatoes are hot and lightly browned, about 30 min.

MASHED POTATOES

Boil: 30-50 min or
Steam: 30-45 min

Yield: 50 portions
Portion: 5 oz (142 g)

Amount		Ingredient	Method
Metric	*U.S.*		
5.44 kg (E.P.)[a]	12 lb (E.P.)[a]	Potatoes, pared	Steam or boil potatoes (p. 502). When done, drain and place in mixer bowl. Mash (low speed) until there are no lumps. Whip (high speed) about 2 min.
1.89-2.37 L	2-2½ qt	Milk, hot	Add milk, butter, and salt to potatoes.
227 g	8 oz	Butter or margarine	
45 mL	3 T	Salt	Whip (high speed) until light and creamy.

[a] Approximately 15 lb (6.8 kg) as purchased.

Notes:
1. Potato water may be substituted for part of milk.
2. 8 oz (227 g) nonfat dry milk and 2-2½ qt (1.89-2.37 L) water may be substituted for the liquid milk. Sprinkle dry milk over potatoes before mashing.
3. 2-2½ lb (0.91-1.05 kg) dehydrated potatoes may be substituted for 12 lb (5.44 kg) raw potatoes. Follow processor's instructions for preparation.

Variations:
1. **Duchess Potatoes.** Add 18 eggs, beaten, to Mashed Potatoes. Add additional milk if necessary. Mix well. Pile lightly into greased baking pans. Bake in a 350 °F (175 °C) oven until set.

2. **Potato Croquettes.** Add 18 well-beaten egg yolks. Shape into croquettes. Egg and crumb (p. 75). Chill. Fry in deep fat at 360 °F (180 °C).

3. **Potato Rosettes.** Force Duchess Potatoes through a pastry tube, forming rosettes or fancy shapes. Bake at 350 °F (175 °C) until browned. Use as a garnish for planked steak.

4. **Mashed Sweet Potatoes.** Use 15 lb (6.80 kg) E.P. sweet potatoes. Add ½ t (3 mL) nutmeg.

5. **Mashed Potato Casserole.** Add ¼ c (60 mL) chopped chives, ¼ c (60 mL) crisp bacon bits, 12 oz (340 g) cream cheese, and white pepper and garlic powder to taste. Mix until blended. Place in greased baking pans. Sprinkle lightly with grated parmesan cheese and paprika. Brush lightly with melted butter or margarine. Bake at 375 °F (190 °C) for 30 min or until light brown.

SCALLOPED POTATOES

Bake: 1½-2 hr   **Yield: 2 pans 12 × 20 × 2 in.**
Oven: 350 °F (175 °C)   **Portion: 5 oz (142 g)**

Amount		Ingredient	Method
Metric	*U.S.*		
5.44 kg (E.P.)[a]	12 lb (E.P.)[a]	Potatoes, pared	Slice potatoes. Place in 2 greased baking pans.
45 mL	3 T	Salt	Sprinkle with salt.
227 g	8 oz	Butter or margarine	Make into Thin White Sauce (p. 458).
114 g	4 oz	Flour	Pour over potatoes.
3.79 L	1 gal	Milk	
23 mL	1½ T	Salt	
170 g	6 oz	Bread crumbs	Sprinkle buttered crumbs over potatoes.
57 g	2 oz	Butter or margarine, melted	Bake.

[a] Approximately 15 lb (6.8 kg) as purchased.

Notes:
1. Potatoes may be partially cooked, and hot white sauce added to shorten baking time.
2. 2 lb (908 g) sliced dehydrated potatoes, reconstituted in 2 gal (7.57 L) boiling water, and 3 T (45 mL) salt may be substituted for the fresh potatoes.

Variations:
1. **Scalloped Potatoes with Onions.** Before baking, cover potatoes with onion rings. About 5 min before removing from oven, cover potatoes with shredded cheese.

2. **Scalloped Potatoes with Ham.** Add 5 lb (2.27 kg) cubed cured ham to white sauce. Cut salt to 1 T (15 mL).

3. **Scalloped Potatoes with Pork Chops.** Brown chops, season, and place on top of potatoes before baking.

Variations in Potato Preparation

Au Gratin Potatoes

Cube 12 lb (5.44 kg) E.P. boiled potatoes (or dice before cooking). Add 1 gal (3.79 L) Medium White Sauce (p. 458) and 2 lb (908 g) grated Cheddar cheese. Place in greased baking pan; top with buttered crumbs. Bake approximately 25 min at 400 °F (205 °C).

Cottage Fried Potatoes

Add sliced, cold, boiled potatoes to hot fat in frying pan. Add salt and pepper. Stir as needed and fry until browned.

Franconia Potatoes

Cook pared uniform potatoes approximately 15 min; drain and place in pan in which meat is roasting. Bake approximately 40 min, or until tender and lightly browned, basting with drippings in pan or turning occasionally to brown all sides. Serve with roast.

French Baked Potatoes

Select small, uniform potatoes and pare. Roll potatoes in melted fat, then in cracker crumbs or crushed cornflakes. Place in shallow pan and bake.

Hashed Brown Potatoes

Add finely chopped boiled potatoes to hot fat in frying pan. Add salt and pepper. Stir occasionally and fry until browned.

Herbed Potato Bake

Pare baking potatoes and cut into ½-in. slices. Place in greased baking pans. Salt. Cover with 1½ c (360 mL) melted butter or margarine, 3½ oz (100 g) dehydrated onion soup mix, and 2 T (30 mL) rosemary and toss lightly. Bake at 325 °F (165 °C) for 1½ hr.

Lyonnaise Potatoes

Cook onion slowly in fat without browning. Add seasoned cut, boiled potatoes and cook until browned; *or* cut potatoes as for French fries. Steam until tender, place in greased baking pan. Cover top with fat and onions. Place in oven and bake until browned.

Lyonnaise Baked Potatoes

Select baking potatoes of medium size. Cut each in 4 crosswise slices; place a slice of onion, salt, pepper, and butter or margarine between slices and wrap each in aluminum foil. Bake at 400 °F (205 °C) until potatoes are almost done. Open foil and return to oven to brown tops.

New Potatoes Parmesan

Scrub small uniform-sized new potatoes. Take 1 in. of peeling off around center of potatoes. Boil or steam until just done. Roll potatoes in melted butter or margarine. Place in baking pans. Sprinkle with parmesan cheese. Bake at 350 °F (175 °C) 20-25 min.

O'Brien Potatoes

Cook cubed potatoes in a small amount of fat with chopped onion and pimiento.

Oven-Browned or Rissolé Potatoes

Pare and cut potatoes in uniform pieces. Place in baking pan containing a small amount of fat. Turn potatoes so that all sides are coated with fat. Sprinkle with salt. Bake in hot oven until browned and tender. Turn as necessary for even browning. Potatoes may be parboiled 10-15 min or browned in deep fat before placing in baking pan, to shorten baking time.

Oven-Fried Potatoes

Prepare potatoes as for French fried potatoes. Place in greased shallow pan to make a thin layer and brush with oil or melted fat, turning to cover all sides. Bake 20-30 min at 450 °F (230 °C) or until browned, turning occasionally. Drain on absorbent paper and sprinkle with salt.

Persillade New Potatoes

Pare and cook uniform, small, new potatoes. Pour over them a mixture of lemon juice and butter, then roll in minced parsley.

Potato Balls

Pare potatoes and cut into balls with a French vegetable cutter. Cook. Season with lemon juice and butter and roll in minced parsley.

Potatoes Continental

Pare and cook small potatoes in meat stock with bay leaves until tender. Drain and season with onion browned in butter or margarine. Garnish with minced parsley and paprika.

Potatoes in Jackets

Wash medium-sized potatoes and remove any blemishes. Steam until tender and serve without removing skins.

Potato Pancakes

Grate or grind 15 lb (6.80 kg) raw potatoes and 4 oz (114 g) onion; drain. Add 6 beaten eggs, 8 oz (227 g) flour, 3 T (45 mL) salt, 1 t (5 mL) baking powder, and ¾ c (180 mL) cream or mlk. Mix. Drop with No. 20 dipper onto a hot greased griddle. Fry until golden brown on each side. Serve with applesauce.

Rissolé Potatoes See Oven-Browned Potatoes.

GLAZED OR CANDIED SWEET POTATOES
Bake: 20-30 min
Oven: 400 °F (205 °C)

Yield: 50 portions
Portion: 4 oz (114 g)

Metric	U.S.	Ingredient	Method
Amount			
9.08-11.57 kg (A.P.)	20-25 lb (A.P.)	Sweet potatoes	Steam or boil potatoes in skins until tender. Peel. Cut into halves lengthwise. Arrange in shallow pans.
794 g	1 lb 12 oz	Brown sugar	Mix sugar, water, butter, or margarine, and salt. Heat to boiling point. Pour over potatoes. Bake.
480 mL	2 c	Water	
227 g	8 oz	Butter or margarine	
3 mL	½ t	Salt	

Note: 3 No. 10 cans sweet potatoes may be substituted for fresh sweet potatoes.

Variations:

1. **Candied Sweet Potatoes with Almonds.** Proceed as for Glazed Sweet Potatoes; increase butter or margarine to 12 oz (340 g); reduce brown sugar to 1½ lb (680 g). Add 1 c (240 mL) dark syrup and 2 t (10 mL) mace. When partially glazed, sprinkle top with chopped almonds and continue cooking until almonds are toasted.

2. **Glazed Sweet Potatoes with Orange Slices.** Add ¼ c (60 mL) grated orange rind to syrup. Cut 5 oranges into thin slices; add to sweet potatoes when syrup is added.

SWEET POTATOES AND APPLES

Bake: 45 min
Oven: 350 °F (175 °C)

Yield: 2 pans 12 × 20 × 2 in.
Portion: 4 oz (114 g)

Amount		Ingredient	Method
Metric	*U.S.*		
6.80 kg (A.P.)	15 lb (A.P.)	Sweet potatoes	Cook potatoes in skins. Peel and slice.
2.27 kg	5 lb	Apples	Pare and slice apples. Place alternate layers of sweet potatoes and apples in baking pans.
454 g	1 lb	Brown sugar	Make a syrup of sugar, salt, butter or margarine, and water.
227 g	8 oz	Granulated sugar	Pour hot syrup over potatoes and apples. Bake.
30 mL	2 T	Salt	
227 g	8 oz	Butter or margarine	
480 mL	2 c	Water	

Notes:
1. 1 lb (454 g) coarsely chopped pecans may be added.
2. During last 5 min of baking, 1 lb (454 g) marshmallows may be placed on top.

Variations:
1. **Sweet Potato and Cranberry Casserole.** Substitute 3 lb (1.36 kg) cooked cranberries for apples; omit brown sugar and add 3 lb (1.36 kg) granulated sugar.

2. **Mashed Sweet Potato and Apple Casserole.** Mash sweet potatoes (p. 519). Delete syrup. Add ⅔ c (160 mL) brown sugar to potatoes. Cook sliced apples in 8 oz (227 g) butter or margarine until barely tender. Spread in 2 pans. Sprinkle 1½ c (360 mL) granulated sugar over apples. Spread sweet potatoes evenly over apples. Cover with topping made of cornflakes, crushed coarsely, melted butter or margarine, and chopped nuts. Bake.

SWEET POTATO AND ALMOND CROQUETTES

Fry: 3-4 min

Temp.: 375 °F (190 °C)

Yield: 50 croquettes

Portion: 3 oz (85 g)

Metric	U.S.	Ingredient	Method
Amount			
6.8 kg (A.P.)	15 lb (A.P.)	Sweet potatoes	Pare, cook, and mash sweet potatoes.
16	16	Egg yolks, beaten	Add egg yolks, seasonings, and almonds. Mix.
10 mL	2 t	Nutmeg	
85 g	3 oz	Sugar	
15 mL	1 T	Salt	
454 g	1 lb	Almonds, chopped	
454 g	1 lb	Cornflakes, crushed	Measure with No. 12 dipper onto tray covered with part of the crushed cornflakes. Chill about 2 hr.
3	3	Eggs	Shape into croquettes or patties, dip in egg mixture, and roll in remainder of cornflakes. Fry in deep fat.
240 mL	1 c	Water or milk	

Note: May be baked. Place on greased baking pan. Spread with 8 oz (227 g) butter or margarine. Bake 30-45 min at 350 °F (175 °C).

BAKED ACORN SQUASH
Bake: 30-40 min total   **Yield: 50 portions**
Oven: 350 °F (175 °C)   **Portion: ½ squash**

Amount			
Metric	*U.S.*	*Ingredient*	*Method*
25	25	Acorn squash	Cut squash into halves. Remove seeds. Bake upside down in shallow pans with a small amount of water, 20-25 min or until just tender.
227 g	8 oz	Butter or margarine	Place squash hollow side up. Add butter or margarine, salt, and brown sugar.
23 mL	1½ T	Salt	
340 g	12 oz	Brown sugar	Bake until sugar is melted, 10-15 min.

Variations:

1. **Acorn Squash with Sausage.** Place 4 oz (114 g) sausage patty or 2 link sausages, partially cooked, in each cooked squash half. Continue baking until meat is done.

2. **Stuffed Acorn Squash.** Fill cooked squash half with No. 12 dipper of the following mixture: 5 qt (4.73 L) cooked rice, 4 lb (1.81 kg) chopped cooked meat, and 4 oz (114 g) sautéed minced onion, moistened with meat stock.

SPINACH SOUFFLÉ
Bake: 40 min
Oven: 350 °F (175 °C)

Yield: 2 12 × 20 × 2 in. pans
Portion: 2½ oz (70 g)

Metric	U.S.	Ingredient	Method
	Amount		
567 g	1 lb 4 oz	Butter or margarine	Melt butter. Add flour, salt, milk, and sour cream.
227 g	8 oz	Flour	Blend over low heat until smooth, stirring constantly. Remove from heat.
37 mL	2½ T	Salt	
1.18 L	1¼ qt	Milk	
1.18 L	1¼ qt	Cultured sour cream	
2.72 kg	6 lb	Frozen chopped spinach, thawed and drained	Add spinach, onion, nutmeg, and egg yolks. Mix.
227 g	8 oz	Onion, finely chopped	
23 mL	1½ T	Nutmeg	
18	18	Egg yolks	
18	18	Egg whites	Beat egg whites until stiff. Fold into spinach mixture. Pour into ungreased counter pans. Bake in pans of hot water until soufflé is set.

BAKED TOMATOES

Bake: 10-12 min   **Yield: 50 portions**
Oven: 400 °F (205 °C)   **Portion: ½ tomato**

Amount			
Metric	*U.S.*	*Ingredient*	*Method*
25	25	Tomatoes (5 oz/ 142 g each)	Wash tomatoes. Cut in halves. Sprinkle each tomato with ⅛-¼ t salt and pepper or seasoned salt.
170 g	6 oz	Butter or margarine, melted	Combine butter or margarine, bread crumbs, and onion.
57 g	2 oz	Bread crumbs, coarse	Place 2 t crumb mixture on each tomato half. Bake.
170 g	6 oz	Onion, chopped fine	

Variations:

1. **Mushroom-Stuffed Tomatoes.** Add 2 lb (908 g) sautéed, sliced, or chopped mushrooms to crumb mixture.

2. **Broiled Tomato Slices.** Cut tomatoes in ½-in. slices. Salt, dot with butter, and broil.

TOMATO VEGETABLE MEDLEY

Yield: 50 portions
Portion: 5 oz (142 g)

Amount		Ingredient	Method
Metric	U.S.		
908 g	2 lb	Celery, cut in 2-in. strips	Steam for 15 min.
908 g	2 lb	Carrots, cut in 2-in. strips	
908 g	2 lb	Onions, sliced	Mix all ingredients and place in 2
454 g	1 lb	Green peppers, cut in strips	greased pans 12 × 20 × 2 in. Cover with foil and cook in
1 No. 10 can	1 No. 10 can	Green beans, cut	steamer for 30 min.
1 No. 10 can	1 No. 10 can	Tomatoes	
30 mL	2 T	Salt	
170 g	6 oz	Tapioca, minute	
284 g	10 oz	Butter or margarine	
4 mL	¾ t	Pepper	
170 g	6 oz	Sugar	

Note: Vegetables may be baked for 1-1½ hr. Do not precook celery and carrots.

BAKED ZUCCHINI
Bake: 10-15 min   **Yield: 50 portions**
Oven: 400 °F (205 °C)   **Portion: 4 oz (114 g)**

Amount		Ingredient	Method
Metric	*U.S.*	*Ingredient*	*Method*
5.44 kg	12 lb	Zucchini	Remove ends of zucchini and cut in halves lengthwise. Simmer in boiling salted water or steam until almost tender. Drain. Arrange in baking pans.
227 g	8 oz	Butter or margarine, melted	Pour melted butter or margarine over zucchini.
5 mL	1 t	Garlic salt	Sprinkle with garlic salt, salt, pepper, oregano, and cheese.
5 mL	1 t	Salt	
5 mL	1 t	White pepper	Bake until lightly browned.
5 mL	1 t	Oregano	
114 g	4 oz	Parmesan cheese, grated	

Variations:

1. **Zucchini Italian.** Slice zucchini. Cook 1½ lb (680 g) sliced onions in 1 c.(240 mL) hot salad oil until tender but not brown. Add 5 lb (2.27 kg) raw tomatoes that have been peeled, sliced, and cooked about 3 min. Combine all ingredients and season with 2½ T (37 mL) salt and 4 t (20 mL) pepper. Cook slowly about 20 min, adding a small amount of water if necessary. Add 1 bay leaf if desired.

2. **Zucchini-Corn Casserole.** Sauté 2 c (480 mL) finely chopped onion, 4 garlic cloves minced, and 4 green peppers, chopped, in 6 oz (170 g) butter or margarine. Combine with 5 lb (2.27 kg) zucchini, cubed, 1 No. 10 can whole kernel corn, drained, and 2 qt (1.89 L) tomatoes. Bake, covered, 30-35 min or until vegetables are done.

BUTTERED APPLES

Yield: 7 qt (6.62 L)
Portion: ½ c (120 mL)

Amount			
Metric	*U.S.*	*Ingredient*	*Method*
5.9 kg (E.P.)	13 lb (E.P.)	Apples	Cut apples into sections. Remove cores. Arrange in pan.
227 g	8 oz	Butter or margarine	Mix remaining ingredients. Pour over apples.
480 mL	2 c	Water, hot	Cover and simmer until apples are tender, approximately 1 hr.
680 g	1 lb 8 oz	Sugar	
23 mL	1½ T	Salt	

Notes:
1. A more attractive product is obtained if apple sections are arranged in a serving pan and steamed until tender, butter or margarine and sugar sprinkled over the top, and then baked for 15-20 min.
2. Hot buttered apples often are served in place of a vegetable.

Variations:
1. **Cinnamon Apples.** Cut apples into rings. Add cinnamon drops (redhots) for flavor and color.

2. **Apple Rings.** Cut rings of unpared apples, steam until tender, add sugar and butter or margarine and bake 15 min.

3. **Stewed Apples.** Use 10 lb (4.54 kg) frozen or canned apples. Heat in steam-jacketed kettle. Substitute brown sugar for granulated sugar. Add 1 T (15 mL) cinnamon.

Suggestions for Seasoning and Serving Vegetables[1]

Asparagus

Asparagus with Cheese Sauce.   Serve 5 or 6 stalks of cooked asparagus with 1 T (15 mL) Cheese Sauce (p. 459).

Fresh Asparagus with Hollandaise Sauce.   Serve 1 T (15 mL) Hollandaise Sauce (p. 469) over cooked asparagus spears.

Creamed Asparagus on Toast.   Add 1 gal (3.79 L) Medium White Sauce (p. 458) to 10 lb (4.54 kg) E.P. asparagus cut in 2-in. lengths and cooked. Serve on toast.

Spices and Herbs for Asparagus.   Mustard seed, sesame seed, or tarragon.

Green Beans

Green Beans Amandine.   Add 8 oz (227 g) slivered almonds lightly browned in 8 oz (227 g) butter or margarine to 12 lb (5.44 kg) freshly cooked and drained beans.

French Green Beans.   Cook 10 lb (4.54 kg) frozen French cut green beans. Drain and season with 1 c (240 mL) mayonnaise, ¾ c (180 mL) cultured sour cream, 2 T (30 mL) vinegar, 2 oz (57 g) onion sautéed in 2 oz (57 g) butter or margarine, and salt and pepper to taste.

Green Beans and Mushrooms.   Add 2 lb (908 g) sliced mushrooms sautéed in 8 oz (227 g) butter or margarine to 10 lb (4.54 kg) freshly cooked green beans.

Herbed Green Beans.   Season 2 No. 10 cans green beans, drained, with 1 lb (454 g) chopped onions, 8 oz (227 g) chopped celery, and 1 t (5 mL) minced garlic, sautéed in 8 oz (227 g) butter or margarine, 2 t (10 mL) basil, and 2 t (10 mL) rosemary.

Spices and Herbs for Green Beans.   Basil, dill, marjoram, mint, mustard seed, oregano, savory, tarragon, or thyme.

Lima Beans

Baked Lima Beans and Peas.   Thaw 5 lb (2.27 kg) frozen baby lima beans and 5 lb (2.27 kg) frozen peas. Combine with 2 T (30 mL) basil, 2 T (30 mL) salt, and

[1] For preparation and detailed cookery methods, see pp. 496-503.

16 green onions, sliced. Place in baking pans. Sprinkle with 1 c (240 mL) water and dot with 8 oz (227 g) butter or margarine. Cover and bake at 325 °F (165 °C) for 45 min. Stir occasionally.

Spices and Herbs for Lima Beans. Basil, marjoram, oregano, sage, savory, tarragon, or thyme.

Beets

Julienne Beets. Shred 8 lb (3.63 kg) cooked beets into thin strips. Season with mixture of 8 oz (227 g) butter or margarine, ½ c (120 mL) sugar, 4 t (20 mL) salt, and 1 c (240 mL) lemon juice.

Beets in Sour Cream. Grate fresh cooked beets and season with a mixture of 1½ c (360 mL) lemon juice, 1½ T (23 mL) onion juice, 2 t (10 mL) salt, and 1¼ c (300 mL) sugar. Toss lightly. Serve with a spoonful of cultured sour cream on each portion.

Spices and Herbs for Beets. Allspice, bay leaves, caraway seed, cloves, dill, ginger, mustard seed, savory, or thyme.

Broccoli

Almond-Buttered Broccoli. Brown slivered almonds in butter or margarine and pour over cooked and drained broccoli.

Broccoli with Hollandaise Sauce or Lemon Butter. Serve cooked spears or chopped broccoli with 1 T (15 mL) Hollandaise Sauce (p. 469) or 1 t (5 mL) lemon butter.

Spices and Herbs for Broccoli. Caraway seed, dill, mustard seed, or tarragon.

Cabbage

Red Cabbage Supreme. Shred finely 10 lb (4.54 kg) red cabbage. Combine with 3 lb (1.36 kg) pared, sliced, tart apples and 1½ lb (680 g) sliced onions. Add 1½ qt (1.42 L) water and cook until tender but still slightly crisp, about 30 min. Add 1¾ c (420 mL) vinegar, 2 T (30 mL) salt, and 4 oz (114 g) sugar. Toss lightly.

Spices and Herbs for Cabbage. Caraway seed, celery seed, dill, mint, mustard seed, nutmeg, savory, or tarragon.

Carrots

Carrots and Celery.   Combine 7 lb (3.18 kg) carrots and 3 lb (1.36 kg) celery sliced about the same thickness. Cook until tender and season with butter or margarine, salt, and pepper.

Spices and Herbs for Carrots.   Allspice, bay leaves, caraway seed, dill, fennel, ginger, mace, marjoram, mint, nutmeg, or thyme.

Cauliflower

Cauliflower with New Peas.   Combine 7 lb (3.18 kg) freshly cooked cauliflower with 5 lb (2.27 kg) cooked frozen peas. Season with melted butter or margarine.

Spices and Herbs for Cauliflower.   Caraway seed, celery salt, dill, mace, or tarragon.

Celery

Creole Celery.   Cook 5 lb (2.27 kg) diced celery until partially done. Add 1 lb (454 g) chopped onions and 4 oz (114 g) chopped green pepper that have been sautéed in 8 oz (227 g) butter or margarine. Add 2 No. 10 cans tomatoes and 1½ t (8 mL) salt. Cook until tender. Serve with 4-oz (114-g) ladle.

Corn

Corn in Cream.   Add 1¼ qt (1.18 L) light cream, 6 oz (170 g) butter or margarine, 2 T (30 mL) salt, and 1 T (15 mL) white pepper to 10 lb (4.54 kg) frozen whole-grain corn, cooked. Bring just to boiling point and serve immediately.

Corn O'Brien.   Drain 2 No. 10 cans whole-grain corn. Add 1 lb (454 g) chopped bacon, 12 oz (340 g) chopped green pepper, and 12 oz (340 g) chopped onion that has been sautéed until lightly browned. Just before serving, add 3 oz (85 g) chopped pimiento, salt, and pepper.

Mushrooms

Sautéed Mushrooms.   Clean thoroughly. Peel all but tender young caps. Sauté sliced or whole small mushrooms in butter or margarine. Allow 2 oz (57 g) butter or margarine for 1 lb (454 g) mushrooms.

Onions

Creamed Pearl Onions.   Cook 12½ lb (5.67 kg) tiny unpeeled white onions in boiling salted water until tender, drain, then peel. Add 2 qt (1.89 L) Medium White Sauce (p. 458) to which 4 oz (114 g) additional butter or margarine has been added. Garnish with paprika.

Spices and Herbs for Onions.   Caraway seed, mustard seed, nutmeg, oregano, sage, or thyme.

Parsnips

Browned Parsnips.   Place 10 lb (4.54 kg) cooked parsnips, cut lengthwise into uniform pieces, in baking pan. Sprinkle with 1½ T (23 mL) salt and 4 oz (114 g) sugar. Pour 8 oz (227 g) melted butter or margarine over top. Bake at 425 °F (220 °C) until browned.

Peas

Creamed New Potatoes and Peas.   Combine 7 lb (3.18 kg) freshly cooked new potatoes and 5 lb (2.27 kg) cooked frozen peas with 3 qt (2.84 L) Medium White Sauce (p. 458).

Green Peas and Sliced New Turnips.   Combine 5 lb (2.27 kg) frozen peas, cooked, with 3 lb (1.36 kg) new turnips, sliced and cooked. Add 8 oz (227 g) melted butter or margarine and salt to taste.

Green Peas with Pearl Onions.   Combine 7½ lb (3.4 kg) frozen peas, cooked, with 3 lb (1.36 kg) pearl onions, cooked. Add 8 oz (227 g) butter or margarine or 2 qt (1.89 L) Medium White Sauce (p. 458) to which 4 oz (114 g) extra butter or margarine has been added.

New Peas with Mushrooms.   Add 2 lb (908 g) fresh mushrooms, sliced, sautéed in 8 oz (227 g) butter or margarine, to 10 lb (4.54 kg) cooked frozen peas.

Peas with Lemon-Mint Butter.   Cream 1 lb (454 g) butter, ¼ c (60 mL) lemon juice, and 1 t (5 mL) grated lemon or orange rind. Add ½ c (120 mL) finely chopped fresh mint. The lemon-mint butter can be made ahead and stored in the refrigerator. When ready to use, melt and pour over hot peas.

Spices and Herbs for Peas.   Basil, dill, marjoram, mint, oregano, poppy seed, rosemary, sage, or savory.

Spinach

Wilted Spinach or Lettuce. To 10 lb (4.54 kg) chopped spinach or lettuce, or a combination of the two, add 2 qt (1.89 L) Hot Vegetable Sauce (p. 465) just before serving.

Spices and Herbs for Spinach. Basil, mace, marjoram, nutmeg, or oregano.

Squash

Mashed Butternut Squash. Cook 15 lb (6.80 kg) peeled butternut squash until tender. Mash and add 1½ qt (1.42 L) hot milk, 8 oz (227 g) butter or margarine, 2 T (30 mL) salt, and 8 oz (227 g) brown sugar. Whip until light. May be garnished with toasted slivered almonds.

Butternut Squash-Apple Casserole. Cook 8 lb (3.63 kg) pared, cored, and sliced apples, 12 oz (340 g) butter or margarine, and 12 oz (340 g) sugar until barely tender. Arrange in baking pans. Cover with mashed butternut squash (use only 10 lb/4.54 kg squash). Top with mixture of crushed cornflakes, chopped pecans, melted butter or margarine, and brown sugar. Bake.

Zucchini and Summer Squash. Wash and slice 5 lb (2.27 kg) zucchini and 5 lb (2.27 kg) yellow summer squash. Cook until just tender. Season with 8 oz (227 g) melted butter or margarine, salt and pepper to taste. Add 2 lb (908 g) cherry tomatoes just before serving.

Spices and Herbs for Squash. Allspice, basil, cinnamon, cloves, fennel, ginger, mustard seed, nutmeg, or rosemary.

Sweet Potatoes

Baked Sweet Potatoes. Select small even-sized sweet potatoes. Scrub and bake 40-45 min, or until done, at 425 °F (220 °C).

Spices and Herbs for Sweet Potatoes. Allspice, cardamom, cinnamon, cloves, or nutmeg.

Tomatoes

Breaded Tomatoes. Add 1 lb (454 g) cubed bread, 8 oz (227 g) butter or margarine, and ¾ c (180 mL) sugar to 2 No. 10 cans tomatoes. Bake approximately 30 min at 350 °F (175 °C).

Creole Tomatoes.   Drain 2 No. 10 cans tomatoes. To the juice add 1 lb (454 g) celery, 4 oz (114 g) onion, and 8 oz (227 g) green pepper, coarsely chopped. Cook about 15 min. Add the tomatoes, 2 T (30 mL) salt, and ¾ t (4 mL) pepper and place in greased baking pan. Cover with 2 qt (1.89 L) toasted bread cubes and bake about 30 min at 350 °F (175 °C).

Spices and Herbs for Tomatoes.   Basil, bay leaves, celery seed, oregano, sage, sesame seed, tarragon, or thyme.

Turnips

Mashed White Turnips.   Cook 15 lb (6.8 kg) turnips, drain, and mash as potatoes. Season with 8 oz (227 g) butter or margarine, 1 T (15 mL) salt, ½ t (3 mL) pepper, and 1 c (240 mL) hot milk or cream.

Part

3

MENU PLANNING

Considerations in Menu Planning

A carefully planned menu is the initial step toward a successful meal. It should provide food for adequate nutrition, tempt the appetite, and result in satisfaction for the guest. For the foodservice, the menu will predetermine the work to be done and largely control the resulting profit or loss. So important is the menu that, without it, there will be no successful foodservice.

Factors basic to menu planning may therefore be divided into two areas: those relating to the clientele and those relating to the foodservice management. The first includes age, sex, and occupation of the group, their nutritional needs, food preferences, and willingness to pay. The second deals with the type of foodservice, number to be served, the food budget, equipment available, number and experience of employees, distribution of work, and availability and seasonability of foods.

Meals outside of the home are eaten in widely diversified places such as school foodservices, child care centers, university cafeterias and residence halls, hospitals, extended care facilities, retirement complexes, industrial and commercial cafeterias, and many types of restaurants. Each of these services is planned to meet the needs of a particular clientele. To insure that a menu will meet the demands of the customer, careful consideration must be given to each of the following factors.

Factors Relating to the Clientele

1. *Age, Sex, and Occupation of Group to be Served.* The menu planner must consider the age, sex, occupation, nutritional needs, food habits, and preferences of the individual members of the group.

   In a situation in which a limited choice of food is offered, as in extended care facilities, child care centers, and retirement complexes, meals must be planned to meet the complete nutritional needs of members of the group and also offer enough variety to minimize monotony and meet, in so far as possible, their food preferences. Including foods from each of the four basic food groups, milk, meat, vegetables and fruits, and bread, in quantities sufficient for the age group will help to provide for their nutritional needs.

   Wherever a multiple choice of foods is offered, care must be taken to provide foods from which the individual patron may choose a well-balanced meal. The choice also must include enough variety to make it possible to select a meal that the patron will enjoy at a price he or she wishes to pay.

Racial, religious, and regional food preferences are important to many individuals and should be considered when planning meals for a group. More and more people, for one reason or another, are following a vegetarian regimen. It is possible to accommodate these individuals in group feeding by offering 1 or more vegetable entrées and a variety of vegetables and fruits. However, care must be given to the selection of the vegetables and accompanying foods to prevent deficiencies of certain essential food elements. A strict vegetarian diet is likely to be missing some essential amino acids and vitamins. If eggs and milk are included, an adequate nutritional balance is more easily obtained.

Planning menus that are acceptable to a group requires that the menu planner be aware of the food preferences of the group and periodically evaluate the acceptance of the foods and food combinations offered.

2. *Climate and Season.* The factor of climate and season is important in the choice of foods. Cool, crisp, fresh foods are often more appealing in hot weather, but at least 1 hot food should be included in each summer menu. In cold weather, the heavier foods high in caloric value may be used. A festive touch may be added on holidays and other special occasions by including foods not served regularly and by adding unusual garnishes and special decorations.

3. *Flavor and Appearance of the Food.* Flavor combinations should receive special consideration. A balance should be maintained between tart and sweet, mild and highly flavored, light and heavy foods. Certain flavors seem to belong together and, if carefully selected, will complement each other. Care must be taken, however, to avoid stereotyped combinations. Foods of the same or similar flavor, such as tomato soup and tomato salad, should not be repeated in 1 menu. A definite contrast in flavor between the foods of different courses is desirable. Tart foods, such as grapefruit, stimulate the appetite and digestion. They are used effectively as a first course or with a bland entrée. Sweet foods are satiating and should be used sparingly. They are served to best advantage as dessert.

Foods selected for a menu should be of harmonious colors that present an inviting appearance on the plate, hospital tray, or cafeteria counter. Just as uninteresting, colorless meals are to be avoided, so should those including foods that clash in color, such as beets and tomatoes. When planning menus for a cafeteria or a buffet meal, foods that are to be displayed together, such as vegetables, salads, or desserts, should offer a pleasing color contrast.

Contrast in shape and form of different foods appearing on a plate likewise lends interest to the meal. Variety in preparation makes it possible to present food shaped in varied forms and sizes. Care should be taken to avoid too many mixed foods of similar shape at the same meal, such as beef stew, mixed vegetables, tossed green salad, and fruit cup. Indiscriminate use of the dippers when serving may cause all the food to assume the shape of tennis balls. A suitable sauce or garnish may be used effectively to give an appearance of unity to the plate.

There should be balance between soft and solid foods. A soft entrée calls for a crisp vegetable or salad. A mashed or creamed vegetable may be served more successfully with a solid meat than with a casserole dish. Two foods prepared in the same manner, such as creamed, buttered, fried, or mashed, should not be served together.

4. *Variety*. Variety is introduced not only in the kind of food, but also in the method of preparation, combinations, textures, and garnishes. With the exception of staples, the same food should not be served too often or repeated on the same day of each week. If the same food must be served often, a change in the method of preparation and the accompanying foods will give desired variety.

Factors Relating to Management

The menu planner, in considering the needs and wishes of the consumer, must also be aware of the problems of management that affect the food offerings. These factors include:

1. *Type of Foodservice*. The menu pattern will be influenced by the type of foodservice. The cafeteria meal planned for the school child will be different from the menu offered in a restaurant catering to business executives.

2. *Number to Be Served*. Besides affecting the variety of food that can be included in the menu, the number to be served also influences the method of preparing the food. For example, it may be difficult, under some institutional conditions, to prepare grilled tomatoes or stuffed baked potatoes for a large group.

3. *The Food Budget*. The amount of income allotted for raw food cost and labor is a determining factor in the type of menu that can be planned and served. The menu planner should not only know how much money is available for food and labor, but should check this amount against the actual cost of the menu as served.

4. *Available Equipment*. To prepare suitable meals with the available equipmnt in a given length of time presents one of the major problems of those re-

sponsible for planning menus. Special attention needs to be given to oven capacity, refrigerator facilities, number and size of steam-jacketed kettles and steamers, and availability and capacity of mixers. Certain combinations of menu items often must be avoided because of lack of pans or dishes.

5. *Number and Experience of Employees*. The man-hours of labor available and the efficiency and skill of employees are important to the successful preparation of any meal. When there is a lack of experienced workers, the menu items must be limited to simple, easily prepared foods.

6. *Distribution of Work*. The distribution of work among the various areas of preparation is of prime importance in meeting a time schedule and in maintaining the morale of the workers. In determining a day's work load, the menu planner needs to consider not only 1 day's menu but any prepreparation necessary for meals for the following day or for several days. Food prepared by the salad and bakery departments are often of the type that require long-time preparation and must be carefully scheduled to equalize the load. On days when the work load is light, some foods may be prepared and stored in the freezer for future use.

The wise planner will make it possible to spread the employee's work load so that a limited number of foods requiring long, time-consuming preparation may be included. To add interest to the menu, foods such as stuffed baked potato, individual salads, fresh grapefruit sections, fresh fruit plates, homemade noodles, and tarts may be included in a menu if combined with other food items that require minimum preparation. The wide variety of ready-to-cook frozen foods, preprepared vegetables, and other convenience foods now makes possible a less restricted menu than can be offered when all food preparation is done in the kitchen. Discrimination in the selection and use of many of the prepared foods is needed to maintain high food standards and to preserve the individuality of the foodservice.

Some foods, including fresh and frozen vegetables, mashed potatoes, hot breads, and certain meats and fish, require last-minute cooking to assure products of high quality. To avoid confusion and delayed meal service, the menu should be so planned that there is a balance between items that may be prepared early and those that must be cooked just prior to serving.

7. *Availability and Seasonability of Foods*. Availability of foods in the local markets will exert a limited influence on the menu items. Although most foods are now available in fresh or frozen form in all sections of the country, fresh foods produced locally are often of better quality and less expensive during the growing season than those shipped from distant markets.

8. *Cooked Foods on Hand*. Unused cooked foods more often are used to effect changes in a menu than as the basis of the original menu. However,

the successful use of foods on hand requires careful thought and imagination to incorporate them in such a way that they will be acceptable. Foods should be used promptly and properly stored until used.

Some foods may be offered in their original form as a choice on a selective menu. Others may be incorporated into combinations such as casseroles, hash, meat roll, barbecued sandwiches, and croquettes. These dishes are often better made from cooked foods than from raw. Cooked vegetables, which should be reused sparingly, may be included in salads and casserole dishes. If suitable, they may be used in soup, or ground and combined with meat loaf or other luncheon entrées. Fresh fruits may be used in fruit cup, gelatins, or mixed salads, and stewed fruits may be combined in an appetizing compote. Cake and bread crumbs often are utilized in puddings, cakes and cookies, and for breading. However used, the food product must be prepared in such a way that it is as acceptable in the combined form as in its original state.

9. *Recipes*. Many a well-planned menu has been a failure because sufficient thought was not given to the selection of recipes. Cooks should be provided with standardized recipes, so that there will be no questions as to the yield or quality of the finished product. If deviations from the original recipes are necessary, great care should be exercised in making substitutions that may affect both quality and yield.

Menu Planning Procedures

The effectiveness of menu planning is largely influenced by the attitudes and ability of the planner, who should recognize that the task is an important one requiring imagination, creative ability, and a deep interest in food. It is important that the menu maker be free of prejudices and food dislikes. Menu planning should not be regarded as a routine duty, but as an opportunity to work through the medium of food to present a three-dimensional picture of food that is attractive, nutritionally sound, and satisfying to the taste.

If at all possible, the menu should be planned during uninterrupted time in a place away from noise and confusion, and at a desk or table large enough to accommodate menu-planning materials. These include:

1. Menu forms as dictated by type and needs of foodservice.

2. Standardized recipe file.

3. Cookbooks, for large- and small-quantity cookery.

4.   Periodicals, institutional and household.

5.   Idea file of pictures and other material clipped from magazines.

6.   Menu suggestion lists, as shown on pp. 580-593.

7.   File of previous menus.

The Planning Cycle

Menus should be planned at least 1 week in advance. Some menu planners prefer a 10-day planning cycle to eliminate the possibility of repeating foods on the same day each week. The trend in institutional meal planning is toward the construction and use of cycle or rotating menus. Such a set of menus is planned well in advance of the time it is to be used and is rotated at predetermined intervals.

Although many factors influence the length of the cycle, many institutions find a cycle of 3-5 weeks satisfactory. School, college, and university foodservices that serve the same clientele for extended periods of time may find it desirable to use a longer cycle than would a hospital, in which the average patient stay is only a few days. With the trend in many institutions toward operating a foodservice with a reduced staff on weekends, a 5-day cycle, with separate weekend cycles, may be useful. To ensure serving of foods that are appropriate to the season, many foodservices have a slightly different cycle for each of the 4 seasons.

Thoughtfully planned menus may be rotated successfully and have many advantages over short-time planning. Such a procedure results in keeping repetition of foods at a minimum, and it aids in the control of food and labor costs. It further facilitates food purchasing, reduces waste, and provides for the effective use of employees' time. Most important, rotating menus are time-saving for the dietitian or foodservice manager, since their use greatly reduces the time spent in menu planning and food ordering. Carefully planned menus offer variety and interest in meals and bring greater satisfaction to patrons or guests. Interest may be added to cycle menus by varying the cookery methods of frequently recurring foods. The cycle menu must be flexible enough to allow for holidays and special functions. To be successful, cycle menus should be reviewed periodically, especially when first developed, to eliminate unpopular combinations and production problems before the menu cycle is repeated.

Menu Pattern

The menu pattern is the outline of food items to be served each meal. A *set* menu consists of a single food item in each menu category, whereas a *selective* or *multiple-choice* menu includes one or more choices in each category.

Menu Planning Form

Menus should be written on a form suited to the needs of the foodservice and should be large enough to contain all food items for the period being planned. Space often is allowed for the insertion of leftovers and last-minute changes of menu items. Notation of acceptance of each food product may be noted and filed for future reference.

Steps in Menu Planning

1. Select menu items systematically, following a definite pattern, about in the following order.

   a. *Meat or Other Entrée*. First, determine the entrées for the entire time for which the menus are being planned, whether for a 1-week or multiple-week cycle. Many managers who plan weekly menus like to schedule the entrées for a longer period, 4 weeks or more. When this has been completed, plan the remainder of each meal around the meat or other main dish. In a multiple-choice menu, the entrées may consist of a roast or other "solid" meat, meat extender, poultry, fish, and a vegetarian entrée. Where no choice is offered, the meat or other main dish must be varied from day to day. Variety may be obtained through the use of different kinds of meat and different cuts and forms, such as roasts, cutlets, chops, ground and cubed meat, and vegetarian entrées. Beef, veal, pork, lamb, poultry, fish, and variety meats may be prepared and served in many interesting ways to offer a wide variety in appearance and flavor.

   b. *Vegetables*. Vegetables appropriate to serve with the planned entrées should be considered next. Although there are a few widely accepted staple vegetables that necessarily must be repeated often, variety may be obtained through varied methods of preparation. Maximum use should be made of fresh vegetables when in season.

   c. *Salads*. The choice of salads is of great importance in adding color, texture, flavor, nutritional value and interest to the menu. There should be a well-balanced distribution of fruit, vegetable, and gelatin salads. Combinations are almost unlimited, and care should be taken to serve a dressing and a garnish that will complement the salad ingredients. On a cafeteria menu, certain basic salads are usually offered daily. These might include head lettuce, combination vegetable salads, relishes, and cottage cheese.

   d. *Bread*. A standard assortment of breads and one or more hot breads are usually offered. Available oven space may be a limiting factor in offering a choice of hot breads.

e. *Desserts*. Dessert is the last item of the dinner and luncheon menu to be planned. The type of dessert offered depends on the other menu items. Where no choice is offered, a light dessert should be served with a heavy main course and a rich dessert with a light main course. When a choice is to be offered, it is customary to plan a 2-crust pie, soft pie, cake, pudding, and gelatin dessert. In addition, ice creams and fruits are usually offered daily.

Complete the menu by adding beverages, first course items, if one is to be served, and breakfast items. Variety in the breakfast menu may be introduced through a choice of entrées, hot breads, fruits, and fruit juices.

2. Check the menu. After the menu has been planned, it should be carefully checked to see if it has met the established criteria.
a. Check for repetition by reviewing each day's meals and then comparing them with the previous and following day's menus.
b. Compare with the previous menu cycle to avoid serving food items on the same day each week. The completed menu should, if possible, have a predominance of familiar and well-accepted menu items, with the introduction of new and less well-liked foods spaced throughout the menu period. In nonselective menus particularly, it is important that the less popular foods be accompanied by foods that are well liked by the majority of the customers.
c. Check individual meals for flavor, texture, and shape combinations.
d. Check for nutritional adequacy in set menus.
e. Check individual meals and daily menus for balance in work loads.
f. Check for scheduling of use of equipment.

3. Evaluate the menu after it has been served and make notations of satisfactory menus and difficulties encountered in production and service of the meals. If it is a cycle menu, make desired alterations. The responsibility of the menu planner does not end with the writing of the menu. The task is completed only when the food has been prepared and served, the reaction of the consumer noted, and the relationship of raw food and labor costs to selling price recorded.

Points to Remember in Menu Planning

1. Leave nothing to chance. Be specific when recording menus. For example, pork chops should be shown as barbecued, stuffed, breaded, or whatever method of preparation is desired.

2. Avoid too many foods with accompaniments, sauces, and garnishes. This will increase the work load and may complicate the service.

3. Watch for "hidden" methods of preparation for different food items; the name may not always be descriptive of the method. For example, breaded pork chops, ham croquettes, cheese balls, browned potatoes, and French fried onion rings are all fried foods, but only one is so indicated by name.

4. Watch for repetition as menus are being developed. Strive for variety through the use of good basic standardized recipes and different methods of presentation, garnishes, and sauces. The menu maker should be aware of ingredients used in all recipes to avoid repetition of any one food. Sunshine salad, vegetable soup, braised liver, vegetable cheese pie, buttered carrot strips, and frozen mixed vegetables all contain carrots, although "carrots" appear in the name of only 1 menu item.

5. Avoid food clichés. Food combinations such as ham and pineapple, pork and apples, are highly acceptable, but should not always be served together. New combinations add interest to the menu.

6. Check completed menu carefully for all factors basic to successful menu planning.

Recording the Menu

After the menu has been planned, a production or work sheet should be developed for each kitchen work center. The food item, recipe, number of servings, time of preparation, sauces, gravies, accompaniments and specific directions for serving should be indicated.

The menu as presented to the consumer will be in a different form from that designed for the preparation and service areas. In preparing the customer's menu, follow these two widely accepted rules: (1) list food items in the order of service, and (2) capitalize all words except prepositions and conjunctions.

In many cases, the menu card is the customer's or patient's preview of the food and service he or she can expect. This emphasizes the importance of the appearance and wording of the menu. Suggestions for writing a menu card are:

1. List the main dish of each course across the center of the sheet. Write 1 accompaniment on the line below, on the right side or in the center. If there are 2 accompaniments, place 1 at the right and 1 at the left on the line below.

Cream of Mushroom Soup
Melba Toast

Cream of Mushroom Soup
Celery Sticks   Melba Toast

2. If more accompaniments are served, balance on sheet.

Breaded Veal Cutlet
Parsley Creamed Potatoes   Buttered Asparagus
Tossed Vegetable Salad
Butterhorn Rolls   Raspberry Jelly
Mocha Almond Frozen Pie
Coffee

3. Write beverage at the bottom of the menu or with the course with which it is to be served.

4. Do not include on the written menu accompaniments such as cream and sugar and salt and pepper or condiments such as mustard, catsup, and vinegar.

5. Use wording that is as descriptive as possible and use terms to indicate the method of preparation, such as candied or honey-glazed. The method of preparation or some descriptive term always should be used for each item on the written menu.

Menus for Schools and Child Care Centers

School Foodservice

The school lunch program has expanded rapidly since the National School Lunch Act was passed by Congress in 1946 and is now an integral part of the total educational program of elementary and secondary schools. The objective of the school lunch program is to serve nutritionally adequate, attractive, and moderately priced lunches. The nutritional goal is to furnish at least one-third of the Recommended Daily Dietary Allowances of the National Research Council for children of various age groups. The original legislation was broadened in subsequent amendments to provide a special milk program, a school breakfast program, and a special foodservice program for children.

Most school foodservices use the Type A lunch pattern, in which foods are selected from the five groups listed below, although alternative methods of planning are being tried. The Type A lunch requirements provide the framework for nutritionally adequate school lunches. The kinds and amounts of foods listed in the Type A pattern are based on the Recommended Daily Dietary Allowances for children 10-12 years of age.

As specified in the National School Lunch Regulations, a Type A lunch shall contain as a minimum:

1. *Fluid Whole Milk:* ½ pt of fluid whole milk as a beverage.

2. *Protein-Rich Foods:* 2 oz (edible portion as served) of lean meat, poultry, or fish; or 2 oz of cheese; or 1 egg, ½ c of cooked dry beans or dry peas; or 4 T of peanut butter; or an equivalent quantity of any combination of the above-listed foods. To be counted in meeting this requirement, these foods must be served in a main dish or in a main dish and one other menu item.

3. *Vegetables and Fruits:* ¾ c serving consisting of two or more vegetables or fruits or both. A serving (¼ c or more) of full-strength vegetable or fruit juice may be counted to meet not more than ¼ c of this requirement.

4. *Bread:* 1 slice of whole-grain or enriched bread; or a serving of other bread such as cornbread, biscuits, rolls, muffins, made of whole-grain or enriched meal or flour.

5. *Butter or Fortified Margarine:* 1 t butter or fortified margarine.

Lesser quantities of the protein-rich foods, the vegetables and fruits, and butter or margarine may be served to children in the elementary grades, provided that such adjustments are based on the lesser food needs of younger children.

To help assure that all Type A lunches meet the nutritional goal, it is recommended that lunches include:

1. A vitamin C food each day.

2. A vitamin A food twice a week.

3. Several foods for iron each day and larger portions of some of these when possible.

To participate in the breakfast program, schools must agree to serve nourishing breakfasts based on USDA nutrition standards. These include fruit or juice, milk, bread or cereal, with a meat or meat alternate served as often as possible.

In addition to meeting the nutritive requirements, meals served in the school should provide satisfaction and pleasure to the pupil and help in the development of good eating habits. Planning menus that meet the nutritive requirements and are attractive, appetizing, and palatable at a price that pupils can afford to pay presents a challenge to the ability of those responsible for this function of the program.

The major factors to be considered by those planning school menus include: variety in texture, color, flavor, and methods of preparation; use of foods in season; number, ability, and experience of personnel; amount and adequacy of equipment and space; time available for food preparation; food habits of the group to be served; nutritional requirements of the students; and amount of money available. Age of the students is also important. As a rule, very young children like plain, identifiable, well-cooked, easy to eat, food that is free from strong flavors.

The cycle menu is used to some extent in school foodservices, and some schools are using multiple-choice menus in which students may select from 2 items of comparable nutritional value for part of the menu; for example, a student may have a choice of 2 vegetables and 2 or more desserts. Some schools offer multiple menus in which more than 1 complete menu is offered, such as a soup and sandwich meal that meets requirements for the Type A lunch and a plate lunch. Some junior and senior high schools offer à la carte menus.

Many foods on the Menu Planning Suggestions list on pp. 580-593 are suitable for school lunches, keeping in mind the nutritional requirements, cost, labor and equipment restraints, and food preferences of the age group to be served. Among the menu items generally well accepted by students are: fried chicken, barbecued spareribs, turkey, beef stew, pizza, spaghetti, lasagne, chili, hamburgers, frankfurters in buns, hot meat sandwiches, French fried potatoes, corn, sliced tomatoes, oranges, orange juice, fresh fruit and fruit salads, ice cream, milk shakes, milk, pies, cakes, and cookies.

Suggested *nonselective* lunch menus are given on p. 552. The nonselective menu is to be found primarily in elementary schools. Older children usually find *selective* menus more acceptable. Many students who have not been exposed to a variety of foods are reluctant to try unfamiliar menu items. Giving these students some choice reduces plate waste and fosters a more positive attitude toward school foodservices. Offering choices is especially desirable when a less popular item is on the menu.

The suggested nonselective menu could be expanded by an additional entrée and a choice of vegetables or by offering a soup and sandwich menu in addition to the plate lunch. In planning a selective menu, care must be taken to offer choices that will contribute equally to the Type A nutritional requirements.

SUGGESTED SCHOOL LUNCH MENUS[a]

1	2	3	4	5	6	7	8
Tomato Juice	Fried Chicken	Pizza	Split Pea Soup	Hungarian Goulash	Fish Squares—Tartar Sauce	Chili—Crackers	Cheese-Stuffed Wieners
Beef Stew with Vegetables	Mashed Potato—Gravy	Buttered Broccoli	Grilled Cheese Sandwich	Buttered Noodles	Scalloped Potatoes	Celery Sticks	Potato Puffs
Pineapple-Marshmallow Salad	Creamy Cole Slaw	Tossed Green Salad	Broiled Tomato	Buttered Lima Beans	Wilted Lettuce	Corn Bread—Butter	Stewed Tomatoes
Hot Biscuits—Butter	Cinnamon Roll	Bread—Butter	Crisp Carrot Strips	Raisin Muffin	Hot Rolls—Butter	Canned Pear—Chocolate Chip Cookie	Honey Buns
Ice Cream	Sliced Peaches	Baked Apple	Chocolate Pudding	Fruit Cup	Cherry Cobbler	Milk	Pineapple Upside-Down Cake
Milk	Milk	Milk	Milk	Milk	Milk		Milk

1	2	3	4	5	6	7	8
Barbecued Chicken	Cheese Soup	Lasagne	Turkey Salad on a Bun	Salmon Loaf	Hamburger on a Bun	Pot Roast—Gravy	Spaghetti with Meat Sauce
Steamed Rice	Submarine Sandwich	Buttered Green Beans	French Fried Potatoes	Creamed Peas	Scalloped Corn	Browned Potato	Buttered Green Beans
Buttered Peas	Molded Fruit Salad	Relishes	Buttered Carrot Rings	Citrus Salad	Sliced Tomato	Buttered Squash	Spinach and Lettuce Salad
Lettuce—Thousand Island Dressing	Snickerdoodles	French Bread Butter	Fruit Crisp	Kolaches	Fruit Gelatine	Apple-Celery Salad	Whole Wheat Rolls Butter
Blueberry Muffin	Milk	Assorted Fresh Fruit	Milk	Oatmeal Cookie	Milk	Orange Rolls	Sherbet
Applesauce		Milk		Milk		Brownie	Milk
Milk						Milk	

[a] Nonselective Type A lunches. May be expanded to multiple choice menu by adding a second vegetable and dessert; or offering a soup and sandwich option.

SUGGESTED MENUS FOR YOUNG CHILDREN[a] BASED ON MEAL REQUIREMENTS FOR CHILDREN 3-6 YEARS

Pattern	First Day	Second Day	Third Day	Fourth Day	Fifth Day
Breakfast					
Juice or fruit	Orange juice—½ c	Sliced banana—½ c	Apricot halves—½ c	Fruit cup—½ c	Grapefruit sections—½ c
Cereal or bread	Toast—½ slice	Cornflakes—⅓ c	Buttered toast—½ slice	Toast—½ slice	Rolled oats—⅓ c
Milk	Milk—¾ c	Milk—¾ c	Cocoa—¾ c	Milk—¾ c	Milk—¾ c
Other food	Baked scrambled egg—2 T Grape jelly			Hard-cooked egg half	
A.M. Supplement					
Milk or juice	Milk—½ c	Tomato juice—½ c	Milk—½ c	Pineapple juice—½ c	Grape juice—½ c
Bread or cereal	Cinnamon toast—½ slice	Cheese toast—½ slice	Rice Krispies—⅓ c	Toasted raisin bread—½ slice	Cinnamon toast—½ slice
Lunch or supper					
Meat or alternate	Meat loaf—1½ oz	Baked chicken—1½ oz meat	Chicken-vegetable soup—½ c (1 oz meat)	Beef patty—1½ oz	Fish sticks—1½ oz
Vegetables and/or fruits	Green beans—¼ c Pineapple cubes—¼ c	Mashed potatoes—¼ c Peas—¼ c Carrot stick	Green pepper stick Canned peaches—¼ c	Carrots—⅜ c Apple wedge—⅛ c	Spinach—¼ c Canned pears—¼ c
Bread	Bread—½ slice	Roll, small	Peanut butter and jelly sandwich—1 T peanut butter	Whole wheat bread—½ slice	Corn bread—1 square
Butter/margarine	Butter—½ t	Butter—½ t		Butter—½ t	Butter—½ t
Milk	Milk—¾ c	Milk—¾ c	Milk—¾ c	Milk—¾ c	Milk—¾ c
Other foods				Chocolate pudding—2 T	
P.M. Supplement					
Milk or juice	Mixed fruit juice—½ c	Milk—½ c	Apple juice—½ c	Milk—½ c	Milk—½ c
Bread or cereal	Peanut butter sandwich—¼	Oatmeal cookie—1	Cheese toast—½ slice	Peanut butter cookie—1 Turnip stick	Rolled wheat cookie—1 Cauliflowerets

[a] From *A Guide for Planning Food Service in Child Care Centers*, FNS 64, Food and Nutrition Service, U.S. Department of Agriculture, Washington, D.C., 1971.

Child Care Centers

An amendment to the National School Lunch Act provides assistance to eligible foodservices for preschool and school-age children in day care centers, settlement houses, recreation centers, and summer day camps. In planning food for children in these centers, the total daily food requirements of children should be considered. The combination of meals and snacks will vary according to the age group, their time of arrival at the center, and their length of stay. It is important that the planner consider the nutritional needs of the children, their food preferences, regional food habits, and equipment, personnel, and other management functions.

Young children need nutritious foods at frequent intervals, but it is important to schedule the service of food to allow sufficient time between meals and supplements. Suggested menus are given on p. 553. Young children enjoy food they can easily handle. Finger food, snacks, and bite-sized pieces are most popular. Apple wedges, banana slices, berries, dried peaches or pears, fresh peach, pear, or pineapple wedges, grapefruit or orange sections, pitted plums and prunes, raisins, cabbage wedges, carrot and celery sticks, cauliflowerets, tomato wedges, cheese cubes, crackers or rusks with peanut butter or cheese, and small sandwiches are examples of finger foods.

Those responsible for foodservice in child care centers should provide the opportunity for children to learn to eat and enjoy a variety of nutritious foods.

Menus for College and University Foodservices

Meals for college and university students may be provided in individual residence halls, large residence hall food centers, university cafeterias, student unions, or smaller living groups.

Residence Halls

The daily menu in a college or university residence hall must be adequate to meet the nutritional needs of the residents. The number to be served is fairly constant, so amounts may be carefully planned; this results in little or no waste. Most residence halls offer some degree of choice in their menus, and many use 4-6 week cycles in their planning.

Foodservice in residence halls generally offers a choice of two or more items in each menu category. Certain salad items, such as tossed salad, cottage cheese, fruit, and gelatin, may be offered each day on a salad bar. Likewise, fresh fruit and soft ice cream may be served each meal, with special desserts added for variety. The trend in residence hall foodservice is toward more variety, more self-service, and informality. Special meals depicting certain themes, such as Hawaiian, Oriental, or German, regional specialties, and ethnic foods are popular. Fast food lines that serve soup and salads, hamburgers and French fries, submarines, or pizza are well liked by students and make it possible for them to eat in a short span of time.

There is little difference in menus planned for men and women. In many universities meals are served to both men and women in a central foodservice. Some selection of menu items and adjustment in size of servings enables the same menus to be served to both men and women students.

SUGGESTED MENU OUTLINE FOR A RESIDENCE HALL

Breakfast	Nonselective Menu Lunch			Dinner
	I	or	II	
Fruit	Main dish		Soup	Main meat dish
Cereal, hot and/or cold	Vegetable		Sandwich	Potato or other starchy vegetable
	Salad or relish		Salad	
Protein dish	Bread, butter		Dessert	Vegetable
Sweet roll or hot bread	Fruit or other light dessert		Milk, tea, or coffee	Salad, ice, or relishes
Toast, jelly	Milk, tea, or coffee			Bread, butter
Coffee, cocoa, tea, or milk				Dessert
				Coffee, tea, or milk

Breakfast	Selective Menu Lunch	Dinner
Fruit or juice (2)	Soup or juice	Meat or other entrée (at least 2; often one is vegetarian)
Assorted cold cereal	Sandwich	
Hot cereal	Hearty salad or salad plate	
Protein dish	Hot main dish	Potato or substitute
Toast, jelly	Salads (2 or more)	Vegetables (2)
Sweet roll, doughnut, or coffee cake	Desserts (2 or more)	Salads (2 or more)
	Milk, tea, or coffee	Desserts (2 or more)
Coffee, cocoa, tea, or milk		Coffee, tea, or milk

Certain standard menu items may be offered every day, such as cottage cheese, peanut butter, tossed vegetable or head lettuce salad, fresh or canned fruit, yogurt, and ice cream. An assortment of breads and beverages would also be offered daily. A week's menus for a residence hall is given on pp. 557-558.

DAILY RECOMMENDED FOOD ALLOWANCES FOR
COLLEGE STUDENTS

1 citrus fruit
2 vegetables in addition to potatoes, 1 of which should be green or yellow and 1 raw
1 pt or more milk per person, in addition to that used in cooking
Fresh fruit
3 whole-grain or enriched cereals, including bread
2 protein foods
   1 meat dish
   1 dish including eggs, cheese, beans, or meat extender
1 T or more butter or fortified margarine
1 egg, or 4 weekly in addition to those used in cooking

SELECTIVE MENUS FOR A COLLEGE OR UNIVERSITY RESIDENCE HALL

BREAKFAST

Monday	Tuesday	Wednesday	Thursday	Friday	Saturday	Sunday
Assorted Fruits	Assorted Fruits	Assorted Fruits	Assorted Fruits	Assorted Fruits	Assorted Fruits	Assorted Fruits
Hot or Cold Cereal	Hot or Cold Cereal	Hot or Cold Cereal	Hot or Cold Cereal	Hot or Cold Cereal	Hot or Cold Cereal	Hot or Cold Cereal
Bacon Slices	French Toast Syrup	Hard and Soft-Cooked Eggs	Poached Eggs	Pancakes—Syrup	Bacon	Toast—Jelly
Scrambled Eggs	Toast—Jelly	Toast—Jelly	Toast—Jelly	Link Sausages	Fried Eggs	Sweet Rolls
Toast—Jelly	Coffee, Cocoa, Milk	Coffee Cake	Sweet Rolls	Toast—Jelly	Toast—Jelly	Coffee, Cocoa, Milk
Sweet Rolls		Coffee, Cocoa, Milk	Coffee, Cocoa, Milk	Coffee, Cocoa, Milk	Bishop's Bread	
Coffee, Cocoa, Milk					Coffee, Cocoa, Milk	

LUNCH

Monday	Tuesday	Wednesday	Thursday	Friday	Saturday	Sunday
Cream of Tomato Soup	Cream of Mushroom Soup	Pepper Pot Soup	Vegetable Beef Soup	Chicken Velvet Soup	Bean Soup	Chilled Fruit Juice
Macaroni and Cheese or Hamburger—Bun	Chicken Pie or Submarine Sandwich—Potato Chips	Spaghetti with Meat Sauce or Chef's Salad	Tuna-Potato Chip Casserole or Reuben Sandwich	Bacon, Lettuce, and Tomato Sandwich or Plantation Shortcake	Pizza or Fresh Fruit Plate	Roast Pork Loin
Buttered Limas	Head Lettuce Salad	Buttered Italian Green Beans	Beets in Orange Sauce	Head Lettuce Salad or Fruit Gelatin Salad	Fresh Spinach Salad or Cottage Cheese	Mashed Potatoes—Gravy
Relish Plate or Pineapple-Banana-Orange Salad	Cucumbers in Sour Cream	Citrus Fruit Salad	Carrifruit Salad or Pear Salad	Caramel Custard	Butterscotch Drop Cookie	French Green Beans Amandine or Browned Parsnips
Brownies	Peach Crisp	Oatmeal Cookie	Tapioca Cream	Beverages	Beverages	Applesauce Mold Salad or Fresh Fruit Salad
Beverages	Beverages	Beverages	Beverages			Kolaches
						Frozen Filled Angel Food Cake
						Beverages

SELECTIVE MENUS FOR A COLLEGE OR UNIVERSITY RESIDENCE HALL

DINNER

Monday	Tuesday	Wednesday	Thursday	Friday	Saturday	Sunday
Roast Beef	Breaded Veal	Swiss Steak or	Fried Chicken	Fisherman's	Barbequed Ribs	
Browned Pota-	Cutlets or	Ham Patty on	Rice Pilaff	Plate or	or	
toes—Gravy	Braised Liver	Pineapple	Buttered Aspar-	Salisbury	Mushroom	
Cauliflower—	Creamed Pota-	Baked Potato	agus or	Steak—	Quiche	
Cheese Sauce	toes	Broccoli Aman-	Buttered Mixed	Mushroom	Parsley But-	
or Green	Breaded Toma-	dine or	Vegetables	Sauce	tered Pota-	
Beans South-	toes or But-	Buttered Whole	Molded Cran-	French Fries	toes	
ern Style	tered Peas	Kernel Corn	berry Salad or	Zucchini Italian	Buttered Car-	
Tossed Green	Stuffed Celery	Head Lettuce	Fresh Spinach	or Buttered	rots or Brus-	
Salad or	or Spicy	Salad or	Salad	Peas	sels Sprouts	
Fruit Salad	Apricot Mold	Beet Pickles	Cloverleaf Rolls	Creamy Cole	Sliced Tomato	
Dinner Rolls	Fan Tan Rolls	Vienna Bread	Cheese Cake	Slaw or	Salad or Head	
Pumpkin Pie	Strawberry	Apple Dump-	Beverages	Salad Greens	Lettuce Salad	
Beverages	Sundae or	ling		with Grape-	Sesame Seed	
	Coconut Cake	Beverages		fruit	Rolls	
	Beverages			Hard Rolls	Fruit Cup or	
				Cherry Cobbler	German	
				Beverages	Chocolate	
					Cake	
					Beverages	

Fruit, yogurt, and ice cream offered daily in addition to desserts listed.

Cafeterias and Student Unions

Additional foodservice is offered by many universities in cafeterias, student unions, coffee shops, or other types of food operations. The cafeteria may be required to be open 20-24 hr a day, 7 days a week. The choice of food items at meal hours resembles the typical cafeteria menu and usually includes a wider range of choices than does the residence hall foodservice. Snacks and short orders fill the need for off-hour operation. Many of these foodservices are also responsible for catering of special functions.

Characteristic of menus planned for a university cafeteria or student union is simplicity in offerings, with emphasis on pleasing combinations and well-prepared food. Menus that meet nutritional needs, offer variety, and can be sold at a moderate cost must be planned for students, faculty, and off-campus guests. The uncertainty of numbers and often unexpectedly small volume of business creates a problem of excess prepared food and food cost control.

The use of a cycle menu is of value in some instances. However, the need for using leftovers and the desirability of including seasonable foods available on the market lead some directors to plan for periods as brief as 1 week, while others prefer a 5-week cycle.

The menu patterns for lunch and dinner in a university cafeteria are so similar that the suggested menus planned for this type of operation (pp. 560-563) may be used for either lunch or for dinner for a 2-week period.

The breakfast menu should offer some choice in food items each day, although there is less need for variety from day to day than is desirable for lunch and dinner. Breakfast should include 2 or more citrus juices and 1 other juice; fresh fruits in season; cooked or ready-to-eat prepared cereals; breakfast hot breads and toast; eggs and bacon, ham, or sausage; jam and jelly; and a choice of beverages.

In addition to the items listed on Suggested Luncheon and Dinner Menus for a University Cafeteria (pp. 560-563), certain other items are available daily. These include:

Entrées: The luncheon and dinner entrées usually include at least 1 meat, 1 meatless entrée, 1 meat extender, and poultry or fish. This variety may be increased or decreased to fit the demands of the foodservice.

Vegetables: Mashed potatoes.

Salads: Cottage cheese, head lettuce, tossed fresh vegetable salad with assorted dressings, and carrot and celery sticks.

Breads: Whole wheat bread, white bread, and a hot bread.

Desserts: Baked custard, fresh fruit in season, fruit juices, yogurt, and a variety of ice creams.

Beverages: Coffee, tea, hot and iced, cocoa, milk, whole, nonfat and cultured buttermilk.

SUGGESTED LUNCHEON AND DINNER MENUS FOR A UNIVERSITY CAFETERIA

Pattern	Monday	Tuesday	Wednesday	Thursday	Friday	Saturday	Sunday
Soup	Vegetable	Barley	Pepper Pot	Mushroom	Bean	Tomato Bouillon	French Onion
Entrées	Swiss Steak Creamed Chipped Beef on Corn Bread Baked Haddock Chinese Omelet	Roast Pork Turkey Loaf Seafood Chef Salad Macaroni and Cheese	Pot Roast Beef Chicken à la Maryland Salmon Loaf Egg Cutlet	Deviled Pork Chop Meat Loaf Chicken Turnover—Mushroom Sauce Russian Salad Bowl	Roast Leg of Lamb Creamed Ham & Celery on Hot Biscuit Fried Whiting Fish Corn Fritters	Country Fried Steak Sweetbread Cutlets Pizza Cheese Soufflé—Shrimp Sauce	Baked Ham with Honey Glaze Fried Chicken Baked Fillet of Sole Beef Stew with Dumplings
Vegetables Mashed potatoes available daily	Baked Potatoes Chilled Tomatoes Broccoli au Gratin Corn on the Cob	Scalloped Sweet Potatoes–Apples Buttered Wax Beans Buttered Asparagus Julienne Carrots	French Baked New Potatoes Cauliflower-Cheese Sauce Buttered Mixed Vegetables Scalloped Tomatoes and Celery	Sautéed Green Tomatoes New Corn in Cream Buttered Spinach with Lemon Mashed Summer Squash	Parsley Buttered Potatoes Baked Tomatoes Braised Celery Buttered Green Peas	French Fried Potatoes Wilted Greens Buttered Zucchini Squash Creole Corn	Baked Sweet Potato Buttered Peas, Rice, Mushrooms Creamed Onions Buttered Baby Limas
Salads	Spicy Apricot Mold Grapefruit–Orange–Red Apple Section Cabbage—	Perfection Stuffed Tomato Waldorf Deviled Egg	Lime Gelatin–Spiced Grape–Celery Cucumber and Onion Sour Cream	Molded Pineapple–Cottage Cheese Tomato–Avocado Sections	Jellied Beet Cantaloupe–Honeydew Wedge–Grape Vegetable Nut	Cabbage Parfait Salad Banana Nut Sliced Tomatoes Carrifruit	Raspberry Ring Mold Fresh Fruit Bowl Sliced Orange—Onion Ring

	Hot Bread	Desserts
Cucumber—Tomato—Green Pepper Beet Relish	Blueberry Muffins	Green Apple Pie / Lemon Pie / Applesauce Cake / English Toffee
Shredded Carrot–Pineapple Mixed Fruit	Dinner Rolls	Raisin Pie / Coconut Cream Pie / Lemon Sponge Cake / Cherry Crisp
Banana Slice–Cubed Pineapple–Orange Sections Cabbage–Green Pepper–Pimiento	Orange Rolls	Apricot Pie / Strawberry Glazed Cream Pie / Angel Food Cake / Apple Brown Betty
Stuffed Celery—Cheese	Bishop's Bread	Cherry Pie / Pumpkin Pie / Fruit Upside-Down Cake / Caramel Custard
	Corn Bread	Blueberry Pie / Frozen Lemon Pie / Burnt Sugar Cake / Blue Plum Cobbler
Green Bean–Pimiento	All Bran Muffins	Apple Pie—Cheese Crust / Date Cream Pie / German Chocolate Cake / Peach Crisp
	Vienna Bread	Fresh Rhubarb Pie / Pecan Pie / Lady Baltimore Cake / Strawberry Shortcake

SUGGESTED LUNCHEON AND DINNER MENUS FOR A UNIVERSITY CAFETERIA

Pattern	Monday	Tuesday	Wednesday	Thursday	Friday	Saturday	Sunday
Soup	Cream of Potato	Creole	Tomato	Clam Chowder	Split Pea	Vegetable Beef	Cream of Tomato
Entrées	Breaded Pork Cutlet Corned Beef—Horseradish Sauce Meat Roll Grilled Cheese Sandwich	Roast Veal Ham Loaf Baked Halibut Baked Beans	Chicken Tahitian Braised Liver Beef Stroganoff Cheeseburger Pie	Grilled Ham Slices Spaghetti and Meat Balls Scalloped Chicken Fruit Plate with Cottage Cheese	Veal Chops in Sour Cream Beef Pot Pie Fried Shrimp Cheese Balls with Pineapple	Barbecued Spareribs Baked Meat Croquettes Chicken Fricassée Tuna Salad	Roast Turkey Mock Drumsticks Hungarian Goulash Steamed Salmon—Lemon Butter
Vegetables Mashed potatoes available daily	Fried Hominy New Peas in Cream Buttered New Cabbage Spanish Green Beans	Green Rice Scalloped Tomatoes Buttered Brussels Sprouts Sautéed New Carrots	Scalloped Corn with Bacon New Potatoes with Peas Buttered Broccoli French Fried Eggplant Succotash with Green Beans	Creamed Potatoes Fresh Spinach with Bacon Corn on the Cob Harvard Beets	New Potatoes in Jackets Grilled Tomatoes Green Peas with Mushrooms Hot Slaw with Poppy Seed	Lattice Potatoes Buttered Green Beans with Celery Baked Onions with Cheese Buttered Summer Squash	Browned New Potatoes Buttered Fresh Asparagus Succotash Buttered Apples

Salads	Molded Grapefruit Cranberry Relish Prune–Apricot Tomato–Cucumber	Frosted Cherry Mold Cabbage Relish Asparagus–Pimiento Green Applesauce	Frozen Fruit Avocado–Orange Sections Cabbage–Pepper Slaw Stuffed Peach	Autumn Mold Pineapple–Cream Cheese–Date Melon Slice–Bing Cherry Tomato–Shrimp	Apple–Grapefruit Mold Green Pepper–Cottage Cheese Orange–Endive Fresh Pineapple–Strawberry	Molded Pineapple–Cucumber Fruit Salad Bowl Raw Spinach–Egg Spiced Apple	Under the Sea Salad Avocado–Grapefruit Stuffed Prune Peaches–Banana–Grape
Hot Bread	Whole Wheat Rolls	Boston Brown Bread	Cinnamon Rolls	Raised Muffins	Butterhorn Rolls	Honey Cornflake Muffins	Butter slices
Desserts	Fresh Peach Pie Custard Pie Chocolate Angel Food Tapioca Cream	Strawberry Pie Butterscotch Pie Jelly Roll Orange Cream Puff	Dutch Apple Pie Eggnog Pie Pineapple–Cashew Cake Apricot Whip	Gooseberry Pie Banana Cream Pie Fudge Cake Fruit Cup–Cookies	Plum Pie Chocolate Cream Pie Lazy Daisy Cake Date Pudding	Cherry Pie—Lattice Crust Lemon Chiffon Pie Chocolate Cup Cake Vanilla Cream Puddng	Boysenberry Pie Mocha Almond Frozen Pie Marble Cake Apple Dumplings

Menus for Health Care Facilities

Hospitals

The basis for successful operation of a hospital department of nutrition and dietetics is the production and service of high-quality foods that not only meet the nutritional requirements of patients and personnel but that are provided at a cost within budgetary allowance. Although often more complex, the principles of meal planning in a hospital are the same as in other types of institutions. For 1 service period foods must be provided for many kinds of diets. These may range from liquid, ground, soft, or regular to bland, low sodium, carbohydrate, protein, or fat restricted, with a wide range in caloric requirements. Often foods must be available 24 hr a day.

When developing a hospital meal pattern, the first step is to plan a regular or normal diet that will supply all food essentials necessary for good nutrition. This pattern then becomes the foundation for most diets required for therapeutic purposes and is the core of all meal planning in a hospital of any type or size. Patients requiring other than a normal diet will receive various modifications of the regular diet to fit their particular needs. A Guide for Planning Normal Diets with Modifications is given on pp. 568-575.

Hospital menus may be nonselective, which gives the patient no choice and does not allow for individual food likes or dislikes; or selective, in which the patient may select from 2 or more menu items. The cycle menu may be either selective or nonselective.

The selective menu adds much to the satisfaction and education of patients and also helps to prevent waste. Choices that appeal to various patients usually can be made available with little extra work, if careful planning is used in pairing items on the menu. The main items on the selective menu are the same as those on the general menu. Some items, such as the choice of meat and vegetables, may be the same as foods prepared for one of the modified diets or for the cafeteria. Other choices may be soup or fruit juice, or fruit or ice cream in place of a prepared dessert. On the dinner menu, choices of light or heavy items may do much to promote patient satiety. "Nutrition education begins as soon as possible after admission as the patient selects a meal regardless of the diet modification, with diet counseling from the dietitian, and continues throughout the hospitalization period. Each individual patient has a variety of basic needs including nutritionally adequate meals, the need for acceptance, understanding, companionship, and a pleasant environment during meal time. Attractive dining rooms located in the patient areas, with patients being encouraged to have guests, helps to promote a successful meal-time experience for them."[1]

[1] *Handbook for Writing Modified Diets,* Indiana University Medical Center, Department of Nutrition and Dietetics, 1976.

Food for hospital personnel usually is served cafeteria style. The menu may be a modification of the patient menu, with a few additions to offer a wider selection than is desirable for the patients.

In planning a normal or regular diet, meals should be planned for each day as a unit. Each day's menu then may be checked to be sure that all essential foods have been included. A suggested 3-meal-a-day menu pattern for a normal diet follows.

Breakfast	*Lunch*	*Dinner*
Fruit or juice	Cream soup or	Soup (optional)
Cereal with milk	Main dish (made with	Meat, poultry, or fish
Egg	meat, fish, poultry, egg,	Potato or alternate starchy
Bread or toast	or cheese)	vegetable
Butter or margarine	Vegetable or salad	Green or yellow vegetable
Beverage	Bread with butter or	Salad: fruit or vegetable
	margarine	Bread with butter or
	Fruit or other simple	margarine
	dessert	Dessert
	Beverage	Beverage

Some hospitals find it advantageous to use a 5-meal plan. Patients like eating smaller meals and more often. Dietitians who use the 5-meal plan claim the cost of food and labor are somewhat reduced because all food requiring skilled cooks can be prepared during one work shift. An outline menu pattern for the 5-meal plan follows.

7 A.M.   Coffee, with toast or sweet roll.

10 A.M.   Breakfast: fruit or juice, cereal with milk, egg or other entrée, toast, coffee, milk, or both.

1 P.M.   Soup, crackers. Cheese, fruit or juice, and melba toast.

4 P.M.   Dinner: fruit juice, meat, potato and other vegetable, dessert, coffee, or milk.

8 P.M.   Sandwich, milk, custard, or ice cream.

Extended Care Facilities

As the number of persons age 65 and older continues to grow, more and more people in this age group are residing in nursing homes and retirement complexes. For these people food is a basic emotional and physical need. Food means different things to different people but, to the older adult, it represents a measure of care others have for them.

Those persons planning meals for older adults should be aware of the problems peculiar to this age group. Their fixed habits and food preferences developed through many years may influence but should not determine entirely the meals planned for them. Healthy adults regardless of age need a well-balanced diet and, in planning the day's food, the basic pattern for the normal diet should be followed. Individual problems of the group members, such as difficulty in chewing solid food and special diet requirements, must also be of major concern. Diminished vigor, limited mobility, and diminished taste and smell also create a challenging problem in planning nutritionally adequate menus.

At least 3 well-planned meals should be served daily, with a hot food at each meal. The menu pattern is similar to that of the regular hospital diet (p. 565), with adjustments in portions and some modification for residents with individual eating problems. The caloric intake or quantity of food eaten usually is smaller because of lessened activity.

The daily food plan should include: (1) at least 1 food of good quality protein at each meal—eggs, lean meat, fish, poultry, or cheese; (2) milk offered at mealtime, with at least 2 c a day for each person; (3) 4 or more servings of fruits and vegetables, including a green leafy or yellow vegetable and a citrus fruit, such as grapefruit, orange, or some other high source of vitamin C; and although chewing may be difficult for some, raw vegetables or fruits should be included; (4) 4 or more servings from the bread-cereal group, which includes in addition to bread and breakfast cereals rice, macaroni, spaghetti, noodles, and baked goods made with whole-grain or enriched flour. Additional foods containing fat, sweets, and flavoring add to the acceptance of the meals. Strongly flavored foods often are not well accepted.

Menus for Commercial Foodservices

Menu planning for commercial foodservices varies according to the size and type of operation, its goals, and the expected check average. Menus range from the fast food chain's limited menu for high volume and speedy service to the elaborate *table d'hote* menu of the hotel or the formal, seated-service restaurant.

Planning the menu for the commercial foodservice has much in common with that for the institution foodservice. Consideration must be given to the basic rules of successful meal planning and food combination and the specific requirements of the clientele. As in any other foodservice, labor is one of the largest items of expense and one of the most difficult to control. The use of preportioned foods such as catsup, jelly, and butter, of prefabricated meat cuts and other portion-ready entrées, of ready-to-cook foods such as French fried potatoes, and of other built-in labor-saving devices is of major importance in effecting economies of time and cost.

Some restaurants have a fixed menu with daily specials featured; others have found the use of rotating menus to be valuable in reducing the time spent in planning and as an aid in the equitable distribution of labor and food. A suggested 4-week cycle menu for an industrial cafeteria is given on pp. 576-579. Breads, sandwiches, salads, desserts, and beverages are planned on a separate menu.

GUIDE FOR PLANNING DIETS[a]
AMOUNTS TO INCLUDE EVERY DAY

Diet	Milk	Meat, Fish, Poultry, Cheese	Eggs	Enriched Breads and Cereals
Normal adult	1 pt	2 servings (2-4 oz edible portions)	1 or more	4 or more servings (1 slice bread, ½ c cooked cereal, ⅔ c dry cereal)
Pregnancy Lactation	1 qt pregnancy 1½ qt lactation	2 servings	1	4 servings
Clear liquid	None	None	None	None
Full liquid	1¼ qt	Finely homogenized meat added to cream soup or broth	Cooked in custard or eggnog	1 serving refined, cooked cereal

[a] Adapted from the *Handbook for Writing Modified Diets,* Indiana Medical Center, Department of Nutrition and Dietetics, 1976.

Potato or Substitute (Rice or Pasta)	Vegetables	Fruits	Butter or Margarine	Miscellaneous (Sweets, Desserts, Beverages, Soups, Seasonings)
1 or more servings	2 or more servings; at least 1 green leafy or yellow	2 or more servings (at least 1 citrus or tomato)	3 t or more	Include amounts to maintain ideal weight
2 servings	3 servings; at least 1 green leafy or yellow	3 servings (2 to be citrus or tomato)	3 t or more	Include amounts to maintain ideal weight
None	None	None	None	Clear broth, consommé, bouillon; coffee or substitute, tea, lemonade, carbonated beverages; grape, apple, or cranberry, juice; gelatin dessert, sugar, hard candy, dextrose
Blenderized, added to cream soup or broth	Vegetable juices (tomato and mixed vegetable) finely blenderized vegetables added to cream soup or broth	3 servings, juice only (1 citrus or tomato)	4 t butter or margarine in soup; cream may be substituted	Flavored gelatins, cornstarch pudding, tapioca, sherbet, plain ice cream

GUIDE FOR PLANNING DIETS[a]
AMOUNTS TO INCLUDE EVERY DAY

Diet	*Milk*	*Meat, Fish, Poultry, Cheese*	*Eggs*	*Enriched Breads and Cereals*
Bland	1 qt or more	2 servings Omit meat extracts, highly spiced or cured meats (except bacon) if not tolerated	3-5 per week	4 or more servings Avoid products with coarse bran or seeds if not tolerated
Restricted fiber	1 pt or more	2 servings: tender lean beef, chicken, lamb, liver, turkey, or veal; crisp bacon and lean pork if tolerated; cream, cottage, or American cheese Highly seasoned meats may cause distress	1	4 or more servings: bread, toast, rolls, crackers made from finely milled whole grain or refined flour; cooked cereals and refined dry cereals Avoid coarse cereals or breads made with seeds or cracked wheat

Potato or Substitute (Rice or Pasta)	Vegetables	Fruits	Butter or Margarine	Miscellaneous (Sweets, Desserts, Beverages, Soups, Seasonings)
1 or more servings Avoid potatoes with skins if not tolerated	2 or more servings, any if tolerated Avoid raw, onions, those from cabbage family	3 servings (1 to be citrus) Avoid raw or those with seeds if not tolerated	3 t or more	Avoid alcohol, black pepper, chili powder, and strong caffeine-containing beverages Avoid chocolate, nuts, coconut, sweets, seeds, and seasonings such as garlic, cloves, mustard if not tolerated May use 6 or more feedings
1 or more servings Avoid potatoes with skins	2 or more servings cooked (at least 1 green leafy or yellow) Omit raw vegetables with tough skins, corn, onions, dried beans and peas, and other strong vegetables not tolerated	2 or more servings (at least 1 citrus or tomato) Avoid raw fruit (except banana and avocado)	3 t or more	Soups made with foods allowed; beverages as desired; seasoning as tolerated Avoid desserts and candy containing nuts, coconut, fruit with seeds or skins; jam with seeds or skins

GUIDE FOR PLANNING DIETS[a]
AMOUNTS TO INCLUDE EVERY DAY

Diet	Milk	Meat, Fish, Poultry, Cheese	Eggs	Enriched Breads and Cereals
Restricted protein (40 g)	1½ c	1 oz	1	3 servings
High-protein high-calorie (100-125 g protein)	1½ qt	6 oz	2	4 or more servings
Controlled fat (1600 cal)	1 pt skim milk	6 oz lean, well-trimmed of fat	3 per week Omit 1 oz meat for 1 egg	7 servings
Restricted sodium (2000 mg, 1800 cal)	1½ pt Avoid buttermilk and chocolate milk	6 oz fresh, frozen, unsalted	1 (maximum)	4 servings; quick breads made with sodium-free baking powder or potassium bicarbonate; unsalted dry cereal

Potato or Substitute (Rice or Pasta)	Vegetables	Fruits	Butter or Margarine	Miscellaneous (Sweets, Desserts, Beverages, Soups, Seasonings)
1 serving	3 servings	3 servings (1 citrus or tomato)	3 T	Sugar and jelly, hard candy, special low-protein products as desired
2 servings	2 or more servings (at least 1 green leafy or yellow)	3 servings (1 citrus or tomato)	2 T	To meet calorie need, add desserts and sweets as desired All foods are allowed Milk shakes, eggnogs, or high-protein feedings
1 serving (½ c)	2 or more servings (at least 1 green leafy or yellow)	6 servings (½ c each) fresh or unsweetened	2 T polyunsaturated only	Fat-free broth, vegetable broths, tea, coffee, spices, and seasoning as desired
2 servings unsalted white or sweet potatoes, unsalted rice noodles, macaroni, or spaghetti	4 servings fresh or frozen, unsalted	3 servings Avoid maraschino cherries, crystallized or glazed fruit	3 t	Omit salt, monosodium glutamate, seasoned salts, meat tenderizer, catsup, Worcestershire sauce, olives, pickles, salted snacks

GUIDE FOR PLANNING DIETS[a]
AMOUNTS TO INCLUDE EVERY DAY

Diet	Milk	Meat, Fish, Poultry, Cheese	Eggs	Enriched Breads and Cereals
Calorie controlled (1200 cal)	1 pt skim milk	7 oz lean, well trimmed of fat	3 per week Omit 1 oz meat for 1 egg	4 servings (1 slice bread, ½ English muffin, roll, or bun; ½ c dry or cooked cereal) May substitute ⅓ c corn, ½ c lima beans or peas, 1 small potato, ½ c squash, ¼ c sweet potato
Calorie controlled (1500 cal)	Same as 1200 calorie diet except 1 pt whole milk may be substituted for skim milk, increase fat to 3 t; add 1 bread exchange			

Potato or Substitute (Rice or Pasta)	Vegetables	Fruits	Butter or Margarine	Miscellaneous (Sweets, Desserts, Beverages, Soups, Seasonings)
No potatoes, noodles, macaroni, spaghetti, or rice except in place of bread	3 servings ½ c cooked or raw; no lima beans or corn except in place of bread	3 servings ½ c fresh or unsweetened	2 t	Use as desired: raw chicory, Chinese cabbage, endive, escarole, lettuce, parsley, radishes, watercress, coffee, tea, clear broth, bouillon, spices, unsweetened pickles

INDUSTRIAL CAFETERIA WEEKLY WINTER MENU CYCLE: MENU 1 [a]

Item	Monday	Tuesday	Wednesday	Thursday	Friday
Soup	Chicken Gumbo	Scotch Broth with Barley	Yellow Split Pea	Turkey Noodle	Clam Chowder
Entrée 1	Creamed Chipped Beef on Toast	Boston Baked Beans—Brown Bread	Baked Eggs and Noodles	French Fried Cauliflower Rarebit Sauce	Macaroni and Cheese Loaf Tomato Sauce
Entrée 2	Salisbury Steak with Brown Sauce	American Chop Suey on Steamed Rice	Barbecued Beef on Bun Plate Potato Chips	Baked Ham Loaf Glazed Pineapple Ring	Deep-sea Scallops Tartar Sauce Cole Slaw
Entrée 3	Roast Leg of Lamb Mint Jelly	Country Smoked Loin of Pork— Sauerkraut	Roast Turkey Dressing Cranberry Sauce Gravy	Potted Swiss Steak with Vegetables	Baked Stuffed Pork Chops— Gravy
Hot sandwich	Roast Pork with Gravy	Roast Veal	Baked Ham	Roast Beef	Corned Beef
Potatoes	Mashed Potatoes	Scalloped Potatoes	Mashed Potatoes	Mashed Potatoes	Parsley Potatoes
Vegetables	Cauliflower Polonaise French Green Beans with Bacon	Julienne Beets Baked Squash	Buttered Frozen Peas with Mushrooms Cream-style corn	Stewed Tomatoes Buttered Lima Beans	Carrots Lyonnaise Buttered Brussels Sprouts

[a] Breads, sandwiches, salads, desserts, and beverages planned as a separate menu.

INDUSTRIAL CAFETERIA WEEKLY WINTER MENU CYCLE: MENU 2

Item	Monday	Tuesday	Wednesday	Thursday	Friday
Soup	Potato and Leek	Navy Bean	Vegetable	Beef Broth with Barley	Mushroom
Entrée 1	Cheese Soufflé Mushroom Sauce	Smoked Link Sausage	Chili Con Carne on Spaghetti	Apple Fritters— Maple Syrup	Scrambled Eggs on Toast
Entrée 2	Braised Beef Stew with Dumpling	Potato Pancakes— Applesauce	Turkey Pot Pie	Spaghetti with Meat Sauce, French Bread	Baked Haddock Fillet—Tartar Sauce
Entrée 3	Baked Ham with Raisin Sauce	Yankee Pot Roast of Beef—Noodles	Braised Liver with Bacon	Quarter Fried Chicken with Baked Rice	Country-fried Steak Cream Gravy
Hot sandwich	Hot Turkey	Roast Lamb	Corned Beef	Roast Pork with Gravy	Roast Beef
Potatoes	Lyonnaise Potatoes	Paprika Potatoes	Au Gratin Potatoes	Mashed Potatoes	Mashed Potatoes
Vegetables	Baked Acorn Squash Spinach Soufflé	Whole Kernel Corn O'Brien Hot Slaw	French Fried Eggplant Harvard Beets	Buttered Broccoli Spears Mixed Vegetables	Buttered Peas Savory Carrots

INDUSTRIAL CAFETERIA WEEKLY WINTER MENU CYCLE: MENU 3

Item	Monday	Tuesday	Wednesday	Thursday	Friday
Soup	Homemade Chicken	Minestrone	Philadelphia Pepper Pot with Spatzels	Green Split Pea	Tomato with Barley
Entrée 1	Oven Baked French Toast with Maple Syrup Link Sausage	Baked Corn Pudding	Mostaccioli—Meat Sauce French Bread	Vegetable Chop Suey Steamed Rice	Scalloped Macaroni and Cheese
Entrée 2	Veal Ragout with Spaghetti	Stuffed Bacon Wrapped Frankfurter on Bun Potato Chips Sliced Tomato	Pork Patties Baked Acorn Squash Applesauce	Baked Meat Loaf—Mushroom Sauce	Salmon Patties with Egg Sauce
Entrée 3	Pepper Steak	Roast Veal Dressing	Braised Short Ribs of Beef with Vegetable Sauce	Roast Loin of Pork—Stewed Apples	Roast Round of Beef—Natural Gravy
Hot sandwich	Roast Pork with Gravy	Brisket of Corned Beef	Roast Lamb	Hot Turkey	Baked Ham
Potatoes	O'Brien Potatoes	Parsley Potatoes	Mashed Potatoes	Browned Potatoes	Rissolé Potatoes
Vegetables	Frozen Baby Lima Beans Zucchini Squash	Fresh Cabbage Glazed Carrots	Acorn Squash Buttered Peas	Mashed Rutabagas Hot Spiced Beets	Cauliflower Polonaise Creole Green Beans

INDUSTRIAL CAFETERIA WEEKLY WINTER MENU CYCLE: MENU 4

Item	Monday	Tuesday	Wednesday	Thursday	Friday
Soup	Lima Bean	Vegetable	Chicken Broth with Rice	Beef Broth with Barley	Clam Chowder
Entrée 1	Ravioli with Meat Sauce and Italian Cheese	Baked Corned Beef Hash	Baked Lima Beans with Salt Pork	Eggs à la King on Crisp Chinese Noodles	Scalloped Tuna and Peas
Entrée 2	Hamburger on a Bun Plate Potato Chips Cole Slaw	Turkey and Vegetable Fricassée— Corn Bread	Stuffed Cabbage Rolls, Creole Style	Braised Lamb Stew with Vegetables	Halibut Steak— Lemon Butter
Entrée 3	Roast Leg of Veal—Baked Peach	Fried Pork Chops Applesauce	Boiled Beef, Horseradish Sauce	Pot Roast of Beef Brown Gravy	Baked Ham Loaf, Mustard Sauce
Hot sandwich	Corned Beef	Roast Beef	Baked Ham	Smoked Pork Butt	Hot Turkey
Potatoes	Cottage Potatoes	Mashed Potatoes	Parsley Potatoes	Hash-browned Potatoes	French Fried Potatoes
Vegetables	French Fried Eggplant Frozen Mixed Vegetables	Buttered Peas Braised Red Cabbage	Glazed Carrots Onions in Cream Sauce	Wilted Spinach Cream-style Corn	Stewed Tomatoes Mashed Squash

Menu-Planning Suggestions

ENTRÉES

MEAT

Beef

Beef à la Mode
Corned Beef
Roast Round
Pot Roast
Chuck Roast
Standing Rib Roast
Rolled Rib Roast
Corned Beef and
  Cabbage
Braised Brisket
Broiled Steak
  T-Bone
  Sirloin
  Filet Mignon
  Club
Cubed Steak
Country Fried Steak
Pepper Steak
Spanish Steak
Swiss Steak
Beef Stroganoff
Yankee Pot Roast
Mock Drumsticks
Barbecued Kabobs
Barbecued Short Ribs
Braised Short Ribs
Salisbury Steak
Beef Pot Pie
Beef Stew with
  Vegetables
Beef Stew with
  Dumplings
Hungarian Goulash
Chop Suey
Meat Loaf
Swedish Meat Balls
Spanish Meat Balls

Meat Balls and
  Spaghetti

Veal

Roast Leg of Veal
Roast Veal Shoulder
Baked Veal Chops
Veal Chops in Sour
  Cream
Breaded Veal Cutlets
Veal Birds
Veal Fricassee with
  Poppyseed Noodles
Veal Scallopini
Veal Parmesan
Veal à la King
Veal Patties
Veal Paprika with Rice
Curried Veal with Rice

Lamb

Roast Leg of Lamb
Roast Lamb Shoulder
Broiled Lamb Chops
Lamb Stew
Braised Lamb Riblets
Barbecued Lamb
  Shanks
Lamb Patties
Curried Lamb with Rice
Lamb Fricassee with
  Noodles

Pork (Fresh)

Baked Fresh Ham
Roast Pork Loin
Roast Pork Shoulder

Roast Pork with
  Dressing
Baked Pork Chops
Breaded Pork Chops
Deviled Pork Chops
Barbecued Pork Chops
Stuffed Pork Chops
Breaded Pork Cutlets
Barbecued Spareribs
Sweet-Sour Spareribs
Spareribs with Dressing
Pork Birds
Sweet-Sour Pork

Pork (Cured)

Baked Ham
Baked Ham Slices with
  Pineapple Rings
  with Orange Sauce
Grilled Ham Slices
Baked Canadian Bacon
Ham Loaf
Ham Patties
Glazed Ham Balls
Smoked Pork Chops

*Miscellaneous or
Variety Meats*

Baked Heart with
  Dressing
Liver and Bacon
Braised Liver and
  Onions
Grilled Liver and
  Onions
Liver with Spanish
  Sauce

ENTRÉES (continued)

Sweetbread Cutlets
Weiners and Sauerkraut
Cheese Stuffed Wieners
Barbecued Wieners

MEAT EXTENDERS

Baked Hash
Corned Beef Hash
Stuffed Peppers
Beef Roll
Spaghetti with Meat
  Sauce
Creole Spaghetti
Cheeseburger Pie
Beef and Pork
  Casserole
Spanish Rice
Creamed Beef
Creamed Chipped Beef
Chipped Beef and
  Noodles
Veal Croquettes
Meat Turnovers
Veal Soufflé
Creamed Ham
Creamy Noodles with
  Ham
Ham à la King
Ham Croquettes
Ham Soufflé
Ham Timbales
Ham and Egg Scallop
Ham-Cheese Casserole
Creamed Ham on
  Spoon Bread or
  Biscuits
Ham Biscuit Roll
Ham Turnover with
  Cheese Sauce
Ham and Cheese
  Quiche
Egg and Sausage Bake
Sausage Rolls

Sausage Cakes
Fried Scrapple
Bacon and Potato
  Omelet
Pork and Noodle
  Casserole
Baked Lima Beans
Boiled Lima Beans with
  Ham
Baked Lima Beans with
  Sausage
Baked Navy Beans
Chili Con Carne
Chili Spaghetti
Ranch Style Beans
Baked Eggs and Bacon
  Rings
Pizza
Lasagne

Poultry

Roast Turkey
Baked Turkey Roll
Turkey Divan
Turkey-Noodle
  Casserole
Baked Chicken
Broiled Chicken
Fried Chicken
Barbecued Chicken
Chicken Cantonese
Chicken Tahitian
Chicken Cacciatore
Breast of Chicken with
  Ham Slice
Chicken à la Maryland
Chicken with Black
  Olive Sauce
Fricassee of Chicken
Chicken with
  Dumplings
Chicken with Noodles
Chicken Pie
Chicken or Turkey Loaf

Chicken Soufflé
Chicken or Turkey
  Tetrazzini
Chicken or Turkey
  Turnovers
Chicken and Rice
  Casserole
Chicken à la King
Hot Chicken Salad
Singapore Curry
Creamed Chicken,
  on Biscuit
  in Patty Shell
  in Toast Cups
  on Chow Mein
    Noodles
  on Spoon Bread
Chicken Croquettes
Chicken Cutlets
Scalloped Chicken
Chicken Timbales
Chicken Chow Mein
Chicken Biscuit Roll
  with Mushroom
  Sauce
Chicken Crepes

FISH

Fresh and Frozen Fish

Fried Salmon Steaks
Poached Salmon
Baked Halibut Steak
Poached Halibut
Fried Halibut Steak
Fried or Baked Fillets
  of Haddock, Perch,
  Sole, Whitefish,
  Catfish
Fried Whole Fish
  Whiting
  Smelts
  Trout
French Fried Shrimp

ENTRÉES (continued)

Creole Shrimp with
  Rice
French Fried Scallops
Fried Clams
Fried Oysters
Scalloped Oysters
Deviled Crab
Broiled Lobster

Canned Fish

Salmon Loaf
Salmon Croquettes
Creamed Salmon on
  Biscuit
Salmon Biscuit Roll
  with Creamed Peas
Scalloped Salmon
Salmon and Potato Chip
  Casserole
Tangy Topped Salmon
Casserole of Tuna and
  Rice
Tuna Croquettes
Creamed Tuna on Toast
  or Biscuits
Tuna Soufflé
Scalloped Tuna
Tuna Biscuit Roll with
  Cheese Sauce
Tuna-Cashew Casserole
Tuna and Noodles
Tuna and Potato Chip
  Casserole

MEATLESS ENTRÉES

Cheese Rarebit
Cheese Balls on
  Pineapple Slice
Cheese Croquettes
Cheese Soufflé with
  Shrimp Sauce
Cheese Fondue

Macaroni and Cheese
Rice Croquettes with
  Cheese Sauce
Chinese Omelet
Rice with Mushroom
  and Almond Sauce
Fried Mush
Baked Eggs with
  Cheese
Curried Eggs
Cheese Lasagne
Spinach Lasagne
Creamed Eggs
Eggs à la Goldenrod
Egg Cutlets
Noodle Casserole
Noodles Romanoff
Hot Stuffed Eggs
Eggs à la King
Scalloped Eggs and
  Cheese
Scrambled Eggs
Omelet
Potato Omelet
Spanish Omelet
Vegetable Timbales
Cheese Puff
Spoon Bread
Corn Rarebit
Welsh Rarebit
Scalloped Corn
Hot Potato Salad
Creamed Asparagus on
  Toast
French Toast
Fritters, Syrup
Corn Fritters
Fruit Fritters

SANDWICHES

Baked Ham
Ham and Cheese

Ham Salad
Bacon and Tomato
Bacon and Tomato on
  Bun with Cheese
  Sauce
Hamburgers on Buns
Barbecued Hamburgers
Wieners with Meat
  Sauce on Bun
Oven Picnic Buns
Hot Roast Beef
Hot Roast Pork
Barbecued Ham, Pork,
  or Beef
Western Sandwich
Toasted Chipped Beef
  and Cheese
Reuben
Submarine
Hot Turkey
Chicken Salad
Sliced Turkey
Hot Tuna Bun
Tuna Salad, Plain or
  Grilled
Grilled Cheese
Egg Salad
Peanut
Runzas

MAIN DISH SALADS

Chef's Salad Bowl
Chicken and Bacon
  Salad
Chicken-Orange-
  Avocado Salad
Baked Ham with Potato
  Salad
Russian Salad Bowl
Chicken or Turkey
  Salad
Chicken Salad in
  Raspberry Mold

ENTRÉES

Crab Salad
Lobster Salad
Seafood Chef Salad
Shrimp Salad
Tuna Salad
Salmon Salad
Cold Salmon with
   Potato Salad

Fruit Plates
Cottage Cheese Salad
Deviled Eggs
Macaroni Salad
Brown Bean Salad
Stuffed Tomato Salad

VEGETABLES

POTATO OR SUBSTITUTE

Potatoes, Irish

Au Gratin
Baked
Browned
Buttered New
Chips
Creamed
Croquettes
Duchess
Fried
French Fried
Lyonnaise
Mashed
O'Brien
Potato Cakes
Potato Pancakes
Potato Salad, hot or
    cold
Rissolè
Scalloped
Stuffed Baked

Potatoes, Sweet

Baked
Candied or Glazed
Croquettes
Mashed with Apples

Pasta

Macaroni and Cheese
Macaroni Salad
Buttered Noodles
Poppyseed Noodles
Buttered Rice
Curried Rice
Fried Rice with
    Almonds
Green Rice
Rice Croquettes

Other Starchy Vegetables

Corn
    Buttered
    In Cream
    On Cob
    Corn and Tomato
    Corn Pudding
    O'Brien
    Scalloped
    With Celery and
        Bacon
    Succotash
Lima Beans
    Buttered
    In Cream
    With Bacon
    With Mushrooms
    With Almonds
Parsnips
    Buttered
    Browned
    Glazed
Squash
    Baked Acorn
    Baked Hubbard
    Mashed Butternut
    Mashed Hubbard

GREEN VEGETABLES

Asparagus
    Buttered or Creamed
    With Cheese or
        Hollandaise Sauce
Beans, Green
    Buttered
    Creole
    Herbed
    With Almonds or
        Mushrooms

With Dill
    Southern Style
Broccoli
    Almond Buttered
    Buttered
    With Cheese Sauce,
        Lemon Butter
    Hollandaise Sauce
    Crumb Butter
Brussels Sprouts,
    Buttered
Cabbage
    Au Gratin
    Buttered or Creamed
    Creole
    Fried
    Hot Slaw
Celery
    Buttered or Creamed
    Creamed Almond
    Creole
Peas
    Buttered or in Cream
    With Carrots,
        Cauliflower, or
        Onions
    With Mushrooms or
        Almonds
Spinach
    Buttered
    Wilted
    With Egg or Bacon
    With New Beets
Squash, Zucchini

OTHER VEGETABLES

Beets
    Buttered
    Harvard

VEGETABLES (continued)

Julienne
In Sour Cream
With Orange Sauce
Hot Spiced
Pickled
Carrots
Buttered or Creamed
Candied
Glazed
Lyonnaise
Marinated
Mint Glazed
Savory
With Celery
With Peas
Parsley Buttered
Sweet-Sour
Cauliflower
Buttered
Creamed
French Fried
With Almond Butter
With Cheese Sauce
With Peas
Eggplant
Creole

Fried or French Fried
Scalloped
Mushrooms
Broiled
Sautéed
Onions
Au Gratin
Baked
Buttered
Creamed
French Fried
Stuffed
With Spanish Sauce
Rutabagas
Buttered
Mashed
Squash, Summer
Buttered
Creole
Tomatoes
Baked
Breaded
Broiled Tomato Slices
Creole
Scalloped
Stewed

Stuffed
Vegetable Medley
Turnips
Buttered
In Cream
Mashed
With New Peas

FRUITS SERVED AS
VEGETABLES

Apples
Buttered
Fried
Hot Baked
Bananas
Baked
French Fried
Grapefruit
Broiled
Peaches
Broiled
Pineapple Ring
Broiled
Sautéed
Glazed

SALADS AND RELISHES

FRUIT SALADS

Apple and Celery
Apple and Carrot
Apple and Cabbage
Banana
Carrifruit
Cranberry Relish
Cranberry Sauce
Frozen Fruit
Grapefruit-Orange
Melon Ball-Orange
Mixed Fruit
Peach Half
Pear-Orange
Pineapple
Spiced Apple
Waldorf
(See p. 402 for
    additional
    suggestions)

VEGETABLE SALADS

Beet Pickles
Beet Relish
Brown Bean
Cabbage Relish
Cabbage
Cabbage-Carrot
Cabbage-Marshmallow
Cabbage-Pineapple
Carrot-Raisin
Celery Cabbage
Cole Slaw
Creamy Cole Slaw
Cucumber-Onion in
    Sour Cream
Hawaiian Tossed
Head Lettuce
Potato
Red Cabbage

Salad Greens with
    Grapefruit
Spinach-Mushroom
Stuffed Tomato
Tossed Green
Tomato
Tomato-Cucumber
Triple Bean

GELATIN SALADS

Applesauce Mold
Arabian Peach
Autumn
Beet
Bing Cherry
Blueberry Mold
Cabbage Parfait
Cranberry Ring Mold
Frosted Cherry
Frosted Lime
Ginger ale Fruit
Jellied Citrus
Jellied Vegetable
Jellied Waldorf
Molded Grapefruit
Molded Pear
Perfection
Molded Pineapple-
    Cheese
Molded Pineapple-
    Cucumber
Molded Pineapple-
    Relish
Molded Pineapple-
    Rhubarb
Raspberry Ring Mold
Ribbon Mold
Spicy Apricot
Strawberry Rhubarb
Sunshine
Swedish Green Top

Tomato Aspic
Under-the-Sea

SHERBETS AS SALAD

Cranberry
Lemon
Lime
Mint
Orange
Pineaple
Raspberry
Tomato

RELISHES

Burr Gherkins
Carrot Curls
Carrot Sticks
Cauliflowerets
Celery Curls
Celery Fans
Celery Hearts
Celery Rings
Cherry Tomatoes
Cucumber Slices
Cucumber Wedges
Green Pepper Rings
Olives
    Green
    Ripe
    Stuffed
Onion Rings
Radish Accordions
Radish Roses
Spiced Crabapples
Spiced Peaches
Spiced Pears
Stuffed Celery
Tomato Slices
Tomato Wedges
Watermelon Pickles

DESSERTS

CAKES AND COOKES

Cakes

Angel Food, Plain,
  Chocolate, and Filled
Applesauce
Banana
Boston Cream
Burnt Sugar
Chiffon
Chocolate and Jelly Roll
Coconut
Cup Cakes
Fruit Upside Down
Fudge
German Sweet
  Chocolate
Gingerbread
Lazy Daisy
Marble
Pineapple Cashew
Poppy Seed
Praline Gingerbread
Prune
Spice
White

Cookies

Brownies
Butter Tea
Butterscotch Pecan
Butterscotch Squares
Chocolate Chip
Coconut Macaroons
Coconut Pecan Bars
Date Bars
Oatmeal
Fudge Balls
Ginger
Marshmallow Squares
Oatmeal-Date Bars
Peanut Butter
Sandies
Sugar Cookies

PIES AND PASTRIES

One-Crust Pies

Apricot Cream
Banana Cream
Butterscotch
Chiffon
Chocolate Cream
Chocolate Sundae
Coconut Cream
Coconut Custard
Custard
Date Cream
Dutch Apple
Frozen Lemon
Frozen Mocha Almond
Fruit Glazed Cream
Ice Cream Pie
Lemon
Pecan
Pineapple Cream
Praline Pumpkin
Pumpkin
Sour Cream Raisin
Rhubarb Custard
Strawberry
Strawberry-Cream
  Cheese

Two-Crust Pies

Apple
Apricot
Blackberry
Blueberry
Boysenberry
Cherry
Gooseberry
Mincemeat
Peach
Pineapple
Plum or Prune
Raisin
Rhubarb
Strawberry

FROZEN DESSERTS

Ice Creams

Apricot
Banana
Butter Brickle
Caramel
Chip Chocolate
Chocolate
Coffee
Lemon Custard
Macaroon
Peach
Peanut Brittle
Pecan
Peppermint Stick
Pineapple
Pistachio
Raspberry
Strawberry
Toffee
Tutti Frutti
Parfaits

Sherbets

Apricot
Cherry
Cranberry
Green Gage Plum
Lemon
Lime
Orange
Mint
Pineapple
Plum
Raspberry
Rhubarb
Watermelon

PUDDINGS

Apple Crisp
Apple Dumplings
Apple Brown Betty

DESSERTS (continued)

Apricot Whip
Baked Custard
Banana Cream
Bavarian Cream
Bread Pudding
Butterscotch Pudding
Caramel Custard
Caramel Tapioca
Cheese Cake
Cherry Crisp
Chocolate Cream
Coconut Cream
Cottage Pudding
Cream Puffs
Date Cream
Date Pudding
Date Roll
Éclairs
English Toffee Dessert
Floating Island

Fruit Cobblers
Fruit Gelatin
Fudge Pudding
Lemon Cake Pudding
Lemon Snow
Meringue Shells
Peach Crisp
Peach Melba
Pineapple Cream
Pineapple Refrigerator
  Dessert
Royal Rice Pudding
Rice Custard
Russian Cream
Shortcake
Steamed Pudding
Strawberry-Sour Cream
  Crepes
Tapioca Cream
Vanilla Cream

MISCELLANEOUS DESSERTS

Cheese, assorted, with
  Crackers and Fruit
Fruit
  Baked or Stewed
    Apples
  Pears
  Rhubarb
Fresh Pineapple with
  Lemon Sherbet
Fruit Compote
Canned or Frozen
  Apricots
  Berries
  Cherries
  Figs
  Fruit Cup
  Peaches
  Pears
  Pineapple
  Plums or Prunes
  Rhubarb

SOUPS

CREAM SOUPS

Asparagus
Celery
Cheese
Chicken
Chicken Rice
Chicken Velvet
Clam Chowder,
    New England
Fish Chowder
Mushroom
Oyster Stew
Pea
Potato
Potato Chowder
Spinach
Tomato
Vegetable Chowder

STOCK SOUPS

Barley
Navy Bean
Beef Noodle
Beef Bouillon
Brunswick Stew
Chicken Bouillon
Chicken and Noodle
Chicken with Spatzels
Chicken Gumbo
Chicken Mushroom
Clam Chowder,
    Manhattan
Consommé
Creole
French Onion
Julienne
Lentil

Minestrone
Mulligatawny
Pepper Pot
Rice
Spanish Bean
Split Pea
Tomato Bouillon
Tomato-Rice
Vegetable-Beef

CHILLED SOUPS

Gazpacho
Jellied Consommé
Jellied Madrilene
Orange
Vichyssoise

GARNISHES

YELLOW-ORANGE

Cheese and Eggs

Balls, Grated, Strips
Rosettes
Egg, Hard-cooked or
   Sections
Deviled Egg Halves
Riced Egg Yolk

Fruit

Apricot Halves,
   Sections
Cantaloupe Balls
Lemon Sections, Slices
Orange Sections, Slices
Peach Slices
Peach Halves with Jelly
Spiced Peaches
Persimmons
Tangerines

Sweets

Apricot Preserves
Orange Marmalade
Peach Conserve
Peanut Brittle, Crushed
Sugar, Yellow or
   Orange

Vegetables

Carrots, Rings,
   Shredded, Strips

Miscellaneous

Butter Balls
Coconut, Tinted
Gelatin Cubes
Mayonnaise

RED

Fruit

Cherries
Cinnamon Apples
Cranberries
Plums
Pomegranate Seeds
Red Raspberries
Maraschino Cherries
Strawberries
Watermelon Cubes,
   Balls

Sweets

Red Jelly
   Apple, Cherry,
   Currant, Loganberry,
   Raspberry
Cranberry Glacé, Jelly
Gelatin Cubes
Red Sugar
Beets, Pickled, Julienne
Beet Relish
Red Cabbage
Peppers, Red, Rings,
   Strips, Shredded
Pimiento, Chopped,
   Strips
Radishes, Red, Sliced,
   Roses
Stuffed Olives, Sliced
Tomato, Aspic, Catsup,
   Chili Sauce, Cups,
   Sections, Slices,
   Broiled

Miscellaneous

Paprika
Tinted Coconut
Cinnamon Drops "Red
   Hots"

GREEN

Fruit

Avocado
Cherries
Frosted Grapes
Green Plums
Honeydew Melon
Lime Wedges

Sweets

Citron
Green Sugar
Gelatin Cubes
Mint Jelly
Mint Pineapple
Mints

Vegetables

Endive
Green Pepper, Strips,
   Chopped
Green Onions
Lettuce Cups
Lettuce, Shredded
Mint Leaves
Olives
Parsley, Sprig, Chopped
Pickles
   Burr Gherkins
   Strips, Fans, Rings
Spinach Leaves

Miscellaneous

Coconut, Tinted
Mayonnaise, Tinted
Pistachios

WHITE

Fruit

Apple Rings

GARNISHES (continued)

Apple Balls
Grapefruit Sections
Gingered Apple
White Raisins
Pear Balls
Pear Sections

Vegetables

Cauliflowerets
Celery Cabbage
Celery Curls, Hearts,
    Strips
Cucumber Rings,
    Strips, Wedges, Cups
Mashed Potato Rosettes
Onion Rings
Onions, Pickled
Radishes, White

Miscellaneous

Cream Cheese Frosting
Sliced Hard-cooked Egg
    White

Shredded Coconut
Marshmallows
Almonds
Mints
Whipped Cream
Powdered Sugar

BROWN-TAN

Breads

Crustades
Croutons
Cheese Straws
Fritters, Tiny
Noodle Rings
Toast, Cubes, Points,
    Strips, Rings

Miscellaneous

Cinnamon
Dates
French Fried
    Cauliflower

French Fried Onions
Mushrooms
Nutmeats
Nut-covered Cheese
    Balls
Potato Chips
Rosettes
Toasted Coconut

BLACK

Caviar
Chocolate-covered
    Mints
Chocolate Sprill
Chocolate, Shredded
Chocolate Sauce
Olives, Ripe
Prunes
Prunes, Spiced
Pickled Walnuts
Raisins, Currants
Truffles

UTILIZATION OF SURPLUS PREPARED FOODS

Bread and Crackers

Bread Crumbs, for
crumbing Cutlets,
Croquettes, and other
fried food; thickening
steamed and other
puddings
Canapés
Cinnamon Toast
Croutons, as soup
accompaniment
Desserts, Bread
Pudding, Brown Betty
French Toast
Hot Dishes, Cheese
Fondue, Scalloped
Macaroni, Soufflé,
Stuffing for Meat,
Poultry or Fish
Melba Toast
Toast Points, as garnish

Cereals

Chinese Omelet
Fried or French Fried
Corn Meal Mush or
Hominy Grits
Meat Balls with Cooked
Cereal as an Extender
Rice and Tuna
Rice Croquettes
Rice Custard
Soup with Rice,
Spaghetti, or Noodles

Cakes and Cookies

Baked Fruit Pudding
Cottage Pudding
Crumbs to coat balls of
ice cream
Crumb Cookies
Icebox Cake
Spice Crumb Cake

Eggs

Boiled or Poached, add
to Cream Sauce,
Mayonnaise, or
French Dressing, as a
garnish for
Vegetables, Egg
Cutlets, in Salad
Scrambled, Potato
Salad, Sandwich
Spread
Egg Whites, raw,
Angel Food Cake,
Bavarians, Fluffy or
Boiled Dressing,
Macaroons,
Meringue, Prune
Whip, White Sheet, or
Layer Cake
Egg Yolks, raw,
Cooked Salad
Dressing, Custard
Sauce, Filling or
Pudding, Duchess
Potatoes, Hollandaise
Sauce, Hot Cake
Batter, Scrambled
Eggs, Strawberry
Bavarian Cream Pie,
Yellow Angel Food
Cake

Fish

Creamed, à la King or
Scalloped
Fish Cakes or
Croquettes
Salad
Sandwich Spread

Fruit

Applesauce Cake

Apricot or Berry
Muffins
Frozen Fruit Salad
Fruit Slaw
Fruit Tarts
Jelied Fruit Cup or
Salad
Jelly or Jam
Mixed Fruit Salad or
Fruit Cup
Prune or Apricot Filling
for Rolls or Cookies
Sauce for Cottage
Pudding

Meat

Apple stuffed with
Sausage
Bacon in Sauce for
Vegetable
Baked Beef Hash
Boiled Lima Beans with
Ham
Chili con Carne
Chop Suey
Creamed Ham or Meat
on Toast
Creamed Ham in
Timbale Cases
Creole Spaghetti
Ham Croquettes
Ham or Bacon Omelet
Ham Quiche
Hot Tamale Pie
Meat Croquettes
Meat Roll or Meat Pie
Meat Turnovers
Salad
Sandwiches
Scalloped Potatoes with
Ham
Scrapple
Stuffed Peppers

UTILIZATION OF SURPLUS PREPARED FOODS (continued)

Milk and Cream, Sour

Biscuit Brown Bread
Butterscotch Cookies
Fudge Cake
Griddle Cakes
Salad Dressing
Sour Cream Pie
Spice Coffee Cake
Veal Chops in Sour
   Cream

Poultry

Chicken and Rice
   Casserole
Chicken Crepes
Chicken Timbales
Creamed Chicken in
   Patty Cases
Chicken à la King
Croquettes
Cutlets
Jellied Chicken Loaf
Pot Pie

Salad
Sandwiches
Soufflé
Soup
Turnovers

Vegetables

Combination—Carrots
   and Peas, Corn and
   Beans, Corn and
   Tomatoes, Peas and
   Celery
Fritters
Potatoes—Duchess,
   Hashed-brown,
   Lyonnaise, Cakes,
   Omelet, Salad (hot
   and cold)
Salad in combination
   (when suitable)
Soup
Vegetable Pie
Vegetable Timbales

Glossary of Food Terms

Menu Terms

à la (ah lah), Fr.

To the, with, in the mode or fashion of, or in, as in *à la Crême,* with cream; *à la Newburg,* Newburg fashion; *à la Moutarde,* in mustard.

à la carte, Fr.

On the menu, but not part of a complete meal, usually prepared as ordered.

à la king, Fr.

Served in cream sauce containing green pepper, pimiento, and mushrooms.

à la mode, Fr.

in style. When applied to desserts, means with ice cream. *Beef à la mode,* a well-larded piece of beef cooked slowly in water with vegetables, similar to braised beef.

à la Newburg

Creamed dish with egg yolks added, originally flavored with lime or sherry. Most often applied to lobster, but may be used with other foods.

allemande (al-mângd), Fr.

German; a smooth yellow sauce consisting of white sauce with the addition of butter, egg yolk, catsup, etc.

amandine

Served with almonds.

anglaise (ng-glayz), Fr.

English; *À la anglaise,* in English style.

antipasti (än-tēē-päs-tēē), It.

Appetizer; a course consisting of relishes.

au gratin (o grat-ang), Fr.

made with crumbs, scalloped. Often refers to dishes made with a cheese sauce.

au jus (o zhüs), Fr.

meat served in its natural juices or gravy.

Bardé (bar-day), Fr.

Larded. Covered with salt pork or with slices of bacon. *Un poulet Bardé de Lard,* a pullet larded with bacon.

bar-le-Duc (bar-luh-dük), Fr.

A preserve originally made of selected whole white currants seeded by hand with the aid of knitting needles. Now gooseberries, strawberries, etc., may be used. It frequently forms a part of the cheese course.

Bavarian Cream

A gelatin dish into which whipped cream is folded as it begins to stiffen.

Bavarois (bav-ar-wâz), Fr.

Bavarian.

Béchamel (bay-sham-ayl), Fr.

Refers to a sauce supposed to have originated with the Marquis de Béchamel, maître d'Hôtel of Louis XIV. A cream sauce made of chicken stock, cream, or milk, and usually seasoned with onion. Sometimes applied to all sauces having a white sauce foundation.

beef à la mode (bēf ah lah mōd), Fr.

A well-larded piece of beef cooked slowly in water with vegetables, similar to braised beef.

bellevue (bel-vü), Fr.

A pleasing sight; in aspic. *À la bellevue,* a food enclosed in aspic through which it can be plainly seen.

Bénédictine (bay-nay-dik-tang), Fr.

A liqueur made principally at the Abbey of Fécamp in Europe. *Eggs à la Bénédictine,* poached eggs served on broiled ham placed on split toasted muffins and garnished with Hollandaise sauce.

beurre (buhr), Fr.

Butter. *Au beurre noir,* with butter sauce browned in a pan; *Beurre Fondue,* melted butter.

beurré (buhr-ay), Fr.

Buttered.

biscotte (bis-kot), Fr.

Rusk, biscuit.

bisque (bisk), Fr.

A thick soup usually made from fish or shellfish. Also a frozen dessert. Sometimes defined as ice cream to which finely chopped nuts are added.

blanquette (blâng-ket), Fr.

A white stew usually made with veal. A cheese similar to Roquefort.

bleu (bluh), Fr.

Blue. *Au bleu,* plain boiled; Used with reference to fresh-water fish.

boeuf (buhf), Fr.

Beef. *Boeuf à la lardinière,* "braised beef with vegetables; boeuf kôti, roast beef.

bombe (bongh), Fr.

Also called *bombe glacée.* A frozen dessert made of a combination of two or more frozen mixtures packed in a round or melon-shaped mold.

bonne femme (bong fam), Fr.

Good wife; in simple home style. Applied to soups, stews, etc.

bordelaise (bord-lez), Fr.

Of Bordeaux. *Sauce bordelaise,* a sauce with Bordeaux wine as its foundation, with various seasonings added.

borsch or bortsch (bōrsh), Rus.

A Russian or Polish soup made with beets. Often sour cream or citric acid is added to give an acid taste.

bouillabaisse (bool-yab-ays), Fr.

A national soup of France. The word comes from the verbs *bouiller,* to boil, and *abaisser,* to go down. A highly seasoned fish soup made especially at Marseilles. Served in plates with dry toast.

bourgeoise (boor-zhwâz), Fr.

Middle-class, family-style. *À la bourgeoise* usually means served with vegetables.

brioche (bre-yosh), Fr.

A slightly sweetened rich bread of French origin.

broche (brosh), Fr.

Skewer, spit for roasting. *À la broche,* cooked on a skewer.

café (kaf-ay), Fr.

Coffee; coffee house; restaurant. *Café au lait,* coffee with hot milk; *Café noir,* black coffee, after-dinner coffee.

canapé (kan-ap-ay), Fr.

Originally couch, sofa, or divan; now an appetizer served either hot or cold. Usually fried or toasted bread spread with or supporting a wide variety of highly seasoned foods. Generally used as the first course of a meal as an hors d'oeuvre and eaten with the fingers, unless accompanied by a sauce or otherwise made impossible to eat this way. Often served on a doily.

carte (kart), Fr.

Card; bill of fare. *À la carte,* according to the bill of fare; *carte au Jour,* bill of fare or menu for the day.

Chantilly (shâng-tē-yē), Fr.

Name originally given to savoy cakes, which were scooped out, filled with preserved fruit, and garnished with whipped cream; now applies to anything served with sweetened and flavored whipped cream. *Chantilly cream,* sweetened and flavored whipped cream.

Chartreuse (shar-truhz), Fr.

Having a hidden filling or stuffing, as meat molded in rice or molded aspic filled with vegetables, meat, or fruit filling in the center; also famous liqueur.

chaud (shô), Fr.

Hot.

chemise (sh-mēz), Fr.

Shirt. *En chemise,* with their skins on; generally applied to potatoes.

chiffonade (shēr-fōn-ăd), Fr.

Rags; minced or shredded vegetables or meat sprinkled over soups or salads.

cloche (klosh), Fr.

Bell, dish cover. *Sous cloche,* under cover.

confit or confiture (kong-fee), Fr.

Preserves or jam made from fruit.

Consommé (kon-so-may), Fr.

A clear soup usually made from two or three kinds of meat.

creole (krē'ōl), Fr.

Relating or peculiar to the Creoles, made with tomatoes, peppers, onions, and other seasonings. Applies to soups, garnishes, sauces, etc., so prepared.

crépe suzette (krayp), Fr.

A small, very thin and crisp pancake served for tea or as dessert.

croissant (krwâ-sâng), Fr.

Crescent. Applied to rolls and confectionery of crescent shape.

curry (kŭr'ĭ).

Highly spiced condiment from India, a stew seasoned with curry.

déjeuner (day-zhuh-nay), Fr.

Breakfast, lunch.

de jour, Fr.

Ready to serve.

de la maison, (de-lah-mā-zōn), Fr.

Specialty of the house.

demi-tasse (dŭh-mee-tâss), Fr.

Half-cup; after-dinner coffee served in small cups.

dîner (de-nay), Fr.

Dinner; to dine.

duglère (doog-lâr), Fr.

After French restaurateur who popularized tomatoes. Signifies the use of tomatoes.

écarlate (ay-kar-lat), Fr.

Scarlet; a red sauce containing lobster roe, red tongue, etc.

entrecote (angtr'kôt), Fr.

Between ribs; a steak cut from between the ribs. Supposed to be second in quality only to the fillet or tenderloin.

entrée (âng-tray) Fr.

The main course of a meal; formerly, and still in some countries, a dish served before the roast or between the main courses, as between the fish and the meat.

espagnole (ays-pah-nyol), Fr.

Spanish; brown sauce.

fanchonette (fâng-sho-net), Fr.

Small pie or tart covered with a meringue.

farci (far-see), Fr.

Stuffed.

fermière (fayr-myayr), Fr.

Farmer's wife; in plain country style.

foie gras (fwâ gra), Fr.

Fat liver. Applied especially to the liver of fat geese. *Foie gras au naturel,* plain cooked, whole foie gras; *Paté de foie gras,* cooked livers seasoned with truffles, wine, and aromatics; most popular form of foie gras.

fondue (fong-dü), Fr.

Melted or blended.

Franconia.

Ancient German duchy; in the culinary sense, browned. Franconia potatoes, whole potatoes browned with the roast.

frappé (frap-pay), Fr.

Beaten and iced. Applied to a water ice frozen to a mush while stirring; usually drunk rather than eaten with a spoon or fork.

glacé (glah-say), Fr.

Iced, frozen, glassy, glazed, frosted, candied, crystallized. *Glacé fruit,* fruit dipped in a hot syrup that has been cooked to a hardcrack stage.

gumbo.

Okra; a rich, thick Creole soup containing okra.

haché (hah-shay), Fr.

Minced, chopped.

hors d'oeuvre (or-duh-vr'), Fr.

Side dish or relish served at the beginning of a meal. Used for luncheons, but not for dinners in France.

Italienne (e-tal-yang), Fr.

Italian style.

Jardinière (zhar-de-nyayr), Fr.

The gardener's wife; a dish of mixed vegetables.

julienne (zhü-lyayn), Fr.

Vegetables cut into fine strips or shreds. Named from the famous chef, Jean Julienne, who invented clear vegetable soup with the vegetables cut into match-like strips.

jus (zhüs), Fr.

Juice or gravy. *Au jus,* meat served in its natural juices or gravy.

kippered.

Scotch term originally applied to salmon; now a method of preserving fish, especially herring and salmon. The fish are split, then lightly salted and smoked.

kosher (kō'shēr)

Jewish term. *Kosher meat,* meat from a strictly healthy animal that has been slaughtered and prepared in accordance with the Jewish requirements.

Kuchen (kōō-ckhen), Ger.

Cake, not necessarily sweet.

Laitue (lay-tü), Fr.

Lettuce.

Lebkuchen (lāp'kōō-ckhen), Ger.

Famous German cake; sweet cakes or honey cakes.

limpa.

Swedish rye bread.

lox

Smoked salmon.

lyonnaise (lyo-nayz), Fr.

From Lyons; seasoned with onions and parsley, as *Lyonnaise potatoes.*

macédoine (mah-say-dooan), Fr.

Mixture or medley; usually applied to cut vegetables, but also to fruit.

maître d'hôtel (maytr' dotayl), Fr.

Steward. In the culinary sense, implies the use of minced parsley. *Maître d'hôtel sauce* (parsley butter), a well-seasoned mixture of creamed butter, chopped parsley, and lemon juice. Served on broiled meats, broiled or boiled fish, and on some vegetables, as potatoes.

marinade (mar-e-nad), Fr.

French dressing in which foods, as cooked vegetables and meats, are allowed to stand to render them more palatable. Also used with uncooked meat to soften tough fibers and to keep meat fresh, in which case it may be no more than a brine or pickle solution.

marinate

To treat with a marinade.

milanaise (me-lan-ayz), Fr.

From Milan. Implies the use of macaroni and Parmesan cheese with a suitable sauce, often Béchamel.

Minestrone (mēē-nōys-trō'ne), It.

Famous Italian thick vegetable soup.

Mulligatawny

Derived from two East Indian words signifying pepper water. A highly seasoned, thick soup characterized chiefly by curry powder. Meats, vegetables, mango chutney, coconut flesh, rice, cayenne, etc., may be added to taste.

Napoleans

Puff pastry kept together in layers with a custard filling, cut into portion size rectangles, and iced.

Neapolitan. (Also Harlequin and Panachée)

Molded dessert of two to four kinds of ice cream or water ice arranged lengthwise in layers. The mixture is sliced across for serving. Also applied to a gelatin dish arranged in layers of different colors.

Nesselrode pudding

Frozen dessert with a custard foundation to which chestnut purée, fruit, and cream have been added. Has been termed the most perfect of frozen puddings.

Newburg

Creamed dish with egg yolk added, originally flavored with lime or sherry. Most often applied to lobster, but may be used with other foods.

noisette (nooâ-zet), Fr.

Literally hazelnut; nut-brown color. May imply nut-shaped. A small piece of lean meat. Generally a chop minus the bone (fillet). Potatoes Noisette, "potatoes cut into the shape and size of hazel-nuts and browned in fat."

normande (nor-mând), Fr.

From Normandy. *À la Normande,* a delicate, smooth mixture often containing whipped cream.

pané (pan-ay), Fr.

Covered with bread crumbs or breaded.

parfait (par-fay), Fr.

Perfect; a mixture containing egg and syrup that is frozen without stirring. May be molded, but is more commonly served in parfait glasses.

parmentière (par-mang-tyayr), Fr.

Potato. Named after Baron Augustine Parmentier, who introduced potatoes to France and originated many methods of preparing them. À la parmentière, with or of potatoes.

pastrami (pa-strä'mi), Hung.

Boneless beef cured with spices and smoked.

pâte (pât), Fr.

Paste, dough.

pâté (pâ-tay), Fr.

Pie, patty, pastry. Also a meat preparation packed in earthenware jars and small tins, prepared largely in Germany and France, so called because it was sold in pies or *pâté* form. *Pâté de foie gras,* paste of fat livers.

persillade (payr-se-yad), Fr.

Served with or containing parsley.

petit pois (puh-tee pooâ), Fr.

A fine grade of very small peas with a delicate flavor but of low food value.

petits fours (puh-tee fo͞or), Fr.

Small fancy cakes.

piquant (pe-kâng), Fr.

Sharp, highly seasoned. Applied to sauces, etc. *Sauce piquante,* "a highly seasoned brown sauce containing lemon juice or vinegar, capers, pickles, etc."

plank (plänk)

Hardwood board used for cooking and serving broiled meat or fish. Thought to improve the flavor of foods so cooked. *Plánked steak,* a broiled steak served on a plank attractively garnished with a border of suitable vegetables or fruits.

plat (plah), Fr.

Dish. *Plat au jour,* food of the day, as featured on the menu.

Polenta (po-lĕn'ta), It.

Popular Italian dish originally of chestnut meal, but now often made with farina or corn meal. Cheese is usually added before serving.

polonaise (po-lo-nay), Fr.

Polish. Dishes prepared with bread crumbs, chopped eggs, brown butter, and chopped parsley.

pomme de terre (pom de tare), Fr.

Apple of the earth, potato. *Pommes de terre à la Lyonnaise,* Lyonnaise potatoes.

purée (pü-ray), Fr.

Foods rubbed through a sieve; also a nutritious vegetable soup in which milk or cream is seldom used.

ragout (rag-oo), Fr.

Stew; originally something to restore the taste and tempt the appetite. Generally a thick, well-seasoned stew containing meat.

ramekin (răm'e-kĭn)

Small, individual baking dish or a pastry shell; also a cheesse cake.

ravigote (rav-e-got), Fr.

Sauce seasoned with tarragon vinegar, chives, shallots, etc.

ravioli (rä-ve-o'-le), It.

Little shapes of Italian or noodle paste rolled thin, one half spread with a filling of minced meat or vegetables and moistened with a sauce if necessary, then folded over and poached in stock.

rémoulade (ray-moo-lad), Fr.

Pungent sauce made of hard-cooked eggs, mustard, oil, vinegar, and seasonings. Served with cold dishes.

rissoler (re-so-lay), Fr.

To roast until golden brown; to brown. *Rissolé,* browned.

rouelle (roo-ayl), Fr.

Round slice or fillet.

roulade (roo-lad), Fr.

Roll; rolled meat.

roux (roo), Fr.

Browned flour and fat used for thickening sauces, stews, etc.

Sabayon Fr.

Custard sauce with wine added.

scallion

Any onion which has not developed a bulb.

Schaumtorte (schoum tor'te), Ger.

Foam cake; layers of meringue and crushed fruit.

shallot

Onion having a stronger but more mellow flavor than the common variety.

sorbet (sor-bay), Fr.

Sherbet made of several kinds of fruits.

soubise (sōō-bēz), Fr.

White sauce containing onion and sometimes parsley.

Springerle (spring'er-le), Ger.

A popular Christmas cake or cookie. The dough is rolled into a sheet and pressed with a springerle mold before baking.

table d'hôte (tabl'dôt), Fr.

Table of the host or innkeeper. *Service table d'hôte,* a meal planned by the establishment at a set price, permitting a wide choice of foods.

terrine (tay-reen), Fr.

Tureen, an earthenware pot resembling a casserole. *Chicken en terrine,* chicken cooked and served in a tureen.

torte (tôr'te), Ger.

Rich cake made from crumbs, eggs, nuts, etc.

tortilla (tô-te̅'ya), Sp.

A round thin "bread" made of corn meal.

tortoni (tôr-tōn'e̅e̅), It.

Originally *tortonois,* meaning from the Italian city Tortona. *Biscuit tortoni,* a frozen mixture containing dried, ground macaroons and chopped, blanched almonds.

tournedos (to̅o̅r-nāy-dōz), Sp.

Small round fillets of beef.

truffles (trŭf'ls).

A species of fungi similar to mushrooms, found chiefly in France. They are black and grow in clusters under oak trees, several inches below the surface of the ground. They are rooted out by pigs trained for the purpose. Used chiefly for garnishing and flavor.

velouté (vu-loo-tay), Fr.

Velvety; a rich white sauce usually made of chicken or veal broth. Considered the principal white sauce, just as *Espagnole* is the chief brown sauce, although some confusion exists in the use of the terms.

volaille (vo-lah-yuh), Fr.

Poultry.

vol-au-vent (vol-o-vang), Fr.

Flying at the mercy of the wind; large patties of puff paste made without a mold and filled with meat, preserves, etc.

Wienerschnitzel (vē'nēr shnit's'l), Ger.

An entrée made of thin veal steak (cutlets) breaded and fried slowly in butter.

Yorkshire pudding

English dish, usually served with roast beef, consisting of a popoverlike mixture that may be baked with the meat or separately with some of the drippings.

Zwieback or Zwiebach (tsvē'bäk), Ger.

Twice-baked bread, crisp and slightly sweet. Now used largely as a food for very young children.

Cooking Processes and Methods

See pp. 78–84.

Part

SPECIAL MEAL SERVICE

Planning Special Meals, Teas, and Receptions

Foodservice personnel in schools, hospitals, and other organizations often are called on to provide meals or refreshments for special occasions. Service for these functions may be requested by the administration, another department in the institution, or a community organization. A decision on serving meals to outside groups should be made in accordance with institutional policies.

Preparation procedures for special meals will differ in many ways from those established for the usual routine of daily foodservice, and a temporary service staff may need to be organized. Preparation of the food may be scheduled for the regular cooks, in which case advance preparation should be carefully planned and, if necessary, other meals on the day of the special occasion simplified. Extra service personnel may be needed and, if inexperienced, should be provided with detailed instructions.

Planning Responsibilities

The major responsibilities of the foodservice staff in charge of a special meal or other function are:

1. Confer with representatives of the group to be served to determine the type of function, time and place, number to be served, service desired, and financial arrangements.

2. Plan menu with the organization representative. Suggested menus for special meals are given on pp. 622-634, for teas and receptions on pp. 635-639.

3. Determine quantity, quality, and estimated cost of food to be served.

4. Place food order.

5. Check dishes and equipment on hand. Make arrangements for obtaining additional items needed.

6. Set up temporary organization.
   a. Assign cooks, regular or special, to prepare food.

    b. Assign cooks and other personnel to the serving counter from which the plates will be filled.

    c. Assign and instruct waiters or waitresses for dining room service.

7. Make detailed work schedule for each group of workers, if inexperienced.

8. Supervise the preparation and service of food.

9. Supervise the dishwashing and cleanup of preparation and service areas.

10. Write a detailed report including information concerning numbers served, income and expenses, and useful comments for service of similar meals in the future.

Dinners, Luncheons, and Other Special Meals

Planning

It is desirable that the person acting as manager for the special meal confer well in advance with an authorized representative of the group to be served. Such a conference provides information as to the menu to be planned, the estimated or guaranteed number to be served, the price to be charged for the meal, the type of service, and the date, time, and place the meal is to be served. It is well also to discuss program arrangements and responsibility for table decorations.

    Duplicate copies of the menu plans should be signed and kept by the group's representative and the food director. This confirms the agreement and may prevent a misunderstanding of details and avoid last minute changes. Suggested menus are given on pp. 622-634.

    After the menu has been planned, the next step is to determine the kind and amount of food to be purchased. It is especially important that orders for special or unusual foods be made early enough to ensure delivery.

    A carefully planned work schedule is important to the success of any special meal. The number of workers and time required for preparation will depend largely on equipment available and the experience of the workers. A detailed work schedule includes prepreparation, cooking, serving, and cleanup assignments. If workers are inexperienced, the schedule should indicate time allotted for each task, detailed procedures, and other special instruction.

    A list including the amount and kind of linen, dishes, silver, glassware, and serving utensils required should be made by the manager and arrangements made for assembling these at least 1 day before they are to be used.

Preparation of the Dining Area

All personnel assisting with the service of the special meal should be given definite instructions. A mimeographed sheet of detailed procedures and instructions should be given to everyone new on a job.

The first step toward the service of a meal is the preparation of the dining area. It should be thoroughly cleaned, lighted, and ventilated, and the temperature should be regulated, if possible. The tables and chairs must be placed so there will be adequate space for serving after the guests are seated. If there is to be a head table, it should be placed so that it is easily seen by the guests. A podium and microphone should be available for the program. Audiovisual equipment, if needed, should be properly placed and adjusted. Serving stands, conveniently placed, facilitate service. Such provision is especially important when the distance to the kitchen is great.

Arrangement of the Table.   In order that the food may be served properly, great care must be taken to follow certain accepted rules for table setting. The physical setup, help available, or other conditions may demand some deviation from the rules given. However, there is often more than one right way.

1. *Tablecloth.* Lay the tablecloth, unfolding it carefully on the table to avoid creases. Place the cloth on the table so that the center lengthwise fold comes exactly in the middle of the table and the 4 corners are an equal distance from the floor. The cloth should extend over the table top 6-12 in. and should not touch the chair bottom. For some types of meals served to large groups, plastic and paper cloths are entirely acceptable. The use of these practical covers often would be limited to informal meals where labor and overall costs must be kept at a minimum.

2. *Place Mats.* Place mats make an attractive table setting when the finish of the table top permits. They are often used in institutions where no linen is available. They should be chosen for the attractiveness of their design, color, and the way in which they enhance other table appointments. Paper napkins also vary widely in quality, color, and design and are now acceptable for use on many occasions. Rectangular place mats may be sufficiently large that a single one will provide protection for the entire cover. If the mats are small, however, it is necessary to have enough paper doilies, of assorted sizes, to put under glasses, cups and saucers, bread and butter plates, and dishes containing food. In many institutions polished wood, lacquered, glass, or attractive composition table tops are used, so the cover may be laid without cloth.

3. *The Cover.* The plate, silver, glasses, and napkin to be used by each person are called a "cover" (see Fig. 4.1). Consider 20 in. of table space as the smallest permissible allowance for each cover; 25 or 30 in. is better. Arrange covers as symmetrically as possible. Place all silver and dishes required for one cover as close together as possible without crowding.

Figure 4.1 Cover for a simple meal. (1) Bread and butter plate; (2)
water glass; (3) napkin; (4) salad fork; (5) dinner fork; (6) knife;
(7) teaspoon.

4. *Silver*. Place the silver about 1 in. from, and at right angles to, the edge of
the table. If the table is round, only the outside pieces can be thus arranged.
Place knives, forks, and spoons in the order of their use, those first used on
the outside with the possible exception of the dinner knife and fork, which
may be placed immediately to the right and left of the plate, thus marking
its position. Some prefer to place the salad or dessert fork next to the plate
as the menu dictates. The trend is away from the use of salad forks when
salad is not served as a separate course.

Place the knives at the right of the plate, with the cutting edge turned
inward. If the menu requires no knife, omit it from the cover. Place the
spoons, bowls up, at the right of the knives. Place the forks, tines up, at
the left of the plate. Oyster and cocktail forks are exceptions to this rule;
place these at the extreme right of the cover beyond the spoons.

The fork may be substituted for the knife at a luncheon where no knife
is needed. Place it on the right side of the plate with the spoon beside it, if
one is used. If more than 1 spoon is needed, the balance is better if the fork
is placed to the left of the plate. With 2 forks and a spoon it may be better
to place the forks in the usual position.

If a butter spreader is used, lay it across the upper right-hand side of the bread and butter plate, with the cutting edge turned toward the center of the plate. It may be placed straight across the top of the plate or with the handle at a convenient angle.

Dessert silver often is not placed on the table when the cover is laid, except when the amount of silver required for the entire meal is small or if it is necessary to simplify service. If a dessert fork is used, it is sometimes placed in the area above the dinner plate, so the guest will use it for the final course.

5. *Napkin*. Place the napkin at the left of the fork with the loose corner at lower right and the open edges next to the edge of the table and the plate. It may be placed between the knife and fork if space is limited.

6. *Glass*. Place the water glass at the tip of the knife or slightly to the right. Goblets and footed tumblers are often preferred for luncheon or dinner and should be used at a formal dinner.

7. *Bread and Butter Plate*. Place the bread and butter plate at the tip of the fork or slightly to the left.

8. *Salt and Pepper*. Salt and pepper shakers should be provided for each 6 covers. They should be placed parallel with the edge of the table and in line with sugar bowls and creamers. Salt shakers are placed to the right.

9. *Nut or Candy Dishes*. Place individual nut or candy dishes directly at top of the cover. Larger dishes for nuts or bonbons are placed symmetrically on the table, usually allowing 1 dish for each six or eight guests.

10. *Chairs*. Place the chairs so that the front edge of each touches or is just below the edge of the tablecloth. The chair should be so placed with relation to the table that it need not be moved when the guest is seated.

11. *Decorations*. Some attractive decorations should be provided for the center of the table. It should be low so the view across the table will not be obstructed. The decoration usually varies in elaborateness with the formality of the meal. Cut flowers should harmonize in color with the menu, the appointments of the table, and the room. The decorations on the table should, if possible, be in charge of someone not connected with the food-service.

Candles should not be used in the daytime unless the lighting is inadequate or the day is dark. When used, they should be the sole source of light. Do not mix candlelight and daylight or candlelight and electric light. Candles often form part of the decorations. Tall ones in low holders should be high enough so that the flame is not on a level with the eyes of the guests.

Place cards usually are put on the napkin or above the cover. Menu cards, or booklets containing the menu and program, are commonly used at banquets.

Seating Arrangement.   It is difficult to lay down arbitrary rules for the seating of guests, since the matter is governed largely by the number and by the degree of formality of the meal. The guest of honor, if a woman, usually is seated at the right of the host; if a man, at the right of the hostess. The woman next in rank is seated at the left of the host. At a women's luncheon, the guest of honor sits at the right of her hostess. At banquets and public dinners, a woman is seated at the right of her partner.

Meal Service

Plate Service.   Food should be served from hot counters if these are available. If there are no hot counters, the utensils containing food should be placed in hot water to keep food hot. Some provision must be made also for keeping plates and cups hot. For serving 50 plates or less, the plan should provide that 1 person serve meat, vegetables, 1 potatoes, and so on. Such an arrangement for serving may be termed a "setup." For 60-100 persons, 2 setups should be provided in order to hasten service. For more than 100 persons it is well to provide additional setups.

It usually is convenient to have the food placed on the hot counter in the following order: meat, potatoes, vegetables, and sauces. Butter, garnish, and relishes are placed on an adjoining table.

The supervisor should demonstrate the size of portions to be given and their arrangement on the plate by serving the first plate and calling attention to the points to be considered.

There should be a checker at the end of the line to remove with a damp cloth any food spots from the plate and to check the plate for completeness, arrangement, and uniformity of servings.

The importance of standardized serving can hardly be overestimated; on this may depend the enjoyment of the guests and the financial success or failure of a meal.

There are various ways in which standard portions may be obtained. Perhaps the first way is by specifying the size or weight of units comprising the purchase if these are to serve as individual portions. Meats such as veal cutlets, chops, or steaks may be ordered 3, 4, or 5 to the pound, as desired, thus providing for standardized service.

Many foods cannot be brought under this plan because they are mixtures or combinations of various foods, or are served in a form quite different from that in which they are purchased. Meatballs, croquettes, mashed potatoes, pudding, cakes, and pies all illustrate this point. Several different methods are followed to obtain standardized individual portions in foods belonging to this group.

1. Portions may be determined by weight during the process of preparation, as is sometimes done in the making of chicken pie.

2. Portions may be determined by the use of dippers of standardized size (p. 64). This method is commonly used in the preparation of foods such as meatballs and sandwich ingredients. Dippers also are used for serving puddings and salads; ladles are used for soups and sauces.

3. Foods that take the form of the container in which they are prepared, such as gelatin salads, desserts, cakes, pies, and meat loaf, are prepared in pans of uniform size, and the prepared product is cut into uniform portions.

To obtain standardized portions by any of these methods, it is essential that the recipe used be standardized.

Table Service

1. Service personnel should report to the supervisor to receive final instructions at least 15 min before the time set for serving the banquet.

2. If the salad is to be on the table when the guests arrive, it should be placed there by the service personnel not more than 15 min before serving time. It should be placed at the left of the fork (Fig. 4.2). If space does not permit

Figure 4.2 The salad is placed at the left of the fork when salad and beverage are both served with the main course. If space does not permit, place salad plate at tip of fork and bread and butter plate above the dinner plate. (1) Bread and butter plate; (2) sherbet dish; (3) water glass; (4) salad plate; (5) dinner plate; (6) cup and saucer.

this arrangement, place the salad plate at the tip of the fork and the bread and butter plate if used, directly above the dinner plate between the water glass and the salad plate.

3. Place creamers at the right of sugar bowls.

4. Place relishes on the table, if desired.

5. For small dinners, the first course may be placed on the table before dinner is announced. For large banquets, however, it is best to wait until the guests are seated. Soups or hot canapés are always served after the guests are seated. To simplify service and to create an atmosphere of cordial hospitality, a first course of fruit or vegetable juices and accompaniments may be served as the guests arrive in the reception area.

6. Place butter on the right side of the bread and butter plate. If no bread and butter plate is used and the salad is to be on the table when the guests arrive, place the butter on the side of the salad plate. This is often necessary where dishes and table space are limited.

7. Place glasses filled with ice water on the table just before guests are seated.

8. When the guests are seated, service personnel line up in the kitchen for trays containing the first course. Two persons work together, one carrying the tray and the other placing the food. Place the cocktail glasses, soup dishes, or canapé plates on the service plates, which are already on the table.

9. Place and remove all dishes from the left with the left hand, except those containing beverages, which are placed and removed from the right with the right hand.

10. Serve the head table first, progressing from there to the right. It is preferable to have the head table the one furthest from the kitchen entrance.

11. When the guests have finished the first course, service personnel remove the dishes. Follow the same order in removing dishes as in serving.

12. For serving the main course, plates may be brought to the dining room on plate carriers or on large trays holding several plates and set on tray stands. Each worker serves the plates to a specified group of guests.

    An alternate method is often used in serving large groups. A tray of filled plates is brought from the kitchen by bus personnel to a particular station in the dining room, from which the plates are served. The dining room service personnel remain at their stations during the serving period.

13. Place the plate 1 in. from the edge of the table with the meat next to the guest.

14. As soon as a table has been served with dinner plates and salad, specially appointed workers should follow immediately with rolls and coffee.

15. At a large banquet, when serving a sherbet with the dinner course, carry it in on trays and place directly above the plate. Two service personnel work together as for first course.

16. Serve rolls at least twice. Offer them from the left at a convenient height and distance. Plates or baskets of rolls may be placed on the table to be passed by the guests.

17. Place the coffee at the right of the spoons with the handles of the cups toward the right.

18. Refill water glasses as necessary. If the tables are crowded, it may be necessary to remove the glasses from the table to fill them. Handle the glass near the base.

19. At the end of the course, remove all dishes and food belonging to that course. Remove dishes from the left of the guest.

20. If the silver for the dessert was not placed on the table when the table was set, take in on a tray and place at the right of the cover.

21. Serve desserts two at a time and in the same order that the plates were served. When pie is served, place it with the point toward the guest.

22. Coffee is served by service personnel who served it with the dinner course.

23. If possible, the table should be cleared except for decorations before the program begins.

24. The handling of dishes should cease before the program begins. Rattling dishes has ruined many banquets and is an unnecessary offense to the guest.

Buffet Service. Buffet suppers and luncheons are increasing in popularity as a means of serving relatively large groups of people. They may be formal or informal with an atmosphere of friendliness, which extends their appeal to people in every age and occupation group. The menu may be simple or elaborate. In general, the buffet meal is limited to 2 courses, but an assortment of hors d'oeuvres and a refreshing beverage may be served to the guests before they go to the buffet.

The success of a buffet meal depends not only on the quality of food, but on the attractiveness of the buffet table. Interesting colors may be introduced in the table covering, the serving dishes, the food, or the decorations. A bowl of fruit, gourds, and nuts may replace the more usual floral decorations in the buffet service. Consideration must be given to contrasts in colors, shapes, and sizes in the food and to the combining of food flavors. It is important to limit the kinds of hot foods to those that can be prepared and served easily.

ARRANGEMENT AND SERVICE

Food in a buffet service is arranged in the order in which it usually is served: meats or other entrées, potatoes, vegetables, salads, and relishes. Fig. 4.3. If more than one kind of cold meat or cheese is included in the menu, a pleasing grouping of the various kinds of food of this type is usually made on one platter. Coffee may be served at tables.

For large groups, a double line will speed service (Fig. 4.4). More space and duplicate serving dishes would be required.

Desserts may be placed on a table other than the one containing the main course, from which the guests will later serve themselves. Usually if the guests are seated, the dishes from the first course will be removed and the dessert served.

The type of service depends largely on the equipment available. If ample table space is provided, places may be set with covers, rolls, and water, and provision may be made for the beverage to be served by service personnel. In this case, the guests need only to pass before a buffet table and select the foods desired. Hot foods at the buffet may be served by a host or hostess, by service personnel, or the guests may serve themselves. When their plates are filled, they

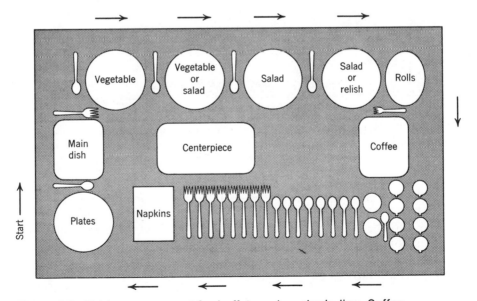

Figure 4.3 Table arrangement for buffet service, single line. Coffee may be served at tables.

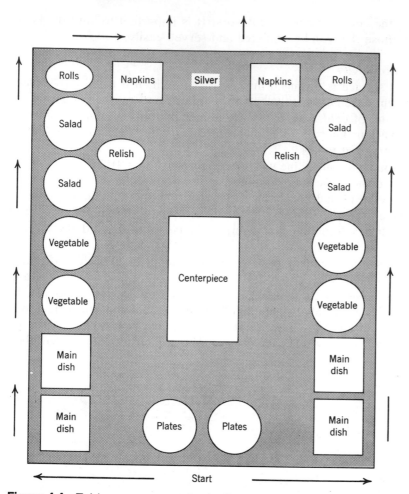

Figure 4.4 Table arrangement for buffet service, double line. Coffee is served at tables.

take their places at the covers prepared. If table room for all is not available, each guest may be given an individual tray on which to place silver, napkin, water glass, and the plate containing the assembled food. Hot beverages and rolls are then commonly served by a foodservice worker.

Menus for Special Meals

Dinners or Banquets.   The Selective Menu Planner (pp. 622-628) is designed as a guide for those responsible for planning dinners for special occasions. Food combinations suggested here may be suitable for community meals, special occasions in residence halls, school banquets or holiday meals, or wherever a special meal for a group is being planned.

Seven entrée groups, arranged according to similarity in flavor and texture, are included in the Menu Planner. Salads, vegetables, breads, and desserts suitable to serve with entrées listed in that group are suggested. To use this guide, first decide on the entrée, then select any vegetable, salad, bread, and dessert given in that group. For example: with roast leg of veal and dressing, you may use herbed green beans, mint-glazed carrots, or any of the other vegetables in that column; then make a choice of salad, rolls, and dessert from those listed in the adjoining columns. Any combination of items within a group, with minor adjustments, is designed to make a well-balanced dinner menu.

A first course of a fruit or seafood cocktail, juice, or clear soup may be added if a three-course dinner is to be served; or a first course of juice or punch with hors d'oeuvres may be served before the guests are seated.

SELECTIVE MENU PLANNER

Beef and Veal—Roast

Entrée Group I	Vegetable	Salad	Bread	Dessert
1. Roast Top Round of Beef O'Brien Potatoes Brown Gravy	Mint-Glazed Whole Carrots	Spinach-Mushroom	Raised Muffins	Chocolate Mint Parfait-Sandies
2. Roast Leg of Veal Dressing Mushroom Sauce	Butternut Squash	Mixed Salad Greens Parisian Dressing	Sesame Twists	Cheese Apple Crisp
3. Standing Rib Roast Parsley Buttered New Potatoes	Herbed Green Beans	Tomato Aspic Campus Dressing	Cornflake Muffins	Walnut Chiffon Cake Praline Topping
4. Roast Sirloin of Beef au Jus Yorkshire Pudding	Asparagus Polonaise	Frozen Fruit	Orange Rolls	Sour Cream Raisin Pie
5. Beef Rump Roast Small Corn Fritters	Zucchini Italian	Hearts of Romaine with Anchovy French Dressing	Whole Wheat Twin Rolls	Fresh Fruit Plate Assorted Cheese and Crackers
6. German Pot Roast Egg Noodles in Casserole Gravy	French Fried Eggplant	Grapefruit Sections–Avocado Strips Poppyseed Dressing	Cloverleaf Rolls	Lemon Sherbet with Fresh Strawberries Butter Tea Cookie

SELECTIVE MENU PLANNER (CONTINUED)

Beef and Lamb—Broiled Entrée Group II	Vegetable	Salad	Bread	Dessert
1. Broiled Center Cut Lamb Chop Creamed New Potato Chutney	Buttered Frozen Peas with Mushrooms	Pineapple, Melon and Orange Celery Seed-Fruit Dressing	Fig Coffee Ring	Ice Cream Pie
2. Broiled T-Bone Steak Corn Pudding Parsley	Baked Stuffed Tomato	Spicy Apricot Mold	Hard Rolls	Pineapple-Cashew Cake
3. Broiled Sirloin Strip Steak Parmesan New Potatoes	Green Beans Amandine	Marinated Carrots	Butterhorn Rolls	English Toffee Dessert
4. Filet Mignon Baked Potato with Sour Cream and Chives	Cauliflower Whipped Lemon Butter and Paprika	Crisp Green Salad Bowl Roquefort Dressing	Cranberry Nut Muffins	Peach Melba
5. Porterhouse Steak Stuffed Baked Potato Green Corn Relish	French Fried Onion Rings	Head Lettuce with Avocado and Grapefruit Sections Piquante Dressing	Hot Cheese Biscuits Jelly	Date Torte Whipped Cream
6. Broiled Rib Eye Steak Duchess Potatoes	Creole Celery	24-Hour Salad	Butterflake Rolls	Fudge Pudding

SELECTIVE MENU PLANNER (CONTINUED)

Beef and Veal—Braised *Entree Group III*	*Vegetable*	*Salad*	*Bread*	*Dessert*
1. Savory Swiss Steak Mashed Potato	Brussels Sprouts Brown Butter Sauce	Hearts of Romaine and Fresh Mushroom	Biscuits Jelly	Fresh Fruit Compote Coconut Macaroon
2. Country Fried Steak Mushroom Gravy Stuffed Baked Potato	Whole Kernel Corn O'Brien	Melon and Grapefruit	Sesame Seed Bread	Brownie à la Mode
3. Baked Veal Cutlets in Sour Cream Glazed Sweet Potato	Jumbo Asparagus Spears Hollandaise Sauce	Green Salad Bowl Avocado Dressing	Orange Rolls	Pineapple Refrigerator Dessert
4. Pepper Steak Buttered Fluffy Rice	Buttered Julienne Carrots	Head Lettuce Thousand Island Dressing	Parkerhouse Rolls	Red Cherry Tarts
5. Mock Drumsticks Potatoes au Gratin	Fordhook Lima Beans	Molded Spiced Fruit	Whole Wheat Rolls	Hot Fudge Sundae
6. Beef Stroganoff Buttered Noodles or Rice	Spinach Soufflé	Sliced Tomatoes on Leaf Lettuce	Texas Toast	Apple Pie with Streusel Topping

SELECTIVE MENU PLANNER (CONTINUED)

Fresh Pork

Entrée Group IV	Vegetable	Salad	Bread	Dessert
1. Stuffed Pork Chops Broiled Fresh Pineapple Slice with Chutney	Cauliflower Cheese Sauce Pimiento Strip	Grapefruit and Orange Sections on Curly Endive French Dressing	Corn Sticks	Chocolate Sundae Pie
2. Roast Loin of Pork Sage Dressing	Broccoli—Drawn Butter	Cranberry Ring Mold	Butterhorn Rolls	Meringue Shells Ice Cream and Fresh Strawberries
3. Pork Chops Supreme Duchess Potatoes	Buttered Green Peas	Guacamole and Tomato	All-Bran Muffins	Pecan Pie
4. Breaded Pork Tenderloin Sweet Potato and Cranberry	Sautéed Zucchini and Yellow Squash Rings	Bibb Lettuce Chiffonade Dressing	Crown Rolls	Fruit Sherbet Fudge Balls
5. Baked Pork Chops Scalloped Potato	French Green Beans	Hawaiian Tossed	Cinnamon Knots	Frozen Filled Angel Food Cake
6. Barbecued Spareribs Baked Potato	Fresh Corn on the Cob	Arabian Peach	Italian Bread	Warm Baked Apple Hard Sauce

SELECTIVE MENU PLANNER (CONTINUED)

Cured Ham

Entrée Group V	Vegetable	Salad	Bread	Dessert
1. Baked Ham Slice Mustard Sauce	Mashed Sweet Potato	Waldorf on Pineaple Slice	Oatmeal Muffin	Rainbow Ice Cream Balls
2. Broiled Ham Slice Cranberry Relish	Creamed New Potatoes	Ginger Ale Fruit	Poppyseed Twin Rolls	German Sweet Chocolate Cake
3. Glazed Baked Ham Currant Jelly	Buttered Whole Kernel Corn– Green Pepper Ring	Combination Fresh Julienne Vegetables	Parkerhouse Rolls	Strawberry Shortcake
4. Baked Chicken Breast on Ham Slice Glazed Apple Ring	Green Lima Beans in Cream	Molded Blueberry	Pecan Rolls	Chilled Fresh Fruit Cup with Lime Sherbet Tea Cookie
5. Glazed Ham Loaf Horseradish Sauce	Southern Style Green Beans	Head Lettuce Roquefort Dressing	Pan Rolls	Fresh Peach Cobbler Hard Sauce
6. Ham Croquettes Creamy Egg Sauce Broiled Peach with Chopped Pecans	Broccoli Spears Lemon Butter	Tossed Green Chilean Dressing	Butterhorn Rolls	Pineapple Upside-Down Cake Whipped Cream

SELECTIVE MENU PLANNER (CONTINUED)

Poultry

Entrée Group VI	Vegetable	Salad	Bread	Dessert
1. Chicken Breasts Black Olive Sauce Noodle Casserole	Buttered Julienne Beets	Head Lettuce with Florida Fruits and Mint Leaf	Hot Biscuits Honey	Orange Chiffon Cake
2. Roast Turkey Dressing Giblet Gravy Cranberry Relish	Glazed Carrots	Creamy Cole Slaw Green Pepper Ring	Parkerhouse Rolls	Russian Cream Berry Sauce
3. Barbecued Chicken Wild Rice Casserole	Fresh Frozen Peas with Sautéed Mushrooms	Peach Apple Salad Pecan Garnish	Prune-Date Coffee Ring	Praline Pumpkin Pie
4. Country Fried Chicken Cream Gravy Mashed Potatoes Spiced Apricot	Buttered Fresh Asparagus	Sliced Cucumbers in Sour Cream Watercress Garnish	Bran Rolls	Lemon Sherbet Melba Sauce
5. Chicken Tahitian Fried Rice with Almonds	Chive Baked Tomato	Mixed Salad Greens Chiffonade Dressing	Dinner Rolls	Strawberry Pie
6. Oven Crusty Chicken Corn Pudding	Green Beans Amandine	Caesar Salad	Pan Rolls	Fudge Cake Chocolate Frosting

SELECTIVE MENU PLANNER (CONTINUED)

Fish

Entrées Group VII	*Vegetable*	*Salad*	*Bread*	*Dessert*
1. Baked Salmon Steak Tartar Sauce Parsley New Potatoes	Fresh Green Beans Dill Sauce	Stuffed Apricot Sliced Orange and Glazed Prune	Cornmeal Muffin	Cherry-Glazed Cheese Cake
2. Broiled Fillet of White Fish and Mushrooms Lemon Butter Corn on Cob	Sliced Buttered Zucchini Grated Italian Cheese	Cucumber Soufflé	Hot Buttered French Bread	Apple Dumpling Nutmeg Sauce
3. Poached Halibut Amandine Sauce Green Rice	Broiled Fresh Tomato	Fruit Salad Bowl Poppy Seed Dressing	Tea Biscuits	Lemon Chiffon Pie
4. Baked Stuffed Fillet of Sole Cucumber Sauce Pimiento Baked Idaho Potato	Fresh Green Peas Drawn Butter	Tossed Fresh Salad Bowl Roquefort Dressing	Braids	Chilled Melon Lime Wedge
5. Creole Shrimp with Rice	Broccoli Polonaise	Pear on Orange Slice with Lime Gelatin and Cherry Garnish	All-Bran Rolls	Vanilla Ice Cream Hot Mincemeat Sauce
6. Shellfish Newburg in Patty Shells	Parsley Buttered Carrots	Spinach-Avocado Slice	Hard Rolls	Sherbet Bouquet

Luncheons

(1)
Turkey Divan
Parsley Buttered Carrot Rings   Broiled Tomato Half
Fresh Fruit Salad Bowl
Raised Muffins
Angel Pie
Coffee

(2)
Individual Glazed Ham Loaves
Spinach Soufflé   Buttered Whole Kernel Corn
Broiled Fresh Pineapple Slice with Chutney
Celery and Olives
Bran Muffins
Strawberry Tarts
Coffee

(3)
French Onion Soup   Toasted Crackers
Cheese Soufflé with Shrimp Sauce
Buttered Italian Green Beans   Salad Greens with Grapefruit
Hot French Garlic Bread
Lemon Sherbet with Frosted Raspberries
Coffee

(4)
Hot Consommé   Assorted Crackers
Chicken-Orange-Avocado Salad
Buttered Asparagus
Whole Wheat Muffins
Filled Angel Food Cake
Coffee

(5)
Cheese Soup   Melba Toast
Fresh Fruit Plate[1]
Chicken Sandwiches[2]   Nut Bread Sandwiches
Chocolate Chiffon Pie
Coffee

[1] Suggested combination: orange slices, pineapple wedges, honeydew melon and cantaloupe wedges, peach half, banana chunks; grapes, cherries, or strawberries in season.
[2] Sandwiches should be small to be attractive on the plate; cut in triangles, fingers, or rounds for variety.

Buffets. A greater variety of food generally is included in a buffet menu than can be offered at *table d'hote* meals, although the extent of the variety will depend on preparation time and space on the buffet table, among other factors. The menu may be built around 1 main dish, with 1 or 2 vegetables, a salad, relishes, hot bread, dessert, and beverage. The menu may consist of a more elaborate offering of main dishes, such as sliced cold meats, a chicken or fish casserole, and a hot meat, with accompanying vegetables, a variety of salads and relishes, bread, and dessert. An assortment of breads is often used to add interest and variety to the buffet table. Dessert for a buffet meal should highlight the meal and should be appropriate to the type of service that will be used for the dessert.

In planning a menu for a buffet, certain precautions should be observed.

1. Keep the service as simple as possible (i.e., avoid foods difficult to serve or that are soft or "soupy" on the plate). Foods that require extra utensils, such as bread and butter spreaders and salad or cocktail forks, should be avoided. If the guests will be eating from a tray, plan a main dish that can be cut with a fork.

2. Include a few attractively decorated foods, assorted salads, and an assortment of relishes. Attractive garnishing is important.

3. Plan hot foods that can be kept hot easily. Large or individual casseroles, chafing dishes, shells for deviled fish and similar foods, or heated trays are essential if hot food is to be served.

4. Plan the arrangement of the table at the same time the menu is planned to be sure of adequate table space and suitable serving dishes (see pp. 619, 620).

Suggested Foods for Buffet Menus

Main Dishes

Shrimp Creole
Scalloped Salmon
Deviled Crab
Scalloped Oysters
Tuna-Cashew Casserole
Chicken Cacciatore
Chicken Loaf
Chicken-Almond Casserole
Scalloped Chicken
Hot Chicken Salad
Chicken or Turkey à la King
Chicken Pie
Chicken Tahitian
Turkey Tetrazzini
Turkey Divan

Barbecued Beef Brisket
Veal Birds en Casserole
Beef Stroganoff with Noodles
Curried Veal with Rice
Swedish Meat Balls
Sweet and Sour Pork
Ham Loaf
Ham Patties with Pineapple Ring
Creamed Ham and Mushrooms
Creamed Sweetbreads and Mushrooms
Sliced Ham and Turkey
Tomato Stuffed with Crab or Shrimp Salad
Singapore Curry
Veal Scallopini

Vegetables

Scalloped Potatoes
Potatoes au Gratin
Sweet Potatoes and Apples
Green Rice
Scalloped Corn
French Fried Onions
Broccoli Casserole

Baby Limas in Butter
Green Beans, Almond Butter
Shredded New Harvard Beets
Buttered Peas, Rice, and Mushrooms
Broiled or Baked Tomatoes
Creole Eggplant
Zucchini Italian

Salads and Relishes

Stuffed Tomato Salad
Potato Salad
Frozen Fruit Salad
Orange and Grapefruit Sections
Stuffed Cinnamon Apple Salad
Fruit Combinations

Molded Fruit Gelatins
Avocado Ring with Fresh Fruit
Cranberry Relish
Spiced Peaches
Assorted Relishes

Salad Bowls

Julienne Vegetables
Creamy Cole Slaw
Salad Greens with Grapefruit

Tossed Green Salad
Hawaiian Tossed Salad
Celery Curls and Carrots

Desserts

Filled Angel Food Cake
German Sweet Chocolate Cake
Lemon or Other Chiffon Pie
Pecan Pie
Ice Cream Pie
Meringue Shells with Ice Cream or
Fruit Filling

Strawberry Shortcake
Peach Melba
Orange Cream Puffs with Chocolate
Filling
Assorted Fresh Fruits
Assorted Cheese and Crackers

Buffet Menus

(1)
Hot Chicken Salad
Buttered Broccoli
Marinated Carrots   Relishes: Celery, Olives, Zucchini Strips
Cloverleaf Rolls
Warm Fresh Peach Cobbler—Hard Sauce
Coffee

(2)
Pork Cutlets with Mushroom Sauce en Casserole
Buttered Cauliflower with Peas   French Baked Potatoes
Spinach-Mushroom Salad   Applesauce Mold
Celery Curls—Olives—Watermelon Pickles
Garlic Bread
Blueberry-Glazed Cream Pie
Coffee

(3)
Veal Paprika with Poppyseed Noodles
Glazed Carrots
Molded Pear Salad   Sliced Tomatoes
Whole Wheat Rolls
Praline Pumpkin Pie
Coffee

(4)
Chicken Tahitian
Broiled Tomatoes   Green Rice
Sliced Cucumbers in Sour Cream   Spicy Apricot Mold
Orange Coffee Ring
French Vanilla Ice Cream   Assorted Toppings
Coffee

(5)

Creole Shrimp on Rice   Oven-Baked Crispy Chicken
Buttered Asparagus Spears   Creamy Cole Slaw
Hawaiian Tossed Salad
Assorted Hot Breads
Old-Fashioned Strawberry Shortcake
Coffee

(6)

Sliced Turkey Roll
Ham Loaf—Horseradish Sauce   Deviled Crab
Green Beans with Herb Butter
Potato Salad   Creamy Cole Slaw   Fresh Fruit Plate
Celery—Radishes—Green Pepper Rings
Crown Rolls
Almond Blitz Torte
Coffee

(7)

Singapore Curry
Fresh Raspberry Parfait   Sandies
Tea

Brunches.   Brunch, a cross between breakfast and lunch, is becoming more and more popular as a way of entertaining. The meal may be served to guests seated at tables or it may be served from a buffet table.

The menu may be made up of foods normally served at breakfast or may resemble a luncheon menu, depending partly on the hour of service. The menu may be quite simple, consisting of fruits, hot breads, and coffee, or it may be a more filling meal that will replace lunch.

Brunch usually starts with fruit or juice placed on the table just before the guests are seated or served to guests from a punch bowl before they go to the buffet table. The main dish may be bacon, ham, sausage, eggs in some form, or a luncheon-type entrée of chicken, turkey, or fish. Attractive trays of bite-size fruits and an assortment of small squares of coffee cake, small sweet rolls, and other hot breads enhance a buffet table set for a brunch. A dessert may be served if the meal is scheduled late in the morning, but it should be light.

Suggested Menus for a Buffet Brunch

(1)
Orange Juice
Canadian Bacon   Sausages   Scrambled Eggs
Blueberry Coffee Cake   Pecan Rolls
Small Banana Bread Sandwiches
Fresh Fuit Tray
Coffee

(2)
Tomato Juice
Grilled Ham   Small Egg Cutlets
Hot Chicken Salad
Broiled Fresh Pineapple Slice
Scotch Scones   Small Orange Rolls   Glazed Donuts
Bowl of Fresh Strawberries—Powdered Sugar
Coffee

(3)
Honeydew Melon
Sausage Patties on Apple Rings
Chicken-Mushroom Crepes   Strawberry-Sour Cream Crepes
Coffee

Suggestions for a Sit-Down Brunch

(1)
Hot Consommé
Ham Slice and Sliced Hard-Cooked Eggs on Toasted English Muffins—Cheese Sauce
Green Rice   Broiled Peach Half
Hot Rolls   Strawberry Jam
Fresh Fruit Cup   Pound Cake
Coffee

(2)
Broiled Grapefruit Half
Ham or Mushroom Quiche
Buttered Broccoli   Cherry Tomato-Olive Kabob
Cranberry Bread
Ambrosia
Coffee

Teas, Coffees, and Receptions

Coffees, teas, and receptions may vary widely in degree of formality or informality and may accommodate a few guests or a large number. The menu must be planned and plans made according to the type of event, the time of day, and the number to be served. Certain general rules apply to all of these events.

A table set for tea or coffee service depends on its attractive appointments for its charm. The table covering, centerpiece, tea service, silver, and serving dishes should be the best available, and the food should be colorful, dainty, and interestingly arranged. To prevent a crowded appearance, there should be a limited amount of silver, china, napkins, and food on the tea table when the serving begins. A small serving table with extra china and silver near the tea table is a convenience. Replacements of small dishes and appointments are brought on trays from the kitchen. Cookies, sandwiches, and other foods should be arranged so they do not present a crowded appearance. It is best to use small servingplates and replace them frequently so there is an assortment of food at all times.

Teas and Receptions

Tea and coffee may both be served. They are placed on either end of the table and served to guests, who then help themselves to the accompaniments. (Fig. 4.5) In warm weather an iced beverage may be served to replace one or both of the hot drinks.

Formal teas and receptions generally are used for entertaining large groups. The occasion may be a wedding anniversary, introducing someone to a group, an open house, or honoring one or more individuals. The degree of formality will vary with the occasion and the desires of the host or hostess.

Foods served at a formal tea or reception are of the same type as those served at an informal tea, except that they are often more elaborately prepared and of greater variety.

A formal tea served in place of supper is sometimes called a high tea. It is more elaborate than afternoon tea and is similar to a buffet supper.

Types of food served at a tea follow.

Beverages

HOT
Coffee, tea, Russian tea, spiced tea, French chocolate, spiced cider.

ICED
Tea or fruit punch (plain or with sherbet).

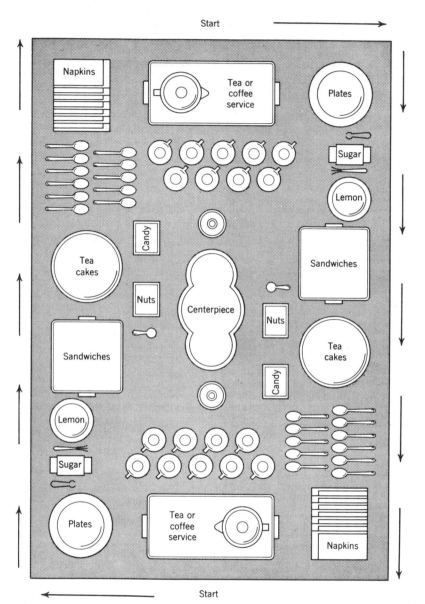

Figure 4.5 Tea-table arrangement.

Bread and Miscellaneous

OPEN-FACE SANDWICHES
Assorted fancy shapes spread with desired filling and decorated.

CLOSED SANDWICHES
Assorted breads such as nut, orange, banana, date, cheese, or plain with suitable filling. Rolled, ribbon, checkerboard, pinwheel sandwiches.

MISCELLANEOUS
Cheese wafers, cheese straws, party crackers, miniature cream puffs filled with cream cheese or chicken salad.

Cakes and Cookies.   Petits fours, small cupcakes, macaroons, kisses, shortbread, chocolate or date bars, small tea cookies.

Ice Creams, Sherbets, or Ices.   Any desired flavor—served in individual cups in which frozen or in sherbet glasses.

Nuts and Candies.   Salted, toasted, spiced, or crystallized nuts, preserved ginger, candied orange or grapefruit peel, mints in pastel colors and various flavors, chocolate mint patties, small hard candies, and stuffed or candied fruits.

Miscellaneous Accompaniments.   Cube or loaf sugar, plain or decorated. Orange or lemon—cut into thin slices, sections, or fancy shapes and often garnished with whole cloves.

Informal Tea Menus

(1)
Cheese Pinwheel Sandwiches   Nutbread Sandwiches
Fudge Balls   Miniature French Pastries
Pastel Mints
Hot Spiced Tea

(2)
Meringue Shells filled with Strawberry Whipped Cream
Sandies   Tea Brownies
Salted Mixed Nuts
Tea   Coffee

(3)
Pecan Tea Time Tarts
Ribbon Sandwiches   Raspberry Thimble Cookies
Candied Orange Peel
Tea

(4)
Banana Bread Finger Sandwiches
Frosted Tea Cakes   Chocolate Spritz
Butter Tea Cookies
Toasted Nuts
Jasmine Tea

(5)
Nut Bread Sandwiches   Two-Tone Cheese Sandwiches
Red Cherry Tartlets   Butterscotch Squares
Mints
Fruit Punch   Coffee

Formal Tea Menus

(1)
Small Cream Puffs filled with Chicken Salad
Assorted Open-Face Sandwiches
Scotch Shortbread   Caramel Marshmallow Squares
Orange Sherbet Cups
Spiced Pecans   Mints
Tea   Coffee

(2)
Christmas Tea
White Meat of Turkey on   Glazed Shrimp Canapés
Midget Parkerhouse Rolls
Norwegian Christmas Bread Tea Sandwiches
Assorted Christmas Cookies from Foreign Lands
Fruit Cake Slices   Mints   Salted Nuts
Sparkling Cranberry Punch

(3)
Wedding Reception
Strawberry Ice Cream in Pastel Cups
Bride's Cake   Groom's Cake
Wedding Punch   Coffee

(4)
Wedding Breakfast
Creamed Chicken and Mushrooms in Timbale Cases
Spiced Peaches   Ripe Olives
Lemon Buttered Asparagus Tips
Assorted Hot Rolls
Raspberry Sherbet   Wedding Cake
Punch   Coffee

Morning Coffee

A morning coffee is becoming more and more popular as a way to entertain. The food served is usually more substantial and the variety more limited than is the tea menu. There is always an ample supply of hot fresh coffee served with one or more hot breads. These may include pecan rolls, glazed marmalade rolls, doughnut holes, Bishop's bread, quick coffee cake, Kolaches, Danish pastry, and toasted English muffins. Fresh fruit or juice may also be included on the menu. A fruit tray, with bite-size pieces of fresh fruit arranged on a silver or wooden tray, is an attractive centerpiece and an interesting addition to a coffee hour.

Morning Coffee Menus

(1)
Blueberry Coffee Cake
Assorted Cookies   Date Bread and Cream Cheese Sandwiches
Sprigs of Frosted Grapes
Coffee

(2)
Slivers of Virginia Ham on Hot Party Biscuit
Small Sugared Doughnuts   Orange Bread Sandwiches
Fresh Fruit Kabobs
Coffee

(3)
Apricot-Filled Kolaches   Cinnamon Puffs
Tray of Bite-Size Fruits
Coffee   French Chocolate

(4)
Small Pecan Rolls   Toasted English Muffins with Jam
Brownies
Fresh Strawberries
Coffee

International Meals

Interest in international foods has increased, as indicated by the many books dealing with food habits and the choice recipes available from various countries. Buffet meals featuring foods from foreign countries afford a ready means of introducing variety and interest into meals that might become routine.

When planning an international meal, menu items should be selected that are typical of the country being featured but that can be prepared in quantity with the personnel, equipment, and ingredients available. Ideas for menus and recipes are easily obtainable from the many international cookbooks on the market today. Small-quantity recipes should be tested first before being enlarged. If some of the ingredients listed in authentic recipes are unavailable, recipes may need to be modified. Special meals are enhanced by the presentation of menu cards, decorations, or posters with names of the various foods being served and an explanation of the typical foods of the country or region being represented.

Suggestions are included in this section for a Swedish Smörgåsbord, Singapore Curry, and Chinese and Hungarian dinners. Many other countries offer foods that are well accepted by Americans; among those that are popular are meals based on Italian, German, Greek, Mexican, and Spanish foods.

Swedish Buffet Suppers

Sweden is famous for its Smörgåsbord, or hors d'oeuvres, which is an ancient tradition and an important accompaniment to all Swedish dinners. The hors d'oeuvres for a family of moderate means are grouped in the center of a long table laid with a spotless white linen tablecloth, plates, and silver. The guests are seated at the table and the hors d'oeuvres are passed and eaten just before a regular meal of 2 or more courses is served. An employee removes the dishes from the first course. Typical food for the family hors d'oeuvres might include: meats and fish—cold spiced tongue, smoked venison, smoked salmon (sliced), fish in aspic jelly, anchovies, herring served in two ways, large shrimps with Thousand Island dressing, parsley, and dried beef; vegetables—radishes, sliced tomatoes, salads (two or more kinds), and a scalloped dish; bread—rye bread, white bread baked in ornamental shapes; cheese—served in a big piece on a cheese plate with a cheese knife.

Hors d'oeuvres for a family, or for a hotel, might be arranged on a separate table as for a buffet supper. Guests would help themselves and then take their places at the dining table. A wide variety of hors d'oeuvres would be offered, including 20-125 articles—Rye Krisp, butter curls, 6 or 7 kinds of cheese, very small Swedish meatballs fried in deep fat, a hot scalloped dish of fish or vegetable, pickled onions, pickled beets or cucumbers; vegetable salads, similar to our own, a bowl of mayonnaise; jellies and marmalades. A regular 3- or 4-course dinner is served after the hors d'oeuvres are eaten.

The use of colorful foods or decorations is an outstanding feature of the Swedish table. Candles are not used for decorations except for banquets. Flowers are always used and often 2 or more bouquets are placed on the table if long.

A Swedish buffet supper suitable for service in this country is planned to include only the Smörgåsbord and the dessert, omitting what the Swedish diner would regard as the main part of the meal.

Swedish Smorgåsbord

Pickled Herring   Canapés
Pickled Beets   Celery Curls   Radish Roses
Deviled Eggs with Parsley Garnish   Sliced Tomatoes
Cucumbers in Sour Cream
Cottage Cheese   Assorted Cheese
Swedish Meat Balls   Potato Sausage
Cold Sliced Baked Ham
Parsley Buttered Potatoes or Potato Salad
Swedish Brown Beans or Green Beans with Mushrooms
Fruit Salad Mold   Swedish Green Top Salad
Cabbage Slaw
Swedish Salad Bowl
Rye Bread   Swedish Tea Ring
Ost Kaka (Cheese Pudding) with Thickened Grape Juice
Lingenberry tarts
Swedish Apple Cake   Assorted Cookies
Swedish Mints
Coffee

Bordstabbel Bakels (Lumberpile Cookies)

½ c butter
1 c light brown sugar
1 egg
½ t vanilla

1¼ c flour
½ t soda
¼ t salt
½ c chopped nutmeats

Cream butter and sugar. Add well-beaten egg and vanilla. Add flour sifted with soda and salt, then nutmeats dredged in portion of flour. Mold dough. Let stand in refrigerator overnight. Cut into strips, 3 in. × 1 in. Bake in a moderate oven. When done, cover with Fluffy Frosting (p. 178) and sprinkle with chopped almonds, caraway seed, or candies. Pile like lumber on serving plates.

Sandbakelser (Sand Tarts)

1 lb butter
pinch of salt
⅓ t baking powder
5 c flour (about)

1 c white sugar
1 T cream or milk
2 eggs
3 T almond extract

Cream butter and sugar. Add eggs. Blend well, add extract, then flour. Press into small "picture" tins or put through cookie press. Chopped almonds may be added to dough if "picture" tins are used. Turn out of tins at once after baking or they will stick.

Smörbakelser (Butter Cookies)

1 c butter (sweet)
1 c powdered sugar
2 c flour

Mix and pat out in 2 10-in. baking tins. Bake in a moderate oven approximately 20-30 min. Cut as soon as removed from oven. This is the same as Scotch Shortbread.

Svenska Kringlor (Swedish Kringle)

1 c butter
1¼ c brown sugar
½ c milk
2 eggs

3½ c flour or enough to make soft dough
2 T baking powder
1 T cinnamon

Sift dry ingredients. Cream butter and sugar. Add egg yolks and flour and milk alternately. Fold in beaten whites. Bake as drop cookies.

Svenska Pepper Nötter (Swedish Peppernuts)

The oldest of all cakes we know today are the peppernuts. They were in popular use long before the eleventh century.

4 eggs
2 c sugar
1 c butter
1 t cinnamon
1 t cloves
1 t pepper

1 t cardamon (ground)
½ c nuts
½ c raisins
4 c flour (bread)
1 t soda
2 T hot water

Drop on cookie sheet and bake at 450 °F.

Fattigman Bakels (Poorman's Crullers)

2 eggs
2 T sugar
⅛ t salt

f.g. cardamon
3 T heavy sweet cream
1¾ c flour (or less)

Beat eggs until light, add sugar, salt, spice, and continue beating. Add cream and enough flour to make a soft dough. Turn out on floured board, roll very thin. Cut into diamond shapes. Slash opposite ends. Pull end through slit, or cut in star shapes. Fry in deep fat. Drain on heavy paper. Dust with sugar.

Swedish Salad Bowl

1 can of pineapple (size 2½)	1 stalk celery
1 tart apple	5 tomatoes
lettuce	½ cucumber

Cut the pineapple and tomato into wedges, dice the apple and celery, cut the cucumber en julienne. Mix with Pineapple Dressing just before serving and add shredded lettuce leaves.

Pineapple Dressing

Mix 2 raw egg yolks with the juice drained from the can of pineapple, stir constantly, and cook over a low heat until thick. Cool, then add 1 mashed, cold, hard-cooked egg yolk that has been mixed with ¼ t mustard and 3 T vinegar. Fold in 2 c whipped cream.

Serve salad in a salad bowl. Yield approximately 10 servings.

Ost Kaka (Cheese Pudding)

2 gal milk	6 eggs
2 c flour	1½ qt cream, coffee
½ cake of cheese rennet (purchased from drug store)	½ c sugar

Heat the milk until lukewarm and stir into it the flour that has been smoothed to a paste. Add the cheese rennet that has been dissolved in 2 T water. Stir well and let stand. As soon as the milk has set, stir gently to separate the curds and whey. Let stand a few minutes, then pour off whey or use a strainer to remove curds. (The curds should be quite moist.) Place curds in 2 medium-sized casseroles and pour over them a custard mixture made from the eggs, cream, and sugar. Sprinkle nutmeg over the top. Bake and test as a plain custard. Serve warm with strawberry jam or grape juice thickened to the consistency of thick cream.

Singapore Curry

Singapore Curry, an unusual combination of foods, is popular not only in the Far East where it originated but has been well accepted by those persons interested in "something different." Basically, this is a curried meat served over rice with a variety of accompaniments.

For the curried meat, a good combination is chicken and fresh pork. However, other meat, such as lamb or veal, fish, such as shrimp, may be used. For a generous serving, allow about ½ lb meat per person. The guests serve themselves rice in the center of their plates, dip curried meat over the rice, and then add accompaniments. A well-served plate will be nicely rounded and self-garnished. Only a dessert need be added to make a complete meal. Fruit, melons, sherbet, or sundaes are especially good for dessert. Hot tea should be served. A recipe for Chicken Curry and suggestions for serving are given on p. 361.

Chinese Buffet Suppers

Americans find Chinese dishes enjoyable and unlike those of any other nation except possibly Japan. Food items desired by a Chinese cook might include: litchi nuts, mushrooms, dry lotus seeds, bamboo shoots, lotus roots, bean sprouts, shark fins, very fine noodles, rice, millet, rice flour, ginger root, bean meal, shell fish and other fish, chicken, pork, chestnuts, almonds, and walnuts. Preserved eggs, condiments and preserved fruits and ginger are frequently used. Chinese sauce or soy sometimes take the place of salt in Chinese cookery. Peanut oil is used for frying.

Tea is the popular beverage and is served without cream or sugar in small covered cups without handles. A party menu usually contains several meat dishes, including chicken, fish, goose, pork, lobster, crab, or shrimp. Each dish is said to be 1 course. Tea may be served with each course. Almond cookies and fruits are common desserts.

Chinese Menu and Recipes

Boo Loo Gai (Pineapple Chicken)	Plain Boiled Rice
Hop Too Guy Ding (Almond Chicken)	Celery Hearts
Egg Foo Yung (Omelet) (p. 212)	Kumquat and Ginger Preserves
Chow Lon Fon (Fried Rice) (p. 190)	Soy Sauce
Fried Shrimp	Litchi Nuts
	Fortune Cookies
	Fruit: Fresh and Candied
	Jasmine Tea

Pineapple Chicken (Boo Loo Gai)

Cut a young chicken as for fried chicken, season with soy sauce, salt, and sugar, and let stand 1 hr. Drain, dredge with flour, and brown in hot fat. Add a little hot water and simmer until tender. Add 1 small can of diced pineapple and 1 t soy sauce. Thicken liquid with flour and serve as soon as flour is cooked. Garnish with parsley.

Almond Chicken (Hop Too Guy Ding)

Fry 2 c shredded onions, 2 c shredded water chestnuts, and 2 c shredded celery until slightly browned, then add chicken broth or white stock to cover, and cook until vegetables are tender. Add 1 young chicken that has been cut into cubes and cooked in peanut oil (or vegetable oil). Thicken liquid with a little cornstarch and water mixed. Add 1 T soy sauce and place in a hot casserole. Add 1 c toasted almonds just before serving.

Almond Cakes (Gum Loo)

1 c flour	1 egg, beaten
¾ c powdered sugar	3 T vegetable oil
¼ c almonds, chopped	

Mix dry ingredients. Add oil and then the beaten egg. Mold into small balls, brush with egg, garnish with a whole almond, and bake in a moderate oven.

Litchi nuts have a characteristic flavor and may be purchased dried or canned.

Hungarian Buffet Suppers

Knowledge of Hungarian cookery is, for many people, restricted to the more or less enthusiastic acceptance of Hungarian goulash, a dish said to be "the savory ancestor of all stews."

The vegetables in common use are similar to those in the American diet and include beets, red and white cabbage, sauerkraut, carrots, cauliflower, kale, kohlrabi, peppers, and lettuce. The popular fruits include apples, apricots, cherries, melons, peaches, pears, and bananas. The large role of cereals in the diet is shown by the appearance of noodles and bread dumplings in many menus along with rye breads and fancy rolls.

Cheese is used freely in cooked dishes and in its natural state; butter (unsalted) is used sparingly. Sour cream is widely used both as a garnish and as an ingredient in cooking. Its use with paprika is regarded by many as the characterizing feature of a Hungarian dish, so popular are both with Hungarians. Paprika, although popular is only one of the numerous condiments used; the Hungarians are fond of spicy foods. A suggested menu for a buffet follows. Recipes are included in Part II.

Hungarian Buffet

Paprika Chicken with Spatzels

Stuffed Squash   Green Beans with Dill Sauce

Cucumber Salad—Sour Cream Dressing

Poppyseed Crescent Rolls   Sweet Butter

Cheese Cake   Fresh Fruit Compote

Coffee

Index